D1297253

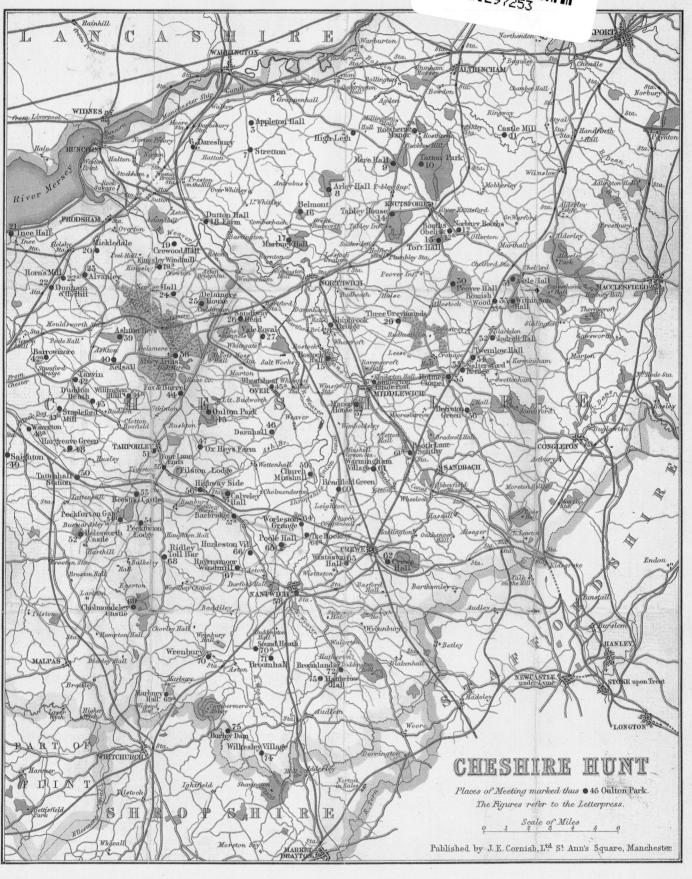

CHESHIRE HUNT.

Places of Meeting marked thus ● 45 Oulton Park.
The Figures refer to the Letterpress.

Scale of Miles

Published by J. E. Cornish, Ltd St. Ann's Square, Manchester.

THE GREEN COLLARS

The Hon. John Smith-Barry with Bluecap, from an oil painting by James Cranke, 1776.

THE GREEN COLLARS

THE TARPORLEY HUNT CLUB AND CHESHIRE HUNTING HISTORY

Gordon Fergusson

Foreword by H.R.H. The Prince of Wales

also incorporating

HUNTING SONGS

by

R. E. Egerton Warburton

(11th Edition - Selected and Annotated by Gordon Fergusson)

and

A MISCELLANY OF SPORTING VERSE BY CHESHIRE AUTHORS

Quiller Press
London

First published 1993 by Quiller Press Ltd
46, Lillie Road, London, SW6 ITN

British Library Cataloguing in Publication Data
1. Social and Fox-hunting history (Cheshire)
1. Fergusson, Gordon
2. Sporting verse
2. Egerton Warburton, Rowland Eyles
3. Miscellaneous Sporting Verse

Set in Ehrhardt by Cambridge Photosetting Services

Produced by Book Production Consultants Plc,
25–27 High Street, Chesterton, Cambridge, CB4 1ND

Book One designed by Tim McPhee and Gordon Fergusson
Book Two designed by Jim Reader and Gordon Fergusson

Printed in Milan, Italy by Rotolito Lombarda

ISBN 1 870948 89 0

To Trushi, John, Didi, James and William,
as well as Samantha and Charlie, Hamish and Polly
and also to the species *Vulpes Vulgaris*;
destiny permitting and common sense prevailing,
long may it be preserved as a beast of the chase.

IN CHESHIRE *there be,*
Egertons and Leighs
As thick as fleas,
As many Massies as asses,
Crewes as Crows,
and Davenports as dog's tails.
— Cheshire Proverb

WM. CAMDEN (1551–1623) *says Cheshire is "the most surpassing nursery of ancient gentry above any other County in England".*
J. C. Bridge, Cheshire Proverbs, 1917.

THE SHIRE *may well be said to be the Seedplot of gentilitie, and the producer of many most ancient and worthy families; neither hath any brought more men of valour into the Field than Chesse-shire hath done, who by a general speech are to this day called the chiefe of men; and for Nature's endowments (besides their own noblenesse of mindes) may compare with any nation in the world: their limmes strait and well-composed; their complexions faire; with cheerful countenance; and the women of a grace, feature and beautie, inferior unto none.* – John Speed, county historian and map-maker, *Theatre of the Empire of Gt. Britain,* 1606. Born at Farndon, 1552.

WHEN LAWS *can check the autumn leaves*
From falling as they die,
When fences in November
Are as blind as in July,
We then will strip our collars off;
But till that day be seen,
We Cheshire men we'll stick till then
To wearing of the Green.
R.E.E.W.

HRH The Patron of the Tarporley Hunt Club and J.J.O'Shea. '*... from Cholmondeley Castle, where we tasted fly fences, ditches and timber, with hounds running brilliantly all day on a sizzling scent, with that consummate huntsman Johnny O'Shea carrying the horn in great style. The Prince of Wales recalls that as one of his red-letter days, ...a day of sheer riding fun.*'
Michael Clayton, *Country Life* (Jan.2nd 1992), 'Prime Country for Crossing.'

As Patron of The Tarporley Hunt Club, I have been asked to write a foreword to this most enjoyable book. I doubt if I can do it much justice for it speaks for itself. It is full of the most wonderful stories about Cheshire country life and about the truly remarkable characters who added such zest and colour to that life. And what characters they must have been! The kind of people who, throughout the centuries, have made our country what it is, and have made it great.

Their stamina was prodigious, their feats of equestrianism extra-ordinary; their ability to endure pain and discomfort exemplary and their capacity for linguistic exuberance heart-warming. How sad it is that our contemporary age makes it ever more impossible for such larger-than-life characters to exist.

The countryside, with its unique way of life - one of the last outposts of a truly British culture - is under constant siege. Countryside sports are daily threatened by the agents of ignorance and prejudice. The delicate web of family farms, passed on from one generation to another and forming an intricate system for the longterm stewardship of our beloved British landscape, is facing a looming crisis.

We seem to think ours is the only generation to have inhabited this piece of Earth. But it is not. We are part of a timeless pattern, of which wise men have always been aware. We shall all be the poorer if this pattern is broken on the wheel of fashion and convenience, and we find ourselves deprived of those cultural roots which have always inspired this country's greatness.

The Cheshire. The Hunted Fox.

Contents

Book One

THE GREEN COLLARS

Part One

Book Two

Part One

THE HUNTING SONGS OF ROWLAND EGERTON WARBURTON

Part Two

A CHESHIRE MISCELLANY OF HUNTING SONGS, POEMS, BALLADS AND VERSE.

Acknowledgements

His Royal Highness the Prince of Wales has written such a forceful Foreword, which succinctly sums up so much of what I hope *The Green Collars* expresses, and by that I am greatly honoured. Although the book is essentially about Cheshire, it is intended for a much wider readership and as a contribution to the social history of England.

It is entirely due to the generosity of the Countryside Foundation by supporting the whole project that I have been able to have the book published at such a reasonable price and to its Chairman, Committee and all concerned I am exceedingly grateful. The Countryside Foundation is a registered charity, established in 1986: 'To research and provide information, knowledge and insight, for a largely urban-based population, about the contribution of country sports, pastimes and leisure activities to the rural environment and economy.' It has been pleased to support the publication of this book as a result of a generous donation and considers it to be a valuable and fascinating piece of social history, connected with an ancient country activity.

As Secretary of the Tarporley Hunt Club and Keeper of the Cheshire Hunt's archive I have had complete access to a fascinating collection of papers and I wish to thank my fellow Members of the Club for their approval of the project, as well as the Cheshire Hunt Committee; nor do I forget my predecessors and former Hunt Secretaries for having recorded and preserved all the books, documents and letters from which I have gleaned the substance of this history.

The reference section at the Chester Library and the County Library itself have been immensely useful, and Ian Dunn's staff at the Chester Record Office has also given every assistance. It is always highly rewarding to a researcher when a little bit of serendipity takes a hand. One such instance concerned a discovery of a Rent Account among the Egerton of Oulton Papers. It had been written on the back of Mr Philip Warburton's letter about Trinket. I must also thank the librarian at the Bodleian. The Henry Higginson Collection of books on hunting at the London Library is a most valuable source, to which I am extremely grateful to have had access. The British Library Newspaper Library at Colindale supplied me with photocopies and illustrations from various articles most efficiently.

Many kind friends have allowed me to look through their bookshelves, as well as others too numerous to mention, who have confirmed facts, given me little bits of information and general encouragement. The late Francis Moore Dutton's enthusiasm was unbounded and Lord Kenyon, a collector of R.E.Egerton Warburton's works, was especially helpful. Among others to give me free range of their libraries were David Brooke, Randle Brooks, the late David Fildes, Frank Lathom and Carolin Paton-Smith, to name but five. Dining one evening with Tony and Dini Hanbury-Williams I spotted a rare edition of Major Guy Paget's *The Flying Parson and Dick Christian*. and thanks to Anthony Barbour, I was able to borrow Mr Geoffrey Shakerley's hunting diary and the Barbour family hunting scrapbook.

Best of all was the time I spent going through the relevant shelves in the magnificent panelled library at Arley, with a number of benign ghosts of the family looking over my shoulder, as I sat, huddled in an overcoat, reading at the desk on two dusky winter afternoons. Piers Egerton Warburton's hunting diary was most fruitful and Charles and Jane Foster were extremely kind and hospitable. Having received the blessing of Viscountess Ashbrook, I am so delighted to be the Editor of another edition of *Hunting Songs*. And Major Peter Egerton-Warburton has allowed me to reproduce some of his grandfather Piers's drawings and two rare photographs of his great grandfather Rowland.

I wish I had more space to describe my day at Inwood, where I was so courteously received by Count Guy de Pelet and his gracious Countess. During the comparatively short time available I was able to skip through nearly a hundred manuscript diaries written by the first Duke of Westminster's parents and their youngest daughter, Lady Theodora Guest, coming across several rewarding passages.

Another great find were the three volumes of the late Mr Harry Rawson's diaries, for the loan of which and the circumstances of their discovery I have acknowledged in a footnote in Chapter XIV.

I apologise for not giving source references or a bibliography, but I will be happy to correspond with anyone requiring further information.

Miss Daphne Moore has given me constant inspiration and allowed me to make use of her extensive hunting library.

Mrs Jane Hampartumian of the Staffordshire Record Office, Mrs S.M.Tonking, the Lichfield Diocesan Archivist, Roger Custance of Winchester College, Simon Bailey of Oxford University Archives, Dr A.S.Bendall of Emmanuel College, Cambridge and Canon Roy Barker of Chester Cathedral have all assisted me to glean as much as I have been able about the Club's first President, the Rev.Obadiah Lane. Miss Jennie Slater of the Derbyshire Record Office produced information about Captain John White, as did Peter Bacon, the Secretary of the Derbyshire Yeomanry Old Comrades Association. Major W.Grant, 9th/12th Royal Lancers has also helped. Before I forget, I must pay tribute to Lysons' *Magna Britannia*, Ormerod's *History of Cheshire*, and Raymond Richards's *Old Cheshire Churches*, all invaluable sources, besides my constantly having recourse to *The Complete Peerage, Burke's Peerage, Baronetage and Knightage, Debrett's* and *Who Was Who*, and not omitting *Baily's Hunting Directory*, founded in 1897.

Once again Michael Saunby, formerly of the Metropolitan Police, now residing in the Belvoir country, has proved to be a veritable fount of knowledge concerning Hunt Servants and has replied to my queries most punctiliously, as well as supplying the odd photograph. I am so very pleased to have the consent of Peter Wright and other members of the family of Joe Wright, the late Cheshire huntsman, to include long extracts from his tape-recorded reminiscences. Bert Maiden and Charlie Johnson are other celebrated huntsmen to have helped me.

Among those who have shown me most interesting family diaries and memoirs are Michael Griffith, Hugh Wilbraham and Michael Jodrell. Seventy-two Members of Tarporley have been M.P.'s and the Right Hon. Alastair Goodlad very efficiently sent me copies of the entries for many of them included in the History of Parliament Trust's scholarly work, *The House of Commons*, and answered other questions with the utmost patience. The Right Hon. David Howell also most kindly found time to write to me in connection with my vignette about Sir Walter Bromley-Davenport.

I also wish to thank Anne, Duchess of Westminster, Lady Mary Grosvenor, Lavinia, Marchioness of Cholmondeley, Penelope, Countess of Lindsay, Rona, Dowager Lady Broughton and Mrs Detmar Blow, Diana Baskervyle-Glegg, Lord Leverhulme, Richard Tomkinson, Geoffrey Churton, Michael Higgin, Sebastian and Naomi de Ferranti, Lord Tollemache, Quentin Crewe, Sir Richard Baker Wilbraham, Bill Spiegelberg, Michael Flower, Peter Greenall, Bill Bromley-Davenport, Harold Cunningham, Sir Derek Bibby, Sir John Grey Egerton, Tim Heywood-Lonsdale, Brian Jenkins, Jack and Margaret Lakin, Peter Ormrod (Col.Rivers Bulkeley's grandson), John Richards, Lord Grey of Codnor, Thomas Woodcock (Somerset Herald), William Dodd, Roger Heaton, and Philip Hunter and his two sons, Peter and John, who have contributed and encouraged in their several ways and to them all my warmest appreciation.

In connection with Tarporley Races, I spent a morning at Haydock Park looking up *Steeplechases Past*, thanks to Charles Barnett, and Weatherbys arranged for other gaps in my records to be filled by Steve Boxall. *The Sporting Life* also deserves credit. Chubb Paterson, an enthusiastic and most competent steeplechase rider in his day, gave me much inspiration for this chapter of the book. Frank Wilson of Tiverton told me his childhood memories of Tarporley Races. Geoffrey Webster, a Director of the Tote, put me right on my erroneous belief that Tarporley was the first race meeting to have a Totalizator. And just as I was wondering at the page-proof stage how to fill up the end of the chapter, Charles Hurding turned up out of the blue with a copy of the last race card.

Many others have also replied most courteously to my letters and I would like to mention Lord Anglesey, Lord Combermere, Lord Delamere, Lord Glendevon, Lord Hesketh, Lord Langford, the Baroness Mallalieu, Q.C., Lord Melchett, the Right Hon. John Needham, Lord Newton, Sir Humphrey de Trafford, Sir William Gladstone, Lady Lucinda Worsthorne, A.H.B.Hart, Secretary to the M.F.H.A., Major Basil Heaton, David Howard of Heirloom and Howard, Major John Clark Kennedy, Major Nigel Kearsley, J.S.K.Mainwaring, Rafe

Cavenagh-Mainwaring, Christopher Naylor, Miss Philippa Glanville, the Curator of the metalwork department at the V&A, Mrs Pat Knight and Miss Eileen Simpson of the Grosvenor Estate, Mrs Didy Grahame and Major A.J.Dickinson, Secretaries of the Victoria Cross and George Cross Association and of the Royal Humane Society respectively, the Librarians of Gray's Inn, Inner Temple and Lincoln's Inn, Roy Bird of Peterborough Royal Fox-hound Show Society, D.K.Smart, the Civil Engineer of Intercity, Tony Priday, *The Sunday Telegraph* bridge correspondent, Julian Treuherz of the Walker Art Gallery and Gregory Way, the Newmarket bookseller.

A letter I wrote to *Country Life* in an effort to trace Sir Harry Mainwaring's gold medal for attending the dinners fifty consecutive years, put me in touch with Peter Lole, an authority on Jacobite customs. I hope many of my readers will have had their appetites whetted by an article I wrote for *The Field* (January, 1993), commissioned as a result of my spending a day in that periodical's former offices at Windsor, looking through the old numbers.

I am greatly indebted to *The Chester Chronicle* for allowing me to examine its file copies, deposited at the County Record Office. During many visits I acquired a plethora of information and particularly in connection with the Empress of Austria's hunting trips to Cheshire, a great deal of which intelligence has not hitherto been included in her biographies. Despite sympathetic aid from Frau Caroline Gudenus, the First Secretary at the Austrian Embassy, my enquiries at the Court and State Archives at Vienna to trace her letters to the Emperor from Cheshire came to nought, apart from discovering the existence of some receipts from English firms. The correspondence is in private hands and has only partially been published – *Letters of Emperor Franz Joseph to the Empress Elisabeth*, edited by Georg Nostitz-Rieneck, Vienna, 1966. According to the preface, the Empress's replies are kept in the same place, but without explanation in the *Anmerkungen* no letters dated between 1875 and 1886 have been included in the book.

I am obliged to the *Institut Français* for information concerning George Wilbraham's incarceration in Paris, as well as M.Philippe Guillemin, the Cultural Counsellor at the French Embassy and himself a fox-hunting man.

I wish to thank Andrew Dobrzynski for telling me about the Northern Rangers, Lieutenant-Colonel Denys Rowan-Hamilton for his information about the Down Hunt Club, J.P.Scarratt, Clerk to the Shrewsbury Hunt Club and especially Dr Simon Rees, the Chairman, and the Members of the Charlton Hunt Club for a memorable lunch at Boodle's.

Miss Pamela Clark, the Deputy Registrar of the Royal Archives, checked through the names of various Members about whom I had enquired, but unfortunately drew blank in each case.

Jim Basker of the Chartered Institute of Bankers went to a lot of trouble to write to me about the origin of Banker's Orders, which have existed since at least 1603. Allan Flowers of the Central Statistical Office also supplied useful information. Michael Skinner and David Cook of Dege & Co., Savile Row, have also produced answers to my various questions.

By some strange synchrony Mrs Marilyn Heenan arrived one day from West Yorkshire with a letter dated 1876 from Geoffrey Shakerley, about whom she was enquiring. It seems that for some private reason he had made regular payments to her forebear.

Thanks to the Duke of Westminster I have spent several happy hours of perusal in the Grosvenor muniment room, and His Grace has also lent me transparencies of his paintings and given permission for them to be reproduced. At the end of the book I gratefully acknowledge the copyright holders and photographers, who have done work for me, those who have allowed me to have their paintings reproduced and the sources of other illustrations. Here I would like to give thanks to Messrs. Sotheby's (in particular Tim Wonnacott and David Moore-Gwynn) and to Richard Green of Dover Street for producing transparencies for me. Mrs Judi Egerton has also lent me a transparency. I have a special thank you for Mrs. Anthony Villiers, who has inherited the Smith-Barry Collection, for allowing me to have her paintings photographed. Tom Wright of Oakmere has meticulously copied many photographs from the Club's albums and I give my recognition here for all he has done.

I am delighted to be able to include various poems and songs in Book Two Part Two, thanks particularly to Mrs Hugh Whittemore, Keith Rae, Simon and Gemma Dewhurst, Tom Haynes and the exors. of the late Phil Stevenson.

Christopher Hibbert, the favourite historian of my godmother, Dame Barbara Cartland, has most generously found time to read my typescript and go through it in detail with me, giving every encouragement. Dermot Daly is another to have saved me a red face. My son, William, has also read it through most meticulously, so that any mistakes, whether factual or typographical, are entirely of my own making.

G.F.
Sandy Brow,
Tarporley, CW6 9EH

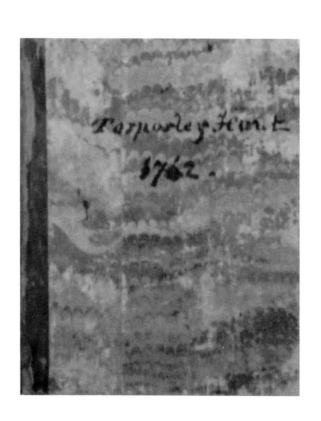

Tarporley Hunt
1762.

Introduction

THE REASON FOR WRITING THIS BOOK is to put on record the annals of the oldest continuously surviving hunt club in England and to republish with them Rowland Egerton Warburton's *Hunting Songs*. The two are inseparable, if one is to appreciate both of them fully, though the atmosphere of the Tarporley Dinners is impossible to capture on paper. Lord Willoughby de Broke described the songs as breathing 'a spirit of good fellowship in the hunting field and conviviality in the Club, to the accompaniment of a jolly jingle of bits, spurs and claret glasses and the music of the hunting horn'.

But by introducing the Hunting Songs to the modern generation and recounting some of the deeds of the Cheshire hunting field, it is hoped that the book will provide a better appreciation of the sport of fox-hunting. There has always been a misunderstanding, not entirely unjustified, as to why the premier sport of the English countryman should be to follow on horseback all over the countryside a pack of hounds intent on killing a wild animal which has no other apparent use. It is certainly inedible, even if the 2nd Duke of Northumberland once set an example, after a particularly good run, by having the fox's head devilled and eating the greater part of it.

Hunting has proved to be the most effective way of controlling what is otherwise a pest and above all, as well as providing healthy enjoyment, it has contributed in a very great measure to the rural economy. There have, and always will be, and now more vociferous than ever before, an element of the population in both town and country, who see it as the height of decadence. But let it be known that fox-hunters are preservers, both of the fox and the countryside as we know it. Were fox-hunting to be abolished, the species would be virtually wiped out and not without a great deal of cruelty and suffering. There is plenty in these pages, in the poetry in particular, to give the antagonists second thoughts.

This is a history of Cheshire Fox-hunting up to the outbreak of the Second World War and is especially intended to be a contribution to the social history of the County Palatinate. It is essentially about people and I hope the reader will get pleasure from studying the *curricula vitae* of all the Members at Appendix A.

I suppose my first recollection of the Club, apart from going to Tarporley Races as a child, was when I went to the Tarporley Jumps a few years after the War and saw Old Mo and his fellow Members in their grey bowlers and thinking what a splendid lot of old buffers they were. Little did I think that the Club would become an integral part of my life.

I first became intimately involved when Dick Verdin approached me at a cocktail party in July, 1962 and asked me if I would care to help him by writing a short history of the Tarporley Hunt Club for the Bicentenary dinner menu. I decided to compile a list of the Presidents as well, showing where they lived. The research for this and two hundred years of history meant the burning of a great deal of midnight oil, but I enjoyed every minute and used to go over to Stoke to read my typescript to the Honorary Secretary for his approval.

I had mentioned the fact that in 1805 the Club had employed a careful man to pour out the wine. 'Scrub that out,' said Dick. 'Who cares about the bloody butler?' I was somewhat taken aback, but had the last say by putting it in a footnote.

At the dinner, to which Dick had very kindly squeezed me in, the Earl of Halifax responded for the Guests. Dick had sent him an advance copy of my history and the only reference he made was to begin by saying: 'Your Grace, My Lords and Gentleman, I see you used to have a careful man to pour the wine. I am afraid tonight he has been far from careful!' Dick had the grace to catch my eye and guffaw with laughter.

On Dick's retirement as Secretary I had the honour to be elected in his place and it is rather nice to think that there have only been him and one other since my godfather, Brian Egerton, undertook the duties from 1897 until his death in 1937. My first President as Secretary was Ronald Antrobus, aged 86. I certainly had my baptism of fire. He declined to take the Business Meeting, leaving me to act as both President and Secretary, remaining seated in my capacity as the former. At one stage I glanced down at him to find that he had nodded off, his beard in his chest. That evening, whilst I was struggling into my stiff collar, his chauffeur telephoned to say his ancient motor car had broken down irretrievably. With but half-an-hour to spare I had to get the Vice-President to deputize and he was eighty-eight. Spurred by his beloved Marjorie, Sir Harold to the rescue came. There were but a few minutes before the King of the Hellenes was due to arrive. Nevertheless the Acting President insisted on being taken up to the Hunt Room to sit in the President's chair to rehearse a speech I wanted him to make, as it was the Royal Caledonian Hunt Club's Bicentenary and we had sent our greetings. Thereupon he dropped his glasses and I all but split my breeches, retrieving them from under the table. We got downstairs just in time.

I

The Reverend Obadiah takes the chair

ON NOVEMBER 14TH, 1762 NINE YOUNG SPORTSMEN met for the first time at The Swan Hotel, Tarporley, and those who had them brought their hounds with them to hunt hares in the neighbourhood. Whose idea it was, where it originated and what they all had in common have never been revealed, apart from their desire to indulge in the pleasures of the chase and enjoy each other's company at what was to become a regular social gathering. As it turned out, their choice of Tarporley was to make it the metropolis of the Cheshire Hunt in the years to come.

They solemnly undertook to keep to their Rules by signing the first page of their record book beneath the following resolution:

> We whose names are hereunto subscribed do agree to meet (at Tarporley) twice annually. The first meeting to be held the Second Monday in November & the second to be fixed by the Majority of the Members who shall meet at the first, Each meeting to last for the space of seven days.+ We do likewise agree to submit to all the underwritten Rules & to all such Rules as shall be thought necefsary by the Majority of the Society for the better keeping of the Same.

> +The first <u>hunting day</u> is meant by the 2nd Monday, the Gentlemen having agreed to meet overnight.

In the pages which follow, the names and signatures of subsequently elected Members are recorded and twenty-four such rules are defined, regulating dress, imposing fines for non-attendance and generally laying down the conduct of their meetings. Indeed the 5th of these original rules reads:

> Any Members that shall cause or make any disturbance during the Meeting (upon refusing to submit to the sentence pass'd on them by the majority of the Society) shall be immediately expell'd.

And in February, 1764 it was:

> Voted that no member shall be entitled to any Priveledge [*sic*] of this Hunt that has not signed his Name in the Book, in his own hand writing.

THE FOUNDERS WERE:

The Rev. Obadiah Lane of Longton, Staffordshire, aged 29, the first President.

He was a scholar of Winchester and a graduate of Emmanuel College, Cambridge. In 1764 he married Sarah, the sister of John Crewe, later 1st Baron Crewe of Crewe. In 1779 he resigned owing to ill health and was made the Club's first Honorary Member and died the following year, aged 47. He was perpetual Curate of Blurton, near Longton, from 1758 to 1772 and was a Prebendary of Lichfield (Gaia Minor) from August, 1767 until his death.* He had two daughters, Elizabeth, married to the Bishop of Peterborough, and Frances, whose husband was a General Watson.

John Crewe, aged 22. The son of the Rev. Dr Joseph Crewe, Rector of Astbury, and a cousin of John Crewe of Crewe and of the President's wife.

---

* Le Neve's *Fasti Ecclesiæ Anglicanæ* gives no reference to any other benefice. He is described in his banns of marriage as 'clerk of Barthomley', his bride being rather puzzlingly a 'spinster of Malpas'. In his will dated September, 20th, 1779 he described himself as: 'of the City of Chester, Clerk' and the document is witnessed by 'S.Leet, Pyed Bull, Chester' and a maid servant, but there is no trace of him in the Chester Diocesan records. Regarding his academic career, although he was in VI Book, the highest class at Winchester, he failed to get into New College. Nevertheless there is an entry for him in *Alumni Oxonienses* as follows:

> LANE, OBADIAH, *of Emmanuel College, Cambridge (B.A., 1756) M.A., 1759; in corp. 7 July 1759.*

He was a sizar at Emmanuel in November, 1751 and became pensioner in November, 1752 and graduated as above, but strangely rated no entry in *Alumni Cantabrigienses*.

The Hon. Booth Grey (3)   *George Wilbraham (5)*   *Roger Wilbraham (9).*   *The 1st Earl Grosvenor.*
                                                                  (From a portrait in oils by   *(From a portrait in oils by*
                                                                  Pompeo Batoni)   *Henry Morland, RA)*

Dr Crewe had been previously Rector of Barthomley and before that of Mucclestone. In 1763 John bought Bolesworth Castle from James Tilson, the original builder, but sold it again in 1785 to Oswald Mosley. He was Secretary to the Club until his death in 1786.

The Hon. Booth Grey of Wincham, also aged 22.

The Deputy Secretary, who on occasions signed himself '*locum tenens* Secretary'. He was the second son of the 4th Earl of Stamford. One-time M.P. for Leicester, he frequently stayed with his brother at Steward's Hay to hunt with the family's private pack of hounds at Bradgate in the latter part of the century.

Sir Henry Mainwaring, the 4th and last baronet of Over Peover, a thirty-six-year-old bachelor.

He had inherited both the title and the property at birth, the posthumous son of Henry, the younger brother of Sir Thomas, the 3rd baronet, who lived at Baddiley Hall. Henry had bought Peover from Thomas, but died in July, 1726, three months before Thomas and four months before Harry was born. In 1788 Sir Harry was invested with a gold medal for having attended fifty meetings.

George Wilbraham, aged 21, the son and heir of Roger Wilbraham of Townsend, Nantwich, who had died in 1754.

He had been to Trinity College, Cambridge. He built Delamere Lodge, Cuddington, later known as Delamere House, from designs by Wyatt. He was 'heir male of this ancient and knightly family, the elder line of Woodhey having terminated . . . about the end of the XVII Century'.

The Rev. Edward Emily, aged 23.

He came from Woking in Surrey and only attended two meetings. He had just succeeded his brother to the family estate at West Clamdon. He was later appointed Dean of Derry but subsequently exchanged his Irish Deanery for several English benefices, mostly in the Diocese of Salisbury, which he enjoyed as well as holding office in the Exchequer.

Richard Walthall, aged 29, of Wistaston, Crewe.

He died unmarried in 1766.

Robert Salusbury Cotton of Combermere Abbey, aged 23.

He succeeded his father as 5th Baronet in 1775 and was also later M.P. for the County of Chester. His hospitality at Combermere was renowned. He was the father of Field-Marshal Lord Combermere, who distinguished himself in the Peninsular War and in India, also a Member of the Tarporley Hunt Club, 1800 to 1836, his campaigns preventing him from being President.

Roger Wilbraham, George's younger brother aged 19.

He was up at Trinity College, Cambridge, of which he was later a Fellow. Like his brother, he spent some years on the Grand Tour. He became a celebrated bibliophile and was the last of the nine founders to die.

Elected at this first Meeting were Richard and Arthur Barry from Marbury, the second and third sons of Lord Barrymore, and Thomas Cholmondeley from Vale Royal. All three were over forty, considerably older than the others, whose average age was twenty-five including Sir Harry, the eldest at 36.

The Members had assembled at The Swan to enjoy hare-hunting and those who kept harriers brought out their packs in turn. Rule 8 provided that:

> If no Member of the Society keeps hounds or if it should be inconvenient for him to bring them, a Pack must be borrowed and kept at the Expense of the Society.

By Rule 3 it was already decreed: 'The Harriers never to wait for any Member after eight o'clock in the Morning.'

So far as their prandial arrangements were concerned, Rule 4 and Rule 9 respectively stated:

> If the majority of the Hunt prefent are at home on the hour Dinner is order'd they are not expected to wait.
>
> Three Collar Bumpers to be drank after dinner & the same after Supper. After they are drank, every Member may do as he pleases in regard to drinking.

But in November, 1763 it was 'voted that after supper but one glass is obliged to be drank'.

A 'bumper' is a wine glass filled to the brim. The definition of a 'collar glass' is obscure, but supposedly contained what was then a bottle of claret. The 'collar' was possibly simply a quilling round the glass. The Club possesses four large faceted-stemmed goblets, engraved 'To All True Sportsmen' within a beaded border, but they are of a date two or three decades later and probably replaced the 'Admittance' Glasses. They hold half a pint. These in turn were superseded by rummers of a much smaller size, engraved on one side 'Success to the Tarporley Hunt' and the Club's motto '*Quæsitum Meritis*' on the other, each with open branches of oak leaves and acorns.

It is a tradition of the Club to drink the *Quæsitum* on admittance.

By Rule 12:

> The houfe Bill must be payd the Seventh day of Each meeting, & after that is done every Member has the liberty of going after his own Inventions.

And they laid down that thenceforward 'all single, or private engagements must yield to the time fixed for the Meeting of this Society'. Eight years later they 'voted that the Club in general do not dine out by invitation'.

It is clear that before proceeding at all they agreed that the Reverend Obadiah should be their first President and appointed Crewe as Secretary with Grey his Deputy. As recorded at the back of the book it was the duty of the latter to carry out two preliminary orders, the procurement of a Balloting Box with eighteen black and eighteen white balls, and also

> for this Society two Collar Glafses, & two admittance Glafses of a larger size. O.LANE Pres:
> Mem:ᵐ An Exprefs was sent this meeting to Chester for a Chine of Mutton by Obadiah Lane Clerck.

It was also ordered that 'Mr Coton [*sic*] have the thanks of the Society for a set of Silver Bottle Tickets. In February, 1763 'a deep snow occasioned this meeting's breaking up on the fourth day.' In November Mr O.Lane was thanked for his present of two dozen of Doyly's [napkins] – a small indication that he was to some extent of private means.

Booth Grey was ordered after the 11th Meeting to procure a book case for the small library they had, consisting of

> 17 volumes of Heber complete
>   ditto.   Annual Register
> Pocket Library
> Oxford Magazine
> Howard's Thoughts
> Oxford Sausage
> Hunting book

Heber, the forerunner of *The Racing Calendar* had been given by Arthur Barry. In addition to the Annual Register they also voted to take a Court Calendar annually. *The Oxford Sausage*, first published in 1764, consists of select poetical pieces written by the most celebrated wits of the University of Oxford. By 1799 two London Papers were provided during each Meeting and this continued into the XX Century. In Edwardian times the following order was sent each year to Wyman & Sons, Newsagents at Crewe Station, to be sent daily to Beeston Castle:

Manchester Guardian	Times
Morning Post	Daily Graphic
Daily News	Standard
Daily Telegraph	Daily Mail
Liverpool Courier	Daily Express
Sporting Life	Sportsman
Sketch	Tatler
Chester Courant	

'Also please send Bradshaws for October and November'. In November, 1782 there was evidently quite a ceremony when:

> This Hunt. Mr Beckford's Book on hunting being presented in due form by Mr J. Arden, the Secretary and two Alderman attending, Mrs Egerton's Health was drank in a Bumper in a goblet.

William Egerton of Tatton was President and his wife had presented him with a daughter a fortnight previously. At this same Meeting her father, Richard Wilbraham Bootle, had been made an Honorary Member, but the connection between Peter Beckford's *Thoughts Upon Hunting*, first published in 1779, and the President's wife is obscure.

In February, 1764 they had decided that each President should provide 'two Dozen of Franks during his meeting for the use of the Society'. These were envelopes bearing the signature of a person entitled to send letters post free.

It having been Proposed in November, 1766 that the Rules of the Hunt 'be written and hung up in the Room during the Meeting, it was carried in the negative, but that any member has a right to take a copy of the Rules for his own private use'.

In February, 1775 the Secretary was to order two dozen of the Hunt tumblers, but none has survived.

Despite the high-stake wagers of that era, there is no mention of bets in the annals until November, 1784, when

> Mr T.Brooke having been detected in making a wager in the dining Room contrary to the rules of the Club of £1. 1. 0. to half a Crown with Sʳ Pʳ Warburton forfeited the Wager.

The year before, Booth Grey had 'moved that no Cards or Dice be allowed after the first toast after Supper, each Member so offending against this Rule must pay two dozen of claret. The above rule was carried by a Majority of four, the President being counted as two'.

Out hunting they had soon changed their quarry to the fox, the chase of which was to provide infinitely more excitement. Hugo Meynell's Quorn regime was already well under way with the new Leicestershire style of riding up to the hounds and flying the fences as they came. In *A Description of the Country from thirty to forty miles round Manchester* Dr. J. Aitkin wrote of Tarporley in 1795 as

> chiefly remarkable for being the place where a number of the principal gentlemen of the county meet at an annual hunt, equally consecrated to the pleasures of conviviality and those of the chase. The neighbouring open heaths of Delamere Forest afford a favourable ground for the latter pastime.

From Tarporley quite a lot of the sporting activity was indeed in the Delamere Forest area as well as the immediate vicinity, within a hacking radius of which was then as now some of the best dairy district, much of it yet to be fenced in.*

But in Patent Rolls, dated 1425, at the Public Record Office there is 'Confirmation of a Charter (dated 1285) to the Abbot of Chester, granting the right to course foxes and hares throughout all the forests of Cheshire', which must be the earliest known reference to fox-hunting in the county. And further proof, were it needed, that foxes are indigenous to the area, came to light in a bog at Lindow Moss in 1984, when the only clothing on the body of a man, battered, garrotted and with his throat cut about 2000 years ago, was a fox fur band.

Delamere Forest was not the only place in Cheshire where there was 'an annual hunt'. There used to be the 'Nantwich Annual Hunt' followed by a ball at the Crown Inn and a notice dated 1791 advertised the Malpas Hunt. 'The Presidents hope to be honoured with the presence of their friends at the Red Lion – dinner on the table at half-past two o'clock.' In 1790 the same time was advertised for dinner at the 'Whitchurch Annual Hunt: *N.B.* Harriers will throw off near the town on Tuesday and the next morning R.P.Puleston's (Esq.) fox-hounds will turn out in Horsemere Bog at seven.'

Several hunts lay claim to having the oldest established pack of fox-hounds. It is virtually impossible to establish who holds the crown. The West Norfolk dates from 1534, but as now constituted only from 1892. The South and West Wilts., according to *Baily's Hunting Directory*, 'is probably the oldest pack of fox-hounds in England, for the 5th Lord Arundell of Wardour Castle kept a pack of hounds exclusively to hunt foxes between 1690 and 1700'.

The oldest by name, however, is the Berkeley which in the XVI Century had its kennels at Wormwood Scrubs and hunted all the way through Hertfordshire to Gloucestershire as far as Bristol. The Brocklesby, kept as a private pack by the Earls of Yarborough and their Pelham ancestors, can claim to be the oldest in the kingdom, dating from before 1700, whilst the Sinnington together with the adjacent Bilsdale country was first hunted in about 1680 by the 2nd Duke of Buckingham from kennels at Helmsley Castle. Mr Thomas Boothby hunted the Quorn country with what is said to have been 'the first pack of fox-hounds then in England' from 1698 to when Meynell founded the Quorn in 1753. His hunting horn came into the possession of his descendant, Reginald Corbet (189)† of Adderley. Eighteen inches long of buffalo-horn and silver it bears the following inscription:

> Thos.Boothby, Esq., Tooley Park, Leices.[*sic*]. With this horn he hunted the first Pack of Fox-hounds then in England 55 years – born 1679, died 1752, now the property of Thos.d'Avenant, Esq., County Salop, his Grandson.

---

* In *The Book of the Horse* S. Sidney writes on the origin of fox-hunting:

> The discovery of the value of bone-dust in fertilising pastures, and the profits from potato growing, made farmers insist on dividing their improved fields from waste land with which the county was intersected until war prices, after 1798, stimulated and made universal enclosures and reclamation.

† A Member of the Tarporley Hunt Club. The figure in parenthesis after a member's name refers to Appendix A.

Oulton Park Lodges, built c. *1775.*

However when Melton Mowbray was in the womb of time, Charlton was the fashionable place to hunt. With its origins in the 1670's, when two packs of fox-hounds were kept by the Duke of Monmouth and also a Mr Roper as Master and Manager. The Old Charlton became the Goodwood Hunt in 1750 and continued until the 1820's when the hounds were slaughtered on an outbreak of rabies, incidentally soon after the 4th Duke of Richmond himself had died from hydrophobia, having been bitten by a pet fox when Governor General of Canada.

It was on Sunday January 19th, 1738 that twenty members of the Charlton Hunt formed a dining club at the Bedford Head Tavern in London, thus becoming the first of its kind. It was reconstituted two hundred and fifty years later as a luncheon and dining club, its twenty members all active hunting men.

So of the surviving hunt clubs in the British Isles the Down Hunt Club is the senior, having been founded in 1757, still holding dinners annually in their Hunt Room at Downpatrick. The Down Hunt toasts, besides the Loyal, are 'Our Noble Selves', 'The Colt' (if the newly elected Member is present), 'Hunting' and, according to a former Treasurer, 'any other excuse for a glass'.

Seven years junior to Tarporley is the Shrewsbury Hunt Club, with a membership of 100, dating from 1769. Whilst promoting fox-hunting in the county, its prime purpose has been the holding of an annual ball. The members wear a blue coat, scarlet velvet collar, single-breasted buff waistcoat and either buff knee breeches with white stockings or black breeches with black stockings. It has never owned its own pack or organized its own hunting.

Of the others, Ireland's Northern Rangers were founded at Dundalk with a trencher-fed pack in 1774, when it was the custom to move from house to house in Louth and the northern parts of Meath during the season, spending a few days with each Member, hunting and depleting his cellar. From 1817 after the county packs came into existence, it became virtually just a dining club. In Scotland The Hunters' Club was instituted in August, 1777 and changed its name to Caledonian Hunt in January, 1778. It was granted the Royal prefix by George IV on his visit to Scotland in 1822 and the following year at the Aberdeen, Forfar, Kincardine and Banff race meeting the Caledonian Hunt used the Royal prefix for the first time. It is a tradition for its Members attending the Royal Caledonian Hunt race meeting on the Scottish circuit each Autumn to wear the club uniform.

In Cheshire in 1682 Sir Willoughby Aston of Aston-juxta-Sutton was out hunting nearly every day, with his accustomed quarries, the hare and the buck, as was an earlier Sir Thomas Mainwaring of Peover, whose diaries also frequently mention hunting and coursing. And by the XVIII Century more people were keeping private packs of hounds than might readily be supposed.

Paper was then at a premium and old letters and notices were kept to be used up for jotting down accounts, *etc*. on the reverse. One such letter in the Egerton of Oulton papers has thus fortunately survived. It clearly shows that the fox had been reinstated as a worthy quarry in Cheshire long before the Tarporley Hunt Club came into being and decided to change their allegiance from the hare:

GRANGE Nov.ʳ 2, 1740

DEAR SIR,

Last Sunday there arrived from Staffordshire the remainder of my black tans, so that I can now bring into the field nine couple of my own & have whelps to enter besides.

It is with the utmost sense of gratitude for the favour, that I now send you back the Hounds you were pleased to lend me, all except Trinkett, who suits our little pack so well that I must beg the continuance of her a while longer if you think proper.

We concluded our fox hunting yesterday with a very smart pace & shall now enter upon the more sober & less laborious diversion of Hare Hunting, & it shall be as fatal for any Hound of mine to run fox as mutton.

Heartily wishing you all the Diversion of the Season, I am

Silver mounted nautilus shell snuff box (maker's mark ID)

This was Philip Henry Warburton, aged 40, of Hefferston Grange, a distant kinsman of the Warburtons of Arley. The recipient was Mr Philip Egerton, aged 46, who had inherited Oulton from his uncle, the builder of the Vanbrugh mansion, and was descended from the younger son of the 1st Baronet, Sir Roland Egerton of Egerton and Oulton, whose wife was the co-heiress of Lord Grey de Wilton. Mr. Egerton died in 1776. The property passed to his brother John's second son, also Philip, who died aged 54 in 1786. This Philip's eldest son succeeded to the baronetcy in 1814.

In 1936 the Club acquired a silver-mounted nautilus shell snuffbox made by James Dixon of Chester and dated 1775.* The inscription on the hinged cover reads:

> The gift of Philip Egerton, Esq. of Oulton to Henry Belasyse Earth Stopper General to the Tarporley Hunt.

Beneath is engraved a crossed pick-axe and spade with a lantern below and a fox's brush and a pad above.

The inscription is a mystery for neither Philip Egerton nor his nephew were members. Although not recorded, it is likely that the Tarporley Hunt drew the Oulton coverts and the gift of the snuffbox box was a pleasant bit of 18th-century humour. It would have been sent to Belasyse by his old friend, as a memento of the rough night when, after a few glasses of port, they ventured out to stop the earths for their young guests' sport on the morrow.

A further inscription round the rim, 'And perpetual to Caerwys Aetatis 65 1775' indicates it was probably also a birthday present and commemorates their association with the Caerwys Hunt, of which Philip Egerton was the Comptroller that year. As well as an annual ball, the Caerwys Hunt also held coursing meetings. From records in the National Library of Wales Mr Egerton of Oulton is known to have been present at one on Sunday, November 13th, 1774. Belasyse lived in Chester and was an uncle to the 2nd Earl of Fauconberg. The Caerwys Hunt was an organization with Jacobite tendencies. The Corwen Hunt was another.

Fox-hunting was clearly established, but the first reference to 'the fox-hounds' in the Tarporley Hunt record of proceedings was in 1765. As hare-hunters the Club had chosen blue for their original uniform, which was not changed to the orthodox scarlet of fox-hunters until 1770. Some historians use this as the date fox-hunters adopted scarlet,[†] but by 1762 the Grosvenor Hunt at Eaton was well established and its uniform was a red coat with a green collar and waistcoat.

---

* It had come into the possession of a Mr Dunstan White of Swindon, who offered it to the Club. The Committee (in reality the Secretary) found it interesting 'but much deplore its condition' and made an initial offer of three guineas. After further haggling he let them have it for ten, as, for a feeling he could not possibly explain, he wanted the Club to have it.

† W.C.A.Blew, the editor of F.P.Delmé Ratcliffe's *The Noble Science*, commenting on a suggestion that it had its origin from one King Henry equipping, in the royal livery of scarlet, a corps for the destruction of foxes, wrote:

> I have been unable to discover any satisfactory reason for the adoption of scarlet. . . . At the time when even the eighth Henry was gathered to his wives, the fox was regarded as vermin; and the king, whichever Henry he was, would have been as likely to array the royal ratcatcher in scarlet as his band of fox-killers.

John, 1st Baron Crewe of Crewe, from a mezzotint by William Say after Sir Thomas Lawrence – courtesy National Portrait Gallery.

Mr John Crewe's hunters, from an oil painting by George Stubbs. The groom appears to be wearing something akin to the Club's original uniform.

The 1st Lord Grosvenor, later created Earl Grosvenor, was elected to Tarporley in November, 1764, but resigned five years later. He had succeeded his father in 1755 and been elevated to the peerage in 1761 in the Barony of Grosvenor of Eaton. Horace Walpole wrote at the time:

> Sir R. Grosvenor is made a lord, viscount or baron, I don't know which; nor does he, for yesterday, when he should have kissed hands, he was gone to Newmarket to see a trial of a racehorse.

During the previous decade, as Sir Richard Grosvenor, he had established his own pack of hounds at Eaton, hunting hares, foxes, deer and occasionally a carted stag in the company of a few close friends, notably Sir Roger Mostyn, Bt. and Mr Bell Lloyd.[‡]

Both are featured with Lord Grosvenor and his brother, Thomas, in Stubbs's famous painting, dated 1762. The scene depicts a stag after it had been brought to bay in a stream, where it has characteristically 'soiled', having had enough. Grosvenor, members of his field and the hunt servants are grouped around a gnarled oak on the bank and the scene has been generally thought by art historians to be in the vicinity of Eaton, the river being the Dee. Beeston Castle is prominent in the background, but it is impossible to view it thus from Eaton. Unless the artist took complete licence, the river is the Gowy at a spot near the Brock Hole at Newton-by-Tattenhall. At this time Beeston Castle was part of the Mostyn estates. In any event it is hardly likely that a carted stag would have been brought to bay within such a short distance of its release.

The huntsman, not hitherto named, is Peter Thomas, who was in charge of the kennels for at least ten seasons up to 1769. From lists of his annual disbursements, the Grosvenor Hunt's activities included hunting foxes at places like Halkin [*sic*] and Wruithin [*sic*] on the vast family estates. Besides millers' bills, *etc.*, his expenses included such items as:

p[d.] for a Fox	0. 5. 0
Diging for a fox	0. 5. 0
Bringing hounds home that was lost	0. 9. 0
p[d.] Paul Panton's Bill for Carron for Dogs	3.14. 8
p[d.] for Stoping Earths	3. 7. 0
p[d.] Earthstopers for striving to preserv the cub fox's	2. 6. 6

and even:

p[d.] for mending Partridge nets	0. 5. 0

For seven seasons Sir Richard rode a blood hunter called Belford. Got by a thoroughbred stallion called Cade it was said to be the best hunter ever known in Cheshire. But Stubbs had come on from Goodwood to Eaton in 1760, originally commissioned to paint a horse called Bandy, possibly a stable name, as it is not indexed in Heber, though he is mentioned in the agent's disbursements for 1760, a payment having been made to a Mr Thos. Smith 'for drawing pictures of Bandy and Trajan'. Stubbs is said to have stayed 'many months' and, in addition to his 'Mares and Foals in a wooded landscape' and other tasks, he worked on this large 'Hunting Piece' (59 in. × 95 in.), which, if an annotation in a Society of Artists catalogue is accurate, was exhibited there in 1764 and cost Lord Grosvenor 300 gns.[§]

In a small painting dated 1755 in the collection at Tabley House, near Knutsford, Sir Peter Leicester, Bt., elected to the Tarporley Hunt Club in February, 1764, is also shown wearing a green collar on his scarlet coat, so it is likely that he too was a member of the Grosvenor Hunt along with the three Barry brothers, Thomas Cholmondeley, John Leche and others, whose names,

---

[‡] In 1794 one of Sir Roger's daughters married the latter's son, Sir Edward Pryce Lloyd, 2nd Baronet and later created Lord Mostyn. Sir Roger's son, Thomas, was the sixth and last Mostyn baronet and the only member of the family to be elected to Tarporley. He hunted the Woore Country before becoming the virtual founder of the Bicester.

[§] George Stubbs, ARA (1724–1806) also painted Mr John Crewe of Crewe's hunters with a groom. Hounds with hunt servants in scarlet are seen in the background, but the *locus quo* is unknown. This oil painting, now in America, was sold at Sotheby's in 1969 for £36,000.

The Grosvenor Hunt, 1762, from an oil painting by George Stubbs. l. to r. to right of tree: Mr. Thos. Grosvenor, Lord Grosvenor (on Honest John), unknown, Sir Roger Mostyn, Bt., Peter Thomas (Huntsman) and Mr Bell Lloyd, the others in green livery being hunt servants.

like his, are all subscribed to a race which took place in 1752 at Wallasey,* where Grosvenor kept his racing stable. Apart from this and various lists of disbursements made by Thomas, the huntsman, and Henry Vigars, the agent, there are no records of the Grosvenor Hunt and its activities in the muniment room at Eaton.

But the sport enjoyed by the fox-hunters of Tarporley was by no means exclusive to the Club. *The Chester Chronicle* reported in its issue of November 13th, 1775 – the first year of publication:

> On Saturday last there took place the first subscription hunt of the season at Tarporley. Twenty-three of the Members were present, including the Earl of Stamford, Sir Thomas Broughton, John Crewe, Esq., member for the county, etc., beside a large number of non-subscribers. Each day was spent with the festivity peculiar to the Noblemen and Gentlemen of this Circle and on Thursday a further addition was made to the sports of the day by two races being run on Crabtree Green . . .

> There was an excellent diversion of the chase each day and several Foxes were killed and the whole was supported by the true spirit of the descendants of Nimrod.

---

* Racing under Jockey Club Rules used to take place on Wallasey Sands during the XVIII Century. For a note on the other race meetings in the county *see* Chapter V.

II

Hark to Bluecap!

WHILE THE MEMBERS OF THE TARPORLEY HUNT were planning the first of their biannual gatherings for hare-hunting and camaraderie at The Swan, John Smith-Barry, the fourth son of the 4th Earl of Barrymore, was busy forming and breeding his famous pack of fox-hounds, which eventually he kennelled at Speedwell Hill, off Watling Street between Sandiway and Hartford. He had taken up the sport a decade and more earlier.

His father, General Lord Barrymore, had been one of the Ten Cheshire Gentlemen who met in 1715 at Ashley Hall to decide which side to support during the first Jacobite rebellion that year. It was by the casting vote of their host, Thomas Assheton, that they chose in favour of George I, thus saving their estates and quite possibly their necks. To commemorate the occasion they commissioned full length portraits of themselves and these adorned the walls of the room where they met. The paintings were brought to Tatton Hall after Ashley was bought by the Egerton family in 1841 and are now on the staircase and landing there.*

Lord Barrymore was very much a Jacobite. In March, 1744 he was 'confined to his house [at Marbury] with a strong guard'. He was a close friend of the Pretender, whom he entertained there. In 1743 he had got his second son, Dick, though a Naval Lieutenant at the time and whom he called 'The Flag', to help with the negotiations between the English Jacobites and the French and to rally supporters in London and West-

minster. He even sent him to Dunkirk in January, 1744 to join the expedition the French were preparing against England. The idea was that young Barry with his expertise as a British Naval Officer could assist them in landing on the English coast. Once there, Dick formed a close friendship with the Young Pretender, who, according to the French Marshal in command, '*regarde sans cesse le fils de* my Lord Barrymore *qui a une trés jolie figure, mais qui me parait être une innocent victime des idèes de son pére; ce qui ne m'est de nulle ressource.*' The operation was abandoned.

In spite of this adventure Dick remained in the Navy and was even promoted to Commander in 1745 – this at his father's request to the Duke of Newcastle, Lord Barrymore being under arrest at the time. It was Commander Richard Barry who carried a letter from his father and Sir Watkin Williams-Wynn to Prince Charles Edward Stuart at Derby in December. In it they pledged £10,000, but it did not catch up with him until he had

Captain the Hon. Richard Barry, R.N. from a portrait by an unknown artist. (Private collection: photograph Courtauld Institute of Art.)

---

* The Cheshire Gentry were Thomas Assheton of Ashley Hall, aged 37 in 1715, Sir Richard Grosvenor, 4th Bart. of Eaton, 26, James, 4th Earl of Barrymore of Marbury Hall, 48, Charles Hurleston of Newton, died, the last of his line, in 1734, Amos Meredith of Henbury, 27, Alexander Radclyff of Fox Denton, Lancs., 38, Robert Cholmondeley of Holford, 63, John Warren of Poynton, 36, Henry Legh of High Legh, 36, and Peter Legh of Lyme, who died in 1744 and who had been sent to the Tower in 1694 on suspicion of another conspiracy.

A mural of Marbury Hall, c.1740, discovered at Hall Green Farm, Acton Bridge. (Courtesy Cheshire County Council)

reached Stirling. Sir Watkin, incidentally, sacrificed three fox-hunting seasons for the cause. In 1747 Dick Barry visited the Young Pretender at Avignon and on his father's death soon afterwards, he was returned to Parliament for Wigan, a seat the 4th Earl had held as an Irish peer. Lord Egmont later said of Richard Barry: 'Bred a Jacobite, but an extreme idle man and will attend little . . .'

In 1714 Lord Barrymore had bought Marbury Hall, near Northwich, from the trustees of his father-in-law, the 4th Earl Rivers, and having cased the old black and white structure in brick, added wings and built stables. He settled the property on Richard and his eldest son was left with the main family home in Co.Cork. All four of his sons and two of his daughters were by his third wife. Lady Penelope Barry, the daughter of his second marriage to the heiress of Lord Rivers, married General James Cholmondeley, a younger brother of the 3rd Earl of Cholmondeley and who commanded an infantry brigade in the Jacobite rebellion of 1745. The ceremony had been in the chapel at Cholmondeley and it was from their childless alliance the Rocksavage property passed to the Cholmondeleys. Arthur, the third Barry son was left Fota Island, another family property in Cork harbour, affectionately known as Foaty by the family and acquired by them in the XII Century. James, the 5th Earl, died in 1751, and was succeeded by his six-year-old son. Their seat, Castlelyons, from which at one time the Barrys ruled over 300,000 acres, was burnt down in 1771.*

Rocksavage was on rising ground above the Weaver and was built in the time of Queen Elizabeth I. It was there that John Barry, the youngest son, was born in 1725. In 1746 he changed his name to Smith-Barry on his marriage to the heiress of Hugh Smith of Weald Hall, Essex. At this time his Cheshire residence was Aston Park, near Runcorn, but in 1750 he commissioned James Gibbs to design Belmont Hall, Great Budworth, not far from Marbury. By which time Rocksavage had fallen into such rapid decay that Lady Penelope's half-brother, John Smith-Barry, once had occasion to draw his pack of fox-hounds through it.

Like other members of his family, John was of an extravagant nature and it was his wife, Dorothy, who became a trustee when their eldest son, James Hugh, was made heir to his maternal grandfather's extensive estates. However she died in 1755 at the age of twenty-eight and the boy only ten. John did not re-marry and thereafter concentrated on his hunting and racing. There was a younger son, Richard, about whom little is known, except that he was a bachelor and left Cheshire. John had two unmarried daughters.

---

* The senior line of the Barry family, in direct descent from the 4th Earl of Barrymore's eldest son, was now hell-bent on squandering its fortune. The Earldom became extinct on the death in 1824 of the 4th Earl's club-footed great grandson Henry, the childless 8th Earl, known as 'Cripple-gate', who had succeeded his brother, 'Hellgate'. Their sister, Lady Caroline, owing to the strength of her language was 'Billingsgate' and another brother, the Rev. Augustus, 'Newgate', supposedly the only prison with which he was not acquainted.

With the fox fast becoming a fashionable and superior beast of the chase, altogether a more exciting quarry to follow than the stag and the hare, hounds were being bred for speed. To put them to the test, challenges were made between rival sportsmen to race them on aniseed trails. Running trail scents for hounds had long been the custom and used to be on the programme at certain race meetings, Woodstock being one of them in 1681.[†]

Hugo Meynell, the acknowledged founder of the Quorn Hunt and its Master from 1753 to 1800, was ten years Smith-Barry's junior – his friend and rival. They were the chief exponents of their day at breeding hounds for speed. It was in 1762 that Meynell accepted a Cheshire challenge given in a spirit summed up by the rousing ditty:

> *They talk of Hugo Meynell and what he can do;*
> *We'll ride 'em and beat 'em, this Leicestershire crew.*
> *We've may be forgotten a lot that they knew,*
> *And we'll teach 'em, Eh, ho!*
> *How the Cheshire can go.*

Smith-Barry asked Meynell to produce a couple of hounds to beat his favourite hound, Bluecap, and one of his daughters, Wanton, for a wager of 500 guineas. By then he had his hounds kennelled at Sandiway with Thomas Cooper as his huntsman and Bluecap, whelped in 1758 at Weaverham Wood Farm, was fast becoming a legend in his lifetime. He was used as a stallion hound the season he was entered and his speed was so superior to the rest of the pack that it was necessary for him to be clogged by trailing a drag – a wooden block fastened to a chain secured round his neck with a strap and buckle – to prevent him from outstripping the pack; a handicap also known as 'trashing'. It is said Bluecap was once taken to London and completed the 180-mile return journey within two days.

[†] Robert Vyner in his *Notitia Venatica* quotes a 17th-century book, *Gentleman's Recreation*:

The old way of trial was by running so many *train scents* after hounds... Others chose to hunt the hare till such an hour prefixed, and then "to run the wild goose-chase" [which received its name from the flight] made by wild geese, generally one after the other; so that the two horses, after the running of twelve score yards, had liberty which horse soever could get the leading, to ride what ground he pleased, the hindermost horse being bound to follow him within a certain distance agreed on by the articles, or else to be whipt up by the tryers or judges, which rode by, and whichever horse could distance the other won the match. But this chase was found by experience so inhumane, and so destructive to horses, especially when two good horses were matched, for neither being able to distance the other, till both were ready to sink under their riders through weakness, oftentimes the match was fain to be drawn and left undecided, though both horses were quite spoiled. This brought them to run *train scents*, which was afterwards changed to three heats and a straight course.

The Match at Newmarket, 1762; Bluecap and Wanton beat Mr Meynell's hounds, from an oil painting by Francis Sartorius.

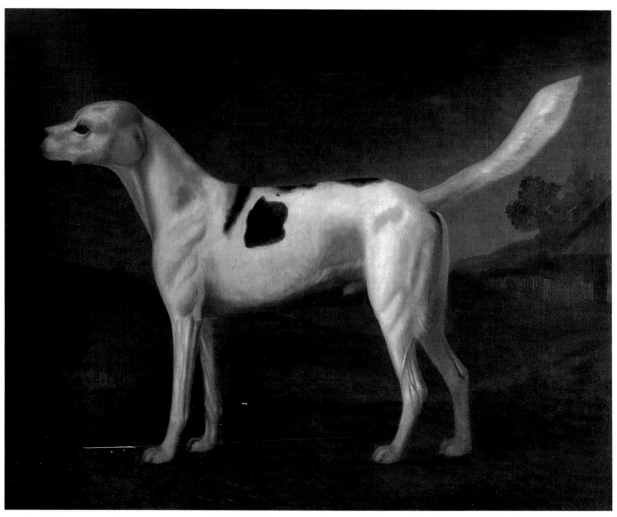

Mr Smith-Barry's Bluecap, 1758–1771, from an oil painting by Francis Sartorius. Symptoms of speed are the forearm under the very foremost part of the shoulder and the hocks well let down.

The match was arranged for September 30th over four miles of the Beacon Course at Newmarket and for two months the Cheshire couple were put into training at Rivenhall in Essex. Their diet comprised oatmeal, milk and boiled sheep's trotters, whilst the Quorn hounds were said to have been fed solely on legs of mutton. Bluecap, a 25" white hound with light blue badger-pied markings, aged four, and his daughter Wanton, aged three, were both seasoned working hounds. As their trainer, Smith-Barry appointed Will Crane, an innkeeper and former huntsman who would have preferred young hounds that had not been entered to fox and could with more certainty be taught to run a drag. He had been huntsman to the 7th Earl of Thanet before taking charge of the Badminton kennels under the 5th Duke of Beaufort and had subsequently been in the employment of Colonel Bullock at Folkborne Hall, Essex. Crane was proved right. At the first trials the hounds took no notice

of the drag, but at length, and after swallowing his pride, he found that by dragging a live fox along the ground and crossing them upon the scent, taking care to let them kill the fox, they became adept at running a drag. He exercised them three times a week on the turf of Tiptree Heath, covering anything from eight to ten miles each day following the drag.

When the match took place, in the face of a brisk wind, there were sixty mounted followers and the Quorn hounds were favourite at 7-4 on. They started from the rubbing-house at Newmarket Town End and ran to the rubbing-house at the starting point of the Beacon Course. Bluecap won, with Wanton a close second, and Meynell's Richmond beaten by upwards of 100 yards, his bitch, said to be Rarity, a daughter of Richmond, failing to run in. The time over the four miles was 'a few seconds more than 8 minutes' – an average speed of just under 30 m.p.h.* Only twelve riders finished the course and Tom

Cooper and Smith-Barry's hounds, from an oil painting by Francis Sartorius.

Cooper was the first up. The mare he rode that day was found to have become blind from her efforts. Crane was twelfth home on a King's Plate horse called Rib.

Bluecap's fame was nation-wide.

Bluecap and Wanton taught fox-hounds to scurry.

He was now almost fêted as a hero locally. 'We viewed him with as much veneration as we did Wellington and Blucher in after-years,' an old fellow once told 'The Druid'. When Cooper, on his way home from hunting, used to stop on the turnpike road to see his lad at school at Gorstage Coppy, the village boys used to rush out of the schoolroom with morsels of bread for Bluecap. They liked to boast they had fed the famous hound. At holiday time, for a treat, the huntsman used to tell his son to 'tak' Bluecap to lie on the bed with thee, if thee would.' It seems the boy Cooper was also a favourite with Smith-Barry, who, when Tarporley Week came round, presented him with a new suit of clothes and six china buttons to adorn it, the set made up of a fox, Bluecap, Wanton, Soundwell, Rockwood and lastly the boy's father mounted on his favourite hunter, Cheshire Cheese, and charging a gate.

Wanton was smothered in a fox-earth, but Bluecap, lived to the ripe old age of thirteen and sired a sufficiently prolific number of litters to make his bloodline truly established. The Fox-hound Kennel Stud Book does not go back to his day, so unfortunately his parentage is unknown; but research has shown that the first record of his offspring, other than Wanton, is five and a half couple entered at the Belvoir in 1765. He was also taken to the Brocklesby and the Milton. When twelve years old he was used at Lord Fitzwilliam's kennel, siring four and a half couple. One of these puppies, Juno, was drafted to the 5th Duke of Beaufort.

On Bluecap's death in 1771 Cheshire's first Master of Fox-hounds had a monument erected to his memory in the form of a small obelisk surrounded with iron railings in the corner of a meadow off Speedwell Hill, close by the old kennels and the cottage where Cooper lived – now

* The record time for The Derby is at an average speed of 35.1 m.p.h. and that for the Grand National 29.8 m.p.h. The fastest recorded time for a racehorse is 43.26 m.p.h. (over 1¼ m.). The highest speed any greyhound has been timed is 41.72 m.p.h.

Bluecap's achievement was bettered about thirty years later by a greyhound crossbred fox-hound bitch, called Merkin, belonging to the eccentric Colonel Thomas Thornton of Yorkshire. She is said to have covered four miles of open country in seven minutes and half a second, an average speed of 34.2 m.p.h. The Colonel sold her in 1795 for four hogsheads of claret and the promise of a couple from her future whelps; but not before he had made an open challenge of 10,000 guineas for anyone to produce a hound the same age to beat her over five miles at Newmarket receiving a furlong start. His dog hound Madcap was included in the challenge, but with half the wager and a reduced handicap of 100 yards. There were no acceptances but the speed of her trial is evidently authentic.

The thoroughly bogus Col. Thornton, a poseur if ever there was one, made a spectacular exodus from Yorkshire when he moved from his other home, Falconer's Hall, to Spye Park in Wiltshire in 1808. A description of his ostentatious cavalcade stretching several miles is given in Michael Brander's *A Hunt Around the Highlands.*

Colonel Thornton's cross-bred bitch, Merkin. (From a small oil painting by Sawrey Gilpin)

known as Blue Cap Cottages. The kennels themselves were converted into caged looseboxes. In 1959 the monument was presented to the Cheshire Hunt Committee by the Cunningham family, who were then selling the property, part of Forest Hill, and it was re-erected at the Forest Kennels at Sandiway, situated on land which was once in the middle of Barry's Wood at the eastern end of Delamere Forest.

The inscription on the brass plate reads:

TO THE MEMORY OF OLD BLUE CAP A FOX HOUND THE LATE PROPERTY OF THE HON^ble JOHN SMITH-BARRY

This obelisk, reader, is a monument rais'd
To a shade, though a hound, that deserves to be prais'd;
For if Life's but a stage whereon each acts a part,
And true greatness a term that's derived from the heart,
If fame, honour, and glory depend on the deed,
Then, O! Blue Cap. rare Blue Cap, we'll boast of thy breed!
If no tear, yet a glass we'll pour on the brute
So high-famed as he was in the glorious pursuit.
But no more of this theme, since this life's but a race,
And Blue Cap has gone to the death of the chace.

Cooper, too, has a memorial. He died on August 28th, 1778. A brass plaque was placed by a later Lord

Bluecap's grave.

Barrymore where his ancestor's faithful huntsman is buried in the south pew of Weaverham Church. Crane was over 90 when he died at Rivenhall.[*]

When Egerton Leigh (214) published his *Ballads & Legends of Cheshire* in 1867, he included his double acrostic, *An Elegy on Bluecap, a Cheshire Hound*:

Bluecap's Grave

BLUECAP's remains, his dust and	**B**one
Lie midst that meadow green and	**L**one
Untired in speed he won his	**U**rn
E'en harder than most heroes	**E**arn
Cheshire will never fox-hound	**C**all
Amongst her pack, that betters	**A**ll
Perfection write on *Bluecap's*	**P**all

The eminent 20th-century authority on the English fox-hound, Miss Daphne Moore, has described Bluecap as 'a beautifully proportioned 25" hound, extremely light of bone and full of quality'. From her research it seems certain that Bluecap's blood runs in the veins of every modern fox-hound, probably multiplied many times.

From Bluecap's deeds on classic heath,
To Sceptre and the rest;
Hounds, horses, all have fallen low
Before a Cheshire best.

* * *

Thomas Cooper, Huntsman to the Hon. John Smith-Barry,
c.1762, from a portrait in oils by Francis Sartorius.

[*] His brother and nephew, Tom, were in turn Stewards at Emral to Sir Richard Puleston, founder of the Wynnstay. The latter served with his master when he commanded the British Fencibles in Ireland in 1798 and saved his life by leading up a replacement when his horse was shot under him. Private Tom Crane transferred to the Coldstream and on Sir Richard's recommendation hunted Wellington's Fox-hounds during the Peninsular War.

IN NOVEMBER, 1765 an entry in the Society's Record Book reads: 'Mr John Barry, having sent the Fox-hounds to a different place to what he was ordered & not meeting them himself at that place, was sent to Coventry, but returned upon giving six bottles of claret to the Hunt.' The next reference to fox-hunting is in November, 1769 when the Club decided to alter the rule that 'instead of three collar glafses only one shall be drank after dinner except a fox is killed above ground and then after [two words obliterated (?the Club)] & Lady Patroness another collar glafs shall be drunk to Fox-hunting'. This, the second time that fox-hunting is mentioned in the record book, shows that by then they had clearly begun to give up their hare hunting.

Twelve years later a most serious offence was perpetrated when

> Offley Crewe & P.Warburton were found guilty of a most heinous offence in having cros'd a Hare's Scut with a Foxes Brush, & fined one gallon of claret each, a very light fine for such an offence. Mr R. Wilbraham Prosecuted, Mr Baugh [landlord of the Inn] was Evidence, together with Mr Peter Heron.

In November, 1775 the Club 'paid Earthstopper £1.1.0' for the first time, though doubtless Smith-Barry had long had the fox as his quarry. By 1777 fox-hunting was the order of the day as the following entries show:

> Ordered that a Cover or Covers on the Forest be made from the Stock Purse under the direction of Sr Pr Warburton, George Wilbraham and Mr Pr Heron, if leave can be obtained.

At the next Meeting in November it was 'Ordered that Mr Wilbraham is paid for sowing and enclosing a Cover £16: 0: 0 (Bill Mr.Wilbraham will deliver)': and then in February 'That Mr Wilbraham gives Mr Stevens as a Compliment for drawing the Lease of a Cover on the Forrest the Sum of five guineas'.

They evidently chose a place at the Old Pale on Eddisbury Hill near the 'Chamber in the Forest' where once stood the old hunting lodge of the Dones, the site of Queen Ethelfleda's 10th-century stronghold, for in November, 1780:

> At this Meeting a Fox was found for the first time in the New Gorse Cover near the Old Pail [*sic*]; being the maidenhead of the cover it was unanimously Xsend [*i.e.*christened] Snipe Hills.

Cooper with Cheshire Cheese, Bluecap and Wanton at Marbury, from an oil painting attributed to Thomas Stringer.

The Hon. John Smith–Barry and his hounds, 1749, from an oil painting by James Seymour.

The Hon. John Smith–Barry and his hounds, showing Bluecap trashing, from a painting by Francis Sartorius after the original by Seymour.

In 1779 John Smith-Barry, known to his friends as Jack (his name is written as 'Jack Barry' more than once in the Minute Book), was President for the second time, 'every member of the Hunt having passed the chair'. It was in 1773 that it was 'Voted unanimous that Mr John Barry is desired to sitt for his Picture for this Hunt. Mr John Barry very politely consents.' And the accounts of 1779 show that every Member subscribed 1 Guinea that year to pay the chosen artist, James Cranke (1746-1826) of Warrington, for the 'Grand Master's picture', the cost of which was £21-0-0 with £9-0-0 for the frame, £1-19-0 for the case and £2-1-0 for carriage, the balance of £8 12s 0d being defrayed by the Club purse. It has always taken pride of place at the end of the Hunt Room and measures 93 in. by 57 in. Smith-Barry is seated full length in a landscape wearing evening dress uniform of a scarlet coat with green collar, high green waistcoat, green breeches, white stockings and buckled shoes. Though portrayed not so successfully as his master,* Bluecap is at his feet with his head adoringly on his lap. Even so, several of the artist's works, including this, were at one time mistakenly attributed to Gainsborough. *See* frontispiece.

Other portraits of the great hound exist, including one dated 1774 by Thomas Stringer (1722-1790) showing him with a terrier and a groom standing behind a horse, possibly Cooper and Cheshire Cheese, with Marbury Hall and the mere in the background. The Club missed an opportunity to buy this picture when it was sold in 1977. The family possesses another very similar painting attributed to Sartorius with the subject purported to be the Honourable John. It is dated 1772, unsigned. The background is not the same and depicts a different horse with Bluecap and Wanton and no terrier, but it is almost certainly also by Stringer and from his pose the figure is a groom, or possibly Cooper, and certainly not Smith-Barry. The confusion has arisen by cataloguers misreading Stringer's FS monogram and he has often wrongly been called Francis.

The famous match was put on canvas for posterity, albeit somewhat fancifully, by Francis Sartorious (1734-1804), who also painted a handsome portrait of Bluecap. There are other paintings by him of Smith-Barry with Bluecap and Wanton, showing Marbury, and also of Cooper with the hounds and a portrait of the huntsman as well.

There is a painting by James Seymour (1702-1752) of John with his hounds in full cry across the Cheshire

countryside. It is dated 1749. There is a copy of it by Sartorius, distinguished, among other details, by one of the hounds being given Bluecap's markings and showing his drag chain. From the evidence of Seymour's painting, it is clear that Lord Barrymore's son had formed his pack of hounds at least a decade before Bluecap was whelped. There is also a mezzotint, *The Chace* by T.Burford, of this painting.

The family is still in possession of the Seymour original. A slightly altered duplicate by the same artist and the copy by Sartorius depicting Bluecap recently passed through a London auction house. It is an interesting reflection on the complexities of the art world that the undated Sartorius copy was sold for £35,000 (with no mention in the catalogue of it being a copy of the painting by Seymour with the substitution of Bluecap), whereas the former fetched £20,000 four months later.

John Smith-Barry died in his 60th year in 1784 and his eldest son, James, took over his father's pack of hounds. He had been elected to Tarporley in November, 1769 on coming down from Brasenose, had been President in 1771 choosing a Miss Byron as his Lady Patroness, but had resigned in 1780. As well as Belmont from his father, he inherited Marbury from his Uncle Dick in 1787. He also came into Fota, had houses in Tipperary, Dublin and Harley Street, London, an apartment in Paris and a villa in Naples, besides which he had Swearford Park in Oxfordshire where he established his Common law wife, Ann Tanner 'a gentle and refined woman', and their two sons and three daughters. It seems that his two spinster sisters, Anne and Catherine, and bachelor brother continued to live at Belmont. Kitty had been Lady Patroness to John Crewe in 1766 and her elder sister to John Arden eighteen months later.

Like his father, James Hugh was free with his money and it was in his young days that he formed most of his considerable collection of marbles and paintings, housed originally at Belmont and later at Marbury. Just before the next Meeting after he had been President, he set out on the Grand Tour with an introduction from Charles Townley (22) to his principal dealer, Thomas Jenkins, with whom he visited Pompeii the following May.

Jenkins wrote to Townley of his new client: 'As this Gentleman is well disposed and has spirit to pay for fine things I hope he will not purchase things of mediocrity.' This did not discourage him the following year from selling Smith-Barry the very restored *Equestrian Paris* for the vast sum of £300. However James's most expensive purchase was the large Antinous he bought from another dealer for £1,000. It proved to be the highest price for

---

* *cf.* Smith-Barry's portrait by Francis Cotes (1726-1770) at Tabley House. The similarity is remarkable.

James Smith-Barry poses in his Tarporley uniform for Pompeo Batoni
with a view of Rome beyond.

any antiquity brought back from Rome in the XVIII Century. Later in 1772 the twenty-six-year-old Barry was joined by Townley, his fellow Tarporley member, some ten years his senior in age, and they added further to their collections. He also went to the Levant, Greece, Constantinople and Egypt and did not return until 1776 to design a sculpture gallery for Belmont, but despite a financial crisis he was off again to add to his collection which he eventually moved to Marbury. The sculptures were moved to Fota House in 1936.

It seems that James also returned with a dark-haired Egyptian lady, who remained at Marbury for many years as a housekeeper and his occasional mistress. It was she who gave rise to the legend of the White Lady of Marbury. She expressed a wish for her body to be embalmed and buried inside the hall. The mummy was duly buried in a coffin beneath the spiral staircase, but when it was disinterred and taken to the family vault at Great Budworth, apparitions started. Taken back to Marbury, the hauntings ceased, but began again when a later generation also had a distaste for it in the house and removed it once more. Returned yet again, it was eventually buried in a lead casket in the rose garden after the house was sold in the 1930s and supposedly many were the instances of her ghost being seen. At least some of the sightings were more likely of a latter-day housekeeper, who lived there alone and walked about the grounds at night.*

Charles Townley became a member of the Society of Dilettanti, which James joined two years later. Sir Watkin Wynn was elected in 1776 – they were mainly noblemen and gentlemen with a taste for the arts and the antique, usually stimulated by the Grand Tour. It was founded in about 1733 as a dining club and had complicated ceremonies and dress, the President attired in a scarlet toga.

Townley, who signed himself Chas. Townley and not Towneley as some authorities give his name, much enjoyed entertaining friends and visitors in his home at Park Street, Mayfair, where, it was said, 'his marbles were so arranged with such accompaniments that the interior of a Roman villa might be inspected in our own metropolis.' He also designed a gallery at Towneley Hall for his marbles and terra cottas which the Trustees of the British Museum were to purchase from his executors in 1805 for £20,000. His gems, coins, bronzes and other items from his collection were added in 1814.

For each year abroad James Barry, like Townley and the others, was obliged to pay a guinea forfeit, but he evidently took his uniform with him. In a large canvas, 93 in. by 60¾ in., painted on one of his visits by Pompeo Girolamo Batoni (1708–1787), he stands, full length in a somewhat arrogant pose. With his tricorn hat and gold-tipped cane in his left hand and a view of Rome behind, he wears a scarlet velvet coat, gold-braided green velvet waistcoat, green breeches, white silk stockings and gold buckled shoes. The painting was sold by the Smith-Barry Estates at Sotheby's in 1988 for £95,000 and is in a private collection in Germany. The two Wilbraham brothers had also each been painted by Batoni.

During his father's lifetime James Hugh had started his own pack of fox-hounds and appointed an old retainer, called Bratt, as his huntsman. He had leased a hunting box at Ruloe, near Cuddington, and had plans to rebuild it extensively. But he was not at all popular in Cheshire and got himself warned off most of the estates over which his father had been accustomed to hunt and after a while was restricted to the family's own land.

There is no indication of what had happened when he and his uncle had resigned from the Club in 1780, four years before his father's death. The entry merely reads: 'Mr R. Barry and James Jnr. Barry having desired to withdraw their names, the same was complied with.' He did, however, continue to hunt despite the general dissent and it was even alleged that he persuaded Richard Bratt, to get a man to run a drag line in the early hours of the morning from his kennels at Ruloe to a covert he knew was to be drawn later in the day by his former fellow-sportsmen.

Despite this, when canvas Honours Boards were made some eighty-five years later to commemorate the Presidents, like that of his illustrious father his name was painted in red as a former Manager of the Cheshire Hounds. But this is not strictly correct and due to the artist following faulty information.

Jack Smith-Barry, his young wife, his sister, Lady Ann Taylor, his two brothers, Richard and Arthur Barry, his sons and daughters and a score or so of his descendants down to Arthur, the first and last Lord Barrymore and his children, lie entombed together in the family vault beneath the Lady Mary Chapel at Great Budworth. With them, too, is sixteen-year-old John, one of his great grandsons, who died at Burney's School at Greenwich in 1834, as a result of flogging for dressing up in the Master's cap and gown or some such minor misdemeanour.

---

* The family notes written by the mother of Robert Smith-Barry (283) make no mention of this legend, but they do include an authentic account of Marbury's other celebrated ghost, the Marbury Dun. The legend goes that the mare galloped from London to Marbury between sunrise and sunset to fulfil a wager. Lady Charlotte's version is that the horse was going to be run in a race at Doncaster, when news came that Marbury was going to be searched in connection with Lord Barrymore's Jacobite activities. It was galloped to Marbury, swam the mere, brought the warning in time and was buried in silver shoes on the banks of the mere. Lady Charlotte's husband, however, looked upon it as simple legend, and an excavation in the equine necropolis in the spinney produced no silver horseshoes.

Bluecap at Marbury.

TARPORLEY HUNT CLUB
RULES, NOVEMBER, 1993

Patron	**H.R.H. THE PRINCE OF WALES, K.G., K.T., G.C.B., A.D.C.**
President	**PHILIP JOHN McLEAN BODDINGTON, ESQ.**
Lady Patroness	**MISS SARAH BODDINGTON**

I.—The Annual Meeting of the Club shall commence on the last Monday in October, should there be five; otherwise, on the 1st Monday in November, and shall end on the Saturday following.

II.—Each Member shall appear at Dinner in strict uniform, *viz.:* Scarlet Coat with Green Collar, Waistcoat, and Breeches or Black Trousers, or forfeit Five Sovereigns.

III.—Any Member appearing on the Field with the Hounds without a Scarlet Coat and Green Collar during the Hunt Week, shall be fined One Sovereign for each offence.

IV.—The business of the Club shall be conducted by a Committee, composed of the President and four elected members, one of whom shall be Honorary Secretary. On the death or resignation of one of them, another shall be appointed at the ensuing Meeting.

V.—The number of Members shall not be more than forty, being qualified by Property, Family or Residence in the County. Any member qualified by residence only shall, on his ceasing to reside, cease to be a Member of the Club.

VI.—Each Member shall be proposed in advance to the Secretary. If no more than two Members object, all having been notified, he shall be elected by Ballot; fifteen Members or more must be present and ballot; three black balls shall exclude.

VII.—Each Member on his Election shall pay One Hundred Pounds, whether married or single; and each Member marrying after his Election, on each event, Twenty Pounds.

VIII.—The charge for guests and dining fees for Members will be settled by the Committee each year and notified to Members when notices of the Meeting are distributed.

IX.—The Members shall meet on Wednesday Morning in the Hunt Week to settle the business of the Club.

X.—Each Member shall be President in rotation, assuming office on May 1st, and the following year Vice-President. Should the President be unable to attend the Annual Meeting in his proper turn, his term of office may be deferred at the discretion of the Committee, and the next in order shall become President.

XI.—Each Member of the Club shall give an Annual Subscription of Twenty Pounds.

XII.—Each Member is requested to fill up, sign and forward to his Bankers a printed authority for payment of the Annual Subscription on or before 1st October in each year, to the credit of the Committee.

XIII.—Every Member on his election is requested to send his Photograph before the next Meeting of the Club.

XIV.—If any Member's Annual Subscription, or the fines imposed by the Club, are not paid on or before the Wednesday of the next Meeting of the Club, the Member's name may be removed from the Club at the discretion of the Meeting.

XV.—Any person appointed Master or Joint Master of the Cheshire Hounds, not being a Member of the Tarporley Hunt Club, may be invited to become an *ex-officio* Supernumerary Member of the club during his or her term of office only, and any such persons at the termination of their Masterships may be invited to become Honorary Members of the Club so long as they continue to reside and hunt in the Cheshire Country. Ladies elected under this rule will be excused from wearing the Hunt Uniform as set out in Rules II and III except for a green collar on their Hunting Coats and will not be eligible to attend the Hunt Dinners.

XVI.—No new Rule, or any rescinding or alteration of an old one, shall be made unless ten Members are actually present and voting; and two-thirds of those voting shall be in favour of such new Rule, rescinding, or alteration.

MEMBERS, NOVEMBER, 1993

1949	Viscount Leverhulme, K.G.	1975	Lord Tollemache	1985	E. M. W. Griffith, C.B.E.
1951	C. R. Tomkinson	1977	Duke of Westminster	——	Hon. R. H. Cornwall-Legh
1956	A. D. Paterson	1978	S. P. Dewhurst	——	P. J. P. Hunter, M.F.H.
1957	Col. G. V. Churton, M.B.E., M.C.	1979	Major P. G. Verdin, M.C.	1986	R. J. McAlpine
1961	Major P. Egerton-Warburton	——	P. J. M. Boddington	——	D. M. Stern
1967	M. E. S. Higgin	——	R. C. Mosley Leigh	——	Randle Brooks
1970	E. G. M. Leycester-Roxby	1980	Sir Richard Baker Wilbraham, Bt.	1987	G. B. Barlow
1972	Capt. J. G. Fergusson	——	A. W. A. Spiegelberg	——	Major W. R. Paton-Smith
——	Sir John Barlow, Bt., M.F.H.	1981	R. J. Posnett	——	R. A. Gilchrist
1973	R. C. Roundell	——	Hon. M. L. W. Flower	1990	W. A. Bromley-Davenport
1974	M. G. Moseley, D.F.C.	1982	R. D. C. Brooke	——	A. G. Barbour
——	S. Z. de Ferranti	1983	H. D. Wilbraham	——	W. H. Midwood
		——	Hon. P. G. Greenall, M.F.H.	——	Marquess of Cholmondeley

HONORARY MEMBER 1985 Lord Grey of Codnor, C.B.E. (1935)

SUPERNUMERARY MEMBERS	**HONORARY MEMBERS** *(Rule XV)*
Mrs. R. F. Windsor, M.F.H. R. S. Williams, M.F.H.	P. G. Hunter Mrs. S. Z. de Ferranti J. Heler
D. H. Woolley, M.F.H.	Lt.-Col. P. B. Sayce J. G. Cooke

COMMITTEE

Capt J. G. Fergusson, *Hon. Sec.*   R. C. Roundell   H. D. Wilbraham   Viscount Leverhulme, K.G.

III

The Rules of The Tarporley Hunt Club

RULE I

THE ANNUAL MEETING

THE FIRST RULE OF THE CLUB was to fix the date for the Meetings and it has been strictly kept. It now reads:

> The Annual Meeting of the Club shall commence on the last Monday in October, should there be five; otherwise on the first Monday in November, and shall end on the Saturday following.

This traditionally sets the opening of the hunting season in Cheshire. The last day was changed from Friday in 1953, otherwise it has been the same since before 1799.

By the original rule the Society met twice annually, 'the first meeting being held the second Monday in November. (By the second Monday is meant the first hunting day, the gentlemen having agreed to meet overnight). The second Meeting to be fixed at the previous Meeting. Each Meeting to last a week. All single or private engagements must yield to the time fixed for the Meeting of this Society.'

But one exception was made in 1768 when there were six parliamentarians in the Club: 'Oct. ye 30th. Parliament meeting sooner than common this meeting by the consent of the majority was held a week sooner than appointed by Rule.' In 1766 it was agreed that the second Meeting should take place the last week in January, and was held annually until 1786, after which it was abandoned. For a few years, after 1766, the November Meeting was extended to a fortnight, but the second week was never well attended and soon lapsed.*

Letters were sent individually from the landlord, *viz.* in this case to his own Landlord, John Arden at Stockport:

> SIR,
>
> YOU are desired to meet your President, at *Tarporley*, on *Sunday* the ~~sixth~~ ___ Day of ~~February~~ ___ next.
>
> *** Dinner at Four o'Clock.
>
> I am, SIR,
>
> Your most obedient,
>
> TARPORLEY,   humble Servant,
>
> ~~January 15, 1780~~   *Joseph Southon.*
>
> *Please to let me know whether you will come, and what Stalls you will want.*

A notice like it also appeared in the local newspaper the week before. This one before the 1786 Meeting:

TARPORLEY HUNT

The Gentlemen are desired to meet their President at the house of John Southon, 29th October – Dinner on the table at four o'clock.

JOHN BOWER JODRELL, ESQ.
PRESIDENT.

---

*On rare occasions in recent decades a dinner for Members only has been held in the Spring, notably for Sir Richard Verdin on his retirement as Secretary of the Club.

or another if frost and snow were likely to interfere with sport; *e.g.*, on January 13th, 1767 when there was a deep snow:

> Meet at W. Baugh's, The Swan in Tarporley, 25th January. Meeting postponed till 1st February as further notice "on account of the weather."
>
> J. Smith-Barry. President.

Throughout the XIX Century the Club still met to hunt as well as to dine. In 1834 it was resolved

> That the President and each Member must attend or send an excuse on or before Tuesday under pain of being fined as before for not attending or sending an excuse before Wednesday. And that the hunt breaks up (in future) on the Friday morning.

Thursday was then the last hunting day. However, in 1871

> It was resolved that unless 5 Members put their names down as intending to dine on the Friday night the Club will be closed on Friday instead of Saturday.

On Thursday, November 5th, 1896 the entry in the Guest Book reads: 'Hard Frost. Members could not Hunt, so all returned home. No-one dined.' By then the number of Members staying at The Swan for the week had long since dwindled to a handful, but a few continued to dine together there on the Monday and Thursday nights in addition to the main dining nights of Tuesday and Wednesday. The last Thursday dinner was in 1904 when Sir Humphrey de Trafford (230)[*] and his guest, the novelist and sporting writer, Raymond Carew, had Mosley Leigh (245) as their sole companion. His father had once dined alone on the Friday back in 1837.

Lieut.-Colonel O. Mosley Leigh (245). 'Old Mo.'

The last-named, 'Old Mo', lived for Tarporley and it is no surprise to find his name in the Guest Book as one of the six members who joined their President and the Hon. Sec. to dine on Monday, October 31st, 1938, the last time the Club dined on the Monday. He was one of the die-hards who maintained the tradition of staying at The Swan,

invariably requiring assistance to his room. Thereafter dinners have only been held on the Tuesday and Wednesday with traditional toasts being drunk to 'Fox-hunting', to 'the President' and to 'the Guests' on the Wednesday night.

In the early days the majority would have stayed at The Swan, but as the years went on, many would spend the night with friends living nearby, such as the Egertons at Oulton. But this was not necessarily the case, no matter the distance involved. For instance in 1823 Lady Belgrave, formerly Lady Elizabeth Leveson-Gower, daughter of the Duke of Sutherland and mother of the future Duke of Westminster, who was born at Eaton two years later, wrote in her diary:

> Thurs. 6 Nov. B. went to breakfast at Tarporley & returned before 2... B. went at $\frac{1}{2}$ p. 3 to dine at Tarporley.

Eaton to Tarporley by the main road via the Old Dee Bridge is a distance of at least 15 miles. However such journeys were not always without frustration, especially after dining well at The Swan and the coachman had perhaps also imbibed a little too freely. In 1826

> . . . They all went hunting at Page's Wood. B. rode Lady. They had a good run but B. did not see it being 5 mins. late. He went to Tarporley & dined there & set out to return home in the Britchka[†] soon after 10 but in consequence of the coachman missing the way in Tarvin they went the wrong road & got to near Sandiway Head in the Forest and consequently did not get home till past 2 in the morning.

In the original Rules there were important conditions regarding non-attendance, the 1st rule being:

> Any Member that abfents himself must pay the Sum of One Guinea unless his excufe shall be allow'd of by the sitting Members. [To which was added] & if he shall attend any Part of the Time he must pay his share of the house bill for the whole, unless as above his excuse was allowed of— NB. Attendance for one day only the Forfeiture is One Guinea.

---

[*] Sir Humphrey, a strict Roman Catholic, was partial to his port and preferred to drink a tumbler of it as a nightcap instead of a whisky and soda. Bend Or's brother-in-law, George Cornwallis-West, stayed with him at Hill Crest for the hunting and one evening, late in the season, he noticed that, instead of vintage, wood port was on the tray. His casual enquiry if his host had run out of the former received the reply: 'No. It's Lent.' It was highly appropriate that his Presidential Gift to the Club should have been vintage port. In 1876 his father had given the Club a dozen large vine, leaf and hound-head pattern silver decanter labels, four sherry, four claret and four port. He was a celebrated whip and had a team of greys.

[†] A new type of travelling carriage, introduced from Austria in 1818. It had an unusual flat bottom and by the movement of different parts it formed an agreeable open carriage by day and a convenient bedchamber by night.

This fine was increased to two guineas at the 6th Meeting and to four at the 10th. And by the 23rd Rule: 'All forfeitures to be applyd for the benefit of the Society attending the Meeting when they are forfeited'.

By Rule 24 the President himself was liable to a fine of Five Guineas. This was voted to Ten Guineas at the 5th Meeting, though later made 5 gns., if President's excuse allowed, and it was also added that: 'If any Member absents himself for a night during the Meeting he shall forfeit one guinea for every such night of absence unless he shall have leave of the majority of the Hunt present.' In practice minor forfeits were incurred even when excuses were 'allowed'. In addition a rule was made for 'Any Member who advances the money for an Absentee, to be reimbursed by the Society in case of such absentee refusing to pay him, and the absentee to be expelled.'

One of the rules appertaining in 1799 required every Member to write his Excuse to the Landlord of the Inn, instead of the President, one fortnight before each Meeting; in Failure of which, to be subject to a Fine to be determined upon by the Members settling the Business.

The fine for non-attendance had been doubled in 1764 and again in 1767 and in 1818 increased to five guineas. These fines brought in considerable revenue and in 1766 it was voted 'Five Guineas out of the forfeits be given to the poor'.

It was recorded that in 1855 'the Rule imposing a fine of One Sovereign for non-attendance at the annual Meeting be rescinded.' But in 1864 a fine was imposed for not attending the Business Meeting. Not until 1895 were all fines for non-attendance abolished.

In the early years 'Mr Crewe and Mr Whitworth fined for lying out one night without leave', 'Lord Grosvenor having quitted the Hunt on the Tuesday without leave was fined five guineas' and conversely 'Leave granted to Mr Lane to go home on the Saturday night to do duty the next day' are typical entries in the register.

Illness sometimes accounted for absence. Dick Barry was a martyr to gout and his brother, Jack, and George Heron, Senior were also fellow sufferers. Charles Townley, James Smith-Barry, Ravenscroft and Sir Thomas Broughton were among those who were sometimes abroad, as well as the Wilbraham brothers. A rule had been passed at the 4th Meeting: 'Voted – that if any Member absents himself for two succefsive meetings the Secretary shall write an admonitory letter as per Marg. He shall be expelled the third unless he appears'. The preamble of the Admonitory Letter was to read as follows:

BY ORDER of the President & the rest of the Tarporley

Hunt I am to inform you that having absented yourself for the two last meetings you have incurred the penalty of the second Vote made at the fourth Meeting, which is as follows . . .

Although the strict rule was later altered to absolve those Members who 'were outside these Kingdoms', they still had to pay a guinea on their return. Before that it had been voted that

Any Member of this Hunt who shall absent himself three successive meetings on account of his being out of England shall submit to a fresh ballott.

'Every Member that does not attend must send his reasons in writing to the President' was an original rule and although no longer specified it is a time-honoured courtesy so to do. For instance in November, 1764:

Mr Wilbraham being on his travels [the Grand Tour which lasted another two years] could not attend.

Sir J. Stanley detained in Wales in expectation of an heir. [His wife was the heiress to Penrhôs, Anglesey].

Mr Cholmondeley, being just married, cd not attend.

Mr R. Wilbraham, pursuing his studies at Cambridge, could not attend. [In 1771 he, too, was to go on the Grand Tour.]

Mem. Mr President John Crewe had leave given to go to Chester to take a Flyer – but broke down.

These excuses were all accepted, although Sir John's son and heir did not arrive until November 26th. At the next Meeting he was fined for absenting himself four nights and for the 7th Meeting it is recorded: 'Sir John Thomas Stanley not altogether approving of the Proceedings of the last meeting, desired his name to be put out of the Book, which we altogether approved of.' The same year George Wilbraham, still on his travels, was allowed as was George Heron's excuse 'on account of his wife being near her time.' John Crewe was fined for lying out one night without leave but 'Obadiah Lane, having company at Home, cd not attend – allowed'.

George Wilbraham (a year or so after his return), Roger Wilbraham, Mr Arden, Mr Townley and Mr Crewe of Crewe (each more than once), Thomas Cholmondeley, Sir Peter Leicester, Stephen Glynn (signifying that he would have been expelled but for the intervention of the Secretary), Mr Ravenscroft, Lord Archibald Hamilton and 'Sir Watkin Williams' were all recipients of admonitory letters one year or another.

Despite having two foxes in saltire on his quarterings, the last named might just as well have not joined. Someone once a little unfairly described him as 'no sportsman'. He was only sixteen months when he succeeded his father, the 3rd baronet and the first 'Sir Watkin', a well known Jacobite, who was killed from a fall on the way home from hunting.* In November, 1767 when he was elected, '"Sir W. W. W." was fined 3. 3. 0 for absenting himself three nights without leave of the majority.' In February, 1768 '"Sir W. W. Wynne" having wrote, but his excuse not allowed, pays two guineas.' In October, 1768 '"Sir Watkin Williams" fined 4. 4. 0 for not writing to President' and again the following February. In November 'Sir W. W. Wynne not Appearing after having received an admonitory letter subject to the Vote of the 4th Meeting held . . .'

The next words are obliterated, but this meant expulsion. However it might be noted that in a list of amusements in which 'men of fashion delight in' given in *The Morning Herald* in 1782, Sir Watkin's is given as 'Acting' and Lord Grosvenor's was 'the Turf', a pastime said to have cost him £250,000. He was the only other Member of the Club to be mentioned. For all that, Sir Watkin was a jolly fellow, very musical and had his own private theatre at Wynnstay. He once rode on stage as St. David, mounted on a Welsh goat. He was a friend of Garrick and in 1775 he was elected a member of the Dilletanti Society.

In those days it was a custom for the ladies and gentlemen at Wynnstay to dine in separate rooms, so that those who sat at the horseshoe table need have no restraint on their potations.

'Dick' Whitworth was also a frequent absentee, but one of his fines was reduced to a guinea because he was attending Parliament. Neither he nor his Vice-President turned up for his Presidential Meeting and consequently 'Richard Whitworth, President, fin'd ten Guineas for not writing to the President. Lord Archibald Hamilton fin'd one Guinea, his excuse being allow'd & one Guinea as Vice-President.' In the absence of both the President and the Vice-President the Junior Alderman, in this instance Jack Smith-Barry, took the chair.

The Staffordshire M.P. must have been a popular fellow for on his resignation from the Club in 1779 he

Sir Henry Mainwaring, Bart. from a portrait in oils by Pompeo Batoni – courtesy National Portrait Gallery. This painting was sold at Christie's in 1975.

and Obadiah Lane became the Club's first two Honorary Members, the Rev. Edward Emily apart. It was 'the unanimous wish of the Society that the Revd. Mr Lane, as an Original Member, whenever he finds his health sufficiently re-established, may be considered as a Member of this Society.' That was the year the Club elected two more sporting parsons, George Heron, Junior and Offley Crewe.

The Rev. Edward Emily from Woking, one of the original nine, only attended twice and in November, 1764 it was voted he 'be no longer a Member of this Hunt, it being thought inconvenient for him to attend'. The Secretary wrote in 'Honorary' against his name on an earlier page, so by rights he must be regarded as the first Honorary Member.

The future Duke of Hamilton and Brandon failed to turn up on three more occasions and although his excuse of illness was accepted the third time, when he took no notice of his admonitory letter the fourth time he was excluded.

In February, 1774 it was noted 'Lord Killmorrey [*sic*] by his own desire is no longer a Member, but voted a Letter to be wrote to him that it is the wish of the London Hunt, that if he is in Town he will try the bond street

---

* Sir Watkin's second wife, who was a Shakerley and his own god-daughter, dreamed that he would be killed out hunting next day and besought him not to go. Her eloquent pleading had all but persuaded him, when a friend intervened and off he went, unable to withstand the ridicule and leaving his pretty young wife in an agony of tears. He got safely through a long run with Mr Leche's Hounds, only for his horse to stumble in Acton Park near Wrexham on his way home. His head struck what proved to be the only stone in the field and he never spoke again.

Covers [*sic*] as a member.' In November Charles Townley 'desired to resign, it not being convenient to him to attend' and it was hoped 'he will reckon himself of the Number of the London Hunt'. Although he had carried out his duties as President, his choice of Lady Patroness did not turn out to be a good example. Lady Almeria Carpenter, daughter of the 1st Earl of Tyrconnell, became the mistress of the Duke of York and acquired from him an obscene vocabulary.

In 1847 when the Rules were re-inscribed in the new register, it still applied that

> a Member not attending for two succefsive years, and not having written an excuse allowed by the Members present to be sufficient to be excluded.

But when it came to regular attendance it was to Sir Harry Mainwaring that the Club gave a Gold Medal. Although there is no record book for the year in question, fortunately the resolutions for this event exist on a separate sheet, probably a draft. In 1787 it was:

> Resolved
>
> That, to encourage and reward a regular and constant attendance at the Tarporley Hunt, each member, who shall have attended at fifty succefsive meetings without intermission, be intitled to a gold medal of the value of 5 Guineas to be paid for at the expence of the Society, which he shall solemnly engage to wear, during each meeting of the Hunt, pendant to his neck by a red Ribbon and that this honourable distinction be called the Order of Merit.

RESOLVED

That Sir Harry Mainwaring Bar^t. having attended for forty-nine succefsive meetings, and there being the greatest probability, from the strong & vigorous health which he at present enjoys, that he will with his accustomed exemplary punctuality appear at the fiftieth meeting, that a Committee of members of this Hunt be appointed to prepare such gold medal with an inscription thereon, expressive of the high sense entertained by the whole Hunt of his meritorious conduct. And that on some day in the Tarporley meeting in 1788 he be solemnly invested with the Insignia of such order, and that he be stiled [*sic*] and called the Grandmaster thereof.

RESOLVED

That on the first day of the meeting of the Tarporley Hunt in 1788 a Committee be appointed to fix the order and method of proceeding as to the forms and ceremonies to be observed in the solemn investiture of Sir Harry Mainwaring, Bart. with the aforesaid Order of Merit and that the day of the investiture being on the fiftieth meeting of the Tarporley Hunt be on that account intitled the first Jubilee of the aforesaid Hunt and be celebrated accordingly.

RESOLVED

That the Earl of Stamford, Sir Robt Cotton, J. Crewe, Esqre, Wm Egerton Esqre, Thomas Brooke & Roger Wilbraham Esqre form such committee.

Five years after the Investiture Sir Harry sent in his resignation. He was staying at the time with his old friend, Harry Stamford, with whom, in their younger days before the Club was founded, he had shared many adventures on the Grand Tour. In two caricatures by Thomas Patch (1725-1782) at Dunham Massey they are depicted together, studying monuments in 'The Voyage from Venice to Pola' and in the other at an inn in Florence enjoying more than just the visual delights of the city.

This is his letter of resignation:

Dunham Massey,
Oct.27th 1793.

Dear Sir,

It is with the greatest Reluctance that I find myself under the disagreeable Necefsity of desiring you to withdraw my name from the Tarporley Society. The repeated Returns of a complaint in my stomach renders me totally unfit for the enjoyment of so social a Meeting, which I have so long and so agreeably and happily attended, and shall ever retain a grateful Remembrance of the many Favours and obligations received from it. I sincerely wish you all every Pleasure and Happiness and am,

Dear Sir, your most faithful and obedient humble Servant
Henry Mainwaring

RULE II

EVENING DRESS

THE SECOND RULE OF THE CLUB is that: 'Each Member shall appear at Dinner in strict uniform, *viz.*: Scarlet Coat with Green Collar, Waistcoat, and Breeches or Black Trousers, or forfeit Five Sovereigns'.

The wording dates from 1890 before which the collar had been velvet.

It was the 1st rule, as recorded in 1799, except the fine was then five guineas, and this was the first mention of wearing hunt uniform at dinner. The collar was then velvet and it was also customary to wear a green velvet waistcoat until late Victorian times. From 1847 the fine was in sovereigns. However the very first Minute in 1762 reads as follows:

> The Lady Patroness of this meeting not having been appointed by the President himself, the obligation in Rules 14 & 15 is adjudged not binding, & Mr Wilbraham being one of the Society, who has got his drefs'd uniform made up, is thought the most proper person for that purpose –
>
> By Order of the Society
>
> J.CREWE, Sect*y*.
> B.GREY, Dep. Sect*y*.

Rule 15 stated: 'Should the Members of this Society in a party attend any of the Neighbouring afsemblys the President must ask the Lady Patroness for the time being to dance, should she be there.' Rule 14: 'All single or private engagements must yield to the time fixed for the meeting of this Society', later obsolete.

Although the field uniform was stipulated, no description of the proper dress clothes was given. But Mr Whitworth was fined two guineas 'for appearing in the Club Room in a Black Coat and Waistcoat' and Mr R.Barry a guinea the same year, 1767, 'for not having on a proper uniform waistcoat'.

Smith-Barry, when he sat for his portrait between 1773 and 1778, was wearing evening dress uniform of scarlet coat with green collar, green high waistcoat, green breeches and white stockings. He has a lace jabot and ruffs and cloth buttons. This was after the original field uniform had been altered. Sir Peter Warburton, in his portrait dated 1810, is similarly attired except that he has no lace at the wrists and his waistcoat is cut lower.

James Smith-Barry's version with a richly embroidered waistcoat, but with no jabot and only a hint of lace at the cuffs is shown in Batoni's portrait.

Although not officially recorded, it seems that a scarlet wool cape with a green velvet collar came into vogue in late Georgian or early Victorian times, but the only one known is that given to the present Secretary by Mrs Muriel Antrobus. It was formerly worn by her husband's ancestor.

It was in 1828 that Lord Belgrave had a motion carried that 'Trowsers be allowed in future' and they have remained a permissible alternative to knee breeches and stockings ever since, though those who wear them are very much in the minority.*

This is a convenient rule for any Member having the misfortune to lose a leg, notably Major Cyril Dewhurst (277) and Sir Evelyn Broughton (320). The former had four different artificial limbs, a riding leg, a golfing leg, a dancing leg and a bridge leg. He was Hunt Secretary and once had a bad fall into the brook at Page's. When he

Major Cyril.

Evelyn.

clambered out his foot was back to front to the consternation of Christo Codrington, a young visitor from the Beaufort, who, white as a sheet, was about to ask where the nearest doctor could be found. The Major vented a variety of oaths making it clear that he had broken his leg. His lone companion went a shade paler. (In later life he had a plum complexion.) 'Don't just stand there, man,' shouted Cyril, 'Go and telephone Tarporley 8 and tell my chauffeur to bring me out my spare!' There were few better men to hounds in his day, in spite of his 'swinger'.

Not so permissible are soft evening shirts which some Members, quite senior ones at that, have taken to wearing during the latter part of the present century.

---

*It is interesting that it was the future 2nd Marquess of Westminster who brought in this rather revolutionary change from tradition. Some twenty years later in the House of Lords, he used to wear a shirt collar 'of such extraordinary dimensions as to denote the most prodigal disregard for the cost of French cambric'.

When asked by Sir John Barlow (305) in 1978 to give a ruling, the Secretary said it was quite clear that 'strict' uniform meant a stiff shirt. However he did state that the amount of starch could be proportionate to the seniority of the Member in reverse ratio, but (looking at Ronald Langford-Brooke) for a Member to wear a completely soft shirt and get away with it, he would have to be very senior indeed. Following this ruling, in 1979 'Micky' Moseley was fined £1 for wearing a soft shirt the previous evening and a further £2 for announcing his

HENBURY HALL

intention of committing a similar offence the second night. By rights it should have been five times as much and that is without taking inflation into account.

Members have often been exhorted to wear club uniform when dining in each others' houses, though since the dinner jacket came into fashion this has seldom been observed except before going on to hunt balls. However, several such dinner parties were given at the time of the Bicentenary, when hostesses vied with each other in producing red and green menus. In recent years club waistcoats have been worn with dinner jackets when Presidents have given a Club Dinner, notably at Lord Tollemache's Presidential party in 1989 in a resplendent marquee at Peckforton Castle, following its sale. When

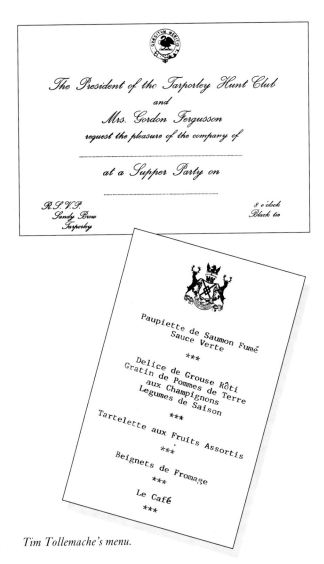

The President of the Tarporley Hunt Club
and
Mrs. Gordon Fergusson
request the pleasure of the company of
....
at a Supper Party on
....
R.S.V.P.   8 o'clock
Sandy Brow   Black tie
Tarporley

Paupiette de Saumon Fumé
Sauce Verte
***
Delice de Grouse Rôti
Gratin de Pommes de Terre
aux Champignons
Legumes de Saison
***
Tartelette aux Fruits Assortis
***
Beignets de Fromage
***
Le Café
***

Tim Tollemache's menu.

Sir Philip Grey-Egerton, 12th Baronet of Egerton and Oulton, from a portrait in oils by Edoardo Gioja.

Mr & Mrs de Ferranti entertained the Club at their newly-built Henbury Hall, based on Palladio's Villa Rotunda, the Members wore uniform although it was not during the hunting season. There was a precedent for this when the Committee conceded to the wish of 'the Father of the Hunt', Lord Egerton of Tatton for members to wear their evening dress uniform at the Tatton & Knutsford Ball in 1903. Although not the custom, it was not against the Rules of the Club.

But in the days when white ties were still worn for dinner, Lord Grey recalled to the author the time when, as a young man home from Ceylon on his first leave in 1930, he was present as Brian Egerton came downstairs at High Legh in a black tailcoat. The Secretary, over from Oulton and staying in the house, was a stickler for etiquette. He saw that his host had donned his Tarporley coat and breeches in his honour and so he hastily went up to change into his regalia, which his valet had prudently packed.

Rule III

Hunt Uniform

'Every member must have a Blue Frock with plain yellow mettled Buttons, Scarlet Velvet Cape, and double breasted scarlet flannel waistcoat, the coat sleeve to be cut and turned up' was laid down as the 2nd rule in 1762. A single-breasted waistcoat was later substituted and the uniform was completely changed at the 16th Meeting in 1770. The blue coat was in accordance with the prescribed uniform for hare-hunting clubs.

At Mere Hall there is a head and shoulders portrait attributed to George Morland, believed to be of Peter Brooke in a blue coat with brass buttons and a scarlet waistcoat. But he was never a Member and his sons were elected after the uniform had been changed, so either the clothing is coincidental or the identity of the sitter must be in doubt. When they moved back across the road from Mere New Hall to the Old in 1908, the family sold it and bought it back in 1984. No other portrait showing the original uniform is known.

It was in November, 1764 that a fine of one guinea was voted for any member not appearing in the amended <u>strict uniform</u>, *viz*:

a Plain Blue Frock with cuff turn'd up one button, with Mohair Buttons & unbound a [red X'd out] scarlet velvet cape with double breasted [red X'd out] scarlet waistcoat; a scarlet saddle cloth bound singly with blue; & the Bridle lapt with scarlet [& blue X'd out before 1770].

The original metal buttons had been changed to 'basket mohair' at the Third Meeting when: 'for the future - Goldsmith of Knutsford & John Dutton of Namptwich [*sic*] be appointed breeches makers to the Hunt'.

In November, 1770 the uniform became '. . . a red Coat unbound with a small frock sleeve, a green Velvett [*sic*] Cape & Green Waistcoat & that the sleeve has no buttons ["but" X'd out] in every other form to be like the old uniform & that the saddle cloth to be bound with green instead of blue and the fronts of the bridles remain the same as at present. The Buttons Baskett same color [*sic*] as the coat and waistcoat [buttons the] color of waistcoat. Every one not appearing as above liable to the old forfeitures.'

They were thus adopting the only orthodox colour for fox-hunting,[*] the first reference to which had been made five years previously.

As Rowland Egerton Warburton was to have Farmer Dobbin put it:

'They'd aw got bookskin leathers on, a-fitten 'em so toight,
As roind and plump as turmits be, and just about as whoit;
Their spurs wor maid o'siller, and buttons maid o'brass,
Their coats wor red as carrots and their collurs green as
grass.'

A curious rider was made to the rule that same year: 'Riding a hack to cover, or a shooting or upon an accident happening, or a horse on tryal, not to be fined according to the strictness of Rule made in regard to uniforms.' In his meticulous notes on the records Col. Geoffrey Egerton-Warburton, Hon. Secretary, 1937-1961, commented that this exception has never been repealed, but doubted if a present-day Member, appearing improperly dressed, could plead 'a horse on tryal', much less 'a shooting'.

By 1799 the rule read:

Any Member not appearing in the Field with the hounds, or upon the Course during the Meeting, with a Scarlet Coat and Green Velvet Collar, be fined One Guinea.

Lord Grosvenor was the first to fall foul of the dress regulations in November, 1765 with his waistcoat, saddle cloth and bridle all wrong. He was probably wearing his own hunt uniform. Other offenders the next year were:

Mr John Barry	– for having a binding to his coat and fined again for a binding to his waistcoat.
and again	
	– fined for not having taken the binding off the button holes of his waistcoat.
Mr Crewe [the Secretary]	– for having his bridle lapt with red and blue.
Mr Whitworth	– for having his saddle cloth bound with purple.
Lord Grosvenor	– for riding to cover with a white saddle cloth and likewise for having his bridle lapt with white. [As in the Stubbs painting.]

---

[*] The Duke of Beaufort's blue coat with blue collar and buff facings with hunt servants in green plush and the yellow livery of the Berkeley hunt servants are notable exceptions. The green servants' livery of the Heythrop dates from the days the country was hunted by the Duke of Beaufort. The Atherstone at one time had an orange coat. A green coat became almost universal for harriers and beagling. The Cheshire Hunt has always had a plain red coat. As Mr Jorrocks said, 'there's no colour like red.' In the U.S.A., where there are well over a hundred long-established packs of fox-hounds, many hunts rejoice in going against the accepted rule.

Mr John Crewe — for riding a hack to cover with saddle cloth not uniform and bridle not lapt with scarlet.

Mr R. Wilbraham — for riding a hack on the field without a proper saddle cloth and bridle.

And that year even the President, himself, John Crewe of Crewe, was fined – for leaving us on the Fryday [*sic*] and for a bridle not properly fronted.

Sir Peter Leicester was another later culprit with a saddle cloth not according to rule. Arthur Barry had improper pockets and Crewe his pockets wrong cut which cost him a double fine.

A more modern President to fall foul of Rule III was Lord Cholmondeley (279), who appeared throughout Hunt Week in tweed. However the Secretary regarded it as a single offence and it only cost him 'one sov'.

When the Rule was reformed in 1891 the velvet collar had been discarded and it was made clear that the fine was payable on each offence during the Hunt Week, otherwise it had remained the same since the uniform was changed:

> Any Member appearing on the field with hounds without a scarlet coat and green collar during the Hunt Week shall be fined one sovereign for each offence.

The first to appear without his uniform and be fined was Bo Littledale (241) in 1893, the year after his election.

Equally this rule has applied to Members attending the Tarporley Week meets on foot, including also that of the Cheshire Forest Hounds who still meet traditionally at the Bluecap Hotel (Sandiway Head) on the Monday. Trousers are worn with the Club's field coat and waistcost. A grey bowler hat is considered *de rigueur* together with a thumbstick or blackthorn.

It was also customary by rule for Members to wear their uniform at 'Tarporley Jumps' – the Club's Horse

'What are we having for dinner tonight?' Lord Cholmondeley and the Secretary at Ox Heys.

Show held on the Wednesday of Tarporley Week for the purpose of entertaining the farmers. The last occasion was in 1953. Members only wore their uniform at the races when it was an Autumn Meeting in Hunt Week. A special resolution was made when the Opening Meet was cancelled in 1967 owing to the outbreak of Foot & Mouth Disease, for the same formalities to apply on the postponed date, which, as it turned out, was never arranged and the Lady Patroness, Miss Gemma Dewhurst, stayed in office another season.

Very few further fines under this rule have since been recorded, except in recent times when members have failed to wear uniform when attending the Tarporley Week meets on foot or following by car. In 1976 the newly appointed Secretary came upon the senior Joint Manager at Highwayside in an overcoat and trilby hat. It transpired that Mr Tomkinson had been on patrol with a posse of police to disperse a party of hunt saboteurs. This was the only time the fine has been waived, even though there had fortunately not been a shooting.

At the suggestion of the Sub-Committee reviewing the rules in 1894/95 two shades of green cloth were approved, a dark shade for the collar of the Hunting coat and waistcoat and a lighter shade for the Evening coat collar, vest and breeches. At that time Messrs. Poole of

A Meet at the Blue Cap, c 1908

At a recent Tarporley Week meet at Highwayside. l. to r. Peter Sayce, Geoffrey Churton and the Secretary.

Savile Row were the Club's tailors. They are now J.Dege & Sons Ltd.

As fashions changed the Club conformed and monogrammed brass buttons were introduced. It seems there was an earlier version. In a letter to the Secretary to the Cheshire Hunt, Rowland Egerton-Warburton, dated May, 1867, the Manager, Mr H.R.Corbet of Adderley, wrote from his hunting box at Cotebrook as follows:

> I am very anxious that we should have a new hunt button, the present one being so very bad. I enclose some designs. I do not know that any of them would be approved of. I think Tarporley Hunt Club in similar letters to those on the Eglinton[*] Hunt button which I enclose would look very well (without the coronet of course). A button might also be struck with only C.H. for the subscribers who are not Members of Tarporley. Lord Grosvenor had the drawings in <u>button shape</u> done. A friend of mine sent me the others and the button came from the makers.

And two days later:

> Pray help me in the matter of the button. I confess I do not think sport will be <u>improved</u> by adopting a new button at the same time the present one is so hideous that I think it might be improved upon. Anne [his wife, Sir Philip Grey-Egerton's daughter] will sketch out a better whip, horn and bit and I will send it for your inspection.

On June 1st from Adderley in another letter about kennel maintenance:

> P.S. I am still <u>Button Mad</u>, could you try and like one of the enclosed in preference to our old one.

Fortunately the whip, horn and bit motif was not chosen.

Silver tie pins with the Tarporley Swan and motto, *Quæsitum Meritis*, were also made sometime after 1870.

It was Regie Corbet, Jnr. who suggested in 1913 that the club buttons be changed for a pattern with the club crest and motto, but nothing came of it.

Wives of Members and Lady Patronesses for their season of office took to wearing the green collar and black monogrammed buttons, though at one time, by resolution, the privilege of wearing the green collar was somewhat starchily not accorded to the wives of Honorary and Supernumerary Members. The question of widows being allowed to continue the privilege was even brought up, but the line was drawn at divorcees. It has now become the practice, for identification purposes, for Lady Managers to have brass buttons. And former Lady Patronesses may continue to wear their Tarporley buttons, even after marriage, though their collar is for their year of office only. In common with general hunting tradition it became the custom for subscribers to hounds and members of the covert fund to wear three buttons on their coat with two on their cuffs, Masters of Hounds four-button front (five if hunting hounds) and two-button cuff, and hunt servants six with two cuff buttons.

Apart from Winifred Rocksavage, Mrs (later Lady) Cotton-Jodrell was one of the very few to wear scarlet and a green collar with her black habit skirt. She had a very good figure and small waist. One or two other lady members of the Cheshire field, who kept Mary company, included Mrs Gordon Houghton of Gardenhurst, but the fashion did not catch on.

The top hat was first worn in 1797 and soon became the correct attire in the hunting field and it was not until decades later that Masters took to wearing the black hunting cap, which at one time was only worn by the hunt servants. And correctly only they and active Masters themselves should leave their ribbons unstitched. Known as 'the flash', these are a legacy from the days when pigtails were secured to the cap by ribbons. A hatguard, a black cord sensibly introduced to secure the silk top hat to a small ring inside the coat-collar, went out of fashion in the second half of this century.

Piers Egerton Warburton was told by his grandfather, Sir Richard Brooke, that it was he who, in Sir Harry Mainwaring's time, first suggested that the huntsman and whippers-in should abandon the hats they had worn

---

*The 14th Earl of Eglinton started his own pack in Ayrshire in 1861 and his livery button was used until 1922. The design then became a running fox inside a belt inscribed 'Eglinton Hunt'.

hitherto and adopt the fashion then in vogue with the Quorn of wearing black velvet caps. Sir Harry refused to incur the expense, but told him he could do so if he wished. This Sir Richard did. Having previously had their heads measured, he drove to the meet with the new caps in his gig and popped them on at the covertside much to the surprise of the Master on his arrival.

A discussion took place in 1983 when hunting caps and various forms of safety helmet were gradually becoming the necessary headgear for all fox-hunters and replacing the traditional silk hat, the cost of which was by then becoming prohibitive and was in any case of scant protection. The black velvet hunting cap, common enough for all sportsmen in the mid-XIX Century, became the prerogative, besides hunt staff, of Masters, ex-Masters of some years standing and ex-Masters who had themselves hunted hounds. But in Cheshire, and doubtless elsewhere, it has long been a privilege accorded to Farmers who had been given their hunt button. Strictly the only ladies entitled to wear a hunting cap used to be wives and daughters of active Masters.

Either a green velvet covered cap or a green silk cover for a riding helmet to be part of the modern club uniform was one suggestion not readily accepted. The Cheshire Hunt Committee had recently approved the wearing by gentlemen of a light grey hunting cap and this seemed even less in accord with most members' tastes. Major Sandy Grant (307) rather confused the issue by bringing ladies' headgear into the discussion, evidently forgetting that it was only the ladies of the Wynnstay who are obliged to wear bowler hats. Whereupon he donned his own infamous brown billycock for the rest of this lighthearted debate, the outcome of which was a decision to leave the matter on the table along with Sandy's hat.

Since 1859 at the instigation of Earl Grosvenor (174) the Hunt Servants of the Cheshire Hounds have worn the Tarporley Hunt Club's green collar by invitation to

successive Masterships. The custom gave rise to a misconception that the hounds were the property of the Club. In 1989 Johnny O'Shea was presented with a club pin at the beginning of his twenty-fourth season as Huntsman, the year before his last. John Jones, Huntsman from 1869 to 1895, is also shown wearing one on his hunting tie in a coloured engraving. It was after Jones's death in 1895 that the Hunt Servants first wore white cord breeches instead of brown.

RULE IV

THE COMMITTEE

AN ORIGINAL RULE OF 1762 enacted that 'The President must manage all the business of the Society during his term of office.' But this was expunged before 1772 and thereafter it would have been left to the Secretary, who by then no longer had his Deputy to assist him. John Crewe died in 1786 and the first two books are in his hand, more often than not signing himself 'Alderman and Secretary'. (Obadiah Lane signed himself 'Sen. Ald.') Booth Grey signed himself 'Dep. Sect.', even when President, but 'Secretary' when Crewe was in the chair and for the next four Meetings thereafter 'Secretary and Alderman' after which he appears to have given up his duties.

It was always the task of the Secretary to collect fines and 'acquaint every Member of their election as soon as chose'. Apart from that, the most important duty was to buy the claret. It was for the President to 'acquaint Mrs Joseph Southon [the landlord's wife, subsequently amended to Mr Baugh] of the time appointed for each meeting'. In 1769 it was voted the Landlord of the house's duty to send out reminders for the next Meeting as follows:

Torpoley Hunt

You are desired to meet your President at Torpoley
the first Sunday in February Next. Dinner at 4 o'clock.
J. CREWE – Secretary

Or November as the case may be and it was necessary to give a month's notice. The landlord kept the letters sent as excuses for absence to show the President. Even up to the time of Geoffrey Egerton-Warburton, members were

Sandy's hat in 1962.

asked to write to the landlord of The Swan, stating the days they proposed to dine.

Notices in a similar vein were also inserted in *The Chester Chronicle* a week before the Meeting.

After John Crewe of Bolesworth died, there is no record of the proceedings for the next sixteen years. The Club's first book is octavo, bound with marbled boards and the second a plain grey quarto notebook. In addition to the draft resolutions for the presentation of Sir Harry's Order of Merit, the only other record is of the wine drank from 1796 onwards.

On the first few pages of the Club's third register book (bound in suede with a red label with TARPORLEY HUNT ACCOUNT BOOK in gilt lettering) a copperplate List of Members as at November 10th, 1799 was inscribed, followed by a list of the previous Presidents and Lady Patronesses, and on the last few pages, reversed, the Rules then applicable. The accounts and proceedings to be written in the hand of the next Secretary for the first time are those of 1802 and on his resignation from his duties in 1808, it was:

> Resolved that the thanks of the Hunt be given to H. A. Leicester Esq. for the trouble he has taken as Secretary to the Hunt and that the Business of the Hunt in future be conducted by a Committee consisting of Sir H.M. Mainwaring Bart, Revᵈ Wᵐ Drake & Chaˢ Cholmondeley Esqʳ.

This was ratified in 1847, with new Committee Members to be chosen at the ensuing Meeting on the death or resignation of one of them. Printed notices for Members' dues had been sent out in the name of all three members of the Committee for payment to be made 'to one of us'.

Apart from the appointments of successive Committee Members this rule remained in force until 1975 when it was decided that a fourth member should be elected and that it was only right that the President should have a say in their deliberations. In 1976 Rule IV was changed to read as follows:

> The business of the Club shall be conducted by a Committee, composed of the President and four elected Members, one of whom shall be Honorary Secretary. On the death or resignation of one of them another shall be appointed at the ensuing Meeting.

The Secretaries of the Club and the Committee Members are listed in Appendix B.

RULE V

QUALIFICATION FOR MEMBERSHIP

ALTHOUGH NO HINT IS GIVEN IN THE RECORDS as to whose idea it was to meet at The Swan for a week's hunting and convivial companionship, the nine bachelor friends formed the 'Torporley Hunt' with no other purpose in mind.

In the past most of their forebears, together with other Cheshire and Shropshire gentry, had indeed met at both Delamere and Wallasey 'under the colour of Hunting and Race matches' for political reasons in the days after the Restoration.* And a considerable number were at one time or another Members of The Cycle of the White Rose. But the motives of the Tarporley Hunt were totally different from those of this Jacobite Society, which had been instituted at Wynnstay on June 10th, 1710 (White Rose Day, the birthday of James II's son).

Originally these gentlemen used the pretext of hunting to cover up their more subversive activities. Mainly from the Welsh, Shropshire and Cheshire Borders, their uniform was dark blue velvet with a primrose vest. However, from about 1780 until the last cycle in 1864 their meetings were entirely social. They took it in turn to meet each month at one another's houses and they, too, had a Lady Patroness, the Lady Williams-Wynn of the day. She wore the great Jewel of the Cycle† at the dinners. The Caerwys Hunt, The Confederacy Hunt and 'The Fraternity of the True Blue Hunt' in Shropshire were similar organizations, dedicated to keeping themselves in condition for the coming of James Stuart.

The gathering at The Swan was purely a group of sportsmen bent solely on the pleasures of the chase and each other's company, its particular politics being best

---

*Of those races the Rev. Matthew Fowler wrote from Whitchurch on September 11th, 1682:

> To-morrow being the Race-day there will bee a meeting of the Loyall gentry of Cheshire and these adjacent parts... upon the Forrest of Delamere... They meet under colour of Hunting and Race matches, but ye designe is to bee in readiness to prevent any ill attempts; God almighty give them wisdom and sobriety, that they may manage their meetings to the advantage of his Majesty. They will have their spies upon the racers at Wallacy from whom I am promised the best account they can get. But I lately heard that the D.[Duke of Monmouth]intends to putt off Wallacy Races till Thursday and to come to hunt with the Gentlemen at the Forrest. If so God keep them, from quarrells, for though the Gent. know how to behave themselves to a person of his High Quality, yet I am sure they love not his company under his present circumstances. And since it is too late to wish he had not come amongst us, wee heartily wish we were well freed from him.

conveyed by Egerton Warburton in his Tarporley Hunt Song of 1855:

> *Though scarlet in colour our clothing,*
> *Our collars though green in their hue,*
> *The red cap of liberty loathing,*
> *Each man is at heart a True Blue;*
> *Through life 'tis our sworn resolution,*
> *To stick to the pigskin and throne;*
> *We are all for a good constitution,*
> *Each man taking care of his own.*

Even so, bumpers were often drunk to highlight a toast – this was especially a Jacobite custom. (Just to confuse the issue, at a banquet to celebrate Fox's return to parliament in 1784 the Prince of Wales jokingly gave the toast "True Blue and Mrs Crewe!") But again, not only are there symbolic oak branches on the Quæsitum, but white roses are interspersed with the foxes' masks and the swans on the Club's coffee cups and saucers. Quite possibly the designer had mistaken Tarporley for an old True Blue Hunt and the Club did not bother to have them changed, or more likely did not even notice them. Their date is thought to be *circa* 1820 and they were retailed by Sharpus & Cullum, 13, Cockspur St., London. Some two dozen remain.

A Cycle wheel dated 1770 shows six who were also Members of Tarporley, about 25% of the Club at the time, including Grosvenor, who had just resigned. The list of names thus printed meant that no one person could be considered more blameworthy than any other. In 1823 a sham wheel of 'A List of the Members of, and those who occasionally Hunt with, The Old Cheshire Hounds' was produced by John Twemlow of Hatherton with his arms in the centre and Sir H. Mainwaring, Bart. at 12 o'clock. Of the twenty-nine names only himself, Lord Hugh Cholmondeley, the twenty-three-year-old younger son of the 1st Marquess, and Dan Ashley of

Top: Legh shows a coffee cup to Dallas Waters.

Frodsham were not T.H.C. Members. He later published Wicksted's song, *The Cheshire Hunt*, in book form with lithographs of Bluecap, his race and monument, dedicated to J.H.Smith-Barry (147). Another wheel of forty-four members of the Cycle of the White Rose, dated 1825, shows only half-a-dozen Tarporley names.

Geoffrey Egerton-Warburton took the view that his grandfather, Rowland, as a young man would have known the last surviving Original Member, Roger Wilbraham, who died in 1829, and would thus have become aware of any Jacobite sympathies had there ever been any. Geoffrey was three years old when his grandfather died.

There is one further enigma. Rosettes are carved on each of the spandrels of the President's chair – 'the Great Chair' made for the Club by John Wilkinson, carpenter of Tarporley, in 1774.

The present Rule V reads as follows:

> The number of Members of the Club shall not be more than forty, being qualified by Property, Family or Residence in the county. Any Member qualified by residence only, shall, on his ceasing to reside, cease to be a Member of the Club.

The restriction to this number has been in force since 1806, the amendment to make it *no more than* forty having been made in 1966. It was in 1764 that a limit was

† A circular gold broach, enamelled on both sides in green with the name of the Lady Patroness and in the centre a serpent round a button in True Blue enamel with a white rose and the word CYCLE, it is surmounted with a lover's knot of diamonds.

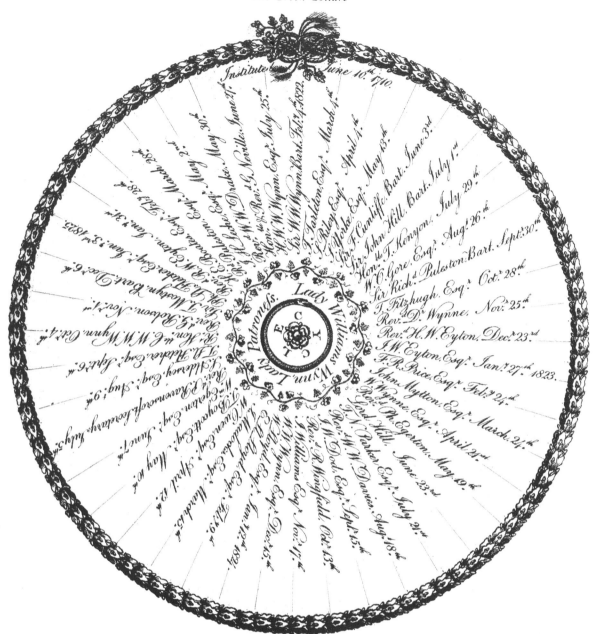

made to twenty and in 1769 it was 'Agreed that the Number of this Hunt shall be enlarged to twenty-five Members, but shall <u>never</u> exceed the same'.

Notwithstanding this vote it was increased to Thirty-Six in 1788 and the qualifications were introduced either then or before 1799 when they are first mentioned. At one time the Members were known amongst the farming community as 'the Green Collars' and at one time in jest by their friends in the county as 'The Forty Thieves'.

With unwitting prophecy Rowland Warburton put it rather better:

> *The sport they began may we still carry on,*
> *And we forty good fellows, who meet at The Swan,*
> *To the green collar stick, tho' our breeches be gone.*

and it is a little sad that now towards the end of the XX Century, a mere 25% of the Membership still appear in the hunting field, though 60% have been hunting men in their day.

In 1803 some discussion took place as to whether Sir Stephen Glynne and Sir Watkin Williams-Wynn were eligible. It was finally agreed that their fathers having been Members was sufficient justification for their election. This Sir Watkin, known affectionately as Bubble, stammered badly and was a big clumsy fellow. He was particularly fond of whist. (His brother was Squeak.) In Sir Watkin's case one would have thought him highly eligible, having ten years earlier reconstituted his family pack of fox-hounds. His hospitality was sumptious. To mark the occasion he had provided a cold collation for all in the morning and the day's sport was followed by an elegant dinner on their return and a ball in the evening. But this was nothing compared with his father's coming-of-age celebrations on April 19th, 1770, when 15,000 people are said to have been seated at the same time in the park, for which three coach loads of cooks had been sent from London. Much of the food and wines and a great deal else came by sea to Chester.

Nevertheless so far as the Tarporley Hunt Club was concerned, 'Family' was to become by far the most important qualification and Geoffrey Egerton-Warburton calculated that it accounted for the election of five-sixths of the Membership, though many of these were qualified by Property and Residence as well.

The Grosvenor family takes pride of place being represented for all but seventeen years of the Club's existence. Sir Peter Warburton (35) and his heirs come second, missing twenty-five and only twelve since his election in 1775. But if the Egertons of Oulton are included with the Egerton-Warburtons their joint total deficit is only the thirteen years prior to his election. There was no Wilbraham in the Club during thirty-four years, but the present head of the family is the sole direct descendant of an Original Member still represented. He has two sons to his name.

There have been twenty-nine instances of fathers and sons being members together. They are marked with an asterisk in Appendix A. George Heron (18) had two sons with him in the Club, as did William Egerton of Tatton (40). Admiral Tollemache and his son were both elected at the same meeting and in the case of the Langford-Brookes, Thomas the son (158) was elected a year before Thomas his father (161). In spite of Estate Duty and Inheritance Tax there have only been six occasions this century when a son, who had had his father's landed estate handed over to him, was elected, having become qualified by 'Property'.

James Smith-Barry (24) was elected with two uncles as well as his father in the Club.

There have been twenty-seven occasions when brothers have been members together, including the three Barry brothers, three Leicesters and three Tarletons. Of the four de Trafford brothers, J.R. resigned before Cecil and Augustus were elected, but all of them had been contemporary members with their eldest brother, Humphrey.

These are all shown in Appendix A by a dagger.

'Property' has never been quantified, the ownership of Cheshire's larger estates having almost invariably been vested in someone qualified by 'Family'. The generally accepted figure of a minimum of 500 acres applied to the rules of the Cheshire Hunt, in so far as special subscription rates were concerned. Recently elected members in the 'Property' category, with varying acreages, include Sir J.R. Barlow (305), Lord Leverhulme (313), G.C.Dean (332), J.G.Fergusson (339) and Randle Brooks (366). Clearly hounds should always be welcome on a 'Green-collar' estate even though the foxes and pheasants conflict. This has long been a contentious issue. As the Club's own Poet Laureate pointed out:

We hold in abhorrence all vulpicide knaves,
With their gins, and their traps, and their velveteen slaves;
They may feed their fat pheasants, their foxes destroy,
And mar the prime sport they themselves can't enjoy;
But such sportsmen as these we good fellows condemn,
And I vow we'll ne'er drink a quæsitum to them.

The third qualification of 'Residence in the County' makes the Membership broadly based. The rider that a Member ceasing to reside and solely so qualified should cease to be a Member, has not been so strictly adhered to as it once may have been, though the matter is first mentioned in 1894 when a Minute reads:

After some discussion it was proposed by H.R.Corbet, seconded by James Tomkinson and unanimously resolved that in the opinion of this Meeting Rule XI[*] does not apply to the case of Ld. Enniskillen so far as it relates to non-residence!!!

Known to his friends as 'Coly' – and in later life to the younger generation as 'Lordy' – Viscount Cole (218)[†] had succeeded to the Earldom in 1886 and had of necessity to spend more time at Florence Court in Co.Fermanagh. He left Cassia Lodge, where on a number of occasions he had entertained the future King Edward VII, but kept on the stables there for a time and stayed with Captain Park Yates (198) at Sandiway Lodge. On the latter's death he moved to Vale Royal and then lived at Cuddington Grange for the last year of his Managership of the Cheshire Hounds, afterwards establishing himself at Heysmere when in Cheshire.

---

[*] The non-attendance rule of which the rule for non-residence was then part. A sub-committee consisting of H.R.Corbet, Henry Tollemache, C.H.Poole and Piers Egerton Warburton was appointed that year to revise the Rules.

[†] Eldest sons of peers normally take as a courtesy title a family title one rank lower, i.e. the son and heir of the Marquess of Cholmondeley takes the title Earl of Rocksavage and his son, the Viscount Malpas. In the case of the Earldom of Enniskillen, the Viscountcy is also Enniskillen, so this rank is chosen with the family name instead of the barony which is Mount-florence. The same principle applies to the Duke of Westminster, whose heir apparent, though ranking as a Marquess, uses the title Earl Grosvenor and the grandson is styled Viscount Belgrave and ranks as an Earl. (see *The Complete Peerage, Vol.V, Appendix H*)

Apart from the entertaining he did in his hunting boxes he was ever popular with the ladies and had his feet under many Cheshire tables. He got rather more than his feet there in one house, as it is known that he made love to his hostess under the dining room table while the butler was laying it for dinner.

There was some embarrassment in the case of Otho Shaw (231). He failed to send an explanation for his absence when he was Vice-President in 1902. The truth was he had funked it, as in those days the Vice-President was involved in speech-making and he felt as President his 'poor endeavours had been received with such evident disapproval'. A pompous letter, afterwards regretted, was sent to him pointing out that as he had left the county and sold his property, his Membership had lapsed. To make matters worse he had been a regular attender and did in fact still own valuable property in the county. He duly sent in his resignation, but asked the Club to accept a handsome two-handled silver cup.

Christopher Roundell (306) and his son, Charles (340) were among the members who resigned when they left the county. The Secretary advised Christopher Roundell, who was settling in London, to follow in Lord Kilmorey's and Chas. Townley's footsteps by joining the London Hunt and drawing the Bond Street Coverts as a Member. Others, such as Dick Poole (297), who went to live in Berkshire when the family sold Marbury, and John Baskervyle-Glegg (321), who moved to London, retained their membership and were always welcome faces on their annual pilgrimage to Tarporley, which they seldom missed. The latter even had his dining room decorated green to match the Hunt Room and added red leather chairs. Although their main residence was in Kenya, Hughie Delamere (240) and his son Tom kept a Cheshire estate and retained their membership. Their native staff at far-off Soysambu wore long khaki tunics and trousers with green tarbooshes and cummerbunds.

In 1949 Lord Cholmondeley (279) tendered his resignation because he was living in Kensington Palace Gardens or at Houghton in Norfolk and had handed over Cholmondeley to his son who had just been elected. 'I would like to have left the Club "feet first" which is the normal procedure but we are not living in normal times,' he wrote. 'I do not grudge my son being at Cholmondeley one little bit, it's having a pistol put to one's head & <u>having</u> to do a thing ...you will want my place & as Rocksavage is a resident & large landowner & <u>hunts</u> he should have the green collar in my opinion.'

It would seem that Lord Cholmondeley did not consider 'Family' as the paramount qualification and was probably unaware that sons had in the past been elected while their fathers had still been members. Egerton-

Warburton prevailed on him to remain. Notwithstanding that the other two new Green Collars were a Bromley-Davenport and the newly-appointed Lord Lieutenant his reply began:

> DEAR CHOLMONDELEY
> As you will no doubt have heard Rocksavage was unanimously elected... and we are delighted to have him. It is a long time since we had the opportunity of electing someone of the old Cheshire stock and someone who hunts and lives here and is so suitable in every way.

It was not the first time that the Marquess had sent in his resignation. In 1936 he had written to Brian Egerton expressing his strong disapproval of the appointment of a new Master, but subsequently withdrew it. He was under a misapprehension and the Secretary had written back:

> The Tarporley Hunt Club has nothing whatever to do or say in the management or control of the Cheshire Hounds... The Tarporley Hunt Club is a purely social one and has nothing to do with the Hunting regime.

Hubert Wilson, a former most popular Master, did, however, resign twice for totally different reasons. He had been commanding the Yeomanry since mobilization and in October, 1915 wrote from Barmere:

> . . . The outlook is so vague & I am so terribly hit in business by my absence & general collapse of trade [He was Chairman of Wilson's Brewery, which owned the Blue Cap Inn.] that I do not feel justified in keeping on any club subscriptions. I fear that my hunting days are over.

and a fortnight later from Lowestoft:

> MY DEAR BRIAN, So many thanks for your kind letter. I feel however that after the war we shall all, or at least many of us, be so poor that hunting will be out of the question. I have always held the opinion very strongly that the membership of T.H.C. should be synonymous with <u>active</u> support of Cheshire hunting & therefore sad as I am to give up my green collar, I feel that it is my duty to do so & make room for someone who will be able to help sport which I fear will want all the assistance anybody can give it. Thank you all the same, old chap, for your very kind thoughts. I have given Barbour and Tomkinson leave [for Tarporley Week].

At the first meeting after the War he was re-elected. But the saga of his unselfish desire to resign began again in 1932 with almost an annual exchange of letters between Barmere and Oulton. Quoting a speech he had read, he wrote "'I prefer to resign now when I am young enough for people to ask why he has resigned rather than wait until folk ask why he doesn't resign." That decided me.' He was by then 72 and was still tenanting the County Council Ridley property for the benefit of hunting. In 1933 Brian wrote again emphasizing the strong persuasion of Sir William Bromley-Davenport, the then Father of the Hunt, and the entire meeting.

By 1936 Hubert was adamant despite the following reply:

> You're a nice cup of tea you are, you old blighter. Just as everybody has been enthusing that there would no election taking place at Tarporley this year, you throw this bombshell in the midst to upset all the harmony – too bad of you, really it is. I have said so much before that I could only repeat myself & that I totally fail to see why you are "quite certain that I am doing the right thing this time". I disagree with you entirely. Age and non-hunting doesn't enter into the question, you can still chat and laugh with the best of 'em and you most certainly have not got one foot in the grave so don't be stubborn by considering yourself an old crock.

The reclusive Lord Egerton of Tatton on his return to Cheshire in 1953 used 'the withdrawal of the relief from Super-Tax' as an excuse to cancel his banker's order, thus severing, as the Hon. Secretary pointed out to him in reluctantly accepting his resignation, a family association dating back to 1780.

RULE VI

ELECTION OF MEMBERS

EACH MEMBER to be chofe but by Ballott, and none but the Members present at the Balloting to have a Vote: which Ballott must be the first night of the Meeting

was the 11th rule laid down by the Original Members. This remained the same until 1771 when it was changed to the last day. The first order given by Obadiah Lane to Booth Grey, the Deputy Secretary, was to 'procure for the use of this Society a Balloting Box with eighteen black & eighteen white Balls'. Another rule in 1762 was that the Club Book 'must be kept in the Balloting Box & the President, for the time being, must keep the key'. The balloting box shown on the mantelpiece in the painting of the Club Dining by Goodwin Kilburne is possibly a true representation. But the original was lost during the Second World War. The book measures 8 in. × 6½ in. The

box was replaced by a square mahogany one with an aperture at the top and two drawers below.

The number of black balls required to exclude was not stipulated until 1774 when it was decided that 'Two black balls [were] necefsary to prevent the election of a Member proposed.' This was changed to three in 1881 with a minimum of fifteen Members being present. It remained the same until 1989 when by the narrowest possible margin the members present voted to abolish the Ballot Box and the two vacancies were not filled. A new system was devised on the lines of that used in modern times by the Jockey Club. However by another minimal majority the Club decided at the next Meeting that the rule should not be altered after all. But the guidelines by which the names of proposed candidates for vacancies are to be circulated in advance were retained.

There is no recorded instance of anyone being blackballed, but it is known that such a thing did happen just before the Second World War. It was probably this which determined the decision of the gentleman concerned to leave the county. The normal procedure was for candidates to be discussed before any election, for instance in 1871:

> Several candidates were proposed but no election took place.

It was most unfortunate, perhaps due to a misunderstanding caused by an indiscretion on the part of his would-be proposer or just possibly by a Committee Member, when, in 1884, Arthur Knowles turned up at Sandiway Head for the Opening Meet wearing a green collar before the election that year had taken place. He lived at Alvaston Hall, Nantwich, and had many close friends in the Club, but he was not elected to join 'the green collar men' that year or ever. It was not until 1896 that he was invited to become a Subscriber to Hounds.

The question was raised in 1912 of Members being permitted to propose candidates by letter instead of being present to nominate them, but it was unanimously agreed that both Proposer and Seconder must be present when the election takes place.

In early years the Secretary would write to the new Members 'informing them they are chosen'. In most

The Tarporley Box.

cases this century the telephone has been used and more often than not the New Member has come to drink his Quæsitum that night, it being customary for him not to wear breeches and not to bring a guest.

In 1990, owing to the arrangement made at the previous Meeting, the four new Members were elected on a Proposal by the President. The only other time the election by ballot has been waived was in 1961 in favour of Captain Peter Egerton-Warburton (329) with a unanimous show of hands as a tribute to his father, Colonel Geoffrey Egerton-Warburton, late Honorary Secretary.

The Ballot Box

RULE VII

JOINING FEE AND MARRIAGE FINE

DURING THE FIRST TEN YEARS of the Club there was no admission fee for unmarried Members, but a fee for married Members was introduced in 1763. They had to give each member of the club a pair of Doeskin Gloves and this was voted to 'two pair' a year later. In 1772, instead of gloves, it was:

> Voted – that any person, who shall be hereafter elected a member of this Hunt, & is a married man, shall pay £10.10.0 on his admission by way of Stock purse, & if a Batchelor six guineas.

The single man's entrance fee was increased to ten by 1785.

In 1812 the joining fee for married men was doubled and the accounts show that pounds were substituted for guineas by 1839. Thereafter no change was made to the entrance fee until 1979 when it became £100, whether married or single. This more or less represented a fortieth share of the wine in the Club's own cellar at The Swan Hotel.

The marriage fine of twenty pounds, incorporated in the same rule, has been the same amount since 1772,

except that guineas were altered to sovereigns. Originally a Member marrying after his election was required to give a pair of buckskin breeches to each member. They were then a guinea a pair and there were twenty members. Initially 'Stiff Top'd, well Stich'd Buckskin Gloves' was written down but these were subsequently changed to buckskin breeches and in 1764 an entry reads:

> Voted. That each member when he marrys instead of providing Breeches for every Member of the Hunt, does pay into the hands of the Secretary for the use of each Member the sum of one guinea to be spent in Leather Breeches.

'Buckskin's the only wear fit for the saddle', as the Club's laureate was to proclaim.

This fine did not, however, go up when the Membership was increased, but in 1766, when the question of a second marriage was discussed without the occasion actually arising, it was 'Voted: that any Member of this Hunt that marries a second time, shall give two pair of Leather Breeches to each Member of the Hunt'.

In November, 1772 it seems they no longer got their breeches when a fellow member was wed – 'Instead of breeches [to each Member] 20 Guineas is Voted to be paid [to the Club]' and in 1779 it was resolved that all fines 'be applyd to the Fund'.

By 1799 the words 'on each event' had been inserted for the Marriage Fine and the club has benefited by an extra twenty sovereigns many times throughout the years from Members' marital arrangements. Since 1946, although the rule was not altered, a Member marrying within a year of his election, has only been required to pay a marriage fine of 10 sovereigns.

Among those to have married more than twice are William Egerton (40), who outlived four wives, one of whom he married as Wm. Tatton before he changed his name to Egerton, John Kennedy (238), who also married four times, and the 2nd Duke of Westminster (248). He was divorced three times before marrying Miss 'Nancy' Sullivan, who in later years was to earn fame as the owner of the triple Cheltenham Gold Cup winner, Arkle, and many other good National Hunt horses, including the 1985 Grand National winner, Last Suspect. Those Members who have married three times are the Rev. Sir Thomas Delves Broughton (26), Lord Combermere (78), Lord Delamere (293), Lord Daresbury (300), Richard Tomkinson (315), Sir Evelyn Delves Broughton (320), Peter Egerton-Warburton (329), Ralph Midwood (336) and Quentin Crewe (352). Only Colonel Stapleton Cotton, Bend Or and Richard Tomkinson were bachelors on election. Egerton had married for the second time the week before.

RULE VIII

GUESTS

IT HAS ALWAYS BEEN A TRADITION of the Club for members to bring guests and the original rule reads:

> Every member has the liberty of introducing his friend, but must pay for him as far as his ordinaries.

But the following year it was 'voted, that no strangers be asked upon the last day of the Meeting, either to dinner or supper'.

The amount to be paid for a Visitor has varied, at different dates, as follows:

	1 night:	2 nights:	4 nights:	6 nights:
1773	nil	1 gal. Claret	2 gal. Claret	3 gal. Claret
		('three hunting days one dozen')		
1779	nil	1 Guinea	2 Guineas	3 Guineas
1799	nil	1 Guinea	5 Guineas	Share of Bill
1809	1½ Guineas per Night			
1847	£1 per night			
1927	£2 per night			
1963	£5 per night			
1973	£5 on Tuesday and £6 on Wednesday			

Since 1978 all Dining Fees have been paid at cost.

At one time the landlord collected the money from each Member. For instance in 1877 Mr Daine was authorized to charge a pound *per diem* for each person, whether Member or Guest, the balance credited to the Club towards the overheads. Dinner then was 7/6d for Members, 10/- for Guests and breakfast, tea and supper 2/- each. Then dinner was served at 7 o'clock.

In 1773 a gallon of Claret, consisting of four bottles, cost 24/-.

The Members own expenses, after deduction for fines, were shared until subscriptions were introduced. Astonishingly, considering the relatively small revenue from fines for the past century and a half, a nominal dining fee was not made until 1976. The rule was altered in 1978 so that Members also pay a guest fee set by the Committee each year which, with the members' own dining fees, covers the catering cost and the replenishment of the wine consumed.

The Club has always taken a pride in its cellar, its port and claret especially. The use of the Club's cellar itself dates from 1805 when it was 'Agreed that Mr Egerton [this would be the Rev. Philip (76)] be requested to apply to Mr Arden [(20), who had resigned in 1800,] for the lease of a Cellar for the Tarporley Hunt'. From time to time it has been necessary to replenish its contents with a levy and that same year a subscription of six guineas was levied for... One Pipe of Port, One Hogshead Claret, One Hogshead

"Good fun how rare it is," The Tarporley Hunt at The Swan', from an engraving published by A. Baird Carter of Jermyn St., London, c.1833.

New ballot box, right, cheese cradle left, with various club decanters and glasses and the new and old coffee cups. The glass on the extreme right is as a set given to H.R.H. The Patron as a wedding present.

Madeira.* Between 1803 and 1810 £1,006. 4s. was spent on wine.

In the early years Members were called upon to contribute to a 'Claret A/c' with an occasional payment amounting to 2 gns. It is in the minutes of 1766 that 'Claret be never admitted to the House-bill; but that wagers laid in claret may be paid in claret.'

In his notes on the Rules, Geoffrey Egerton-Warburton took this to mean that, since the Club bought its own wine, any claret supplied by the landlord to individuals had to be paid for by them and not put on the bill. It was ruled in 1778 that 'the deficiency of the claret account after the share is paid for strangers to be inserted in the bill'. The entry goes on:

> . . . the Secretary's accounts were settled & allowed, being on the Clarett[*sic*] A/c 15. 5. 6., and on the house acct. 2. 2. 0. No more is now left in his hands. Voted that each Member of this Hunt do deposit 2 gns. in the Secretary's hands for a fund to purchase claret and that Mr Roger Wilbraham be requested to order it down, and that the Secretary do answer Mr Roger Wilbraham's draft for that purpose.[†]

The following year it was 'agreed to allow Mr Southon [the innkeeper of The Swan] '15d a bottle and the bottles for drinking our own claret.' The landlord was allowed two guineas for his cook but had to pay his own clerk for writing out his accounts. The cook's wage was reduced to two sovereigns in 1847, but the corkage went up by 3d. It ceased by agreement with Miss Hayes in 1885.

It had been the custom for the owner of the winning horse at the Club's race meeting to present a dozen of claret, but this was rescinded in 1785, the same year that Booth Grey moved that 'no Cards or Dice be allowed after the first Toast after Supper, each Member so offending against this Rule must pay two dozen of claret'.

---

* 1 Pipe = 2 Hogsheads = 105 Imperial Gallons. There were of course 20 shillings to the pound and 12 pence to the shilling. In 1762 a pound would have purchased goods which in 1992 would cost £70. However the value of the 1762 pound was only £1 16s (£1.80p) by 1914. It was not until the 1970's that inflation hit the Tarporley Hunt Club. Up to then Members had been dining without fee and only paying £5 for a guest. At the beginning of the Century inflation was virtually non-existent. The local upholsterer used to charge £2 10/- for preparing the Hunt Room, but when one year he charged £2 12/- he was immediately asked to account for the difference. It was perhaps this universal parsimony that kept the prices down.

† As judges of claret the Wilbraham family has retained that aptitude to the present day. Roger was a man of many talents. He was largely responsible for collecting much of the Delamere House library, which contained four First Folio editions of Shakespeare.

The Rules, as transcribed in 1799 state that 'a careful man be provided, each Meeting, to give out the Wine and attend the Hunt at Dinners and Suppers; and that he is allowed Five Guineas for the Week'. Forty-eight years later the butler got 'two sovereigns for his attendance.'

In 1806 each Member agreed to subscribe £3 3s for the purchase of silver forks, some six dozen being obtained in rat tail pattern made by R. Crossley and engraved 'Tally Ho' on a ribbon over a fox courant. R.E.Egerton Warburton, commented in 1877:

> It may appear strange to our ideas that a luxury, now so universal, should not have been introduced at Tarporley until the year 1806; but I am assured by a lady now living, [this was probably Lady Combermere,] that so late as 1809, in one of the most hospitable houses in the county, a silver fork was never seen on the dinner table.

Two-pronged steel forks with long sharp tines had been in normal use previously, sometimes with silver-plated handles, known as game forks, but there is no record of what had been provided at The Swan by way of cutlery or china. In former times knives had sharp points to spear gobbets of food, a spoon being used for the gravy.

Some decanters were bought in 1814 for £7 11s 6d An item in the same accounts is 'Sundry people to drink – 18/-'. It was in 1867 that the Club bought 6 Magnum decanters engraved with stars and the monogram. These cost £6 1s, including package from Daniell & Co. of New Bond St. Three are left.

In 1847 the Landlord was allowed to charge each Member one sovereign for a single bed in his house and each Guest 7 shillings a night, half-a-crown a stall for a horse for one night, 5 shillings for two or more and each gentleman to give the Waiter and the Chambermaid half-a-crown to half a sovereign according to the time he remains. The Committee were of the opinion that 10 shillings to 30 shillings should be charged for Lodgings, according to the time they are occupied.

These charges were notified annually to Members and remained the same until 1913.

The following is a random table of wine consumption:

	1797	1802	1814	1828
Sherry	13	1	20	26
Madeira	101	61	29	17
Claret	201	226	153	66
Port	120	71	43	20
Total Bottles:	435	359	245	129
Numbers Dining:	No record	152	166	124
Average consumption of bottles per person per night:-	No record	2.3	1.4	1.0

	1884	1906	1960	1979	1989
Sherry	13	12	12	6	
Chablis/Hock			12	22	28
Champagne	54	25	24	26	39
Claret	21	47	27	32	41
Brandy, etc.		9	14	4	1
Port	6	20	26	28	30
Total Bottles:	103	106	105	121	144
Numbers Dining:		61	54	81	101	112
Average consumption of bottles per person per night:-	1.7	2.0	1.3	1.2	1.3

NB The wine and sherry drunk at the President's Reception downstairs before dinner is not included in these figures, nor is the ale consumed at supper.

The first reference to Champagne was in 1876, when it was proposed that it should be used on the Tuesday and Wednesday nights.

The Cellar Book in use dates from 1909 when there were still 4 doz. Cockburn 1868, but the Croft's '75 was finished off first. The claret was Ch.Latour '93 and the champagne Louis Roederer '89. In 1904 a total of 19 doz. Veuve Clicquot '98 & '99 and Lanson 1900 was laid down. It would appear that the last bottle of the '68 was

The two Loving Cups and a Staffordshire brown-glazed pottery beer jug

drunk by Brian Egerton and his guests, Ossy Moseley and Jock Fergusson, the author's father, on the eve of the latter's wedding; but by then the Club was chiefly drinking Cockburn '81.

In the previous book dating from 1887 they were still drinking 1847 port (Cathcart).

In 1927 some Dow's '12 (9 doz.) was put in the cellar and this was not touched until 1947. The last 6 bottles were polished off in 1952. Ch.Cheval Blanc '48, Bollinger '52 and Gould Campbell '27 were drank at the Bicentenary Dinner. Other noteworthy vintages to have passed through the cellar include Martinez 1911, Graham's '20, Ch.Latour '26, '34, & '52, Ch.Lafite '34, Ch.Giscours '43 and Krug, '49. Though still conservative with its port shippers, in recent decades the Club has become more adventurous with its clarets and, to the chagrin of certain Members, it is some time since vintage champagne was consumed.

Brandy is also served for those not addicted to port. A present of 3 doz. Liqueur Brandy was made to the Club in 1922 by Lord Wavertree (268).

In time, outside caterers were employed. Mr Gunter, the celebrated confectioner of Berkeley Square and himself a hunting man, provided the cook for the 1848 Meeting at The Swan. 'His good office and attention gave satisfaction.' The cost was £12 4s (including Truffles) and £24 16s 8d the second year, including his journey and bill for fish. The arrangement with the Royal Warrant holders, Gunter & Co., continued until well into the 1880s. (Founded in 1757, the tea shop moved to Curzon Street in 1936 and closed down in 1956. The catering side of the business had been moved to Bryanston Square, where it continued until 1976.) In 1898 Agars of Manchester were brought in and provided a staff of waiters for the next seventy years.

The Club also bought its wine from London. In 1853, for instance, 12 doz. East Ind. Madeira, 8 doz. Gold Sherry, 4 doz. Pale Sherry and 6 doz. Château Margaux, costing £123 4s 6d, was delivered by Messrs. Griffiths' of Pall Mall. Port and Claret was also being bought from Mr Barnes of Lincoln's Inn Fields.

The financial arrangements for Guests were altered in 1870 when all the arrears of fines due for guests were done away with and the Landlord was to be informed by

(photo. *Hal Mullin.*)

a Member having a Guest and paid 'the sum of One pound *per diem*, half to go to the landlord and the other half to the Club'.

The names of 'visitors' are recorded between 1802 and 1839 and from 1874 onwards a book has been kept for members to sign in themselves and their guests, many of whom were in due course elected members. One regular, between 1806 and 1834, was John Ireland Blackburne of Hale Hall, Lancs., coming on eleven occasions. He was one of the oldest members of the House of Commons and extremely absent-minded. His father had been a visitor in 1785 and in 1846 his son, John Ireland Blackburne, a serving officer in the 5th Dragoon Guards, was elected but resigned immediately. His marriage took place the following week. Perhaps it was the pending marriage fine that put him off.

In 1810 a keen Meltonian and wit, William, the bachelor 2nd Lord Alvanley, was a guest for three days of Wilbraham Egerton (84). Friend of the Prince Regent, he was a nephew of John Arden (20), whose Cheshire estate he inherited, and uncle of the future Lady Haddington. It was from him that Major Tomkinson (133) acquired the Willington Estate. He occasionally hunted in Cheshire, but as a non-resident was never made a Member. He was also an addicted card player.[*]

He was a Meltonian first-flighter, despite his 16 stone, and it was he who said 'What rare fun we should have, if it was not for these damned hounds.' But he was a terrible man for butchering his horses, with spurs well-home and a slack rein. 'Harden your hearts and tighten your girths,' he would cry at the 'View Halloo'. He used to wear boots with the tops well above his knees to keep thorns out when jumping the hairy bullfinches. He once went out of his way to have a shy at the widest part of the Whissendine and justified his action by lisping: 'Whath the uth of giving seven hundred guineas for a hoth, if he's not to do more than other hothes?'

He was once hunting the same day as Mr Gunter, the famous pastry cook, whose considerable patron he was and who was out on a pulling horse and complaining bitterly of the hotness of his mount. Amid laughter from the field, Lord Alvanley called to him: 'Ith him, Gunter, ith him!'

---

[*] It has been said that he composed his own epitaph:
Here lies Lord Alvanley, waiting for the last trump.

But this story correctly appertains to the 22nd Baron de Ros, who in 1837 was found guilty in a libel action of cheating at cards by reversing the cut. When he died two years later he was said to have been given the epitaph:
Here lies England's Premier Baron, patiently awaiting the last trump.
When asked what action should be taken by those who detected Lord de Ros cheating, Lord Alvanley replied: "Back him!"

After John Arden had resigned in 1800, and possibly before that, it was customary for a list of all those who dined to be sent each year to him as the owner of The Swan. Lord Alvanley received a similar report. The lists are to be found in the Arderne Papers and also included the names of guests and the programme for the races. They were sent by a clerk called J. Cookson who would write:

MY LORD,
It being an antient custom to send to Pepper Hall a list of Gentlemen who attend the Tarporley Hunt...
I believe the gentlemen have had good sport & [were] highly gratified with the entertainment and accommodation at the Inn.

Lord Alvanley was a lifelong Subscriber to the Cheshire Hounds by his own resolution to pay £20 a year when he inherited the Arderne estate.

In 1886 it was resolved that W.H.Starkey should be asked each year as a Club Guest. In 1891 Walter Starkey, although not a Member, 'was asked to undertake the duties of Assistant Secretary at an annual salary of £10'. This was chiefly to run the Stallion Account. He lived with his brother at Wrenbury Hall and was agent for the Marbury Hall Estate for thirty years. He hunted regularly with the South Cheshire Hounds and assiduously kept a hunting journal, ten large suède-bound volumes of which from 1890 to 1935 are in the Cheshire Hunt Archive; but he rather restricted his remarks to the numbers of foxes found and killed and the runs they gave. He was eventually presented with a massive silver inkstand and a purse for his gratuitous services looking after the Poultry Fund.

Walter Starkey, cub-hunting at Poole, 1935.

Of the regular guests, not subsequently elected, mention must be made of Captain 'Ap' Griffith of Tiresford, who as a subaltern of the 7th Royal Fusiliers, before he transferred to the 1st Royal Dragoons, had whipped in to the Calpe Hounds in Gibraltar back in

1859. He married the sister of his brother-officer Captain Edmund Park Yates (198). He and his son, Captain 'Ned' Griffith, appear in the Guest Book no less than thirty-seven times up to 1921, one or the other, and sometimes both, often dining every night of the week. Major Gilbert Cotton, long-time agent at both Peckforton and Oulton,* and for fifty years Clerk of the Course at Bangor-on-Dee and a National Hunt Inspector of Courses, holds the record as an habitué with twenty-nine appearances, often as a Club Guest. Like him, Jock Fergusson, leading Gentleman Rider at the turn of the century with over 500 winners to his credit, was a frequent guest of Brian Egerton, the Secretary, being second in this particular league table, dining twenty-seven times at Tarporley. Micky Moseley (342) was one less. It gave the author great pleasure when Moseley was elected in 1974, for it meant that he was not to have any more free dinners at Tarporley and possibly top the list. He, with Gilbert Cotton and the author, were among the guests at the Bicentenary Dinner and his father, Ossy Moseley of Agden, was often a fellow diner with Jock Fergusson. The author's son-in-law, John Hunter, a former Joint Master and Honorary Secretary of the Cheshire Forest Hounds has to date dined twenty-four times as a guest. John Stringer was another pillar of the Cheshire Forest to have been invited twenty times.

As well as bringing sons, sons-in-law and other relatives or close friends to dine at Tarporley it has long been the custom to invite prominent members of the Cheshire hunting field and the Hunt Secretary of the day has often been a Club Guest if he was not already a Member of the Club.

One interesting name which appears several times in

Captain Billy Baldwin.

the Guest Book is that of Captain 'Billy' Baldwin, the pioneer big-game hunter and author of *African Hunting and Adventure*.† His hosts were doubtless regaled by The Lion's tales after a glass or two of port. He tended to speak gruffly in short sentences. The fortune he had made from ivory had by then, the early 1880's, been dissolved in the Leicestershire hunting fields, where he had also lost an eye from a thorn in a bullfinch. He was mounted on small T.B. chasers and won the Open Race at Tarporley on Reckless in 1871 and on one occasion went through the card at Croxteth, doubtless inspiring his steeds with his own headstrong nature. There must have been a bit of Jack Mytton about him as he had another old point-to-pointer, British Oak, with which he also fetched the coal and ploughed a straight furrow and on occasions rode it round the dining room table. Short and stocky with a luxuriant growth of beard, he lived with his housekeeper at Cotebrook.

Returning once unexpectedly from his travels, he arrived at Beeston Castle & Tarporley Station too late to find a fly to take him home. So he set out to walk the mere six miles carrying his baggage and on arrival in the early hours failed to arouse Mrs Matthews. He fetched a ladder and climbed in through the bedroom window. Without lighting a lamp or candle, he kicked off his boots

Gilbert Cotton.

---

* He was at the scene of the fire at Oulton on February 14th, 1926 when six lives were lost. He was in the salon when the lead water tanks came crashing through the ceiling. As it was a cold blustery morning he was fortunately wearing a heavy trenchcoat and he escaped from the holocaust of plaster and blazing beams by hurling himself backwards through the plate-glass french windows onto the balcony to save his own life. He was 91 when he died from a heart attack driving his car.

† In his younger days W.C.Baldwin had been quite fearless, reckless for sure, once having every intention of kicking a slumbering twenty-foot crocodile in the ribs 'as a memento'. His companion had stopped him from shooting it and just dragged him back in time to prevent his legs being cracked off like pipe stumps as the brute awoke and whirled its tail.

MENU.

Tortue Claire.
Palestine.
—
Turbot Sauce Homard.
Blanchailles á la Diable.
—
Cotelettes de Mouton á la reforme.
Haricot Verts.
—
Dindoneau Rôtie.
Hanche de Venaisan.
—
Pouding de Grouse.
—
Pouding a Cabinet.
Peches Melba Glaces.
—
Auges a Cheval.
—
Fromage Cuit.
—
Dessert.

SWAN INN.
TARPORLEY.   NOVEMBRE 2nd, 1910.

MENU.

Tortue Claire.
—
Merlans Frit Sauce Anchois.
—
Dinde Braze à la Chipolata.
Hanche de Venaison.
—
Perdreaux Salade.
—
Fruits.   Salade.   Glacé.
—
Œufs a l'Indienne.
—
Fromage Cuet.
—
Dessert.

SWAN INN,
TARPORLEY.   NOVEMBRE 4, 1919.

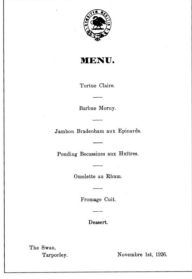

MENU.

Tortue Claire.
—
Barbue Morny.
—
Jambon Bradenham aux Epinards.
—
Pouding Becassines aux Huitres.
—
Omelette au Rhum.
—
Fromage Cuit.
—
Dessert.

The Swan,
Tarporley.   Novembre 1st, 1926.

MENU.

Tortue Claire.
—
Merlans Frit.
—
Pouding Bécassine.
—
Omelette au rhum.
—
Möelle de Bœuf.
—
Fromage Cuit.
—
Dessert.

OCTOBRE 31st, 1932.   SWAN INN,
                            TARPORLEY.

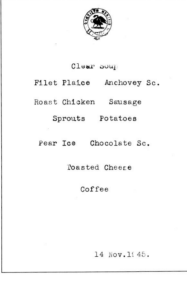

Clear Soup

Filet Plaice   Anchovey Sc.

Roast Chicken   Sausage

Sprouts   Potatoes

Pear Ice   Chocolate Sc.

Toasted Cheese

Coffee

14 Nov. 1945.

MENU

Tortue Claire
—
Scampi Meuniere
—
Faisans Roti
        Pommes Chip
—
Apricot Semoulè Eugénie
—
Fromage Cuit
—
Dessert

SWAN HOTEL
TARPORLEY   6 NOVEMBRE, 1957

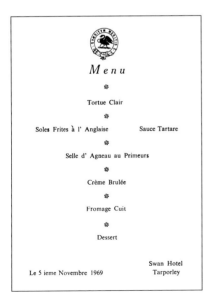

Menu
✿
Tortue Clair
✿
Soles Frites à l' Anglaise   Sauce Tartare
✿
Selle d' Agneau au Primeurs
✿
Crème Brulée
✿
Fromage Cuit
✿
Dessert

Le 5 ieme Novembre 1969   Swan Hotel
                               Tarporley

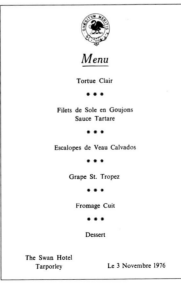

Menu

Tortue Clair
* * *
Filets de Sole en Goujons
Sauce Tartare
* * *
Escalopes de Veau Calvados
* * *
Grape St. Tropez
* * *
Fromage Cuit
* * *
Dessert

The Swan Hotel
Tarporley   Le 3 Novembre 1976

Menu

Turtle Soup
Gonzalez Byass La Concha
* * *
Butterfly King Prawns
Chablis 1989
Perrier-Jouet, N/V Brut
* * *
Roast Venison
Chateau Langoa Barton 1975
* * *
Toasted Cheese
* * *
Dessert
Graham 1975

The Swan Hotel
Tarporley   Wednesday 31st October 1990

and got thankfully into bed. He gave the prostrate form beside him a prod and announced his return. To his surprise the flesh he touched was cold and stiff. It transpired that there had been an accident on the road outside and the injured man, after being carried up to the Captain's bedroom, had expired. Not wishing to be alone overnight with a corpse in the house, Mrs Matthews had gone to stay with her sister. 'So what did you do about it, Billy?' they would ask when he told this story. 'I heaved the corpse out onto the floor and went straight to sleep. The bed was no good to him,' he used to reply in his gruff voice, though another published version, perhaps even more typical of The Lion, relates that on finding the dead man in his bed, he merely laid himself down on the floor and slept soundly until morning.

Captain David Longfield Beatty, 4th Hussars, came many times. The first time was in 1876 with 'Regie' Corbet (189) and often with Lord Combermere (157). Lord Shrewsbury, who used nearby Shavington Hall, Crewe, as a hunting box, had leased to him Howbeck Lodge, Stapleton, near Nantwich, where his second son, the future Admiral of the Fleet Earl Beatty, was born. Later, when living at Beeston Lodge, Tiverton, near Tarporley, he was usually the guest of 'Jack' Cotton-Jodrell (225), the last time in 1900. He had eloped from

Baron William von Schröder of The Rookery.

Ireland with a brother officer's wife, whom he had not been able to marry until June, 1871, by which time their first two sons had been born.

That first occasion in 1876 there was some consternation when the Club's faithful butler, Serg[t]. Corrivan of Chester, entangled his feet in a bell rope while serving and crashed to the ground. He broke his leg and the Club next morning voted him an extra £10. That was also the year the Club agreed that champagne should not be drunk at supper time.

Other notable guests before 1900 included the future 8th Duke of Atholl, invited by William Schröder (224) when Marquess of Tullibardine in 1894, and Lord Hopetoun, who became the 1st Marquess of Linlithgow. He was a close friend of Rock Cholmondeley, who let him take Higginsfield for many years as a hunting box. Another of the German Baron's guests was Capt. F.H.Fetherstonhaugh, who at one time lived at Tilstone House with his wife, the formidable Beatrice Ellerie, and was the King's Racing Manager prior to 'Mouse' Tomkinson (271). The Hon. George Keppel came in 1883 when he was eighteen.

One of Mr Booth Grey's 'Orders' in 1762 had been to 'procure for this Society two Collar Glasses and two Admittance Glasses of a larger size.' These are no longer in the Club's possession. As mentioned there is a collection of engraved rummers, the glasses from which New Members drink the classical *Quæsitum* and the four cut-glass goblets, but this glassware is thought to be of a later date, the former most likely being the item in the Disbursements for October, 1834:

Bill for Quæsitums & Carriage £2 5s

However some differ slightly and are probably older.

Each New Member, on being introduced, has to quaff off his 'Quæsitum' and may elect to do so in port, claret or champagne. In 1921 Sir Arthur Stanley (274), under doctor's orders at the time, drank his in water. This was a strange coincidence, for his uncle, the bachelor 3rd Lord Stanley of Alderley, had embraced Islam and, in the unlikely event of this very boring man having been elected, would perforce have drunk his Quæsitum in water. When he was buried in Alderley Park, the Imam of the Turkish Embassy performed the Moslem rites. The story goes that as his nephew respectfully removed his hat at the graveside, Stanley's brother snapped: 'Not your hat, you fool, your boots.'

One of the original rules was:

Three Collar Bumpers to be drank after dinner, and the same after supper. After they are drank every member may do as he pleases in regard to drinking.

By 1799 the Collar Toasts were

SUCCESS to the Meeting, Lady Patroness and Absent Members . . . . the Rest at the discretion of the President. And these were the same in 1847. The traditional toasts evolved, with FOX-HUNTING becoming the principal one, to which it was incumbent on the Manager to reply and give an account of the sport. That to the LADY PATRONESS was rather ungallantly dropped and in due course, besides the Loyal Toast and apart from THE NEW MEMBERS, the only two other toasts eventually became THE PRESIDENT and THE GUESTS.

The oldest list kept reads:

Toasts 1896

The Queen & rest of Royal Family..............The President
Fox-hunting & the Managers....................A. Smith-Barry
Father of the Hunt ....The President
New Members..J. Tomkinson
The President..H. R. Corbet
Fox Preservers ....Enniskillen
  coup. with H. Tollemache
The Guests, coupled with Ld. Hopetoun
& Prince Adolphus of Teck ....Hon. Alan Egerton
The Committee..H. R. Corbet

The last record of glasses being raised to the Father of the Hunt was in 1922 when Lord Barrymore (200) responded. In 1896 it had been Francis Elcocke Massey (163), the year before he died. It was traditional for the junior Member to propose this or otherwise the President. In 1922 there was still a toast to the Covert Owners.

It is a sad reflection that in the decades to follow fewer and not all shooting Members of the Club could put their hands on their hearts and swear their keepers had never shot foxes. For fox preservation was and is what this toast is all about.

It was after dinner that the hunting songs were sung. There is no record of when the custom was introduced, but at an early stage of the Club's history, the fare for Supper became traditionally 'black puddings and bones', the latter usually being devilled pheasant legs or wings or perhaps poultry instead of game. After their previous indulgence few of those supping would probably care. *See* Appendix H.

The evening begins downstairs at 7 o'clock with oysters and chablis, while the President greets his fellow members and their guests. The earliest mention of oysters in the accounts is a payment to Goodwin of £2 5s 4d in 1841; thereafter Jas. Lynn of Liverpool and Fleet Street became the purveyor, but they were usually sent

from Bentley & Co. of London. They got through eight or nine barrels of Natives. The price fluctuated, 26/- a barrel in 1883, but 18/- two years later. The Club used to possess its own oyster table, the gift of Wellington Cotton (157) in 1873. In more recent times smoked salmon and champagne has also been served before dinner at what in the XVIII Century was timed 7½.

Captain F.V.Hughes-Hallett, a guest of Sir Humphrey de Trafford, early in the Edwardian era, gave this description in a newspaper article:

. . . At the end of dinner without any preamble whatever, the members of the club proceed to burst into song, one by one, all round the board, everybody remaining seated, and no accompaniment whatever is provided. This over, the whole of the company adjourns for about twenty minutes to allow the board to be cleared; then up we all come again for *supper (!)*, to partake of an age old custom – to wit, "black puddings" and old beer, the latter handed round in a loving-cup, of which everybody present, members and guests, is expected to absorb his share.

Now after a first-rate dinner of umpteen courses, washed down by a perfect vintage champagne and copious bumpers of glorious old port, this pigs' blood confection, with or without the "old October," comes as a terrible stomachic shock to the hardiest diner-out. But it is so old a custom, and one is so evidently expected to acquiesce, that nobody dreams of "burking" for a moment. With as little a wry face as possible, gentlemen, down *must* go a mouthful at least of the (to me) black beastliness and a sip of the ancient brew. (*Chacun à son goût!* I remember that I nearly regurgitated my dinner, as I watched my host slowly and methodically consume an *entire plateful* of the "pudding"!)

To give him his due the gallant sailor was out next day mounted by his host on a beautiful-looking grey, but 'with a mouth like a fouled anchor'. He took himself home after being in danger of over-riding hounds and a short while later nearly jumping on top of the Duke of Westminster, who had taken a toss into a ditch and broken his wrist.

Turtle Soup has invariably been on the menu, usually on the Wednesday. It is first mentioned in the accounts in 1858 – 'preparing a turtle: £5-2-6'. For many years the turtle soup was sent out by train from the Queen's Hotel, Manchester. In 1991 a move was made by the President to abolish the tradition, mainly on 'green' grounds, having canvassed a number of Members beforehand. Lord Tollemache spoke first. Mr de Ferranti saw it as excuse to have caviare on the menu. The President himself did not regard the soup as the culinary delight others did and spoke volubly on the conscience of the Nation. However those in favour of its retention aired their views with sufficient force to bring

Tony.

Hugh.

Dick.

Geoffrey.

FOUR CARICATURES BY NOËL DEWHURST

a frown on the President's fair countenance, notably Mr Wilbraham, who defended its place on the menu as one of the Club's great traditions. When the Secretary, having been briefed by Messrs. Fortnum & Mason pointed out that turtle meat was imported under special licence and that the majority of snapper turtles used for the purpose were farmed and were not an endangered species, his chief argument was rather thwarted. The motion was defeated by 23 votes to 9.

The savoury which has long been an established tradition is *Fromage Cuit* or Toasted Cheese. The waitresses still offer: 'Wet or dry, sir?' For the choice of 'wet', the toast has previously been dunked in mulled ale.* Loving cups filled with mulled ale are also passed round, Members and Guests standing to receive them, though this custom now seems to have lapsed. For many years a certain Mrs Woodward used to loan the Club a special two-handled 'Hot Ale Mug' for this purpose and presented it in 1900. In 1926 the Club was indebted to Capt. the Hon. Evan Baillie of Bass for a consignment of strong ale. *See* Appendix H.

In the 1890s a billiard table was put up for the benefit of Members and their Guests and bridge was also played after dinner.

When William Schröder brought the twenty-eight-year-old Prince Adolphus Alexander of Teck in 1896, it was the first time there had been a Royal guest. He was a frequent member of Mr Corbet's field in South Cheshire and two years previously had married Lady Margaret Grosvenor, the Duke of Westminster's fourth daughter. His sister had married the Duke of York, the future King George V. His Serene Highness, known to his friends as Dolly, was created Marquess of Cambridge in 1917. His and Meg's home was in Shropshire, but when in Cheshire they lived at Saighton Grange and were regular subscribers to the Cheshire Hunt Covert Fund.

The next time was not until 1977 when Sebastian de Ferranti (343) brought ex-King Constantine II of The Hellenes as a private guest.

In 1979 the Prince of Wales dined with the Club for the first time. He was afterwards approached informally and following an exchange of letters between the Secretary and the Prince's Private Secretary, the latter confirmed that the Prince of Wales was 'delighted to agree to become Patron of the Tarporley Hunt Club'. The Club thus enjoys the Patronage of the Heir to the Throne as well as that of its own annually-appointed Lady Patroness. When dining he had worn Windsor Uniform and had stayed at Cholmondeley Castle. He dined again in 1988, whilst staying at Henbury Hall, the new rotunda built by Sebastian de Ferranti, and that time wore a Tarporley evening dress coat and waistcoat. In the hunting field and whenever he has hunted with the Cheshire Hounds, almost invariably on at least one day a season, he has worn his Windsor Uniform hunt coat.† He carries a silver-mounted cutting whip, with the Club's silver badge mounted on the handle.

For the Bicentenary Dinner private guests had to be limited. Apart from the President, who brought his eldest son, they were limited to the Committee and the next senior Member able to attend, Col. Langford-

---

* Sir Philip Grey-Egerton, Secretary to the Club from 1896 to 1937, used to serve 'wet or dry' at his own dinner parties at Oulton, dishing it out from a silver toasting stand, heated by hot bricks, which the butler or footman would place before him. The footmen at Oulton still wore powdered wigs prior to the Great War and, so, attired, even attended the family in their pew at Little Budworth Church at the turn of the century.

† In the summer of 1990 the Secretary wrote to offer the Club's commiserations on his painful accident on the polo field and added a postscript sending on a personal message from O'Shea the retiring huntsman, hoping that His Royal Highness would be well enough for a day with the Cheshires before the end of his last season. Back came a reply from the Private Secretary stating that the Prince had written on the letter with his left hand: 'Tell O'Shea it is the only reason I want to get better!!'

Brooke, who naturally invited Micky Moseley, and the Manager invited Mr Justice Stable, who wore his Bullingdon coat. The Duke of Beaufort himself responded to Sir John Dixon's toast to 'Fox-hunting', three new Members drank the Quæsitum that night, having been elected at an extraordinary Meeting in July.

The Earl of Halifax, MFH replied for the Guests, who also included: Sir Peter Farquhar, Bart., Sir Watkin Williams-Wynn and Sir Guy Lowther, the neighbouring Joint Managers, Brigadier A.H.Pepys, representing the British Field Sports Society, Lieut.-General Sir 'Ted' Howard-Vyse, Mr Harold (later Lord) Woolley, the President of the N.F.U., and regulars like Major Gilbert Cotton, whom the Secretary had thoughtfully included with the Club Guests, Frank Spiegelberg and the much respected Tarporley solicitor, A. W. 'Chips' Chambers. The author was also privileged to be one of them , having written a short history of the Club for the occasion. Gilbert Cotton had been at the Sesquicentennial Dinner in 1912, though at the time there was no special celebration. (A ball was held fourteen months later.)

Their letters of thanks to the Secretary give but one impression that it was a memorable evening. Many stayed on for 'bones'. Rowland Egerton Warburton's great grandson, Peter, was prevailed upon to sing more verses of the Hunting Songs he had sung after the speeches and glasses were raised to Obadiah Lane (1).

It was for long the custom to invite garrison officers from Chester and later the Army Commander from Western Command and newly appointed Chief Constables, and on occasions Bishops of Chester or members of the judiciary, including Lord Chief Justice Goddard and Lord Trevithin and Oaksey. A distinguished cleric to come in 1992 was the Right. Rev. Michael Mann, who was the guest of Major Philip Verdin. In 1922 General Beauvoir de Lisle responded for the Guests, as did General Sir Henry Jackson, who was Commander-in-Chief from 1936 to 1939. Right to the end of his life at the age of 93, he had cherished memories of dining at Tarporley, regarding Cheshire as the best scenting country he had ever hunted in. Lieut.-General Sir Brian Horrocks came in 1946 and General Ted Howard-Vyse on other occasions. The latter, like Brigadier 'Christy' Grimthorpe, used to hunt regularly in Cheshire in their day. The former 8th Army Commander, Lieut.- General Sir Oliver Leese, was brought by his brother-in-law, John Leicester-Warren (301). In 1977 Major-General 'Robin' Brockbank replied for the Guests when he was Director of the B.F.S.S.

The toast to 'Fox-hunting' has often been proposed by a visitor, including on more than one occasion Captain Ronnie Wallace himself. Lord Margadale, Colonel Sir Harry Llewellyn and Sir Bernard Waley-Cohen are other great fox-hunters to have spoken in the Hunt Room. Owen Williams-Wynn, the 10th Sir Watkin, replied to this toast the year it was given by the author. Colonel Sir Andrew Horsbrugh-Porter, Bart., one-time hunting correspondent of *The Field*, was a guest on several occasions, his predecessor being Captain John Smith-Maxwell, a 'regular' when a prominent member of the Cheshire Hunt in the 1930's. Lord (John) Oaksey, in his inimitable histrionic way, and Michael Clayton, editor of *Horse and Hound*, also made memorable speeches, the latter in the author's Presidential Year, which coincided with that magazine's centenary. Max Hastings was invited as Guest of Honour when the Duke of Westminster (347)was President.

It was appropriate that 'Toby' Daresbury (301) should respond to the main Toast the first time he dined at Tarporley, forty-two years after his election. (He had been brought as a guest in 1936.) Whilst his Limerick green collar matched the Club uniform, he failed to borrow a green waistcoat and had to be fined.

Colonel Sir John Miller came with the Prince of Wales the first time he dined. Mr John Beveridge, QC, Joint Master of the West Meath, spoke that night. On the second occasion Mr Winston Spencer-Churchill was the speaker. Alastair Goodlad (Eddisbury) and Wing Commander Robert Grant-Ferris (later Lord Harvington) and Sir Nicholas Bonsor (Nantwich) are other politicians to have been invited. Clough Williams-Ellis was a guest when he was making improvements at Bolesworth in 1936 and Lord Zuckerman once came with Sebastian de Ferranti.

When the author sat in the President's Hard Chair, his friend, the racecourse commentator and biographer, Michael Seth-Smith, was invited to respond for the Guests. He concluded his speech with his own version of a Tarporley Hunt Song:

> *Oh! give me that man with a heart that is loyal;*
> *Who loves all sport, but has no fear of toil;*
> *Who hunts in scarlet, collared in green*
> *And I'll tell you then that the man I have seen*
> *Is of character noble and countenance clear,*
> *And dines at The Swan in the Autumn each year.*
>
> *So to that man whose honour is true*
> *Who believes in tradition, but shirks nothing new*
> *We guests raise our glasses – in friendship indeed*
> *Wishing him health, good sport on his steed.*
> *Quæsitum! Quæsitum! Fill the glass to the brim*
> *For we'll drink deeply a bumper to him!*

On this occasion the Guests all rose and drank a bumper to their hosts.

RULE IX

THE BUSINESS MEETING

ORIGINALLY ALL BUSINESS WAS TRANSACTED on the Sunday, the day of assembly, except for the balloting for New Members which, after 1771, was done on the last night. The written rules of 1799 do not specifically mention when the business was to be dealt with but it was clearly still on the last day.

In 1818 it was 'resolved that in future Wednesday shall be the Race Day and Members to meet that morning for business...' In 1819 they decided to race on the Thursday in Hunt Week and to meet for business at 10 o'clock. In 1834 the race day was in future to be Wednesday and the Business Meeting continued to be that morning. When the date for the races changed again the Business Meeting was still on the Wednesday, 10 o'clock from 1848, 11 o'clock from 1889 and 10.30 o'clock from 1892 until 1955 when they went back to 11 a.m. with the time being omitted from the printed rules.

In 1864:

> It was proposed by Earl Grosvenor and seconded by Lord Egerton that any Member not attending the Meeting for the purpose of the Club business, or not sending an efficient excuse on the Wednesday morning, "be fined" a sum not exceeding 5£, besides the usual subscription of £5.0.0 as paid by absent Members. – The motion was carried.

This was abolished in 1895 but for many years afterwards it was an unwritten rule of the Club that members who habitually failed to attend the Business Meeting should resign their membership. This appears to have lapsed in post-war years. But nevertheless the Business Meeting is regarded as a three-line whip.

Up to 1785 the average attendance when the business was done was thirteen or fourteen Members.

After 1785 the excuses of members sending their apologies to the President have seldom been recorded. In the previous two registers John Crewe of Crewe is shown as frequently not sending a letter and once had 'too idle to write' against his name. The 20th-century representative of his family, Quentin Crewe, the wheelchair-bound travel writer, explorer, restaurateur and *bon vivant* was also not always punctilious about writing in and is variously shown as being in the Sahara Desert, Kenya, India, promoting his latest book on South America, Africa and 'whereabouts unknown'.

In more recent times the Meeting has frequently clashed with the Opening of Parliament, necessitating the absence of whichever Marquess of Cholmondeley was Lord Great Chamberlain. Since it has become customary once again to record the excuses, some admissible and some not so laudable have been:

Sir John Barlow sent a telegram from Kuala Lumpur in 1963
 – Finding himself outside the Kingdom.

Lord Tollemache – At Helmingham in preparation for a visit by the Monarch and her Consort that week-end.

and again – In Washington at the Treasure Houses of Great Britain Exhibition.

Sir Randle Baker Wilbraham
 – Attending the 700th Anniversary of Congleton in his capacity of Lord High Steward.

Michael Griffith – Attending an Investiture.

Sir Evelyn Broughton – Defending a lawsuit brought by one of his wives.

Randle Brooks – In the Divorce Court.

Michael Higgin – Owing to a fall at the Opening Meet.

and (twice) – Hunting with the Wynnstay.

'Chubb' Paterson – Ordered by his wife to gallop her racehorses. (Aside from Sir Randle: 'Who wears the breeches?')

Richard Tomkinson – Committing an unforgivable sin.
and again (as Vice-President)
 – Horse-coping.
and (after he had ceased to be
Master and was running his
home, Willington Hall, most
successfully as a hotel)
 – On a wine-tasting tour of Burgundy.

and perhaps the most poignant of all

Geoffrey Dean (telephoning later in the day)
 – Because Foot & Mouth Disease had been confirmed on his farm that morning and his champion herd of pedigree Jerseys had had to be destroyed.

In 1968 the President, Sir Walter Bromley-Davenport,

Tony and Hugh listening to Walter

The three Joint Managers, Gerald, Philip and Richard.

well known as a gourmand, did not attend the Business Meeting, 'suffering from a heavy cold and remaining in bed to ensure his presence at the dinner that night'. At the reception downstairs before dinner it was by no means easy to count the number of oysters he consumed. On occasions his prodigious appetite enabled him to guzzle, when available, two platefuls of crab as well, complaining most vociferously to the Secretary if none was produced or it was not properly served with all the right trimmings, including beetroot. It had been at his specific request that this crustacean had been added to the menu.

Champagne is served in the Hunt Room after the meeting and the majority of members then have lunch downstairs still wearing their club uniform field coats and waistcoats, which are as much obligatory at the Business Meeting as on the field with hounds. Amazingly until 1976 this meal was without cost to individuals, being covered by the annual subscription.

When the arrangements were made to celebrate the

The Lord President with the Secretary and the Senior Committee Member, Sir John Dixon

Bicentenary, it was decided to commission a group portrait of the Business Meeting. The artist chosen on the recommendation of Lord Leverhulme was Terence Cuneo, who accepted for a fee of one thousand guineas on condition he would be allowed to pose the members appropriately after the meeting, rather than have them all seated. He found it one of the most difficult compositions he had ever attempted, the Royal College of Surgeons giving the artist his greatest problems. He dined on the Tuesday to meet his sitters and next morning, after the meeting, tackled the formidable task of marshalling them into position for his preliminary sketch, and then during the next few months each member visited the artist's studio near Esher for a sitting and was painted direct onto the canvas. Even 'Sandy' Grant's infamous brown bowler hat was recorded for posterity.

Back at the studio, as the artist recalled in an article for *The Field* a year later when the picture was given pride of place on the front cover, 'a frequent difficulty was having to complete one isolated portrait in a part of the canvas that was barely started and at the same time establish correct proportions between a background and a foreground figure. This at a time when the intermediate characters had not even visited the studio'. His famous mouse sits attentively on the edge of Lord Rocksavage's chair, 'determined,' as Cuneo put it, 'to share the joke in Sir Walter's lively tale'.

Three Members were absent – Lord Cholmondeley at the Opening of Parliament, Lord Delamere in Kenya and Lord Daresbury hunting the Limerick Hounds. Some years later Cuneo went to Ireland and painted Toby on his grey hunter.

Sir Richard Brooke, by 1962 'Father of the Hunt' following the death that year of 'Peter' Tatton, was unable to come from Jersey, but asked to be included. As

The Business Meeting of the Tarporley Hunt Club, 1962, from an oil painting by Terence Cuneo.

1. Viscount Ashbrook, M.B.E., *President*
2. Lt.-Col. Sir Richard Verdin, O.B.E., T.D., *Hon. Secretary*
3. C. L. S. Cornwall Legh
4. G. C. Dean
5. Capt. R. V. Wilbraham, M.C.
6. A. D. Paterson, T.D.
7. Lt.-Col. J. Baskervyle-Glegg
8. C. W. Roundell
9. Sir Evelyn Delves Broughton, Bt.
10. Major D. P. G. Moseley
11. Capt. P. Egerton-Warburton
12. Lord Tollemache, M.C.
13. Lt.-Col. R. W. Whineray
14. Sir Randle Baker Wilbraham, Bt.
15. Sir Richard Brooke, Bt.
16. Earl of Rocksavage, M.C.
17. Sir Walter Bromley-Davenport, T.D., M.P.
18. Major A. L. Grant, T.D.
19. G. H. Rigby, O.B.E.
20. Col. T. M. Brooks, M.C., T.D.
21. Col. R. P. Langford-Brooke, T.D.

22. Lt.-Col. J. D. Waters, C.B., D.S.O.
23. Sir John Dixon, Bt.
24. Sir Harold Bibby, Bt., D.S.O.
25. Col. G. V. Churton, M.B.E., M.C., T.D.
26. Col. G. H. Grosvenor, D.S.O., M.F.H.
27. Viscount Leverhulme, T.D., M F.H.
28. C. R. Tomkinson, M.F.H.
29. Lt.-Col. C. D. F. Phillips Brocklehurst
30. Major H. W. Griffith, M.B.E.
31. Col. B. W. Heaton, M.C.
32. Lt.-Col. J. A. Dewhurst, T.D.
33. Col. G. N. Heath, C.B.E., D.S.O., T.D.
34. Sir John Barlow, Bt., M.P.
35. Lt.-Col. J. L. B. Leicester-Warren, T.D.
36. Col. R. D. Poole
37. Lt.-Col. R. H. Antrobus, M.C.

Absent Marquess of Cholmondeley, G.C.V.O.
                    (*Attending Opening of Parliament*)
Absent Lord Delamere (*In Kenya*)
Absent Lord Daresbury, M.F.H.
                    (*Hunting Hounds in Ireland*

Philip – now the Father of the Hunt

he anticipated, the artist ran into difficulties fitting everyone in to the agreed composition, notably Colonel Dallas Waters, Humphrey Griffith and 'Chris' Brooke himself, who was the only one not to turn up for a sitting. 'Dick', with masterly tact and masterful control of the situation steered it all through in the end and everyone was fitted in, the oldest member writing that he preferred not to comment on the final position allocated to him. But there was nothing wrong with 'Chris' Brooke's likeness. The only trouble was that, with artist's licence, Cuneo had eventually depicted him quietly pouring out for himself another glass of champagne. Sir Richard, though not a lifelong teetotaller, was more than a little hurt by the implication.

RULE X

THE PRESIDENT

WHY THE OTHER ORIGINAL MEMBERS appointed the Rev. Obadiah Lane as their first President is not known, unless it was because he was a parson. He and Richard Walthall were seven years younger than Sir Harry Mainwaring, the oldest of the nine at thirty-six.

The 6th rule laid down on November 14th, 1762 was that 'if the society consists of an equal number, the President has a casting vote' and the seventh that 'A new president for the following meeting to be ballotted [*sic*] for the last day of the preceding meeting. [And then, subsequently X'd out:] The president must manage also

the business of the Society during the time of his office.'

This custom of electing the President continued until 1866 when the practice of the next Member in succession becoming President was finally adopted. Sometimes a Member other than the Vice-President would take his place. In 1832 Lord Grosvenor, who had himself been in London when he was President two years before, wrote in his diary:

> T. 30. O. Went with Mr Tomkinson and canvassed with him. Slept at Dorfold.

> W. 31. O. Went with Mr Tomkinson to canvass about and drove in his carriage at 5 to Tarporley where I acted as President of the Hunt. We dined about 7-30.

In 1837 there had been a rule that 'if the President for the year does not attend himself, he must appoint a Member to attend in his stead, and in default of his so doing or such Member so appointed not attending, the President to be fined 5 sovereigns.' Ten years later it had been agreed that on the failure of both to attend the next in succession would act as President.

In 1895, when fines for non-attendance were abolished, Rule X from then on read:

> Each Member shall fill the office of 'President' in rotation and the following year that of 'Vice-President'. Should the President be unable to attend the 'Annual Meeting' in his proper turn, his term of office may be deferred until the next year (but no longer) and the next in turn shall become President.

In 1972 discussion took place as to whether the President and/or President-in-Waiting should be *ex officio* Members of the Committee and then in 1976 when Rule VI was changed to include the President on the Committee this rule was amended so that he took office from May 1st and the length of deferment of a Member becoming President was thenceforward at the discretion of the Committee.

In the days when there were two Meetings a year nine Members had the honour of being elected for a second term, in Lord Kilmorey (30)'s case, consecutive Meetings; 'his mild and pleasant administration was approved not only by his second Election, but by his health being Drank in three Gobblets [*sic*].' He even 'accepted the Chair a third time', but when November came round he was unable to come and subsequently resigned 'by his own desire'. In November, 1772 it was recorded:

> As Mr President has done this Hunt the honor of his Picture, their thanks are returned for the same.

John, 10th Viscount Kilmorey, from a portrait in oils by Thomas Gainsborough, c.1768 (courtesy Tate Gallery). Could this be the portrait he meant the Club to have and he then changed his mind? The glass on the right is similar to the set given to H.R.H. The Patron as a Wedding Present.

But, but apart from the above, there is no record of this or any other portrait of Lord Kilmorey having been in possession of the Club. His portrait by Gainsborough, *c.*1768, is in the Tate Gallery.[*]

A unique ceremony had taken place the first time he was in the chair at the 21st Meeting in 1772:

> During this meeting, on the 5th of Nov^br. the Lord President was pleased to signify his intention of investing Thos. Cholmondeley, Esq. of Vale Royal in this County with the most Noble order of the Belt. Accordingly he was introduced to the Lord President by two Senior Aldermen. The Whip of State was borne by the Secretary and the Belt carried on a cushion of State by the Master of the Fox-hounds; Sir Thomas's train was borne by the Junior Member & the President's by the Coverer. Great attention was paid during this ceremony, every member standing & Sir Thomas returning to the Chair his health was drunk with three Cheers. Ordered that he always appears in the insignia of his order during the meeting.

Thereafter the squire of Vale Royal signed himself: 'Thos. Cholmondeley, Alderman and Knight of the Belt.' Of those present the senior were Obadiah Lane and Booth Grey and all were Aldermen, *i.e.* Past Presidents, except for Kyffyn Heron and Thomas Ravenscroft. The Master of the Fox-hounds, who bore the Belt, was Jack Smith-Barry, sometimes referred to as 'the Grand Master'.

No others have been President twice, but it was planned that for the Bicentenary Year the Secretary, Colonel Geoffrey Egerton-Warburton, reluctant though he was, should take the chair, but he died in 1961.

In 1945, when there were seven Members elected, the order of seniority was decided by drawing lots. It was thanks to 'Dick' Verdin that it became one of the Club's unwritten rules that Members should take their seniority by age in the year in which they were elected and not by the actual order of election. Had this applied when there were seven New Members in 1915, Lord Wavertree (268) would have been President in 1928 as the oldest of them. As it was, he died twenty-one months before he was due to be President. Members who were next in line to be President when they died were Richard Walthall (7), aged 33, Edward Tomkinson (97), aged 46, Henry Hervey-Aston (103), 29, John Leche (139), 39, Baskervyle Glegg (140), 37, Arthur Davenport (182), 45, Lee Townshend (246) but for the War, aged 46, Lord Royden (287), 79, John Glegg (321), 51, Lord Tollemache (322), 65, and, but for the new arrangement which had just come into force on his election, Charles Brocklehurst (327), aged 73.

George Walmsley (128) and Colonel Tomkinson (133) both resigned just about when they would have been likely to be President – the latter for domestic economy – but their resignations were not minuted, the Secretary merely indicating the dates in the register at the beginning of the book.

Lord Grosvenor (19) was never elected President and he resigned in November, 1769, explained by the facts.

---

[*] As well as his son, Robert, his great grandson Robert was also to be elected to the Club in 1843. This Robert was the second son of 'Black Jack Kilmorey, the Wicked Earl,' whose father General Kilmorey, John Kilmorey's youngest son, had been made an Earl in 1822. The 2nd Earl abandoned Shavington in 1839, and went to live in a 'palace' at Isleworth, London, where he kept a succession of mistresses. His favourite was Prucilla Hough, for whom he built an Egyptian mausoleum of pink and grey granite when she died in 1850. It was connected to the house by a tunnel painted to look like a trellised avenue and he would rehearse his own funeral, dressed in white and lying in his coffin, pushed on a bier by his servants. When he died in his ninety-third year, he was laid beside his beloved Prucilla in her crimson velvet-covered coffin, embossed with gold, and his corpse was in a dressing gown of rat fur. – (As lucidly described by Lady Lucinda Lambton in her *Alphabet of Britain* on BBC2.)

21ᵗʰ Meeting held Novᵇʳ 1ᵗ
1772

6 : 11 : 6
40 15 10
47 : 7 : 4

Lord Kilmorey President Named for Patroness

Miss Jenny Alcock   Reelected President &
„meeting adjourned till _____   the first Sunday in Febᵖˢ

Zoforth   pᵈ by

Stephen Glynne	not excused	2 . 2 . 0	Geo Wilbr̄
Sʳ Thoˢ Broughton	abroad as V: P:	2 . 2 . 0	Geo Wilbraham
Tomkinson	do	1 . 1 . 0	Geo. Wilson
James Barry	do	1 . 1 . 0	J. Barry
Ashton	do	1 . 1 . 0	G Wilbraham —
R. Wilbraham	do	1 . 1 . 0	G. Wilson / do
Ardern	Excused	0 . 10 . 0	Geo Ardern
Crewe	not excused	2 . 2 . 0	Jⁿ A. Mainwaring

12 . 12 . 0   11 : 11 : 0

During this meeting (on the 5ᵗʰ of Novᵇ) the Lord President was pleased to signify his intention of investing Thoˢ Cholmondeley Esqʳ of Vale Royal in this County with the most Noble order of the BELT. Accordingly he was introduced to the Lord President by two senior ~~Members~~ Aldermen — The Whip of State was born by the Secretary, the belt carried on a cushion by

Kyffyn Heron (28), from a portrait in oils at Arley Hall. Two large silver cups previously owned by him were loaned to the Club by Capt. R.H.G. Tatton from 1951 until his death in 1962.

Peter Tatton

He evidently attended the year he was elected, his signature appearing against the date November 4th, 1764. He attended but one night in November, 1765 and was fined for his waistcoat, *etc*. He was fined for sending no excuse in February, 1766 and in November, as mentioned, he was fined for his horse being turned out in Grosvenor Hunt tack and quitting on the Tuesday without leave. Again he sent no excuse for the next Meeting and absented himself for three nights in November, 1767. However he was excused on payment of one guinea three months later, but in October he turned up two days without uniform, being fined for each as well as for absenting himself one night without leave. He was fined four guineas for not writing to the President to excuse himself from attending in February, 1769. Little wonder that in November the entry reads 'Lord Grosvenor: Out by his desire & his letter received – Arthur Barry has promised to speak to him about his arrears.' The accounts show that the £4 4s was collected by the landlord, Wm. Baugh.

What was far more puzzling was why his descendant, the 2nd Duke of Westminster, failed to take up his Presidential duties. When the Notices for the dinners and the List of Rules and Members were sent out for the 1919 Meeting his name was printed as President with Miss Barbara de Knoop as his chosen Lady Patroness. He had been President Elect since 1914 on the death of Lee Townsend, but in the event John Baskervyle Glegg (251) took over and neither an apology for absence nor explanation is recorded in the Minute Book by Brian Egerton. No correspondence on the matter has survived. He had just been divorced that June. His second marriage to Mrs Violet Rowley did not take place until

November 20th the following year. In 1921 Bend Or's elder daughter, Lady Ursula, was Lady Patroness and he dined on the Wednesday – his first appearance at The Swan since 1909.

As Lord Belgrave, he dined as a guest of his grandfather in 1898, a year before he succeeded. During his fifty-two years of membership Bend Or[*] only dined with the Club on six occasions in all – in 1901 when he drank his Quæsitum and brought Henry Chaplin[†] with his step-father, George Wyndham, as guests, in 1904 (bringing Lindsay Fitzpatrick), 1909 (his step-father again and Percy Wyndham, his half-brother, known as 'Perf') and in 1929 and 1932 (with his Private Secretary and *aide de chasse*, Colonel Charles Hunter). His Grace is not recorded as having sent his apology for absence from the Business Meeting, except in 1945, 1946 and 1948, although it is mentioned in the Minutes that he was abroad in 1903, 1905 and 1906 and that in 1907 'the Duke of Westminster has received a "Command" so could not attend'.

It was a happy quirk of fate that the turn of his grandfather to fill the chair coincided with the Centenary

Bend Or. There is no record of him being fined for wearing a yellow waistcoat. From a portrait in oils of the 2nd Duke of Westminster by Sir Oswald Birley.

EARL GROSVENOR'S CHAIR BY ROGERS.

Year. As mentioned elsewhere, the chair itself was known as 'The President's Hard Chair', so dubbed by Rowland Warburton. Perhaps for this reason Earl Grosvenor was motivated to commission a craftsman and woodcarver called Rogers to make a new one which he duly presented as a Presidential gift. It is not known if he actually sat in it that year – the club records contain no reference, but

The Secretary's chair presented in the Centenary Year by Earl Grosvenor. It is the same height at the President's Chair, 56 ins., made in oak and upholstered in calf with padded arms and seat. It has double baluster and vase feet. The arched back and top-rail is carved in relief TARPORLEY HUNT with a fox's mask either side and with two Grosvenor talbots supporting the Club's garter and swan badge in the back, with 'Established AD 1762 on a shield above the motto, QUÆSITUM MERITIS. The garter is inscribed STILL SWINGING AT HER MOORINGS WITH A CABLE ROUND HER NECK. At the base is a plaque with the chorus from Egerton Warburton's Tarporley Hunt, 1833:

> *Fox preservation,*
> *Throughout the whole nation,*
> *Affords recreation,*
> *Then drink it each man.*

> *Quæsitum Meritis!*
> *Good fun how rare it is!*
> *I know not where it is,*
> *Save at The Swan.*

A fox's pelt and mask are carved on the shaped seat-rail.
In relief at the base of the back is DONO DEDIT GROSVENOR and HOC FECIT ROGERS on the reverse with the words interspersed with crossed mallets and chisels.

---

* He derived his lifelong soubriquet, so the 4th Duke told the author, because as a small child his hair matched the light chesnut mane and tail of his father's Derby winner, which in turn had been given the name in commemoration of the family's heraldic shield, *Azure, a bend or*, which they had lost to the Scrope family in the Court of Chivalry after a case lasting five years in the XIV Century. Neither the heraldic term nor the Derby winner's name has an apostrophe, but strangely the 2nd Duke himself used one, Bend'or [*sic*]. His biographers are at variance – Bend'Or (Gervas Huxley), Bend Or (Michael Harrison), Bendor (Anita Leslie and Lesley Field) and Bend' Or (George Ridley). The King of Spain wrote to him as "Bend'or!" thanking him for 'the pretty polo whip' and promising to use it in important tournaments. Churchill usually called him 'Bennie' but in one typewritten letter signed by himself he addressed him as 'Bendor'. Clementine used 'Bend'or'. This signature is on a letter from Capetown, a few month's after he came of age:

† The Squire of Blankney was still active in politics. It was he who said it was harder to find a good huntsman, than a good Prime Minister. His wife had been a niece of Bend Or's grandmother. When at Trentham he occasionally came over with his daughter to hunt with the Cheshire. He was not created a Viscount until 1916.

*Sir Louis Delves
Broughton, Bt.*

in due course it became 'The Secretary's Chair' and the author can vouch for any discomfort of the old 18th-century chair as being a fallacy.

The identity of the maker is uncertain, but it is most probably William Gibb Rogers, rather than an estate craftsman. There is no record at Eaton nor in the Club papers. W.G. Rogers had exhibited at the Great Exhibition of 1851.

To add to the mystery a photograph of the chair in an unupholstered condition was found recently in the papers at Keele Park, Staffs., the seat of the Sneyd family, who were friends and neighbours of the Sutherlands.

Other Presidential Gifts include:

Four doz. Coburg Shell pattern crested Silver Table Spoons and four doz. Dessert Spoons, dated 1823:
in 1903 from Sir Delves Broughton (233), exchanged in 1980 with his grandson, Sir Evelyn (320), for two paintings of the Club by Goodwin Kilburne (1839–1924), *The Meet at The Swan* and *The Club Dining*, Sir Evelyn retaining them during his lifetime for his London house and bringing them to Tarporley each year.

Silver-gilt Two-handled Porringer and Cover in Charles II taste:
in 1910 by the Earl of Shrewsbury and Talbot (243).

Two Staffordshire part brown-glazed Beer Jugs, applied with hunting scene and other motifs:
in 1977 (belated) by Lord Grey of Codnor (296).

Silver Fox's Mask Stirrup Cup, engraved T.H.C. badge and inscription:
in 1979 by Peter Egerton-Warburton (329), to commemorate H.R.H. the Patron dining with the Club on 31st October, 1979.

Six Crystal Sherry Decanters, engraved with club monogram:
in 1983 by E.G.M.Leycester-Roxby (338).

Portrait sketch in oils by H.Calvert of Tom Rance, Whipper-in:
in 1984 by J.G.Fergusson (339).

Vice-President's Chair: the Duke of Westminster (347).

A doz. bottles Liqueur Brandy: Major Philip Verdin (349).

The Club was also given its silver-mounted ebony gavel, inscribed as follows:

Tarporley Hunt Club, 1908
President
Col. Henry Tomkinson
Presented by
Alfred Henry Tarleton of Breakspears
both of the above being Great Grandsons
of Thomas Tarleton of Bolesworth Castle
President 1788
and Grandsons of Thomas Tarleton, Junior
President 1805.

In 1912, after fifty years' membership, Colonel C.H.France-Hayhurst (193) gave a large Silver Circular Punch Bowl, embossed with peasant scenes after David Teniers, Jan Steen and Van Ostade.

Among those declining to fill the post of President were Lord Egerton of Tatton (280), who resigned the same year, Lord Newton (284), Jimmy Tinsley (288), who never attended after the War, 'Robin' Grosvenor (289), Richard Barbour (294), Lord Daresbury (300), always hunting his hounds in Ireland, and Gavin Clegg (333). Richard Barbour, although he did not send in his resignation until 1957, had strong views about hunting and post-war agriculture in Cheshire and wished to be passed over when his turn came in 1954. Stating that he regarded the President of the T.H.C. as the official Cheshire host to fox-hunting, he declined the second offer a year later. 'My time is more than fully occupied trying to make good the prestige of property ownership on the Bolesworth Estate where others in bygone years have failed to do repairs, galloped away the good grass which pays for such work and fritted main-tenance on the erection of hunting hatches etc. As property own-ership is the primary qual-ification for membership... I feel that by my works I am upholding the high and nec-

*George Richard
Barbour, from a
portrait in oils by
Frank Eastman.*

essary traditions to the existence of the club,' wrote the ex-Manager somewhat incongruously.

Two years later he resigned in an irretrievable mood of irreconciliation so far as hunting and farming were concerned.

Gavin Clegg, who suffered from ulcers as well as infirmities of old age, wrote to the Secretary:

> There have been a stream of octogenarian Presidents lately ...and I don't want to add to their number.

He resisted the Secretary's efforts to persuade him that it would not have been the amphytrionic ordeal he envisaged from an oratorical, gastronomic, bibulous or even temperate point of view. The Club sent him a bottle of burgundy to enjoy at home. (Such a gesture has often been made for Members unable to attend through illness.)

In 1980 when 'Sim' Wilbraham was President in his eighty-seventh year he had been unable to take the chair at the Business Meeting and missed the dinner. He had been taken ill during the Tuesday dinner and had a bad fall at his home that night. After his health had been proposed *in absentem*, his son, Hugh, the seventh generation of his family in the Club, read out his intended reply. That night 'Chris' Brooke had hoped to be present on the 60th anniversary of his election but was not fit enough to travel from Jersey. He died the following February in his ninety-third year, at the time the oldest ever Member of the Club. However he was overtaken in this distinction by Sir Harold Bibby (324) who was born on February 18th, 1889 and died on March 7th, 1986. He had been 68 when elected.[*]

It was not invariably the custom for the President to take the chair at the Business Meeting. The practice of signing the previous year's minutes did not start until 1876 and from then until 1890 Lord Combermere (157) seems to have taken the chair and thereafter Henry Tollemache (204) or whoever was the senior Committee member.

The average age of the President during the first fifty years was 33, including the congenial Lord Kilmorey (30) who was 62 the first time he was elected. But George Heron (18) was the oldest at 67. Between 1812 and 1900 the President's average age rose to 41 and from 1901 to 1938 it was 54 and has been 58 since 1946. The first septugenarian was Hubert Wilson (249) owing to his resignation and subsequent re-election. When the octogenarian Colonel Noah Heath took the chair in 1966, the Secretary added to the Minutes before signing them as President the next year:

> Members noted that the President, aged 85, was ten years older than any previous holder of the office. At Ox Heys . . . he had been accompanied by his daughter, grandson and great grandson.

Colonel Noah Heath

Rowland Egerton Warburton was a Member for forty-eight years and a further eighteen as an Honorary Member. Harry Brooke (111) was sixty-three years a Member with four as Honorary. But Sir William Bromley-Davenport (235) achieved sixty-three and three months. The first time the Club dined after the War, Lord Cholmondeley (279) and the twenty-two others present signed a letter of congratulations in which there was what seems rather an unenterprising reference to Sir Harry Mainwaring's Gold Medal:

> We should now have liked to present you with a Diamond Medal, but present circumstances forbid and, in any case, we feel that you would probably prefer this expression of our deep regard and affection for you and of our continued good wishes for your health, which we drink tonight.

It was and has remained so by an original rule, now unwritten, that the President must appoint a Lady Patroness for his meeting, 'she being a spinster'.[†] It was

---

[*] A remarkable link with the past is formed by Field-Marshal Combermere's third wife, Mary, who died aged 90 in 1889, the year Sir Harold was born, in that her husband was contemporary with George Wilbraham, an Original Member. Lady Combermere was thus living in the lifetime of seven Members who celebrated the Club's Bicentenary, the last of whom died in 1986.

[†] Besides the Cycle of the White Rose, other notable neighbouring institutions to appoint Lady Patronesses are The Ancient and Loyal Corporation of Ardwick, founded in 1763, and the Anglesey Hunting Club (which also has a green collar), founded 1815, and the Anglesey Hunt Balls dating from 1757. The mock Aldermen of Ardwick used to send six pairs of gloves to their Lady Patroness, an unmarried daughter or near relation of the old Mayor. It was stipulated that 'if the Lady Patroness gives birth during her year of office, the new Mayor presents her with a silver cradle for the child.' D.P.G.Moseley (318) was Mayor, 1970-71.Current members include Michael Flower, Richard Cornwall-Legh and Bill Bromley-Davenport.

Coursing Clubs were also institutions which appointed Lady Patronesses.

The young Lady Patroness, from a sketch by Piers Egerton Warburton.

his first duty. And 'Should the Members of this Society in a party attend any of the Neighbouring aſſemblys the President must ask the Lady Patronefs for the time being to dance, should she be there.' It became and still is the custom for the permission of the Tarporley Hunt Club's Lady Patroness to be sought by the Manager of the Cheshire Hunt before hounds move off from the Opening Meet at Ox Heys. Other duties occasionally performed on behalf of her President over the years have been the presentation of the prizes at the Horse Show and the T.H.C. Cup at the Cheshire Hunt Point-to-Point.

It is the normal practice to choose the daughter or grand-daughter of a Green Collar and during her season of office she too wears the green collar. Lady Patronesses are now entitled to wear the Club button for life. Until comparatively recent years before the Second World War she was expected to ride side-saddle.

Apart from the five years for which the records were lost and the thirteen years when there was no President, a Lady Patroness was for some reason not appointed on another thirty-seven occasions. This was deplored in 1859 and minuted that 'such want of gallantry, it was hoped, would be remedied for the future'. This accounts for the years 1842 to 1859, but there was a further lapse from 1883 to 1897 with one exception – naturally enough

Lord Enniskillen, who chose Miss Cholmondeley. Of the young ladies who thus missed out during the former period, the two most notable were Mary Alice and Mary, the daughters of the Poet Squire, Rowland Egerton Warburton, who for some reason made but one reference to the Club's traditional appointment and that was in his *Farewell to Tarporley*.

> *The classical* Quæsitum *and the President's hard chair,*
> *Each year's succeeding Patroness whose charms were toasted*
> *there;*
> *The inevitable wrangle which the Farmers' Cup provokes,*
> *Sir Watkin cracking biscuits and Sir Harry cracking jokes.*

Six ladies have been appointed for a 2nd Term, but in 1948 it was agreed that a lady should not hold office more than once. One of the six was Miss Mimi Poole, who in later life, as Mrs Bache Hay, later Lady Hay, was a prominent National Hunt owner and enjoyed a lot of fun with a Grand National contender, Goosander. The youngest Lady Patroness, it seems, was Lord Delamere's daughter, Sybil, chosen by Lord Richard Grosvenor (197) in 1879 when still seven years old. In 1896 she married a future Master of the Quorn, Algy Burnaby of Baggrave Hall, Leics., but divorced him in 1902. (She was only 39 when she died in 1911 and is buried at

Whitegate, Cheshire.) Lord Arthur Grosvenor (226) was the first member to choose his own niece (the future Countess of Shaftesbury), Lord Rocksavage (312) his own daughter and 'Teddy' Leycester-Roxby ((338) his grand-daughter. The author's grand-daughter, Samantha Hunter, at 12, was the youngest since Sybil Cholmondeley and therefore this century.

The ladies are listed in Appendix A, showing their relationship, if any, to Members of the Club.

The last word of this chapter can be left to the last member of the Arden family to be President. In his letter to the Secretary when Tarporley Week was over in 1937 offering him 'thanks that I am quite unable to voice as I would':

DEAR AND KIND FRIEND,
Thank you for your letter. It is, of course, a <u>shocking</u> thing that the President should have to pay for his guests!! I enclose my £2... [Referring to] the groundwork of my speech, I must confess that I had it mind to "fire off" some really good stories of happenings in the hunting field; and at some propitious moment, to sing a rattling good (old) hunting song which in long byegone days, had appeared in the "Pink 'Un". All this "went by the board" – very naturally ... The Hunt Club – and the Hunt Room –; small wonder that our guests look round the walls – as you and I have seen – with feelings of astonishment and admiration, aye; and something that goes deeper still. I've felt it myself, whenever – and that is often – I find myself irresistibly drawn in to the "Swan"; to stand and think of all those whose names are most fittingly inscribed in letters of gold.

Ever yours –
HENRY

As a postscript, he discovered at Arderne, just after the War, a carved wooden saltbox, which had been there for over seventy years and had previously belonged to the Club. It gave him special pleasure to ask the Club to receive it back.

Miss Samantha Hunter, Lady Patroness, 1984, with her father and grandfather at Ox Heys Farm.

The Salt box

RULE XI

ANNUAL SUBSCRIPTION

IT WAS NOT UNTIL 1867 THAT AN ANNUAL SUBSCRIPTION was introduced. Up to then the cost of each meeting was shared amongst the Members present. The 12th rule of 1762 had been:

> The House bill must be payd the seventh day of each Meeting & after that is done every Member has the liberty of going after his own Inventions.

The fines, especially those for non-attendance, had always been considerable and as 'forfeitures were applyd for the benefit of the Society attending the Meeting when they were forfeited', these fines represented a fair contribution towards the expenses.

Besides the House bill, there was as already mentioned, in the early days, a Claret A/C to which all Members contributed, whether present or not – a levy which was made whenever necessary, usually amounting to two guineas. In 1805 there was the levy of six guineas for wine, but the Secretary notes that he was unable to collect it, – 'N.B. Six Pounds only appears to have been brought to account and collected.'

There had been various subscriptions levied, such as that for 'the Grand Master's' picture in 1779, the forks in 1806 and other amounts for the 'Race Fund' and the 'Show Fund', but in 1867 it was decided:

> that each Member of the Hunt shall, after this year, give an annual subscription of TEN POUNDS and shall not in future be liable to any payments towards the Racing Fund or Horse Show.

It was agreed to contract with the Landlord of The Swan for one specified sum (£15) to be paid out of the subscriptions to the house servants, in lieu of the charge for attendance. The ostlers were excluded from this arrangement.

In 1908 it was increased to £11 'to cover the £1 which had to be collected separately for the Hunt Horse Nomination'. (*See* Appendix G.) It remained at this figure until it became £20 in 1970.

Over the years donations were made to worthy causes.

In 1849, for example:

> Ten Pounds was voted to be given by the Club in aid of the Funds collecting to rebuild the Tarporley School House and Two Pounds annually towards the School expenses. The above amount was given to the Rev. Mr [Richard] Statham, Rector, at the Meeting.

A Meeting of the Club was held on October 4th, 1939 at Bostock Hall with eleven Members present, when it was decided that the subscription would be reduced to £2 until further notice.

RULE XII

BANKER'S ORDER

IT WAS IN 1867 THAT A RULE WAS ALSO BROUGHT IN for each Member to pay his Annual Subscription on or before 1st October by forwarding a written authority to his Bankers.

The Club's bankers were originally The Union Bank of Manchester (Northwich Branch), taken over by Barclay's in 1942. The Cheshire Hunt account was formerly kept with Messrs. Parr & Lyon at Warrington.

RULE XIII

PHOTOGRAPH

THE YEAR AFTER THE CENTENARY CELEBRATIONS the President, Colonel Richard Brooke (151), seconded by Rowland Egerton Warburton (125) proposed:

> That each of the present and all future Members of the Club be expected to present to the Club a coloured Photograph Portrait of himself in the hunting uniform of the Club – in size Eight inches by Six.

It was then further proposed by Lord Egerton (132) and seconded by Mr Glegg (94) that the portraits be kept in a book or case and not to be put up on the walls – the book to be selected by the Club.

The huge album in which these portraits were kept was rebound, because of its excessive weight, into two large red leather volumes at the time of the Bicentenary celebrations. There had been much consternation when it was first produced and talk of a stand to put it on, but this never materialized.

However, from the 1890s onwards fewer and fewer Members complied with this rule. Up to then seventy-four Members out of a possible eighty-eight are recorded and between then and 1938 out of sixty only some

Right*: Sir Richard Brooke, Bt. (151)*

Below: *David Brooke (358), from a portrait in oils by Raymond L. Skipp.*

Above right: *Frank Massey by Piers Egerton Warburton(163).*

Right: *The Rev. William Armitstead, Vicar of Goostrey and editor of* Portrait Sketches of Cheshire Hunting Men.

Diana Russell Allen.

fourteen produced photographs of themselves for posterity, not all of them in club uniform. Various attempts have been made by the Secretary of the day to maintain the custom, but with limited success. Fortunately at the time of the bicentenary, photographs of all the Members were taken at the Tuesday dinner and after the Business Meeting to assist the artist, Mr Terence Cuneo, to commemorate the occasion on canvas. Specially bound and cased albums of these were made, for those Members requiring them. There is also a separate collection of coloured photographs mounted in a small album. Since 1962 less than half have honoured the rule.

On the resignation of Sir Richard Brooke (91) in 1863, the new 'Father of the Hunt', John Baskervyle Glegg (94) was the first to have his portrait in the Album, although Rowland Eyles Egerton-Warburton (125) is now on the first page. Mr Glegg, one of those who chose to wear

evening dress, has a velvet waistcoat, which by then had gone out of fashion. The President, whose idea it was, presented a small gouache of himself standing beside his grey hunter. He is not, however, wearing a green collar, unlike his great great grandson, David (358), who chose the club evening uniform for a recently commissioned portrait of himself, as did Ricky Roundell (341).

In 1899 Colonel the Hon. Richard Stapleton-Cotton, the second Lord Combermere's younger son presented the album of original hunting sketches collected by his father. Several are copies of ones contained in *Portrait Sketches of Cheshire Hunting Men (1850-1890)*, which was published in 1903. This was edited by the Rev. W.G.Armitstead, the hunting Vicar of Goostrey, who presented a copy to the Club. The artist was Frank

Johnny Dixon, the Hunt Secretary and dedicated Committee Members of the T.H.C., who, although he started hunting late in life, frequently invited the Master to 'be sure to draw my bottom', which he assured him had lots of good lying. His language could be as blue as a very ripe Cheshire

Massey (163) of Poole Hall and a leather-bound volume of all the original water-colours also came into the possession of the Club. The first sketch is of Massey himself, dated 1876 by Piers Egerton Warburton (194). In 1991 David Clegg gave another copy in memory of his parents, Gavin and Angie Clegg, who came to live at Poole in the 1950's.

Another volume of drawings, called *Cheshire Cats and Cheshire Cheeses* was published in 1937. These were by *Hard Hide* (Miss Mildred Brown) with text and captions by *Tough Skin* (Diana Russell Allen). Several are reproduced in this volume.

The Roundells – the modern generation at Dorfold, from an oil painting by Howard Morgan.

RULE XIV

FAILURE TO PAY

THE TWENTIETH RULE IN 1762 READ: 'Any Member who advances the money for an Absentee to be re-imbursed by the Society in case of such absentee refusing to pay him, & the absentee to be expelled.'

It never happened.

By the 5th Rule it was already decreed that:

Any Member that shall cause or make any disturbance during the meeting (upon refusing to submit to the sentence pafsed on him by the Majority of the Society) shall be immediately expelld.

This rule has yet to be invoked.

The present rule was passed in 1891 as follows:

If any Member's Annual Subscription, or the fines imposed by the Club, are not paid on or before the Wednesday of the next Meeting of the Club, the Member's name may be removed from the Club at the discretion of the Meeting.

RULE XV

SUPERNUMARY AND HONORARY MEMBERS

see Appendix C

THE PRESENT RULE IS AS FOLLOWS: 'Any person appointed Master or Joint Master of the Cheshire Hounds. not being a Member of the Tarporley Hunt Club, may be invited to become an *ex officio* Supernumerary Member of the Club during his or her term of office only and any such persons at the termination of their Masterships may be invited to become Honorary Members of the Club so long as they

Johnnie Glegg (94).

Harry Brooke (111)

Sir Philip de Malpas Grey-Egerton, Bt. (130).

Lord Egerton of Tatton (132).

Sir Humphrey de Trafford, Bt. (144).

Capt. H.H. France (153).

Tom Aldersey (183).

William Legh of Lyme (188).

Sir Philip le Belward Grey-Egerton, Bt. (191)

Gus de Trafford (192).

Willie Tomkinson (195).

William Langford Brooke (199).

Capt. G.J.Shakerley, Jnr. (201).

The Earl of Haddington (202).

Henry Tollemache (204).

T.H.Marshall (208).

Major George Dixon (213).

Lieut.-Col. Henry Cornwall-Legh (219).

The Hon Alan de Tatton Egerton (232).

Colonel Henry Tomkinson (239).

Johnnie Baskervyle-Clegg (251).

Captain Cuthbert Leicester-Warren (267).

Captain George Wilbraham (290).

Sir Philip le Belward Grey Egerton, Bt. (298).

continue to reside and hunt in the Cheshire Country. Ladies elected under this rule will be excused from wearing the Hunt Uniform as set out in Rules II and III except for a green collar on their hunting coats and will not be eligible to attend the hunt dinners.'

RULE XVI

ALTERATION OF RULES

NO LESS THAN TWENTY-FOUR RULES WERE MADE at the Inaugural Meeting and these have been added to, rescinded and altered from time to time ever since. At the 9th Meeting in 1766 'it having been Proposed that the Rules of the Hunt be written & hung up in the Room during the Meeting, it was carried in the negative – but that any Member has a right to take a copy of the Rules for his own private use'.

The oldest printed list of Rules and Members in the possession of the Club is dated January 1st, 1814 and addressed to Wilbraham Egerton, Esq., M.P., Tatton Park and stamped KNUTSFORD. By then there were fourteen Rules and the first eleven have virtually remained in the same order, covering the same aspects ever since.

In the fold of this particular sheet are written the conditions for two races due to close and a debit note for Mr Egerton's 1813 subscription. It was later the practice to send out these lists of rules and members prior to the Annual Meeting. Apart from 1926 and 1927 the Club has a complete set of them from 1887 onwards. They were not printed for the wartime years nor for 1947.

In 1847 the present rule came into force, namely that

No new Rule, or any rescinding or alteration of an old one, shall be made unless ten Members are actually present and voting; and two-thirds of those voting shall be in favour of such new Rule, rescinding, or alteration.

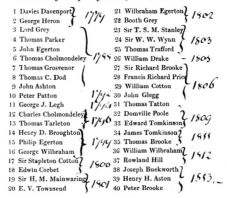

RULES

OF THE

TARPORLEY HUNT,

January 1st, 1814.

1. The Meeting to commence on the last Monday in October, if there are five, if not, on the first Monday in November.

2. Each Member to appear at Dinner in strict Uniform, viz. Scarlet Coat, with Green Velvet Collar, and Green Waistcoat, and Breeches, or forfeit Five Guineas.

3. Each Member not appearing in the Field with the Hounds, or upon the Course, with Scarlet Coat, and Green Velvet Collar; also, with a Red Ribbon in front of his Bridle, be fined One Guinea for each offence.

4. The business of the Hunt to be conducted by a Committee of three Members, and on the death, or resignation of either, another to be appointed at the ensuing Meeting.

5. The number of Members to be Forty, and confined to the County, being qualified by property, family, or residence.

6. The Members to be elected by ballot, and two black balls to exclude.

7. Every Member on his Election to pay, if married, Twenty Guineas; if single Ten Guineas.

8. Each Member marrying after his election, to pay Twenty Guineas, each time.

9. Any Member introducing a guest, to pay for each, if he stays one day, One Guinea; if two days, Three Guineas; and Guinea and Half each day afterwards.

10. The Members to meet at ten o'clock on Thursday morning in the Hunt week, to settle the business of the Hunt.

11. The President to be elected by the Majority of Members present, on the Thursday, and fined Five Guineas for non-attendance if his excuse is not allowed of.

12. Any Member not attending the Hunt for two succeeding years, and not having written an excuse, allowed by the Meeting to be sufficient, is excluded.

13. Any Member not attending on or before Wednesday, or having sent no excuse, is fined Five Guineas; and any Member absenting himself from the Meeting afterwards, without leave of the President, to be fined at the discretion of the Hunt.

14. Every Member is fined One Guinea of course, for not attending the Meeting, and more if his excuse is not deemed satisfactory.

Members of Tarporley Hunt, 1st Jan. 1814.

1 Davies Davenport	*1779*	21 Wilbraham Egerton	*1802*
2 George Heron		22 Booth Grey	
3 Lord Grey		23 Sir T. S. M. Stanley	
4 Thomas Parker		24 Sir W. W. Wynn	*1803*
5 John Egerton		25 Thomas Trafford	
6 Thomas Cholmondeley	*1788*	26 William Drake	*1805*
7 Thomas Grosvenor		27 Sir Richard Brooke	
8 Thomas C. Dod		28 Francis Richard Price	
9 John Ashton		29 William Cotton	*1806*
10 Peter Patton	*1794*	30 John Glegg	
11 George J. Legh	*1792*	31 Thomas Tatton	
12 Charles Cholmondeley	*1796*	32 Domville Poole	*1809*
13 Thomas Tarleton		33 Edward Tomkinson	
14 Henry D. Broughton		34 James Tomkinson	*1811*
15 Philip Egerton	*1799*	35 Thomas Brooke	
16 George Wilbraham		36 William Wilbraham	*1812*
17 Sir Stapleton Cotton	*1800*	37 Rowland Hill	
18 Edwin Corbet		38 Joseph Buckworth	
19 Sir H. M. Mainwaring	*1801*	39 Henry H. Aston	*1813*
20 E. V. Townsend		40 Peter Brooke	

CHAPLAIN.
REVEREND PHILIP EGERTON.

COMMITTEE.
SIR H. M. MAINWARING, BART.
REV. WILLIAM DRAKE.
CHARLES CHOLMONDELEY, ESQ.

J. FLETCHER, PRINTER, CHESTER.

IV

'Shades of Sir Peter and Barry Look Down'

THE CLUB'S USE OF A PRIVATE ROOM at The Swan was acquired from the outset but the present Hunt Room was built in 1789, when extensive alterations were carried out. This date over what was an open Market Hall, when the Inn had its Georgian façade added, is on the lead rainwater heads. It was during the period for which the Club has no records. The old Corn Market had been built in 1711 by Sir John Crewe with masonry from the old hall at Utkinton. That the original room, probably in another part of the building, was in need of re-furbishment, is borne out by an item in the club accounts for November, 1773:

Paid Mʳ Yoxall for survey of intended alterations and plans £2 2s

The work was done by the next Meeting, each Member paying £1 11s 6d and Mr Arden, himself, who owned the property, contributed £6 14s 0d. The total cost was £73 7s 6d of which Mr Scarrott of Namptwich was paid £19

2s 0d for supplying the eating room with a Scotch Carpet & Green Moreen* Curtains and the balance was

Pᵈ. Wilkinson on acct of Bill delivered Febʳʸ.1774
£20. 9s.6d.
Settled with him for Room and Paid him   £33.10s.0d.

The former amount was for making two Dozen Common & two Arm Chairs & two Cradles for Port, as ordered by the Club at their meeting in February, 1773, so the rest is likely to have been for the installation of new doors, window shutters, mantelpiece, panelling or dado rails or the like.

Such features were incorporated in the new room and later were added a new-fangled bell-wire system, with a bell-pull either side of the chimney-breast, and a wrought-iron grate, chased with foxes, vines and bunches

* A stout woollen or woollen and cotton material, either plain or watered .- O.E.D.

A corner of the Hunt Room as it was in 1912, showing the 'President's Hard Chair'on the right. From a photograph in the 9th Edition of HUNTING SONGS.

Peter Egerton-Warburton and Col. Gerald Grosvenor. Note the wicker firescreens.

69

of grapes, believed to be 18th-century Coalbrookdale. Though sealed off, the extensive back-ovens are still there in the pantry behind. Although cane screens were provided for the backs of the chairs, those seats were always the most unpopular and invariably the cause for a grumble. In recent years because of central heating, the fire has only been lit for supper.

The room measures $37\frac{1}{2}$ ft. by 26 ft. with three doors leading off, one into the upstairs passage, one into an ante room, now used as a bar by the hotel, and one into a pantry. In the old days the ovens would have been put to good use. Until the arrival of modern equipment it was a miracle for food to arrive hot on the table. This was by no means always achieved and plates were often cold. The quickest access from the hotel kitchen to the Hunt Room is by means of an outside staircase across the cobbled yard, making life a misery for the catering staff, especially in inclement weather, sometimes even in snow and ice.

In November, 1774 it was noted 'Wilkinson to take back the great chair and either to alter it to the approbation of the Hunt or to make a new one, charging nothing for the same; on this condition the gentlemen agree to paying him for the great chair'.

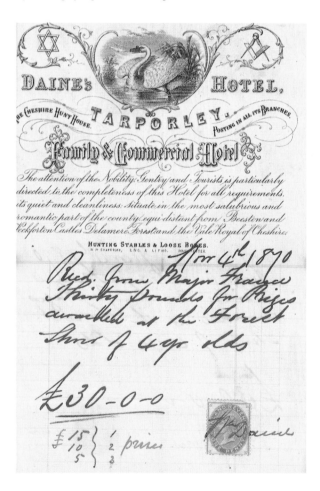

And in the account:

Wilkinson Joiner for the little chairs — 18: 08: 6.

In February he was paid a further 14=0=6 with a note in November, 1775 that he was still to be paid for the Great Chair, his bill being finally settled in April, 1776 for 18=7=6.

There are entries in the Parish Register for a 'John Wilkinson, carpenter of Tarporley', so it would be this local craftsman the members had commissioned to make a suitable chair for their President and it is believed that this is the one still in use with its ornamental urn and recumbent foxes on its arm supports. But there is an unexplained entry in February, 1784:

Ordered that the President's Chair be presented by the Torporley Hunt to the Rev^d. Crewe Arden, the very worthy Rector of this parish, as a Testimony of their high respect and regard.

There is no record of a second chair, so it was probably returned to the Club after the death of John Arden (20)'s youngest brother in 1787. Either that, or he declined the gift. A further possibility is that the rejected chair was palmed off on the parson and Wilkinson made a bigger and better one without further charge.

The Club now has a harlequin set of forty dining chairs with two open armchairs, each with a fox's mask carved in relief on the top-rail, with four slightly differing Chippendale-style patterns, including Wilkinson's 'little chairs'. They have been mentioned at various times, usually in dire need of repair, first in 1807.

Forty years later:

The Committee called the Members' attention to the distressed state of the room furniture etc. when it was voted that the room should, be painted – carpet and new curtains provided of the hunt colours, the chairs new stuffed and repaired and the picture frames re-gilt.

In 1848 'the new furniture and painting was approved of and Members sat much easier in their seats, if not longer than formerly'. It was in 1870 that they were in need of repair again and others of a similar pattern were ordered to be made.

The Founder Members would have chosen Tarporley not only for its central location, close to Delamere Forest, but for being within hacking distance of what was then, as now, some of the best pasture land in the county. The Swan, as a Coaching Inn with ample outlying stabling, was a well-established staging post on the road to Chester and Holyhead and the turnpike road North.

Wilkinson's Great Chair, which cost £18:7s.:6d. It is mahogany, 56 ins. high. The rectangular back is surmounted by a double-scroll broken pediment with dentilling, centred by an urn with fluted pilasters pierced with an arched floral apse, vertical splats, the lower part with spindles. Two small rosettes are placed in the spandrels. The heads of the recumbent foxes, carved in relief on the moulded scroll arm-supports, are somewhat crude, probably due to their ears being worn away or damaged over the years. The padded seat with a fluted shaped seat-rail is on fluted square legs, joined by an H-stretcher, with brass castors. It is upholstered in black horsehair with brass nailhead borders.

The oldest part of the building dates from 1565 and the main part of it had been rebuilt after a fire in 1735.* Like many others, this hostelry took its name from the collars of white embroidered swans which Queen Margaret of Anjou, the Consort of Henry VI, got their six-year-old son to distribute to Lord Audley, the commander of the Lancastrian forces, and to all the Cheshire gentry before the Battle of Bloreheath, near Muckle-stone in Staffordshire, in 1459. They were to be worn by them in token of their attachment to herself, the King, and the ill-fated Edward, Prince of Wales. As Egerton Warburton put it in his *Tarporley Swan-Hopping* (1862):

The emblem of the fettered white swan was in turn adopted by the Club as its badge, encircled by a garter

> *Heralds say she is sprung from the White Swan of yore*
> *Which our Sires at Blore Heath to the Battlefield bore;*
> *When* Quæsitum meritis, *loyal and true,*
> *Their swords Cheshire men for Queen Margaret drew.*

---

* A twenty-six-year-old pot boy was trapped in what is now the Club's cellar and asphyxiated. A psychic investigator has confirmed the presence there of his troubled spirit, which has caused poltergeist activity, though fortunately without detriment to the port.

inscribed *Quæsitum Meritis.* It was in 1870 that a die was ordered to be made for stamping the Club's writing paper and envelopes. It is not known when and at whose suggestion this motto came into being, but it was in the XVIII Century, as some of the rummers engraved with it date from then. A literal translation is 'That which is sought to those who merit it'. It is derived from the XXX Ode of Book III of Horace (65-8BC): *Sume superbiam quæsitam meritis).*

In 1956 the Hon. Secretary asked Prof. Robt.W.Lee, DCL, FBA, a Latin scholar of some repute, for a translation. He agreed with another version of Horace: 'Won by their merits', which had been suggested by Sir Leonard Stone of Salterswell House when responding for the Guests. Another academic gave it as 'The Quarry through merit'. That of Colonel Geoffrey's grandfather is preferred – 'The Deserving Alone'.

The premises were part of the Utkinton Hall estate which the Arderne family of Alvanley Hall and Harden Hall (near Stockport) had inherited through marriage to a Done.* John Arden, Jnr., the first to live at Utkinton Hall, the seat of the Dones, was elected a Member of Tarporley in November, 1765, not resigning until 1800. It was doubtless at his instigation that the inn was rebuilt and this close tie with the Club's interests was maintained by the Baillie-Hamilton family, which succeeded on the death of the last Lord Alvanley in 1857.

---

* With this property goes the office of Hereditary Chief Forester and Bowbearer-in-Chief of the Forest of Mara and Mondrem (Delamere Forest) dating from AD1123. This bailiwick was granted by the 3rd Earl of Chester to Ranulf de Kyngeslegh by tenure of a horn, held in sergeantry, the black horn itself now being in the Grosvenor Museum, Chester. *Circa* 1244 it passed from the Kyngeslegh family to the Dones. The eventual heiress of that family married a Crewe in the mid-XVII Century. After passing for the fifth time with the spindle to the Ardernes, John Arden, Jnr.(20) became the twenty-seventh Hereditary Chief Forester, his grandfather having married an aunt of the Miss Done who had married a Crewe. On John Arden's death it passed in turn to his nephews, the 2nd and 3rd Lord Alvanley, and going on to their great-niece, who married Lord Haddington (202). His great great grand-daughter, Desmond O'Brien's elder daughter, Mrs Karen Cowan, became the thirty-sixth holder of this ancient office.

From 1863 a Mr William Daine was the tenant and the inn was known as Daine's Hotel as may be seen from the bill-head. His predecessor was a Mr Edward Hepper, who had taken over from a Mr Prideaux, who had succeeded a family called Bull. At the beginning of the century people called Baines kept the house and a Mr White was the landlord in 1811 and handed over to Mrs Elizabeth Bull in 1823. Daine also farmed 106 acres with the hotel. After he gave up the licence in 1884, Lord Haddington engaged Miss Hayes as his successor. Mary Ann and Alice Hayes were helped by their sisters until they were married. With their aging father living there as 'the Man about the House', it meant that the licence could be granted to a woman. It was on Daine's departure that Lord Haddington gave his consent that 'in any agreement with an incoming tenant, the exclusive use of the Hotel should be reserved for the Club during the Hunt Week'.

By an agreement, dated 1885, with Mary Ann Hayes the Club provided Turtle, Punch, Oysters and Ice and paid her £100 for all other charges except the Wine Butler, the menu to be approved each morning by the Committee. Bedrooms were to be charged on the same conditions as previously and in addition the Committee was to pay Miss Hayes £25 for the Farmers' luncheons up to 200 with an extra 1/- a head above that number.

To make life more difficult for her, Members had until 6 p.m. each day to sign in their guests, but in practice the numbers were fairly constant over the years, with 6 on the Monday, about 30 on Tuesday and Wednesday and 12 on the Thursday.

In due course the estate was left to Lord Haddington's youngest son, Henry, who, a few years before he died in 1949, began selling off parts of it. It was an anxious time for the Committee, for it was clear that The Swan Hotel would soon be sold. And the running of the hotel and the Club's requirements for Hunt Week were far from being back on an even keel after the intervening war and immediate post-war years.

The first idea of the Club buying The Swan on a mortgage was dismissed. Clearly the best solution was for Greenall, Whitley & Co., Ltd. to buy it. The Chairman, Lord Daresbury (300), and another of their Directors, Humphrey Griffith (299), were both Members, and after being approached, they generously gave their assurance that if it came on the market Greenalls would buy it at any cost for the sake of the Club.

After Henry had died, a letter was received from his niece Lady Helen O'Brien's solicitors announcing her intention to sell, at the same time wishing to protect the interests of the Club. Doubtless under the strong

A Meet at The Swan.

influence of her redoubtable aunt, Lady Grisell Arden-Baillie-Hamilton, she proved a stalwart ally, keeping predators at bay and augmenting Humphrey's efforts to safeguard the Club. 'I have all my life been interested in its old traditions & have heard so much about it from my grandfather and uncle,' she wrote. She even gave Geoffrey the impression she was protecting the Club against its future Members, evidently not trusting them

The Club Dining, also from an oil painting by George Goodwin Kilburne. The Hunt Room is depicted after the portrait of Mr Chas. Cholmondeley was presented in 1848 and before the Presidents' Boards were put up in 1865. Note the old balloting box on the mantelpiece.

Presidents of Tarporley Hunt				1772	S.T.Broughton
	1762	Obadiah Lane		1772	Lord Kilmorey
	1763	Booth Grey		1773	Lord Kilmorey
	1763	R.S.Cotton		1773	Lord Stamford
	1764	S:P.Leicester		1774	Peter Heron
	1764	John Crewe		1774	Asheton Smith
	1765	S:H.Mainwaring		1775	T.Ravenscroft
	1765	Mr. Arthur Barry		1775	Stephen Glynne
	1766	Mr. Richard Barry		1776	Rogr Wilbraham
	1766	Mr. Crewe		1776	S:P.Warburton
	1767	Mr. John S.Barry		1777	Robt Needham
	1767	Mr. Heron		1777	Richard Brooke
	1768	Mr. Ardern		1778	James Croxton
	1768	Lᵈ Archᵈ Hamilton		1778	Thos Brooke
	1769	Richd Whitworth		1779	Hon.J.S.Barry
	1769	Chas Towneley		1779	Hon.Booth Grey
	1770	Geo.Wilbraham		1780	S.H.Mainwaring
	1770	T.Cholmondeley		1780	Davs Davenport
	1771	James Barry		1781	George Heron
	1771	Lord Stamford		1781	Offley Crewe

	1782	Jonas L.Brooke		1798	C.W.J.Shakerley
	1782	Willm Egerton		1799	Thos Crewe Dod
	1783	S:P.Warburton		1800	Chas Leicester
	1783	S:Thos Egerton		1801	Col.Broughton
	1784	John Crewe		1802	Peter Patten
	1784	S:W.Stanley		1803	C.Cholmondeley
	1785	T.H.Ravenscroft		1804	George J.Legh
	1785	P.R.Heron		1805	T.Tarleton, Junr
	1786			1806	E.V.Townshend
	1787			1807	Philip Egerton
	1788	Thos Tarleton		1808	S.H.M.Mainwaring
	1789			1809	Edwin Corbet
	1790	Lord Grey		1810	W.W.Drake
	1791			1811	S:W.W.Wynn
	1792	T.Cholmondeley		1812	Wilbr Egerton
	1793	Thos Parker		1813	Geo.Wilbraham
	1794	H.A.Leicester		1814	Booth Grey
	1795	John Egerton		1815	S: Richd Brooke
	1796	Thos L.Brooke		1816	J.B.Glegg
	1797	John Asheton		1817	F.R.Price

to maintain the standards were the Hunt Room ever to be altered. In the days when planning restrictions were not so rigid, she had visions that the place would be pulled down and 'a road house erected in its place with neon lights and jazz-bands', as the Secretary put it to the Business Meeting of the Club in 1950, expressing horror at the very thought.

The Committee's time of anxiety and toil, and an exchange of at least eighty-five letters during the year,* had culminated in a satisfactory sale to Greenall Whitley with an agreement being signed for the Tarporley Hunt Club to have amongst other things, the exclusive use of the Hunt Room for two whole days in Tarporley Week

and 'for the rights, privileges and services hitherto granted to the Club to be maintained in perpetuity.'

The terms of the sale included the retention of the sitting tenant, Charles Hayes and his wife, Eva, who stayed on until 1976. He had been landlord for forty years, taking over from his mother. His father, Bertie Hayes, brother of Mary Ann and Alice, held the licence from 1906 until 1923. The Members presented Mr and Mrs Hayes with an inscribed onyx clock in appreciation of the ninety years' service the family had given to the Club.

It was realized how much the Club had relied on the goodwill of the Arden family and their successors, the proprietors of The Swan, and its Members are, or should be, ever conscious of a profound sense of gratitude for all that has been and is done for them. In the last part of the XIX Century the Club used to hold its own annual ball

---

* The Colonel also had to cope, in his usual courteous manner, with Tom Baugh from Cotebrook, who was descended from one of the 18th-century landlords of The Swan, laying claim to title.

1818	Thos. Trafford.	1838	Egerton Warburton
1819	Will. Tatton.	1839	S.P.G.Egerton.
1820	Domville Poole.	1840	W.Tat.n Egerton.
1821	L.Col.T.Brooke.	1841	G.Cornwall Legh.
1822	Peter L.Brooke.	1842	Geof.y Shakerley.
1823	R.Town.d Parker.	1843	Humph.y de Trafford
1824	Thomas Legh.	1844	L.d R.Grosvenor.
1825	Law.e Armistead.	1845	Ja.s H.S.Barry.
1826	James F.France.	1846	Lord de Tabley.
1827	Henry Brooke.	1847	T.W.Tatton.
1828	Chas. Wicksted.	1848	John Dixon.
1829	El.d Swettenham.	1849	G.F.Wilbraham.
1830	Vis. Belgrave.	1850	Henry France.
1831	J.S.Barry.	1851	S.W.W.Wynn.
1832	Henry Hesketh.	1852	William Court.
1833	Lord Grey.	1853	Thos. L.Brooke.
1834	Edm.d Antrobus.	1854	Thomas Booth.
1835	Charles Ford.	1855	Hon.Wel.r Cotton.
1836	J.W.Hammond.	1856	Francis Massey.
1837	Gib.t E.Antrobus	1857	John Sidebottom.

1858	W.Worthington.	1878	Bolton Littledale
1859	S.Thos.Hesketh.	1879	Lord Rich.Grosvenor
1860	John Fox.	1880	Cap.t Park Yates.
1861	John H.Leche.	1881	A.H.Smith Barry.
1862	Lord Grosvenor.	1882	G.J.Shakerley.
1863	Rich.d Brooke.	1883	H.Tollemache.
1864	Hon.ble T.G.Cholmondeley	1884	Earl of Haddington
1865	Gen.Sir J.Scarlett.	1885	J.H. Smith Barry
1866	Hon.A.Lascelles.	1886	Cudworth H.Poole.
1867	Thos. Aldersey.	1887	James Tomkinson
1868	Charles G.Cholmondeley	1888	George Dixon.
1869	Hon.ble Wilb.m Egerton	1889	Egerton Leigh.
1870	Cecil de Trafford.	1890	Samuel H.Sandbach
1871	William John Legh.	1891	Christopher Kay.
1872	Henry Reginald Corbet	1892	Earl of Enniskillen.
1873	Thomas Henry Lyon	1893	Henry Cornwall Legh
1874	Angus.te de Trafford.	1894	Reginald Corbet
1875	Philip le B.Egerton	1895	Marq.s of Cholmondeley
1876	Chas. H.France Hayhurst	1896	B.tn Will.m Schroder
1877	Piers Egerton Warburton	1897	C.T.D.Cotton-Jodrell

in the Hunt Room, usually about one hundred and fifty being present. There was a large green and red awning from the front door to the pavement and a crowd would gather to see the guests arrive. The hotel was illuminated with gas jets displayed in the shape of a large star and crown. If the Lady Patroness was not present, the Secretary's wife would act for her.

Quite apart from the Tarporley Meetings and Dinners, the old Club Room (Room 10 at The Swan) has been the scene of many and varied functions – hunt balls and assorted dances and discoteques, property auction sales, conferences, lectures, committee meetings, wedding receptions, club, regimental and private dinners,[†] Christmas lunches, cocktail parties, funeral wakes, exhibitions, commercial presentations, charity fairs, Masonic ceremonies even. One particular Masonic Lodge to use it is the Sylvania, a special Cheshire 'Hunting' Lodge founded by John Paterson (314). In the mid-XVIII Century the Forest Troop of the King's Cheshire Yeomanry Cavalry used to have their annual dinner at The Swan, just as the Earl of Chester's Yeomanry does in modern times.

One regular party used to be the dance held by the Century Club, founded in 1926. It was limited to one hundred members and strictly 'white tie' in keeping with the dignity of the room. (From the 1930's to the years just after the war the favourite place for less formal affaires – the word is used advisedly – was the Four Ways

---

[†] At some Rotary Club or local business men's dinners in aid of charity in recent times guest speakers have included: Bill Beaumont (rugby football), Les Dawson (comedian), Sir Richard Hadlee (cricket), Emlyn Hughes (football), Barry McGuigan (boxing), Lord Oaksey (racing) and Cynthia Payne, (ex Brothel keeper).

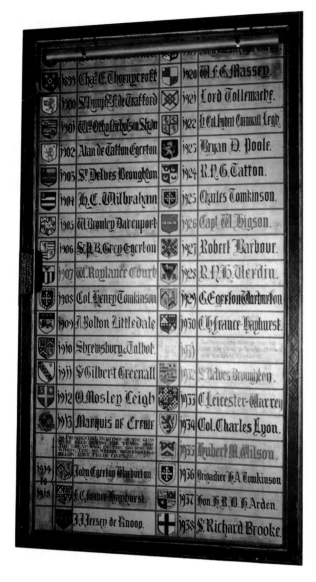

Country Club next to the old Oakmere Court House.) The Cheshire Hunt Pony Club also held a Christmas party in the Hunt Room each year when Frances, Lady Darebury presided. There was usually a conjuror and a film of the previous Grand National was shown and then run backwards.

Most of the hotel bedrooms are now named after prominent Cheshire families associated with the Club.

* * *

IN HIS LETTER OF THANKS to the Secretary in 1937, Henry Arden had referred to 'names inscribed in letters of gold'. He was perhaps writing metaphorically for the 'Presidents' Boards', the framed canvas panels on which the names and arms of the Club's Presidents are displayed, have the names in black. The canvases themselves are gold-leafed. Those who were Managers of the Cheshire Hounds are in red, a custom introduced in 1874 when rails were also put up to protect them. These were removed when the room was redecorated after the Second World War and unfortunately never put back.

The first three Honours boards are not contemporary. In 1865 an entry reads:

> A proposal from "Mr Morris", Chester, to be allowed to "decorate" the Tarporley Hunt Dining Room was accepted and Mr E^ton. Warburton was requested to see the arrangements carried out...

This was Mr John Morris, the Chester paint manufacturer, recently retired and with time on his hands. It was he who had painted the 'Tarporley Room' and gilded the frames in 1848 at a cost of £25. Judging from the year-long correspondence he had with R.E.E.W., it seems that this time it was a labour of love and a gift to the Club. The actual heraldic painter was a 'Mr Turner'. No cost is shown in the accounts. At the same time he undertook to have the room redecorated. His light green shade card, preserved in his clip-fastened letters, has, on the principle of authenticity taking precedence over taste, enabled the walls to be painted the same colour a century later. What the room looked like before this redecoration is shown in Goodwin Kilburne's painting, the precise date of which is not known, though it was after 1848 when the Calvert sketch of Chas. Cholmondeley (68) was presented by Harry Brooke (111). The painting also shows the chandelier which then existed, together with the two large canvases then in the Club's possession, and the dentil cornice picked out in red. The Club also carried a proposal that 'the Landlord of The Swan Hotel be strictly ordered not to use Gas in lighting the sitting room'. Indeed it was well into the XX Century before anything but candlelight was tolerated.

Mr Morris wanted to paint the cornice imitation oak and the doors and dado in walnut, but this was overruled. The chandelier he noted had been pink and white and proposed to do it in white only with a little gilding. It was in 1890 that the magnificent mid-Victorian thirty-six light chandelier of rococo design with chased foliate scroll branches was presented for the Hunt Room by Lord Combermere (157), the year before he died. It was wired for electricity in 1971, as a result of repeated complaints, mostly from Johnnie Dixon (281), about candle grease dripping on coats and down people's necks.

In 1952 R.E.E.W.'s grandson was trying to establish the date of origin of the Boards and only surmised they might have been included in Mr Morris's offer 'to decorate'. Before he discovered the file of letters, his eagle eye spotted some mistakes. He found ample proof that the names were taken from the Minute Books. For instance:

1763 Booth Grey but 1779 Hon.Booth Grey (same person)
1767 Mr John Barry but 1779 Hon.J.S.Barry (same person)

In each case these styles are in the Minute Book. There are many other inconsistencies and mistakes. Domville Poole (96) is shown as 'Dumville' both on the board and in the book, as pronounced.

It was then that Geoffrey Egerton-Warburton worked out the most likely names of the missing Presidents for 1786, 1787, 1789 and 1791, still shown blank in the Hunt Room.

Although there are four blank spaces, five Presidents are missing from the records, since it is known the last

February Meeting was in 1786, not shown on the canvas. The last Meeting in the second book, February, 1785, is numbered the 46th, whereas the November, 1802 Meeting, the first in the next book, is clearly named the 'Sixty Fifth'. Contrary to this seemingly irrefutable evidence, 1788 is recorded in the draft resolution as the Fiftieth Meeting, the occasion for Sir Harry Mainwaring's Jubilee medal. There must therefore have been two additional Meetings in the intervening years between 1788 and 1802. From an annotation and other internal evidence in the book listing the Rules and Members as at 10th November, 1799, it seems probable that no records had been kept and unlikely that the book has been lost or destroyed. The successor to John Crewe (2) could well have been Booth Grey, the Deputy Secretary. He died in 1802 and must have resigned some years before as he is not listed as a Member in 1799. So it is a mystery why no book was kept.

Bower Jodrell's Presidency is confirmed as November, 1786 by a notice published in *The Chester Chronicle*, and similarly Hervey Aston is shown as President in a notice in *Adams's Weekly Courant* for 1789, but there were no notices in the other years. Domville Poole was elected in 1784 and died in 1795. He was senior to Leicester and Grosvenor, who were both elected in 1788, the latter being likely to have been given the chair in 1791 in preference to Tom Grosvenor, whose military duties prevented him from being President at a later date. But on his return from overseas and after the records were resumed he attended at least five more times before his

The Coalbrookdale firegrate

resignation,[*] so he is the most likely one to have been President for one of the extra meetings, provided it was after 1788.

The fourth was James Mainwaring (44), who was unmarried when elected, attended both meetings in 1783 but was absent for the next three, his reason being that he was abroad. He married in France (date not stated by Ormerod), but at least one of his two children were born at Avignon. It is known that he resigned before 1799, and since he would presumably have returned by 1793 when England was at War with France, his marriage must have taken place before that. In all probability he was permanently resident abroad and unlikely to have been President between 1786 and 1791.

The President in 1787 must therefore have been somebody holding office for the second time.

As an addendum to G.E.W.'s notes, if the chair was not taken by somebody for a second time at these additional meetings, the only other possible candidates are Mainwaring of Bromborough after all or Major John Crewe (64) if his military duties permitted and the extra meetings were after 1794.

When a new board was required in 1898, there was a lengthy discussion about the re-arrangement and despite many thinking it an indignity to Obadiah Lane, it was decided that 'he and his contemporaries should be placed on the left hand side of the fireplace (proper right), the other boards to be moved back in rotation'. In the course of time the Club's first President took his rightful place at the head of the room. Gilt description plates were also put on the Club's pictures.

Besides the Presidents the names are inscribed of those Members who lost their lives in the Great War of 1914-18. After the Second World War the name of Major Cyril Dewhurst starts off the sixth board.[†] He would have been President in 1939, two years before his death, had the Meeting been held. By a quirk of fate the name of his eldest son, Tony, fell immediately opposite. No President was appointed nor Meeting nor dinners held in 1947 owing to food and petrol restrictions. A small crest of the Prince of Wales's feathers shows the years the Patron dined with the Club.

During the Second World War the President's Boards, the pictures and the rest of the Club's possessions were removed for safekeeping to Arderne Hall. This Gothic red and blue brick building was built by Lord and Lady Binning in 1867 on the site of Eaton Banks,[‡] commanding the view across to Beeston Castle and beyond. (It was demolished in 1958 and eventually replaced with a double towered house, originally designed for Lady Helen O'Brien's son, Desmond, and now the clubhouse for the Portal Golf Course.) Living there with Henry were his two surviving sisters, Lady Ruth and Lady Grisell. The Club's possessions, stored in the capacious cellars then serving as a household Air Raid Shelter, could not have been in better hands. Every time the sirens went, Grisell saw to it that the ancient Horn of

---

[*] Between 1802 and 1808 five Members were Generals, Grosvenor, Crewe, Broughton, Cotton and Heron. The only recorded instance of Lord Combermere dining was in 1825. He conscientiously paid his fines for absence throughout the thirty-six years he was a Member.

[†] Owing to post-war shortages gold paint was used on the new canvas instead of books of gold-leaf. In due course it turned a rather nasty brown. There was a serious, nearly disastrous fire, in the early hours of January 6th, 1988, caused by an electrical fault in the pantry off the Hunt Room. The Club's handmade russet velvet chenille curtains with a fringed selvedge of orange and blue design, dating from 1891 (Harvey Nicholls & Co., £16.6s.6d) and stored in a chest to be hung annually, were destroyed and practically all the Club's property and pictures had to be restored from severe smoke damage. The post-war board, just by the pantry door, which had been left open, was too badly scorched to be restored and a new canvas had to be created with all forty arms, dates and names, this time with proper gold leaf. From that point of view the fire can be said to have been a blessing in disguise, but had the door been left shut, the resident manager would not have been roused by the smoke fumes in time to save the entire premises.

[‡] The previous tenant of this small white house had been one of Rowland Egerton Warburton's uncles, Lieutenant-General Richard Egerton, CB, who, as a lieutenant-colonel in the 34th Foot, had been General Lord Hill's First A.D.C. at Waterloo. The youngest of the nine sons of Philip Egerton of Egerton and Oulton, he was married to the youngest sister of the Tomkinson brothers. He had a distinct look of Mr Pickwick about him with his bald head and spectacles; he was always cheery and very kind to children. He took an immense pride in the park around Eaton Banks, landscaping

General Richard Egerton of Eaton Banks, from a portrait in oils by Wm. Salter.

it and building follies. The 2nd Lord Alvanley once sent word to his agent to fell £1,000 worth of timber there. The outraged General settled his landlord's gambling debt on that occasion and thus saved his beloved oaks, many of which dated from the time of James I. He died in 1853 and his wife seven years later. They had no children.

Delamere Forest was taken from its ornately carved oak board in the hall to join them until the *ALL CLEAR* was sounded. She died in 1957 in her 97th year.

* * *

TWICE RECENTLY a psychic investigator, Mr Stanley Rowley-Goodall, surveyed the Hunt Room in the presence of the Secretary and the names of the Presidents were called as he concentrated on each one on the boards in turn. The following members were among a score or so found to be visitees to the Hunt Room on various occasions: John Crewe (2), Thos. Cholmondeley (12), Lord de Tabley (50), whose name is not inscribed, Wilbraham Egerton (84), whose manifested himself in a vibratory sense to Mr Rowley-Goodall while we were there, Sir Richard Brooke (91), Cornwall Legh (137), Lord Tollemache (254), Bryan Davies Poole (257), Peter Tatton (259), Robert Barbour, (262), Chris Brooke (275), Sir Walter Bromley-Davenport (311) and Sim Wilbraham (330). On the second occasion the complete roll was called to which four members who had not been President responded to the investigator, namely Lord Grosvenor (19), Admiral Tollemache (121), Lyonel Tollemache (227) and John Egerton-Warburton (255). Three, who had given no indication on the first visit, gave vibratory manifestations – Lord Grosvenor, the Rev. George Heron (38) and Puffles Park Yates (198). Any Members who have been re-incarnated would not have shown themselves.

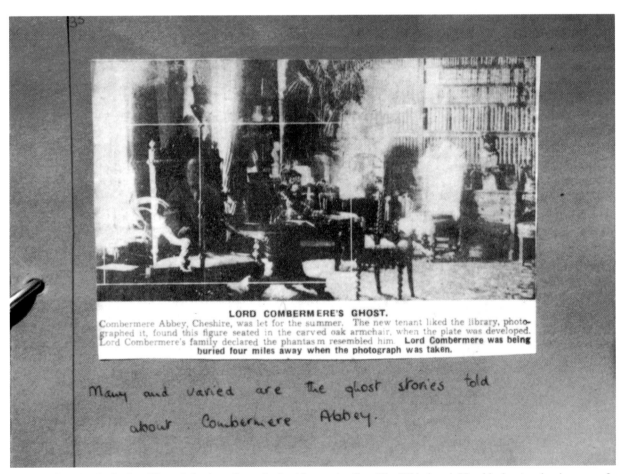

LORD COMBERMERE'S GHOST.
Combermere Abbey, Cheshire, was let for the summer. The new tenant liked the library, photographed it, found this figure seated in the carved oak armchair, when the plate was developed. Lord Combermere's family declared the phantasm resembled him. **Lord Combermere was being buried four miles away when the photograph was taken.**

Many and varied are the ghost stories told about Combermere Abbey.

A page from the Burleydam Women's Institute Scrap-book with a cutting from The Whitchurch Herald, *showing the phantasm of Lord Combermere (157). See page 249.*

Tarporley Hunt Races

SINCE 1740 RECOGNISED HORSE RACING has been governed by an Act of Parliament. The Jockey Club, first mentioned in 1752, formulated 'the Newmarket Rules' and it was under these rules that the Tarporley Hunt Club's own race meeting was run. As a matter of course, Members decided to match their horses against each others' as well as to enjoy their sport in the hunting field. Tarporley Hunt Races and later Tarporley Hunt Steeplechases were to become an annual fixture in the Racing Calendar, but up to 1848 the races were all on the flat under the Jockey Club's Rules.

In the club minutes it went on record that in November, 1774 'Sir Thomas Broughton paid forfeit to Booth Grey for a match to have been run', but a year later:

> This meeting a Sweepstakes was won by Sir Thomas Broughton starting against Mr Crewe of Crewe, Lord Stamford, Geo. Wilbraham and Lord Kilmorey paid Forfeit.

This was one of the two races as reported in *The Chester Chronicle*. The other, a pony race, was won by James Croxton, the new Green Collar.

Although the county's principal race meetings at the time were at Chester, Farndon, Knutsford and Wallasey,[*] there was also a long established course on Crabtree Green, by then part of the estate acquired by George Wilbraham.

Sir Willoughby Aston, the ancestor of Henry Hervey-Aston (46), *inter alia*, noted in his diary after the Restoration that there were monthly race meetings at Delamere Forest. On a map of Delamere Forest drawn for a Crown Commission in 1687, beside the 'Carryer's Road from Chester to Northwych', is marked:

Race ℓ Post

on Crabtree Greene.

This course, according to a map of the Forest dated 1813, consisted of an oval circuit crossing the track running north towards Norley.

In 1776 seven Members challenged each other with their blood hunters for a 10 gn. sweepstake over a 4-mile heat, carrying 13 st. Three paid forfeit and Kyffin Heron

George Wilbraham (5). (From a portrait in oils by Pompeo Batoni)

---

[*] Other Race Meetings in Cheshire, long since defunct, were Cheadle, Hoylake (the Liverpool Hunt Mtg.), Latchford Green, Middlewich, Nantwich, Northwich, Sandbach, Stockport and Wilmslow. The Chester Meeting was at one time described in *The Racing Calendar* as The City of West Chester. Mains of Cocks were held at Chester and Nantwich. In Lysons' *Magna Britannica* (1810) it is recorded that 'there were formerly, about the reign of Charles I, horfe-races near Little Budworth; it was a four-mile courfe, and there was an annual plate of 20 *l*'.

won. The same day Sir Thomas Broughton's Romeo was beaten by Sir Peter Warburton on his Molly-long-legs for 100 gns. They had finished third and fourth respectively in the other race.

These 4-mile races continued for a few years, until it became normal for races to be run in heats, varying once, twice or thrice round, according to the race conditions. 2-mile heats were the norm, although the distances are not always given in *The Racing Calendar* until 1809. The club events, as officially recorded, often resulted in walk-overs. It was noted in November, 1783:

> This Meeting a rule was made that the owner of the winning horse is not to give a dozen of Claret as was customary. N.B. This rule was made before, but was not entered.

In the previous year's accounts an entry reads:

> Received from Lord Stamford, having won the Race   £3 3s.
> Received from S.Cotton, having won the Race   £3 3s.

That was the year one of the Club's senior bachelors, Booth Grey, paid his marriage fine of £21, when he succumbed to the charms of James Mainwaring's twenty-five-year-old eldest sister. He had probably been first enamoured to her when she was Lady Patroness in 1781.

Crabtree Green Races was a colourful occasion with those of the thirty-six Members of the Club who were present being obliged, under penalty of a guinea fine, to wear their green-collared red coats. There were doubtless also unofficial events on the card for local half-bred horses and probably 'all the fun of the fair' for the local populace. Throughout the years there are regular entries in the accounts for 'Whippers-in Clearing Course £1', 'Woman at Gate 5s.' and even one in 1812: 'Mr Jones the Fire-eater ... £2', as well as 'Bad Notes ... £7' in 1817.

In November, 1777 it was ordered that 'the Ropes for Crabtree Green are paid for by the President £5:17.0' and that Mr Grey 'is paid for the repair of the Course £5:19:0 (Bill Mr Wilbraham will deliver)'. The first mention of a stand was in 1805, one Hugh Pavers being paid £3.13s.8d 'for repairing course and stand' with similar amounts in succeeding years, including £2 8s.8d 'To him for Journeys & Trouble'.

Following the race results in 1790 it was reported that 'the hunt was numerous and brilliant and the viands and wines at honest Southon's were of the first order.'

Although its owner had other runners and a winner there, a famous Cheshire racehorse which never ran at Tarporley was The Smoker, bred by the Prince Regent and the property of Sir John Leicester (50). At 4, 5 and 6 yrs. the grey won twelve races from nineteen starts,

Lady Barlow presents the Richmond Cup to Mrs Michael Griffith, winning owner of the Tarporley Hunt Club Open Steeplechase, 1991.

including the silver gilt Richmond Cup of 1792, which Lieut.-Colonel John Leicester-Warren (301) presented to the Club as a challenge cup for the Tarporley Hunt Club Steeplechase, the Open Race at the Cheshire Point-to-Point from 1960 onwards. *See* Appendix K. It has been won several times in recent years by sons and grandsons of Members. The donor's ancestor, who was the founder of the Cheshire Yeomanry liked to use The Smoker as his charger and they feature together in several paintings at Tabley, the family's former home. Colonel Leicester was considered to be the best pistol shot in England. He was incidentally another Tarporley Member to have gone on the Grand Tour.

Colonel Ronald Langford-Brooke (291) left the Club the 'Kilton Cup', another silver gilt trophy won in a match by his ancestor at Knutsford in 1796. Thomas Langford-Brooke (60)'s 5 y.o. horse beat William Tatton (65)'s 3 y.o. Delamere over a 4-mile heat, giving him 31 *lb*. Kilton won twelve races and was thrice second.

The official races were at first restricted to horses owned or nominated by Members, but in 1806 a Silver Cup was given for horses belonging to Cheshire Farmers. The entertainment of the farmers, over whose land they hunted, was always a great tradition of the Club. The meeting was abandoned in 1807 and 1808, and again in 1814.

In 1805 it had been:

> Agreed that a Silver Cup be purchased by the Hunt by a Subscription of one guinea each Member for Farmers renting under £300 *per annum* for Horses, Mares & Geldings to be half-bred & *bona fide* the property of such Farmer Six Months preceeding each Meeting – to be named & a Certificate of their never having been in Training, pd or recd forfeit, to the Secretary of the Hunt on Monday in each Meeting – Heats twice round the Course – 13 stone.

Charles Cholmondeley (66) had several wins at the turn of the century and Sir Watkin also enjoyed a winner. General Grosvenor had a 2nd and 3rd in 1811, one of the years he was able to attend. The Club's first handicap was run the next year – the first known handicap having been run at Ascot in 1790. A three-year-old colt belonging to Sir Watkin, had already run eight times, winning twice, won at Tarporley carrying 6st. against older horses.

As well as their own meeting at Tarporley and the other Cheshire fixtures, many of the Members liked to race at Wrexham and Oswestry. In addition there was the Holywell Hunt which they also used to enjoy. This was another club, of which there were fifty members, who met in October to dine at the White Horse Inn, where they used to have a ball as well as a race meeting. Their uniform was a red cloth coat with a plain gold embroidered buttonhole and a red velvet turndown collar and white waistcoat and breeches. In 1841 six of the twenty-seven Members then existing were also Members or former Members of Tarporley, namely Francis Price, Lord Robert Grosvenor (his father was the senior Member), William Massey Stanley, Lord de Tabley, Sir Watkin Williams-Wynn and John Leche.

In 1814 it was resolved unanimously that no gentleman's servant, jockey or horse dealer should in future ride for the Cup, but only farmers themselves, their sons or servants. Four years later this was repealed and thereafter anyone was permitted to ride.

The last race meeting held on Crabtree Green was in November, 1815, owing to the Act of Enclosure of Delamere Forest. Though still racing on the flat, there was a great deal of grief that year with horses bolting and falling and one being killed. The meeting was held on Billington's Training Ground in 1816 and 1817 before being 'Over the New Course on Delamere Forest'.

Billington's Training Ground was on Lord Shrewsbury's land, adjacent to Seven Lows Farm, and included both a sand and a turf gallop. This area of Delamere and Oakmere have long had a tradition for training horses, though in many cases the credit nationally has often gone to Tarporley, being the postal district.

On the other side of the lane from Billington's Training ground, there was then another gallop near the Fishpool and it was most probably there that the 12th Earl of Derby had his horses trained by W. Saunders, Senr. before the latter moved South. Their successes included The Oaks in 1779 and 1794 and The Derby in 1786 with Sir Peter Teazle. The 14th Earl of Derby, as Lord Stanley, also had his horses trained at Delamere Forest, as did John Mytton, the eccentric squire of Halston in Shropshire, as soon as he came of age in 1817.

John Billington, himself, trained a mare called Catherina which, between 1833 and 1841, established a record, which has never been broken, by winning 79 races, and being placed on almost as many occasions. She ran 176 times under Jockey Club Rules, even carrying George Osbaldeston, the Squire of England, himself, to victory at Heaton Park in her first three races.

The New Tarporley Course was nearby, towards Cotebrook, and incorporated Billington's Training Ground as well as what is now a sand circuit at Gorselands off Racecourse Lane. It was not one of the more picturesque courses and certainly not the best for seeing. His Lordship was paid a rent of £2. At Cotebrook the horses started with their back to the main road (now the A49) and the finish was in front of Stand House. There was an upper room with a fireplace there for the Club's use, with a balcony off it. The unadopted road to it used to be known locally as Starting Chair Lane.

This little hamlet on the turnpike road had previously been known as Colebrook. A cockfight was fought there in 1751 between the Gentleman of Cheshire against the Gentlemen of Lancashire, for five guineas a Battle and 100 guineas the Main, the former winning by fourteen battles to nine. John Crewe (2), Sir Robert Cotton (8) and Sir Peter Warburton (35) were later among the most enthusiastic Cestrian cockers. Mr Price of Bryn-y-Pys (92) and Captain White (159) were others. The most renowned was Dr J. Bellyse of Audlem.

Such matches were invariably on the programme for Chester Races until 1849, when cock-pits were banned by statute. There was hardly a village in the county without one and mains were held furtively for many years afterwards.*

---

* 'Cheshire Piles', a breed of game-fowl evolved in the county, were famed throughout Britain. A spadeful of the purest gravel, fresh from the bottom of the Dee, was what the feeders found the best stimulant for their champions to peck at in their pens. And eggs, sugar-candy water, hot bread and milk, barley, rue, butter and rhubarb formed a diet which few were fated to taste more than once in their lives.

William Yeardsley, the Norley tailor, who made the uniforms for the hunt servants and many of the local gentry towards the end of the XIX Century, was a great breeder and feeder of gamebirds. Bill always boasted that no man could make a better pair of breeches or feed a gamecock better than he.

In about 1877 there had been a big gathering, including a sprinkling of magistrates, at Merebank, Weaverham, in spite of police warnings of a raid. Only the owner, a Mr Marshall, was summoned. Captain Beatty was nearly caught, but managed to scale one of the highest brick walls ever climbed and evaded pursuit. A cockfight also took place in the stable yard at Abbot's Moss, when the Hall was empty in 1912. Delamere House was another place where cockfighting was held during this century. A clandestine meeting was staged at Cotton Edmunds Farm as recently as 1956, but on that occasion a Police raid resulted in a number of Cheshire sportsmen being fined, though quite a few well-known personalities were able to escape across the fields or by hiding in the rickyard.

Tarporley Hunt, 1822.

P. L. Brooke, Esq. President.

First Race.---One o'Clock.

On Thursday, November 7th, the Ten Guineas Stake, (seven subscribers.) Twice round.

P. L. Brooke, Esq.'s Sir Edward, by Friend Ned, 3 yrs old, 7st. 5lb. - *3*
Sir J. G. Egerton names Malgwyn, 3 yrs old, 7st. 3lb. yellow and black cap - *2*
L. Armitstead, Esq.'s b. g. Coxcomb, 4 yrs old, 8st. 1lb. pink and black cap - *1*
W. Egerton, Esq. names Anti-Radical, 6 yrs old, 8st. 13lb. green and white - *4*
Sir Thomas Stanley's Eastham, 4 yrs old, 8st. 5lb. - - - - - *2*

Second Race.---Half-past One o'Clock.

The Five Guineas Half-bred Stake, (14 subs.) Twice round.

Sir H. Mainwaring's br. g. Alonzo, by Peruvian, 12st. 0lb. aged - - *2*
Sir R. Brooke's br. g. Howell, 12st. 3lb. aged - - - - - *3*
L. Armitstead, Esq.'s b. g. 6 yrs old, 12st. 3lb. pink and black cap - - *Disqualified*
J. B. Glegg, Esq.'s b. g. by Sir Oliver, 12st. 3lb. aged - - - - *2*

Third Race.---Two o'Clock.

Farmers' Cup, with 15l. added ; Second-best, 10l. ; Third, Entrance Money. Best of Heats. Twice round.

Mr. Edward Briscoe's ch. g. Little Bob, 4 yrs old, 11st. 4lb. green and white *3 1 1*
Mr. Bolshaw's br. m. by Sober Robin, 4 yrs old, 11st. 4lb. blue and red - *0 3 2*
Mr. Taylor's g. m. Overton Lass, by Hit or Miss, 4 yrs old, 11st. 4lb. - *0 2 2*

Match for One Hundred Guineas each, h. ft.

L. Armitstead, Esq.'s b. m. by Castrel - - - - - received forfeit.
J. B. Glegg, Esq.'s b. m. Milo, (dead) - - - - - - paid forfeit.

Chester, printed by J. Fletcher, Chronicle Office.

From 1818 the Race Day was on the Wednesday of Tarporley Week with the Members meeting that morning for business. Any Member not attending on or before the Tuesday (or having sent no excuse) was to be fined 5 guineas, but the next year they changed both to the Thursday. In 1835 they reverted to the Wednesday.

Curiously in 1818 it was also:

> Resolved that each Member be requested not to name any
> horse belonging to Rev. Nanny Wynne in any Stake to
> which he subscribes.

This was a Welsh parson called Nanney with a passion
for racing and clearly a bit of a reputation. He had
changed his name to Wynne on inheriting some property.

In 1820 Billington was 'paid in full for Stand £145. 0.
9.' and a man called Prince £6. 19. 7½ for 'plastering Race
Stand'. This would have been what is now Stand House,
and the recipient the well-known trainer, John
Billington, who lived nearby. A payment of £1 was made
to him in 1835 for the part expense of a chimney and later
10/- for measuring the course, so it may well have been
his house that was used as a stand each year. The
Sweepstakes in 1820 were won by John Mytton, beating
a horse owned by Lord Derby. Although the accounts
show a charge for the Cup no further meeting was
published in *The Racing Calendar* until 1825, when six
officers of the Prince Regent's Second Regiment of
Cheshire Yeomanry Cavalry competed in three heats for
a Silver Cup, presented by their Colonel, Lord
Delamere. The race took place again the next year.
However in 1823 it had been:

> Resolved that in future the Farmer's Cup be confined to
> Cheshire-Bred Horses. And that the beaten Horses of the
> Cheshire Yeomanry Cavalry Cups may start for it, if be-
> longing to Cheshire Farmers and otherwise duly qualified.

An entry for 1823 reads 'Lost by Revd. Hill . . . £25'.
One assumes he was the victim of a pickpocket and that
the Club was not reimbursing his gambling debts.
Rowland Hill (100) resigned the same year. There were
also payments for the toll-gates, including one at Portal
Lodge.

For 63 years the purchase of the Farmers' Cup, value
about £25, appears annually in the accounts. Those for
1845, 1856 and 1868 were many years later acquired by
the Club either by gift or at auction and grace the dining
table each year. That for 1845 was won by Mr Vernon's
Quicksilver and was presented in 1960 by the widow of
one of his descendants. Of a different design each year,
they were usually supplied by Messrs. Thomas of New
Bond Street.

A collection of race cards is in the Arderne Papers at
the County Record Office, mostly single printed sheets
of paper, showing the first race at 1 o'clock. The oldest
is for 1822. That for 1840 is on a single card.

In 1825 a preliminary event was on the programme for
£100 –

> Foot Race 140 yds.
> Admiral Tolmache's son
> C. Cholmondeley's son

The track had been marked out near Oulton lodge and
quite a number of the latter's supporters from Knutsford
had been arriving at Sandiway Head to fortify themselves
with 'Day and Martin' against the drenching rain before
going on in time for the race at noon.

> Tolmache won the race beating Cholmondeley about 3 yds.

The lightly-built future Lord Tollemache was always
exceptionally athletic, as was his father. His opponent
was over six feet tall and powerful, but was easily
overhauled. The Secretary's son became Rector of
Hodnet.

Prize money for 'Foot Races' is shown in the accounts
in other years.

One of the most prolific winners at this time was James
France (109) who won either the Tarporley Hunt Stakes
or the Half-Bred Stakes on ten or more occasions, giving
the mount on several occasions to John White (159).

In 1833 the Judge had not taken his place when the
Genteel Stakes was run and 'we believe all [seven]
subscribers subsequently withdrew their stakes', noted
Messrs. Edward and Charles Weatherby. They did not
record any results for 1834 or for the years 1836 to 1842
inclusive.

It was unfortunate that after a race was awarded to Sir
Watkin Williams-Wynn in 1846 because the winner was
not the mare described in the entry, his horse was
disqualified after running against the same mare in the
next race without carrying a penalty. That race was given
to the third horse ridden by Captain White (159) for Mr
Glegg (94).

At the Business Meeting that morning a new race was
proposed for the next year, called the Welter Stakes: 'Two
miles, twice round. To carry 13 st. each, horses
thoroughbred to carry 10 *lb* extra – horses to be the
property of and ridden by Members of the Hunt.' But it
did not take place and apart from the Farmer's Cup there
were two walk-overs for a mare belonging to Lord de
Tabley. It was customary then to advertise the Hunt and
the Races twice in each of the Chester papers in July and
October and printed notices were sent to each Member.
At that time the hunting days during the Meeting were
Monday, Tuesday, Thursday and Friday.

In 1848 the Welter Race became a Hurdle Race
over six flights of hurdles, for which Jas. Crank was paid
30/-, and was won by Mr Sidebotham (164). The newly
published annual *The Hurdle Race Calendar* records a
half-length victory over Mr Glegg with Sir Richard

Above: *'What do you think of my man?' shouts Captain White, as he gives Moses a lead to the start.*
Below: *A match supposedly instigated by Captain White and Lord Combermere between Colonel Le Gendre Starkie of Huntroyd Park, Lancs. and Horatio Behrens. The verdict was 'Wins by a nose', but whether equine or human, Frank Massey, the artist, found it a moot point. After hunting for many years in Cheshire, Colonel Starkie later became Master of the Pendle Forest Harriers.*

Brooke third. The next year's race was a walk-over for Mr Glegg. It had been agreed that morning that

> Gentlemen Riders for the Welter Hurdle Race should be extended to Members of the Heaton Park, Croxton Park and Bibury Racing Clubs, to Members of White's, Brooks's, Arthur's, Carlton, Conservative, Army & Navy, Senior & Junior United Service Clubs or of other clubs that the Meeting should agree to before before Wed. at 12 o'clock a.m. on the day of the Race.

From 1850 this race did not close previous to the evening before the Race Day. Although no further meetings were recorded in *The Racing Calendar* under 'Newmarket Rules' as the Jockey Club Rules were known until 'The Rules of Racing' came into force on January 1st, 1877, races were still held each year. Results were published in the volume of *Steeple Chases Past* and *The Hurdle Race Epitome*.

At one time the reports in the local paper included somewhat unctuous accounts of what went on afterwards. In 1849, for instance:

> At the conclusion of the races the members of the Hunt adjourned to The Swan Hotel, where about thirty sat down to a sumptuous dinner prepared in the best style by Mr & Mrs Prideaux. Mr Geo. Wilbraham, Jnr. officiated as President and the duties of Vice were ably discharged by John Dixon Esq. of Astle. The conviviality of the evening was well maintained and the happy party separated highly pleased with the pleasures of the day. The meet on Thursday was at Duddon Heath and after a good run the members returned to The Swan. The comfort of the gentlemen of the Hunt called forth the deserved eulogium of the oldest member, who had attended for forty years; and we sincerely trust the endeavours of Mr Prideaux to comply with the requirements of the Cheshire Hunt will meet with that patronage and support which he is justly entitled.

(The services provided by Mr Gunter from Berkeley Square were not mentioned this year, although the previous year the reporter had given the name of his cook. The landlord was clearly put out that the Club had brought in a London firm to cater for them.)
In 1851

> A sharp frost and a heavy fall of snow prevented the Meeting on the Tuesday. A thaw followed in the night and the Races took place as usual on Wednesday. Seventeen Members attended this Meeting.

The next year the time of closing for the Farmers' Cup was altered from October 1st to 'the last Market Day (Tarporley) but one, previous to the Meeting' and in 1853 it was agreed to alter the weights for for the Half-Bred Tarporley Stakes to 11st.(4 y.o.), 11st 7*lb*. (5 y.o.) and 12st.(6 y.o.). Horses bred by Members of the Hunt were later allowed 3*lb*.

In 1856 the hurdle race reverted to a flat race with 20 sov. added by the Club if there were more than three starters. By 1860 it was called the Welter Hunter Race with horses carrying 14st. Publicans, landlords and tradesmen were also banned from starting horses in the Farmers Cup unless they occupied a farm of not less than 100 acres.

In the Spring of 1859 the Cheshire Steeple Chases were advertised to take place at 2 p.m. on April 2nd in Cheshire over three miles of fair hunting country and were to be 'under the entire control of John White, Esq. of Dale Ford'. The event is not mentioned in the club records, nor were the results published in either *The Chester Chronicle* or *The Racing Calendar*, so they would seem to have been cross-country races organized by 'Leicestershire' White, the former Master of the Cheshire Hounds, then aged sixty-nine. One was for a Cup value £50 with professional riders carrying 7 *lb*. extra and the other was a Steeple Chase for horses belonging to Members of the Cheshire Hunt only, ridden by Gentlemen Riders.

The Club possesses the trophy presented to the owner of the winning horse of the main event. It was a grey horse, Bobbin' Around, carrying the 'Orange Jacket, Cherry Cap' of Captain Edward Sanderson Kearsley, who kept a hunting box at Hartford. The prize was a handsome silver tankard, hall-marked 1774, with domed cover and embossed with the portrait of a horse. It was bought by the Club in 1929 and is engraved with the foregoing details and states 'The above was the first Cheshire Steeple Chase ever held'. The cover has Captain Kearsley's monogram and crest and in 1979 his great great nephew, Captain Nigel Kearsley, came to dine at Tarporley and presented the Club with Bobbin'

William Roylance Court (156)

Getting ready for Tarporley, a sketch by Piers Egerton Warburton.

Around's hoof, mounted as a stamp-box and also engraved with his family crest and the inscription:

> Bobbin' Around, Winner of the Tarporley Steeplechase, 1859.

But the Club has no other record of this race. The horse was painted by Calvert. As to the race being the first Steeplechase held in Cheshire, this was not the case as over a decade earlier the Crewe Annual Steeple Chases took place.

A large chased silver bowl, gilt inside, and two goblets, value £50, were given for the Farmers' Race in 1862 to celebrate the Centenary. A Horse Show was introduced as well to entertain the farmers. There was a long line of carriages outside the railing of the course and across on the far side were numerous drinking booths.

As *The Chronicle* put it:

> Many a poor rustic who had come out for the day with the intention of having his full swing of pleasure was to be seen between two friends whose united and in some cases not too gentle assistance was absolutely necessary to convey him to fresh scenes of action. Amusements provided were 'civil will', 'the Ducal game', Aunt Sally, etc., one and all having their admirers and supporters.

Rowland Egerton Warburton was sent this dialectical description of the day on the lines of *Farmer Dobbin* by Thomas Smelt of Warburton:

TARPORLEY RACES

One morning' i' November, aw sed aw'd av a spree,
And aw'd go an see the reeces on the coorse o' Tarporlee;
For aw thoght as workin' aw the day without a bit o' play
Wud make a chap grow seedy loik, an aw'd av a 'oliday.

So aw drew the plow besoides the doik, and turned ow'd Farmer loose,
An' weshed my feace an donned my best, and started for the coorse.
And theer wot crowds o' folk aw seed as throng as honey bees,
Fro' scarlet coated noblemen to 'umbler folk i' frieze.

There were drinkin' tents, an sta's wi' nuts, an gingerbreds and pop,
Aunt Sally's mugs and brass o' sticks – o' such a goodly crop;
Here wur gipsy folk tow'd fortunes, and grooms as woise as they
Cud tell wich 'orse for sartin sure wud win the coop that day.

Aw seed some four or foive o' these – a downy lot they looked –
Who sed as 'ow the favorite wos just as good as cooked:
One sed as Forester was sure to carry off the proize,
For he'd bin tried wi' racers loik, and when he goos he floies.

Aw ax'd about Matilda, but they said she war'nt no gud,
For why, they sed, she's up to nowt, she's but a weedy blud.
Says aw, young men, doan't gammon me – will yo lay two to one,
In creawns or peaunds, which best yo loik, but ne'er a one sed dun.

A show o' horses next aw seed, a goodly lot they been,
For field, or plow, or breedin' loik, as ever they were seen.
Ralph Percival for 'unters wi his roan cum first for shares
Whilst Austen's pair wos best o' teams, and Whitlow's best o' mares.

Just then the bell for saddlin' rung, the coorse was quickly cleared,
The members race was first to run, and Shakerley was cheer'd.
Next Coort and Trafford mounted, for a match across the sward,
But Coort he cum but second best, for Trafford's run too 'ard.

Then cum the coop, a glorious proize! they sed 'twas lined wi' gowd;
And as each roider oied it o'er, each roider's 'eart grew bowd;
Eight on 'em mustered at the poast, in green or white or red,
Their jackets glisterin' i' the sun, loik poppies in a bed.

High throbbed each 'art as off they flew – and Philo led the band,
But Forester wos in his stroide, and Ploughman close at hand;
And Tetton Horse wos workin' 'ard, Matilda lyin' back,
Hark Forward, an the rest on 'em, a followin' in their track.

Now Forester! now Philo wins! the air wi' shouts wos rent,
As neck and neck they raced along, to gain each 'orseman's bent;
Matilda aw too late to win, cum wi a rush for place,
For Forester had won the yett, tho' he'd na wun the race.

Agen they met, agen they strove, an Ploughman led the van,
Matilda closely followin' – Coort rode her loik a man;
But as they neared the winnin' post she shot ahead o' all,
For blud mun tell when cocktails run – an they wur cocktails all.

Once moor they met, but only two were left upon the field;
This toim 'twas aw for victory, an one o' two mun yield.
*"Neaw Parker theau mun do thi best," Jones whispered in his ear,**
"For Coort is gettin' dang'rous mon – will skill avail thi here

And now loik greyhounds from the slips, they stretched across the plain,
An Forester at topmost speed he troid his moight and main;
But Matilda aw within hersel stuck closely at his soid,
An Coort he knew the race wur his, an wud na be denoid.

Houd, Parker, Houd! 'twur vain they croid, thou canst na do na moor,
Nor whip nor spur can serve thee now; for why the race wur o'er.
Matilda wins! one loud huzza, as th' poost she cantered by,
In deafinin' shouts fro' earth to skoy proclaims her victory!

Then wur the coop o'erbrimmed wi' wine – the goblets passed areaund –
Matilda's health! her owner's too! was drunk upo' the ground;
For th' best o' tits had wun that day, own'd by the best o' men,
And when the next he goos a racing, sirs, may aw be theer agen.

ALPHA.

* Parker rode Forester, and Jones trained him.

IN 1863 BOTH THE FOREST STAKES AND THE WELTER RACE were abolished, but the Farmers's Cup continued with entry forms and conditions made available with the landlord of The Swan Hotel. A year or two later forms for certificates were also left with Mr Daine.

In April, 1867 the Cheshire Hunt held a meeting at Tarporley and this time the results were published in the volume of *Steeple Chases Past*. But the precise location is not given. It took place again the next two years in March with six races on the card.

From 1869 onwards an omnibus was provided 'for the Races, each Member using it to pay 2/6'. This was for the Tarporley Hunt meeting in November, when they were still racing on the flat.

It was in 1870 that Lord Combermere proposed 'that Gentlemen Riders should come under the same rules as they do in the Grand National'. This was a reference to the Grand National Steeplechase Rules, as National Hunt Rules were first known and which had been introduced in 1863. The Grand National Hunt Committee was formed in 1866. At Tarporley changes were made to the Farmers' Race in 1870, mainly that it was no longer to be run in heats, nor, as previously, were the officers from the Manchester Cavalry to be asked (as a regiment) by the Club.

Lord Shrewsbury, who had just been elected, was approached with a view to an additional room being added to the Stand. Three years earlier they had written to his father regarding the £15 charge his estate had been making 'for the use, for one day only, of the Tarporley Race ground'.

The Clerk of the Scales at this time was, incidentally, John Cossins, a tenant of the Cheshire Hunt Subscribers at Blue Cap Cottage where he ran a Hunting Livery Stable. He was paid £2 10s. for the day.

The next year two races failed to fill and a match was substituted between Miss Littledale and Mr Marshall Brooks for £25, given by the Club and won by the latter. Already that morning

> A discussion took place on the subject of the racing, which was generally agreed to be on an unsatisfactory footing and it was proposed that a Committee, consisting of Lord Combermere, Sir Humphrey de Trafford, Philip Egerton, Hy. F. Hayhurst and Bolton Littledale, be appointed, to whom the whole subject be referred for revision, and who were requested to report upon in sufficient time to carry out their recommendations at the next Meeting. The sum to be given by the Club (including £30 for the Horse Prizes as now given[*]) not to exceed £200.

*For the Horse Show, instituted in 1862, *see* Appendix F.

It seems that it was not so much the organization of the meeting as the conditions for the races, which had been considered at fault. The committee reformed the card as follows with the conditions much as before:

1. THE FARMERS CUP of £20 with £30 added or £50 at the option of the winner, for half-bred horses. Entrance 1 sov. Twice round, about 2 miles.
2. THE TARPORLEY STAKES of £5 each with £50 added for *bona fide* Hunters, the property of members of the Hunt. Twice round, over 2 miles.
3. THE CHESHIRE STAKES of one sov. each and £25 added for half-bred horses, *bona fide* the property of Farmers, Innkeepers and Tradesmen resident in Cheshire. Twice round.
4. THE GENTLEMEN'S RACE of £5 each with £25 added for *bona fide* Hunters that have been fairly hunted with the Cheshire, Sir W. W. Wynn's, North Shropshire and North Staffordshire for which racehorse duty has not been paid . . . Twice round, 2 miles.

The races and Horse Show continued at Cotebrook for two more years, but the time had clearly come for a change. Lord Combermere and Sir Humphrey proposed that they should organize a Steeplechase instead two years hence in 1875 and co-opted Messrs. Corbet, Smith-Barry, Court, Piers Egerton Warburton, Henry Tollemache, Lord Richard Grosvenor and Bolton Littledale to help them.

The last named was Secretary and the first official Tarporley Hunt Steeplechase was held in April, 1875 on the fields behind The Swan Hotel, half-a-mile away. As is clear from these letters the landlord helped with the organization.

Sandiway Bank,
Hartford.

2nd April, 1875

DEAR WARBURTON,
I duly received yours of the 1st, enclosing letter from Lord Haddington. The Committee being very anxious to avoid all drunkenness had arranged that no tents should be allowed on the ground excepting Mr Daine's, who had promised to allow no drunkenness and to sell no ale or spirits after the last race.

I have been on the Course this morning and have seen several Gentlemen who are all of the opinion that if no tents are allowed on the ground, they would be put up close to the Course by parties over whom the Committee would have no control. Mr Daine being Lord Haddington's tenant [farmer, as well as licencee] could, of course, be prevented from selling refreshments, but I cannot help thinking, if that were explained to Lord H., and also that many people, who would leave home early, would be away 11 or 12 hours, while even those living a few miles off, being absent from

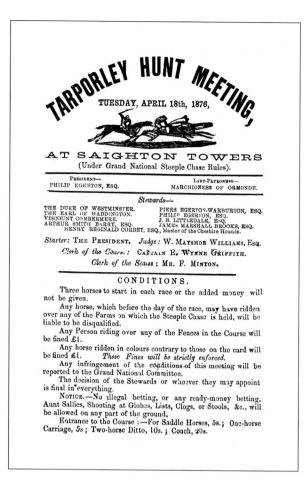

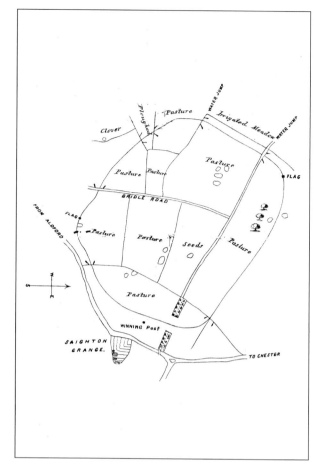

home for at least 8 or 9 hours, would require refreshment, he would no longer object to Mr Daine's tent.

But I think the worst feature of all is that Gentlemen and Ladies would come in their carriages with well-packed hampers and have their lunch as usual while all around them would be literally a starving crowd.

I remain yours very truly
J.B.LITTLEDALE

*

Tyninghame,
Prestonkirk,
April 7th, 1875   N.B.

MY DEAR WARBURTON,
I really am very much indebted to you for your kindness and all the trouble you have taken in trying to have my wishes carried out in regard to the Booths, etc.

I am quite satisfied with the arrangements made by Littledale and the Committee.

His letter rather amuses me and he certainly appears to have a low estimate of the sociable or hospitable qualities of the Cheshire ladies!

Believe me,
Sincerely yours,
HADDINGTON

The first race was the Cheshire Farmers' Steeple Chase Plate of 75 sov. and a Silver Cup for hunters. Five of the seven runners fell. The winning riders included James Smith-Barry, whose brother Arthur also had a winner, ridden by their brother-in-law, Lord Willoughby de Broke, and Major Charles Rivers Bulkeley with a double.

But for Daine the 1876 event would not have filled. After some spirited canvassing on his part, it took place a second time and then the next two years the Meeting was held at Saighton Towers. The first meeting there was not a universal success, according to Mr Harry Rawson, who wrote in his hunting journal:

The so-called Tarporley race meeting was held on April 10th at Saighton & a sorry affair it was. Knew none of the horses which ran & few of the jockeys who rode them. The incident of the day was the following:- Paper Dick was leading a pony through a crowd when the little beast lashed out viciously & caught the Duke of Westminster's horse on the hind leg & lamed it for the time being. The Duke took the thing well & said nothing. Paper Dick took it equally well and was equally silent, & so the matter ended.

The meeting was pretty well attended considering the situation of the course as regards the county in general.

The winning post was just across the road from Saighton Grange with the circuit flagged on the pasture of Saighton Farm. It included two water jumps and a little bit of plough.

For entrance to the course, saddle horses and one-horse carriages were charged 5s., two-horse carriages, 10s. and coaches 20s. No metal badges were issued for Tarporley, but Members were admitted by green tickets.

For the two years the races were at Saighton, the name of the Lady Patroness graced the card, but not subsequently. It happened that on each occasion they were married Ladies, the former Lady Elizabeth Grosvenor, by then the Marchioness of Ormonde, and Mrs Thomas Egerton Tatton, the former Essex Cholmondeley, recently returned from her honeymoon.

After the two years at Saighton began the heyday of the Tarporley Hunt Steeplechases when the meeting was moved to its permanent site on the Arderne Estate near Ash Hill, off the Chester Road from Tarporley. From then on it was always a Spring Meeting in April. Not being in Tarporley Week, club uniform was no longer obligatory for Members. It became the President's duty to act as Starter.

A right-handed circular course was made and in time stands were built, behind which was a small railed parade ring with the weighing room and changing room alongside. With its long climb up to an exceptionally short run-in of 200 yards from the last fence and often tenacious going, Tarporley was considered as good a test as any for a true 'chaser and many good horses and great horsemen did battle over the birch and gorse fences on the Cheshire grassland. It became a most fashionable and popular event in the county's social and sporting calendar. The Members' Steeplechase was for many years ridden in hunting costume and was popularly known as 'the red coat race'.

The roads and lanes to Tarporley and from

TARPORLEY HUNT MEETING,

Wednesday, April 4th, 1888,

AT TARPORLEY,

Under GRAND NATIONAL HUNT RULES.

PRESIDENT:
JAMES TOMKINSON, ESQ.

STEWARDS:

THE DUKE OF WESTMINSTER,	ARTHUR H. SMITH BARRY, ESQ.
THE MARQUIS OF CHOLMONDELEY,	PIERS EGERTON-WARBURTON, ESQ.
THE EARL OF HADDINGTON,	JAMES H. SMITH BARRY, ESQ.
THE EARL OF ENNISKILLEN,	J. B. LITTLEDALE, ESQ.
VISCOUNT COMBERMERE,	JAMES MARSHALL BROOKS, ESQ.
SIR PHILIP LE BELWARD GREY-EGERTON, BART.	

CAPT. E. PARK YATES,
HENRY REGINALD CORBET, ESQ. } Masters of the Cheshire Hounds.

13TH HUSSARS' STEWARDS:

COLONEL T. K. SPILLING,   A. OGILVY, ESQ.
CAPTAIN C. WILLIAMS,   T. PHILLIPS, ESQ.
CAPTAIN K. McLAREN.

STARTER: THE PRESIDENT.   JUDGE: MR. PICKERING.
CLERK OF THE COURSE: T. F. LINNELL, ESQ.
CLERK OF THE SCALES: MR. PICKERING.

CONDITIONS.

Three horses to start in each Race, or the added money will not be given; when only two start, the property of different owners, sufficient will be added to make the value of the Stakes not less than £20.

Any Horse, which, before the day of the Race, may have been ridden over any of the Farms on which the Steeplechase is held, will be liable to be disqualified.

Any person riding over any fence in the course will be fined £1.

The Owner of any Horse ridden in colours contrary to those on the Card, will be fined £1.

These fines will be strictly enforced.

NOTICE.—No illegal Betting, or any ready money Betting, Aunt Sallies, Shooting at Globes, Lists, Clogs, or Stools, &c., will be allowed on any part of the Ground.

The decision of the Stewards, or whoever they may appoint, is final in everything.

Any infringement of the conditions of this meeting will be reported to the Grand National Steeplechase Committee.

Entrance to Course:—Saddle Horses, 5s.; Carriages 5s. each Horse.

To start at the winning post and go twice round for 3½ miles.

Price of Card, SIXPENCE each.

PRINTED AT JEFFS' HIGH STREET PRINTING WORKS, TARPORLEY.

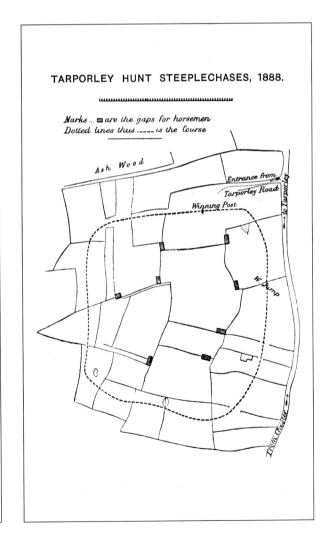

TARPORLEY HUNT STEEPLECHASES, 1888.

Marks ... ◼ are the gaps for horsemen
Dotted lines thus ------ is the Course

Tarporley Steeplechases, 1890, from an oil painting by Archibald Mackinnon.
KEY: r. of flower girl, *Sam Sandbach, Capt.P.H.B. Egerton.* Centre l. to r., mounted, *Mrs Sissie Sandbach, The Earl of Enniskillen, Baron von Schröder, Lady Alexander Paget,* standing, *Viscount Combermere, Duke of Westminster, Lord Alexander Paget, Capt.E.W.Park Yates, Miss Frances Griffith, H.R.Corbet, Captain Billy Baldwin (in topee)* and further to r. *Cudworth Poole.*

Cuddington and Beeston Castle stations were thronged with all manner of horse drawn vehicles and many rode on horseback from twenty miles and more. Villagers turned out as the coaching horns sounded and children scrambled for coppers thrown from the carriages.

At the course there was always a large marquee where the farmers were entertained by the Hunt to a sit-down lunch. Veal and ham or pork pies of noble proportions with all the trimmings, as well as beer and even champagne, were provided for invited tenant farmers. Picnics were the order of the day, often with liveried servants. Guests were seated with their hosts at linen-

clad trestle tables in front of each crested carriage.

The 1880 event was described by Rawson as:

A very good meeting. Didn't see a single drunken man on the ground.

The next he reported two hay stacks being destroyed by fire.

In late Victorian times a cavalry regiment was often stationed in the county and among those to combine their Race Meeting with the Tarporley Hunt under Grand National Hunt Rules* were the King's Dragoon

Guards (1877 & 1878), Royal Dragoon Guards (1880), 3rd Dragoon Guards (1884), 3rd Hussars (1887), 13th Hussars (1888), 9th Lancers (1889) and the XII Royal Lancers (1893). On some such occasions there were as many as ten races on the card, all steeplechases. Tarporley remained one of the few jumping meetings not to stage hurdle races. At the XII Lancers' meeting Eustace Loder won the Subalterns' Challenge Cup and the Regimental Challenge Cup with the same horse. As Major Loder, he owned and bred the phenomenal Pretty Polly and in 1906 won The Derby with Spearmint. The

regiment had participated the previous year and the Farmers' Steeple Chase was won by Miles Tristram: this fearless subaltern was run away with and won by a distance, the rest all falling.[†]

In 1890 the scene was painted in oils 'with all the fun of the fair' by Archibald MacKinnon (1850-1935), a Scotsman who had settled at Nantwich. It is a magnificent canvas $30\frac{1}{2}$" by 72", a photogravure of which, formerly in the possession of Major Gilbert Cotton was presented to the Club by Colonel Geoffrey Churton and the author. The canvas itself is dated 1896

---

[*] The 'Grand' was dropped in 1890. The Committee, whilst sharing the Secretariat run by Weatherby & Sons, administered the Winter sport entirely separately from the Jockey Club, until the Membership of the two bodies merged in 1969.

[†] Stationed in Manchester, a new purchase also bolted with him when exercising in the grounds of Trafford Park. His mount on that occasion pulled up on the main road after hitting the top bar of a 6-foot gate flanked with iron deer hurdles. Mr Tristam decided to walk back to barracks.

Willy Hall Walker on Raleigh at Tarporley, winner of the Ladies' Purse, 1899, from an oil painting by Adrian Jones.

and signed with the artist's monogram.

Beeston Castle and the Peckforton Hills are clearly shown on the skyline. The flags on tall poles are the winning post with a box for the judge. Note the fire-eater dressed as Mephistopheles (in left middle background); away to the right stands a preacher. The blackboard, centre right, belonging to the gypsy with the parrokeets, reads:

THE WONDERFUL FORTUNE TELLING BIRDS.
TRY YOUR LUCK BEFORE YOU GO IN FOR SPECULATIVE
HORSE RACING LOVE AND MARRIAGE
PREVENT SUICIDE. ONLY A 1D.

The Chronicle reported that there was 'an enormous attendance with an unusually large muster of drags and private carriages' that day which was 'beautifully fine, marred only by one heavy shower although there was an incessant downpour at Chester all day'.

It was still customary for the President to act as Starter, but Captain Eggie Leigh, who had been in the chair the previous November, was absent and the President elect, Sam Sandbach, took his place. Captain 'Bay' Middleton had a ride there that day.

Three years later there was a move afoot to combine the races with the Wynnstay Hunt Meeting at Bangor-on-Dee and to have two days' racing at Tarporley, but nothing came of it. Again there was a splendid crowd and 'an aristocratic line of drags' with much sipping of champagne, as 'itinerant musicians, "niggers", boxers, cripples and blacklegs contributed unflagging entertainment throughout the day, including a man with a cornet and irreproachable lung-power', persistently singing *The man that broke the bank of Monte Carlo.*

The most prolific winner at Tarporley was Mr Arthur Brocklehurst, who rode twenty-three winners there between 1879 and 1892, eleven of them his own and a twelfth ridden by Captain Billy Baldwin, himself no stranger to the winner's enclosure. Brocklehurst lived at Cholmondeley. Both of them and the author's father, Jock Fergusson, each had the distinction of riding four Tarporley winners in an afternoon, in 1887, 1876 and 1899 respectively. The Lion had ridden his Reckless a winner in a 4-mile Hunter Chase at the Cheshire Hunt Steeplechase Meeting in the Spring of 1868. Mr Fred Hassall of Whitchurch was another top Tarporley rider, later turning professional.

Arthur Brocklehurst once rode five winners and a second at the Wirral Hunt Meeting, which was first held at Parkgate in 1884 before being moved to Hooton Park in 1897. A great friend and rival of the pigskin was Massey Harper, who kept The Lion and Swan at Congleton. They were once riding the only two runners in the Tarporley Hunt Stakes and were seen to go slower and slower before eventually pulling up on the far side of the course. A heated argument took place, for one horse would not jump without a lead and the other's rider refused to give it. They were on the point of coming to blows when the Stewards sent across a galloper to let them know the race would be declared void unless it was completed in five minutes. Brocklehurst won on the favourite.

Captain J.M.Gordon, a former 12th Lancer living at The Oaklands, Bunbury, could also be relied on to ride a winner. Arthur Knowles of Alvaston Hall had a good ex-Irish hunter called Jack Tar, which often won at the local meetings, usually ridden by his friend, Jock Fergusson, twice successfully carrying 14st 7 *lb.* at Tarporley. A frequent and popular winning owner in those days was Rock Cholmondeley (222), for whom the great George Lambton rode a double in 1888. One of the most sporting events was the Ladies' Purse. Among those who won it were Willy Hall Walker (268) in 1899,[*] Tom Royden (287), who also rode a treble in 1907, Lord Cholmondeley (Fergusson up), Gilbert Cotton, and Oswald Mosley Leigh (245) for Brian Egerton back in 1888. In later years up to 1914, Mouse Tomkinson (271), Harry Cottrill, who then lived and trained at Cotebrook at Sandiford Lodge, and Jack Anthony all rode winners.

[*] Three years earlier he had been second to a horse owned by his youngest brother. The future Lord Wavertree never did get on especially well with most of his brothers, and on this occasion he objected on the grounds that the horse had not been regularly hunted to conform with the race conditions, but withdrew by permission of the Stewards, his deposit money being returned.

Jock Fergusson after winning the Ladies' Purse on Lord Cholmondeley's Avincourt, 1906.

Tarporley Races, 1905.

Bend Or, himself, was no stranger to the pigskin and had won his fair share of point-to-points. He was on his own much fancied Drumree at Tarporley in 1901 with the Cheshire farmers all on him to a man, not to mention the ladies. He was coming home with a wet sail when the favourite made a desperate mistake at the last, the ducal seat all but being lost. A young lad called Costello on a horse trained by Johnny Cowap on the Cop at Sealand, seized his chance and held on to win by half-a-length. Coincidentally the winner's sire was called Quæsitum.

A particularly notable horse to win its first steeplechase in 1884 at Tarporley was Gamecock, trained locally at Sandy Brow by Jimmie Jordan. The race was the Foxhunters' Open Steeplechase. Captain Bay Middleton was riding in the race and he came head for head up the hill to the last, 'where he came down a buster' and Gamecock went on to win. Three years later, with local professional Billy Daniels up in preference to George Lambton who had wanted the ride, he won the Grand National on the Friday and was saddled again the next day to win the Liverpool Champion Steeplechase, a further three miles round the gruelling Aintree course, which in those days included plough.[†] The second horse in that National was Savoyard, owned by Baron von Schröder (224).

A lesser equine star of Tarporley was Dreadnought, whose owner, Mr Sam Challoner, farmed the Cheshire Farmer's Half-Bred Steeple Chase with him between 1898 and 1906, winning four times and thrice 2nd. Dreadnought also won the Cheshire Farmers' Steeple Chase in 1897, ridden by Daniels, but apart from two other occasions, Jock Fergusson, who headed the G.R.s' list several years, was in the saddle.[‡] The rest of the year Dreadnought worked on his owner's farm near Beeston Castle and was frequently seen at the Cattle Market with a load of pigs or calves and was even driven to the races in his 'shandy'.

Two of Tom Royden's victories in 1907 were on Mr J.E.Shore's Picton II, which also won at Woore. The third was in the Tarporley Steeple Chase with a horse of his own. Riding in the race, besides Vic Herman of Park House, Cholmondeley, and Frank Tinsley, was Baron von Trutzschler from Buerton, who had a reputation as a horse-coper, a breeder of Holsteins and a womanizer.[§]

For the 1914 Meeting a cinder track had been constructed to accommodate the motor cars. The neverending stream of cars, carriages and pedestrians that year formed what was thought to be a record crowd. The stands had been improved and over 1,000 tenant farmers

Mr Thomas Royden on Picton II, after bringing off a treble.

[†] The horse had his final preparation by being ridden four times round a mile figure-of-eight gallop in Oulton Park with a fresh horse jumping in each time round to take him on. That was on the Tuesday. He was given a rest on the Wednesday and was led in hand to Aintree the next day.

[‡] *See* Cheshire Miscellany.

[§] The Baron was not unknown to have defrauded the bookmakers. He once worked a telegram job by taking a pile of forms in to a post office, mostly addressed to himself. The top one, consisted of the first chapter of Genesis translated into German. The old postmistress was having a terrible time getting it off, so he made sure she time-stamped all the rest and went out to a telephone to find out what had won the next race at that day's meeting. He then made an excuse to the poor woman and inserted the name of the winner on the other telegrams while she was still busy with the German one.

N.B. In those days telegrams could also be withdrawn on payment of 6d, which gave rise to other such devious schemes.

and their families were guests at the hunt luncheon.

National Hunt racing was curtailed more and more throughout the Great War with only fifteen days' racing in England by 1916 and ten the next year. (Gatwick staged a substitute 'War National'.) The Tarporley Hunt Meeting was not revived until 1921. With free access to the course the inimitable atmosphere of a country day-out was the same as ever. Crowds still walked from Cuddington and Beeston stations and the village children came out to see the cars and traps go by. Two clowns, Snowball and Jerk, were usually there to add to the fun and would foregather with the locals at the Beeston Station Hotel before catching the last train home. The chief topic would invariably be how the entries for the Farmers' Races had fared, owned over the years by such sportsmen as Barnett, Cummins (Lady Gosland), Dodd, Dutton, Edge, Fearnall, Greenway, Hewitt, Hocknell, Shore, Williamson, Worrall and many another. It had long been the practice of some landlords on race days to provide a communal pie, well-laced with salt. The beer sales were even higher.

The Ladies' Purse was no longer in the revived programme. The Stewards in 1921 were Lord Cholmondeley (222), Lord Arthur Grosvenor (226), the Secretary (236), Major F.H. Fetherstonhaugh and, for the first time, Lord Wavertree (268). The last-named had the pleasure of seeing his home-bred, All White, win the Tarporley Handicap Steeple Chase. He was ridden by the stable jockey, Bob Chadwick, who the previous month had been third on him in the Grand National.

All White was surely the unluckiest loser ever of the famous Aintree race. Two years earlier the mount had been given to little-known Tommy Williams, as Chadwick had broken his wrist. The race was run in torrential rain. The second time round, All White was with the leaders, when his rider was seen to pull him up after jumping Becher's and allow the entire field to disappear before going in pursuit. He finished fifth, full of running to the locally owned Poethlyn. Asked the reason afterwards he said: 'Beg pardon, sir, my lunch did not agree with me and I had to pull up to be sick!'

The 1923 Meeting drew a record crowd and consequent enormous traffic jams, then a rarity. A future Master of the Cheshire Hounds won the Tarporley Hunt Cup, a hunter steeplechase, with his own horse, Edgeley. Its previous owner, a great uncle of Geoffrey Churton (328) had become disgruntled with the horse, which had got beaten too many times when the money was down. John Paterson (314) went over to inspect the horse in its paddock near Whitchurch.' What will you give me for it, Paterson?' asked Jack Churton. 'Nothing,' replied the Scotsman. 'Right, he's yours, take him away!' When he

won at Tarporley, it was quite a triumph, as John was 42 at the time.

A popular winner of the Tarporley Hunt Cup the previous year had been Major Cyril Dewhurst's Conjuror II, who finished 3rd in the 1923 Grand National. Tipperary Tim, the 1928 winner, won the 1924 Open Handicap at Tarporley as a six-year-old. On that occasion he was not ridden by the Chester solicitor, Mr Billy Dutton, who had, however, before his Liverpool victory, gained valuable experience at Tarporley, winning four races there from fourteen rides.

Other 'National' heroes to ride and/or win at Tarporley in the ensuing years included Mr Harry Brown, Fred Rees, George Owen, who won eight races there as a jockey including his first winner, Gerry Wilson, and Messrs. Peter Cazalet, Frank Furlong, Fulke Walwyn and Bobby Petre. The champion Amateur Rider, later Senior Jockey Club Starter, Alec Marsh, rode four winners, including a treble in 1937.

When All White finished third in the National a horse called Turkey Buzzard, owned by the formidable Mrs.H.M.Hollins and ridden by Capt.G.H.Bennet, had trailed in fourth, the only other to finish, having been remounted three times. It was coincidentally by the same sire, Lord Wavertree's White Eagle. The Captain's determination was not appreciated by the owner, who chased him round the paddock brandishing her umbrella for submitting her horse to unnecessary stress. Mrs Hollins hunted regularly with the Cheshire, keeping her horses at Hartford. Three years later, on a soaking wet day, Turkey Buzzard won the Tarporley Handicap Steeplechase with 12 st.8*lb*. and in 1926 it started again for the same race with top weight, this time with the champion jockey, W.Stott, up.

The Racing Calendar reported:

All [six] horses refused at the first fence and the race was declared void.– The Stewards, having interviewed the riders, were of the opinion that the horses refused owing to the state of the course through rain.

What it did not relate was that 'Billy' Stott refused to come out of the Weighing Room afterwards, because old 'Ma' Hollins was waiting outside, umbrella at the ready.

In 1925 Bend Or's son-in-law, Billy Filmer-Sankey, won the United Hunts' Cup* on his own horse, beating Tipperary Tim, and in 1927 the Tarporley Hunt Cup on

---

* This Hunter Chase was first included on the card in 1909 and should not be confused with the long-established United Hunts' Meeting, for many years held at Lingfield. Professional jockeys were allowed to ride in such races, but carried 5 *lb*. extra.

SEEN AT
TARPORLEY RACES

Photos by Crompton

(Above) *Left to Right :* Brockton (winner), Kendal Kid (second), Herodora (third), neck-and-neck at the last hurdle, in the Tarporley Hunt Cup.

(Above) *Sir John Dixon and Mr. Matson.*

(Left) *Mrs. T. Marshall Brooks, Mrs. Noel Brooks, Miss Barbour, Master Brooks.*

(Above) *Running Sand (winner) leads Silver Graid (second) and Torley (third), at the last jump in the Beeston Castle Steeplechase.*

(Left)
Miss "Tibby" Rolt and Mr. "Micky" Moseley.

(Above)
Mr. Eric Williams and Major G. Cotton.

Lady Ursula's odds-on favourite. That year Anthony Crossley, whose father, Sir Kenneth, had bought Combermere Abbey, came home alone to win the United Hunts' Cup. These were not the only races Filmer-Sankey won at Tarporley. In 1931 he got up by a length to beat Pat Moseley riding for John Paterson, who promptly objected on the ground that the Captain was not entitled to ride as he was not a subscriber to the Cheshire Hounds. He was by then Master of the South Notts. It was a difficult moment for the Stewards, whose decision to overrule, and at the same time to return the deposit, had probably been aided, did they but know it, by the rapid exodus from the course of old Albert Matson, the Hunt Treasurer.

However all was not as it should be. The course had become waterlogged in places and there was a notable decline in both the quality and number of entries. In 1925 two races were declared void, because there were no finishers. It had become a go-as-you-please outing for the general public, who had free access. Vendors of all sorts of trifles thronged there and pick-pockets were rife. Many spectators still watched the races from horseback and this added to the chaos.

In 1926 the Members of the T.H.C. decided to form a limited company to run their race meeting with the directors each holding shares in trust for the Club. With its registered office and affairs in the hands of Tarporley solicitor, Chips Chambers, Tarporley Steeplechases Ltd. came into being. Prior to that, since 1875, the Club had financed the races to the extent of £135 *per annum*. It now made a capital investment of £4,000 and the Club Stand and the paddock were enlarged, lavatory accommodation was provided and the finishing post moved to a point by the stand. Most important of all, 20,000 drain pipes were laid round the course with the desired result. The crowds still came and from 1928 paid a shilling to go through the turnstiles.

The Liverpool Cotton broker and Cheshire Master, Walter Midwood, won the Club Cup in 1928, piloted by none other than the future Sir Noël Murless. Another fine local amateur rider in those years was Pat Moseley (318). He won the United Hunts' Cup in 1929 with his father's Agden, on whom he had won the previous year's Liverpool Foxhunters' and rode in the National the following year. Also he won the Tarporley Hunt Cup for John Paterson (314) in 1932. A great judge of pace and a fine finisher, by 1939 he had ridden over 100 winners under N.H.Rules and between the flags. His younger brother, Micky, took over his mantle after the War. In his first race ever Micky finished third on Agden in the Tarporley Hunt Cup when they were both sixteen.

There was always a horse-drawn lorry from Arderne

as a private stand near the winning post for staff and estate workers. In 1930 they were able to cheer home a house guest, when Lord Haddington, the nephew of Henry Baillie-Hamilton Arden and his sisters, rode his own hunter to win the United Hunts Cup. Nor did the wagon go back empty; the gardeners would help themselves to a supply of pea-sticks out of the birch fences after the last race.

This Meeting was the first time the Totalisator was operated – win only to a 2/- stake. Compared to the S.P., it showed a profit of £1 6s 1d to a level stake on the winner of all six races and 17/10d the next year. It had been first introduced on British racecourses in 1929.[*] The machine had come to stay, despite the sound advice of that great character of the Northern bookmaking fraternity, Tom Skelton, who implored the author, on one of his early and almost invariably unsuccessful skirmishes with the Ring: 'Never bet on the Tote, sonny – they slam yer fingers in the windows.'

In 1937 a new stand to accommodate 2,000 and a proper number board were erected. A semaphore system to the far corners of the course worked well and, for the first time, the police had 'walkie-talkie' equipment to keep the traffic flowing.

Sir Thomas Royden, for long a Steward of the Meeting as well as, in his younger days, such a sporting rider, was moved to write to the Directors:

> You go from triumph to triumph. The Tarporley Meeting of to-day under your guidance is as different from the Old Tarporley I knew in the years long past, as is Liverpool from a Point-to-Point. From being literally moribund, it is now one of the livliest meetings in the country and everything goes as if on oiled wheels. The entries, which are always the best evidence of good management, were splendid and I was amazed at the number of runners. The course itself is one of the very best I know of, and I wish I were young enough once more to ride over it.

In 1966 Lord Royden's widow gave the Club the handsome Silver circular punch bowl he had won that day back in 1907, its bombé body decorated with mermaids, tritons, flowers and scrolling foliage. It has lion-mask and ring handles.

A familiar figure was Colonel Mosley Leigh, always a favourite subject for the photographers as he was seen chatting with his cronies. He invariably attired himself in a smart hacking jacket with a red carnation, jodhpurs and a grey bowler.

---

[*] The record win dividend of £341 2s 6d to a 2/- stake was established at Haydock Park in a handicap hurdle on November 30th, 1929 and still stands.

The last race at Tarporley on April 20th, 1939 was won by Mr Luke Lillingston, who was to lose his life in France later in the year. The second was ridden by H. 'Frenchie' Nicholson and George Owen came third.

During the War the course was a P.o.W. Camp, for both Italians and Germans. Afterwards five attempts were made to start up racing again, thwarted mostly by costs and the agricultural needs of the farmers. Wardle aerodrome was considered. The author played a small part in a final attempt to revive the meeting, by offering in the 1950's to lease a new course on the gallops at Abbot's Moss. It was mainly due to the necessity to provide secure racecourse stables that the idea was abandoned. Tarporley Steeplechases Ltd. was finally wound up in 1963 and what was left of the stands, ancillary buildings and iron railings were demolished and sold.

In 1992 the Club decided to present a silver challenge cup to Bangor-on-Dee for their new November fixture to commemorate Tarporley Hunt Steeplechases.

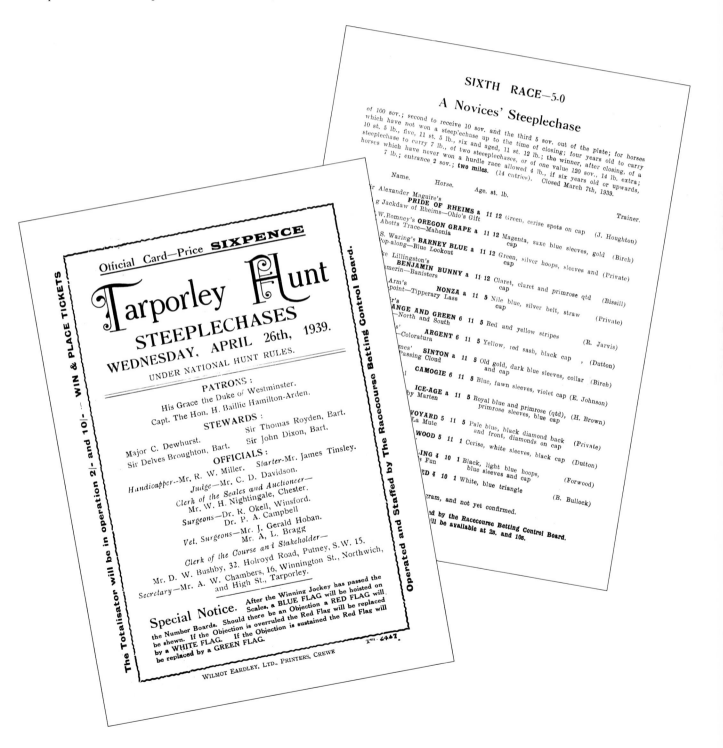

VI

Quæsitiana Primus

THE HEAD OF THE WILBRAHAM FAMILY has kept a *Livre de Memoire* ever since the mid-XVI Century, sometimes more diligently than others. When **Captain 'Sim' Wilbraham (330)** was taken Prisoner of War by the Germans on June 6th, 1940 near Rouen for almost the duration of the Second World War, history was being repeated.

This is part of the entry made by **George Wilbraham, Jnr. (77)**:

> In 1799 I was induced to purchase a Commission in the Army and served as Lieut. in the 4th or King's own Regt of Infantry during the campaign in North Holland. I continued with my Regiment in England till the peace of 1802. Being then at liberty to indulge my taste for travel, I went to France where I was presented to Napoléon Buonaparte then 1st Consul of the French Republic. After travelling through France I returned to Paris and there became one of the victims of that cruel edict of the French Governor which constituted Prisoners all the English within his grasp.
>
> I passed part of my captivity at Verdun, but no inconsiderable portion of it at Paris. I was however fortunate enough to be permitted to come home in 1806.

The circumstances of his imprisonment seem strange, considering that he had been given an audience by Napoléon himself. Various distinguished historians have been unable to elucidate the particulars of this edict. On writing to the French Embassy the author was informed by the Cultural Consul that a reputed British historian of the French Revolution, whom he had consulted, had stated that whilst Napoléon gave the order in 1803 for a surveillance to be maintained on foreigners, he knew of no particular edict. He thought that it would have been likely that on instructions from the *Préfet de Police* a number of British citizens would have been arrested and more often than not kept under house arrest, some being

transferred to Verdun or the surrounding region with orders not to leave the area. However, from information received from the *Institut Français*, in 1803 English officers in the militia visiting France were taken prisoners of war as a reprisal for French citizens and ships which had been impounded by the British when the two countries were not actually at war.

Wilbraham, there as a tourist and no longer a serving officer, albeit an officer of the Royal Cheshire Militia, seems to have taken his incarceration very philosophically. It is a pity he did not go into greater detail.

Another Member, **Frank Jodrell (73)** also had the misfortune to be a *détenu*. He was at Dijon.

Sim

Sim's incarceration began at OFLAG VII C, which was once the Archbishop of Salzburg's palace. In all he was moved three times, from September, 1942 to 29th March, 1945 being held in OFLAG IX A/H, a schloss near Spangenberg. After his liberation by the U.S. Army he arrived at Brook House on April 11th.

* * *

RICHARD BRINSLEY SHERIDAN dedicated *School for Scandal* (1771) to Frances Greville, the year after she married **John Crewe (14)**. She was said to be the most

From a drawing by George A. Fothergill.

William and John, but he died in 1785 just before Dickens's father, John, was born. The widow stayed on as housekeeper for thirty-five years. Lord Crewe arranged for the boys' education and set them up in their careers.

Charles Dickens found his grandmother rather awesome, but was deeply impressed by all the stories she embroidered for him in his childhood in her retirement in Oxford Street – exaggerated reminiscences, legends and fairy tales, just as she had retailed them to Lord Crewe's children by the fire of her little room at Crewe Hall of a Winter's evening She died when he was only twelve. He immortalized her as the wise and genial Mrs Rouncewell in *Bleak House* and drew heavily on all she used to tell him.

*

beautiful woman of her time and was painted three times by Sir Joshua Reynolds. It was once said of her that 'she uglifies everything near her.' It was no wonder Prinny proposed her health.

Coincidentally the youngest of the three beautiful and talented daughters of Sheridan's only son, Thomas, became the Duchess of Somerset. Her grand-daughter, Lady Hermione Graham, had a daughter called Sybil, who married the **Marquess of Crewe (244)** and their daughter, Annabel, was the mother of **Quentin Crewe** (*né* **Dodds, 352**).

Sophie Sheridan, a great grand-daughter of the orator, statesman, dramatist and wit, married **Willie Hall Walker (268)**, in 1896 and lived for a time at Sandy Brow, near Tarporley, where she kept a pack of beagles – some thirty couple, mostly 12"-13".

* * *

DICKENS CONNECTIONS

WILLIAM DICKENS, THE NOVELIST'S GRANDFATHER, was steward at Crewe Hall at the time of **John Crewe** and his beautiful wife and brilliant hostess, Frances, and when Crewe was the scene of most cultivated Whig hospitality with Grillion himself, the founder of the fashionable Grillion's Hotel in Albemarle Street, merely one of the French chefs in the kitchens there and at their Hampstead villa, when they were entertaining in London. Fox, Burke, Canning, Sheridan and Sir Joshua Reynolds were among their guests at both establishments.

Mr Dickens's wife, Elizabeth, bore him two sons,

IT HAS BEEN GENERALLY SUPPOSED that the character, Miss Havisham, was based on an eccentric French duchess Dickens had heard about. However, Dickens is known to have once stayed a short time in Swanlow Lane, Winsford and was told the details of what had happened at nearby Stanthorne Grange. A family called Joule resided there and it is a well authenticated story that the daughter was jilted by her fiancé from Stanthorne Hall. A farmer called Richard Dutton was living at the Hall at the time of Dickens's visit, either as a tenant of the France-Hayhurst family or before it became their property. It is quite likely that Miss Joule's circumstances, also inspired the author when he created the embittered and lonely old maid, Miss Havisham in *Great Expectations*, who died still wearing the shreds of her wedding dress, surrounded by all the tattered trappings of what was to have been her bridal day.

The story long told in Middlewich was that on the wedding morn the young man eloped with another lady as the bride was dressing for her wedding. Her mind unhinged by her lover's perfidy, Miss Joule became a recluse and, as an old and frightened lady, was often seen running from the sight of any man appearing within her vision. It was also known that her parents had sealed the room where the wedding breakfast had been laid out, left to mice and spiders, never to be opened up and used again until after their death.

Charles Leicester (62), who had previously lived at Stanthorne Hall until his death in 1815 at the age of 49, left by his second wife two sons and three daughters. His sons were boys of thirteen and eight at the time. The elder, who became a parson, at the age of 26 married the young widow of his uncle, Lord de Tabley (50), in 1828 the year after he had died. His brother married a distant kinswoman the previous year, aged 20. But the identity of the young man who dashed Miss Joule's expectations has yet to be established.

* * *

BEFORE MARRYING the second of his three wives, the Rev. **Sir Thomas Delves Broughton (26)** once proposed to Miss Clive, his first wife having borne him thirteen children. The lady thanked him for the honour but declined it for fourteen reasons: herself and her own concerns formed the first, the remainder she felt were obvious. He had his portrait painted by Romney, paying

100 gns., half with the order and half on completion, and he built Doddington Hall, which took twenty-two years, from plans by Samuel Wyatt. There was a banqueting house in the centre of Doddington Pool, which ceased to exist in 1813, the year the Rev. Sir Thomas died. The story goes that he was so angry after being marooned there all night after his rowing boat had slipped its moorings, he gave orders for it to be blown up immediately.

* * *

Tom Grosvenor (57) was a real goodhearted, pleasant and amusing old fellow, full of fun and good stories, as recounted by C.T.S.Birch Reynardson in his *Sports and Anecdotes of Byegone Days*. Given his field-marshal's baton at the age of eighty-two, this distinguished officer's first engagement had been as a subaltern in command of the piquet at the Bank of England during the Gordon Riots in 1780. As Brigade Commander he had a narrow escape in the trenches at the siege of Copenhagen in 1807, when a shell, hissing and fizzing, landed on a corner of his cloak, burying it and itself in the sand with the garment still hooked

tightly round his neck. The shell burst, but not before he and his staff had flung themselves face down, 'and not one of us was touched' he was able to recall in his old age. On the march during the Walcheren raid a round shot got into his portmanteau on the baggage-waggon. Amongst his clothes were two bottles of brandy, but neither had been broken.

Of all his escapes, however. he reckoned his narrowest to have been among his own countrymen after an election at his home town. He had been declared duly elected and his Whig supporters had removed his horses from the shafts to drag his carriage back in triumph to Eaton. Opposition ruffians, with their dander up on the far-famed Chester ale, gave chase, intent on hurling him, carriage and all, into the Dee. There was an almighty scrimmage with brickbats flying about instead of cannon balls, and bludgeons being wielded instead of swords. Just as the carriage was being lifted up against the side of the bridge by the Independent mob, the General managed to slip out on the other side and, as supporters rallied round him, he escaped a watery grave as the carriage plunged into the river.

In 1802 he vehemently opposed the suppression of bull-baiting and raised a laugh by observing that 'the higher orders had their *Billington*, why not allow the lower orders their *bull*'. This was a very unflattering reference to Madame Elizabeth Billington, a celebrated

General Tom Grosvenor, from a portrait attributed to Robert Bowyer, c.1820 – courtesy National Portrait Gallery.

singer then at the zenith of her career, living in splendid style at Fulham. (The bill was rejected by 13 votes and bull- and bear-baiting were not finally prohibited until 1835.)

In Rutland he used to entertain very lavishly especially during the hunting season. He was most hospitable and his heart was perhaps a little larger than his purse. As a result some of his tradesmen had to wait a while for their bills to be settled. They all knew the General would pay and never ran him very hard.

However there was a tailor, who, though only a country craftsman – the General was by then living at Stocken Hall, between Stamford and Grantham – was considerably patronized by him. Instead of regarding this patronage sufficient for his own maintenance and that of his family, he, having more than once sent in his little bill, had the audacity to put in a personal appearance. The General, finding no way of escape, received him most courteously. After a great deal of small talk, the tailor, not to be shaken off, drew his bill from his pocket and politely presented it to the General, who paid up with what grace he could muster. After consigning the receipted account to his drawerful of bills he wished him a good day and his parting shot was 'I tell you what, Mr H——, you are a damned bad tailor, and if I had thought that you would have expected to be paid, by Jove, I would never have employed you!'

When he took Anne, the youngest daughter of George Wilbraham (5), as his second wife in 1831, Tom Grosvenor wrote to his friend, the Duke of Rutland. The letter is preserved in the Grosvenor Muniment Room at Eaton:

MY DEAR DUKE,
You, who have children & grandchildren to light up your halls with shining morning faces, can never know what dullness is. But for me it is far otherwise. Now, you are beginning to guess that I have something of a <u>communication</u> to make you; and I think I have. I cannot live alone. And I have been so fortunate as to find a gentle lady that takes pity on my singleness. She is the younger sister of George Wilbraham, the Member for Cheshire, already my cousin, so that we have no new connexions, no new faces to cultivate...

. . . I may have a favour to ask you... to beg the loan of Cheveley Park for a fortnight, always understanding that you have withdrawn yourself from that Chateau . . .

So now I have imparted to you a secret and six months ago I thought you might have had a secret to impart to me. The fact is (I speak for myself) I have done with all politics & public men & measures. I shall shut my eyes to all newspapers And I <u>must</u> open them on something.

Let our old friendship shield me from your saying what I know all the busy world <u>will</u> say on hearing this news I impart to you. But I am easy on that score. Let me have but the continuance of old friends in the circle of whom, none I can value so high as my old & attached comrade & friend, John, Duke of Rutland & God bless him & all his house.
Affectionately,
T.GROSVENOR

Miss Wilbraham was then aged 40 and 26 years his junior. Lady Elizabeth Grosvenor disapproved. 'She is . . . said to be an old maid, disagreeable, cross and peevish,' she wrote to her mother, the Marchioness of Stafford, 'I think they are both crazy.' However she found that the General and his wife got on well together. She herself always found her a bore.

The General was a Meltonian and did much of his hunting from Brooksby. He also enjoyed his racing at Newmarket. He hated sleeping out and was once offered a bed when dining in the Cottesmore country. Indecisive on that occasion, he sent for the housemaid, a tiny little woman, and asked when the bed had last been used. "Why, I slept in it myself, General, only last night," came the reply. "You slept in it?" said he, looking her up and down, "You're not big enough to air a bed. Please be good enough to order my carriage."

He liked nothing better than a bit of horse-coping and if on occasion he got hold of a screw, he was a dab hand at passing it on. Through his persuasive eloquence he sold a partially blind horse to a friend, who did not discover the deficit until he had ridden it several times. On demanding the return of his money the General's reply was simply: 'If the horse had not eyes, you had.' Nor did he give him his money back.

Tom Grosvenor's factotum, Tom Perkins, whose chief job was to look after his racehorses, once applied to his master to stand godfather to a newly arrived daughter. Agreeing to be responsible for the little stranger's sins and wickedness, the General did so on condition she was named Briseïs after their favourite 1807 Oaks winner. In due course Miss Briseïs Perkins became a milliner and dressmaker in London. He won The Oaks twice, but was unsuccessful in The Derby, unlike his uncle, the 1st Earl, who also won The Oaks in three successive years.

During the last few years of his life both he and his wife became almost blind.

* * *

THE ONLY HALF-BRED BROODMARE in the General Stud Book is Lady Catherine, 'Bred by General Grosvenor in —, got by John Bull, her dam by Rutland Arabian out of a hunting mare, not thoroughbred'. The editors of that day bent their strict rule to admit her in

Volume II solely because in 1808 she foaled the chesnut colt Copenhagen, by Meteor and bred by **General Grosvenor (57)**. He was to be ridden by the Duke of Wellington at the Battle of Waterloo and, like his dam, is in the Stud Book on sufferance only, having been granted, as somebody put it, 'a title of nobility for military services'. Lady Catherine herself was on active service as her master's charger at Copenhagen and he sent her back to Eaton, when he discovered she was in foal, hence her famous progeny's name.

When the old warhorse was buried at Strathfieldsaye in February, 1836, Rowland Egerton Warburton wrote the following epitaph:

> *With years o'erburdened, sunk the battle steed;–*
> *War's funeral honours to his dust decreed;*
> *A foal when Cathcart overpowered the Dane,*
> *And Gambuier's fleet despoil'd the northern main,*
> *'Twas his to tread the Belgian field, and bear*
> *A mightier chief to prouder triumphs there!*
> *Let Strathfieldsaye to wondering patriots tell*
> *How Wellesley wept when "Copenghagen" fell.*

* * *

Sir **Stephen Glynne (87)**, 8th baronet and Gladstone's father-in-law, was born posthumously. He bought one of the white chargers which Napoléon rode at the Battle of Borodino outside Moscow in 1811, and brought it back to Hawarden where it is buried.

* * *

ARGUABLY one of the most dedicated and proficient fox-hunters of his day was **Sir Thomas Mostyn, Bart. (70)**, who was hunting the Woore Country at the time of his election. In 1800 he took over the Bicester country and hunted it until his death in 1831. He did not resign from the Club until 1813. Nimrod wrote of him:

> Few men are better qualified to be at the head of a pack of fox-hounds than Sir Thomas. A single man, possessed of a fine fortune and at ease in his circumstances, the expense is not an object to him, and his conduct in the field is particularly gentlemanlike.

His wife's kinsman, the Rev. Griff Lloyd, Rector of Christleton, near Chester, turned his hounds for him and was known as 'the Black Whipper-in'. He thought nothing of catching the coach from Chester to Bicester, arriving at midnight to go cub-hunting at 4 a.m. and returning to Chester the same day as an outside passenger on the coach. A favourite story of the late Lord

Sir Thomas Mostyn, Bart., from a portrait in oils by Thomas Bennett.

Mostyn about him, concerned the time he lost his place in his sermon at Newton Purcell, where also he was curate; and Sir Thomas was in the congregation. As he fumbled about trying to find it, his friend called out: 'Try back! Griff, try back!' Not to be beaten, this hunting parson cried out triumphantly: 'Tally-ho! I've got it.'

Sir Thomas acquired a favourite brood bitch called Lady. She, too, like Bluecap, had an obelisk raised to her memory. Sir Thomas was an enthusiastic whip and delighted in putting together four horses, which had never been in harness before, and then a few days later driving them from Bicester the 150 miles to his Flintshire home. Lady once followed the coach the whole way on her own feet.

* * *

Stapleton Cotton, Viscount Combermere, Field-Marshal (78) is the only Member ever to have had a statue erected in his memory. He is seated on his charger in full dress uniform outside the gateway to Chester Castle with his battle honours on the plinth. In the Peninsula he had been known as 'Le Leon d'Or' on account of his rich uniform of a General of Hussars and the gorgeous trappings of his chargers. As a quick, lively boy, his family had called him 'Young Rapid' and he was always getting into scrapes. He was 'Little Cotton' to his hard-drinking, frequently duelling, brother officers of the 6th Carabiniers, but his good temper and moderation kept him out of trouble.

He became a major-general at 32. From 1811 to 1814 he commanded the whole of the allied cavalry and as second-in-command under Wellington, led the famous charge at Salamanca. After the battle he was hit in his right arm by a stray volley from a Portuguese picket. He had been the host at several balls during the campaign, but he spent that night in a pig-trough and was lucky not to suffer amputation. Throughout his campaigns, his experience as a fox-hunter had stood him in good stead, time and time again.

His bitter disappointment was to be passed over for the supreme cavalry command at Waterloo, due to the intervention of the Prince Regent, whom he had displeased beyond forgiveness many years before. When he was stationed at Brighton with his 16th Light Dragoons, he disclosed to Lady Liverpool the fact that Prinny had sprained his leg when he fell at Mrs Fitzherbert's doorway after a nocturnal visit and the London gossips got hold of it.

But thanks to his friend Wellington, he commanded the allied cavalry after Waterloo from July, 1815 to the end of 1816 to the discomfort of the French. The Duke would have preferred him to Uxbridge at Waterloo and when he appointed him, he instructed him as follows:

> General Cotton I am glad to see you in command of the cavalry, and I wish you to bear in mind that cavalry should always be held well in hand; that your men and horses should not be used up in wild and useless charges, but put forward when you are sure that their onset will have a decisive effect.

In 1817 he was appointed Governor of Barbados where he had a strange experience. For many years, whenever a particular vault had been opened, the coffins had been found in utter disarray, as if from volcanic power. It was opened again soon after his arrival and again there was chaos inside. He went there himself and had the floor sanded and the entrance sealed with his own seal. Nine months later the vault had to be used for another burial. A crowd stood around in awe as His Excellency supervised the reopening. It was with the greatest difficulty that the cemented door, with all the seals intact, was finally pushed open. A massive lead coffin was leaning against it upside down and a smaller one had been flung so hard against the wall that its imprint was on the stonework. The family removed their relatives' remains and abandoned the vault to the poltergeist.

The General called his son and eventual heir, born in Barbados, Wellington Henry after his two godfathers, the Dukes of Wellington and Newcastle. During his years of absence his son, Robert, by his first marriage had been brought up by the latter, but died aged eighteen. Back in Cheshire in December, 1820 the christening took place and the Iron Duke planted an oak in the park at Combermere and attended a Civic Dinner in Chester, but as he was the Tory Prime Minister at the time, the influence of the Grosvenor Whigs prevented him from being given the Freedom of the City.

When the Duke recommended his old friend to the East India Company to undertake the capture of Bhurtpore, he was told: 'But we have always understood that your Grace thought Lord Combermere a fool.' 'So he is,' supposedly snapped the Duke, 'a fool and a damned fool; but I tell you he's the man to take Rangoon.' He meant Bhurtpore; now Bharatpur, it is 100 miles south of Delhi. With a population of 100,000, it

Field-Marshal the Viscount Combermere, G.C.B., &c., &c.

was protected by 25,000 defenders, mostly Pathan. Lord Amherst, Governor-General of Bengal, wrote to Combermere on the eve of the assault:

> . . . We have been for the last 2 or 3 days on tiptoe of expectation of decisive news... but nobody regrets or is surprised at the delay which has taken place. I rejoice to find that you are making things sure. I apprehend the more the Engineers do previously the less will be the expenditure [inserted] of lives... Festina lenté...

Thirteen thousand natives were killed and British casualties amounted to 1,050, including 7 officers killed, 41 wounded. One specific task Combermere had given his Sappers was to cut off the water supply. This they did by stopping up a cut, which had been made to fill the fortress ditches with water. For in addition to the hordes of Pathan warriors, Bhurtpore was protected by an ancient Brahmin superstition that the fortress could only be captured when a crocodile drank the moat dry. And so the prediction came true. The Sanskrit for crocodile is 'combeer'.*

He remained in India for five years and was Acting Governor-General for nine months, during which the Great Mogul bestowed on him the titles, 'Champion of the State', 'Sword of the Emperor', and 'Lord of the World' at his court at Delhi.

General Lord Combermere was sixty-five when he married for a third time. His Irish bride, Mary, was thirty-eight and has been described as 'handsome with flashing eyes and very glossy black hair, very rich, very clever and very witty.'

Once at an investiture of the Bath, as Gold Stick, he nearly put the Duke of Wellington's eye out, presenting the heavy sword to Her Majesty and from then on a lighter weapon was used to dub the knights. He was first pall-bearer at the Duke's funeral. His last public duty was to attend the marriage of the Prince of Wales as Gold Stick in Brigade Waiting in his ninetieth year and seventy-third year of his service.

He sat repeatedly for the Royal Academician, Baron Carlo Marochetti (1805-1867), only a

year or two before his death. His equestrian memorial was sculpted at a cost of £5,000, raised by public subscription in the county. Other equestrian statues by this highly fashionable sculptor include those of Richard Cœur de Lion at Westminster, Lord Clive at Shrewsbury, Her Majesty and two of the Duke of Wellington.

His tomb is at Wrenbury Church, and on high ground west of Combermere an imposing obelisk, erected in 1890, stands proudly in his memory.

* * *

IT WAS ON HIS RETURN FROM FRANCE on St. David's Day, 1815 with his regiment of Militia that **Sir Watkin Williams-Wynn (88)** was presented to the Prince Regent. 'Surely you must be the Prince of Wales!', observed Prinny. 'No, your Royal Highness,' said Sir Richard Puleston, who was present, 'Sir Watkin is the Prince *in* Wales!' The 4th and 5th Baronets both declined an Earldom (Merioneth had been mooted) and the 6th Baronet also a peerage. In his younger days his slim figure had been painted by Batoni, whilst on the Grand Tour. But by the time he was next in Paris after Waterloo with the British soldiery enjoying what the city had to offer for the first time since Agincourt, he had put on excessive weight, all of seventeen stone; so much so it was said of him that he demolished more of the flimsy Louis XVI chairs than anyone else.

The story is told of a tourist in the old coaching days who once joined a coach at Drwsynant Station on its way to Bala. Inside he found a stout gentleman enjoying a nap. When he awoke the tourist asked whose was the farm

---

* Combermere Abbey takes its name from Comber Mere. When Lord Combermere was advanced to a viscountcy, he joined a select band of peers to include a foreign achievement in their title, such as HEATHFIELD OF GIBRALTAR, Baron NELSON OF THE NILE And Earl NELSON OF TRAFALGAR, *etc*. Subsequent titles were to include, NAPIER OF MAGDALA, WOLSELEY OF CAIRO, ROBERTS OF KANDAHAR (Baronies), KITCHENER OF KHARTOUM (Barony, Viscountcy and Earldom), and more recently, MONTGOMERY OF ALAMEIN, ALEXANDER OF TUNIS and MOUNTBATTEN OF BURMA. Not all have invariably used the full style, including the Viscounts COMBERMERE OF BHURTPORE and of Combermere in the county of Chester.

The Prince in *Wales.*

> *"I am monarch of all I survey,*
> *My right there is none to dispute."*

A Punch *cartoon of the 6th baronet by Linley Sambourne, 1883.*

they were passing. "Mine," said his companion, nodding off again. Another wakeful moment, and many miles further on another question: "Who owns that mountain?" "I do," dozing off again. And then again: "Do you know who owns that valley?" "I am not sure, but I think it is mine," came the reply. On arrival the man bolted into the hotel. "I have been riding with either a prince or the devil," he exclaimed. "You are right," he was told, " you have been riding with Sir Watkin, the Prince in Wales and a devil-ish good landlord." Much the same tale has been told in the days of the steam train about Sir Watkin's grandson, the 6th baronet, who also rejoiced as 'the Prince in Wales'.

* * *

Thomas Legh of Lyme (107), the first of Colonel Thomas Peter Legh's seven illegitimate children (all with different mothers), was elected the year after Waterloo. He had the unusual distinction of taking part in that battle as a civilian – and not merely as a spectator. He was up at Oxford and already a Member of Parliament, when he heard of Napoléon's escape from Elba. So off he went to Brussels and volunteered to carry despatches to the outposts.

He had already developed a taste for travel and after visiting the Ægean sailed to Alexandria and thence up the Nile to Nubia, being the first European to reach Ibrim, the capital, a feat he accomplished singlehanded by the sword – the English blade he presented to the Sheik.

Among the many treasures he brought back to Cheshire from his various adventures over the years is the stele of Aristophanes. He was responsible for acquiring for the British Museum the frieze from the Temple of Apollo at Barsac, which he helped to excavate.

'T.P.' Legh, Col. Thomas Peter Legh's eldest illegitimate son, whose birth had to be legitimized by Act of Parliament to enable him to inherit Lyme Park on his father's death in 1797. He became renowned as an explorer and archæologist and was painted in Eastern dress by William Bradley (1801-1857). One of his more alarming adventures was in an underground labarynth in the desert at Amabdi, when he fortunately failed to reach the crocodile mummy pits.

VII

'Ould Sir Harry Wur A Spoortsmon'

Sir Peter Warburton, the fifth and last baronet of Arley, was the true founder of the Cheshire Hounds as a subscription pack. He was up at 'The House' at Oxford when his father died and he had just come of age when he was elected to the Club in 1775, the year after. His mother was Lady Betty Stanley, eldest daughter of the 11th Earl of Derby. By 1784 Sir Peter Warburton kept his own pack of fox-hounds at Arley. Since Jack Barry's former fellow sportsmen were not going to transfer their allegiance after his death to his arrogant and unpopular son, Sir Peter was soon hunting the whole Cheshire country. There is scant record of the sport at that time, nor is it known if he hunted hounds himself, but it is probable that he did during the course of his long managership, which lasted from 1784 until 1810.

It is difficult to glean a clear impression of the sporting activity, for no diaries or lists of meets have survived, merely the occasional entry in the accounts for oatmeal, journeys to Sandiway Head, 'Waggin to Kennel – 6d', sawing timber for hunting hatches (£1.4s. in 1789), etc. Sir Peter's 'hunting dress' cost him 9/6d in 1777. Significantly one Gilbert Clough's disbursements that year included:

Stopping fox earth at Hill Cliff [Appleton] . . . 1s 3d

In 1794 Sir Peter was joined by William Egerton of Tatton (40) and Sir Richard Brooke (33), just prior to his death, after which his brother Tom (34) acted for the heir of Norton. Between them they purchased the site of the Delamere Forest Kennels at Sandiway from the Marbury Estate and built kennels there, close by Barry's Wood, incorrectly known sometimes as Kennel Wood. They also built housing for the hunt staff. All this they did entirely at their own expense.

The hounds were moved from Arley to the Forest Kennels in 1798. What was to become the Cheshire Hunt was now on a sound footing; for the time being, while the country was 'Cheshire', the pack was the 'Delamere Forest'. The generosity of the arrangement was eventually confirmed by the heirs of these three gentlemen in a Deed of Conveyance and Declaration dated 1869, making themselves Family Trustees. By this document, *only in the event of the Hounds being finally given up*, the proceeds of a sale of the property would be divided, one third equally between the Family Trustees and two thirds between the Subscribers to Hounds living at that time, who had been entitled to vote in the election of the Elected Trustees at the preceding Annual Meeting.*

A book, compiled by H.R.Corbet (189) and privately printed in 1882, lists the Cheshire Hounds from 1806, when there were 39 couple in kennel, the oldest of them Traveller (1798) by *Cheshire* Sparkler out of Traffic. Soon there was an average of about 60 couple. The oldest actual hound list in the possession of the Club is dated 1807. In these little booklets the pack was officially listed as 'Delamere Forest' and was not headed 'Cheshire Hounds' until 1826. Until about then it was known as 'The Tarporley Hunt', as opposed to the Cheshire Hunt and which was not to be confused with Sir Thomas

---

* By the Deed relating to the Kennel Property, 'Elected Trustees' were also appointed on behalf of the Cheshire Hunt with power for the Subscribers to appoint new ones, the Deed itself being deposited at Arley Hall with the Mortgage Deed. The original Elected Trustees were Earl Grosvenor, Sir Philip de Malpas Grey-Egerton and A. H. Smith-Barry. In 1963 Cheshire Hunt Properties Limited was constituted to regulate the situation with directors having 'A' and 'B' Shares, reflecting the joint ownership. To bring the company further into line with modern conditions, its Articles of Association were re-constituted in 1990.

'A Huntsman letting hounds out of kennel with view of Beeston Castle beyond'. Possibly either Payne or Leech. From an oil painting by John Boultbee, 1803, sold by Sotheby's in 1983.

Stanley's, whose hunt was confined to the Wirral. Except when the hounds were owned privately in the early days by the Orignal Members or by Smith-Barry, the hounds were always the property of the Subscribers and never the Club, so that Tarporley must be the only hunt club never to have owned a pack of hounds other than its Shropshire neighbour.

Philip Payne is the first known professional huntsman in Cheshire, apart from Cooper and the infamous Bratt and was with Sir Peter from 1801 to 1804. He had been with Sir William Lowther, later the 1st Earl of Lonsdale, at the Cottesmore. He left Cheshire to go to the Duke of Beaufort, one of whose best bitches he crossed with *Cheshire* Nectar '04, 'with rare legs and feet, and long jowels, dewlap and a coarse neck, all features of his ancient Talbot origin'.

Payne was followed by Leech, who, from this letter written in 1865 by John Glegg (94) just before he died, clearly showed some exceptional sport:

In the early days of the Nantwich country from 1805 onwards, there was great sport from Ravensmoor to the Hills. Leech was constantly on them, and we hardly ever failed in finding in the Admiral's covert, and going direct as a line over that fine country. I don't ever recollect to have seen finer sport constantly than at that time and over that country. The hounds then hunted the Woore Country, and had a wonderful run from Buerton Gorse, went through Oakley Park (Sir J.Chetwode's [son-in-law of Lord Stamford (25)]), crossed the Drayton Road below the Loggerheads, just skirted the Burnt Woods, left the Bishop's Woods on the left, Hales on the left, right on through the small wood at Knighton, and killed at Batchacre Park [Mr Whitworth's (16)] in Shropshire. 18 miles as the crow flies, in an hour and forty-five minutes. It was an extraordinary fine run, and to within these few years that fox's pad was on the stable door [at Withington].

He goes on to mention another run at much the same time when hounds found a fox at Old Baddiley and ran through Cholmondeley and Dods-Edge, to the Shocklach meadows and over the Dee. 'Reynard got safe into Wales and it was too late at Night to follow him any further.'

Additional evidence of improvements is in the club accounts:

(1810) Joseph Vernon,   Stopping in Tilston etc.   5/-
       James Teasdale,   Stopping in Peckforton   2 gns.

They were also paying rent for coverts, until such time a Member became their benefactor, for instance:

Williams half yrs Rent for Oulton Lowe to Tarporley Hunt 1808 when Mr Egerton gave it to the Hunt – £4 7s.

Tickell yrs. Rent for Huxley (to Lady Day 1809) from which time Mr R. Wilbraham gives it to the Hunt – £12 17s.

The Willingtons and Darlington Gorse were other coverts for which rent was paid. And at this time it seems a fencing organization was in existence:

Samuel Kirkham repairing fences – – – – 14s.
Mr Tickell Hatches and other exps – – £2 15s.

This was in 1812 and the following Spring a further £23 4s was spent on 'Cutting & Fencing Huxley' and

Fencing [at Darlington Gorse] and men to drink there – 10/s

An incident which occurred in 1807 is recounted in *Rural Sports* by the Rev. Wm.Daniel, citing it as proof that the music of hounds has an overwhelming influence on the horse:

As the Liverpool Mail Coach was changing horses at the inn at Monk's Heath, the horses which had performed the stage from Congleton having been just taken off and separated, hearing Sir Peter Warburton's Fox-hounds in full cry, immediately started after, their harness on, and followed the chase until the last. One of them, a blood mare, kept the track with the whipper-in, and gallantly followed him for about two hours over every leap he took, until Reynard [was] run to earth in Mr. Hibbert's plantation. These spirited horses were led back to the inn at Monk's Heath, and performed their stage back to Congleton the same evening.

The Fox and Barrel at Cotebrook became a regular meet, like so many public houses. It is so named on a map dated 1812. Formerly the King's Head, the inn derived its new name traditionally from a hunted fox taking refuge in the cellar. The incident is likely to have been many years before, but there is no record. The Abbey Arms at Oakmere, the Black Dog at Waverton and the Three Greyhounds at Allostock are the three earliest recorded hostelries with a meet, apart from the Blue Cap Inn, then known as Sandiway Head.

At this time Sir Peter was also hunting the Woore Country with the Cheshire Hounds and used to stay a fortnight at a time at The Swan Inn at Woore.

In 1810 Sir Peter, then aged 56, handed over the reins of office. As for Smith-Barry, the Members of the Club commissioned a full-length portrait of their Manager, paying Sir William Beechey, (1753-1839) £249 18. 10d in November, 1811. The Royal Academician protested about the uniform and declared he might as well be asked to paint a parrot.

When Sir Peter died in 1813, the baronetcy became extinct, but he left his estates to a boy of nine, Rowland Eyles Egerton, his great nephew. Young Rowley was the son of the Rev. Rowland Egerton, the seventh son of Philip Egerton of Oulton, whose eldest son, John, succeeded Lord Wilton as 8th Baronet of Oulton the following year. Born at Moston, near Chester, he was given the name Eyles from his paternal grandmother's maiden name. She did not die until 1821, thirty-five years after her husband. Rowland's own mother died in her hundredth year in 1881.

Sir Peter's youngest sister, Emma, had married James Croxton (36) of Norley Bank and their only daughter, also Emma, became the heiress of her father. In 1800, eight years after James Croxton died, his widow married a man called John Hunt, much to the disapproval of her brother. Miss Emma Croxton married the Rev. Rowland Egerton in 1803 and they had five sons and four daughters. Rowley was the eldest and Sir Peter left the Arley estate to him in his will, thus cutting out his sister and any children she may have had by Hunt.

George Wilbraham, apart from his bachelor brother, the last surviving founder member, also died the same year, having 'been afflicted with some smart fit of the Gout and for the last year or two of his life suffered occasionally from Asthma, which was the beginning of the disorder of which he died Decr 3^d.' Roger survived until 1829, aged 86.

On Sir Peter's death, Rowley's father took the additional name of Warburton. Three of the boys were to go into the Army, and one into the Church. The Rev. James was later given the Rectorship of Warburton and was one of the first Cheshire clergymen to revive the surplice. Both he and Rowland came under the spell of the Oxford Movement in the 1830's.

The Rev. Rowland and Emma lived for a very short

Sir Peter Warburton, Bt., Manager, 1784 to 1810, from an oil painting by Sir Wm.Beechey, RA,
who said he might as well have been asked to paint a parrot.

time at Arley, but spent several summers at Rock Point, which they built, and then took their family to Orleans and did not return to England until the end of the next decade. On coming of age young Rowland did not live at Arley, but rented Ruloe. When he married Sir Richard Brooke's eldest daughter in 1831, he and Mary came to Arley and furnished Birchbrook, a farmhouse in the park, while they rebuilt the Hall.

The Warburton family had held the advowson of the parish of Warburton since 1271, or before, and the Rev. George Heron (38), a true hunting parson,* had been Rector since 1776. In 1810, at the age of sixty-one, he is said to have been told by Sir Peter that he could retain the living on condition that he took over the management of the hounds, not that he could really have been deprived of the former.

The truth was that Sir Peter wished to retire from the burden of organization and, though their identity is not known, several of his fellow fox-hunters contributed an annual sum of money to enable the sporting parson to take over – a sum which in future years was to be known as 'the guarantee'.

Of the thirteen Members of the Club to be clerics, only George Heron became Master, but he did not carry the horn. And only Philip Egerton (76) had been the Club's Chaplain during his membership, before becoming Rector of St.Helen's, Tarporley, next to The Swan. The Club and the Hunt invariably had excellent relations with all the Rectors, at one time paying a rent for the use of the Rectory drive as an overflow car park. It was also the custom between 1817 and 1834 to donate £2 to the Tarporley Poor and 5/- to the 'Woman at the Turnpike Gate'. Long before that, over the centuries, numerous entries are recorded in the parish records of payments for 'Foxes Heds', urchins and other creatures supposedly doing depredations to the parishioners' livestock and crops: but none for foxes since 1762, implying the Rectors' faith in the prowess of the fox-hunting fraternity.

As well as Sir Peter's Delamere Forest pack, mention may be made of the Altrincham Hunt which hunted the North-East corner of Cheshire between 1805 and 1815. They were a large type of harrier, belonging to Mr Francis Astley, the Squire of Dukinfield, and hunted both hare and fox. Its record of accounts is in the library at Peover Hall. This was presumably the same hunt with which the Manchester weavers used to go out in the Cheshire hills, 'true to their country past and oblivious of their proletarian future.' Samuel Bamford in his *Passages in the Life of a Radical*, noted that the huntsman at that time, Sam Stott, used to treat them to a warm ale and ginger. Also active were the Chester Harriers, whose

meets were advertised in *The Chester Chronicle* ranging from Dodleston to Stamford Bridge. *See* Addenda.

The Rev. George's career as a master of fox-hounds was seriously curtailed. To his annoyance advancing years and the effects of a bad fall prevented him from properly enjoying the sport his hounds were showing. There was still plenty of Bluecap blood in the kennels, but he it was who, perhaps just a shade ironically, bought the majority of Mr Meynell's hounds and formed a working pack of fox-hounds, for decades considered among the best in England and their strain was much sought after. The same four or five gentleman, who had put up his guarantee, had also formed a fund, with which the hounds were purchased. And, as 'Cecil' of *The Field* once wrote, their progeny may be considered as heirlooms to the county.

After three seasons he got Sir Henry Mainwaring (81) of Peover Superior to act as Field Master, but still remained at the head until 1818 when Mainwaring took over completely. Sir Harry, who married General Cotton's sister the year after he had been created a baronet, had been entered to hare in his youth and was always a 'regular hound man'. He had been given his green collar on attaining his majority in 1801 and twelve years later, he was 'unanimously requested to wear occasionally the medal presented to the late Sir Harry'.†

The Subscribers guaranteed him £2,000 a season. He made a boast that he never exceeded £500 out of his own pocket and had three kennels. The main pack was at the Forest Kennels and he also kept hounds at his home at Peover Hall, where the decorative Carolean stables are still in fine condition. He also had kennels near Wrenbury at Baddiley Hall, an old Mainwaring property, which, since the death of the previous Sir Harry, had been acquired by the guardians of young Charlie Wicksted. The country he covered was even greater than that of his predecessors. Sir Harry was once described as 'an unostentatious country gentleman and affable to all and was quite the right man in the right place for perhaps the most clannish society in the World'.

Said also to be 'one of the best-tempered men in the World', the new Manager was a zealous sportsman and

---

* Dean Samuel Reynolds Hole of Rochester, who died in 1914 at the age of 95, said there had been many changes in the Church since he was a boy. Then there were only three kinds of parson, the Nimrod, the Ramrod and the Fishing Rod Parson.

† Both at the time of the Bicentenary and recently, the author has corresponded with the Mainwaring family in an effort to trace Sir Harry's 'Order of Merit', to which no reference has been discovered since that entry in the Club's record of proceedings. Not even a letter to *Country Life* produced any direct answer.

a great tactician. With three sets of kennels to cover an extended country and in time fifty gorse coverts, the job required a remarkable skill for organization. Sir Harry launched out in style and his staff were superbly mounted on well-made horses, cheaply bought, as described by Henry Hall Dixon ('The Druid') in *Silk and Scarlet*:

His best hunters were Brown Bess, an eighty pound one-eyed mare called Alice Grey, Virgo, Delamere Lass, and a little chesnut from Shropshire, which he bought for 50*l.*, and sold to the Rothschilds. He also had a wonderful long-tailed brown hack, called Sweetbread, from the fact that she was bought from a Knutsford butcher for 18*l.*, which always kept up a perpetual motion canter to covert, whatever the distance might be.

His stud groom was Charles Davis.

* * *

PRESENT AT THE TARPORLEY MEETING in 1818 were Sir John Grey Egerton and the first Earl Grosvenor's grandson, Lord Belgrave, still a bachelor. The latter, aged 23, was a guest on the first two evenings and was elected the next day. The former had been elected thirty years previously and was by then aged 52. History does not relate whether young Richard Grosvenor had his arm in a sling and was obliged to drink his Quæsitum with his left hand, but it seems likely, since an extraordinary event was reported to have taken place in Chester only the previous week-end. The two gentlemen had been 'out.'

The two Chester parliamentary seats had long been a Grosvenor stronghold and General Tom Grosvenor (57) had held one since 1795. John Egerton had been put forward and duly elected for the other in 1807, but in the June election of 1818 he had finished a distant third to the two Grosvenor candidates. There was little doubt that there had been blatant bribery of a section of the electorate at the local election to unseat him, but it was a few months before matters came to a head. In Tarporley Week the following report appeared in a national newspaper:

A SILLY DUEL. An affair of honour was decided on Saturday morning last on the Flats near Chester between Sir John Grey Egerton and Lord Belgrave. On the first fire Sir John's ball struck Lord Belgrave in the pistol arm, but his Lordship was not wounded dangerously, and is doing well. The cause of the quarrel between the two parties originated, we understand, in certain proceedings which took place the day preceding at the annual election for Mayor for the City of Chester. A Mr Barker in proposing a

Mr Evans, who is in the Grosvenor interest, as Mayor, made what were considered rather pointed allusions to some of the Egerton party and insinuated that they had been stimulated by Sir John Egerton himself. The insinuation was required by Sir John to be disavowed by Lord Belgrave, who was present, but this his Lordship refused. The greatest confusion then arose in the assembly and the Recorder was obliged to adjourn the Court to another day. The meeting between Sir John and Lord Belgrave was immediately afterwards arranged.

Their seconds are not named. Under the heading HOAX, *The Chester Chronicle* made out that it was an impudent falsehood, emanating from a letter from a Chester resident to *The Morning Herald* which had published a denial of 'this witling's contemptible report'. The fact that the two principals were present at Tarporley as if nothing had happened means that honour was satisfied, come what may.[‡] But as a postscript Sir John's entry in the Houses of Parliament Trust's *The House of Commons* concludes:

. . . tried again at Chester in 1820, when he was beaten by only 18 votes. Egerton's electioneering took a heavy toll of his financial resources and forced him to sell land and timber.

* * *

AFTER LEECH, a man called William Gaff had been engaged just before Sir Peter's retirement and remained as huntsman for thirteen seasons; Will Griffiths whipped-in. The Druid referred to him as 'Bill Gaff', but he was sometimes also known as Garfit or Garft. He had an exceptionally fine voice with which he controlled the pack, never once needing to use a horn. One day hounds finished so far from home, he took the least-tired horse and travelled back through the night to be on time for a meet on the Forest early next morning. He left his wearied whippers-in to follow with the

---

[‡] The 2nd Earl of Wilton once gave satisfaction to his opponent in the paddock behind Egerton Lodge, before he went out hunting. His antagonist missed with both shots, whereupon Wilton made him bow; 'I cannot waste any more time,' he said, mounted his hack and rode off to the Meet.

Another of their contemporaries to have been "out" once or twice was Lord Alvanley, on one occasion going to Wimbledon to face Morgan O'Connell, whose father had denounced him in the House as 'a bloated buffoon'. Several ineffectual shots were fired, when the seconds intervened. On the way home Alvanley said: 'What a clumsy fellow... to miss such a fat fellow as I am. He ought to practise at a haystack to get his hand in'. On arrival he gave the jarvey a sovereign, who protested it 'was a great deal just to drive your lordship to Wimbledon.' 'No, my good man,' said Alvanley, 'I give it you, not for taking me, but for bringing me back.'

Sir Harry Mainwaring, Bt., Manager, 1818 to 1837, from an engraving by S.W.Reynolds after C.A.Duval.

exhausted pack at their own pace. He put the kennel boy into a red coat and was at the Meet in time. Finding a good strong fox, the second pack proceeded to run him over the Welsh Border. Will probably had the good fortune to obtain fresh horses *en route* and was with his hounds when they killed in the open at Bryn-y-pys, Overton, the home of Francis Price (92) – a good thirty miles distant.

Gaff left in August, 1820 and lived for some years in a cottage by the Blue Cap Inn. Sir Harry engaged John Jones, who had just been with Lord Scarborough in Nottinghamshire.* But he had no real flare for hounds

---

* Not to be confused with David Jones, who had been head groom, trainer and jockey at Eaton to Lord Grosvenor and his brother, General Tom. As a soldier servant going out to the Peninsula, he had cantered his charges between the guns on deck for exercise. Back home General Grosvenor once sent him to Newmarket toll-gate for hog's lard, when his horse's feet became balled with snow before a match. He had originally been apprenticed to the elder Chifney. He ended his days blind in a Chelsea workhouse, whence a little pauper girl led him by the hand round the green lanes of Brompton. He always returned with a bunch of flowers in his buttonhole, 'just to show 'em I've been in the country'. He has been mistaken for John Jones by several historians.

He had been at Waterloo and he died soon after he heard of his son's death in hospital at Scutari. It was thanks to The Druid that his mortal remains were honoured with decent burial.

and was replaced after three seasons by Will Head, promoted after being 1st Whipper-in with Jones. Head hunted hounds from 1823 to 1832, and 'delighted Cheshire men with his capital ways and bearing'. 'Unassuming, civil and indefatigable, his heart and soul was in the pack and he delighted to see everything as it should be' was another correspondent's appraisal. Someone once wrote that his name was good enough to have been invented. He had received his education under Sir Bellingham Graham at the Badsworth and had whipped-in to old Shaw at the Belvoir. On arrival in Cheshire he found the hounds very wild, but very determined. After nine seasons, Head was to go as huntsman to Lord Hastings.

Even more meticulous than George Heron in regard to hound breeding, Sir Harry visited the Belvoir, Meynell, Grove, and Badminton kennels and was to bring in some more hard-driving blood from Squire Osbaldeston's Furrier and Ranter lines at the Quorn and the Pytchley. In turn other Masters were soon keen to use *Cheshire* Nectar, Champion, Chaser and Harlequin. In 1821 he took on a large draft of Mr Mytton's Hounds when the Squire of Halston gave them up on the formation of the Shropshire Hounds. The Druid once called Sir Harry 'the venerable father' of the Cheshire hunting field:

He was hale and vigorous to the very day of his death; and although the glories and hospitalities of Peover had ended, he was as cheerful as ever at 76 and fond of a little quiet cub-hunting when Sir Watkin's or the Cheshire came within reach of his quiet little village home [at Marbury, near Whitchurch] ... His dynasty, which lasted for nineteen seasons, came to a close in 1837 ... Sir Harry was a capital judge of a hound in kennel, or in his work, and made a tour of the best kennels every year. However promising might be the stories he heard of a hound's work, he would never breed from him, unless the kennel used it themselves; and the excuse, 'we have a good deal of the sort', was wholly lost on him. He liked a large hound, and was most particular about legs and feet. Bedford, Gloster, Gulliver, Bangor, Whynot and Marquis, of the direct blood from the first introduction of hounds into Cheshire, were his favourites, and when he gave up the pack, it would have been difficult to find many superior to them in England; while the Hunt had three or four men among its first-flight dozen who would bow to none. The day was never too long for Sir Harry in hunting, and no man ever kept a country better together or hunted it more fairly. It was his boast that during his Mastership he was never five minutes late at covert side, and yet he had sometimes immense distances to reach from Peover. When there, he would never allow more than five minutes' law. He always wore flannel, never drank spirits – no "pick-me-ups" in the morning, no gins and bitters, no

From J.E.Ferneley's painting of Sir Thomas Stanley's Hounds at Hooton.

small brandies or liqueurs, no "Mahogany ones," and other modern forms of jumping powder – never had rheumatic pain or headache in his life, and was always an early riser.

Sir Harry was a fine man across country, provided the day was not too misty. He was shortsighted and used to carry an eyeglass in the handle of his whip. He needed a horse that pulled at him a little, so as to keep him straight. He liked the Vale of Cheshire and the Nantwich country the best, with Saighton Gorse, Ravensmoor Windmill, Warmingham Wood and Bradfield Green his most popular meets.

In his letter, dated 1865, to Sir Harry's son, J.B.Glegg recalled as good a run in Will Head's time as ever he had wished to see:

> We found at the Long Lane, in Holford, hunted slowly thro' Winnington Wood, the Leonards, Holbrook's nursery ground, up to the ice house at Tabley; here he waited, having been bred in the roof of it. From this point we had one of the most continuous fine runs possible, crossed the turnpike road close to the lodge, to Tabley Walk, over Tabley High Fields, left Mere Moss just to his right, thro' Gleave's Hole, over Winterbottom to Waterless Brook, where Brooke's Gorse now stands, over the brook, which was rather a puzzler for the Field, but I saw where there was good going out and jumped in.
>
> When I got to the top of the bank every hound crossed me at an open rail place. With this bother at the brook, of course, the hounds beat the Field, which did not come [up] until they were crossing Budworth Heath. We then went behind Belmont, crossed the Warrington Road, run down to the Horns at Whitley, where we kill'd, after a first rate run.

Forwarding this letter to Rowland Warburton, Sir Harry's son sent further particulars of 'the palmy days… recollected by Glegg':

> when Doddington, Dorfold, Bolesworth Castle and Bryn-y-Pys were the chief hunting houses, when Crewe, Broughton, Tarleton and (rather later on) Tomkinson, Brooke and Glegg were the heroes, when the Cheshire hunted the Woore Country and the Wyches, when they

used to run as described by Glegg from Woore to Bishop's Wood, and from Hampton Heath to the Duke's Woods, near Ellesmere [way into Shropshire].

This was in Heron's time and Sir Harry's eldest son, the second baronet, born in 1804, went on to state that when his father 'took the Country, and the Wyches were given up, gorses were made in the Nantwich Country and in the Chester Vale. The Middlewich Country, then as now, the best in Cheshire, was hunted the second week in every month, and the Withington Country the last week. The Withington Kennels were given up, and kennels built at Peover'.

In fact the Cheshire only hunted the Doddington coverts until 1812/13, when, owing to the Cheshire gentlemen resenting something that occurred concerning General Broughton (69), Sir John had warned them off. For a time the coverts were hunted by Sir Richard Puleston, by Mr Mytton even and afterwards by a Mr Hay until Charlie Wicksted (112) was allowed to draw them regularly when he had the Woore Country. When he gave up,[†] Sir Thomas Boughey took over and then there was an interregnum before the country was hunted by Mr William Davenport (known affectionately as 'Mr Port'). During that time all was forgiven by the General, and Captain White, by then the Cheshire Manager, was allowed back. But after five seasons, as a result of another misunderstanding with the General just before he died, the Cheshires were warned

---

† Chas. Wicksted eventually moved to Shakenhurst in Worcestershire, where, according to 'Borderer', 'he amused himself with about the most perfect little pack of harriers in Europe'. His second son, Charles Wigley Wicksted, took on the Ludlow Hounds in 1866 for twenty years and carried the horn himself.

The Cheshire Hunt, 1828 from the portrait by J.E. Ferneley, Snr., commissioned by Lord Belgrave, son of the 2nd Earl Grosvenor. l. to r. Major W. Tomkinson, Rev. J. Tomkinson (hat raised), Lord Delamere, Lord Belgrave, Sir Harry Mainwaring, Bt., the Hon. Thomas Grosvenor, Will Head, the Hon. Robert Grosvenor, John Baskervyle Glegg, Esq., and Charles Wicksted, Esq. Groom with hacks in foreground, figure on far right not named. The artist has omitted the green collars which were appropriate except for Major Tomkinson, Lord Belgrave's two brothers and Head.

off again and permission was given to the North Staffordshire, the matter not being finally resolved until 1870 by the Fox-hunting Committee of Boodle's, the Cheshire having unsuccessfully claimed that the N.Staffs. and the others had become illegally possessed of a piece of their country.

Another run in Head's day was described by young Sir Harry, who for some reason was not elected to fill his father's place at Tarporley – he was 56 when his father died, aged 78. He wrote:

We met at Hurlestone, and had drawn all the coverts in the country blank, when (it was late in March) we found at 3 p.m., in a small patch of gorse under Calveley Park wall, a very small fox. The hounds got away close to him, and all went together into the barn at the farmhouse; "the fox is kill'd," we all said, but he got away under the door. Head cast the hounds round the barn, away we went! very best pace! over Wettenhall Green, up to the wood, leaving it and Darnhall on the left, and made a sudden turn to the right, over the very best of the Minshull country, to the river at Eardswick Hall, a mile above Minshull Village. We crossed at the wooden bridge, and ran very fast almost to Bradfield Green, bore to the left, and we run into our fox, a small

vixen without cubs, at Warmingham Rectory, 1 hr. almost without a check. James Tomkinson rode The Pea, and he mounted me on Whizgig.

Lord Belgrave (114) commissioned J.E.Ferneley (1783-1860) to paint the Cheshire field in action. He and his brothers, Thomas, who succeeded his maternal grandfather as 2nd Earl of Wilton* in 1814, and Lord Robert Grosvenor (143), are depicted, along with Sir Harry Mainwaring, Lord Delamere, John Glegg and Charlie Wicksted. Two of the Tomkinson brothers are also prominent. In her diary, Belgrave's wife, Elizabeth, wrote:

Tues. Oct. 28, 1828. Mr Tomkinson came in time for breakfast & to sit to Ferneley for the hunting picture.
Fri. Oct. 31. Major Tomkinson came early to straddle over the bar for his picture. He and Sir Richard Brooke both sat & and afterwards went out shooting with B.

* He remained a Meltonian to the end and would appear at the meets when well in his eighties, his seat and hands as impeccable as ever.

In the 1st Duke of Westminster's time coloured engravings were done, but the key for them shows the huntsman as Maiden, instead of Head, and prematurely promotes Major Wm. Tomkinson to Colonel. There also exists a Ferneley of a Meet at Hooton.

From Eaton they hunted with Sir Watkin's Hounds and Mr Leche's at Carden as well as with Sir Harry, in 1823 going out with both Sir Watkin and the Puleston Hounds. It is clear from Lady Elizabeth's journals that almost every year from the mid-1820s for a decade or so the weather for Tarporley Week was very stormy, often with torrential rain.

> 1824. 3 Nov. B dined at Tarporley and returned before 12. Very stormy, rainy, haily night.
> 1825. Stormy rainy, B set out after 3 to dine at Tarporley & returned soon after 12 with Wilton.

But they did not always go in the comfort of a closed carriage.

> Thurs. 6 Nov. 1829. Wilton, Robt. & Lord Forester & Mr Brooke went shooting at 12 . . . B. set out at 4½ for dinner at Tarporley. B. came back abt. 12. He went in the gig & had no rain.
> 1831. G. [his father had just been created Marquess of Westminster] had had a good meeting at Tarporley & had hunted today.

Some years the Grosvenors were away at Shaftesbury during Tarporley Week.

There was invariably a report each year in *Annals of Sporting* about Tarporley Hunt Races and the Cheshire Fox-Hounds. 'I am inclined to think that few packs in the kingdom... kill so many foxes, or kill them so handsomely as the Cheshire,' gushed Mr Fore's correspondent. Or again: '...those who can get well over Cheshire will get well over any other country.' In 1828 he described a ten-mile point of 1 hr. 5 mins. from Mr Armitstead's Moston Gorse, past Coppenhall and Warmingham, across the Weaver, finally killing at Mr Dod's, Minshull Hall. Mr Tomkinson remarked to him that it was the severest run he ever experienced.

Three years earlier the Annals carried a lengthy account of an extraordinary run of nearly 40 miles [an exaggeration perhaps], Sir Harry and Lord Delamere among the few still hobbling along when the pursuit of reynard was abandoned near Knutsford. He had led them from Moulton Woods near the Winsford Salt-works after hounds had met at Shipbrooke Bridge. The fox was badly headed but with determination was soon away for Hartford Bridge before making for Bostock Park and Leftwich. General Heron had been calmly waiting

for hounds to settle and was soon in the van. After a brilliant 45 mins. the fox gained sanctuary at Holford Moss, but then pressed on past Winnington Wood and thence to Wincham with hounds never far behind and Sir Harry, Lord Delamere and 'the Man from the Annals' up close with Will Head.

The baronet had just had a view and thought it would be only a matter of a minute or two. But as hounds were foiled in a thicket, their quarry eluded them and made ground for Marbury, before twisting back on much the same line towards Winnington. Here he veered off and covered a considerable extent of country to reach Tabley, over the park to Mere and crossed by the toll-bar there and on into Tatton Park. Hounds were sticking to him and on reaching the water on the Mobberley side of the park he turned short up to Knutsford-Town-End, surrounded by the hounds. He escaped by jumping a 6 ft. wall and away past the Knutsford race-ground. He was headed back into the park again and was last viewed going towards Rostherne to save his brush. Everyone had had enough.

The correspondent went on to praise to his Editor the courage and dash of the Cheshire pack, 'uncommonly well crossed and therefore excellent.' He noted that to date (March 14th) they had killed thirty-three brace.

One of the greatest chroniclers of the English sporting scene and contributor to the *New Sporting Magazine*[†] was Charles James Apperley, born in Wales in 1778 and educated at Rugby, by which time he had already become accustomed to driving the Chester & Shrewsbury High Flyer. His father had accompanied the 4th Sir Watkin on the Grand Tour and he himself had fought with the 5th Sir Watkin's Ancient British Fencible Cavalry, known as 'Sir Watkin's Lambs' or 'The Bloody Britons', in Ireland. His *nom-de-plume* was 'Nimrod' and during his 'Hunting Tour' in the 1825/26 Season he was joined by his friend Jack Mytton and they stayed at Marbury with Domville Poole (96) for three nights. Sir Harry also joined the party for a couple of nights. Mytton had brought his 'Hit-or-Miss' mare with him from Halston for the honour of Shropshire.

From Shavington next day 'there was some sharp riding with the Cheshire Hounds' and Nimrod even saw a Cheshire fox clear a five-barred gate just before meeting his end after 40 mins. over country which greatly impressed him on this his first visit. Mytton was hard on

---

[†] Mr Pittman, the proprietor, paid Nimrod £1,500 a year for the keep of five hunters and a hack and a £1 a page for his articles. On Pittman's death in 1827, he was refused a rise and went to Calais to escape his creditors. He returned to London in 1843, dying the same year.

John Mytton, the harum-scarum Squire of Halston, Salop.

and the gentleman suggested Charley had spouted himself in a drain which ran across it. Head stationed himself at one end, while the whippers-in and farmhands set to work. They had scarcely started when Head cried out 'Tally Ho! By God I have his brush, sir!' 'He must be a long fox,' replied the gentleman, 'for I have his teeth fastened in my whip at my end!' Before they finished digging they accounted for two-and-a-half brace.

He observed that there was at least a hare to an acre, but, despite this, found the hounds free from riot, though a bitch called Lightsome (encouraged, but not by Head) did run hare for a mile and lost them their fox. 'There is one peculiarity of the Cheshire Hunt' he went on, '– almost all of them ride in leather breeches–the best protection against thorns – but cold when wet, obviated by the use of flannel drawers' and added:

> The Cheshire Farmers are good preservers of foxes and a blank in their gorse coverts is a rarity. "Go it, my tulips!" is the order of the day with the young followers. The second whipper-in is well bred, being by old Ned out of a neighbouring dairymaid . . .

In the greater part of Cheshire the fence is placed on a very narrow bank or cop and strengthened by a very deep ditch. This kind of fence not only requires a horse to be quick and ready with his legs – as he must spring from the cop when the ditch is from him– but also a good horseman to get him over it with safety when he becomes a little distressed.

It seems that 1828 was a really good scenting year. Old Sir Harry wrote to the young bachelor Squire of Arley:

Peover,
Monday.

DEAR ROWLAND,
You have just exactly missed the best run this year. They found at Holford in a gorze lane; he went away for Wincham, crossed the brook and ran down it to Tabley willow-bed where they had a long check, the fox being some way before them; 50 minutes & consequently slow; however he waited there for them, & away he went through the lodges (no doubt the same fox you ran from Arley) crossed Tabley walk, almost to Mere Moss, turned to the left over those fine fields up to Quakers Farm, & crossed [the] Brook just in the same place you did before. He then went through the Fir Plantation where you slanged Shakespeare Phillips, over Aston Park to Picmere Moss, back very best pace to Arley thro' the willow bed & then away for the Pole & Mr Jackson's and they killed him in the middle of one of those large fields behind Chetwodes' house at Whitley, one hour & 20 minutes from Tabley: the best run this season and you have missed it.

As all our people go to Baslow [Derbyshire] next week

his brush, competing with two of the Tomkinson brothers. He astonished even them by leaping over drops of ten feet or more, and never hesitated for a moment at a fence or gate. Nimrod was able to report:

> I consider the condition of the Cheshire Hounds particularly good, second only to the Duke of Beaufort's in that respect. The brightness of their skins and their general healthy look are worthy of all the praise I can bestow; and the more credit is due to Will for this, having three kennels to boil in –some of them none of the best, and consequently a deal of travelling – to say nothing of being often obliged to feed at irregular hours.

He described Head as being very zealous to kill his fox, 'rides well up to his hounds and has a nice cheering halloo, though perhaps a little too free with it at times.'

So far as foxes were concerned Will became choleric if one got the better of him. A Cheshire gentleman liked to reminisce about the one in Delamere Forest which would invariably disappear in a particular spot and Head said he would see all the foxes ever littered in Hades, before he should be served again in such a fashion. Next time it happened they traced the line to a large farmyard for the fancy ball, which I do not fancy, I will pay you a visit on Monday next if you can receive me; I have a mount on Wednesday at Sandle Bridge.

Yours truly,
HARRY MAINWARING

Despite the age gap, they were already firm friends.[*]

The Cheshire ladies were now occasionally taking part, not merely going out as onlookers in gigs or barouches, like the modern car followers, though it was still the exception. Belgrave's talented bride was allowed out by her husband on a day from Eaton. The entry in her diary reads:

> Went to covert, they drew Wharton's Gorse and found – a slow run. I followed B. during the whole of it, Mic [her favourite mare] jumped beautifully and they gave me the brush on the field of battle – a beautiful day.

But more often than not she was an enthusiastic spectator. It was not always exciting. For instance:

> Mrs Tomkinson, Mary [Lady Wilton, wife of her husband's brother and a daughter of Lord Derby] and I went in the barouche to see them find. They tried Saighton, then a little rough, then Handley Gorse without effect. We waited a long time and then came home but they went on to Huxley and had a good run at last.

On another day she

> Set out at 10 to go with B. to Huxley – went the first 4 miles in the gig, then I mounted Deva and B. The Mite, changed horses again at the Canal Bridge, he for Belvoir and I for Althorp, met the hounds exactly at Huxley – a large field out. They found and then ran very fast up to Duddon Heath, made a ring round Stapleford and then to Major Tomkinson's, the Willingtons, where B. changed Belvoir for Amber that the groom was riding. I waited some time on some high ground while they cast about for the fox but

they could not find him. B. and Major Tomkinson came back and Major T. gave us some luncheon at his home. The run a very pretty and very fast one – and we then came home.

On a December day in 1831 following with her sister-in-law, Lady Robert Grosvenor, a bride of less than six months, she had plenty of excitement:

> . . . went out to see the hunting and had a very long ride and prodigious fun at the end, as the fox crossed the river just by Eccleston, and all the field crossed by the ferry boat after a vast deal of clamour, shrieking and vociferation, as at first they loaded the boat so full they were near sinking it. Others would get in and nobody would get out so the boat was run aground. It got off again with a great deal of difficulty and went over with 18 men and 18 horses and then returned for the rest in detachments. B. was one of the first over and was in time to get up with hounds and to have a very good run straight through our Park and on towards Hawarden. One man attempted to swim the river and was as nearly as possible drowned with his horse, but both were fished out separately. Another man, a farmer on a young horse, rode so unmercifully that the poor beast dropped dead in crossing the Park.

But the greatest spectacle of all was on April 7th, 1829 when, as a result of a challenge made at a large dinner party given by Lord Kilmorey, the famous Joint Meet of Sir Harry Mainwaring's Cheshire pack, Sir Edward Smythe's Shropshire Hounds (with Mr Lloyd of Aston, the manager in charge) and Mr Wicksted's from the Woore Country in Staffordshire was held at Shavington Hall. It seems that Sir Richard Puleston, who had just started to hunt that side of the Wynnstay Country again, was not invited to bring any hounds. The rendezvous was at Wrenbury the night before, where a main of cocks was fought. Since the meet was in their country, and Cheshire being the senior pack, Will Head was appointed huntsman for the day with Will Staples of the Shropshire and 'old Wells'[†] of the Wicksted kennel at Betley in attendance. Each had brought six couple of their fastest hounds for a trial of 'speed, nose and bottom'.

---

[*] Just before leaving for the Continent in November, 1836, Rowland wrote to Sir Harry, sending his subscription to the Cheshire Hounds:

<table>
<tr><td>My springs are braced to carry</td><td>On wheels tho' slowly whirling</td></tr>
<tr><td>My chaise is packed for three</td><td>Am I borne to Germany</td></tr>
<tr><td>But ere we start Sir Harry</td><td>But Dresden, Emms or Berlin</td></tr>
<tr><td>Here's a hundred pounds for thee!</td><td>What are they to Tarporley?</td></tr>
<tr><td></td><td></td></tr>
<tr><td>Here's a smile for every hundred</td><td>Wer't the last drop I could carry,</td></tr>
<tr><td>Here's a sigh for twenty-five</td><td>Ere laid upon my back</td></tr>
<tr><td>And tho' the church be plundered</td><td>One bumper still, Sir Harry</td></tr>
<tr><td>Oh! let the kennel thrive.</td><td>Would I pledge thee to the pack.</td></tr>
</table>

On the Rhine as on the Weaver
Whether hock or port my wine
Prosperity to Peover
And a health to thee and thine.

[†] A huntsman of the old school who adopted the maxim: 'Master finds horse, and I find neck.', he had spent thirty-six years, twenty-four of them as huntsman, with the Oakley before coming to Mr. Wicksted and was with him all eleven years he had the Woore Country.

Will Wells fractured his ribs twice and broke his collar bone seven times. Warburton said of him: 'He doated upon every hound in his pack with as much fondness as a father feels for his children.' He died in 1847 in the service of Sir Thomas Boughey, Bt. of Betley Court, who was then hunting the Woore country.

As to Will Staples, it used to be said of him that he could hunt a Shropshire fox without hounds.

'Now for the honour of Shropshire,' Henry Alken's impression of the Shavington Day.

For 'The Shavington Day' the Field was reported to be more than a thousand horsemen, seven hundred of them in scarlet, not to mention the occupants of carriages without number, there to see the fun. It must have been a brilliant scene, with 'the gentlest blood of three counties, never a man missing, boiling for the chase, every one of them determined to be in at the kill'. Their host was 'that hearty old buck', Lord Kilmorey, by then, at eighty-three, the oldest (though not the senior) General in the British Army. Known as 'the Little General' and a veteran of the American War of Independence and chiefly responsible for quelling the Irish rebellion of '98, he was the 10th Viscount's younger son and had been raised in rank to Earl seven years before. The meet was at eleven, but the united packs were not thrown into the Big Wood in Shavington Park until twelve.

According to the new Hunting Correspondent of *The New Sporting Magazine* a fox broke almost at once and off they went 'at an astonishing terrible pace to Styche, then to Cloverley Gorse, where they came to a check; crossed New Street lane, leaving Ightfield to the left, and lost near Burleydam. This burst lasted about 25 mins.' But his geography is at fault and differs from Nimrod's

account in his biography of Mytton. This states that the fox 'having stood before them for 30 mins. at a very severe pace, was lost near the village of Cloverley.

The rivalry was immense as 'Mad Jack' Mytton,[*] over from Halston, soon took the lead with his mare, Hit-or-Miss, which he had ordered his groom 'to have right fit to go'. He had spent the night at Whitchurch, but not before he had driven over to Wrenbury for the cockfighting and not until after, on his return at no early hour to the Whitchurch hostelry, he had roused a commercial traveller from his bed to help him consume the contents of several more bottles before finally retiring.

However Mytton was to lose the lead when, not far from Cloverley Gorse, he charged a ha-ha with a stiff post and rail on the rising side, 'a regular Squire-Trap', shouting and halloaing 'Out of the way you fellows, here goes for the honour of Shropshire!' He came a terrible purler and was badly hurt by a man jumping on top of him, about two dozen being down at the same fence. The horse crushed him and his hat was not worth picking up. Mytton remounted, bleeding and bare-headed, but did not sufficiently recover to take the lead again. It was in fact the end of his hunting career. He was never out with hounds again.

The pack had been pressed by the large field, 'so that they were drove from the scent; afterwards they hunted a cold scent back to the coverts at Shavington', according to Staple's diary which continues:

> But the gentlemen belonging to the Cheshire were not satisfied, they thought the hunted fox was gone for Combermere. Head made a wide cast on that line, but to no effect. We then went to Combermere, found by the pool and killed him; it was thought he was the fox from Shavington, as he had a good chance of getting away [but was] supposed to have been beat. As soon as the hounds had eat him there was a halloa the other side of the pool by the house. We got away with our fox, and had a very pretty run of twenty-five minutes; when the hounds were running into their fox it was

---

[*] The astonishing exploits of this seven-bottles-of-port-a-day man are too numerous to mention. Nimrod's *The Life of John Mytton, Esq.* is prescribed reading. Within five years of the Shavington Day he had died, aged 37, in the King's Bench prison. He had been removed there after insulting the French when imprisoned for debt in Calais, where, perhaps justifiably, he had taken a surfeit of brandy. But as a footnote, his son, also Jack, was appointed agent to the almost equally eccentric 2nd Earl of Kilmorey at Shavington, not far from where the Squire trap may be seen to this day.

'A squire trap, by Jove!'.

perceived that it was a vixen [heavy in cub]; we stopped the hounds. We drew one covert after, but we did not find. We went to Wrenbury, and spent a pleasant night with our fellow sportsmen, and each party steered for their respective homes the next morning.

Head was awarded the brush, never having left the hounds and being first up, but he forfeited his wager of two sovereigns to Staples, as the Shropshire hounds were the first to taste blood.

Glegg in his old age considered these the palmy days, but Sir Harry was to have another eight seasons before he handed over the reins. In 1832 he engaged Joe Maiden, who was to carry the horn for twelve seasons, serving in all six masterships. Maiden has got to have the glory of being the greatest of all the Cheshire huntsmen.

When Joe was their huntsman, and Tom their first whip,
Who then could the chosen of Cheshire outstrip?

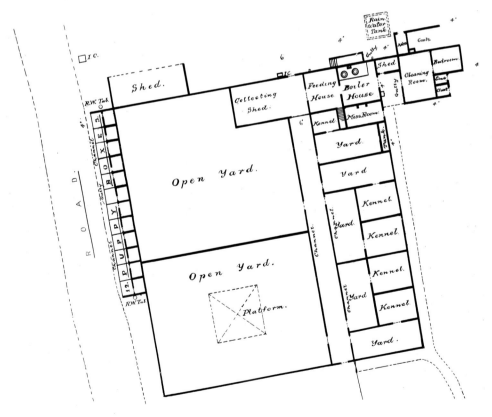

It was not long before the Subscribers decided to build new kennels with 'Lodging Rooms and Courts' as prescribed by Peter Beckford.

VIII

The Maiden Who Rode Like A Man

IN SEPTEMBER, 1829 THE HUNTSMAN TO A MR SHAW, who had a pack of hounds at Cliff, near Tamworth and hunted a portion of what became the Atherstone and North Warwickshire countries, took a day off to go to Lichfield Races. Before leaving, dressed in his best suit, he went down to kennels to check that the boy was preparing the pudding correctly and that the flesh was being properly cooked. As he climbed the few steps to reach inside the boiling copper, he slipped and his left leg got badly scalded. He managed to scramble out in double quick time and still had every intention of going on to the races after a change of clothes. But the application of some homely remedy drove him distracted with pain. Very soon his wife arrived to take charge and when his left stocking was removed, half his calf came away with it, exposing the bone. Thanks to the professional skill of two Birmingham surgeons and a good constitution, he pulled through.

The injury would have kept many a man out of the saddle for life, but not Joe Maiden – 'The Maiden who rides like a man,' as the Bard of Cheshire sport was to dub him. Three seasons later Mr Shaw's huntsman was engaged by Sir Harry Mainwaring and came to Cheshire. He lay sleepless in agony many a night. As his knee tendons contracted, he had to add little strips of leather to the sole of his boot and afterwards found he always had to ride one stirrup shorter than the other. And yet he hunted sometimes six days a week, and seldom less than four. Twice he broke that leg and at one time or another had nine or ten pieces of bone removed from it. In spite of his affliction, he once stayed with his hounds all day in a record point of 25 miles, getting through three horses and a hack and ending with a kill by moonlight, but this was not in Sir Harry's day.

It was not until 1855, long after he had left the Cheshire, that he had his leg amputated below the knee;

not even when he had broken his ankle in Cheshire. He caught a cold one dewy morning while exercising the young hounds from the North Staffordshire kennels and mortification set in the limb. He furnished himself with two new legs, one for walking and one for riding. Sometime later he went to London and bought a dual purpose leg and the same day tested it properly when Mr Edmund Tattersall lent him a hunter from the Knightsbridge ring for a trial spin. He went round Earl's Court and Brompton before having two strong gallops down Rotten Row. Out hunting his leg had a device by which, though fitted to the saddle, it would come free in the event of a fall.

Joseph Maiden was born in 1795 at Linley, near Much Wenlock in Salop. His grandfather hunted Mr George Forester's Hounds and had the celebrated Tom Moody as his whipper-in. As a boy of 14, Joe had whipped-in to a pack of harriers near Bridgnorth, before gaining experience as second whipper-in to Lord Middleton in Warwickshire and afterwards Mr Hornyold in Worcestershire under Stephen Goodall and was for a time with Sir Bellingham Graham at the Albrighton, hunting the Enville country, he and Will Staples whipping-in together and forming a lifelong friendship. One of Sir Bellingham's favourite hounds was Vulcan, which he had brought with him from the Quorn. Few hounds could be so savage as Vulcan when put out. He was once running hare and as Joe Maiden, then 2nd Whipper-in, caught him a heavy broadsider for it, he flew at him and bit him right through his boot and stirrup leather. Then for a time he acted as huntsman to Sir Clifford Constable's Stag-hounds at Tixall before going to Mr.Shaw.

Four seasons later he delivered the hounds to Leicestershire after they had been sold to Sir Harry Goodricke and hunted them there for a week or two in

April. The Duke of Rutland spotted him and wanted to employ him as a successor to his huntsman, Goosey. But Maiden declined and it was at Croxton Races that he was engaged by Sir Harry Mainwaring to go to Cheshire. He rode his little 14 hands Welsh cob back to Cliff and two days later rode it all the way to Sir Harry's kennels at Wrenbury, meeting the Master at 8.30 in the morning at Wells the huntsman's house. He started back next day on the same hack, but met Mr Meynell's hounds at Cannock Chase, hunted with them all day, dined at Lichfield and got home to Cliff that night.

So Maiden came to Sandiway and Rowland Warburton was to say of him that he had never seen his equal as a huntsman and that 'he was, moreover, as pleasant a companion to ride home with after a run as any gentleman could desire'.

Popular though he became with the members of the Cheshire Field, he was not unknown to have a sharp word with his subordinates. A nervous young 2nd whipper-in once complained to him out hunting:

"This 'ere 'orse 'll break me neck."
"'oo ever 'eard of a second whipper-in havin' a neck," came the reply. "You go and turn them 'ounds."

Maiden acquired a high reputation for his judgement of hounds and went great distances to give it. To get his own into condition he gave them a deal of steady work as early as 3 a.m. of a Summer morning. He especially liked getting puppies out to walk with butchers for it meant they got plenty of flesh, an insufficiency of which he considered made hounds prone to the yellows.

Joe's principal lieutenant was Thomas Rance who had joined Sir Harry's staff in 1830 and was to remain at the kennels thirty seasons. Born with the Century, or so he claimed, he served eight Masterships and six huntsmen of the Cheshire pack. He had lost his eye in a shooting accident when he was twelve, and as the Laureate put it:

Tom Rance has got a single oie, wurth many another's two,
He held his cap abuv his yedd to shew he had a view;
Tom's voice was loik th' owd raven's when he skroik'd
out "Tally Ho!"
For when the fox had seen Tom's feace, he thoght it toim to go.

It was Lord Delamere (55) who found Tom and brought him to Cheshire, persuading Lord Rothschild to release him from his duties as his 'pad' groom. Before that Rance had been second horseman to a horsecoper in the Puckeridge country and his very first job had been to whip-in *two harriers* at Yarmouth. One of a family of ten, he himself left ten children behind him, several of whose descendants are still living in the county.

Joseph Maiden, Huntsman, from a portrait presented to the Tarporley Hunt Club in 1982 by Mrs Edgar Hyde of Heswall from her late husband's collection of water-colours. Used as the frontispiece of the 1st Edition of Hunting Songs, *1834.*

Mr Warburton wrote of him:

In the station of life in which he was placed, no one ever did his duty better. I have seen him ride the most unmanageable horses with rare nerve and temper, still keeping his one eye open to detect, and his handy lash ready to reach, any riotous hound. Many a time in the course of a run have I been beholden to him for his active assistance under a difficulty, and there are others, I know, who would, if now alive, gratefully acknowledge his services in the field. If after charging a fence you found yourself on the other side, planted in a pit (a mischance by no means unfrequent in Cheshire), Tom Rance was always to hand to pull your horse out, or if discomforted by the loss of a stirrup leather, Tom was promptly at your side to touch his cap and proffer you his spare or even one of his own.

The Druid recalled:

There was no finer characteristic of the man than his genial tone and polite manner of steering his hounds at the end of his drooping whiplash through a crowd of horsemen in a narrow lane. "Jest stand a' one side, gemmen, if you please; beg yer pardon; a little mossel, to let the 'ounds paass; thank ye sir; now gemmen, be so good; thank ye, sir"; and the feat was accomplished.

Tom may have treated his 'gemmen' with impeccable civility, but to transgressing hounds he was not so polite and 'rigidly included any previous conviction for riot in his sentence'. As a turner of hounds he only had one equal – Tom Moody also thirty years a whipper-in in Shropshire. Rance used to declare that he would rather break stones on the road than be a huntsman. As a horseman he was a wonderful performer and it was said 'the way he would screw his horses through the fences was quite marvellous'.

Tom Rance, 1st Whipper In, 1830-1862.

"We had four horses apiece when I came," he told The Druid on a visit to the Forest Kennels in 1860. "We had no second horse that time of day. We lost the Wrenbury and the Wicksted country; that's all done away with. We used to go to Wrenbury, and stop the week."

He had been engaged under Will Head, whom he considered 'a good little huntsman, a determined little fellow.' Of Maiden he said: '...few could go with him; resolute determined chap was Maiden across country; so persevering; never liked to lose a fox.'

Tom was fortunately an incorrigible gossip. His comments about some of 'his gemmen' who hunted with Sir Harry were set down for posterity by The Druid, the greatest gossip of all:

Talk about riding. I saw Mr Wilbraham Tollemache taking the River Weaver brimming full, close by Nantwich; he had a black, snaffle-bridle mare; she slipped back again, and he

jerked himself clean over her head on to the bank and pulled her out. "That's well done, Tollemache!" said Lord Delamere, and in the next field but one they ran to ground. Mr Tollemache stripped, and met us going on for Aston Gorse in an old farmer's clothes, and rode the run; he rode little thoroughbred things; he was a neat horseman, and had a deal of nerve.

Sir Richard Brooke was a very good one, as long as he could last; he'd go as long as he could; never nursed his horses.

Mr Glegg would take a line to himself, wide, always with the hounds, not as some of these young 'uns do: if they see the hounds a little at fault they go by them and make the fences crash again.

I've seen Mr Warburton go along pretty well; he had his glasses on; he's obliged to take them off and polish 'em a bit, when we get to slow hunting.

Colonel Cholmondeley [(177), a heavy weight who was in the field towards the end of Tom's long career] bruises along; I've heard him make these wire fences rattle a bit.

And of his first Cheshire employer:

Sir Harry. he was a good 'un, coming up with his glass in his whip-handle; his two greys and his bay horse, Briton, I liked best to see him on; he would come on his hack, be it where it would, and his hunters met him from the kennels.

Tom Trafford (89) and Walmesley (128) were in their day also numbered with the hard riding brigade and others of note were 'the pride of all Cheshire, the bold Delamere' and the Tomkinson brothers, 'The brothers three from Dorfold sprung, whom none of us could beat'. They could more than hold their own with anyone. During a run in Leicestershire the riding of two of these brothers provoked the exclamation from Goosey, the Belvoir huntsman: 'How those Cheshire Cheese do trundle long!' Dick Christian, the famous rough-rider, remarked: 'I've seen those two Mr Tompkinsons [*sic*], from Cheshire, ride wonderful here; there was no beating them. It put Goosey right out to see them going as they did.'

Were my life to depend on a wager
I know not which brother I'd back;
The Vicar, the Squire or the Major,
The purple, the pink or the black.

The Tomkinson family had its origins at Knightley in Staffordshire, before one of them came to Bostock in the XVI Century. A grandson, James, bought Dorfold in 1754 from the Wilbraham family, whose affairs he had been managing for many years as their lawyer. As their solicitor he was able to acquire it on the most favourable

Wilbraham Tollemache of Dorfold Hall, a later sketch. In his time he was a brilliant and daring rider in both Cheshire and Leicestershire.

terms. The Dorfold property was inherited by his second son, Henry Tomkinson, born in 1741. He in turn had four sons. Edward, the eldest, died young at Cheltenham, the Rev. James was 'the Black Squire' of Dorfold, the Rev. Henry (the purple), not a Member of Tarporley, was 'the Vicar' of Acton (and Rector of Davenham) and had also been called to the bar. (At this time parsons compromised by wearing purple, rather than scarlet.) 'The Major' was William, the youngest of the four, whose coat may well have been made by Mr Pink, the tailor, had such a tradesman ever existed. He built Willington Hall on land he bought from Lord Alvanley in 1827. Edward and James had been painted by Gainsborough when they were boys.

On the death of his father, Henry, James kept open house at Dorfold in the 'Nantwich Week', as it was called, in each month of the season and, according to his nephew, Jimmie, was 'a wonderfully good man to hounds.' In 1821 William, 'the Major', retired on half-pay from his regiment, the 16th Light Dragoons, shortly after it became a Lancer Regiment when in Dublin, and just before it was ordered to India. He was a very abstemious man, by the drinking habits of those days, and declined membership of the Club until 1829. Soon after his marriage to the beautiful Miss Tarleton in 1836, he decided to give up hunting in the interests of economy and the welfare of his family, and resigned from the Club the year before he was due to become President. 'Yet there was no stinginess or "pinching" in the household for either parlour or servants' hall,' wrote his son, James. '. . . He was delightfully genial, kind and indulgent, too much so indeed to us, who were allowed to run wild and be mischievous as boys.'

After James's day, the family pack of harriers at Dorfold was taken over by Wilbraham Tollemache, who

had married his heiress. Of the latter's daughters, it was Alice, who died a spinster in 1914, that was never very far behind hounds.

Captain Wilbraham Spencer Tollemache, late of the Rifle Brigade and Coldstream Guards, was the second son of Admiral Tollemache (121) and married Anne, the elder daughter of the Rev. James Tomkinson (98), the Squire of Dorfold, in 1844. Her brother in the Blues had died, aged 26, in 1839. Tollemache was descended from the Wilbrahams of Woodhey, a junior branch of which family had built Dorfold in the early XVI Century. He was also a denizen of Leicestershire and it was strange he was never given his green collar, but he was a frequent guest. R.E.E.W. called this inveterate fox-hunter 'Dorfold's invincible squire and summed up his qualities with these lines:

> *Few sportsmen so gallant, if any*
> *Did Woore ever send to the chase.*
> *Each dingle for him has a cranny,*
> *Each river a fordable place,*
> *He knows the best line for each covert,*
> *He knows where to stand for a start,*
> *And long may he live to ride over*
> *The country he loves in his heart.*

His betrothal to Anne Tomkinson was violently opposed by her father and the source of much unhappiness in the Squire's declining years. James Tomkinson once rode over to Willington and took Jimmie, William's baby son, on his knee and then paced up and down the room in distress, muttering: 'That man shall never have my property.' They waited three years after his death before marrying, but it was quite some years before the wound healed and Dorfold made the first call in the late forties. Their son, Henry, was given his Green Collar, at the age of 23. By then Wilbraham Tollemache was 62. He died in 1890, nineteen years after Anne.

As to the quality of the hounds in Sir Harry's time, this was The Druid's analysis in *Silk and Scarlet*:

'Those sons of Old Bedford, so prized by George Heron', were generally black-tan themselves, for they went straight back to the red-tan of the Southern hound. Bedford himself was descended from Meynell's Splendour and Ramper; and Gulliver and Grecian were both badger pies, also of Bedford lineage. Gulliver's stock was generally dark tan, very high-couraged, stout as steel, had long, sensible-looking heads, and large crowns. Victor was another hound of the Bedford line, and quite a fugleman for Joe. He would go a few yards into a covert, and decide at once if there was a fox; and if there was not, he would sit and triumphantly await the confirmation of his opinion at the huntsman's side.

Captain the Hon. Thomas Cholmondeley of Abbot's Moss Hall.

He described *Cheshire* Hannibal '38 as the idol of Maiden's heart. He had immense bone and depth of chest, and measured a good nine inches round the arm.

The Druid mentions two of the bitches in particular. One was Bravery, 'quite a little handmaid to a huntsman'. She would hunt her fox like a beagle, and when they were breaking him up, she would give just one snack and then sit up and be the first to move off again. She was given to Maiden and was no doubt his best hound. The other was Bonny Bell (bred from one of Mr. Wicksted's good, short-legged hounds), one of the fastest bitches that ever a huntsman rode to. She got completely spoilt in a run from Mobberley Wood, for she came out with the fox, ran close to his brush for four miles and killed him in Tatton Park after 8 mins. – shades of Bluecap. Rowland Warburton refers to 'this race over Tatton Park' and its palings as 'an extraordinary performance'.

Such coursing as this ruined her and Maiden found she could never be got to stoop to the line again, and was always dancing about to get a view. She was drafted to the Wynnstay her third season, but according to a letter received by Lord Delamere, Sir Watkin did not mind her antics. 'Send us all the Bonny Bells you've got. We've such racing; away goes the fox, and then goes Bonny Bell,' he wrote.

The great Manager was all the while intent on providing good hunters for himself and his staff. To quote G. T. Burrows (*The Cheshire Hunt*):

The well-bred horses of the Cheshire Hunt in Sir Harry's day attracted universal attention and comments. Such bloodlike sires as Speculator, Sir Oliver and Cheshire Cheese gave the hunters of the county brevet rank. Speculator got them small, but particularly stouthearted; Sir Oliver got a lot of leggy browns, all good gallopers; but Cheshire Cheese's offspring were thick and stout and true as steel. Astbury, the gallant heat-winning racehorse, had very few good mares sent him, but he got some wonderfully game hunter stock, although they were a bit leggy. He, however, was the sire of Joseph Maiden's celebrated mount, Pevorette, a fine 16 hands bay with a short back, always 'blowing his nose', as high-couraged horses do.

This horse was bred by Mr James Pevor, steward to Mr Wilbraham at Delamere Forest, and was secured by Maiden for the hunt at £35. His price had been £80, but as he was always clumsy on the road, he fell and broke his knees when being taken to Nantwich Fair. A few days later, after his spill, he heard hounds cub-hunting in the Forest, and leaping out of his paddock, ran loose by Joe's side all day. That was a Saturday. He was caught somewhere near to Wettenhall Wood on the Monday, and became Maiden's mount. He never gave Joe a fall the eight seasons he rode him. His stamina was endless, and he always appeared able to make a second effort, a necessity for a horse who had to carry a huntsman across the Vale of Chester, where in those days, the doubles nearly all measured *nine yards*.

Lord Delamere thought so highly of Pevorette and Maiden that he offered to run them for 1,000 guineas a side against any man and horse in England, four miles over Cheshire. Still there were some few men in the Hunt, who would live with them, and Maiden was fairly collared one day by Mr Wilbraham Tollemache (who loved a rushing and pulling horse), just at the finish of a fine run from Combermere Abbey, near unto Whitchurch.

'He had slipped all the rest of the field' says The Druid, who tells the tale in his own droll way in *The Post and Paddock*, 'and finding that the chesnut mare was catching him for speed, he dashed up a green lane and jumped five gates in succession. "Drat you, Joe, you thought to shake me off, did you?" roared Mr Tollemache, as they landed almost together in a large grass field, in the middle of which hounds had run their fox to earth. "Well, Sir, I did; but I'll have no more gates', was the rejoinder as they trotted up to hounds, and decided that it was to be a drawn match.'

Pevorette changed hands with successive masters at £350, £370 and £500, to be sold next to Sir Richard Sutton for 200 gns. He carried the Quorn master for two seasons and was ultimately fed to his hounds.

'The bold Delamere'. Thomas Cholmondeley, 1st Baron Delamere with Vale Royal in the background, from an oil painting by Henry Calvert.

But there were plenty of other good horses to stretch Pevorette's neck. Sir Richard Brooke (91) rode a rat-tailed Irish mare, brought over from Mullingar Fair by Tom Hewitt of Liverpool. Lord Delamere had a favourite mare called Wynnstay and Mr. Leycester of Toft (152) rode another son of Astbury. Rowland Warburton was happiest with small thoroughbreds. Two others of the first flight at this time were Captain France (153), never better than on his steeplechasing mare, Brenda, and Mr Glegg, described as a patient but sure horseman, who steered a 16 hands horse called Kangaroo.

Maiden's other great performer was Corporal, a little 15.1 grey by Irish Starch, and reputed to be faster than Pevorette. He pulled and rushed, but was never tired, even over sticky plough country. He had a constant habit of swishing his tail and Joe had to hold it with his whip handle, while he listened to hounds in covert. Sir Harry had bought him cheaply with broken knees thrown in and he was sold for £500 when the Mastership changed.

Whipcord was another faithful steed, which carried Joe throughout a five hour run to Carden. He lost hounds for 2 hrs. and picked them up running hard by moonlight. It was all he could do to stop them and he and his whippers-in got back to Sandiway at 1 a.m., after getting some lapping for his hounds at Mr Leche's kennels.

It was on a little brown horse called Wonder that in the Vale of Chester he once cleared $33\frac{1}{2}$ feet over some rails.[*]

* * *

M AIDEN HAD BEEN AT SANDIWAY a season when it was decided to build the new Kennels. They were completed in May, 1834 and a stone plaque was mounted on the wall above the feedhouse:

[*] The second best jump on record was in 1870 at Marbury, when Sir Claude Champion de Crespigny covered over 31 feet after clearing a five feet high fence.

On the turnpike road by Sandiway. Maiden on Corporal with the hounds and Rance, his whipper-in. From an oil painting by Henry Calvert, presented to the Club by Mrs Lee Townshend.

These Kennels were built
by the Subscribers
to the Cheshire Hounds
A.D.1834.
Sir H.M.Mainwaring, Manager
Joseph Maiden, Huntsman
John Douglas, Architect.

At this time there were no more than seventeen Subscribers to Hounds. The architect, who was also the builder, was the father of John Douglas (1830-1911), the architect of many buildings in Chester and on the Eaton Estate. The family lived at Park Cottage, Sandiway, later known as Littlefold. Rowland Egerton-Warburton wrote some verses in honour of the New Kennels.

Great names in the Abbey are graven in stone,
Our kennel records them in good flesh and bone;
A Bedford, a Gloster to life we restore,
And Nelson with Victory couple once more.

Besides five hound yards and lodges, the buildings included a draw yard, feedhouse, hospital and boilerhouse, *etc*. One of the two walled exercise yards served as a splendid site for the Puppy Show in the years to come. The new range of loose boxes, saddle room, bothy and mess room were not built until Mr Hubert Wilson's day in 1901.

It was the following season that no less a sportsman than Robert Smith Surtees, the creator of Mr John Jorrocks, took an opportunity to see Maiden at work with his hounds. 'The fixture, Crewood Hall, being so near the Forest, is not in great favour, and we had not above half a dozen pinks in the field,' he wrote in a chapter of his *Thoughts on Hunting*, called 'A Chivey through Cheshire'. He arrived in Chester, hired himself a horse the next day and set off for Delamere Forest, spending that night at the Bear's Paw at Alvanley. The day after, just as he arrived at the meet:

Maiden, attended by two whippers-in and about thirty couple of hounds, came in the contrary direction, and presently a few horsemen joined the party. Maiden is a civil fellow, and notwithstanding my unsportsmanlike appearance, entered fully into the spirit of the thing, and told me all about "the horses and hounds, and the system of the kennel", as the old song says, just the same as though I had been in scarlet and mounted on a 300 guinea nag. Indeed he is a very respectable servant, both in manner and appearance, and seems uncommonly keen and fond of the thing. His hounds were looking extremely well, and as he expected to get into the Forest, he had brought out a large pack, among which were eight or nine couple of young ones. The two whips are also active varmint-looking fellows, and the black-muzzled one [Rance] has an uncommonly knowing screech and holloa of his own, more like the celebrated Dick Barton's [*sic**] than any other man's I know. They were all... on useful-looking horses in capital condition; and altogether the turnout, without the slightest approach of anything flash, was extremely sporting and business-like...

After drawing the banks by the riverside blank, and also several woods in the neighbourhood, Maiden, in the absence of Sir Harry Mainwaring, gave the word for the Forest, and on we jogged, when arriving at the foot of a hill, or rather a young mountain, we serpentined our ways to the top, and the hounds commenced drawing the wild and rugged sides, which appeared much better calculated for the sheltering of a fox than for the working of hounds . . .

After moving on, they did find, 'but after running for an hour they disturbed so many foxes and there were so many holloas in different quarters, that I got tired of riding.' It was three o'clock when Surtees found his way out of the Forest and quietly jogged his chesnut mare back to Chester and the Albion Hotel. Two days later – he had taken a stroll to Eaton on his day of rest –he had a day on her with Mr Leche's Hounds from Carden Hall. Will Head by then had left, but old Joe Sinclair, former huntsman to the old squire and 'a sharp knowing-looking chap (on a thoroughbred chesnut mare) called Gaff' brought the hounds up to the house. 'Mr Leche made his appearance, attired in scarlet and a cap, mounted on a fine old white horse, carrying the horn on the saddle, and took command of the pack.'

---

* Clearly a misprint for Dick Burton, who started his career with Mr Assheton-Smith at the Quorn and Burton before whipping-in to Mr Osbaldeston and serving another two seasons as Lord Southampton's huntsman at the Quorn, finally returning to Mr Assheton-Smith at Tedworth.

It seems to have been a scrappy day with a break for lunch and good strong ale sent out for those who did not go off to a hostelry to eat. Surtees chose to look into the Kennel, until the others were again mounted for the chase, as he put it, 'determined to ride and resolved to be first . . . for, after all is said and done, one spur in the head is worth two in the heel'.

> Another fox was found and lost, and just as it began to get dark, Mr Leche trotted off to a gorse about three miles out of my line, and I trotted off to the Albion at Chester.

A pity the scent was so poor, but no one knew better than he the transient nature of the sport.

A bound volume of 'photostat positives' of the original lists of Places of Meeting of the Cheshire Hounds from 1836 to 1875, together with the collection of Hound Lists, was presented to the Tarporley Hunt Club in 1939 by Frances, Lady Daresbury. The originals had formerly been at Peover. That for Sir Harry's last season is written retrospectively in his hand with this note appended with his signature:

> These may be [used] for a general outline for fixtures, but all places must depend on the number of foxes, as to the times for hunting, the country throughout is now so well stocked with old foxes there will be no difficulty.

It transpired that there had been an importation of foxes from Ireland.

Sir Harry's long and distinguished reign came to an end three seasons later, followed in quick succession by Geoffrey Shakerley (138) of Whatcroft Hall for two seasons, James Smith-Barry (147) with Lieut.-Colonel John Dixon (150) of Astle Hall as Joint Manager for one season before a season in sole charge and then a more senior Member of the Club, Charles Ford (124) of Abbeyfield, Sandbach, just for the season 1841/42.

W.C.A.Blew, editor of F.P.Delmé Radcliffe's *The Noble Science*, stated that when Sir Harry resigned, 'there was not in the whole of England a better pack than the Cheshire'. At the Club's Meeting in November Sir Henry Mainwaring resigned and it was 'unanimously resolved that [he] be made an Honorary Member', proposed by Lord Delamere and seconded by Wilbraham Egerton, the two senior Members – the first since Wilbraham Bootle in 1782. Evidently, perhaps, this precluded his thirty-three-year-old eldest son from filling his place.

IX

Mr Shakerley Takes Over

GEOFFREY SHAKERLEY, a scion of a wealthy Cheshire family whose rent roll had risen tenfold to £30,000 in George III's reign, continued with the good sport. A copy of the proceedings of a Meeting of Subscribers, which form the basis for the terms of his agreement, is the oldest surviving document in the Cheshire Hunt Archive, except for a handwritten list of the seventeen Subscribers to the Cheshire Hounds for the 1835/36 season. The main stipulation of Shakerley's agreement was that he should receive an annual guarantee of £2,000, just as Mainwaring had done throughout his Mastership. He was also to be paid £1,000 'out of the Auxiliary Fund' then set up, for the purchase of horses. This was to be repaid upon his resignation of the management. The Chairman at the time was Lord Delamere, and the Joint Treasurers, Cornwall Legh and R.E.E.Warburton, then living at Norley Bank.

Shakerley's hunting diary, now in the library at Bolesworth, gives a complete record of his two seasons, 1837/38 & 1838/39.

Corporal and Pevorette were still in the stable, the latter having 21 days in the second season – more than any other of the thirty horses used by the Master and his hunt servants. Another sturdy performer was Sir Patrick,

High Billinge from Luddington Hill.

who carried Maiden 'brilliantly' from Wrenbury on November 16th until he failed him by 'the inclosures at the town of Whitchurch' and Maiden 'stopped to bleed him'. (Sir Patrick was taken out again at The Three Greyhounds on the 29th.) Shakerley's diary continues:

> I went on with the hounds until Maiden overtook us at Terrick Hall on Long Tom Hewitt and we went on by Hinton [and] Agden to the top of the Wyches and Wigland and when within a short distance of Malpas he turned and we killed him in the open near Bradley Hall. Mr.Wilmot lives there; he comes from Manchester. The second burst from Magor's Gorse to the end was 2 hrs. 5 mins. and by far the most brilliant day's sport I ever saw.

From the Duddon Heath meet in Tarporley Week 'a gallant vixen' from Waverton Gorse had taken them to the High Billinge in 53 mins., – 'the first 25 mins. splendid'. Four days later there was a significant entry from a meet at Shipbrooke when hounds 'found one of the Irish foxes and unluckily killed him'.*

On December 2nd from a meet at Four Lane Ends, near Tarporley, a fox found behind Tilstone Lodge ran at a good pace across Eaton Bank and on past the High Billinge† into Primrose Hill. Shakerley thought they changed foxes by the Ranger's House, but it was uncertain and away they went to Delamere House. Thence right-handed back to the Kennels at Sandiway at a 'capital pace', they 'skirted Petty Pool, turned over the forest, leaving the Chaise Gorse on the right. Nearly to Over and then Little Budworth on our right to Oulton Park wall and into the stable. It lasted 2 hrs. 35 mins., a capital run'.

This season was spoilt by one foggy day and thirty hunting days lost by frost, but the meet at Moreton Hall on April 19th was the seventeenth. It is interesting that on three occasions during his two seasons hounds met at Duddon Heath on consecutive days, Tarporley Week

Geoffrey Shakerley, Esq. when older.

Did not find in Peckforton Wood, but unluckily killed a bitch fox at the Cholmondeley Gorse and did not find again there or Norbury Heath. At the Cornet's Gorse we went away well [with a good fox], but, on Maiden coming up, he was sulky, cast the hounds wrong, did not give them time, but lifted them and lost us a good run as he went by Woodhey. I have no doubt [he] went on to the hills as he came back by Chester's Wood... he cast to the Cornet's Gorse where he killed a fox with three legs Tollemache had turned out. Here ended the day.

There was another instance late in the season when the Huntsman failed to obey the Manager's orders regarding the draw.

Another remarkable run in Geoffrey Shakerley's day was on December 23rd, 1837 from a meet at Barr Bridge [*sic*]:

No fox at Dorfold or Hurlestone. Two in Radnor ran a short circuit and [we] gave it up leaving the fox in Radnor. Then drew Wardle blank but found at Tilstone and he immediately ran into the dairy through the window. We bagged him, the largest fox I ever saw and turned him beside Wardle Gorse. He went first for Radnor but turned back straight to the canal, left Calveley to the left, through Hill's Gorse bending to the right, crossed Cholmondeston lane by

excluded, usually going over to Waverton and Saighton the first day. On one of these days they ran to Oulton where another fox took them again to the High Billinge 'and we lost him by Jones the trainer's stables after a very long day'.

It seems that at times Maiden behaved no less like a prima donna than a great many of the top members of his profession. In March, 1839 Shakerley records a day from Bunbury Heath:

---

* In the earlier part of the last century foreign foxes were frequently to be found in Leadenhall Market, many from Holland, France and Germany as well as other parts of the United Kingdom. A dealer with an unlimited commission once despatched 75 brace at 15/- a head, 12/6d a small one, all on the same day. The practice was not uncommon in the previous century and Sardinian foxes, even, were once turned down in the Belvoir. It was a miracle that rabies did not become endemic. Captain White (159) himself sent a former Master of the Quorn some very good foxes from Derbyshire, which he kept in training, when cubs, in a barn at Park Hall, with the aid of a terrier and a four-in-hand whip.

† A prominent and beloved feature of the Mid-Cheshire landscape. The tops of the trees are said to be the last bit of England that can be seen when sailing from Liverpool for America. High Billinge was bought by Sebastian de Ferranti (343) ostensibly to preserve the clump of beech trees, but in reality as a gift for his future second wife, so that he would be reminded of her every time he saw it out hunting.

Cornwall Legh, the Cheshire Hunt's first Joint Treasurer.

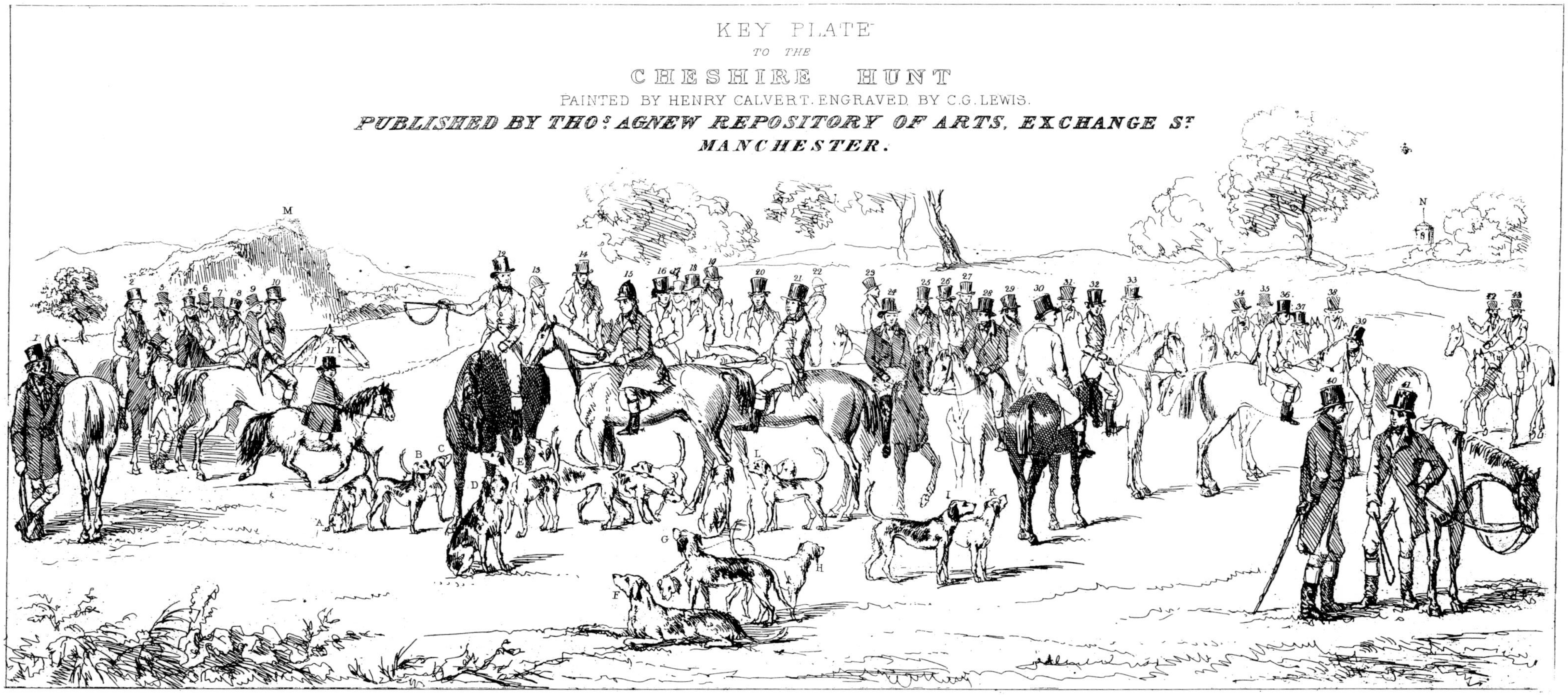

KEY PLATE
TO THE
CHESHIRE HUNT

PAINTED BY HENRY CALVERT. ENGRAVED BY C.G. LEWIS.

PUBLISHED BY THOS AGNEW REPOSITORY OF ARTS, EXCHANGE ST.
MANCHESTER.

KEY PLATE TO THE CHESHIRE HUNT PAINTED BY HENRY CALVERT. ENGRAVED BY C.G. LEWIS. 1839

1. James Royd, Esq.
2. Charles J. Ford, Esq.
3. J.S. Entwisle, Esq.
4. Peter Langford Brooke, Esq.
5. George Cornwall Legh, Esq.
6. Thomas W. Tatton, Esq.
7. R.G. Leycester, Esq.

8. R.E.E. Warburton, Esq.
9. Henry Brooke, Esq.
10. Philip de Malpas Egerton, Esq.
11. Master Egerton
12. Geoffrey Shakerley, Esq.
13. T. Rance, 1st Whipper In
14. W. Worthington, Esq.

15. Mr Maiden, the Huntsman
16. Lt.-Col. W. Tomkinson
17. Lord Robert Grosvenor, MP
18. Lord de Tabley
19. J.H. Harper, Esq.
20. Earl Grosvenor
21. Wilbraham Egerton, Esq.

22. The 2nd Whipper In
23. Wilbraham Tollemache, Esq.
24. John Tollemache, Esq.
25. Humphrey de Trafford, Esq.
26. Col. Thomas Brooke
27. Richard Brooke, Esq.
28. W. Tatton Egerton, Esq., MP

29. J.I. Blackburne, Esq., Snr., MP
30. Lord Delamere
31. Charles Wicksted, Esq.
32. Sir Richard Brooke, Bart.
33. James France France, Esq.
34. J.W. Hammond, Esq.
35. J. Wilson Patten, Esq., MP

36. J.H. Smith-Barry, Esq.
37. Thomas Hibbert, Esq.
38. Rev. James Tomkinson
39. John Dixon, Esq.
40. Chas. Cholmondeley, Esq.
41. John Glegg, Esq.
42. George Clarke, Esq.
43. Thomas Knight, Esq.

A Lounger C Bounty E Waverley G Envoy I General   M BEESTON CASTLE
B Bridesmaid D Bravery F Regent H Clasher K Guider L Hannibal N TARPORLEY CHURCH

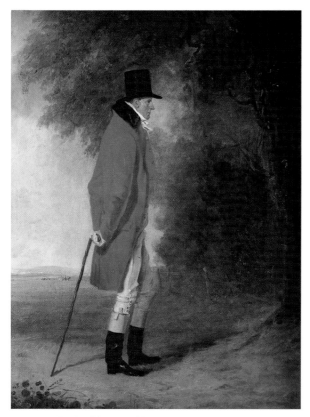

Portrait sketch of Charles Cholmondeley.

Portrait sketch of John Dixon.

Magor's farm house, then crossed the canal opposite the Gorse, which he went into. It was 28 mins. to this place and after stopping five minutes in cover he re-crossed the canal and we killed on the other side... altogether 37 mins.

It became known as the Calveley Run and Rowland Egerton-Warburton duly set it to verse with 'Cheshire Chivalry'. 'Here's a health to the pretty milk maid!' *(See Book Two, Part One.)*

When Shakerley resigned the managership of the hounds the young Manchester artist Henry Calvert (1816-1861) was commissioned to make a portrait of the Cheshire Hunt. It was done at the instigation of Wilbraham Egerton (84), who paid £450 for the huge canvas, 8 ft. x 11 ft., now in the entrance hall at Tatton. By the time the portrait was finished, he was Father of the Tarporley Hunt Club, since Lord Delamere (55) resigned that year, 1839, and his brother, the Secretary, Charles Chol-

Portrait sketch of William Egerton.

mondeley (66), at the following Meeting.

Calvert made portrait sketches, of which the Club possesses three:

Charles Cholmondeley, presented in 1848 by Henry Brooke.

Lieut.-Colonel John Dixon, who succeeded Shakerley as Master that year, presented by his grandson, Sir John Dixon, who also gave the Club the Colonel's silver hunting horn. (This particular painting is only attributed to the artist.)

Tom Rance, the 1st Whipper-in, acquired from his great great granddaughter and presented by J.G. Fergusson in his Presidential Year, 1984.

A fourth one, of William Tatton Egerton, is at Tatton, now belonging to the National Trust.

The artist actually started on his canvas at The Swan Hotel, as described by both Lord and Lady Grosvenor in their diaries, first the former, who had stayed at The Willingtons the night before:

W. 6. N. I rode at $\frac{1}{2}$ past 10 to Tarporley being the business morning of the hunt and at 1 o/c when the others went to the Races sat to Mr Calvert for my likeness in a picture of the Cheshire Hunt till 3 o/c at 4 rode home to Eaton.

T. 7. N. Lady Gros. & I rode by Duddon to Tarporley where I sat for $\frac{1}{2}$ an hour for the picture. Saw some of the gentlemen after hunting. We returned to Eaton by 4 o/c. A rainy day.

Lady Elizabeth goes into more detail:

Thurs. Nov. 7. Very rainy day. It prevented our setting out early for Duddon Heath as we intended but it grew better so I set forth with G. at $11\frac{1}{2}$, I on the little mare... Found the hounds gone from Stapleford so we decided on riding on to Tarporley to see a large picture painting there by Calvert of the Cheshire Hunt. Met Col. & Mrs Tom[k] on horseback as we passed the Willingtons. They rode on with us to Tarporley and we staid [sic] some time at the Inn seeing the picture & a good many people. G. sat for a short time & much enjoyed his portrait. We came home by the towing path of the canal. Rain almost all the way.

Though the canvas was painted in Tarporley Week, the background for 'the Meet' was chosen to suit the artist's licence and shows Beeston Castle and Tarporley Church in the far distance from a place which would be hard to find but probably intended for Four-Lane-Ends. When it was decided to have engravings made, the artist also painted a small water-colour copy to assist the engraver, Chas. G. Lewis (1808-1880), many of whose works were after Landseer. As well as Knight's *The Waterloo Banquet* he also engraved *The Melton Breakfast* by Sir Francis Grant. The water-colour was discovered in Fore's, Piccadilly, in 1913 by Mr W.H.Cooke, who described himself as a 'Lancashire Lad' on presenting it to the Club in memory of forty years' hunting in Cheshire. The original handwritten key was with it.

The prints were published by Agnew's of Manchester in 1842, which gave rise to the picture often being wrongly dated. The canvas itself is signed and dated 1839. The comprehensive key includes the names of the hounds.

Portrait sketch of Tom Rance, 1st Whipper In.

The retiring Manager is mounted on his bay gelding, Tatton, who had carried him thirty-four times during his two seasons in office. His whip is raised, showing Maiden (on Pevorette) the direction he wishes him to move off, and Wilbraham Egerton himself takes pride of place in the centre. Twenty-five Members of the Club are depicted as well as two future Members, including young Philip Egerton (191) of Oulton on his pony next to his father, the President, and six other former Members, Peter Langford-Brooke (104), who drowned whilst skating that Winter, James France (109), Thomas Hibbert (115), the High Sheriff, the Rev. James Tomkinson ('the Squire'), who died two years later and Wilson Patten (134). John Tollemache (124) was still in the mounted field, despite having resigned from the Club five years previously. He is depicted wearing a black cutaway with eight brass buttons.

Calvert was clearly at pains not to give a green collar to anyone not entitled to it, but gives one to the two new Members for 1839, Richard Brooke and Leycester-Roxby. By then, however, Shakerley was no longer Manager, so it seems that the commission dated from the end of the previous season. The artist gets over the fact that Lord Delamere resigned that year by painting him

Calvert's sketch in oils of the hounds in kennel.

in a mackintosh,* though his green collar is just visible. The engraver, however. has put him in a Cheshire coat. Lord Delamere chose to wear his Cheshire coat for a separate equestrian portrait by Calvert with Vale Royal in the background. In fact his Lordship met with 'a severe accident', which had prevented his attendance at Tarporley in 1838.

A portrait sketch of all the hounds was also skilfully made in one of the lodges at the Kennels and cleverly repeated in the main composition. It came into the possession of the new Joint Manager, James Smith-Barry. Calvert has put in about thirteen couple of hounds with Bravery '31, 'the handmaid', in her special pose and Hannibal '38, 'the idol', right by Mr Maiden's side. Five more couple are named portraits.

The only possible criticism about this complicated and masterfully executed scene is the horse with spidery legs galloping off in the distance.

The Club possesses another Calvert, originally the property of the 1st Lord Delamere. It is of Maiden on Corporal, with his hounds and Rance, on the turnpike road near the Forest Kennels. Lord Delamere's grand-daughter, the daughter of Colonel Tom Chol-mondeley (177) and wife of Lee Townshend (246), presented it, together with Maiden's copper hunting horn (engraved J. MAIDEN), on her husband's death in 1914. It has had a somewhat chequered career in recent times, having had to be heavily restored after the fire in 1988. It had been in need of restoration before, having been hung for many years over the fireplace, and it is noted in the Minute Book in 1977 that when Colonel Tony Dewhurst was taking it to the restorer, his labrador, Ginger, caused further damage by jumping through the canvas *en route*.

Tony Dewhurst with Ginger.

* * *

BUT FOR THE BAR SINISTER, the eldest son of James Hugh Smith-Barry (24) would have succeeded to the Earldom. He applied for a renewal and was advised to accept a baronetcy and hope for the peerage later on, but declined.

John Smith-Barry (117), born in 1793, was wild and gay, very hospitable and very amusing. Very good looking, fair with blue eyes and curly hair, he had been sent down from Brasenose after accepting a bet that he would kiss the first woman he met round the next corner in the High who unfortunately proved to be the wife of the President of St. John's. In Cork he was known as 'John the Magnificent'.

He had spent most of his time at Fota, which he built onto extensively, but had come over to Marbury each Autumn, usually to attend Doncaster Races. The family colours were 'Blue, yellow stripes'. He had been elected to Tarporley in 1819 and doubtless enjoyed its traditions hugely, a great quantity of wine being consumed in his day at Foaty where there was a decanter holding nine bottles. He married as his second wife the daughter of General Peter Heron (83) of Moore Hall, but died just over a year later on his 44th birthday.

Although John was seldom in Cheshire, that is not to say he neglected the Hunt's interests. It was a tradition for hounds to be walked by Marbury tenants as part of their agreements, but at one time, to Sir Harry's dismay the young entry was returned in a neglected state, virtually ruined. The Manager mentioned this to Mr Barry's steward and word came back from Ireland for the chief offenders to be given notices to quit their farms. These were not executed, but from then on the hounds were sent in from their walks in the best possible condition.

Elected to Tarporley the year before his father died, James Smith-Barry (147) never cared for Fota Island, disliking his father's habit of keeping open house. He was too good-natured to put a stop to all the hangers-on, but transferred his affections to Marbury, from where he greatly enjoyed the hunting and very soon contracted as Manager. Tall and slight, James Barry was said to have 'a beautiful countenance' and was greatly loved by all who knew him. Once, on returning from one of his many visits abroad with his family, he was met by his mounted tenantry at Hartford Station and escorted home.

Encouraged by his close friend, Rowland Warburton, he employed Salvin, who had designed the new Arley and later Peckforton Castle, and had the house rebuilt.

---

* Charles Macintosh took out his patent for making waterproof fabrics in 1823 and the manufacture of the garments named after him started in Manchester in 1824. The advent of railways caused a recession in the trade as travellers were no longer so exposed to the elements as they had been on the stage coaches.

In 1842 John Glegg wrote to the Secretary, complaining about having to attend subscribers' meetings at The Kennels. It had been snowing hard. '...I turned back being certain of a wetting & very uncertain if there would have been a meeting after the bore of bumping 36 miles in a mackintosh.'

James Smith-Barry (203) going home on his mare Smoke to the comforts of Marbury.

He had it modelled on a French château, despite protestations from John Tollemache (124), who did his best to dissuade him. There was a disastrous fire and the house was never properly finished. For most of the time the family lived in the old West wing and, when there, often had theatricals. His son stated that the works on the house and the landscaping of the gardens cost £80-100,000.

When his turn came to be President of the T.H.C in 1845, Rowland Egerton Warburton, with whom he, and his widow afterwards, corresponded in verse, wrote a special Hunting Song for him which he used to sing himself. It was always greeted with enthusiasm the rest of his days. Like his father he was a member of the Royal Yacht Squadron and the nine verses were very much of a nautical flavour, the last line of the chorus being: 'What tars are half so jolly as the tars of Tarporley?' He was only 40 when he died in 1856. He lost the use of his legs and spent his last two years in a wheelchair at Marbury.

Arthur Hugh Smith-Barry, his elder son, was elected in 1868 aged 25, the same year he married. In later life he recalled his first theatrical appearance at Marbury in 1847 and that in the audience was Lord Douglas, grandson of the 9th Duke of Hamilton (21), who had taken Arley that Winter and had with him Prince Louis Bonaparte, later Emperor Napoléon III, Lady Douglas's second cousin. Arthur started hunting regularly when Jack White was Manager, but a serious accident made him give it up eventually. His favourite hunter was Paintbox. He and his brother James, and his brother-in-law, Lord Willoughby de Broke, were joined by Piers Egerton Warburton, Lord Cole and Lords Alexander and Berkeley Paget in setting a good fashion in both dress and horseflesh. It would be hard to better them and they were a splendid example of the maxim that a hunting field will never have much vogue which does not dress

properly as well as go. They did both.

Arthur was President of the Club in 1881. After being M.P. for Cork and later South Huntingdonshire, he was created Lord Barrymore, but died in 1925 without an heir, as his son, James Hugh, had died aged seven months. His younger brother, also James Hugh, elected the year after him, was President in 1885 and resigned in 1896. One season, despite his delicate health, he hunted every day hounds met and rode a grey mare called Smoke. He had married the 3rd Earl of Enniskillen's daughter, Charlotte Jane, in 1874. Robert, their son, a Colonel in the Royal Flying Corps was elected on the death of his uncle, but resigned in 1932 on selling up Marbury, which he had inherited from Lord Barrymore. 'It is a sad affair altogether, selling Marbury, but there it is,' he wrote to Brian Grey-Egerton, the Secretary, confirming his resignation since he no longer had property or resided in the county. He died without children in 1948.

Mrs Smith-Barry, the Master's widow, stayed on at Marbury for sixteen years. On one occasion Lord Cole (218), her younger son's brother-in-law, – and no mean judge in such matters – on seeing her alighting from a carriage, reckoned she had the most beautiful foot in London, where she was a frequent visitor. She then married Lord de Tabley (145) and was a most charming and accomplished hostess at Tabley. Widowed a second time, she died, aged 93, twenty-eight years later.

* * *

FOR THE 1839/40 SEASON Messrs. Dixon and Barry took control of the kennel with a similar guarantee, paid half-yearly. Mr Dixon, however, withdrew 'his personal subscription', which was £50. At this period the Subscribers took out a mortgage of £1,400 for the property, which included the Kennels Farm. The

Lord Cole and Lord 'Dandy' Paget.

Masters ran this in those days for an annual rent of £30. Sir Richard Brooke was then Chairman of the Hunt.

Maiden and Rance were kept on. According to the latter, when he was interviewed by The Druid, 'Mr Smith-Barry was a fancy rider, he rode to his horse; he was rather on the larking system, jump off and make horses come over gates and stiles after him.' He was only twenty-three and his Joint was seventeen years his senior. His father, John, had died two years previously. Tom did not mention the other Joint Master, to whom the writer of Egerton Warburton's obituary refers as 'Long John Dixon', one of the tallest men who ever rode to hounds.

Under 'The Chase', *The Chester Chronicle* advertised the meets. Hounds met at half-past ten o'clock. Appointments were also published for other hunts, including those in Shropshire, as far afield as the Wheatland, the Ludlow, 'the United Pack' and the Montgomeryshire. Since 1834/35 Mr Leche (139) had been hunting the Wynnstay country on the Cheshire side, just as his father had done, known by some as the Carden Park Hunt.* He had Will Head as his huntsman and Garfit's son as a 2nd Whipper-in. In 1841 Mr James Attey of Lightwood Hall took over the Carden pack for two seasons, whilst Sir Watkin was serving with the Life Guards. The hounds had been bought for 500 gns. by Mr Price of Bryn-y-Pys (92) on behalf of the young Sir Watkin, who came of age that year. The Opening Meet was at Carden as usual. (Francis Price, incidentally, had an amazing 18th-century collection of stuffed birds.)

Barry and Dixon produced ninety-four days sport with a whole month lost through frost. Both resigned at the end of the season. Long John incurred a fine when he married Sophie Tatton in May and Barry was persuaded to stay on a second season in sole charge. Two months were lost owing to frost, but they had some sport in March and April.

There was then, as always, much deliberation as to who should succeed. James France (106) offered to undertake the management in conjunction with Glegg and Shakerley, but Shakerley would not consent to be a member of such a committee. Mr Tomkinson also put his name forward but subsequently withdrew and it was left to the Chairman to approach Sir John Gerard (168). Flattered though he was, Sir John declined. In the meantime Mr Tomkinson had had an interview with Mr Charles Ford who had been a Member of the Tarporley Hunt Club since 1824 and was one of the most active members of the Gorse Covert Committee. The

Subscribers came to an arrangement for him to take on the hounds for the season 1841/42. Ford had an extra £200 for his guarantee, but declined the offer of a £1,000 bond to buy the horses, hoping to make a profit for himself when he relinquished the mastership.

Geoffrey Shakerley was a long serving member of the Committee, serving twenty-nine years and occasionally deputizing as Secretary from his home at Whatcroft.

In his letter to young Sir Harry in 1865, John Glegg reminisces about some more good runs in Maiden's time, but he does not give the dates. 'R. Warburton will also recollect,' he wrote, 'a good run from The Breeches', when one of the twin brothers, Peel, lost his horse directly after leaving the covert; Rowland's advice was

> *May the next time that white horse you bestraddle,*
> *See less of the Breeches and more of the Saddle.*

On another occasion:

> . . . we had a splendid run from Radnor Gorse, when Mr Knight was knocked off his horse at the end of the first field, and was ridden over by the crowd. The fox set his head for Woodhey, left the farmhouse on the left, then up to Chertsey's Wood, crossed the wide green lane at the top, at which point, the pace had thinned the Field very much. Sir Richard Brooke, on a big grey, fell, leaping into the road, and never got beyond. Maiden here stopped the Corporal, and the running was left to Clive of Stych, Coke Gooch and myself; but on going up the field, leaving Aldersey's rough on the left, the Colonel's grey put his foot in a grip, and went heels over head. The field was then quite beat off. We went on to Bunbury, then to the right by Wardle Hall, and killed after an unusually fine run at Reaseheath. Wilbraham Tollemache stopped The Rebel in the first ten minutes.
>
> Don't think this a very boasting detail of sport. The only thing I can do now is to go a little over the mahogany; but a long life of uninterrupted good health enabled me to be constantly out, and to carry my recollections of good runs as far back as most. But I must stop, for every good run were I to record, Sir, I ne'er should have done.

In his letter to R. Warburton, just after he had heard from John Glegg, Mainwaring mentions a meet at Ashley Hall on a cold day in March:

> . . . high N.E. wind, snow fell in the morning. Put hounds in Cooper's Plantation, a small place, and immediately chopp'd a fine dog-fox. Another was halloo'd away at the same time, and away we went at a capital pace almost up to Castle Mill, turn'd to the right, and then over a fine wild country, the best of Mobberley, towards Wilmslow, over Lindon Common, Warford, Little Warford, and up to where Chelford Station now is, left Astle on right, and away straight to Alderley Park, where I saw hounds run into him

---

* A notice in *Adams's Weekly Courant* dated 1786 advertised 'BARNHILL HUNT – Mr Leech's Fox-Dogs will attend. Dinner on the table 2 o'clock.' Barnhill is near Broxton.

Geoffrey Shakerley, Long John Dixon and Humphrey de Trafford.
'Farmer Dobbin', having mentioned 'Zur Umferry', described them thus:
I seed Squoir Geffrey Shakerley, the best 'un o' the breed,
His smiling feace tould plainly how the sport wi' him agreed;
Eh! what a mon be Dixon John of Astle Haw, Esquoir,
You wuldna foind, and measure him, his marrow in the shoir.

under the library window dead beat; about 1 hr., a very good run, and many horses beat.

And a run in March, 1842 when 'Jack' Ford was Manager:

. . . from the "Cobbler" up to the road at Whitley Reed, turn'd over Crowley Moss, straight to Arley, over the bridge at Arley Green to the Gore, on to Tabley through the old foxcovert at Lower Peover where Maiden came up and they killed him at Goostrey; only about eight men with the Hounds, the Field having been thrown out at Whitley Reed.

'These indeed are runs to be remembered,' continued Sir Harry's son, 'without wishing to set myself up as a praiser of past times I ask do we ever hear of such now-a-day? I ask in sorrow, not reproachfully; hounds, horses, and huntsmen are probably as good, if not better than they formerly were, but every succeeding year seems to add some new impediment to Fox-hunting. High farming is rapidly converting our fields into gardens. "Look before you leap," is a precaution more requisite than ever since the introduction of wire fencing.

'The increase of population and of dwellings, prevents a fox, headed at every corner, from making straight to his point, and last but not least in the list of grievances is the scarcity of wild foxes.'

He does not mention the railways. Yet more wire, the internal combustion engine, the motorways, the hunt saboteurs *et al* - even a golf course at 'Wharton' - were still to come. How delighted all those old boys would have been, had they known that a century-and-a-half and more later all those problems, and more, had been contended with and that hunting was still flourishing.

Nor could Warburton have foreseen such hazards of progress that The Chase would manage to survive when in 1840 he wrote the lines:

Still distant the day, yet in ages to come,
When the gorse is uprooted, the fox-hound is dumb.

But in the Spring of 1842 an even greater scourge was to strike the Cheshire kennel that next season – an outbreak of the dreaded 'madness', as the inevitably fatal disease of rabies was known. One of its symptoms was a vicious excitability. The entire pack had to be destroyed, including little Bravery, by then a matronly brood bitch, and Envoy and Hannibal, too.

Jack Ford's only season had been curtailed for a week in January by an outbreak of distemper, but it was over by the time the 'madness' struck. Luckily the puppies were still out at walk, so that 25 couple were entered the next season, retaining the original blood, including that of the mighty Bluecap.

It must have been a dreadful time for Maiden and Rance. Night after night for several weeks the Kennel staff kept watch with long leather gauntlets and badger tongs. The moment a hound showed signs of madness, it was dragged out to its fate. All those good true Cheshire quality hounds, full of bone and substance were put down – some 60 couple in all. They even tried chaining individuals in separate kennels, but to no avail.

As Rance said: '. . . the best we had we lost in the madness. . . We had the sweetest pack before the malady.'

By the end of May they had been replaced by 50 couple bought from the Exors. of Mr Codrington, of the New Forest. Maiden put in for his expenses to Mr Legh:

	£	s	d
May 28 1842 My expenses to London and into Hampshire twice and back with 32 couple of hounds to Hartford Station	26	9	6
Paid the Huntsman his expenses back into Hampshire	3	0	0
Gave him as a present	5	0	0
Tattersalls bill for lodging hounds 1 night	2	8	0
Paid for new couples for hounds	3	2	6
Board wages for myself and the Huntsman to the late Mr Codrington	2	5	0
	42	5	0
July 29 Received the above	£42	5	0

JOSEPH MAIDEN

The hounds themselves cost £400. By June 15th Maiden, on drawing up an inventory of the subscribers' property, saddlery *etc.*, for the new Manager, reported to Mr Legh that 'the hounds are all going on very well.' So evidently the crisis was over.

Drafts of hounds later came from Mr Wm. Drake (Bicester) and the Duke of Beaufort and some of Mr Wyndham's hounds (the South Wilts) were also bought by Ford, for which he was reimbursed with an additional subscription. Writing to Cornwall Legh the following year he gives an account of his expenditure and asked for more money:

> . . . I have been told I made a good thing of the Hounds. I have enclosed their cost the year I had them which was £2,524 18s. 9d. and as this excess of expenditure over income was incurred in a great measure by circumstances over which I had no control and which could not enter into my calculations before taking the Hounds, viz the malady which raged in the Kennel & the large Drafts ordered in by the Subscribers to recruit our losses, I doubt not the subscribers will think it only fair that they should bear the loss of £324 rather than a poor devil like myself, particularly when it is considered I lost more than £300 by the horses.

Ford also wrote to Sir Richard Brooke asking for his authorization as Chairman and added a little bit of gossip:

> We found a fox yesterday at Betley and had a decent 30 mins. towards the Gladding & lost unaccountably, all at <u>once</u> as if the object of our pursuit had been taken into the clouds. So ended this day's fun, except some cold pig and ale at little Rasbottoms on our return home. Sir Chas. was out and as usual [had] much to say, which <u>much</u> he says <u>well</u> He told us Lord Crewe [(146)] fell asleep in his opera box and that the Queen sent to enquire who it was.

Jack Ford was made an Honorary Member for life when he resigned from the Club in 1854, 'free of fees or subscription, whether present or not'.

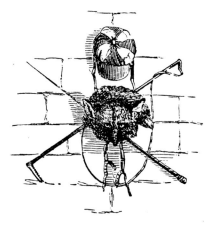

X

Captain White to the Fore

MAIDEN RECKONED THE FINEST HUNT he ever rode with the Cheshire was 1 hr. 20 mins. without check from Stapleford Gorse to kill in the open at Mr Wicksted's residence at Baddiley Old Hall. But on November 26th, 1842 from a meet at Oulton Park he and his hounds had a real marathon.

A fox broke from Darley Gorse at 11.30. It ran northwards in a long loop past Blakeden and then back down past Darnhall Hall, bearing eastwards to Ashbrook Hall and Lea Green and across the London & North Western Railway line by Parkfield House. On it took them past Warmingham, some twelves mile distant from the meet, with the new Master, Captain White, and his field trailing.

It crossed both the River Wheelock and the Trent and Mersey canal, circling by Boothlane Head, before crossing two more railway lines and heading northwards. It doubled into a ditch near Brereton Gorse, where it evidently stayed for nearly an hour. Most unusually both hounds and huntsman were prevented from going on by an irate farmer, who with his men held them at bay with pitchforks. Eventually hounds went in and made it out for themselves and pushed the fox on towards Holmes Chapel. It suddenly bore right and doubled to and fro between the railway line and Sandlow Green, crossing the River Croco three times. Running on, in a double loop it then crossed the Dane in three places and ended up by Rowley Hall, where hounds killed it with the moon shining bright.

The run from point to point was 25 miles, more like 40 as hounds ran. That was the day Joe got through three horses and a hack; Joe had blown them away and he managed to catch up with them in time to sound the worry.

By an extraordinary coincidence a framed map, showing the line hounds ran from Oulton to the kill at Rowley Hall near Swettenham, was acquired in Canada by Ted Clare in the late 1950's when huntsman of the Lake of Two Mountains at Como, near Quebec.* On his return to hunt service with the Cheshire Forest Hounds as Kennel Huntsman, he gave it to the Master, Philip Hunter.

Unfortunately for the reputation of the Cheshire, this remarkable point is explained by a handwritten note on the map to the effect that this was a bagman. Apparently the fox was 'a small vixen caught at Brereton & brought in a sack to the meet the night before.' The statement that 'the run became historic in the county' is therefore tarnished.†

By an agreement dated August 1st, 1842, Captain John White had taken over as Manager at the age of fifty-two. His home during the hunting season was at Dale

---

* The handwriting round the outside of the back of the frame reads: *To mine host of the Hare and Hounds with kind regards from Dick and Pat Oldfield of Salop. We'll come and see it hung one day.*

† On November 30th, 1792 fox-hounds kept by a Mr Roberts found in The Twemlows and, after a run of 60 miles with a 16-mile point, came up with their fox at Tarporley.

In 1804 the Shropshire Hounds had a 50-mile point from Whixall Moss, through Flintshire into Cheshire to Malpas where it was headed and was killed near Wem after 4 hrs. 30 mins, with two of the sixteen to start in at the death.

On December 3rd, 1830 Sir Thomas Stanley's Hounds met at Eastham and had a run of 20 miles also in 4 hrs. 30 mins., although they only achieved an 8-mile point.

In 1915 the Blencathra Hounds ran from 9 a.m until 7 a.m. the next morning. But the longest fox-hunts cannot compare with the stag-hunts of former times. In the reign of Charles II the Royal Buckhounds ran from Windsor to Warley in Essex, a distance of 70 miles. The Duke of York, the future James II, was almost the only rider to be in at the kill. (In 1676 he stayed for the deer hunting at Lyme Park. His grandfather, James I, hunted in Delamere Forest, whilst staying at Vale Royal and at Utkinton Hall in 1617.)

141

Ford, Sandiway, his main residence being Park Hall, near Stockport. The terms included 'the usual guarantee of £2,000' with an additional £100 on this specific occasion with the purchase of the horses his responsibility. This amount was sustained throughout his mastership. In his letter to Cornwall Legh, dated July 22nd, undertaking the management of the hounds, he rather ominously concluded: 'I hear there is not a very good report of foxes in several places.'

Captain John White

During his reign, as Tom Rance told The Druid, Captain White knew that the best way to populate the country with good strong foxes was to drive them down from the hills.

"The foxes are sadly changed" (said Tom, as he was nearing retirement after the Captain's time); "so many of them turned down; very few straight-forward foxes at all now; keepers level the old'uns off, and the young'uns, a hignorant lot of little devils, they know no country; they've no parents to show them, or yet larn them the country, and it ain't likely they can find it for themselves."

"We had very few straightforward foxes in the Wrenbury country. The Chester country was never the same as the Wrenbury country for good foxes; they might chance about Saighton and Waverton to pick up a good one, and take it to the hills. We had two devilish good runs from Wharton Gorse [as Waverton Gorse was called] to The Willingtons, time Maiden was here; the fox from Beech [Bache] House covert, Hurleston Gorse they call it, used to go away regularly at the lower end for Radnor, and on for Peckforton Wood, up by Ridley. We ran him three seasons and killed him at last. He was a greyhound fox; regular leggy one. They used to send me up to the corner at the lower end of

the gorse. He knew us – before hounds got there, you'd see Charley walking off quickish. These foxes on the hills, bless my heart and body, they don't half rouse them. We want two or three days amongst them, then we'd get some better foxes in the country; they want well rousing. That was a great point with Captain White."

'Captain White, he was a clipper; he could ride and keep them in first-rate order, too,' was Rance's appraisal of the new Manager, whose keen black eye, shaggy brow and stentorian tones made many a young man, out from Manchester or Liverpool for a day's sport, shake in the saddle.

Jack White, sometimes also called 'Black' White, was not given the soubriquet 'Leicestershire' by Charley Wicksted for nothing. Quite apart from his exceptional prowess as a cross-country rider, he had, so 'The Druid' wrote, graduated with 'the Squire' in Lincolnshire. And it was he who had acted as go-between for the purchase of the Quorn by George Osbaldeston from Assheton-Smith.[*]

According to an article in *Baily's Magazine* in 1862, John White was born in Lancashire; Willmott Dixon, *alias* 'Thormanby', in his *Kings of the Hunting Field* states he was Cheshire born and bred at Dale Ford, not far from the kennels at Sandiway, and which he used as his hunting box in later life; but this must be incorrect. In his notes on Wicksted's *The Cheshire Hunt: A Song*, John Twemlow states he lived at Sale Hall, the house, according to Ormerod, of the relict of Charles White, FRS on the banks of the Mersey. And yet again, although *Alumni Oxoniensis* shows him as the son of 'Thomas White of Manchester', *The Derbyshire Country House* (volume I, by Maxwell Craven and Michael Stanley) states he was the son of an Irish rake-hell, Captain John White, who built Park Hall, Hayfield in Derbyshire,

---

[*] Tom Smith, as his father, Thomas Assheton-Smith (27), always called him, was acclaimed first fox-hunting man of his day when received by an assembly of 2,000 horsemen at Rolleston in Leicestershire on March 20th, 1840. They had come from far and wide to pay homage to their old Master, despite his brusque manner in or out of the hunting field, on an invitation day there with his hounds. Even at the age of 26 his prowess was far-flung. When after the Peace of Amiens in 1802, he was received by Napoléon in Paris, along with George Wilbraham, Junior (77), the Emperor saluted him and, turning to his staff, said: *Voici, messieurs,* **le premier chasseur d'Angleterre.**

When, after ten years, he handed over the horn at the Quorn to George Osbaldeston in 1816, he had the Burton Hounds in Lincolnshire for eight years. In 1828 Assheton-Smith took over what became the Tedworth country and hunted it up to his death in 1858. Even in his old age he was able to vault from his hack to his hunter without first rising from the saddle. Rowland Egerton Warburton penned some lines: 'On Reading in *The Times* on April 9th, 1860, a Critique on the life of Assheton-Smith' and referred to him as 'the High Priest' of the Meltonians.

Leicestershire White on his shapely mare, Alice White.

about twelve miles East of Stockport. So he may possibly have been born in Ireland. It was in 1846 that Captain Jack White let Park Hall, after he had taken up residence at Sandiway, but the Derbyshire property was apparently not sold until twenty-one years after his death. At the age of five Jack used to ride a pony so small that, to quote his own words, 'with the saddle on him he used to walk under a leaping bar at home and be afterwards galloped over it'. His precocity in the saddle knew no bounds. 'He rode to hounds in "full hunting rig", velvet cap and red coat before he was 12 and drove a coach and four when but a year older.'

After Eton, where he is only registered as being in the Lower Div. Vth Form in 1808, he matriculated two years later at Christ Church, Oxford, where he continued his studies of Diana and never missed a day with the hounds if he could help it. He once made a match overnight to ride his horse against another undergraduate for 500 gns. over the Bibury Course at Salisbury. It was probably fortunate the match fell through. White began his career as a cross-country rider in 1811, when hunting with Mr Osbaldeston, 'little Ossey', in Lincolnshire. Living in the county city he took a fancy to a mare in a post chaise and managed to buy her cheaply from the owner, a Mr Widdowson. He put her into training and called her The Widow, winning five Hunters' Stakes off the reel and was only beaten a head in the sixth at Ormskirk, after he knocked down a man crossing the course. After that she changed hands to Lord Middleton for 500gns.

In 1815 he moved to Melton, which for a decade past had become the metropolis of fox-hunting. The establishment he shared there with James Maxse and their cronies became celebrated as 'Claret Lodge' and in their acknowledged rôle as 'half dandy, half dare-devil' they lived life to the full. (The other establishments were The Old Club, The New Club and Lord Rokeby's Club). White features high in the Meltonians' Honours List, compiled *c.*1820 by Parson Empson, as 'First Class' and as 'Pilot – John White' at the top of the list of 'Hunters, Good and Good-looking', as distinct from 'Hard Riders – not synonymous with good sportsmen'.

In no time Jack White became 'decidedly the best', according to Nimrod himself, which was praise indeed. On a day with the Belvoir, when hounds ran 19 miles point blank, he had been alone with the great Assheton-Smith in a memorable duet. In the ballad 'Rouse, boys, rouse!' by John Campbell of Glen Saddell, 1831, it went:

> *White on the right, sir, 'midst the first flight, sir,*
> *Is quite out of sight of those in the rear.*

In those days they would go slap-bang at the bullfinches, hollering like fun, to cheer up horses and men. They once came to a fence with but a single possible place in it and White got stuck. 'Ram the spurs in and pray get out of my way', says Tom. 'If you are in such a damned hurry, why don't you charge me,' replies Jack. And he did and they went on as if nothing had happened.

'Them's the stitchers,' Dick Christian, the famous Leicestershire rough-rider and raconteur, used to say, '. . . Captain White was a good 'un at that game. How he would holler, to be sure!' and he would mimick the Captain's banter, ' "Haw! Haw! What? Down again, Veteran?" ' Black White himself sustained the most appalling falls, but had an undaunted nerve and above all an elegant seat and fine hands. Heavily-moustached and curly-whiskered, he had a somewhat intimidating appearance, especially as he had a voice like thunder and relished using it.

After a day's hunting it was customary to foregather at the Old Club premises in Melton and quite a bit of

That 'great commander in the saddle,' Captain Whoit.

horsedealing used to go on, known as 'rapping', from the raps on the table which accompanied each bid. . After a couple of bottles of claret, business was quite brisk and the grooms would have bewildered faces next morning as the horses changed stables. An owner was always allowed a reserve, which he wrote on a scrap of paper and placed under a candlestick before business began after dinner. One of White's deals involved Harlequin, which he had bought in Derbyshire for £100. He sold it for £900 cash and a horse, for which he later got a further £250, to Francis Holyoake, one of Sir Harry Goodricke's toadies, 'an Oxford tuft-hunter' as The Squire called him. Harlequin was in fact a brilliant snaffle-bridle hunter and carried hard-riding Holyoake for seven seasons. A sharper deal involved identical liver chesnuts. One day, after a very fast 40 mins., White had a bad fall from one of them into a lane, but his second horseman coming up promptly, he changed horses and went on so well to be in at the kill, that he sold the second horse for £400 that night.

If there was serious business next morning, Black White liked to be at his best at the covertside and when the bumper toasts were proposed at the Old Club house at Melton, he had discreetly tipped out many a glass of best claret under the table.

Wearing silks he was a formidable force at such popular meetings of the day as Heaton Park, near Manchester, (three days) and Croxton Park (Leicestershire) and rode many winners for Lord Durham, as well as wearing his own 'pink, black sleeves and cap'. For the former meeting* he would stay with his friend and fellow Meltonian, Lord Wilton, brother of Lord Grosvenor, and grandson of the 1st Earl (43). His finest piece of jockeyship was when he won the 200 sov. Gold Cup there in 1833 by a head, beating his host, the owner-rider of the hot favourite, which had won the 100 sov. Gold Cup the first day. The young Lord Wilton was regarded as invincible over his own course. Jack had managed to shed 10 *lb.* to get down to 10 st. between the Wednesday night and Friday morning. He had been much teased when he returned from his energetic jogging accompanied by a Scottish piper. The man happened to pass by as he was resting exhausted at a gate.

---

* A portrait of John White by John Ferneley, Snr. riding Euxton at the Heaton Park Meeting of 1829 is in the Paul Mellon Collection. Euxton had been schooled by Dick Christian and was one of the savagest horses he ever saw. He won the Foresters' Stakes that year, but had previously carried off five cups on Euxton, including the Matilda Gold Cup at Heaton Park the previous year.

Another story about him relates to the days when he went in for walking matches on the road. He met a regiment of soldiers and they formed into two lines and let him pass, they thought so much of him. He was also a patron of a pugilist, one Henry Pearce, known as 'The Game Chicken'.

In his cockfighting days he once won a main at Melton by one battle against Smith-Barry for £1,500. The Earl of Derby was another of his great protagonists and the Knowsley cocks would be brought to the pit in silk bags, embroidered in gold with the Stanley arms. Rowland Warburton remembered his voice sounding above all others at the old Chester cockpit behind the Royal Hotel and Sir Tatton Sykes used to say that to hear Jack White's laugh at Tattersall's did him more good than anything else in the year.

At the races he sometimes also acted as starter for the two-year-old scurries and his voice could be heard right down the course at the winning post. If they got off too slowly, his loud 'Tally-ho's' would bustle them along. He became a familiar figure at race meetings all over the country, but it was on the flat that he liked to exert his jockeyship and was as conscientious as any professional to keep his weight down. His services were in demand annually at Tarporley and he was by no means without success. But for such a fearless cross-country rider, it seems strange that as a jockey he had a contempt for steeplechasing, although the sport was in its infancy.

Perhaps his most prodigious feat was the day he rode over from 'Claret Lodge' to Uffington, a good 25 miles away, to meet Lord Lonsdale at a favourite covert, had two 'capital runs, one of 40 mins., one of 70 mins., killing both their foxes'. He left off '24 miles from Melton' after his long day's hunting, rode back there, changed his clothes, had a chop and cup (?glass) of tea, rode home to Hayfield, a distance of 75 miles, crossing the Peak of Derbyshire in a snowstorm, and reached Park Hall at 11 o'clock at night. He had got over some 160 miles of country since his breakfast. Unbelievable though it is, there are several reliable sources for the Captain's extraordinary achievement.

His Captaincy had been in the Derbyshire Volunteer Cavalry. In 1819 he raised the North High Peak Troop, following riots which had taken place in those parts of Cheshire and Lancashire which border Derbyshire. During the Reform Riots of 1826 his troop was ordered out to quell a disturbance at Glossop. A raid was about to be made on some mills with the intention of preventing the use of power looms. Captain White received the order to disperse the mob. Before ordering his men to draw their swords and charge, he rode out alone, his piercing eyes blazing, into the thick of them.

He must have been a fearsome sight in his white plumed shako as he addressed them tersely in his best stentorian tones from behind his bushy whiskers:

> Look here, my lads, I want to give you one more chance before there's bloodshed. The Riot Act has been read, get away peaceably like sensible chaps. I don't want to kill my fellow countrymen. But, by God! if you don't clear off, I'll cut you down as if you were so many bloody Frenchmen, make no mistake about that. Now clear off.

And clear off they did.

In time for his first season as Manager of the Cheshire, new drafts of hounds were purchased from the Duke of Beaufort and Mr Drake's and the kennel was back at full strength with 63½ couple. White's standards must have been as high as anyone's in the land and in a letter to the Treasurer at the end of the season, asking for the £800 due to him from the hunt's banker's, Parr & Lyon of Warrington, he goes on to write:

> . . . I am glad to say we are having <u>most excellent</u> sport, indeed I may say in my experience I do not ever recollect seeing so much with any one pack of hounds for one month, as we have had in February – <u>every day</u> & killing our foxes. Sir P.Egerton was out on Friday when we ran from Saighton <u>through</u> all the <u>festivities</u> at Carden to some rocks in Bickerton – will you tell him, as I supposed [*sic*] he is returned to London, that several hounds got into the rocks after the fox. Tom Rance followed them with a candle & lantern and in a cavern [†] found the hounds lying by the fox which they <u>had killed</u>. <u>All were</u> got out safe.

In the Summer of 1844, the time had come for Maiden to leave the Cheshire Kennels and was appropriately given the job as landlord of the Blue Cap Inn at Sandiway Head.‡ They gave him a cup and £250 at a dinner there. But he remained pulling pints for a mere two years before he was back in hunt service, this time with old 'Mr Port' of Maer Hall in the North Staffordshire country. And there he remained for nineteen seasons, showing sport as always, despite his afflictions. The legs he had spent his money on proved unsatisfactory. With the 3½*lb*. 'Palmer's patent American leg', bought on his trip to London, he

---

† Mad Allen's Cave, below the Iron Age Hill Fort known as Maiden Castle on land for centuries the domain of the Egertons.

‡ Known as 'Sandy Lane Head' when Celia Fiennes baited (lunched) there on her travels in 1697, the present building dates from 1716. She was thirty-five when she accomplished her ride around England. She had only one encounter with a highwayman and that was near Beeston Castle, when '2 fellows with great Coates dogg'd' her and her servants. Her father was a Cromwellian colonel and her grandfather the 1st Viscount Saye and Sele.

went about his business in comfort at last. Better still was the embossed tankard, brim full with 750 gold sovereigns, which he received at Mr Davenport's house on his final retirement.

The fact that Maiden continued his career so successfully after leaving Cheshire gives credence to the idea that the main, if not the sole reason he left, was due entirely to a clash of Titans. But no evidence has survived

Joe Maiden at the North Staffordshire.

and at least Fox Rance was discreet about what went on between the Captain and his huntsman. The probable reason was that the Captain occasionally liked to hunt hounds himself and perhaps took the horn off his huntsman once too often.

So long as the old fellow was able to cross a saddle with his artificial limb he kept in touch with Mr Warburton, who generally heard from him at the beginning of each season. On November 17th, 1862 Maiden wrote from Wolstanton:

Sir,

I have taken the liberty of sending you a list of our hounds. It has been the worst scenting season I ever saw. These hounds will be leaving here shortly to go to Trentham, the seat of the Duke of Sutherland. I don't go with them. I shall stop here the winter and I don't intend going with hounds any more. I have Rheumatic very bad at times and cannot ride to hounds, this being my 54th season with Hounds.
I have a very good entry and they are all going on well.

I remain, Sir,
Your obedient Servt.
J. MAIDEN.

He was in his sixty-ninth year. His last good day was in February, 1863 with a run of 1 hr. 40 mins. The report in *The Field* concluded:

. . . From the elevated ground at the finish might be seen the jaded steeds tailing off, some one or two miles, the pace, considering the state of the ground, having been very severe. The pack was hunted by Joe Maiden, who had a rather singular mishap in the middle of the run, riding with his neck against a clothes line with such force as to break the cord, and, as the veteran jocularly remarked, proving that he was not born for the hangman's noose.

Maiden died just before the opening of the 1864/65 Season and his wish was granted to be buried in Maer churchyard, 'so that foxes might sometimes come and sport over my grave'. Within a year hounds killed a fox on the very spot.*

Joe's successor at Sandiway was William Markwell, who was to remain for ten seasons. Tom Rance gave his opinion that 'no-one knew better how to handle a pack of hounds than poor Markwell'. John Ferneley, Jnr. painted him with his hounds on the Captain's grey, Magic.

Maiden had left, but fields were getting larger and it seems the fox population was also on the increase with more and more complaints coming from the farmers. Part of the trouble was the increase of the fields, swelled with sportsmen from Liverpool and Manchester, seeking glory in the Cheshire pastures when the covertside was within easy reach of the nearest railway halt. Markwell once did something which would have made him the envy of his peers before and since.

The meet had been at Lord Stamford's place, Dunham Massey. Cecil of *The Field* continues the story:

When drawing the coverts in the park, and more and more so after having found his fox and got him well away,

---

* There have been many instances of this phenomenon. See *Strange Stories of the Chase*, collected by the Countess of Feversham (1972). Maiden left four sons, three known as Will, in hunt service. The first started as 2nd Whipper-in to his father in 1849 and was killed through a fall with the H.H. The second Will Maiden ended up as huntsman in South Dorset with forty-six years' service to his credit and the third was 1st Whipper-in to the Meynell, whilst Jim hunted hounds mostly in Ireland. Harry Maiden, Jim's son was a whipper-in at the Belvoir. Bert Maiden, of the third generation, was with his father Will in South Dorset before eventually succeeding Stanley Barker as Huntsman of the Pytchley in 1960. He was huntsman of the North Staffs. in 1971 and then Kennel Huntsman to Philip Hunter, before looking after the Cheshire Beagles in 1976 and then became Kennel Huntsman of the Eton Beagles in 1979 retiring in 1993. His son, Christopher, became huntsman of the Berkeley in 1981. When hunting the North Staffordshire Hounds Bert actually killed a fox on Joe's grave.

William Markwell on Captain White's Magic, from an oil painting by John Ferneley, Jnr.

Markwell was greatly annoyed by the pressing attentions of a gentleman evidently determined to acquire fame at any hazard, that he might take back to Manchester an account of his daring, which the huntsman would corroborate.

Markwell had ridden over several fences of considerable magnitude, without being able to shake off his 'customer'; but like a game fox, determined to make good his point, and knowing his country, as the hounds were approaching the River Bollin –a dark, sullen stream, with treacherous banks, hidden from view by an embankment – he rode straight towards the place the fox had made for, but not liking the aspect, turned away which caused the hounds to check. With well-feigned resolution the Huntsman continued his course to the very banks, as if in the act of charging the stream, from whence he suddenly turned his horse.

At this instant the Manchester hero, burning with ambition, and feeling that it was the moment to gain distinction, drove his horse at it and plunged headlong into [the Bollin below]. When or how he got out is a tale as yet untold. . .

But in the Spring of 1847 White was put out by a formal complaint to the Hunt Chairman from Sir Philip Egerton about a day in January, when hounds ran to Oulton from a meet at Darnhall. He accordingly tendered his resignation. At a meeting of Subscribers it was unanimously considered to be groundless and Sir Richard Brooke was called upon to write to Sir Philip to withdraw his complaint in a personal letter to Mr White. After much correspondence between those who mattered, White's feathers were unruffled and he was back in office.

This was not surprising, as many years later one historian considered:

A better Master was never known, even in Cheshire. His popularity, readiness of resource, and thorough knowledge of both horse and hound were wonderful, while his riding "to be with them I will" was much more easy to admire than to imitate.

Sir Philip's complaint was doubtless justified, but another verse about him went:

Ever-honoured White,
The farmers' favourite, who was never known
To cross a clover-field except his own.

However, owing to 'the high price of provisions' White asked for new terms to be agreed, whereby only three days a week were to be advertised and ten couple of hounds were to be sold to defray the cost of some new beds. But he bound himself to restore the old order of things, once conditions allowed.

There was also a problem at this time of some hounds being poisoned, as well as a considerable correspondence about a disputed bill of £25 from a Mr F.C.Calvert of the Royal Institution at Manchester for analysing the contents of the dead hounds' stomachs.

It was in 1847 that the future Emperor of the French graced the Cheshire field with his presence. H.I.M. Napoléon III was fated to fall – constantly in the hunting field in both Cheshire and Lancashire and eventually from his throne when defeated by the Prussians. He was staying with Lord Douglas at Arley, shortly after it was rebuilt, Rowland and Mary Egerton Warburton having gone to the continent for a few months. It was typical of the Poet-Squire later to record in verse the death of Arley's Royal guest's son, the Prince Imperial, who had

"Manchester" Skittles with Tom Jones of Denbigh, from the 2nd Viscount Combermere's album of original drawing and sketches.

gone out as an observer to the Zulu War and was killed while out with a reconnoitring party before the decisive Battle of UluNdi in 1879,

> *By savage foeman screening their advance*
> *To wash their spears that princely heart was rent . . .*

Although nineteen years White's junior, one of his fellow Meltonians and senior to him at Tarporley, was Rowland Errington (136). He may not have been one of the greatest Masters of the Quorn, but was said to have been one of the most likeable and he did hunt the country single-handed. In the young Cheshire squire's days at Melton, the cry was 'On Stanley, on!' He went as fast as the good things of life could go and acquired a reputation for hospitality exceeded by none of his predecessors. Both he and his brother Massey-Stanley (129) feature in Sir Francis Grant's picture, *The Melton Breakfast. The*

Sporting Magazine reckoned it was 'a faithful representation of eleven of the best sportsmen in the world'. It was originally commissioned for presentation to Sir Rowland on his giving up the Quorn. Grant painted another version which is at Belvoir.

Errington gave a Quorn Hunt Ball at Leicester in 1835, the first since one given in 1760 by 'Hugo Meynell, Esq. and the gentlemen of the Leicestershire Hunt.' But the custom lapsed until the present century, apart from a revival for two years in 1877 and 1878.

Another distinguished Master of the Quorn, who also wore the green collar was Harry Stamford, the 7th Earl, the owner of a considerable estate in the Tuesday country. Some years after giving up the Albrighton, he was persuaded to take charge of the Quornites from his Leicestershire home, the newly-built Bradgate. As was his wont, he was prepared to do the thing in style, but was not always assiduous in his attendance. Indeed when he arrived in January during his first season in 1856, he and his party indulged in a tremendous week's shooting with a total bag of over 5,000, including 'one large snake', with a predominance of rabbits over pheasants. But he proved to be a generous Master. This was the year White gave up the Cheshire and as an 'old and long-loved sportsmen' he, too, had been considered for the post on the death of Sir Richard Sutton.

In the Summer of the previous year Lord Stamford had taken the daughter of a Norfolk gamekeeper as his second wife. The fact that her previous career had been as a circus equestrienne no doubt caused raised eyebrows, but the presence in the field of the new Countess would have to be accepted with good grace.

It so happened that back in Cheshire in the early years of that decade another most decorative character of the hunting field, and future 'denizenne' of the Quorn, was making her début. Scant details have survived about the background and upbringing of Catherine Walters, known affectionately throughout England as 'Skittles' for many years to come.* But this Mersey tidewaiter's daughter was bold enough to come out hunting with the Cheshire Fox-hounds in the Captain's day before she was seventeen and, from the evidence of a sketch in Lord Combermere's collection, most probably a little later with the Wynnstay as well, for it shows her graceful form coyly riding home with a certain Mr Tom Jones of Denbigh. This would have been on a later visit. She is reputed to be the first of her sex to wear a shiny top hat for hunting.

She became a highly accomplished rider and, when she went out with the Quorn, it was her habit not to flaunt herself at the Meet but to steal to the covert-side and appear in the course of a run, up with the first flight. She did, however, delight, when the occasion arose, in out-riding the Master's wife. Few could have hard words for her, except of course for Lady Stamford, who eventually made a scene at a meet and told her husband

to send Miss Walters home at once, or she would go herself and never hunt with his hounds again. Catherine overheard and promptly turned for home to save embarrassment. But she had not gone far when a fox crossed the road in front of her with the hounds in full cry. It was too much for Skittles, who jumped the hedge and gave pursuit. At the end of the run she had gone so straight and well his Lordship went out of his way to congratulate her and told her she must always come out with the Quorn. 'Damn all jealous women!', said he, when asked about his wife. At least that is one of the versions of what happened.

Thereafter she stuck to her own strict rule never to visit any member of the hunt in his house and, for her part, Lady Stamford never hunted with the Quorn again when Catherine Walters was in the field.

On hearing of this decision, Skittles's indignant comment was:

> I don't know what right Lady Stamford has to object to me. She's not even head of our profession – Lady Cardigan is.[†]

An interesting new Member at Tarporley in White's day as Manager was James Yorke Scarlett, who two years later was in the Crimea commanding the Heavy Brigade

General the Hon. Sir James Yorke Scarlett (179).

---

* See *Skittles, the Life and Times of Catherine Walters, the last Victorian Courtesan* by Henry Blyth (1970), for whom the author carried out some research before he was aware of the existence of this sketch, which puzzlingly, since her family's origin was Liverpudlian, names her as 'Manchester Skittles'. When she died in her West End home in 1920, at her bedside was her faithful friend, the Hon. Gerald de Saumarez, whose sister married Piers Egerton Warburton (194). He had been her lover ever since he was a boy of 15 at Eton and she a woman of 35. Skittles left him most of her possessions, including a large selection of her love-letters and private papers, which his spinster sisters subsequently burnt.

† The hero of Balaclava's second wife and former mistress, the notorious Miss Adeline de Horsey, not to be confused with the first Lady Cardigan, who died in 1858 and was the eldest daughter of Admiral Tollemache (121).

at Balaclava. There he rode up the valley at the head of his troops. 'What are all those funny pointed things on the ridge on the left?' he asked his aide-de-camp. 'Thistles, sir,' came the ready reply. The 'thistles' turned out to be the lance-heads of 2,000 Russian cavalry. In the ensuing pocket battle the General became so tightly wedged amongst the enemy that he escaped being hurt. He afterwards succeeded Lord Lucan to the command of the Cavalry Division. Despite his appearance, florid features and bushy whiskers, however, he was rather a colourless character – but hard working and conscientious. Unlike so many of his contemporaries, he was a good cavalry officer, though not exactly brilliant.*

Meanwhile, before the smoke of battle had dispersed, it was to a future Member of the Tarporley Hunt Club that the Governor of Balaclava Fort, a certain Col. Monto, surrendered his sword. Lieut. Philip le Belward Egerton (191), then serving with the Rifle Brigade, had captured it with a small band of men. He got through the War unscathed but had had a narrow escape at the Alma when a bullet passed through his trouser leg, lucklily missing the limb.

Leicestershire White continued as Manager and replaced his huntsman, Markwell, in 1854 with George Whitemore, who had been with Lord Henry Bentinck. On the Friday of Tarporley Week of what turned out to be his last season in charge, a match was arranged at Highwayside on the Friday between Thomas Langford-Brooke (158) of Mere and John Sidebottom (164) of Harewood. The loser was the first man to fall or whose horse refused a second time and the umpire of this unusual contest was Mr Davenport Bromley, the father of William Bromley-Davenport (207). Rowland Warburton recorded the event in his inimitable way in *The Cheshire Jumpers*. It was clearly a bit of larking arranged before hounds moved off with the Master fully enjoying the spirit of the thing. Sidebottom's experience in the Shires won him the day, but it was a bit of an anti-climax when his opponent was eliminated at the second obstacle.

* Brigadier-General Sir Harry Flashman, VC, KCB, KCIE, then a Colonel, and who was present with him just before the charge, describes General Scarlett in *The Flashman Papers* as 'a fat cheery old Falstaff, mopping his bald head with a hideously-coloured scarf, and dabbing the sweat from his red cheeks.' As stated in another volume, the former regarded hunt suppers among the best things of life, but there is no evidence that Flashman ever dined at Tarporley. However the first nine pages of the club Guest Book, prior to November, 1873, have been mysteriously cut out with a pair of scissors. In his *Farewell to Tarporley*, dated 1872, it has always been assumed that Warburton was referring to Sir Harry Mainwaring in the line '*Sir Watkin cracking biscuits, Sir Harry cracking jokes*'.

Whether breeches white, or breeches brown, the more adhesive be,
And which the more effective spur, Champagne or Eau-de-Vie?
These alas! and other problems which their progress had reveal'd,
Remain unsettled questions for the future hunting field.

So it is all the more surprising to discover that White's popularity was beginning to wane. But as so often happens in these affairs, the Subscribers, as fickle as ever, decided a change was needed. There is no evidence that it was the new huntsman who was at fault. At a Meeting at Arley in March, 1855 they passed a resolution, which makes sad reading in the Minute Book:

> That the Conduct and general management of the Hunt of late years has been unsatisfactory.

Ten days later they met at the Crown Inn at Northwich and 'after much discussion', they finally decided that 'Mr White be requested to resign the management of the hounds'. The Chairman sent a suitable letter, concluding:

> . . . It is sincerely hoped, though our connection with you as Manager must of necessity cease, that our long intimacy may not be interrupted but that we may still have the pleasure of meeting you in the field.

He was elected President for 1856, but for some unrecorded reason old White was absent when the time came, his name thus sadly not destined to be recorded for posterity in red in the Hunt Room. It was still a few years before he finally retired from the chase, and he is known to have had an occasional day with the Wynnstay at the age of 68. The Druid was present on another frosty bye-afternoon to witness him helping Sir Watkin to dig out a fox and standing stick in hand at a bolt hole, ready, as the 'immortal Captain' told him, 'to nobble him'.

At the age of seventy he had yet to give up his hunting. In 1860, when leading a run from Wettenhall Wood, he jumped into a pond, overgrown with weeds. Unfortunately Mr Egerton Warburton, whose sight was none too good, jumped on top of him, and both went under. Rowland recalled what happened:

> Giving him precedence at a fence, and having allowed him time, as I thought, to get clear away, I put my horse at the same place, and found, when too late, that he had jumped into a pit. I, of course, fell upon him; but we never knew whether the slight injury which he received was caused by the struggling of his horse or mine. I saw him home, and we often had a laugh over this misadventure.

After being attended to by a bone-setter, he was back in the saddle in three weeks and remained as active as many a man twenty years his junior, and as upright as ever on his hack at Newmarket, where he was, as always, never averse to a tilt at the Ring. He nearly brought off a nice touch at Chester in 1858 when his own colt Jordan, on which he had £10,000 to £110, got beat half a length in the Cup, then known as the Tradesmen's Plate, carrying 5 *lb.* overweight. It was beaten a neck in the Dee Stakes next day and went on to be unplaced in The Derby. Jordan won the Liverpool St. Leger, but did not train on. Had he won at Chester, the old boy would have been chaired up Watergate Street.

The Manchester Guardian once reported his death and he had the pleasure of reading his own obituary when staying at the Rutland at Newmarket. He then wired his wife: I AM ALL ALIVE AND KICKING STOP YOU ARE NOT TO MARRY YET STOP.

He concentrated on the Turf and besides organizing Cheshire's first steeplechase meeting and often officiating as Judge at Tarporley Races, he had a most successful association with Richard Christopher Naylor (178), who won the 1863 Two Thousand Guineas and The Derby with Macaroni (bred by Lord Westminster) and The Oaks the previous year with Feu de Joie. At that time Mr Naylor was standing his recently acquired champion stallion, Stockwell, at Hooton, exacting an unheard-of stallion fee of 200 gns.† Naylor had bought Hooton in 1848 from Massey Stanley 'when the embarassments of that popular sportsman compelled him to abandon house and home for the Continent'.

White was Racing Manager, too, for Lord Stamford (175), who had become a force on the Turf, winning both The 2,000 and The 1,000 Guineas Stakes. And there was none better than John White at hood-winking the touts about a trial.

His taste for claret, convivial company and his fund of stories never became impaired. But on October 30th, 1865 he wrote to The Swan Inn, Tarporley:

> MR PRESIDENT,
> SIR,
> In consequence of my very severe illness I am obliged to give up Hunting; under these circumstances I do not think it would be fair to deprive a candidate from becoming a Member of the Tarporley Hunt Club.
>
> I therefore beg my name may be taken off the List of Members.
>
> Your Obd Serv[t].

He had been suffering from dropsy, but it was said to be the effects of eating a mutton pie which brought on the short illness from which he died in February.

His old friend George Osbaldeston died the same year.

---

† Two other most prolific and successful stallions bought by Members were the 1st Lord Grosvenor's Pot-8-os, which was the best son of Eclipse, and the 1st Duke of Westminster's Doncaster, a son of Stockwell. The former had been bought at 5 yrs. and carried until he was 11 the original Grosvenor 'Orange', which later became 'Orange, Black Cap' before the 'Yellow jacket, black cap' was registered. The latter was sold to the Austrian Government in 1884 at the express wish of the Empress, who had seen him when she was in Cheshire one hunting season and told the Duke she would like to buy him, if he was ever for sale.

Maiden's grave at Maer, Staffs.

XI

Quæsitiana Secundus

THE TOLLEMACHES HAVE AN INTERESTING DESCENT from both the Plantagenet and Tudor Kings of England. They have owned land in Suffolk from the XII Century, but inherited much of their Cheshire property through the marriage of Lionel Tollemache, 3rd Earl of Dysart, to Grace, the co-heiress of Sir Thomas Wilbraham, Bart. of Woodhey, co. Chester.

In 1770 Lady Jane Tollemache, the younger daughter and co-heiress of the 4th Earl of Dysart, eloped with her first husband, a young captain in the Light Horse, John Delap Halliday of Castlemaine, Kirkcudbrightshire, who was on the point of marrying Miss Byron, the daughter of Commodore (later Admiral) the Hon. John Byron, and aunt of the poet. Perhaps she took consolation in being James Smith-Barry's Lady Patroness the following year, if she was the same Miss Byron.

They went to live in Worcestershire and in due course their eldest son, John Delap Halliday, inherited the Woodhey Estate and a large property in Northampton-shire, along with his father's not inconsiderable fortune.

John Halliday's wife was only sixteen when he married her and, despite his long naval career at sea, they had twelve children. In 1810 he was commanding the seventy-four-gun H.M.S. *Repulse* off Toulon. In his book, *The Tollemaches of Helmingham and Ham*, Maj.-Gen.E.D.H.('Teddy') Tollemache, grandfather of Lord Tollemache (345) wrote:

> . . . his look-out man reported a French squadron of eight ships of the line and four frigates looming out of the mist in close pursuit of the British brig *Philomel*. The rest of the British fleet were out of sight.
>
> John crowded on sail and placed the *Repulse* between the *Philomel* and the enemy. His broadsides so raked the French van... that they abandoned the chase.

The Captain's youngest son, Augustus, commemorated his bravery in verse, which ends:

> *The fight was short, the Brig was safe*
> *In less than half an hour,*
> *Saved by the gallant Tollemache*
> *On board his Seventy-four.*
>
> *Alone he faced the Toulon fleet,*
> *No British ship in view,*
> *But his sole reward for his daring feat*
> *Was a cheer from the Philomel's crew.*

He had immense muscular strength. Just after the War he was at Calais and happened to be playing the pocketless game which the French call billiards. As he was making a stroke, a French bully nudged his arm. A repetition of the offence made it evident that it was no accident. He picked up the Frenchman and threw him out of the window, and then, warned by the landlord that this Frenchman was the leader of a gang of notorious cut-throats, he and his friends beat a hasty retreat to his ship.

As a further instance of his fiery temper, he once put his sixteen-year-old sister-in-law over his knee and gave her a severe spanking for laughing at him. His mother-in-law, Lady Aldborough, also present, protested, but prudently said no more when he threatened to mete out the same treatment to her. He was promoted Rear Admiral of the Blue Squadron* in 1819.

The Admiral (121) and his eldest son, **John (124)**, who was created Baron Tollemache of Helmingham in 1876, were unique in the annals of the Tarporley Hunt

---

* Since the re-organization of the Royal Navy by Charles II, there were Admirals, Vice-Admirals and Rear-Admirals of the Red, of the White and of the Blue. Ships in the vanguard flew a white ensign or index, centre red and rear blue. Admirals of the Red took precedence over all others, the centre being the proper place for the commander-in-chief, and so on, the head of the line being senior to the rearguard.

John Tollemache (124), from a sketch by George Richmond.

Club, in that they are the only father and son ever to have been elected at the same Meeting (1823). They had by then changed their name to Tollemache in *lieu* of Halliday. It was the future Lord Tollemache who later inherited the moated Helmingham, with its drawbridges, and the 7,000 acres of Suffolk estates from his great-aunt, Louisa, Countess of Dysart. As mentioned, the Admiral's second son, Wilbraham Spencer Tollemache, married Anne, the heiress of the Rev. James Tomkinson of Dorfold Hall.

Like his father, John Tollemache, was strong, extremely athletic and robust. His constitution was such that it became a sign of a severe winter if he wore a waistcoat to his club. His aristocratic features were invariably adorned with a pleasant smile. Strangely he took to wearing a wig quite early in life, even though he allowed his curly hair to grow beneath it. It once fell off, unnoticed by him, at a dinner party in London and the butler picked it up and quietly placed it firmly and slightly scew-whiff on the only bald head in the room, that of a parson.

John Tollemache married twice and had eleven sons and a much longed-for daughter.

He was thirty-two when the Admiral died, leaving him about 26,000 acres in Cheshire. There were, in addition, 15,000 Halliday acres in Antigua, which he later sold to Lord Combermere, and a fine house in

Piccadilly, next to Apsley House, No.1, London. This he sold to Lord Rothschild. He bought the Mostyns' Beeston-Peckforton Estate in the late 1830's, soon after his father died.

It is no exaggeration to say that Lord Tollemache became the leading agriculturist of his day. Though a strong Tory, his liberal-mindedness caused him to be dubbed the Labourers' Lord. He was one of the first to introduce allotments for his workers and the old phrase 'Three acres and a cow' can truly be ascribed to him. He, his eldest son and his nephew, Henry Tollemache of Dorfold, were to represent Cheshire constituencies for sixty-five consecutive years. When he died, aged ninety-two, Henry was the oldest magistrate in Britain.

By 1882 John had spent £280,000 building or re-building over a hundred of his Cheshire farmhouses and cottages. But, as the 5th Earl of Dysart had pulled down Woodhey Hall, the family felt they had no suitable home in Cheshire, having used Tilstone Lodge when staying in the county, for the time being. It was an old farmhouse they had re-built.

He chose a breathtaking site at the northern end of the Peckforton Hills, facing Beeston Crag and its ancient ruin with a view over eight counties. With Cheshire sandstone from his own quarries and timber from his own woodland he had built an astonishing replica of a mediæval castle. Designed by Anthony Salvin, who embodied all the characteristic details John, himself, had suggested, it contained a hundred rooms, a chapel, and stabling for forty horses. The scale was enormous. Work began in 1844 and Peckforton Castle was completed in 1852 at a cost of £67,847 9s. 7½d.

The servants' livery matched the coat of arms, in the Winter black with silver buttons and white facings, in the Summer white with black facings.

He was a much respected whip and, in London, always gave way with his four-in-hand to the struggling omnibus horses, whose drivers would salute him. He is said to be the last to drive a curricle in London. Once, a Japanese delegation, staying with him at Peckforton *en route* to Ireland, missed their train at Beeston Castle Station. John galloped them in his coach the fourteen miles to Chester and they caught their connection. His prowess at driving a coach and four at a canter over the tricky canal bridge at Bate's Mill is recounted in *The Two Wizards*. He was a great horsemaster with a penchant for liver chesnuts with long manes and tails and would not have a horse docked. He insisted on the minimum and plainest of brown-leather harness, unadorned.

Lord Tollemache delighted in taking his grand-children every morning to feed the horses, sitting on a bench in the long stables at Peckforton, and calling their

Bob at Dorfold, from an oil painting at Willington Hall.

names as the groom unloosed each one from its stall in turn. There was a stable cat that used to jump from one horse's back to another all down the stalls, but always jumping clear of a bad-tempered one, called The Czar.

There have been several Cheshire families that can boast a polo team. But, on his Helmingham cricket ground, Lord Tollemache delighted in putting in the field against all comers an eleven composed entirely of his sons and his daughter as scorer. In fact his wives had borne him yet another dozen sons, who had all died in infancy or childhood.

He was asked, when over eighty, if his family had come over with William the Conqueror. "No, my family was here a hundred years before the bastard was born," came the reply, referring to Athelmarche, who fought the Danes.

* * *

ONE OF THE MOST FASCINATING AND AUTHENTIC ACCOUNTS OF THE PENINSULAR WAR is *The Diary of a Cavalry Officer*. The manuscript diaries kept throughout the years 1809 to 1815 by **William Tomkinson (133)**, the youngest son of Henry Tomkinson of Dorfold Hall, were not published until 1895. They were edited by the second of his four sons, **James Tomkinson (209)**.

At the age of seventeen William was gazetted to a cornetcy of the 16th Light Dragoons and joined his regiment in April, 1808. A year later he embarked for Lisbon with his bay horse, Bob. When they went on board at Falmouth, Bob kicked himself out of the slings and nearly killed the second mate by knocking him overboard. Unfortunately the tide was out. Of his

father's military adventures James wrote in his preface:

> He was thanked in the General Orders of the day of January 22nd, 1811, and recommended for promotion in the Duke of Wellington's despatch to the Horse Guards in May the same year. In 1812 he was gazetted a Captain in the 60th Rifles, from which he exchanged back into his old regiment without leaving it. It is somewhat remarkable that, while severly wounded in four places in almost his first skirmish, he passed unscathed through four years' service in the Peninsula and the Waterloo campaign, although under fire, to the best of his recollection, on nearly one hundred occasions.

The 16th was in the brigade commanded by **Major-General Cotton (78)** and Tomkinson's Troop leader, when he was wounded, was **Clement Swetenham (113)** of Somerford Booths, near Congleton. He was shot in the neck and both arms with musket balls and also received a bayonet wound. He had been at the head of affairs, galloping to attack 3,000 French infantry, who were scattered all over the field. Poor Bob got a bayonet stuck in him too and he 'turned short round' and went full gallop to the rear until his helpless rider fell off when Bob pulled up under a tree. On such occasions the sky was filled with vultures soaring and gliding above ready

Lieut.-Colonel William Tomkinson (133), from a portrait in oils at Willington Hall.

to swoop. William expressed a horror at the thought of men lying wounded with out the strength to fend them off.

His horrible flesh wounds healed within a month, by which time both Swetenham and Cotton himself had written to Dorfold to assure the family that William was in good spirits and that they would soon see him at home for some convalescence. A surgeon removed from his arm what he thought was a bullet. It was a jagged button off his jacket and probably saved his life.

When he returned to the Peninsula in March, 1810, Lieut.-General Sir Stapleton Cotton was in the same party, going back out to take the Cavalry command. Two years later, whilst waiting to return to the 16th on his promotion, he served for a time as an Extra A.D.C. to Cotton, and noted on his second day, when the Peer inspected the cavalry brigades:

> Sir Stapleton put them through some movements, contrary to the desire of Lord Wellington, who said he had no wish of the kind. After doing one or two things, the affair got confused, the Peer rode off in the midst of it, expressing what he thought, "What the devil is he about now?"

Shortly afterwards General Cotton got shot in the arm by 'friendly fire' when he went in front of the picquets after dark. He failed to answer when challenged on his return and both he and his orderly dragoon got hit.

The action which caused William to be mentioned in the Cavalry Division Orders had been on his 21st birthday. He sold the three horses he captured that day for $256 (£64). Two months later, with a sergeant and twelve men, he took 64 prisoners and spared the life of a Frenchman who had tried to shoot him at point blank range. Another of his adventures had been with a guerrilla chief and 600 mounted peasants.

The Captain returned home in September, 1813 and took Bob with him. They had been re-united, though Tomkinson had found him much neglected when he got back to the Peninsula in 1810. Bob's portrait is still at Willington. Especially interesting is James's footnote in the diary:

> After five campaigns and an absence of four years and a half [Bob] returned safe and sound to his old home, the servant reporting that he knew his way back to his stable at Dorfold perfectly. He lived for many years to carry his master with the pack of harriers kept by him.

In April, 1815 both Swetenham and Tomkinson left Hounslow for the Netherlands and the Waterloo campaign, each commanding troops of 55 horses. The latter's brother, Henry ('The Vicar'), came out to join them and remained to see the battle; he even bivouacked with them, leaving the field only after the firing had begun, though William makes scant mention of him in his diary and the editor none at all.

In the battlefield with William was his future brother-in-law, Lieut.-Colonel (later General) Richard Egerton, youngest brother of **Sir John Grey Egerton (53)** and the **Rev. Philip (76)**. He was A.D.C. to General 'Daddy' Hill and they met just after William had been thrashing a peasant with the flat of his sword for pulling the boots off a guardsman before he was dead.

William was elected to Tarporley in 1829, just after he built Willington Hall on the property he had acquired from Lord Alvanley. There is no evidence to support the rumour that it was as a result of a gambling debt, a theory that is extremely improbable. Soon after his marriage to his young and beautiful bride he gave up hunting and set himself deliberately to economize and save for his children, as mentioned.

Only the male line of the Willington branch of the family was to continue, the Tomkinson head stock from Bostock having long since ended in the second generation back in the XVI Century. Dorfold and Reaseheath passed with the spindle, the family at one time also owning property at Wettenhall and Hall-o-Coole as well as an estate at Nuneaton.

'Willie' (195), the Colonel's eldest son, was 6 feet 4, very handsome and athletic, but died aged 30 from a brain tumour. During the few years he was a Green Collar, his rich baritone voice gave much delight at the Hunt Dinners. He and **Wellington Cotton (157)** were the two principal performers.

The celebrated TOMKINSON TOUCH exploit of Jimmie, William Tomkinson's second son, when he crossed the canal at Hurleston by copping on and off a barge is described in Chapter XIV and also his excessive zeal in the hunting field. He was highly delighted when, in his sixty-fifth year, he won the race between the Cheshire and Lancashire regiments at the Yeomanry Point-to-Point at Eccleston in 1905, leading the two miles and winning as he liked. The dashing young Duke of Westminster was on the favourite, which had won the Cheshire Point-to-Point the previous week, fell ignominiously.

As a seventy-year-old Privy Councillor and M.P. for Crewe, he broke his neck at Epping in 1910, when his horse, May Day, fell when leading half a mile out in the House of Commons Light Weight Steeplechase won by **Col. W. Hall Walker (268)**, M.P. for Widnes. Another Member of the Club to win this race was **Col. Wm. Bromley-Davenport (207)**.

Sir Philip de Malpas Grey-Egerton (130), the 10th baronet of Oulton, as well as being a Cheshire M.P. for many years, was an eminent palæo-ichthyologist and Trustee of the British Museum which houses the collections of fossil fishes he and his friend Lord Cole, father of the **4th Earl of Enniskillen (218)**, amassed on their travels all over Europe from about 1830 onwards. Sir Philip's part of the collection contains over 275 specimens, some named *Egertonia* after him. They were all kept at Oulton until his death. Before 1830 the two companions had explored some of the caverns of Franconia and their scientific researches resulted in a rare collection of the Cave Bear remains and other Pleistocene Mammalia.

In 1838 Philip Egerton read a paper to the Geological Society of London on some prehistoric sandstone casts, which he had acquired from his uncle, General Richard Egerton of Eaton Banks. They had been found in a quarry on Lord Alvanley's estate in 1824. The imprints were the hind feet of a gigantic cheirotherium, a 230 million-year-old four-footed animal, whose footprints resemble a human hand.

He pointed out the differences between them and others found at Hessberg in Germany and at both Lymm and also Storeton in the Wirral. He concluded that the Tarporley specimen, which measured 15" from heel to the point of the second toe, was a distinct species and proposed for it the name Chirotherium Herculis.

It was accepted as the holotype, Isochirotherium Herculis, after which all subsequent finds of the same species are to take their name. Found in Triassic Keuper Sandstone like this and the ones at Storeton and Lymm, cheirotherium was originally thought to be a mammal. It was subsequently identified as a pseudosuchian reptile and more tangible remains of the creature have been discovered in Brazil.

It was his father. the 9th Baronet, the Rector of Tarporley and one-time Chaplain to the Club, who was granted by Royal warrant the rare distinction of having supporters to the family's arms. The baronetcy is currently eighth in seniority.

* * *

It has been said that old **Hungerford Crewe (146)**, a shy bachelor and a bit of a religious neurotic, had an almost manic aversion to meeting any of his servants and it was woebetide any housemaid who was seen on the family's side of the green-baize door at Crewe Hall after 10 o'clock in the morning.

He was in fact a very generous man and liked to attend Charity Dinners. The Duke of Portland was astonished to see him at two in one week, on each occasion wearing a 'red-hot poker' in his buttonhole – he normally wore an orchid. 'I am very fond of society,' he told the Duke, but I am so old that nobody invites me now, so unless I attend dinners like this, I am obliged to stay at home.' He once caused some consternation by turning up at a Levée with his eccentric floral adornment pinned to his uniform and warded off attempts by various courtiers to remove it.

On a cold January night in 1866 Crewe Hall was ablaze. Pictures and furniture were strewn on the snow-covered lawns. Lord Crewe turned to his shivering sister, Annabel, and remarked: 'You've always said Crewe was a cold house, but you can't call it that now!' He then settled himself down at a writing table under the stars and drafted a telegram to his architect, Edward Blore, describing the disaster and asking him to build Crewe up again. There too, helping to rescue the family's precious things, was Annabel's eight-year-old son, Bob, the future first and last **Marquess of Crewe (124)**.

Soon afterwards R.E.Egerton-Warburton sent Hungerford Crewe these lines:

> *May fire which well nigh overthrew*
> *This Hall be ne'er more known at Crewe;*
> *Save that which on the hearthstone here*
> *Is lit each welcome guest to cheer.*

* * *

DIARY OF TWO MELTONIANS

Captain John White (159) was not elected to Tarporley until he took over the Managership of the Cheshire Hounds in 1842 at the age of fifty-two. He had spent his youth hunting in Leicestershire and, as this extract from 'Diary of Two Meltonians' (Maxse and White) shows, they sought their amusements in Town as well as indulging in the thrills of the chase:

CLARENDON HOTEL

Anniversary of Allsop's Corse Run, Ash Wednesday, 1818.

11 o'clock: Came downstairs; picked the brains of the Waiter; looked thro' the third page of the *Morning Post* and then looked out of the window; breakfasted; stretched ourselves, and arranged our cravats at the glass, not a bad glass; water closet out of order.

12 o'clock: Went to Milton's stable. examined his horses and examined the groom [Dick Christian] and had a closet audience of Mat who may tell lies to other people, but dares not to us; Mat hates us more than he hates Steward, but two of a trade never agree.

Rose, great grand-daughter of Richard Wilbraham Bootle (45) has a mishap at Arley with Mary and Piers.

Rose Bootle-Wilbraham mounting the 'Mad Hatter' at Arley.

4 o'clock: Started a Bristol coach and the Reading Fly from Gloucester Coffee House; walked down St.James's Street, nodded to an exquisite at Boodles and smiled in reply to a semi-dandy. Called in Pall Mall at Stockdale's for the last editions of the Pigeons, the Greeks and Modern Belles.

5 o'clock: Paraded Bond Street; Saw Crockford who whispered in our ears the pedigree of our nag for the Croxton Stakes; memorandum to hire a Yorkshireman with a stonehewer face [supposed to be a big fool] to make our bets; Crockford goes halves.

6 o'clock: Sat down to dinner; Jacquier [Head Waiter at Crockfords] very civil, likes frost and snow, and inquired after our little parson [Rev.John Empson, known as the Flying Parson, the Lincoln Crow and also 'the Man in the Oilskin Hat, one of the leading Meltonians], must not know anything of his reverence since he has become slack; toasted Val Meadows, Allsop's Gorse and Assheton Smith; asked Jacquier to go down to Lincoln to see frogs, fens, and Miss Burton [engaged at one time to Geo. Osbaldeston, married Sir Richard Sutton]; under waiter stared, and did not know where Lincoln was.

9 o'clock: Went to a silver Hell, fiddled with a stranger, old birds not to be caught.

10 o'clock: Stole off to the Play; too late to see Kean, our loves gone by mistake to the other House; followed them, laughed at Grimaldi but could not find Charlotte [a celebrated demi-mondaine].

12 o'clock: Took a Jarvey to Crawfurd Street [a brothel], and thought of a Tea Pot on the way; found Parry gone out for the night; sent for our clothes and persuaded Bertram [the brothel keeper] to send for her sister; when I see my friend's old woman in the North, must not tell of Jack's infidelity, and amour with BANG . . .

* * *

*R*andom entries, extracted from the ARLEY HALL WEIGHT BOOK:

	st.	lb.		st.	lb.
1844 R.E.E.W. (Nov)	10	3	1860 P.E.W. (Aug)	11	0
1845 Piers W.	2	12½	1860 P.E.W. (Sep)	10	10
1845 Mr Salvin	13	4¾	(after the Servants' Ball)		
1846 H.Mainwaring	11	8½	1866 Mrs Warburton	9	3
1847 Lord Douglas	12	2	(after journey to Spain)		
1847 G. Shakerley	13	4½	1870 P.E.W.	11	6
1851 Gen. Egerton	14	11½	(in hunting dress, how dreadful)		
1852 H. de Trafford	14	0	1870 P.E.W.	10	0
1853 Lee Townsend	15	2	(1st day downstairs after illness)		
1853 Mrs Smith-Barry	8	6	1889 R.E.E.W.	11	11
1853 Mrs Warburton	8	8	1899 Geoffrey E.W.	5	5½

and the last entry, on August 11th, 1911, was the heaviest in the book: B. R. Lascelles 16st. 10lb.

* * *

ACCORDING TO HIS STUD GROOM, Richard Chapman, the **Duke of Westminster (174)** 'spent practically all the money his horses won – and it averaged about £25,000 a year – on church building, estate improvements and charity'. He was approached by the Trustees of the new Royal Alexandra Hospital at Rhyl just after Flying Fox had won him his fourth Derby. They had run into difficulties. 'If Flying Fox wins the Eclipse, you can have the stakes.' he told them. The horse duly won and he kept his word, the stakes amounting to £9,285 – nearly £4,000 more than the value of The Derby. To commemorate the gift, a 'Flying Fox' weathervane adorns the building. He won six races that year, including The 2,000 Guineas, The Derby and The St.Leger, of a total value of £37,415, making the Duke the only man to have bred and owned two Triple Crown winners. The other was Ormonde.

Foaled at Eaton that same year, the year the Duke died, was the incomparable Sceptre, the only filly ever or ever likely to run in all five classics, winning four of them.* But for some injudicious riding, after she had dwelt at the start, she would also have won The Derby, in which she finished 4th. Most unusually for a classic contender, her first race as a three-years-old was when she was beaten a head in the Lincolnshire Handicap. But sadly she was not destined to carry the Grosvenor 'Yellow, Black Cap'.

Hugh Lupus, Duke of Westminster (174)

The Duke's death necessitated the dispersal by public auction of all his bloodstock the following summer. Flying Fox went to France for 37,500 gns. Although the young **Duke of Westminster (248)** secured seven of the yearling colts, he was underbidder for Sceptre when, to trainer John Porter's profound disappointment and against his urging, the Duke's agent, the Hon. Cecil Parker, dropped out after 'Bob' Siever bid a record £10,000. Bend Or himself had minutes earlier established a record for a yearling by paying 9,100 gns. for the subsequently disappointing colt, Cupbearer.

When he was Master of the Horse, the Duke wrangled constantly with the Queen, who insisted on the bearing reins never being relaxed when the carriage horses were waiting about. They were necessary for control when in moving traffic, but Hugh abhorred cruelty to horses. He occasionally hacked his racehorses and was once seen in

Rotten Row on his entire horse Whipper In, valued at £3,000 at the time, and on which Fred Archer had won some good races, including the Dee Stakes at Chester. As A.D.C. to the Queen, it had even been his original intention, with Porter's assurance the horse would not be upset, to ride the unbeaten Ormonde in the Jubilee Procession.

* * *

THE EARLS OF STAMFORD are descended from the younger brother of the Duke of Suffolk, father of the ill-fated Lady Jane Grey, who was proclaimed Queen on the death of Edward VI. It became a tradition for the eldest daughter of the family to take her name. The sister of the 10th and last Earl, Lady Jane Turnbull, died in 1991 aged 91.

The 7th Earl of Stamford (175), a fine shot and a first class cricketer, as well being Master of the Quorn was a Leading Owner on the Turf with sixty or more horses in training with Joe Dawson at Newmarket, with whom he was to fall out badly. He kept as many as 89 horses in condition as hunters or hacks at Bradgate, whither he and Lady Stamford delighted in having the apprentices sent for the Winter months to further their education. It was said of Lord Stamford that 'he never abuses a horse, has a remarkably good eye for country, and sees more foxes than any man alive, but a keeper or earth-stopper.'

* * *

BEFORE HE FINALLY WENT TO LIVE IN DORSET, **Lord Stalbridge (197)**, formerly Lord Richard Grosvenor, the Duke's youngest brother, had a rather peripatetic life, renting a variety of homes prior to his mother's death at Motcombe in her 95th year. These included Wilbury and Knoyle House, both in Wiltshire, and Middleton Park in Oxfordshire. He had a London house in Upper

Lord Richard Grosvenor,
later Lord Stalbridge

---

*A filly to win both The Oaks and The Derby was Signorinetta in 1913, ridden by William Bullock, whose daughter, Bertha, married **George Wilbraham (290)** as his second wife.

Brook Street. Before settling down to his political and family life, he had experienced quite an adventurous youth. He was present at the sacking of the Summer Palace in Peking in 1860, before which he had spent some time in America, living for a time with the Mormons in Salt Lake City, as well as with the Sioux Indians somewhere near Chicago in its infancy. When he was later Vice Chamberlain of the Household, the Princess of Wales used to call him 'Dick the Devil'. In Cheshire he lived mostly with Regie Corbet at Dale Ford, renting a little cottage nearby. He once swam the Dee and on another occasion was with the hounds on a run of 27 miles from Crewe to the Lancashire border. He also became a familiar figure with the Queen's County, Kilkenny, Whaddon Chase, Bicester and Lord Portman's.

* * *

'*Clever*' — *Statesman of the Day, Lieut.-Col. Wm. Bromley-Davenport, from a cartoon by Spy in* Vanity Fair.

Lieutenant-Colonel **William Bromley-Davenport (207)**, parliamentarian for twenty years, had most varied talents, including acting, quite apart from being a sporting poet on a par with Whyte-Melville and Egerton Warburton. (*See* Book Two, Part Two for his *Dream of an Old Meltonian*.) He was a first-rate shot and efficient fisherman as well as being a fearless rider. He did most of his hunting with the Quorn where his acute shortsightness did not prevent him taking the boldest of lines. He invariably wore a black coat and a white hunting tie. Once, a visitor, seeing him slip quickly through a gate as hounds found and went away, decided he was a useful sort to follow. Before long the stranger found himself committed to being given a lead over some of the hairiest fences he had ever seen. 'How did you get here?' he was asked. 'I f-

followed that p-parson,' he stammered, pointing to B.-D., who, according to Whyte-Melville, 'never seemed to remember that he had a neck to break.'

* * *

MEMBERS OF THE FOUR-IN-HAND CLUB, founded in 1856 wore their brown coats with brass buttons in the Royal Enclosure at Ascot. 'Their boxes, strapped on the back of the coaches, contained the necessary toppers,' wrote the Duke of Portland in his *Memories of Hunting and Racing*. His chapter on Coaching, headed by two verses of Warburton's *The Tantivy Trot*, relates an indiscretion of the **Marquess of Cholmondeley (222)** from his younger days. A very senior member, who could not pronounce his *r*'s, addressed a Committee meeting thus:

Rock

My Lords and Gentlemen, I wish to weport to you the conduct of Lord Wocksavage. Well, my Lords and Gentlemen, as you all know, it is a standing wule of the club that the owner of any coach using the Four-in-hand Enclosure at Woyal Ascot should either dwive his coach himself or else be sitting on it when it enters the enclosure. But, my Lords and Gentlemen, what do you think Lord Wocksavage did? He hired a howwible old wattle-twap machine, with hardly any paint on it, and with the spwings all tied up with stwing! You would not believe it, my Lords and Gentlemen, but he actually placed that howwible old wattle-twap in the enclosure, and used it to entertain his fwiends to luncheon. I think a message of disappwoval should be sent to Lord Wocksavage.

The Committee was too convulsed with laughter to be able to pass sentence.

* * *

Lord Arthur Grosvenor (226) was an ardent big game hunter. In 1884 he walked from the borders of India through the Himalayan Mountains to Tibet. He killed six tigers as well as rhinoceros, ibex and other game the year he spent in India and in 1897 he added wapiti and bighorn sheep to his trophies in the Rocky Mountains. In his letter two days out from New York in R.M.S. *Teutonic*, sending his excuse for Tarporley, he had been hoping to get Grizzly Bear and Elk. 'This is a splendid boat and fairly flies, & warm weather and calm sea.'

* * *

Hugh Delamere (240), the 3rd Baron, has gone down in history as the founder of Kenya, if not actually the earliest settler, and during his lifetime the bulk of the Vale Royal Estate was sold to enable him to develop his property in that colony.

His father was fifty-nine when he was born and he spent his childhood at Vale Royal. As a ginger-haired, fiery-tempered lad with a large nose and piercing blue eyes, Hughie did not exactly excel himself at Eton, on one occasion wrecking a shoe-shop in Windsor and hurling the boots and shoes all over the High Street. He had another flogging when he was caught at Ascot races. While he was at a crammer's, with the idea of going into the army, his father died and he returned home to live with his mother and indulged in a passion for hunting.

Hughie.

He was never happier than when his adrenalin was flowing and the chances he took resulted in many a toss. At one time he delighted in charging down a hill on a bicycle, usually a borrowed one, towards a wall and throwing himself off at the last moment.

The London season and the social round bored Hughie to tears. He could scarcely wait to come of age and go off big-game hunting. However, at nineteen he went to Corsica and the next year persuaded his mother to accompany him to New Zealand and had a spell in Australia, where he learnt the rudiments of sheep-farming. By 1894 he had already made three trips to Somaliland. Meeting him on the platform at Hartford Station from a later trip, his mother failed to recognize him behind a thick red beard.

Whenever he returned home, he found Cheshire far too tame, even with the fox-hunting. On occasions he would even resort to creeping down the drive at dead of night to Whitegate Church and ring a violent peel of bells to see what the reaction of the villagers would be.

But despite his quick temper, he was a man of immense charm. He spoke in a soft voice and had that great gift of making people with him feel that their opinion really mattered. He liked to do things in style and kept far more hunters than he needed himself, purely for the pleasure of mounting his friends. He also had his own small pack of beagles and enjoyed inviting a few friends to follow on horseback. In the house he had engaged a chef from White's Club, who, the day after he arrived, produced seven hot dishes for breakfast, as well as a cold sideboard, even when there was but one guest in the house.

Never a good horseman, his pluck made up for it and one day in the Chester Vale he took thirteen falls, one of them into the canal at Waverton. He was not the least hurt that day, but later he had a bad toss near Calveley, injuring his spine and causing him to remain prone for six months. That was the end of his hunting. It was during his convalescence that Hughie fell in love with Lady Florence Cole, the younger of Lord Enniskillen's surviving daughters. They were married in 1899 when she was 21.

They were off almost at once for the East Africa highlands, followed by a further attempt to settle at Vale Royal, but it was no good, the Maasai called. Back again in the East Africa Protectorate he had a crashing fall, resulting in severe concussion and spinal injury, which laid him low, but no less indomitable, for many months; typically he was still on a stretcher when he and Florence moved into Soysambu. She was only thirty-six when she died in 1914.

An innovation he could, in truth, ill afford, was for the

rest of his life to issue his Maasai herdsmen with an umbrella twice a year to protect them from both sun and savage rain which lashed down from the Mau. He never returned to Vale Royal. He had given his heart to his new country, where, in 1931 on a rocky knowl above the lake at Soysambu, his bones were laid to rest. Elspeth Huxley described the scene:

It was a strange assortment which followed the bier across the veld. Old timers, whom Lord Delamere knew 25 years before, came in in torn and stained clothes, shorts and khaki bush shirt, bearded Dutchmen, officials in white uniforms and decorations, clergymen in surplices and sun helmets. Copper-skinned Maasai stalked the procession in their hide cloaks and oily pigtails, carrying their long spears.

An early game of Polo in Cheshire, October, 1872, from a drawing by
Piers Egerton Warburton in Rose Bootle-Wilbraham's scrap-book.

XII

The Cheshire Difficulty

FOLLOWING CAPTAIN WHITE'S FORCED RESIGNATION at the end of the 1854/55 Season, a suitable letter of appreciation for all his services was composed by Sir Richard Brooke, the Chairman. By then, the name of Sir Harry Mainwaring's youngest son, Captain Arthur Mainwaring, had been put forward as his successor with strong backing from his father. He had gone on half-pay in 1844 and retired in 1848 from the 66th Regt.(later Royal Berkshire Regt. – the Biscuit Boys), which he had joined in 1833. He was living in a fine Georgian house at Worting, on the outskirts of Basingstoke. He had been married to a doctor's daughter for twelve years. They had no children.

In April a six-man committee (Glegg, Harry Brooke, Lascelles, Shakerley, de Trafford and Warburton) 'was appointed to correspond with Mr A.Mainwaring and arrange matters with him in case he consents to undertake the management of the Hounds'. Whitemore was told he could stay on and Tom Rance also.

Before handing over in July, White had been much offended and 'demanded the reason for his "dismissal" and complained of his not having had more notice'. Sir Richard Brooke firmly replied that 'no intended discourtesy was contemplated but that the dissatisfaction was very general...' A private letter to the Secretary from Sir Philip Grey-Egerton makes it clear what the trouble was. Rejoicing in the decision to find a replacement, he continued:

> ... The want of common courtesy and civility, the outbreaks of passion and the recurrent profanity of language in [the] head of the establishment, combined with the decadence of our sport and the general dissatisfaction render a change absolutely necessary.

It later transpired, not that it was really relevant, that the Captain had kept the hounds on economic lines, feeding them on Indian meal. For all that, he was not unknown to have drunk the broth from the kennel boiler.

On August 1st Warburton and Shakerley met Mainwaring at the Kennels and gave him possession, but not before an agreement had been drawn up guaranteeing him £2,100 *per annum* with, after a further £100 the first year had been negotiated. *Despite urgent advice to the contrary from Shakerley, it was to be for three seasons.*

The new Master wanted to build himself a house on land belonging to the Hunt, but the idea was turned

The Hon. Arthur Lascelles of Norley Bank.

162

down and he moved into Oakmere Lodge instead, the name he gave to what became the Stud Groom's house at The Kennels. All was fine this first season and Mainwaring's eldest brother recorded that there was very good sport on and after February 16th. There had been four weeks lost through frost. 'A famous run' was noted from a meet at Broomhall on January 9th.

Sir Charles Shakerley, however, had been killing foxes at Rudheath, Byley and Somerford and a deputation, which did not include his younger brother, Geoffrey, the former Master, went to see him to try to persuade him to withdraw the restrictions he had placed on his coverts. Thomas Booth (160) reported to the Secretary that the elderly first baronet had been paying his men a sovereign for each fox. He also enclosed a copy of a letter he received from Mainwaring the previous August about a Rudheath man in Sir Charles's employ. 'Ask him to the dinner,' he had written, '& will you give him a sovereign from me when you see him.' There had followed an exchange of letters between Sir Charles and the new Manager, the former accusing the latter of interfering with his servants and the latter strongly denying it. But all this was the least of the Subscribers' worries, compared with what was to happen before the next season got under way.

As nephew of the one-time Cheshire Manager, it was ironic that Sir Charles, the 2nd Baronet, should also turn out to be a vulpicide. As it happened he was a child of his father's second marriage and succeeded to Somerford in September, 1857. The first Mrs Shakerley, Angelique, daughter of the Duke d'Avaray, was considered by Nimrod the most graceful woman he had ever seen on a horse. When in 1825 he saw her out with the Warwickshire 'on a superb horse called The Golden Ball,' he wrote of her:

> . . . Her hand as well as her seat, is quite perfect, and I understand she has gone very well once or twice in Leicestershire.

There were at this time some thirty-two Subscribers to Hounds, a list of whom was printed annually on a smart card. All but two were Members or past Members of the Tarporley Hunt Club, the only exceptions being Sir Arthur Aston, GCB brother of H.C.Hervey-Aston (103) and Lord Alvanley. The hunting of the country was vested in them. And being virtually all green collar men, though their organization was entirely separate from the Club, they usually took advantage of having their meetings and discussions in Hunt Week at The Swan, many of which were informal and not minuted, certainly not in the club records.

It should be emphasized that these Subscribers were

SUBSCRIBERS TO
The Cheshire Hounds.
January, 1854.

ASTON, Sir Arth. Ingram, G.C.B., Afton Hall.
ALVANLEY, The Lord, Pepper Hall, Yorkshire.
BARRY, James Hugh Smith, Marbury Hall, Esq.
BOOTH, Thomas, Twemlow Hall, Esquire.
BROOKE, Sir Richard, Norton Priory, Baronet.
BROOKE, Colonel, Norton Priory.
BROOKE, Henry, Foreft Hill, Esquire.
BROOKE, Thomas Langford, Mere Hall, Esquire.
CHOLMONDELEY, Hon. Thomas, Abbot's Mofs.
CREWE, The Lord, Crewe Hall.
DAVENPORT, Arthur Henry, Capefthorne, Esquire.
DE TABLEY, The Lord, Tabley Houfe.
DE TRAFFORD, Sir Humphrey, Trafford Hall, Baronet.
DIXON, John, Aftle Hall, Esquire.
EGERTON, Sir Philip de Malpas Grey, Oulton Park, Bart., M.P.
EGERTON, Wilbraham, Tatton Park, Esquire.
EGERTON, William Tatton, Mere Hall, Esquire, M.P.
FOX, John Wilson, Statham, Esquire.
GLEGG, John Baskerville, Withington Hall, Esquire.
LASCELLES, Hon. Arthur, Norley.
LEIGH, Egerton, High Leigh Hall, Esquire.
MARE, Charles, Broomlands, Esquire.
MASSEY Francis, Poole Hall, Esquire.
NAYLOR, Richard Christopher, Hooton Hall, Esquire.
PATTEN, John Wilson, Bank Hall, Esquire, M.P.
SHAKERLEY, Geoffrey Joseph, Whatcroft, Esquire.
SIDEBOTTOM, John, Harewood Lodge, Esquire.
STAMFORD, The Earl of, Dunham Maffey.
WARBURTON, Rowland Eyles Egerton, Arley Hall, Esq.
WESTMINSTER, The Marquis of, Eaton Hall.
WILBRAHAM, George, Delamere Houfe, Esquire.
WORTHINGTON, William, Brockhurft, Esquire.

the owners of the Cheshire Hounds, the equivalent in modern times of the Members of the Cheshire Hunt, who are individually elected and are entitled to wear the CH hunt button. The gentlemen and ladies, who are now known as Subscribers to Hounds were formerly 'Members of the Cheshire Hunt Covert Fund', a list of whose subscriptions was later also printed privately each year.

Long before Tarporley Week the minutes of two Subscribers' Meetings and the correspondence which ensued with their Manager had been circulated to all concerned in a printed notice as follows:

Meeting of Subscribers to the CHESHIRE HOUNDS at the Crown, Inn, Northwich, October 4th, 1856.

Present:- SIR RICHARD BROOKE (CHAIRMAN)

Lord de Tabley, Col. Brooke, Thomas Booth, Esq., Geoffrey Shakerley, Esq., Hon. A. Lascelles, Thomas Brooke, Esq., Hon. Thomas Cholmondeley, G. Wilbraham, Esq., John

Glegg, Esq., Sir Humphrey de Trafford, F. E. Massey, Esq., Cecil de Trafford, Esq., R. E. E. Warburton, Esq.

RESOLVED

That in consequence of a letter from Captain Mainwaring, addressed to Mrs Robert Parker, which had been brought before the public in a circulated letter from Captain Parker to Captain Heron, and the impression produced thereby on many Subscribers, it is the unanimous opinion of this Meeting that Captain Mainwaring can no longer, with propriety, carry on the management of the Hounds.

The Secretary be requested to forward the above Resolution to Captain Mainwaring.

The Secretary received the following reply:

Oakmere Lodge,
October 5th, 1856

Dear Warburton,

I beg to acknowledge the receipt of your letter of yesterday's date, enclosing a copy of a Resolution passed at a Meeting of the Subscribers to the Cheshire Hounds, held at Northwich yesterday.

With the greatest respect for the Members of the Hunt present at the Meeting, I hope I may be allowed to state that I do not recognise their right to judge my private conduct, more particularly in a matter which, grave as I allow it to have been, is entirely unconnected with the management of the Hounds, and has been finally arranged by an apology, which was duly accepted; and at the same time the letter, upon which rests the Resolution, was promised to be returned to me; and the affair having been concluded, I contend that nobody has any right to revert to it.

Believe me,
Yours truly,
ARTHUR MAINWARING

To R.E.E.Warburton, Esq.

A second letter, as below, was written by the Secretary, and the reply following received by him on October 13th.

DEAR MAINWARING,

On reference to your letter to me in reply to the Resolution of October the 4th, I think it would be more satisfactory to all parties could I lay before the next Meeting definitively what your intentions are; you merely deny their right to judge your private conduct, but as the purport of the Resolution, however worded, was to request you to resign the management, I should be very much obliged if you would enable me to state what course you have decided to adopt.

Yours truly,
R.E.E.W.

Oakmere Lodge,
October 13th, 1856

DEAR WARBURTON,

In answer to your letter of yesterday, asking me to state my intentions and what course of action I have decided to adopt, with respect to the Resolution of the Subscribers, passed at their Meeting on the 4th inst., a copy of which I received from you on the 5th and replied to on the same day, I have to say that I have nothing to add to my answer.

Believe me,
Yours truly,
ARTHUR MAINWARING

Meeting of Subscribers to the CHESHIRE HOUNDS at the George Inn, Knutsford, October 14th, 1856.

Present:- SIR RICHARD BROOKE, (CHAIRMAN.)
R.E.E.Warburton, Esq., J. Dixon, Esq., G. Shakerley, Esq., Hon. T. Cholmondeley, Sir H. de Trafford, E. Leigh, Esq., W. Worthington, Esq., G. Wilbraham, Esq., Thomas L. Brooke, Esq., Cecil de Trafford, Esq., Thomas Booth, Esq., Lord de Tabley, Hon. A. Lascelles.

The Resolution passed at the previous Meeting and Captain Mainwaring's answer were read.

The following resolutions were then passed.

RESOLVED 1st. – That in consequence of the indefinite answer made by Captain Mainwaring to the Resolution passed at Northwich, October 4th, Captain Mainwaring be requested to say whether he will resign the management or not.

The Subscribers are willing to hold Captain Mainwaring harmless from all pecuniary loss he may sustain in resigning the Hounds; should he however, taking advantage of his agreement, persist in retaining the management, the Subscribers protest against such determination, and regret that he should consider himself justified in remaining in his present position in opposition to their unanimous wishes.

RESOLVED 2nd. – Whatever course Mr Mainwaring may adopt the Subscribers will not in consequence of these unpleasant circumstances, withdraw their support from the Establishment, nor absent themselves from the Hunting Field.

(*Signed*)

RICHARD BROOKE	A. LASCELLES
G. J. SHAKERLEY	THOMAS BOOTH
CECIL DE TRAFFORD	W. WORTHINGTON
G. F. WILBRAHAM	T. G. CHOLMONDELEY
HUMPHREY DE TRAFFORD	WARREN DE TABLEY
EGERTON LEIGH, JNR	R. E. E. WARBURTON
JOHN DIXON	THOMAS L. BROOKE

The first of these Resolutions was forwarded to

Captain Mainwaring, and the following reply has been received.

Oakmere Lodge,
October 16th, 1856

MY LORDS AND GENTLEMEN,

Having received a copy of a Resolution passed at a Meeting held at Knutsford on the 14th inst., I have the honour most respectfully to state my reply thereto, that it is not my intention to resign the management of the Cheshire Hounds.

With submission I would take leave to inquire from you, my Lords and Gentlemen, for what purpose the Agreement guaranteeing to me the Hounds, the Country &c., &c., and a certain amount of Subscription for a certain term was ever tendered by you to me, if not to ensure the due observance by both parties, of a Contract entered into to Hunt this Country; therefore may I be allowed to express my astonishment at your now protesting against the fulfilment of your own act and deed, which being both by law and honour as binding upon you as it is upon me, not one word can in justice be said against my taking advantage of it.

The act upon which you have founded your Resolutions of the 4th and 14th October, *viz:*- The letter I addressed to Mrs R. Parker, having already been settled by my having complied with all that was required of me by the usages of society in such cases, it cannot be urged as a plea for your requesting me to resign the management of the Hounds; and as I have, I hope, in every respect acted up to my part of the agreement and am fully prepared to continue to carry out the same for the remainder of the term as agreed upon, I trust you will be found equally willing to fulfil yours.

I have the honour to be,
My Lords and Gentlemen,
ARTHUR MAINWARING

To the Subscribers to the Cheshire Hounds.

The Subscribers did not meet again until November 29th but in the meantime there had been much lobbying, a vast exchange of letters and every conceivable advice sought and given. The Cheshire Hounds had continued to meet their Manager, who in turn had shown what sport he could under the restrictions inevitably imposed.

One of the first letters to arrive at Arley was from Lord Westminster, the 2nd Marquess, by then over sixty and Lord Lieutenant. 'MY DEAR MR WARBURTON,' he wrote from Buxton on October 24th, acknowledging the printed circular,

. . . I hope I shall not be thought too critical if I venture to give as my opinion that never was a *non-sequitur* more fully developed than by those Resolutions.

For see how the case stands – you first call upon Captain Mainwaring to resign – & then you go on to say you will not withdraw your support from the establishment nor absent yourselves from the hunting field – and this after the unanimous opinion . . . that Captain Mainwaring can no longer with propriety carry on the management of the Hounds.

And yet after this you still mean to countenance (as by your personal appearance you must do) his immoral conduct & unblushing effrontery in supporting him by your presence in the Field – in what way you are to mark your displeasure at his behaviour, & yet join him in his amusements, I am at a loss to imagine.

But I must protest in the only way I can to give effect to my views, by withdrawing the permission to hunt my coverts, & by stopping my subscription except so far as it may be implicated by any agreement with you.

For I do think it is our bounden duty to act with consistency and to maintain the credit of the County by a determination to renounce every amusement, rather than to appear to sanction what you have so properly condemned.

It is Captain Mainwaring that has by his conduct occasioned the rupture, & it is obvious that no feeling of shame will influence his actions – and I hope that another meeting will soon be held, at which the subscribers will not content themselves merely with protesting, but will feel the necessity of acting with more decision in this painful affair.

Believe me to remain,
Very truly y^rs.
WESTMINSTER

This then set the tone. Others with similar views, who immediately notified the Secretary that Hounds had been warned off their estates so long as Mainwaring was Manager, followed, including James France, who wrote again a week later, astonished to hear that hounds had drawn some of his coverts from the meet at Shipbrooke in the second week, despite his ban.

John Tollemache wrote three times, firstly announcing his ban and secondly after pondering that Mainwaring, having refused to surrender the Hounds, would be likely to ignore requests not to draw any coverts. So accordingly he had sent his agent with strict instructions to the Huntsman. He went on to confirm his desire to continue to preserve foxes and to suggest that Sir Watkin 'be invited occasionally to meet at Beeston or this place for the purpose of hunting my coverts'; and thirdly, when sure enough Mainwaring had drawn Page's Wood and Wettenhall Wood, he confirmed that the matter was now in the hands of his solicitor. (It seems he blamed Rance among others for not telling the Manager those coverts belonged to the Peckforton Estate.)

Then Wilbraham Tollemache's letter made it clear, as an Exor., he had denied the Toft Property to Arthur Mainwaring, whose 'conduct is such an outrage on all decency and right feeling that I feel compelled to raise my voice against it and to do what I can to get rid of such a Manager.

Lord Cholmondeley, the 2nd Marquess, was equally indignant. In his somewhat shaky hand, he let it be clearly known that the coverts on his estate were not to be drawn.

Lord Delamere, too, had warned Mainwaring off his coverts at an early stage, as did Lord Combermere. The Field-Marshal himself posted a note on plain paper from 'C. Abbey' confirming that he had 'sent by Post to Capt. Mainwaring a regular notice not to draw the Coverts upon my estate and when the Hounds were last at Wrenbury, my Steward delivered to the Huntsman a duplicate thereof.'

In a lengthy epistle from Venice, mostly about the weather and his visit to Austria and Switzerland, William Tatton Egerton, gave staunch support and hoped the matter would be resolved by Mainwaring's resignation, come the season's end.

Westminster wrote again reiterating much of what he had written previously and asking Rowland to be the medium to convey to Captain Mainwaring that he and his servants were not to enter on the Eaton Estate. He ended with a by no means mild rebuke that he was, 'as others have been, much surprised at the familiar manner in which you addressed Captain Mainwaring in apparently an official communication.'

'Depend upon it there is but one way to deal with a Person like Mr Mainwaring, which is to hold no communication with him, and to stop the supplies' was his advice the next time he wrote.

Meanwhile Lord de Tabley, writing on heavily black-edged mourning paper from Windsor Castle, had offered much sound advice.

What then had the cad the effrontery to write to Mrs Parker to cause such a furore?

As always in such matters, his chief crime had been to be found out. Robert Townley-Parker, the second of Townley Parker's (106) five sons, had been a Captain in the 53rd Regt., known as the Old Five and Threepennies (the King's Shropshire Light Infantry), and was a veteran of the Battles of Aliwāl and Sobrāon in the First Sikh War. In 1850 he had married a Miss Judith Caroline Augusta Panton from Anglesey and by 1856 had a house at Hartford. They had two sons, aged four and one. On July 31st he had gone to visit his father in Lancashire and left instructions with the Northwich postmaster to forward his mail, making no mention of his wife's letters. Unfortunately for EVERYBODY, a letter addressed to his wife was redirected three days later to Cuerdon Hall and inadvertently opened by him that Sunday. And this is what was written:

Worting, Friday.

MY DEAREST CARY,

I have been very ill ever since I wrote to you. I am rather better today, but very weak. I will try to get to you tomorrow: but I don't know till the morning whether I shall be well enough to travel so far; I trust I may, for I fret so about you, and long to be with you. I have just got your note; I conclude <u>you received mine</u> on Wednesday, directed to Mrs T. Roberts, Post Office, Northwich. I shall try to get to Hartford by 3.45. I may not be in time at Wolverhampton for that train: if so, I shall not get to Hartford till 5.30. I think perhaps it would be as well if I was not to appear at your house until <u>Monday</u> or <u>Tuesday</u>, as he is sure to hear what day I go there, and it will <u>look better</u> if I don't go there so soon after his going away. Therefore, dearest, perhaps you had best walk up the road at 3.45 toward's Woolley's, where I shall see you. If I do not see you from the bridge I shall go down to your house – <u>but please yourself</u> I am so glad he is gone. I expect a <u>letter</u> from you today, telling me what the row has been – I am rather disappointed; but you thought, no doubt I might be on the rail.

GOOD BYE, DEAREST LOVE, EVER, EVER THINE.

The letter was unsigned, but, in addition to being dated from Worting, the envelope bore Mainwaring's seal and his handwriting was readily recognized. The outraged husband wasted no time. Clearly he demanded that honour should be satisfied. The next day he sent his 'friend', Frederic Gerard, JP,DL of Aspull House, Wigan, to see Mainwaring, acting on his behalf.

On the Wednesday Gerard wrote formally to Mainwaring:

Having seen Captain Parker yesterday on the subject of my visit to you on Monday, I am desired by him to ask you to name your friend, and let me know at your earliest convenience.

Mainwaring replied from Forest Kennels, Northwich, naming 'Captain Richard Pelham Warren as my friend, whose address I will forward to you by to-morrow's post'. The next day, writing from Boodle's *en route* to Basingstoke, he reported Warren, his brother-in-law, still to be in Norway, his permanent address being at Worting House, the same as his own.

. . . I have written letters requesting him to come to England, and to put himself in immediate communication with you. These I shall send off tonight, if he is at any place to which there is an electric telegraph.

On arrival he discovered that Warren had left Christiana, but was returning there in a few days, where his letter would be waiting for him, urging his return. 'There are

Mr Robert Parker.

steamers twice a week to Hull taking about two and a half days, so I fully expect Captain Warren in London by the middle of next week.'

This did not satisfy Gerard, who wrote on Sunday the 10th demanding him to name another 'friend' forthwith, as Warren's 'return to England is a matter of the greatest uncertainty'. Mainwaring replied:

I beg to say that my particular reasons for naming Captain Warren as my friend were, that it is important that I should arrange with him family affairs previous to any meeting that may take place. I beg further, that it may be clearly understood that I do not shrink from the consequences of any act that I have committed, but that I merely wish to arrange my affairs, which it will be impossible for me to do without seeing Captain Warren.

On August 21st Frederic Gerard wrote again at some length in exasperation:

No less than sixteen days having been permitted by you to elapse without any result, since I waited upon you in Cheshire, at the request of Captain Parker, and urged you to name a friend with whom I could confer upon the insult

you had offered him, I must now remind you of the circumstances as they have occurred within that time.

He then gave a detailed resumé of the letters they had exchanged and continued:

. . . By post on the 14th instant, I wrote to you a third time, induced to do so by consideration for the honour of my friend, and the ordinary practice in unfortunate occurrences of this nature; in which, though it is most unadvised to act with precipitation, there ought to be no delay having the appearance or character of indifference... I was astonished at not having heard from you, relative to Captain Warren's return to England... [and] that if I did not do so in the course of a few days, I should consider that you were withholding that satisfaction which one gentleman expects from another in a case of this sort.

Seven days having expired . . . and still receiving no communication from Captain Warren, I am under the necessity of writing to say that I have advised Captain Parker no further to pursue the course which, as a Gentleman of honour and of offended feelings, he had at first adopted; because I think he and others must be convinced that in no part of a transaction, which ought to have been discussed without the slightest delay, has there been any promptness to afford him the satisfaction it was my privilege, as his friend, to require, and which I must conclude he has not a reasonable prospect of obtaining.

Still at Basingstoke, Arthur Mainwaring replied indignantly that the delay was not of his making, adding 'I must also correct you as regards your assertion that I told you at that interview that I had no friend in Cheshire to whom I could refer you, you not having ever mentioned the subject of a friend at that time. . . I was under the impression that you were satisfied to await [Captain Warren's] arrival... You are quite at liberty, in the meantime, to advise your friend to adopt any course which he may think proper.' Clearly the Captain had no intention of 'going out'.

He had, however, been taking further action and had brought in another friend, Lieut.-Colonel Henry Bowles, formerly of the Rifle Brigade, who wrote from the Army and Navy Club on August 23rd to make an appointment with Gerard on his way up to Scotland. They duly met at the Royal Hotel, Wigan, two days later. Mainwaring had in fact first consulted him on the 12th. At their interview the following Memoranda were reduced to writing:

> . . . it was agreed that in the matter of Captain Parker *versus* Captain Mainwaring, that as Captain Mainwaring has, in the most positive manner, declared that nothing has ever taken place between him and Mrs Parker of an objectionable nature, further than the correspondence which was intercepted by Captain Parker; and that as Captain Mainwaring is willing to forward to Captain Gerard a written apology, declaring that he deeply regrets that anything of the kind should have taken place, Captain Gerard declares that he is, therefore, willing to accept of this apology on the part of his friend, Captain Parker; and Captain Gerard does by this declare that, on receipt of this apology from Captain Mainwaring a sufficient satisfaction for any injury or insult committed by the said Captain Mainwaring. And Lieut.-Colonel Bowles engages to communicate the result of this meeting to-day to Captain Mainwaring, and to guarantee that Captain Mainwaring shall immediately, by return of post, forward to Captain Gerard his apology. In witness to the above we the undersigned subscribe our names.

On August 27th Gerard received the following letter:

> Boodle's Club[*], St. James's Street, London, August 26th, 1856.
>
> Sir,
> With reference to a letter addressed by me to Mrs Parker, and the communications which have taken place between

you, on the part of Captain Parker, and my brother-in-law, Lieut.-Colonel Bowles, in consequence, I beg to say that I am quite conscious that it was couched in terms of which Captain Parker might reasonably complain, and which I had no right to address to a married lady. I beg to express my unqualified regret, and I rejoice that the letter did not reach her hands. I should be glad to have it returned to me, that it may be destroyed.

> I have the honour to be, Sir, your obedient servant,
> Arthur Mainwaring

This letter was not shown to the injured party until the afternoon of the 28th. 'I could not be otherwise than of the opinion,' Parker wrote later to Captain Harry Heron (169), 'that all direct apology to me was studiously evaded in the above.' Gerard thought the same and he sent him back his letter with a note indicating what form the apology should take.

> Your letter of the 26th is not satisfactory [he wrote]; nothing short of the note on the other side can be so; if that apology be addressed to me at this place, on or before the 8th of September, which will allow you time to consult Colonel Bowles, and received by me in due course, I shall be prepared to accept it on the part of Captain Parker. I must otherwise consider the affair as having reverted to the situation it was before I had the honour of seeing Colonel Bowles on the subject. The letter which came into Captain Parker's hands being the occasion of his intended separation from Mrs Parker, and justifying that course, he must certainly retain.

The proposed form for Captain Mainwaring's adoption read:

> I request you to offer for the acceptance of Captain Parker my unqualified apology for the insult I have offered to him

---

* The Secretary of Boodle's insists that the establishment has invariably been so called, but this is not the case as throughout this particular correspondence letters and documents have been headed 'Boodle's Club'.

† *i.e.* Adultery. In polite and legal circles it was referred to as 'Criminal Conversation'. The old procedure was to sue the co-respondent for heavy damages for the loss of the wife's society and affection. There was a celebrated case in 1770 when the Duke of Cumberland was tried for having committed just such an offence with Lady (Harriet) Grosvenor, wife of **Lord Grosvenor** (19). No less than sixteen incriminating letters, in some of which, incidentally, she referred to him as 'My Dearest Carry', were produced in evidence, as well as many other witnesses. Part of the deposition was that Lord Grosvenor's brother broke open a bedroom door at an inn in St. Albans to find H.R.H. 'sitting on the bedside along with Lady Grosvenor with his waistcoat loose, and the lady with her dress unbutton'd and her breasts wholly exposed'. The jury awarded the husband £10,000 damages. After a separation Lord Grosvenor settled £1,200 a year for life on his errant wife, but apparently his own conduct had given her 'no slight grounds for alienation'.

in addressing Mrs Parker by letter in the manner he has noticed, and which has been the subject of your correspondence with me. I desire at the same time to express my regret that I did so, and to declare on my honour that any suspicion of criminality [†] would be without foundation, and that I pledge my word that neither in writing nor personally, directly or indirectly, will I have any further communication with that lady.

Mainwaring waited until the 8th before acknowledging this, stating that he had forwarded it at once to Bowles at Inverness and not having heard from him had written again. 'No doubt you will hear from him before I shall.'

Gerard was away for a few days, but the Colonel's reply from Rovie, by Golspie, Sutherlandshire [*sic*] was forwarded on his return and received at Hartford on the afternoon of the 12th. He was not giving in:

> . . . I consider that I must inform you how surprised I am at finding that there should be anything still to settle in this matter, it having appeared to me that on the day of our interview everything was definitely settled, and according to the written agreement signed by both of us, and by which we are both of us bound to act. I forwarded one copy of that agreement to Captain Mainwaring the same evening, and informed him that the affair was arranged upon the condition specified in that agreement. You will excuse my reminding you, that I asked you whether you were prepared to act for Captain Parker, and that whatever you agreed to, he would comply with, and you informed me that such was the case. I then informed you that I could act in the same manner for Captain Mainwaring.
>
> The agreement was then drawn up, in which it is stated that you declare that Captain Parker shall consider a written apology, according to the words of the agreement, from Captain Mainwaring, as a full and entire satisfaction for any <u>insult</u> or <u>injury</u> offered to him. Therefore, as Captain Mainwaring has sent an apology according to the words of that agreement, I consider that he complied with what I required him to do, and it will be impossible for you to refuse to receive his apology, and there cannot be any question as to the affair reverting to the position in which it stood previous to my interview with you; that, of course, it cannot do, as you did <u>then</u> and <u>there</u> agree, in the name of your principal, to be satisfied with such an apology as was specified in the agreement, and having so agreed to that mode of arranging the affair, which mode has in all respects been acted up to by Captain Mainwaring, the affair must be considered as satisfactorily arranged.
>
> Captain Mainwaring having again requested me to speak to you on the subject of the letter written by him to Mrs Parker, which you assured me you would endeavour to obtain from Captain Parker and return, I must again request that this letter is returned to him; <u>not that I consider it of much consequence</u>, as, by the words of the agreement, it specifies that, when Captain Parker shall have received a written apology as stated in the agreement, this apology shall be considered as a full and entire satisfaction for any insult offered to him by Captain Mainwaring. I shall inform Captain Mainwaring that, as he has forwarded the apology demanded of him in the agreement signed by you, nothing more can be required of him in this matter.
>
> I regret having to write again on this subject, and the [necessity of] having to inform you that the agreement must be acted up to by both of us, the parties who have signed it; and that as my principal has performed his part, I shall most certainly require that, on your side, the conditions therein specified be fulfilled. The affair is closed, and I shall be prepared, if necessary, to publish the whole correspondence, in the firm opinion that in every respect I have acted both on account of Captain Mainwaring, in the advice I gave him, and in what took place at our interview, in a matter perfectly justifiable.

It was at this juncture that Gerard withdrew, declining to press the matter further, after Parker had expressed his continued dissatisfaction with the 'so-called apology'. 'It was impossible for me,' he wrote to Captain Heron in his letter making public all the correspondence, 'to consider myself bound to accept the very qualified expressions with which Captain Mainwaring noticed the greatest insult a husband could receive at his hands, or to be satisfied with them, as Colonel Bowles suggests, for <u>any injury</u> received.

Accordingly Bob Parker turned to another 'friend', one Henry Alison of Park Hall, Lancs., who went with him to Cheshire the next day to find Captain Mainwaring. Yet another lengthy letter was added to the circular, minutely detailing all that took place on September 15th when Mr Alison called at the Cheshire

Kennels to confront Arthur Mainwaring, and taking up a closely printed page of foolscap.

After introducing himself as Gerard's successor, he asked him to sign the proscribed apology, in default of which to name a friend, with whom he might communicate; to which Mainwaring expressed his extreme surprise, saying that he considered the matter was at an end, having tendered his own apology and – as it was later printed – that HE UNDERSTOOD *that Captain Parker considered himself satisfied with that apology*.

Alison reminded him that his presence indicated this was not so and pressed his proposition or the alternative. It happened that Colonel Bowles was out in the yard and the Manager left the room to consult him. Forty-five minutes later Bowles came into the room and would not budge on what he had agreed with Gerard. Alison told him that as he had not been formally named to him by Mainwaring, he was not at liberty to discuss the matter with him and asked to see Mainwaring again.

By then Bowles wanted nothing more to do with the matter. After first suggesting that Captain Warren was sent for, Mainwaring declined a further supplication to sign the document, which Alison said he should do, 'acting entirely according to the dictates of his own sense of propriety'. The latter was perfectly willing to wait at Hartford until the arrival of Warren or any other friend he cared to name. But it was all to no avail. Mainwaring left the room again to consult Colonel Bowles and on his return announced that he had been advised to proceed no further. Ultimately the following conversation to took place:

HENRY ALISON – 'Captain Mainwaring, do you, having deliberately read this apology, refuse to sign it?'

ARTHUR MAINWARING – 'I decline to act any further in this matter, and I shall commit my answer to paper.'

H.A. – 'Do you, having declined to sign this apology (for your last answer is more than tantamount to a refusal to do so), undertake to name a friend who will, within a reasonable time, repair to Cheshire, with a view to enabling you to afford Captain Parker the satisfaction which he, in the first instance, demanded from you?'

A.M. – 'I decline to proceed any further in the matter; I have apologised; and the matter is at an end.'

H.A. – 'You must understand that no further explanation will be entertained by Captain Parker, and that all correspondence and negotiation upon the subject must be considered as at an end. I shall proceed straight to Captain Parker, and state to him the result of my interview. It is my duty to forewarn you that Captain Parker will denounce you to the world as an arrant coward, and at the same time publish the full particulars of all that has taken place.'

A.M. – 'He is at liberty to adopt any course he thinks proper. I shall meet his statement with my own version of the case.'

Robert Parker chose Captain Harry Heron (169) of Manley Hall to whom to address his circular letter denouncing Captain Mainwaring, enclosing printed transcripts of *all* the relevant correspondence.

DEAR HERON, (he had begun, writing from Cuerdon on 16th Sept.)

You and others, I believe, are aware that a separation has taken place between Mrs R. T. Parker and myself, and as misrepresentations on the subject have, I understand, been current, I am desirous of making you and all my friends fully acquainted with the circumstance . . .

His concluding paragraph read as follows:

And now having arranged all these particulars for perusal, rendered, I fear, tedious in their detail by a protracted correspondence, and length-ened by my desire to put you in possession of the facts which my friend, Mr Henry Alison, carefully noted immediately after his interview with Captain Mainwaring. I will only further allude to the letter addressed by the latter to Mrs T.Roberts. [This does not appear to be mentioned elsewhere. Perhaps it was a trap they set for the hapless Cary.] The Postmaster at Northwich has informed me that it was delivered to a female, and Mrs Parker has admitted that she received it. In conclusion, I will say, that although nothing further can reconcile me to the unhappy event which has taken place, yet I trust I shall have satisfied you – and others, I hope will be so – that I have endeavoured in this affair to conduct myself with propriety; and that in proclaiming the *arrant cowardice* of Captain Mainwaring, who after insulting my honour, has evaded giving me satisfaction, I do not outstep my duty to society.

Believe me sincerely yours,
R. TOWNLEY PARKER, JUNIOR.

To CAPTAIN HERON,
Manley Hall,
Near Chester.

So much for the injured party. It can, however, be added that Captain and Mrs Robert Parker did have a further son to their name, born in September, 1858, and two daughters, the second of whom died in 1867, aged six months.

* * *

THERE WAS LITTLE WONDER that within just over a fortnight of the distribution of this missive the Subscribers met to pass their resolution 'that Captain Mainwaring could no longer, with propriety, carry on the management of the Hounds.' On September 24th the Manager himself circulated the Subscribers, writing ironically from Boodle's, and sending a letter in his defence from Colonel Bowles, stating that he had advised Mainwaring to remain firm on his original determination. And a further letter was sent by Parker to Heron, as a result of this, condemning Bowles for not having tendered an apology to Gerard, *etc., etc., etc.*

It was then that Rowland Warburton began to be inundated with letters. Once it became clear that the Manager was going to stick by his contract and as more and more landowners closed ranks on him, the time had come to seek Counsel's Opinion – this at the Chairman's behest. Lord de Tabley's advice had been to approach Lord Redesdale and get the Fox-hunting Committee of Boodle's, of which he was a prominent member, to adjudicate. Boodle's, founded the same year as Tarporley, is much favoured by country gentlemen and its fox-hunting committee, recently formed in 1856, became the recognized body which laid down or interpreted the 'laws' of fox-hunting, much as the M.C.C. did for cricket. Until the Master of Fox-hounds Association came into being in 1881, it also dealt with disputes. The Chairman endorsed the Secretary's opinion that Mainwaring must abide by Boodle's decision.

The Meets were advertised as usual at the beginning of the season and, quite non-plussed, Mainwaring even wrote to Warburton on November 1st to report dampness in the Kennels. The hounds were suffering from 'kennel lameness' and apparently it was attributed to salt having got into the mortar, due to a practice in Markwell's day to spread salt on the floor.

A new huntsman had been engaged, David Edwards from the South Berkshire, who had spent his formative years at the Tedworth kennels. It was going to be a difficult time for the hunt servants, especially Rance, with so many familiar figures missing from the field, and not knowing quite where their loyalties lay.

But on November 9th the Manager wrote to confirm over whose estates he had been forbidden to hunt, namely the Lords Westminster, Cholmondeley and Crewe and Mr Tollemache, Mr W. Tollemache, Mrs Tomkinson at Dorfold and Sir Charles Shakerley. Of these only Lord Crewe was a Subscriber, Westminster having recently withdrawn his subscription. The Manager wanted to notify him that 'Hounds will meet at the usual fixtures, or at any other points the Subscribers can find land to sport over'.

At the same time there began between Rowland Warburton and Lord Redesdale a correspondence which was to last over the next eighteen months. Writing mostly from his home at Batsford Park, the former Master of the Heythrop, despatched to Arley and to Tabley no less than seventy-five letters, crammed with advice, comments, queries, answers and eventually decisions, to the dedicated and patient Secretary of the Cheshire Hunt; and these did not include the official replies and acknowledgements sent on behalf of the Fox-hunting Committee.

Lord Redesdale had recently ended a Mastership of eleven years and more and he was active in the House of Lords, eventually being given an Earldom. He was, as it happened, a theologian of some distinction and he had strong and narrow-minded views on divorce. And he was old fashioned to the extent that to the end of his days he invariably wore a tail-coat with brass buttons.

At first Lord R. did not think it was a fox-hunting matter and did not want to get involved. And the fact that Mainwaring was a Member of the Boodle's Committee further complicated matters. But he did give a ruling at an early stage that 'it would be quite out of the question for a neighbouring M.F.H. to come in to hunt the country or any part of it'.

Lord de Tabley was having doubts by mid-November and wrote to Rowland:

. . . There cannot I think be the slightest doubt that we are honourably bound... to abide by our agreement... I am very glad you are coming to town. Pray talk on the subject to come as uninfluenced by Cheshire breezes.

Meanwhile the opinion of Mr Edwin James, QC, Temple, was sought. In his brief he was given all the reasons why 'the prospects of Sport in Cheshire for the present and following Season are gloomy'.

Several modes of compelling Captain Mainwaring to resign have suggested themselves to the Subscribers: and it has been anticipated that the withholding the next subscription (payable 1st March next) might have the desired affect; but if Captain Mainwaring were then to retire without even contesting the question, this Season's hunting would be sacrificed.

A more speedy and efficacious mode has also been suggested . . .

In the *Case for the Opinion* it was also even stated that it was contemplated to take the Hounds away from the Kennel Premises, but could they legally deprive the Manager of the Hounds and would they be Trespassers?

It might be mentioned that James looked more like a prize-fighter and had that Spring been a Leading Counsel for the Prosecution employed in the trial of Palmer, the notorious poisoner, whose trial at the Old Bailey lasted 12 days and during which Mr John Tollemache happened to have been present. Not long after this, James was disbarred for professional misconduct.

For his fee of £5 10s., learned Counsel scribbled his opinion that the agreement was binding and that the Manager had every right to remain at the head of the establishment for three years. And further, 'the conduct imported to Capt. Mainwaring is not sufficient ground in point of law to justify the Subscribers in rescinding or putting an end to the agreement – but if proved, it will reduce to almost nominal damages any claim he might make at law for a breach of it.'

But he went on to recommend the serving of a formal notice determining the agreement and demanding immediate possession of the hounds and property with 'as little force as possible so as to avoid a breach of the peace.' He advised them in conclusion that should an action be brought it would be a matter for consideration what sum, if any, should be paid into Court to meet any damages that might be recovered.

The Chairman had not liked the idea of taking forceful possession and wrote to Rowland acknowledging James's opinion, which he had found 'much the same as Hostage gave us'. (Hostage was their Northwich solicitor, whose

bill to the Subscribers, including Counsels' fees and many other disbursements, eventually amounted to £147 7s 10d.) Sir Richard Brooke, then seventy-two, concluded:

I have not been out hunting since Tarporley and I think shall not at present appear in the Field, sad as it is not to get a few more days sport in my old age.

On November 29th the Subscribers met to hear from the Secretary the result of his correspondence with Lord Redesdale, Mr James's Opinion and an account of his interview with him in chambers. It was essential that both parties must agree to be bound by the decision from Boodle's, whatever it might be. Unfortunately Captain Mainwaring had refused to be a party to the reference on the ground that the dispute was between the Subscribers and the Landowners who had warned him off.

Little wonder they went off a week or two later to seek a further opinion, this time from Sir Frederick Thesiger, also of Temple and within two years, as Lord Chelmsford, to be Lord Chancellor. His fee was no different, but his somewhat inconclusive opinion was. He admonished them for not having 'provided for the occurrence of circumstances which render it highly desirable that Captain Mainwaring should not be continued in the management'. There was little they could do and he considered the removal of the hounds 'most hazardous', leading to litigation and defeat. He could find no solution. He even ended:

Deeply regretting as I do this result of my attentive consideration of the case, I cannot help in conclusion offering perhaps an unnecessary caution as the experience of what has occurred will necessarily have suggested it that in any future agreement...

and he went on to repeat at length what he had said in the beginning:

. . . as a remedy against the possibility of the occurrence of such a state of things as now cramps and embarrasses the action of the Cheshire Hunt.

Already no less than 68,000 acres of Cheshire were denied to the unrepentant Manager and his field. Now it was up to the Committee at Boodle's, to whom a full statement of the case had been sent. They had already pronounced that

Mr Mainwaring, being a member of the committee, is bound by the rules to refer his case to our decision if those with whom he has dispute desire such reference.

Portrait of an unknown gentleman arriving at a meet of the Cheshire Hounds at Ravensmoor Windmill; note Acton Church in distance. (Who was he?) From an oil painting by J. E. Walker [fl. *1855-66.*]

The case was now being reported in the gossip columns. Even the *South Bucks Free Post* ran an article:

DELICATE DISCLOSURES IN HIGH LIFE

THE following account of a case which has excited great sensation in Cheshire in which many persons of very high rank and great fortune are concerned, we abridge from the Court Circular, suppressing of course the names of the parties who are most painfully affected.

The Cheshire Hunt is composed of the first gentlemen in that aristocratic county. To hunt the hounds and to keep up the sport in a becoming manner they appointed a master of the hunt, to whom they bound themselves to pay £3,000 a year [*sic*] for three years certain, on certain specified conditions.

The gentlemen in whom their confidence reposed is Captain M–g; and on the score of activity, vigilance and energy there has not, we believe, been any fault found with his conduct as manager of the hunt. Among the members of the Cheshire is Mr T–y P–r, a gentleman of large fortune

and high connections. His wife unfortunately attracted the notice of Captain M–g, whose attentions to her were rather more assiduous and tender than was consistent with prudence. At length came a letter addressed to the lady which by the usual fatality of these little affairs of the heart, the husband opened by mistake. It began in very endearing terms and spoke of the rapture of meeting.

This billet-doux did not afford that evidence of guilt which would guarantee proceedings in the courts of law. But the husband conceived himself entitled to proceed in the court of honour and a hostile message was delivered which the gallant manager of the Cheshire Hunt considered it indiscreet to accept. And we cannot blame him. Duelling is a sin and a crime.

On the other hand, if the liaison went no further than a billet-doux how wrong it would be to expose two lives to the perils of heartless lead and 'villainous saltpetre' for an epistolary peccadillo. So reasoned Captain M–g. The husband was not so reasonable and he had recourse to the Hibernian fashion of 'posting'.

The Marquess of Westminster, the Egertons, and other

large landowners in Cheshire, conceiving that a gentleman who could be so imprudent as to address his neighbour's wife in such amorous terms was not a proper person to preside over the kennel, forbade the hunt from riding over their estates. The captain was required to retire but this step also he declined to take. It must be allowed that the members of the Cheshire Hunt were very unpleasantly situated. They could not enjoy the noble national sport in the fine open weather because their manager had wounded the religious sentiment of the great landlords; and they could not get rid of the obnoxious manager because they omitted to reserve the right of dismissal on giving due notice.

What mischief comes from crinoline! It would be a pity if the pleasure of the fearless fox-hunters of the land of cheese had suffered by this luckless episode. But we learn that a compromise has been entered into with Captain M–g, he having resigned his post on receiving £2,000 to cover the expenses he has incurred.

Not long afterwards the inevitable **ALPHABET** was produced:

A will fit **Arthur B** will **Bob** suit
C is the **Circular D** the **Dispute**
E is the **End** which we'll talk of hereafter
F is the **Fox** who is bursting with laughter
G the **Gent** who as second was sent, number two,
H the **Husband** who opened the wife's billet doux
I is the **Injury** still unredress'd
J is the **Jealousy** which is a **jest**
K the **Kiss** of the Serpent consoling the Dove and
L the **Love-letter** which **lost** him his **love**
M is the **Manager** very contrary
N is the **Name** which he spelt "dearest Cary"
O is the **Oatmeal** he bought for the pot
P is the **Powder** which buy he did not
Q is the **Quibble** by which he holds on
R is Lord **Redesdale** who bid him begone
S is the **Shooting** to which he is partial
T the **terrible threat** which he sent the Field-Marshal
U is the **Uncle** too near him of kin
V the **Vengeance** he'd take if it were not a sin
White is the **W** pleased at this brawl
X that e**X-Manager** damning us all
Y the "**Yoicks tally-ho**" which no longer resounds
Z the **Zeal** and the **Zest** with which France supports hounds.

When the time came for the Boodle's Fox-hunting Committee to adjudicate, the thirty-two-year-old Duke of Beaufort took the chair with Lord Southampton, 52, Lord Redesdale, 51, Sir Bellingham Graham, 67 and Henry Greene, a Lancashire man, aged 40.* These Stewards had been carefully briefed on a large printed paper, post size. It gave details of the Agreement and pointed out that in September, 1856, 'in consequence of

Captain Mainwaring's conduct in an affair unconnected with fox-hunting, he became personally offensive to almost every Gentleman in the County' and went on to list the estates from which he was subsequently warned off, having refused to resign, claiming a right under the original agreement to continue in the management for three years. With 'upwards of one half of the customary fixtures... rendered impractical by these warnings-off' of which the sole cause was Captain Mainwaring's conduct, the Subscribers, on whose behalf R. E. Egerton Warburton, was the only signatory, just as he had signed the agreement for them, now desired a decision from the Stewards on the following points:

1stly. Does it not appear on the face of the original agreement that equally, as it was never meant to bind Captain Mainwaring to continue in the management of the Hounds, contrary to his wishes or ability, so it was never meant to bind the Subscribers to continue him as Manager should circumstances arise to prevent his discharging the duties devolving upon him therefrom?
2ndly. Have not circumstances now arisen by which Captain Mainwaring is rendered incapable of discharging those duties which he undertook by the original agreement?
3rdly. Is not this inability to fulfil his contract caused solely by Captain Mainwaring's own conduct? and
4thly. Ought not therefore the original agreement to be declared null and void, and the contracting parties respectively set free from all future liabilities, subject to any such conditions as the Stewards may lay down as fair and equitable between the two parties?

This was referred to the Stewards on December 20th. The Secretary had their Decision circulated, closely printed on three pages of a similarly sized 15" × 19" sheet and not before the proof had been carefully vetted by Lord Redesdale. It was dated January 8th, 1857, and, at Redesdale's suggestion, included a copy of the original Agreement, which he stated privately to be 'a slovenly composition'. After a long preamble, re-stating the case before them and pointing out that hunt agreements were never meant to be legal documents, but are 'framed in a great degree on a mutual understanding'.

For instance, the country having been hitherto hunted four days a week, and the pack, which belongs to the subscribers,

---

* The 8th Duke of Beaufort was Master of his own hounds (sometimes known as the Badminton at that date) from 1853 to 1899.
   Lord Southhampton, M.F.H. (Grafton, 1842-1861).
   Lord Redesdale, formerly M.F.H. (Heythrop, 1835-1853).
   Sir Bellingham Graham, 7th Bart., one time Master of theBadsworth, Atherstone, Pytchley, Hambledon, Quorn, North Shropshire and Enville & Albrighton Fox-hounds between 1815 and 1825.

having been delivered to Mr Mainwaring strong enough for that amount of work, there are no words to be found in the agreement restraining the manager, who has power to draft at discretion, from reducing the pack to twenty or thirty couple, and hunting only one or two days a week, if it should so please him, taking the £2,100 a year. There are no words securing an annual entry of young hounds by breeding or otherwise. There is nothing to prevent his crossing the pack entrusted to his care with other than pure fox-hound blood. Yet no one can doubt that any one of the above-mentioned acts, if done by the manager, would be a breach of necessarily implied contracts . . . which would justify the hunt taking immediate steps to get rid of him.

They went on to make the valid point that:

A good understanding with the proprietors is a *sine qua non* for fox-hunting, and if any manager so conducts himself as to deprive the hunt of the privileges usually conceded by them, he disqualifies himself for the office by becoming incapable of performing his part of the contract...

The Stewards continued at length to describe how they had come to their conclusion before they gave their 'decided and unanimous opinion that Mr Mainwaring can no longer perform his engagements with the Subscribers...' It was on the understanding they had been influenced *solely on fox-hunting reasons* and confidently expected Mr Mainwaring to acquiesce.

In the meantime, Rowland's good friend, 'young' Harry Mainwaring, the Manager's eldest brother, had written from Peover, hoping

that Arthur will be moderate in his <u>Bill of Rights</u>. In both my letters I urged upon him the great desirability of his yielding to the decision, of giving up the Hounds with a good grace . . .

The intention was for the Subscribers to accept Mr M.'s resignation as from April 1st with indemnity for losses he may incur and his submission to the decision was duly forwarded to Redesdale from Boodle's. Needless to say it was not going to be that simple.

An anxious Lord Redesdale continued to write to the Hunt Secretary, strongly advising him not to act in any further dispute with Mainwaring without reference to the Stewards. Rowland in turn had been exchanging letters with the Manager. A month after the Stewards' decision had been given, this letter appeared in *Bell's Life in London*:

MR EDITOR, With reference to your observation that "the Cheshire Difficulty is settled," I beg to say that I have done my best towards a settlement, upon condition that the Subscribers do theirs; whether they will do so or not remains to be seen. It is an entire mistake to say that "the best part of the country has been sealed to me" or that "Edwards has been perpetually obliged to stop the hounds." The warns-off were confined to a very small corner of the county, and were not sufficiently important to interfere materially with the sport, even in that small corner. I will venture to say that the sport has never been more uniformly good than during the present season, and the hounds have never, on any one single occasion, been stopped while I was out with them, nor in my absence, except once only.

I request therefore, you will correct your statement where erroneous in point of fact.– Your obedient servant,

ARTHUR MAINWARING.

A fortnight later the Stewards thought it right to state how the matter stood and to make public their judgement, which was published in full in *Bell's Life* with a covering letter stating the only thing to be settled was the amount the Subscribers should pay to the Manager on his retirement. Redesdale advised extreme caution all along, but privately had a liberal attitude towards Mainwaring.

No response came from Mainwaring to the terms he had been offered and he in turn on March 14th wrote another lengthy screed, addressed to the Stewards and

Mr W.V. Fox

causing it to be published in *Bell's Life*. And the Boodle's Committee was asked by the Cheshire Subscribers to give a further opinion as to the fairness of their terms, which, as well as various financial considerations, absolved the Manager from any further expense after May 1st; but he was as obdurate as ever. It was clear that once again it was going to get into the hands of the lawyers.

Having agreed to give up at the ending of the 'Hunting Season', rather than August 1st, the end of the 'Management Season', Mainwaring submitted his account, which in simple terms came to £1,600 plus £80 for the keep of his horses for April. This was twice the amount the Subscribers were prepared to pay. Their final offer was £850 less £156 12s 10d, 'an earth-stopping payment they would themselves take charge of'.

Mainwaring wrote to Warburton that unless he received the payment he had stipulated, he would immediately place the affair in his lawyers' hands.

Again Counsel's Opinion was sought; this time of Mr J.H.Lloyd, QC, a Cheshire man with high reputation as a jurisconsult. This time the advice turned out to be very positive. Very simply he gave it that on purely legal grounds they had no chance of preventing Captain Arthur Mainwaring from remaining in charge of the hounds for yet another season, if he so wished.

This was despite the fact that all concerned took the view that, he must be considered bound to obey the decision of the Stewards of the M.F.H. Committee, of which he was himself a member and which everybody regarded as 'a twin foal with the Committee of the Jockey Club'; and notwithstanding the comment in his brief that:

It will be seen, from a Perusal of the accompanying Papers, that Captain Mainwaring has, by his conduct, subjected himself to, and tolerated from all Parties, language and treatment which, to a Person in his Position, ought to be hard to endure.

The simple mistake the Stewards made was to give their judgement without bearing in mind that the basic charge was not a fox-hunting question, and therefore, by their own rules, not within their jurisdiction. It was no wonder Captain Mainwaring now refused to acknowledge their decision.

And in the meantime the Stewards took up another half-column of *Bell's* typeset, making public their reply to the recalcitrant M.F.H. An exasperated Lord

Redesdale told Rowland Warburton privately:

> I think he will hardly be able to show his face in society again, or expect to be treated as a gentleman by anyone. We have done our utmost to save him, but he refuses all advice at the last and must take the consequences.

'I hear he calls us cowards,' he wrote later in one of his almost daily letters.

With his approval, the long-suffering Secretary then took to print. (He had still found time to publish *Three Hunting Songs* and sent a copy to Redesdale at Batsford Park.) In *Bell's* he refuted the Manager's claim that the 'warns-off' were of no consequence. They include 'the very cream of our country and the very choicest of our covers', he concluded. By then it was mid-April and Mainwaring replied with another salvo, stating that the country banned to him was a mere tenth of the whole. On and on he whinged: 'I cannot conceive that I can be justly accused of unbecoming or ungentlemanlike conduct, such as the Stewards insinuate – though they have not the courage to state it plainly...'

He sent the Secretary his ultimatum that, as the Subscribers had taken no notice of his claim for the indemnification he would require to give up at their request, and as he no longer intended to submit to the interference of the Boodle's Stewards, he was reverting to his former position to continue to hunt the country as before until the end of his agreed term.

Naturally enough at the hastily convened meeting Mainwaring's request for a further half-year's subscription was refused.

Arthur Lascelles (181) foresaw that if he did not go, they would be 'in a more awkward position than we were last [season] for the country will be equally open to him, and I cannot see how we can well hunt with a man to whom we have refused our subscription'. He surmised that Mainwaring must either be carrying on by his own means, with assistance from an unknown source or 'which I suspect is the case, upon <u>Tick</u>. Bring pressure to bear by making it known to his creditors that he was no longer supported by the Subscribers, was his advice in a letter to the Hunt Secretary. 'I think this would produce a sensation amongst meal-sellers, horse dealers and other classes of the community to whom he owes money.' He even hinted they were going to consult the old and trusted whipper-in. 'If I can get a talk with Tom Rance I will, but it will be very difficult to do casually.'

Old John Glegg, Harry Brooke and Cecil de Trafford were among those vehemently against going to law. 'My impression is that <u>we are beaten</u> decidedly <u>beaten</u>, bemoaned Lord de Tabley. Even Lord Alvanley, William's younger brother, who had inherited the title in 1849, sent his apologies, but he did not fully understand what was going on.

As can be imagined, all sorts of angry discussions were still to follow. Legal proceedings were instituted and withdrawn at the last moment, and the case ended in Mainwaring continuing in possession of the hounds and country for his third season as originally agreed upon.

Captain Arthur Mainwaring was now himself 'The Cheshire Difficulty' with a vengeance.

John Wilson Fox (172).

C. G. Cholmondeley (184), father of the 4th Marquess.

Henry Lyon (185).

Hon. Wilbraham Egerton (186), later Earl Egerton of Tatton.

XIII

Le Gros – Veneur

ALL THE WHILE HOUNDS HAD BEEN MEETING the Master the past season as if nothing was amiss. And, unbelievably, the same was to apply for his last. Not even the Tarporley Week Meets were changed. A cursory glance through the list shows but a few unfamiliar places, such as 'Eddisbury Turnpike' and 'Bradley Orchard, Frodsham'. The Manager's brother noted for 1857/58: 'Very excellent sport all season, but none of the "Cheshire Hunt" went out with the Hounds.

1857 was John Sidebotham's year as President. The entry in the book reads:

> The Members of the Hunt having declined to hunt whilst Capt. Mainwaring continued to act as the Manager of the Hounds, the Meeting was confined this year to two days only – the Meeting commencing on the Tuesday which was very numerously attended and carried on with much animation. It ended on the Thursday.

They ordered some light claret @ 12/- a dozen and the races took place as usual.

With fields largely made up with Manchester and Liverpool businessmen, an interesting Member of the Covert Fund during this time was Friedrich Engels, who, when he was not running his family cotton-thread factory in Manchester or plotting revolution with Karl Marx, took time off for a day with the Cheshire. For Christmas, 1856 his father had sent him some money to buy a hunter. A year later on he wrote that on Boxing Day 'I spent seven hours in the saddle with the fox-hunt... confident that exercise in the hunting field would soon restore my health to normal.' The meet had been at Bucklow Hill, relatively local to the terraced house he shared with his Irish common-law wife. He continued in his letter:

> [Translation] . . . It is the most magnificent bodily pleasure that I know. In the entire field I saw only two better ridden

than I, but they also had better horses. At least twenty fellows fell from their horses or were thrown, two horses were destroyed and a fox was killed (I was at the death)...

Some months later, on a visit, the father of Communism himself was persuaded to go out riding with him.

The Field correspondent[*] gave a slightly different version of the Boxing Day sport from Bucklow Hill:

> . . . I think Edwards, as a huntsman, displayed great patience and perseverance throughout. He, in the absence of the Master, Captain Mainwaring, had to rule a most reckless field of riders, many of whom seemed to know neither their own place nor that of others – [who] apparently were out for the day, or rather the Christmas days – but of course there were several out who did honour to the hunt, and could well appreciate the beautiful hunting of the hounds. . . The brush was handed to Mr James Greaves of Oldham, a keen sportsman; the head to a juvenile boy, son of a sporting boot-maker; but the brush might have been freely presented to Master Newton, who unquestionably displayed throughout the boldest and neatest horse-manship.

In the previous Spring the whole matter of 'the Cheshire Difficulty' had been bandied about in the columns of *Bells's Life* and in April the Stewards had issued a 1,500-word resumé of the proceedings, washing their hands of the whole sorry affair. At one stage it seems that Mainwaring had claimed that he was no longer bound by their decision because he had not paid his subscription to Boodle's. But he later wished to be exonerated from attempting to withdraw from their jurisdiction 'upon so paltry a quibble'. Mainwaring had evidently withdrawn his valid point that the matter

---

[*] Apart from 'Cecil', who was Cornelius Tongue, they varied. This report was by 'A.D.' Others about this time were 'Evergreen', 'Not a Cheshire Man', 'E.B.', 'Black Coat', 'Leather Leggings' and 'The Roan Rider'.

under discussion was not a Fox-hunting one, outside the Committee's brief, and had conceded that he was being judged purely as a result of the warnings off he had been given, rather than the reason for them. But he was stubborn to the end on the matter of indemnity, making out that he would make a profit on his last season to recoup some of his previous losses. The Subscribers, on the other hand, were only prepared to consider the short term.

Hence the final impasse.

In June the Stewards' judgement and award had been unanimously confirmed at Boodle's with seventeen Masters of Fox-hounds present. They saw no grounds for reopening the case and they expressed their approval of the way the Cheshire Subscribers had acted throughout.

And all the while the indignant and ever-helpful Lord Redesdale continued his correspondence with Rowland about the man he regarded 'as so little like a gentleman'. On August 8th with Sir Bellingham Graham's approval he wrote to Rowland, recommending another stand by the Subscribers:

MY DEAR SIR,

The use of the notice in the paper would be to create some public action on the subject. Of course if the subscribers intend after all to kneel under to Mr M. & to hunt with him this season when he has proved himself ten times more a blackguard than he did last when they refused to hunt with him or allow him to come on their estates, nothing more is to be said. But in my opinion a general rising against him should be got up, & almost universal warning off and for that purpose public agitation is necessary . . .

Both the Duke of Beaufort and Sir Bellingham agreed such action and the continued witholding of the subscription until such a time as M. was forced to obtain a decision from the courts, of which he still seemed to be shy. In a further letter adding extra incitement, he hastened to implore:

Pray bear in mind that all that I have suggested is subject to your better judgement or that of others... – and further that all is given as my <u>private</u> advice only, and that for obvious reasons my name must not be mentioned in the business – the same in regard to the Duke & Sir B.Graham . . .

An expostulation and a gentle retort. Sir Gresley Puleston, Bart., Philip Godsal. Esq., M.H. and Sir W. W. Wynn, Bart., M.F.H.
W.W.: *"I say, Godsal, they tell me your hounds have been hunting my foxes."*
P.G.: *"Well, Watkin, if they have, they tell me your hounds often hunt my hares!"*

The Secretary hastily obtained signatures on individual statements copied to each Subscriber and a month later a printed notice from thirty-three of the Subscribers was circulated to all interested parties and published in the local Press with the full list of signatories. It read

> WE, Subscribers to the Cheshire Hounds, notify to all Persons, who have kindly allowed us to sport over their Lands, that despite the decision of the Stewards of the "Master of Fox-hounds Committee," (by which Captain Mainwaring, as a Member of such Committee, was bound) unanimously confirmed by the General Meeting of that Committee "that Captain Mainwaring is bound as a gentleman," to resign; and despite our unanimous request to Captain Mainwaring to resign the management of our Hounds, and our offer to him, repeatedly and recently made, of indemnity from all pecuniary loss, Captain Mainwaring persists in continuing such Management, and in attempting to hunt the Country. In consequence, therefore, of such conduct on the part of Captain Mainwaring, we hereby declare that we no longer acknowledge him as Manager of our Hounds, nor will we again meet him in the hunting field.

Rowland Warburton had not received unanimous agreement. Johnny Glegg did not sign without first protesting about its wording, which he thought was making a dangerous precedent which could result in freeholders warning hounds off of their own accord in the future.

Fox of Statham, who was to take the chair at Tarporley in 1860, argued that there was a gross want of consistency if he signed the repudiation. "I like to think twice before I act once . . .," he wrote, "I cannot agree with you that I am ever likely to regret my present determination either as a Cheshire man or a Member of Tarporley, but be the consequences what they may I must decline to include my name. . ."

And Wilbraham Tollemache reported to Rowland:

> I know not what you are doing respecting the Hounds, but I had a letter from Lord Combermere in which (among other things) he says " I am over run with Foxes, and if the Cheshire Hounds do not draw my Coverts soon, I must destroy half of them. I wish you would let Warburton know this; I cannot be expected to preserve, if <u>nobody</u> draws my coverts"

However, the letter, 'from thirty-three of the most influential men in Cheshire', received supportive editorial comment in *The Chester Courant*:

> "What is a gentleman without his recreations?" asks the old

play. . . We have therefore noticed with much regret that the fine old English sport of Fox-hunting is suspended in this county... under circumstances of a most unpleasant and painful nature. . . We sincerely hope. . . we may soon have to announce Captain Mainwaring's resignation.

It turned out to be some hope indeed.

Not surprisingly *The Chronicle* rallied to Mainwaring at some length and concluded:

> . . . Here the matter rests; and as the Captain does not choose to be socially tabooed, and pecuniarily mulcted, here it is likely to rest until the expiry of the present season.
>
> Under the peculiar circumstances of the case, we cannot account for the virtuous sensitiveness of our Cheshire purists, "the thirty-three of the most influential..." They seem to us more exacting than Mr Townley Parker was. That gallant gentleman only required a supplemental apology. . . Mr T.Parker refused to conform to the opinion of his own friend and of Colonel Bowles. Are "the thirty-three. . ." justified in taking higher ground than Mr T.Parker? It is very well to give a dog a bad name, and hang him; but in the name of all that's fair do not apply the same rule to the hound's master. . .

On the eve of the 1857/58 Season an influential group of the some twenty landowners, such as Tomkinson, Swetenham, Harper, Lyon, Townshend, Starkey of Wrenbury and Crawfurd Antrobus of Eaton, took the unprecedented step of publishing a letter addressed to the obstinate Mainwaring, publicly warning him off their coverts and lands. This was following a letter he himself had written to *The Chester Chronicle* the week before, announcing the usual Tarporley Week meets and giving his own version of what had happened. He even alluded to the Secretary withholding the subscription due to him since February and brought the whole thing up all over again.

> . . . in consequence of a personal difference between myself and a gentleman residing in the county, not a member of the Hunt, a certain party among the Subscribers... assembling behind closed doors, listened to an *ex parte* statement, and, coming to the conclusion I was no longer a fit person to manage the Cheshire Hounds, required me forthwith to resign . . . blackening my character . . ., *etc., etc.*
>
> I have now finished cub-hunting, and have found promise of ample sport in the ensuing season through which I am fully prepared to hunt . . . If, however, I should be prevented from doing so . . . in consequence of the Subscribers' notice... the fox-hunters of Cheshire will have to attribute the loss of their favourite amusement, and the subscribers the probable ruin of a first-rate pack of Hounds, to the unsportsmanlike conduct of those among them who have prevailed upon the rest to sacrifice their own sport and

that of their neighbours to the dictates of an overbearing and unreasonable combination.

Thus Mainwaring started his third and last season–

Away, away we go
With a tally, tally-ho!
With a tally, tally, tally, tally, tally, tally-ho!

* * *

MEANWHILE LETTERS were still being exchanged between his solicitors from Lincoln's Inn and Hostage and Blake at Northwich.

FRERE GOODFORD & CO.: We beg to remind you. . . This extremely fair offer the Subscribers rejected. . . Capt. Mainwaring feels... the matter... one of a purely domestic nature, with which a knot of Gentlemen associated for the purposes of sport had no right to intermeddle. They had no right to make the relations. . . the means of prosecuting the cause of private enmity, and he considers himself ill-used from the commencement. . . He cannot be expected to enter upon the mere question of money, whilst the reflexions upon his character, *etc., etc.* . . . without prejudice to the Action.

HOSTAGE & BLAKE: It is obviously undesirable that we should point out the incorrectness of several of the statements . . . to the extraordinary intimation which Capt. Mainwaring coveys through you, we answer it is simply ridiculous. We may add that... Boodle's would appear much more amenable to the imputation of having endeavoured to place a stigma on Captain Mainwaring's reputation as a gentleman than the Subscribers to the Cheshire Hounds. . . . conclude without prejudice to all Proceedings.

And so on and so on. In an earlier letter they had pointed out that the Boodle's Resolution

is overwhelmingly powerful with those who recognize the Rules, which are held by Gentlemen, to bind Gentlemen more strongly than Acts of Parliament.

The Cheshire Subscribers and the Committee at Boodle's were not alone in their condemnation of Mainwaring. Back in March the North Hants. Hunt Club had held a meeting, which the Captain and his brother-in-law had attended, and, despite their protestations, a resolution was passed requesting his resignation. It was not until Boxing Day that an indignant Mainwaring poured out another effusion in *Bell's Life* on the subject, eighteen column inches of it, addressed publicly to the Hon. Sec. of the N.H.H.C. He concluded:

I understand that very unfounded assertions have been circulated in order to discredit me, such as that I have been expelled from Boodle's and other clubs. I merely mention this to warn those who feel hostile to me, that they must take care what means they use in indulging their vindictive feelings.

This subject is, in one respect, painful to me, and I am desirous it should be at rest for the sake of others. I do not want to rake up again that unfortunate occurrence to which I have alluded, and which must inevitably form a part of every discussion of the question...

The true, original and only cause for all this annoyance has been set at rest by the reconciliation of the parties principally concerned. The Cheshire Subscribers have seen their error, and have agreed to pay the arrears of their subscription with interest, and the expenses attending the necessary whipping, which, after long forbearance and some inconvenience I was obliged to administer. The Cheshire Hunt never had better sport. We have now a large and respectable field, and it is to be hoped that the Subscribers, when they have swallowed their bite, will not keep their horses to fatten in the stables, and themselves on their sofas, whilst we are enjoying ourselves in the air, hunting their country at their expenses, but will come out like men and join in the laugh against themselves, and have an end of it...

But there was still more copy for the ever patient Editor of *Bell's* to fill his correspondence columns. The Stewards of Boodle's thought it wise to reply to the above diatribe, repudiating what he had written and clarifying the true position. It happened that some verses appeared beneath it, under the heading:

HIGHWAYSIDE.–A CHESHIRE "FIXTURE" WITHOUT A "DIFFICULTY."

Highwayside is one of Cheshire's traditional Tarporley Week meets. but this was different. These were the first three verses:

What a chance for the Cheshire! – warn'd out of the field –
To find that the road such diversion can yield;
That the huntsman can still, with no covers to draw,
Blow his horn at the toll without breaking the law.

'Twixt highways and byeways still ringing the change,
Now from cinder and sand to McAdam they range;
When quite on the pavé, *their speed they restrain,*
And enjoy their jogtrot down a hard Cheshire lane.

Earth-stoppers, whose night occupation is gone,
Now stop the road ruts and rake gravel thereon;
The use of the milestone, now coaching is done,
Is to measure exactly the length of a run.

The full text may be found in Book Two, but this

version even had another verse, which went:

Sometimes, as the saying is, "coming to grief,"
They may follow the hearse, and act mourners in chief;
How apt then, the terms of the hunting field sound,
Either "in at the death," or else "running to ground."

This produced the following rejoinder from A FOX-HUNTER, written to *The Field*:

THE CHESHIRE HOUNDS

SIR, – *Bell's Life in London* . . . published some verses respecting the Cheshire Hounds. . . evidently written by some untruthful individual. I regret not having a copy of these verses; but, as they have been much commented upon, I have no doubt all your readers who are interested in hunting matters will remember them. As they were calculated to give sportsmen in general a wrong idea of the sport in this county, and knowing from personal observation (having hunted in Cheshire this season) that they were false in every particular, I wrote to the paper they appeared in, and contradicted the statements; no notice has been taken of my letter – I conclude because it spoke the truth, and favourably of the management of these hounds. The injustice is manifest of a paper that claims the lead in sporting matters publishing falsehoods about a pack of hounds, and not inserting the refutation. May I ask you, then, to allow this note to appear. . . ? The Cheshire Hounds never have had better sport or killed more foxes; the way the men are mounted, and the blooming condition of the hounds, is perfection; the warns-off have not affected sport in any way; the men have always been with their hounds, and have never been compelled in one single instance to ride roads. These are simply facts I can vouch for, utterly at variance with the statements of the "poet"; so I leave your readers to judge what he is. I am not connected in any way with the county or the master of the hounds; I merely went with them for the sake of sport, and obtained it; and am only induced from a sense of justice and fair play to make these remarks and not allow this mendacious poet to pass uncontradicted. I enclose my card.

Little did he realize that 'the mendacious poet' was none other than the bard of Cheshire sport and country life himself, the overburdened Secretary to the Subscribers, who, for one, had kept his sense of humour to the end.

Months after the season was over Lord Redesdale could not resist a final word about Mainwaring to Rowland:

If I was a Cheshire landowner he should never set foot on my ground again, and as you have paid him, you can now do as you please that way. He has a sort of triumph with the vulgar by going on blackguarding everyone and hunting as

Major the Hon. W.H. Stapleton-Cotton.

before. It w^d. be well that he sh^d. close the season in evident disgrace with all the gentlemen of the county.

It seems strange that Fox Rance never left for posterity his views on Captain Mainwaring, nor even gave The Druid any account of the sport for those two clandestine seasons. Nor does there seem to be much mention of the Cheshire gentleman going out with their neighbour, Sir Watkin, but no doubt a lot of them did. It was in March, 1858 that Wynnstay Hall was destroyed by fire, with many cherished heirlooms and works of art, due to the gale that was blowing at the time. Virtually all that was unimpaired was the £40,000 worth of wine in the cellars. Sir Watkin took his wife abroad for a year while the place was rebuilt and Major Wellington Stapleton-Cotton took on his hounds for a season.*

All that remained was to find a new Manager and who better than the one Rowland called *Le Gros-Veneur* for his song at Tarporley the next Autumn? He announced to the Subscribers at their meeting on March 20th that Lord Grosvenor had consented. (There was only one other applicant, a Mr Henley Greaves from Pontefract, who had kept hounds for ten years – and who was to take the Warwickshire Hounds instead.) A new agreement

---

* Major Wellington Cotton and and his wife were staying at Wynnstay at the time of the fire and lost £2,000 worth of jewellery. Captain Charles Rivers Bulkeley was also there. The Wynnstay Hounds then became a subscription pack for a season and Major Cotton was an extremely successful and popular Master, especially with the tenant farmers. He was well-experienced, for at one time he had kept a pack of harriers, as well being keen to turn out with the otter-hounds every Spring. His first venture with the Cheshire Hounds had been when he was blooded by Will Head, cub-hunting at Ravensmoor where his father had sent him on a pony.

was drawn up, though not before Lord Redesdale had had a look at it. Nothing was being left to chance and the new Manager, highly respected though he was, was going to hunt the country four days a week, 'weather permitting'; and there was a lengthy clause firmly assuring that any possible dispute would be dealt with by reference to Boodle's; so far as any difference of opinion with the Subscribers was concerned, the new Manager wisely added 'or any of them' as a rider in a letter to Warburton. In return he was to receive £1,050 on September 1st and £600 the following March, but this was on the basis that he gave up the following May 1st and not August. His lordship had been quick to point out he 'rather thought the subscription had been £2,200!'

The heir to the Grosvenor empire in those days was not so wealthy as might be thought, and his father tended to be parsimonious with him. Years later he told Regie Corbet he was £1,000 out of pocket, not taking into account his own hunting.

Earl Grosvenor, Manager of the Cheshire Hounds, from a portrait in oils by Sir J.E.Millais.

And Corbet later discovered, from a perusal of White's accounts lent to him by his widow, that the Captain had been spending an average of £2,800 in spite of feeding Indian meal instead of oatmeal.

As well as engaging Edwards, Lord Grosvenor had already written to say he had taken on Thomas Rance at a wage 'of £80 *per ann*: & house and the Second Whip £65 *per ann*: House, firing & candles – which is I suppose correct'. He had taken a lease of Calveley Hall from the Davenport family shortly after his marriage in 1852 and writing from there before moving his horses into the Kennels, he went into detail on the state of the place and its drains and even condemned a wooden bedstead and bedding as 'also quite useless'.

The floors were to be concreted. A letter in October from Captain Heron, whose advice the Master had evidently sought on this subject, describes what had happened previously. It would seem that he had had something to do with the running of the Kennels for he also kept hounds himself. For some years Heron had had his own harriers, which he hunted in Delamere Forest. So here is a possible explanation why Captain Robert Townley-Parker had chosen to address his open letter to him.

But all that was in the past and a letter appeared in *The Field* from GONE AWAY announcing to its readers 'that the matter of "The Cheshire Difficulty" had been arranged with the hounds given up to the worthy new master, Lord Grosvenor; and I assure you much good sport is anticipated, as I understand he intends doing the thing in good style.'

Or as the song went at Tarporley in November:

> 'Tis a maxim by fox-hunters well understood,
> That in horses and hounds there is nothing like blood:
> So the chief who the fame of our kennel maintains
> Should be born with the purest of blood in his veins!
> The man we now place at the head of our Chace
> Can his pedigree trace from Le Gros-Veneur!

The young nobleman lived up to this reputation by having a graceful seat and 'as proof of his determination to be with his pack', noted a scribe in *Baily's Magazine*, 'we witnessed him breasting the Dee in a flood when only four others out of a large field were found to follow him in his Leander trip to Wales'.

In December Cornelius Tongue gave the Cheshire Hounds and Country the full treatment in the Hunting section of *The Field*:

The great popularity and extensive influence of the Earl Grosvenor paves his lordship's way to success as a master of hounds to an extent which few of his contemporaries can hope to enjoy [wrote Cecil, the future Duke, being then aged 33]. Always in the front rank when hounds are running, he appears delighted when they are having sport; though the extremely large fields pretty generally in attendance, frequently pressing upon hounds, must cause him great annoyance, which he seldom expresses, and never in terms of irritation.

Of the country he wrote unctuously:

There are not any large woodlands in Cheshire, but it contains many very splendid gorse coverts and plantations which hold foxes, and they are plentifully preserved. It abounds with parks and mansions, and the aristocracy have from time immemorial been most devoted patrons of fox-hunting; indeed there is no country in England where that feeling can prevail more universally among the higher classes. The land is principally devoted to pasture, though there is much sandy soil; the plough has not made those innovations so frequently complained of in Leicestershire, Warwickshire, Northamptonshire and other grazing districts. . .

Eastward of the river Weaver there are numerous noblemen's and gentlemen's parks, full of pheasants and foxes; and throughout the country the wily animal is preserved.

He went on to give a detailed description of the hounds and their origins, commenting that he had not seen on his rounds a leveller lot than the young entry of fifteen couple, 'a family likeness throughout, greatly enhancing the appearance of the pack'.

Mr Tongue gave a short account of the sport that had been enjoyed that week, during which he had been invited to dine with 'one of Cheshire's most highly respected and worthy country squires'. Not disclosing his name, he went on to describe his inspection of his host's unrivalled collection of terriers, kept in miniature kennels, and how he witnessed 'a huge monster' rat, being 'very quickly despatched by a little bitch only six months old; and although the rat caught her by the cheek, she did not even utter a whimper.' The clue to the Squire's identity is Cecil's mention of the painting by Baraud in the dining room, depicting him and his little pack 'destroying the depredators of the rick-yard'. This would surely have been seventy-one-year-old Domville Poole at Marbury, host all those years ago to Mytton, Nimrod and Sir Harry. The painting is now with his descendant in Australia.

All was not entirely as it should be, however. In February Harry Mainwaring, Junior wrote privately to Rowland, complaining that the country was not being hunted properly and sent a draft showing how it had been done in his father's day. The new Master had

arranged consecutive meets in the same area several times and, for example, had met at Ravensmoor Windmill twice in a fortnight.

"Seeing weekly the wonderfully bad arrangement & system of hunting the Country, so very inconvenient to the Fox-hunting & to the non-Fox-hunting squires of Cheshire; seeing also that the plan of meeting two weeks together in the same country & stopping the earths, so very injurious to sport. . . I wrote out a plan," he began.

The point he was really making was that 'Cheshire woods & coverts, being all small, will only bear to be drawn once in a month'. With the same earths stopped 'week after week', as he put it, the old foxes were driven away. 'The system as adopted this season cannot go on: the whole country will be ruined if it is continued.' He admitted in a later letter that 'Railways have made a difference'.

His father died in 1860 and the new Sir Harry tried again, sending his comments on that season's arrangements, but evidently to no avail, as at the end of the 1861/62 Season he recorded:

Very bad sport this year again – as last year. Country very badly hunted as will be seen by the fixtures. The Withington and Peover country virtually given up.

There had also been complaints about the earth-stopping and at a meeting of the Subscribers at the Kennels 'it was agreed that the old system of employing a man to go the rounds was preferable to the uncertainty of the post.'

But nobody but a Master knows a Master's cares and afterwards, having agreed to continue, the young Hugh Lupus had written to the Hunt Secretary in March, 1859:

I presume the list of fixtures you gave me yesterday for next season is not to be strictly but generally followed. It seems to me that some discretion must be left to the Master in making the fixtures both in suiting as far as possible the convenience of the subscribers both with regards to their arrangements and to the ball weeks, but also with some regard to sport. Bye-days are arranged in the list, but it seems to be of little use either rattling the hills or Forest unless we find foxes scarce in other places which has not proved to be the case this season until lately when we went to the hills. There are some fixtures on the list such as Wrenbury and Wilkesley put on consecutive days which we cannot manage, as the hounds sleep out for those meets, but I conclude the list is for general guidance. . .

I do not quite understand whether the decision arrived at at Tarporley [at the Subscribers' Meeting] to hunt two days in the Nantwich Country is reversed and that, as before, it is decided to hunt there three days? I hope it is for two, otherwise by frost we may be shut out of that country for half the season!

Come September, he wrote:

Edwards thinks well of the young hounds in their work. Somebody is a vulpicide to some extent at & about Minshull and I have a near neighbour with some similar propensities – but generally speaking I think we shall do.

From February onwards the Master had to be in London, busy raising his Westminster Volunteers. He had some comments to make to Rowland in the various letters he wrote requesting him to look after the arrangements:

... if Edwards has the meets at the Kennels on the <u>Sunday</u> he will have them put in all the Papers.
... if when out, you could try and keep Hornby in order (an impossibility) you will confer a very important service upon the hounds!

On his return from town he reported 'a capital run of 45 mins. & fast – no casting required' from Philo through Eaton Banks with a kill at Tilstone Moss and went on:

I asked Edwards whether he would prefer remaining & changing his system of hunting, but he prefers leaving under the circumstances as I anticipated, & leaves this day month, so that I must look out for a good man without delay.
    I have no doubt that this will be satisfactory to the country, tho' I lose in Edwards a very good servant, but he was very often wrong in his casts and certainly his manner & temper in the field are very disagreeable.

He later gave his opinion that 'what we want is a harum scarum sort of fellow like Jem Hills of the Heythrop to gallop his hounds <u>forward</u> – we should have more fun but lose scientific hunting... We never manage to <u>kill</u> our foxes, 10 brace only have fallen this year, not that numbers are a criterion of sport, but we hardly ever run into our foxes.'* As a postscript to another letter he put:

I suppose you heard of one of the hounds caught in a large trap near Cholmondeley on Saturday & two very good hounds poisoned. I have written a strong remonstrance upon these proceedings to Lord Cholmondeley. The

keepers there have long been in the habit of destroying foxes and I hope this crisis may eventuate in a stop being put to their work, if not we cannot take the hounds there again.

The custom of the Cheshire hunt servants wearing a green collar by invitation of the Tarporley Hunt Club was introduced in Lord Grosvenor's second season, which must have pleased Tom Rance. Edwards was replaced by a man called Henry Nason, late of the South and West Wilts.

The Master heard from Wellington Cotton, who was just handed back the reins of office to Sir Watkin. It had been proposed that Shavington, Adderley and Kent's Rough were to be neutral draws for each and for the North Staffordshire as well.

Ld. Kilmorey is such an odd man that it will not do to run the risk of offending him, [wrote Col. Cotton], and I am told he would never hear of allowing the Cheshire Hounds to draw Shavington owing to some quarrel he had years ago when he warned them off. Under these circumstances it is not worth while writing to Watkin upon the subject we discussed at Tarporley. There is no reason however that you should not carry out the arrangement with Corbet and Davenport as regards to Adderley & Kent's Wood. Glad to hear you had such a good run yesterday from Baddiley. There is nothing like rattling coverts!!

Grosvenor concurred it would be imprudent to have 'the impudence to write' and thus incur 'that Lord's displeasure'.

On March 28th, 1861 hounds met at Duddon Heath. After a brisk 15 mins. to Waverton, a fox from Cotton Gorse gave them a 'never-to-be-forgotten' 1 hr. 50 mins. ending at Philo, lineal distance 10 miles, distance run about 16, as reported in *The Field*. Four horses were dead, and not more than twenty riders up at the end.

It was the most brilliant hunting... over the cream of the vale . . . until we came to a brook with posts and wire fencing. I verily believe that this fence of iron wire was put up to prevent the decay of blasphemy. I heard several very improper expressions as the posts were surveyed with so much irony. After going five miles in twenty-five minutes, full cheery, to be pulled up by a confounded invention not so big as your little finger, put in mind of the Irishman who fell from a house. "Did the fall hurt you, Pat?" "No," says Pat, "it wasn't the fall – it was being stopped so sudden that hurt me." However, as there was no use in looking at the wire, we saw hounds through it and we had to divide and find the end . . .

By then Mr Fox was heading for the Peckforton Hills, but changed his mind, hard pressed by the hounds and 'badly accompanied by scarlet runners'.

---

*The revered Jem Hills used to send his whippers-in on ahead to view the hunted fox. It is known as the telegraph system, which resulted in hounds paying little attention to the scent and coursing like greyhounds. Whilst his method may have produced good sport, it was certainly not in accordance with the proper art of venery.

It was impossible to have better sport, better country, better day, or better horses, better men, better hounds or better scent. "How were you pleased?" said I to a friend. "Pleased!" said he, "Pleased!! Pleased!!! Is that the mild way you speak of it? Ah! I can now die a happy man. I'll not do anything for several days, for fear of disturbing the state I am in. Hurrah for fox-hunting!" So say I.– PORT.

First the railways, now the wire.*

*Still distant the day, yet in ages to come,
When the gorse is uprooted, the fox-hound is dumb.*

The time had come for the one-eyed whipper-in to retire. Rance had been with six different huntsmen in eight Masterships in Cheshire since the day, as The Druid put it, Sir Harry met him at Vale Royal and handed him his seals of office thirty-one seasons before. And now his eyesight was failing him. In the course of that time he had his fair share of accidents. He broke the bridge of his nose on a bough, when his horse ran away with him. 'I could not blow it again for weeks,' he minded. 'And then a stub got in my blind eye, and I pulled it out. But when I broke the corner of my rib I was in furious pain all the day. I still never gave up.'

He once told Nimrod he had had 'three ribs broken one side, two on t'other, both collar bones and been scalped.' He recalled a horse called Valentine – 'a dunghill brute' – which lay on him for half-an-hour and when he did get up he kicked him on the head till the skin hung down all over his eyes and face. 'And do you know, Sir, when I gets to Wrexham, I faints from loss of blood!' Talking of his good eye, he mentioned that he felt it bad at feeding time and said:

. . . the hounds and everything looked like a cloud of sulphur. The Manchester doctors have been trying their hands on it; I think they've cleared it a little; fire seemed to come out of it; and something like a bottle screw, a black wavy thing from the eye to the ground. I could hardly see a fox at last; I dare say I missed some of them my last season.

But he was game to the end. One of his red-letter days was March 28th, 1861 when hounds met at Duddon Heath with Stapleford the first draw as usual. A fast 14 mins. to 'Wharton' Gorse was a pipe-opener for the test to follow. Tom then tally ho'd a fox away from Cotton Gorse and hounds raced past Waverton to Saighton, Aldersey and on to Bolesworth. The pace was

tremendous, as this gallant fox sought no refuge in the hills and hounds sped on behind him, skirting Pennsylvania, Peckforton and Beeston Castle. Most of the horses were long since blown, and but a handful of riders saw hounds run their quarry by Tilstone Lodge and Page's Wood and thence to ground in Philo Gorse. A brilliant 1 hr. 40 mins. without check.

Rance's last comment to The Druid had concerned the country:

I beg your pardon, gemmem, there are great changes; men and country; they were all small fields, ditches never cleaned out in that Saighton country; now its like a garden; for two miles round these cops are kept high and narrow, cut sharp as the ridge of your hand to keep the harriers off; they're getting a little flatter, horses get their hind feet on them; there's a deal of bone-dust about this country now; it alters scent; the hounds stop and peck at it, it's a bad fault these bone-dust fields; and there's so much goano used. I beg your pardon, gemmem, I've some earthstopping to do.

After old Tom, sometimes known to his friends as 'Fox', had bestowed on him a mask and some foxes' teeth to make into breast pins, this was the last that H. H. Dixon saw of him, as he 'watched his thin, upright form disappearing through the mist on his midnight errand'.

At the end of the 1861/62 Season a subscription raised £483 for his retirement. Not that he left the hunting scene. So long as he remained alive and hearty he continued to do good service to his 'country' as superintendent-general of earth-stopping.

Lord Grosvenor made up his gratuity to £500 and invested it for him in the Liverpool Docks @ 4¼% in the names of Lord Grosvenor, Henry Brooke and R. Egerton Warburton with the interest to be paid to Tom. Lord Grosvenor was to be repaid the £17 from out of any future subscriptions, but four years later he gave Tom a silver teapot, engraved:

Tom Rance
from
Earl Grosvenor
1866

With a London hall-mark dated 1801 and boxwood handle and finial it was well used by Tom and his family and is on display at the Grosvenor Museum with the crop of his Cheshire Hunt hunting whip, presented by one of his many descendants. He died in 1875 and was buried at Whitegate, his age given as 72.

Meanwhile at Tarporley there had been much discussion how best to celebrate the Club's Centenary 'in a manner worthy of noting the duration of a Society of

* The first wire to line the fences and ditches was of a stout rusty make, ¼ or ⅜ of an inch thick, never seen to-day. It had the merit of being sufficiently visible for a horse to rise at occasionally, if the posts were not too far apart.

'Fox'Rance

Cheshire gentlemen, which had continued to hold its Meetings annually for so long a period'. At the 1861 Meeting:

> The sum of Four Hundred Pounds was voted for the purpose of giving a Ball, to be held at Chester, to providing a Cup value £50 for a race for Farmers' horses, and £50 for prizes to be given to the best young horses bred by farmers for hunting and agricultural purposes.

The Club being full, each Member subscribed £10 and two separate committees were appointed. Thus started the Tarporley Hunt Club Horse Show, which came to be known as 'Tarporley Jumps'. (*See* Appendix F.) An Extraordinary Meeting in February at the Hartford Railway Station Inn, attended by only eight Members, appointed de Tabley, Lascelles, Wilbraham Egerton, Rowland Warburton and old Shakerley with the Lord President Elect as Chairman to make all the arrangements for the Tarporley Hunt Ball. Ten dozen Château Lafitte @ 96/- per doz. had been laid down in 1860, incidentally, (vintage not stated).

Nason left to go to the Warwickshire after two seasons and the Earl brought in Peter Collison from the North Warwickshire. He had contemplated promoting John Jones, the 1st Whipper-in, who had already been huntsman to both the Kilkenny and the Meath before coming to Cheshire in 1861 and who had started his career as 2nd Whipper-in to his father at the Old Berkshire. But his lordship decided against it when he heard he had been seen drunk in Northwich. 'I hope I have frightened Jones into sobriety, & [will] give him another trial.' Jack Snaith was the 2nd Whipper-in.

Collison's first season was the first time that Rowland's twenty-three-year-old son, Piers, kept a diary. He was out at the Blue Cap Inn for the Opening Meet on a chesnut, which had not seen hounds before.

> . . . I spent ½ an hour at the 1st fence with the mare, she gave in after a long fight and jumped the next six fences to the best of her ability... I came home early and went to Tarporley with my father. My Aunt Charlotte Brooke gave me a bed at Bowmere Lodge. I dined at The Swan.

Next morning was wet and muggy and he was out again riding Valentine for the first time – a young horse which 'never refused once, but pulls devilish hard. I think he will tire my father very much when he comes to ride him.'

Also at Ox Heys was PEREGRINUS, staying with a friend for Tarporley Week and who reported the Club's festivities and sport in full to *Baily's Magazine*:

> . . . The field was not so large as I had been led to expect; and among them the Master, Lord Grosvenor, and other members of Tarporley were conspicuous in their collars of green. Collison, who hunts hounds for the first season, looks exactly like the sort of servant that a Master of Fox-hounds would wish to possess – light in the saddle, a good and temperate horseman, quick in getting away to his fox and very keen for sport. His hounds were in fine condition, and seemed as fit for work as himself.

It was a poor scenting day, but the visitor was impressed with what he saw and enjoyed a circuit from Page's Wood through Philo to Oulton Park and to ground and another skurry from Oulton Lowe back to Oulton, whence the quarry escaped by running along the park wall, causing quite a lapse of time before hounds could pick up a cold scent, only to lose him heading for Wettenhall.

Piers again dined at The Swan, where there was a great gathering that night to hear his father read the song he had written for the occasion – *Tarporley Swan-Hopping.*

> *When a Swan takes to singing they say she will die,*
> *But our Tarporley Swan proves that legend a lie;*
> *For a hundred years past she has swung at this door,*
> *May she swing there and sing there a thousand years more!*

Piers Egerton Warburton of Arley

His diary continues:

. . . [He] was much applauded. Old Glegg tried to sing one of my father's old songs, he is very plucky to attempt it, but I can't say much for his voice; his health was afterwards drunk as Father of the hunt. He made a short speech and was much affected by it even to tears.

On the Wednesday PEREGRINUS rode to Cotebrook and noted how keen the farmers were to win the Club's awards for the best pairs of Shire horses and single cart mares, judged with some difficulty by Colonel Cotton and old Captain White. At their discretion the Committee had also spent the allotted money on cups for Dairy Cows, the best Boar and the best Four- or Five-year-old Colts likely to make a Hunter; 'all to be bred and owned by *bona fide* Tenant Farmers residing within the limits of the Cheshire Hunt.' The Hunters' Stakes were won by Mr Shakerley's Witch; and 'a capacious silver bowl, with two goblets and fifty pounds added, was carried off by a well-bred chesnut mare belonging to Mr Kay.'

Kay was 'my father's tenant from Warburton, and a right good man too,' noted Piers. 'After the races I drove

to Hawarden for the Tarporley Centenary Ball and didn't hunt again that week.'

By a happy coincidence it was Hugh Grosvenor's turn to be President for the celebrations.[*] But there had been little business to transact that morning, other than to discuss the arrangements for the ball the next day, so on a lovely sunny morning they had all gone off to the races.

These were the numbers, surprisingly low perhaps, at The Swan that week, according to the landlord's bill to the committee:

	Mon.	Tues.	Wed.	Thurs.	Fri.
Breakfast @ 2/-		10	24	23	4
Luncheon @ 1/-	1	10	24		
Tea @ 2/-	10	24	23	4	
Dinner @ 7/-	10	24	23	4	
Supper @ 1/6d	10	24	23	4	

Mr Hepper also charged 10/- for venison, 2 gns. for 'Fire Hunt R$^{m.}$', 1 gn. for 'Chase to Race course' and, among other sundries, a total of £8 2s. for corkage @ 1/6d. Gunter & Co.'s bill for £18 8s 6d was not on a *per capita* basis and included 5 gns. for their cook.

PEREGRINUS was present along with nearly 300 other guests on the Thursday evening at the old Royal Hotel, Chester.[†] He was much impressed, especially

. . . as regards the decoration of the room. Many of your readers may probably have seen how often such attempts at decoration degenerate into vulgarity. The embellishments usually are limited to "Tally-ho!", a "Success to Fox-hunting!" and to a pair of fox's brushes, sticked and stiffly crossed over the chimney wall.

On entering the ballroom at Chester, the general effect was particularly agreeable to the eye, and though on examination every detail was appropriate . . ., there was yet nothing which could offend the most fastidious taste, or

---

[*] Apart from John Smith-Barry, others to be President during their Managership of the Cheshire Hounds were Regie Corbet, Snr., Puffles Park-Yates, Richard Tomkinson and Pat Moseley.

[†] Once The Golden Talbot, this was the swan-song for this fine Georgian building. Demolition started the following June and the Grosvenor Hotel took its place as part of the Eaton Estate. The Royal had been built by the supporters of John Crewe (2) after he had unsuccessfully challenged the Grosvenors for the Independent cause in the 1784 election and it remained that party's headquarters until Lord Grosvenor, the first Earl's son, bought it. Its assembly room was the scene of a banquet given for Lord Combermere (78) and Lord Hill on their return from the Peninsula. The Grosvenor Hotel provided the catering service for the Club at The Swan from 1981 to 1985, by then the Chester Grosvenor and still the county's most fashionable hotel, where the Cheshire Forest Hunt Club has always held its annual dinner and the Mid-Cheshire Pitt Club meets.

which did not add to the harmony of the colour that pervaded the room. At the extreme end were hung two full-length portraits, one of Mr Smith-Barry and one of Sir Peter Warburton, which had been removed for the occasion from the Tarporley Club-Room. Over each chimney-piece was a large oil-painting representing the badge of the Hunt: a white swan, encircled by the motto, *Quæsitum Meritis*. Other scrolls, both on the walls, and on the orchestra front, were inscribed, in illuminated letters, with quotations from the hunting songs of their poet-laureate, Mr Warburton of Arley, among which I read:

> *May the sport we ensure, many seasons endure,*
> *And the chief of our chase be* Le Gros-Veneur!

In the centre of the orchestra was a circular wreath of gorse flowers, from which projected a fox's head in full relief. The music was supplied by Horabin's quadrille band.

The red coats of the Members helped much to enliven the scene, and I observed that several ladies did honour to the occasion by adopting the Hunt colours for their ball dresses. All from the Lord Lieutenant of the County [the President's father, who, as he had resigned twenty years previously, was presumably not wearing the club uniform] down to the youngest ensign from the barracks, appeared fully to enjoy the evening. The Chancellor of the Exchequer, [Mr W.E.Gladstone, over from Hawarden Castle with his house party, the son-in-law of Sir Stephen Glynne (87)‡]..., seemingly as free from care as the merriest dancer in the room, looked as if he shared in the happiness all round him. Possibly, though no fox-hunter himself, *he may have been calculating with inward satisfaction the amount which a pack of fox-hounds and the number of horses necessarily contribute to the resources of the country*. [My italics. – G.F.] I did not forget to drink "Success to Tarporley Hunt!" in a bumper of champagne, which I found well worthy of the commendations bestowed upon it by my companions in the supper-room.

Mr Gunter was still doing the catering at Tarporley, but for the ball the famous Chester firm of Bollands excelled themselves with an elaborate menu at the Royal Hotel, including four choices of soup, a lavish cold side board, including truffles and lobster, and a mouth-watering display of trifles, gateaux, jellies and ices.§ Dancing began at 9-30 p.m.

In her diary, now kept with those of her mother and father at Inwood in Somerset,‖ Lady Theodora Grosvenor, the youngest of the 2nd Marquess's children, gives a vivid account of the Eaton House Party:

> Rode by Belgrave and Poulton in the afternoon, came in at 4-30. Kept on my riding habit & about 5 o/c we received Lord and Lady de Tabley & the two Miss Warrens & Mr Warren, Lady Egerton of T. & two eldest daughters,

Earl Grosvenor, later 3rd Marquess and 1st Duke of Westminster.

‡ His laconic diary reads: '... Went in evg to the Tarporley Hunt Ball. Saw [*inter alia*] Col W.Patten on the Distress. Back at 12½.' This referred to Wilson Patten (134), long since resigned from the Club and M.P. for N.Lancs. 'Famine fever' had broken out in Preston and there were riots in Blackburn.

§ Mr John Blackburne of Chester, the purveyor of wines to the Club at that time, was given strict regulations by Mr Warburton to prevent the export of bottles from the Supper Room. A man at the door was to be paid 5/- for the night and a penny a piece for the empty bottles and he was to refund a shilling for every bottle that went missing. Twelve dozen champagne to be iced ready for use, two dozen claret to be made into Cup and six bottles of sherry were to be placed on the table along with an initial two dozen champagne. 'The man in charge not to give out any other bottle until he receives back an empty one which will be mark'd.' No champagne or other wine was to be given in the tea room or anywhere except the Supper Room. The wine bill amounted to £73. At that time, incidentally, it was normal for wine merchants to make a charge of 2d for the bottle.

‖ This Victorian mansion next to the Grosvenors' Stalbridge estate near Shaftesbury was a wedding present to Lady Theodora from her mother when she married the Hon. Merthyr Guest, Lord Wimbourne's younger brother and Master of the Blackmore Vale from 1884 to 1900. At one time he kept eighty horses, all greys. Both he and Lady Theodora did much for the promulgation of the Hunt Servants' Benefit Society. _

The Inwood Collection includes a charming painting by Basil Nightingale of Lady Theodora being piloted over a double Dorset bank. Their only child, Elizabeth Augusta Grosvenor Guest, was born in 1879. Miss 'Aura' Guest devoted much of her life to fox-hunting and the Blackmore Vale and was succeeded both at Inwood and in the Mastership by Count Guy de Pelet.

'Failure' & 'Beauty' [*], Mr & Mrs G. Shakerley & 2 daughters, Lady Gertrude Talbot [the Lady Patroness] and her brother Capt. Walter Talbot, Mr & Mrs Warburton & last and best Grosvenor and Constance. Also Mr Robt Bourke & Mr Harris Temple. At 7 we dined and about 9 we all went to the Ball in many carriages. Ma, Pa & self, 2 Miss Shakerleys & Mr Warren in own. It is the Tarporley Hunt Centenary Ball given by invitation from the Committee of whom Grosvenor is President. I danced with Mr Bourke, Mr L[eopold] Cust [of Leasowe Castle] & Mr H. Temple – a country dance, Mr Warren, Mr W. Egerton and Mr Tollemache. . .

Pa and Ma went home in the Brougham before 2 & the others soon after and L[d] Shrewsbury, Gertrude, Mr Warren & myself got home in our 'bus at 3 o/c precisely having enjoyed a very good ball – had supper & retired to bed.

Friday 7. Grosvenor, Capt[n] Talbot & Mr Bourke went hunting, the meet at Saighton. We sat with the ladies in the morning & walked in the garden in the afternoon. Mrs Warburton and some young ladies going one way & Constance & I took Gertrude & Mr Warren & Mr Temple over the garden & then by road to Eccleston & back by the yew tree walk. Then Con. & I sat together in Hugh's room till dressing time. The hunters came in soon after 4 having had a pretty good run. L[d] Shrewsbury 2 falls. In the evening we had conversation and a game of curling.

The next Monday at Shipbrook Bridge Piers rode his young mare with a ticket on his coat – the practice of red

---

* Elizabeth, Lord Egerton of Tatton's eldest daughter, died a spinster in 1890, aged 53, and Alice died in childbirth in 1868, the year after her marriage to Reginald Cholmondeley of Condover Hall, Salop., the descendant of Charles Cholmondeley (66).

ribbons on horses' tails was not yet in general use. When she fell and got away from him for some time, he felt very foolish running across the ploughed land with 'She kicks' on his back. He was out the next day at Tatton, as was Prince Henri of Orléans, the Duc d'Aumale, later to be the Inspector General of the French Army, 'who seemed to enjoy himself'. The deer fouled the scent and the fox was killed near the house and 'broken up and worried in front of the hall door'.

[Wednesday 12 (cont.)]... I lunched at Tatton and rode back to Tabley where I was staying for the ball at Knutsford.

Thursday, 13. The hounds met at Tabley, but the frost was too severe to hunt. Ld. Grosvenor never sent word to Collison so the hounds were kept in the cold till 1 o'clock. I think he ought to have come over or at least have sent [someone] over, but he went out shooting instead.

Friday, 14. Frost gone, rain and mist instead. Waited for Ld. G. till 11 $\frac{1}{4}$ then drew two small coverts in the park at Tabley. Lord G. came just as we were going to the Smoker covert. Everyone felt foolish at having started without the Manager, but it had been given out that he was gone to Wales. I think it a pity we did not find at once and leave him as he came so late, it would have been a lesson to him to come punctually in future. We never found till we got to Arley Wood where there were three foxes on foot. . .

The next month at Oulton:

There was great quantity of ruffians out from L. & M. as usual. What a curse they are to hunting in Cheshire.

And on Boxing Day from Dutton Hall when a fox pointed for Cobbler's Gorse near Belmont:

Meet at The Smoker Inn, Plumley, from an oil painting by George Goodwin Kilburne.

Moses, Cecil de Trafford, Collison, Lord Grosvenor and Augustus de Trafford

It is a curious thing that the old cobbler who looked after the covert died the night before (Xmas) and was lying in the cottage at the time we came there. When the fox left the gorse he went straight through the garden and close past the door of the cottage, a line he had never before taken while the old man was alive.

Lord Richard Grosvenor (197) used occasionally to act as field master in his brother's absence, no easy task with fields often exceeding two hundred. During his brother's last season he was present at the kennels to show round 'B', *The Field's* Special Commissioner, who was impressed by the eight horses kept for the whippers-in. He found them a credit to Waddington, the Stud Groom, who was 'a strenuous advocate for indoor summering, and giving gentle exercise throughout the year'. Cecil de Trafford (187) was another who acted as Grosvenor's deputy in the North. 'He is known to everyone out, is always the first man up with the hounds, knows the country, is liked and is the "right man in the right place", besides which he hunts regularly – all these considerations led me to ask him,' the Master wrote to Rowland the week after Tarporley with the proviso that he wanted Piers to take a hand on his return from America.

In February, 1865 Hugh Grosvenor hinted to Rowland that the next season would most probably be his last. It was as a postscript to a letter suggesting that Cotton covert be given up and asking if he might write to his father's agent 'enclosing its death warrant'. Fortunately nothing came of it. On the subject of a possible successor he took the view that 'there is no one else except a "professional" who could be found to keep the hounds just now'. He wanted Rowland 'to look about quietly', just in case.

Before the next season began, the Hunt Secretary was to get involved in another controversial, if not quite so protracted, correspondence as he had with the Cheshire Difficulty. This time it was 'To divide or not to divide'. In September Lord Grosvenor wrote from Dunrobin Castle:

A strong feeling exists "down South" [he meant South Cheshire] in which I share, that the country is too large to be hunted properly by one pack of Hounds, that it would ensure more regular hunting and more conveniently for everyone in the County by dividing it.

I write therefore to ask you to give me yr. sentiments on the subject. What we should propose would be to bring the matter before the Tarporley public for discussion at the next meeting – we might then appoint a Committee of two or three of each side of the County to draw up a report to be submitted as soon as possible to a meeting of landowners to be held at some central place.

I take it for granted that on consideration it will be found that some such change is desirable. There will remain the question of how the country should be divided, whether into two divisions of East and West divided by the line of the Weaver which could necessitate two new Kennels & would be the most <u>complete</u> arrangement probably, giving 3 days hunting a week on each side – or by the line (more or less) of the Chester & Crewe Railway keeping the Kennels where they are for a 4 days a week country & making a <u>two</u> days a week country in the South with a new Kennels in some central place.

There will be the question (all important) of funds which I understand there will be no difficulty in raising on <u>our</u> side, on yours there is no fear of any deficiency. I do not think I can continue the management as now constituted after this next season as I have difficulty in getting to the North side.

There will I think be no difficulty in finding <u>masters</u> for either side. A line will oblige me on these points.

Rowland was vehemently opposed:

My Dear Grosvenor,
I had heard rumours of your proposal and am sorry to find them confirmed by your letter of yesterday. I am sorry because I do not admit the reason you give for the change. The country has never hitherto been found too large for a pack hunting 4 days a week. Both in White's and Sir Harry Mainwaring's time more country (particularly by the latter) was satisfactorily hunted than we now attempt.

The idea of moving our Kennels and making the Weaver a division is I should say quite impracticable. The second plan, that of taking sufficient country for a 2 days a week pack, is not so objectionable, though for that I see no necessity. Should that, however, be the general opinion I think it should be done on the understanding that the portion of country when no longer required should be returned to the old Cheshire County Pack. I do not think the arrangement would be an improvement. I cannot give you in a letter the many objections I feel to the scheme. Not only would it be a fatal blow to the County Pack which has so long been a bond of union but I feel that so far from promoting sport, it will be a very great injury to it.

He then convened a Subscribers' Meeting and Lord Egerton of Tatton was the first to reply, saying he would come to talk the matter over beforehand. He felt, like Rowland, that both the Hunt and the Country would be destroyed. Geoffrey Shakerley wrote, anxious for the Secretary to canvas John Tollemache's support: 'I think it would be wise to ask him not to pledge himself in any way as his property is of such consequence to us and I

Lord Grosvenor.

have little doubt he will be a friend and [on] that side of the country it is very desirable to have friends.'

There was a prompt answer from Helmingham:

. . . My fox-hunting days are over and I am not even a subscriber to the hounds, therefore, I feel I have no right to express an opinion or a wish . . . & all I can say is that as long as I live I shall be a staunch preserver of foxes. I can quite understand you, Tatton Egerton & others being opposed to a change. At one time I know that Sir W. Wynn wished the Peckforton Hills to be considered as neutral ground for himself and the Cheshire Gentry, but I felt a delicacy in naming this to any of the Subscribers.

The idea of division was not entirely new and 'young' Sir Harry jotted down 'some suggestions that have been made at various times', briefly:

1. That the Country should be kept as it is with hounds meeting five days a week and £500 added to the subscription. (He gave a sequence for the arrangement of meets.)
2. That the Country be divided into two districts, North and South, the River Weaver from Nantwich to Weston Point being the boundary; with two Masters, kennels to be built near Knutsford and another near Tarporley, each pack to hunt three times a week.
3. 'The Cheshire' to give up <u>all</u> the country on the South and West of the Turnpike road from Nantwich to Chester to Sir Watkin or some other Pack.
4. The Cheshire to give up all the country on the East and North of the Turnpike road from Brereton Green thro' Knutsford to Warrington, (to be abandoned).

He hoped that No.1 would be carried. It was the only way for the country to be fully and fairly and regularly hunted. He thought No.2 would receive strong support, despite the fact it would break up the country altogether and that, in his opinion, it would be next to an impossibility to build two Kennels. No.3 was foolish and No.4 a non-starter.

Lord Grosvenor was at pains to write again at length on the eve of the Meeting:

> I hope you will understand that in bringing forward the question of a division... I do so in no spirit of <u>hostility</u> to the North, but solely on the general ground of greater convenience to the public and more especially to the men of the South who are blessed with a good country <u>not</u> in their opinion sufficiently hunted even by the present Master who lives at Calveley and perhaps has some little bias in their direction. <u>What</u> they would feel with a more central or Northern Master is impossible to say!
>
> ... Down here we say we have money to support a second pack and I conclude that you in the North, so rich & rich millionaires!, will find no difficulty...

After outlining various possibilities he added that he had no wish 'to fire the first gun of secession to take Fort Sumter by a *coup de-main*!' He concluded by saying how very sorry he was to hear of Sir Richard Brooke's illness. Rowland's father-in-law died shortly afterwards. Rowland replied:

> I read your letters to the meeting yesterday. Ld. Egerton was in the Chair. There were present some of our main supporters and I had received from others, who were unable to attend, their opinions on the proposed division... The matter was fully discussed and I was myself somewhat astonished at the unanimity that prevailed. All without a single exception were against any change.

A committee of four was appointed "to talk the matter over with Lord Grosvenor in the hope that he may reconsider his determination". It was composed entirely of Green Collars, so Warburton looked forward to meeting him at Tarporley for the further discussion. General Yorke Scarlett was to have presided, but missed the meeting as he had just taken up duty at Aldershot.

The Cheshire Hunt Servants, 1866/67, l. to r. Jack Snaith, 2nd Whipper In, Huntsman's 2nd Horseman, Peter Collison, Huntsman, John Jones, 1st Whipper In. From a photograph formerly in the possession of Sir P.H.B.Grey-Egerton, Bt.

In any case hunting matters were seldom put down in the Club's record book and in the event the idea was dropped and Grosvenor wrote that, after all, he was willing to take the hounds for one more season, though still expressing a hope one day to hunt the South for a few seasons without a subscription.

In December a letter came from Dorfold:

> I did not know that my trumpet had given an uncertain sound. I have always advocated the *quieta non movere*, [wrote Wilbraham Tollemache]. The present system has prospered for above a 100 years and a division of the Country would, I think, be fatal. I have told Lords Grosvenor and Combermere [the Field-Marshal had died that year], my brother and many others, my views in the matter. I hope the subject is not to be revived. I had fancied it had been let at rest.

It was Farmer Dobbin who really had the last say, as may be read in *Hunting Songs:*

> *As to haulving the Hunt betwixt owd pack and new,*
> *Oi'd as soon think o'cutting moi missus in two;*
> *To our Queen and our Country let aw on us stick,*
> *To th'oud Pack, to th'oud Kennel, and four days a wik.*

Lord Grosvenor's last season in office ended on a sad note with the Cheshire countryside smitten with the cattle plague. Hunting was stopped in February, a month after the outbreak. Urgent meetings had been held by the Subscribers and there had been a numerously attended meeting of farmers at the board of guardians of the Nantwich Union, where the disease had struck severely. The unanimous opinion of the board at that stage was that hunting should not be stopped and in a letter to *The Chester Courant* the Master stated he had received but one letter from a farmer objecting to hounds crossing his land.

The Cattle Plague was taking its grim toll in January and the Master was most anxious to do the right thing by the farmers. The Combermere estate was one of the first to be hit. A meeting was called. Sir Harry Mainwaring took the view that with the cattle all up, there was no likelihood of hounds spreading the disease and only the odd stray hound ever went through a farmyard. Some farmers thought farm dogs 'a deal more likely to spread it than hounds.' Anxiety was also expressed about the puppies at walk who at the beginning of Spring had a tendency to go off hunting together.

Hugh Grosvenor could not attend the meeting he had called as he had an engagement with the Prince and Princess of Wales at Lilleshall, Staffs. He sent the one letter he had received objecting to hounds on his land; it was from a Mr Robert Parkinson of Dutton Lodge.* He mentioned that Sir Watkin 'expected he would be obliged to stop hunting shortly' and that the N. Staffordshire 'have been hunting occasionally in certain districts, without advertising!, but intend to resume operations on the 1st February!'

A month later they stopped hunting. 'It is not so much a risk of infection as a feeling of dislike to be riding over the farms of those whose welfare in the world in many cases is seriously compromised,' wrote the Master to the Secretary. But as Piers put it in his diary:

> The farmers as a body do not wish the hounds stopped at all, but there is so much distress in the county and men like that disgusting radical John Bright have made such a talk about the hounds carrying infection that it is better to stop and not give occasion to the enemies of fox-hunting to blaspheme.
>
> I have had 26 days hunting and have not been stopped by frost once,

As it happened the last day was described as 'glorious' in *The Field.* 'The meet was at Belmont, the seat of Squire Leigh, a strict preserver of foxes. Unfortunately a vixen (heavy with cub) was chopped in the covert close to the hall. Trotted off to Arley...' The main sport of the day was provided by a fox found in Cobbler's. He saved his brush after 1 hr. 20 mins.

But what, understandably, was little known at the time was an outbreak of rabies among the young entry. It was ascribed to one puppy in from walk. Six and a half couple were put down, but fortunately they were isolated from the working hounds.

On March 1st Rowland received a letter from Adderley. Mr H. Reginald Corbet confirmed he was willing to be Master of the Cheshire Hounds. When he had heard from his father-in-law, Sir Philip Grey-Egerton who happened to be Chairman, that his name had been favourably suggested, he had lost no time in writing to Grosvenor, who in turn had written back:

> ... I was surprised at your proposal as it had never occurred to me for a moment... I write at once to say that as far as I am concerned, I could not wish to see the management in better hands ...

The Vote of Thanks to Earl Grosvenor must surely serve as an exemplary model:

---

* He also enclosed, in his own hand, a copy of the lengthy letter he had sent to the local paper.

That the Subscribers beg to express to Lord Grosvenor their very great regret on hearing that he intends to resign the management of their hounds.

Aware of the many demands upon his time, they are the more grateful to him for having in compliance with the unanimous wish of the County continued to retain the Mastership at so much personal inconvenience.

Looking back with much pleasure to the sport he has shown they are still more impressed by the recollection of the kindness and urbanity that has endeared him to all.

It is very gratifying to them to feel assured that they will still have the pleasure of meeting him in the hunting field and they most cordially hope that he may long continue to share with them the sport of the old Pack of which for the last eight years he has been so popular a Manager.

Hugh replied from the House of Commons:

I feel sure that no Master of Hounds ever had an easier berth or a nearer approach to a bed of roses if there is such a thing in this "vale of grief" than myself.

But that was by no means the end of his hunting. He rode right up to his death and was often out with the local packs when well into his seventies and used to take the family out cub-hunting and later to the meets. He adored being with his young children and grandchildren, played 'Fox and Hounds' with them all over the Eaton gardens and took them for picnics to Beeston Castle and to play games in the gorse and heather round Halkyn Castle. He would take them and their friends for afternoon rides in the Park. Then, without warning he would give a loud 'View-halloa' and jump a low fence and they would all go charging helter-skelter after him, little Bend Or among them.

YE PROGRESS OF DON QUICKTROT & SUCH A PANTER
A DRAWING BY PIERS EGERTON WARBURTON FOUND IN THE
TARPORLEY HUNT CLUB PAPERS

'A Corbet To Lead Us'

WHEN OLD LORD KILMOREY DIED a few years after the Shavington Day, the hall and estate fell into the hands of his son, 'Black Jack', the 'Wicked' 2nd Earl, who himself was to live to the age of 92. But he had few friends in either Cheshire or Shropshire and mainly consorted with his butler. The glories of the Needham connection with Shavington were now almost at an end.

When he was there, he liked to exchange lands and properties with his neighbours, Lord Combermere and Sir Corbet Corbet included, as often as not over the dinner table. Before Jack Kilmorey left for good in 1839 he caused to be built the great wall round the park, some seven miles in length. His purpose was to keep out fox-hunters and the Corbets in particular, but unfortunately the builders started the wrong way and by the time they got back to the Adderley boundary the wall became lower and lower owing to a lack of funds until it petered out altogether. Lord Kilmorey departed to London for a life of debauchery in his 'palace' at Isleworth. Shavington Hall was abandoned, to be rat-infested for almost half-a-century.

The 3rd Earl, Black Jack's grandson, sold Shavington in 1885 to Arthur Heywood-Lonsdale, whose family remain in possession, though the Hall itself was demolished in 1958. A biography of the latter in *Baily's Magazine* mentions the 2nd Earl's desire 'to shut out forever fox-hunters from his domains' and goes on to state that Shavington 'by the irony of fate, became the property of an M.F.H. [N.Shropshire, 1883/97*], and one of the staunchest preservers of foxes.' When Heywood-Lonsdale took over as new squire, he already

knew that he was to assume the Kilmoreys' part in a centuries old feud with the Corbets of neighbouring Adderley, so rife were the rumours of these ancient differences which came to his ears.

The Corbets had once claimed a heriot on the alienation of Shavington, which was supposed to have been held of the manor of Adderley by an eighth part of a knight's service and twelve shillings and sixpence rent, though neither side really knew the details, so remote in time had it first cropped up. The case went before the Court of Wards and Liveries in 1609, with evidence produced from the time of Edward III. Then there was the matter of the road from Shavington to Adderley and the question of who was to keep it in repair. Another row concerned the best hunter of a former Viscount, who alleged it had been taken by the Corbet of the day who then got the crier of Market Drayton to proclaim its loss and announce a reward for the discovery of the perpetrator of the theft.

They were ever in dispute, even with the 11th Viscount and Sir Corbet Corbet of Adderley each being married to sisters of Lord Combermere. Both families are buried in the same churchyard at Adderley, where there is a Kilmorey chapel, yet another cause for animosity. The dispute over this came before the Court of Arches in 1630. Three years later, just after the 2nd Lord Kilmorey had won his appeal against their decision, he had to petition the Earl Marshal after Sir John Corbet had caused an Irish footboy to be buried in the chapel only four feet from where the late Viscount was laid to rest. Corbet had thought it appropriate since the widow was Irish; but the remains of Darby Maghkillary were duly removed from the chancel. Even in recent times, the head of the Corbet family, who had long since demolished Adderley and sold the estate, refused to bury the hatchet when the reigning Needham

---

* In 1920 this pack was taken on by Brigadier-General Hugh Cholmondeley (252), then aged 68. He married for the second time in 1931 and when his new wife gave birth to their daughter the following year, their combined age was 120. Mrs Violet Cholmondeley died aged 100 in 1993.

had the misfortune to be a little late at the church for a ceremony to reopen the chapel.

But Heywood-Lonsdale had also in his day un-wittingly fallen foul of Mr H.Reginald Corbet, Squire of Adderley and in his twentieth season as Manager of the Cheshire Hounds, when the new owner of Shavington arrived. Not long afterwards a couple of puppies had been sent out to walk with his tenant at Castle Hill Farm near the Shavington estate and had been found dead. Corbet came storming round and accused Heywood-Lonsdale's keepers, but he could not deal with the matter there and then as he was just off to dine at Tarporley and would be back in a week's time.

Whereupon Arthur Lonsdale had the corpses exhumed and skinned and got veterinary evidence that there were no pellet holes in the hides and that the hounds had in fact died from distemper. On his return Regie was furious and remonstrated with his new neighbour for desecrating his hounds' grave. He nevertheless then had their remains rendered down and was able to produce a quantity of lead shot. This they may or may not have acquired by consuming dead pheasants or rabbits, but he would have none of it and so the feud continued.

* * *

THE MOMENT HE WAS APPOINTED Manager at the age of 34, Mr Corbet undertook to hunt the country five days a week. His own estate was over the Shropshire border in North Staffordshire country, but throughout his managership it was on loan to the Cheshire. In due course he took Dale Ford as a hunting box to be near the Kennels, but for the time being he rented Sandiford Lodge, close by the racecourse at Cotebrook, previously occupied by a horse dealer called Murray. The rest of the year he and his wife returned to Adderley, where his father was still residing. In the summer he liked to go over to judge at the Dublin Horse Show.

Rowland Warburton, for one, had expressed grave doubts about his desire to hunt five days a week.

If the majority of the Foxes departing this life do so by the mouths of hounds and not by the hands of velveteen slaves, I think you would soon see the advantage of the fifth day. A thoroughly hunted country is without doubt always better preserved than a partially hunted one... Peter [Collison] told me a while back that he should like to do 6 days a week. I am convinced he could do it well, a man who is so much accustomed to be on horseback never feels tired, how many men are there hunting regularly their six days a week? In

my own case no distance on horseback tires me and the more hunting I get the keener I get . . .

came the reply and Corbet added in another letter:

Whilst on the subject of a fifth day yesterday, I quite forgot to mention that the best sport I ever saw in Cheshire was the year Arthur Mainwaring was warned off a very large portion of the country. He nevertheless continued to hunt 4 days a week and, as I said before, had wonderful sport.

His appointment, however, had not had unanimous backing. Despite his impeccable fox-hunting ante-cedents,* he was not after all strictly a Cheshire man, as those hitherto. The Senior ex-Manager did not think 'Corbet a good man for the hounds':

. . . and I feel confident it is part of the game that was played last Tarporley Meeting to get Liverpool and Manchester men subscribers to which I, like you, strongly object and

Corbet, aged thirty.

hope never to see. . . [†] I think Grosvenor has no right to be in such a hurry. . . I have no doubt we can get another person to take them on and why not your son?? I think we could not have a better and he will be on the right side of the county. I do not for many reasons like the idea of Reginald Corbet but when I see you I will say more.

> Believe me Dear Warburton,
> ever truly yours
> GEOFFREY J. SHAKERLEY

But the Manager elect had already given his assurance that

> . . . no one is more alive to the importance of keeping as select as possible the number of Subscribers to the Hunt – it is also far from my wish to endeavour to alter the old rules in any way.

Lord Egerton of Tatton had also had misgivings; and several Subscribers, including Roylance Court and Lord

Delamere, were reducing or discontinuing their payments owing to the Cattle Plague.

According to Piers, Corbet did not get off to a very good start, despite being 'very keen to do the thing well'.

> This has been the worst season I have seen. There was much frost and snow and a total absence of scent the whole year. Corbett [*sic*] has done the management very well but now wants more money. He gets £2,100 but he wants another £300. I think he ought to have counted his cost before doing everything so extravagantly.

Piers had started the season by winning both the Tarporley Hunt Stakes on his chesnut mare, Firefly, and the Hunter Stakes with Valentine. His father had won the former three times in succession, as well as once dead-heating with Henry France.

Harry Rawson, who hunted with the Cheshire for many years and lived at Sandiway Cottage, Hartford,‡ had some better sport and was more positive about the scent, but noted only four good days, none before Christmas. From Twemlows there was

> not a fox in any covert of w^h France has the shooting. A slow hunting run from Rudheath and thence home in a bad temper.

However Rawson did mention some incidents, one concerning a poor fellow who disappeared in a mud-hole crossing Whitley Brook and was ridden over by several men who did not know he was there. From the Fox & Barrel 'Julius Behrens rather distinguished himself':

> Whilst riding quietly at a fence [wrote Rawson] heard "Hey! hey!" shouted in frantic tones. On looking round saw Julius coming at the rate of 500 miles an hour. Pulled on one side to let him pass. Pass he did, but directly the horse reached the obstacle he stopped short & landed its rider head foremost into a bramble bush to the infinite amusement of a damsel who witnessed the performance.

He had 86 days with five horses, taking only eleven tosses. His resumé of the four good runs was:

> Marbury to Barnton & thence across the river to Hartford Grange where the fox was killed.
> A fast five and twenty minutes – Cotton to near Tarvin, where the fox got to ground, a ring.
> Cogshull to High Leigh, three quarters of an hour. Peckforton Hills to Saighton Gorse – fox to ground. A fast 40 mins. As far as Tattenhall the hounds had the run to themselves.

The day before a meet at Poole on March 1st Francis Elcocke Massey (163), aged 46, had married Mr

---

* In just the same way that traditionally Sir Harry Mainwaring's ancestor was Ranulphus, a companion in arms of William the Conqueror, and as the Grosvenor family descends from his chief huntsman in Normandy, so Regie Corbet's Norman forbear was a 'cunning marksman against hart or doe'. His valour at Acre was rewarded by Richard Cœur de Lion with the privilege of bearing ravens on his shield. One Peter Corbet was given letters patent by Edward I to take wolves in the Royal Forests, not to mention the close family connection with Thomas Boothby, recognized as the founder and first Master of the Quorn, 1698-1753, until Meynell took over.

Not only that, at Harrow and Magdalen, Oxford, he had had his own pack of beagles, which very quickly developed into harriers. He ran them for four or five seasons, giving amusement to his family and friends and gaining himself valuable experience as a huntsman. He had in addition been a student of Lord Macclesfield with the South Oxfordshire. Jem Hills was another from whom he had gained knowledge of the noble science.

† For one, Friedrich Engels was still enjoying the sport. Receipts for his £10 subscriptions to the Cheshire Hunt Covert Fund for 1867/68 and 1868/69 and some Meet Cards are deposited in the International Institute of Social History at Amsterdam. He left Manchester in 1869.

‡ The second son of his father, who came from Lancashire and fought at Corunna. A second son, Harry Rawson died without issue in 1888. His calf-bound manuscript hunting journals in three volumes, from 1866 to April 1888, passed into the possession of his great nephew, the Hon. Simon Warrender, who emigrated to Australia and whose great grandfather was a brother of Lady Haddington, the heiress of the Arderne Estate. Volumes I & III were found on a bookstall at Peterborough. It is a mystery as to how they got there, for Volume II is still in Mr Warrender's possession. The author is grateful to the Hon. Mrs Simon Warrender for arranging for it to be copied for him and to John Boddington (350) for his being able to borrow the other two.

There is scant mention of the Tarporley Hunt Club throughout their pages, a clear indication that the Club had little bearing on the Cheshire Hunt, other than by its individual Members as Subscribers and officials. It must be noted, however, that the Club occasionally donated substantial sums in these decades towards repairs and improvements which were carried out from time to time at the Kennels.

Harry Rawson sees Frank Massey in trouble.

Harry Rawson in trouble himself.

Hornby's daughter and it seems the celebrations were still in full swing.

> There was a g^t crowd out. The row & confusion caused by the foot people were indescribable. They ran one fox to ground themselves without the least assistance from the hounds.
> To get rid of them Corbet trotted off to Hurleston.

Corbet's Puppy Show that summer was a great success, as later described in detail in *The Field*, with silver cups for the winners, a silver tea pot for the best bitch and silk dresses for the farmers' wives who walked the runners-up. *Leather Leggings* then reported on the cub-hunting, which began at Philo on August 26th. Hounds migrated from the Forest for a fortnight at Adderley. They found eleven litters at Combermere and killed 8½ brace there. Much credit went to Goring, his lordship's keeper, for after hounds had been through the coverts one morning, 112 head of game were shot by Lord C. with a small party in the afternoon. But again poor scenting conditions prevailed at the beginning of the 1867/68 Season.

During the second week, hounds were at Arley and Piers wrote:

> . . . A party in the house for the Knutsford Ball§]. . . Corbet is a great glutton for blood; he digs out too many to please me.

The Master's great maxim about foxes was: 'The more

you kill, the more you have.' However, in a letter to Piers's father, confirming arrangements for cub-hunting at Arley, Corbet had written:

> I promise not to be very blood thirsty but to be satisfied with a brace of cubs.

Like all good masters of fox-hounds he believed his hounds should always be rewarded. Many years later, in 1896, hounds ran a fox into the canal near Calveley and killed him in the water. He sank, but was got out with a drag-hook and eaten.

Rawson noted that during 35 mins. from Marbury in the North in the cub-hunting season, 'Corbet got an ugly fall at wire,' but he was even more critical about the Master's methods. Hounds met at the Abbey Arms on Oct.13th: 'A d–d stupid day – nothing whatever to do.' Then followed four days at Peckforton the week before the Opening Meet:

> Out all four days. One run in the period. A fox w^h took to the open went to Cholmondeley & was there lost. Five others were dug out & cruelly done to death. The murder was called driving foxes into the Vale! Perhaps the vale of death was meant by the facetious authorities.

In Tarporley Week: 'Corbet sold the crowd who were all round Stapleford by trotting off to a willow bed near Tarvin. We found at once and had a 12 mins. run up to The Willingtons.' (P.E.W.) H.R. continues:

> [Thence] over Primrose Hill, by the Abbey Arms & across Leather's Farm [close to what became Delamere Golf Course] to Hunt's Hill . . . to ground. It was dug out & done to death much to the disgust of nine people out of ten. Time 1¼ hrs. . . . The day ended in the forest.

Jones, the whipper-in, had been hunting hounds

§ It was at just such a ball, attended by Reginald Corbet, that the wife of a member of the Covert Fund, recently arrived in the 'county', made her presence known. Right over her ample bosom, glittering under the chandeliers, was a diamond necklace of a fox with a pack of hounds in full cry. 'What do you think of that?' someone asked the Master. 'By Jove!', replied Regie, 'they have to hunt across a very hilly country.'

Frank Behrens of Worleston Grange. 'I am forty, I look sixty and I feel a hundred!'

instead of Corbet some days, as the Master had hurt his knee.

Piers also mentions that at Worleston: 'The Jews had a great breakfast as usual.' 'Sumptious' was the word Harry used. The host was the ever popular Mr Frank Behrens (alias 'The Infant') of Worleston Grange, who once said of himself: 'I am forty, I look sixty and I feel a hundred'. He was hacking home at the time, drenched and perished with cold. The central heating in his house was so efficient that it was advisable to discard what items of clothing one could when dining there.

His newly-arrived neighbour at The Rookery, Baron William von Schröder (224), also renowned for his hospitality, was always immaculately turned out with a bunch of violets in his buttonhole. Although his father was the founder of the family merchant banking business, he concentrated far more on his sport than running the Liverpool branch. He often invited distinguished soldier friends to stay for the hunting. His son Willie was a 9th Lancer and came out regularly. The Baron liked lightweight horses and, like Behrens, was adept as a coachman. Behrens hunted five or six days a week and used to drive to the meets in a broughham, whatever the weather, and had it put up somewhere handy to drive back in.

There was a large stud of hunters at Worleston Cottage and he usually found a mount for visiting aristocracy. Behrens himself was not at all a thruster, though, and did not trouble the fences much. He employed a first class rough-rider called Downes. His brother Horatio, known as 'Moses', and he used to be denizens of Leicestershire and were great admirers of Skittles. Their father had been a successful Manchester industrialist. At Melton they secretly kept Ms Walters' chesnut hack for her during the winter, having it exercised only at night, not wishing their father to

discover the liason. One day she was following Horatio when he fell in a brook. She blew him a kiss as she sailed over both man and water and called: 'Moses in the bulrushes, I see.'

The day after the Worleston meet was from Tattenhall. 'Billy Baldwin charged the Gowie twice & went overhead both times' but Rawson noted 'that P. Warburton and Arthur Barry both finished in gallant style.'

[P.E.W.:] Sat.Mar.7th MICKLEDALE. Lord Shrewsbury's Gorse blank. A vixen went away from Manley, the hounds close on her. I was close and certain she was a vixen. I told Jones but he assured me it was "as fine a dog fox as ever he saw in his life". Lying butcher – those men would run their grandmothers, I believe. After 1 hr.'s good run through Ashton Hayes the poor little vixen was killed at Kelsall with 3 cubs in her. They will be in want of foxes next year if they do much of this work.

and then, surprisingly:

Cecil de Trafford tells me he has been trying to get Sir H. Mainwaring [the 2nd Bart.] to get out some foxes on his side of the country, but I fear it is no use, he does not care for hunting the least.

It never was, or will be, an easy task for a Master to give total satisfaction to the subscribers. Despite such criticism, plenty of sport was shown that season, during which hounds had been stopped by frost 14 times and there were 6 blank days and a total of 59½ brace of foxes accounted for.

In October, 1868 Corbet wrote to Warburton about his finances:

. . . I feel quite sure I must be greatly out of pocket by the hounds, and next year I shall have to give you a Jorrocks hunt, hounds fed on <u>Indian meal Brown paper</u> top boots &c, that is to say if I can go on at all, I am not joking. I am glad to say I find a very good show of foxes throughout.

Moses.

'A very melancholy couple,' Corbet and Collison. They had just had their fox safe in a garden, when Jack Snaith left the door open and he escaped.

To give him his due he always gave his servants two coats a year. Corbet used to sell his horses at a profit annually, which helped, but in November he had been into it carefully and felt he would be compelled to resign at the end of the season. 'I am quite aware that a <u>Handley Cross Hunt</u> may be carried out at a considerably reduced rate, but I could not undertake that kind of thing.' However all was well when the Subscribers decided to increase his subscription to £2,500 and he wrote, whilst staying at Oulton over Christmas, to acknowledge the good news.* There had also been some grumbling about Collison's horses being sold. His horses fetched an average of £128 that season, £600 the highest bid.

I may as well add, (concluded Corbet after giving his explanation) Jones told me that if <u>he was a gentleman</u> with £10,000 *per an.* he would not wish for a better stud and I have always given the huntsman his choice . . . all warranted <u>made</u> hunters before I bought them.

It was a highly successful ploy to have an annual or bi-annual sale, and one followed by many other Masters of Hounds.

Hunting a lot at this time before she got married and became 'Queen' of the Blackmore Vale country, was Lord Grosvenor's youngest sister, Lady Theodora. She was very often out with her brother Dick, still a bachelor and back from his adventures abroad.

In her diary of 1869 she described what happened from Tattenhall Station with her groom, Frank, to pilot her:

. . . at the first fence a man & his horse rolled over just in front of me, so I had to pull Pursuit in, & she jumped a little short with her hind legs in, but got up again cleverly – this lost a little time, but now soon got forward again & then began a most delightful succession of fences, gallops, hedges, ditches of every kind, Pursuit going like a bird, clean over anything. I was close after Rich^d. all the time, & we went over one rattling place, a laid down fence and big ditch with a lane & up a place out again, & on! on! on! it was too delicious! From Tattenhall to Hargrave out of the lane & over lots of fences to Duddon Heath & on to Stapleford. Here was a slight check but Collison soon got them on the scent again and we went away again & faster now than before. I got well forward here and astonished Dick by keeping well with him & when we got to Ashwoods I was in

---

* 'I hope your eyesight is well,' enquires Corbet at this time. Six years later Rowland contracted the glaucoma which led to his tragic total blindness.

the first flight & not very many up either. Here he went to ground, after a most <u>capital</u> hunting run of about 50 mins. with which everybody was delighted. A heavy shower came on then.

. . . we went on to draw Clotton Hoofied along a <u>very</u> dirty lane! and over a respectable fence or two, which puzzled that noisy "Tom" Aldersey considerably. Drew Clotton blank & went on over another field or two and a good fence as a finale to Huxley gorse when I settled to go home if they ran <u>from</u> Eaton, which they did, and turned homewards having had the most <u>delicious</u> ride possible . . .

There was not a single blank day in 1868/69, according to Rawson who was out 109 times, only 19 of them cub-hunting. It was Collison's last. That season he had a bad fall, which the Laureate set to verse; but the real reason for seeking new pastures in Yorkshire[*] he gave in a letter to Mr Warburton acknowledging a cheque for disbursements:

. . . I am sorry to leave the Cheshire Gentlemen & the Country. But I really could not put up with Mr Corbet. He would not leave me alone in the Hunting Field.

Ever since Corbet had his own harriers, it was his ambition to carry the horn again himself. And in the course of time he was to gain the reputation of being the Premier Amateur Huntsman of England.

There was alternative sport to be had at this time. Rawson recounts the days he was out with 'The Harriers' but gives no indication whose they were, nor were the meets advertised. However, recently home at Ince from his service with the Royals was Captain Edmund Park Yates, a thirty-four-year-old parson's son, still a bachelor. He had decided to sell out soon after inheriting the Ince estate from his mother. (His father was the Rev. Wm. Park who married Elizabeth Jane, the heiress of the Ince Estate, which lies in the angle between the Mersey and

Seen at Tatton Park, February, 1869.

the Gowy. The Commanding Officer of the Royals had been an enthustiastic fox-hunter and the District Commander was one of those who rightly and fervently believed in the hunting field as a school for soldiering. As a result young Park Yates had been able to enjoy many a day with the Pytchley and Atherstone, their fields often swelled by as many as a score of officers from The Royals.

It was not long before he acquired Captain Harry Heron's pack of harriers, which were large blue-mottled ones of the Nugger type from Lancashire, slow but with plenty of tongue and the best of noses, always accounting for their hare. He soon crossed them with fox-hounds to improved their speed and occasionally laid a drag for a sharp 40 mins. over the difficult dyke country round about Ince and was apparently allowed to have the odd scurry across the pasture of the Chester Vale. Piers used sometimes to join him:

Tues. Apr. 2nd 1869. I went out with Park Yates's Harriers. He turned out a stag at Huxley, but it was not much fun. We afterwards had a drag.

On another occasion a deer had escaped from Oulton and found its way to Ince marshes. The harriers hunted it back but it was so hard pressed that it soiled at Oak Mere, afterwards being returned to Sir Philip. Another was sent over from Croxteth by Lord Sefton and was lost after a great hunt in Delamere Forest.

Perhaps best of all was the fun they had with the drags, especially one of which the young Squire of Ince had no idea what the finale would be. He had much enjoyed riding in Military steeplechases, and was on close terms with some of the greatest G.R.'s of the day, who would come to stay for the sport he had on offer. On the day in question much talent was out, including the great Captain 'Bee' Coventry, winner of the 1865 Grand National, Captain A.C. Tempest, who had been a close 2nd in that race, and Captains Boyce and Riddell, who had ridden Rifleman to victory for Park Yates in the Grand Military Gold Cup of '61 as well as several other crack soldier performers.

He went to draw for a fox at Picton Gorse, two or three miles North of Chester, but no fox was ever viewed. However, hounds went away carrying a great head over a most intricate country. Even all those intrepid riders had the greatest difficulty in keeping the little pack in view. Eventually hounds marked to ground at Sandiway

---

[*] A vacancy had occurred with the York & Ainsty, following a tragedy at Newby Ferry when six lives were lost, including that of the Master. For full details see Rowland Egerton Warburton's note to his lament, *Newby Ferry*, published in the 5th and subsequent editions of his *Hunting Songs*.

J.Bolton Littledale, viewing away two foxes from his own gorse.

on land belonging to Mr Littledale. An exhausted field came up one by one after their 20-mile run and Bolton Littledale stood there insisting on the fox being dug out as he claimed it had been doing a lot of damage to the local poultry. The Captain's guests took off their coats in turn and set to with a will and took it in turns until they dug out a neatly buried case of champagne and three dozen tumblers!

Captain Park Yates's nephew, Edward Waldegrave Griffith the father of H.W.Griffith (299), jotted down his memoirs in 1934 and recalled his Uncle Edmund telling him that his harriers used to settle down at once to hare or fox after such excursions. He had put this down to the old harrier blood, which for generations had been bred to hunt with great perseverance. Ned Griffith's own earliest recollection of hunting in Cheshire was as small boy being led to a meet at Four Lane Ends in 1877 from his father Captain 'Ap' Griffith's home at Tiresford. His mother was an enthusiastic hunt follower. Their daughter Frances, later Lady Darebury, known as Tiny, once wrote:

She saw a great deal of the sport. There was no more familiar sight than Mrs Griffith, driving her galloping thoroughbred chesnut mare in her dogcart round the lanes she knew so well.

But the Ince Harriers were not the only ones. Long John Dixon, whose health prevented him from driving after the hounds, wrote to Rowland to let him know his eldest son, recently home from his army service, intended to hunt. He mentions casually:

Some gentlemen at Chelford have got some beagles and have got leave from Lord Egerton and other gentlemen to hunt over their ground, and to-day they threw off at Mere Hills and drew the fir plantation near there and found a fine fox, but could not run him.

Jones had been appointed huntsman and in due course shared the horn with the Master. A fellow called George was also still kept on as 2nd Whipper-in, notwithstanding a strong comment from Piers the previous season:

George is a regular fool – he looked half drunk all day. [He had annoyed him by cutting off a brush Piers had wanted for his young nephew] . . . The ass cut it off bone and all instead of drawing it.

It was another very bad scenting season with a great deal of frost. Lord de Tabley's keeper was also rebuked in the diary:

. . . [he] takes no trouble about stopping. He spends his time at the public house.

Nor did Rawson enjoy himself much, reporting more than the usual number of falls, including a nasty one

A dejected Mr Corbet hacking home with his hounds after a foxless day. 'They trail their sterns behind them'. A sketch by Frank Massey.

John Jones, his huntsman, whose favourite hounds were Viceroy, Mistletoe, Gildermire and Linkboy. Woebetide any fox when he had them on his line.

Wilbraham Tollemache in his old age.

when he caught his chin in a clothes line between two trees and bit a piece out of his tongue before being trodden on by his mare. Incidentally Wilbraham Tollemache, who in his youth had charged an oxer and swished at a rasper with the best of them and now over sixty, was still active. Earlier in the season from Highwayside, Rawson observed that 'Young Broughton killed his steed, Wilbraham Tollemache was ridden against & had his knee a good deal hurt & Brocklebank broke his collar bone.'

Other instances of grief described in his diary include:

. . . Tom Brooks got a fall & was seen with his foot in the stirrup hanging head downwards. Helped to release him from his uncomfortable position.

. . . Much grief – amongst the victims was T. Marshall whose horse jumped into the river ag^t his rider's inclinations.

[After a sharp 70 mins. from Aston Gorse in March, '71, his own horse,] Tivoli done to a turn, but not overdone as were many other horses. Lord Willoughby de Broke's died on the way home.[*] Augustus de Trafford had to leave his for the night at Cassia Lodge and Royds did not get his to Sandiway till nine o'clock. Distance covered about 12 miles.

. . . Got bogged down, as did Littledale. In difficulties for upwards of half an hour. Fellows very good natured in helping us out. L^{d}Rich$^{d.}$ one of the most so.

Tivoli gave her master a fall and then trod on him. She then got an over-reach and later in the day got kicked.

. . . Tivoli's rider used strong language to the kicker, who, like a gentleman, apologised for the kick. Whereupon Tivoli's rider withdrew strong expressions and there was peace and anmity.

. . . Mare fell back into a ditch & was there for a quarter of an hour. The rider escaped unhurt but his hat and pocket suffered grievously – the one was crushed flat and filled with mud & water, the other emptied of 9/-.

Rawson also describes the demise of one of his favourite hunters which got tetanus:

Lawson vetted the poor brute after Dunn had tried his hand. The latter blistered the spine w^h the g^t man from Manchester said was the very worst treatment that could have been devised.

Lawson's treatment was as follows. The patient was put in a darkened box & kept as quiet as possible. No one allowed to go near him except to administer his wants. Thirty drops of prussic acid in a wine glass of water administered every 8 hours. The acid administered immediately after the dilution. It rapidly loses its properties by exposure.

Lawson said at once on seeing his patient that he had been called in too late. The theory of this treatment was that the complaint was on the nerves & the horse required sedatives and quiet. The cause of the attack was owing to his having trodden on a nail w^h ran into his foot, when out at exercise.

The horse was shot.

* * *

A HIGH LEIGH FOX was once killed in Arley Park. 'A second fox in Arley led to a catastrophe. The fox after running a ring returned to the Park & crossed the lake. Five or six couple of hounds in attempting to do likewise got off the ice into the open water & four were drowned before assistance arrived.'

2nd Horsewoman and Lady.

---

* Henry, the 18th Baron, aged 26, who had married James Smith-Barry's daughter, Geraldine, was Master of the Warwickshire from 1877 to 1900 and one of the greatest hound breeders of all time. He acquired a reputation for extreme invective.

In his diary, Piers once noted that 'Augustus de Trafford got kicked below the knee by Baldwin the Lionkiller's young horse'.

Harry Rawson seemed to have a hatred for Wrenbury days. Although now long recognized as one of the Cheshire's most popular meets, he once wrote 'this accursed country has produced a run at last' and at the end of the 1869/70 season, also from Wrenbury:

> In that detestable place, Combermere, all day nearly, but did not do any good, although there were plenty of foxes on foot. Did nothing either with a fox found in the afternoon in Court's Gorse. Miserable work!

Hounds were at Wrenbury again nine days later. 'Fifteen shillings worth of bad fun' was his comment that time. It must be remembered that, because of the convenience of the station, Wrenbury was on the *tapis* more often in those days. However trains did not always run on time. 'Thanks to beautiful railway arrangements, did not reach Wrenbury till after 12 o'clock,' Rawson once complained. But for all that he had enjoyed 104 days with the fox-hounds with only two blank days. A day had been missed in November for the Marquess of Westminster's funeral.

In October, 1870 Corbet had grumbled to Warburton: 'I find the honour and glory of being M.F.H does not compensate for the sum I am annually out of pocket. This rain will now set us up.'

One thing H.Reg^d Corbet, as he invariably signed himself, had strong views about was the observance of the Hunt's boundaries. 'I consider it to be the duty of a master of hounds when a country is entrusted to him that he should to the best of his ability prevent an encroachment from any other pack . . .,' he once wrote to the Secretary.

Sir Watkin, who incidentally rode at fully 17 stone,[†] had been claiming a portion of the Combermere Park coverts, perhaps not entirely surprisingly, since Wattie and Cheese had been together in the Tins. Out hunting the baronet had never been a flyer,

> but he had an extraordinary knack of getting over a country [his obituarist was to write]. He would creep through blind places, drop his horse into a road, jump the Aldersey Brook at a stand, and never lose the line of his hounds. In his heyday he always rode big horses, but latterly he preferred strong cobby ones, and tested their understandings down all sorts of roads that younger and lighter men would have shuddered at with a loose rein at full gallop.

The village children used to shout: 'Sir Watkin for ever!' as he rode by and he would gallop down the lanes on his cob with his red coat unbuttoned and everything flying. He had a habit of having one end of his bandana handkerchief in his pocket and the other in his mouth, and he held his hunting whip by the end of the thong and it waved about perilously behind him. In fact the crook once caught in the bridle of a child's pony he was passing and he towed them along some way. He was puzzled what was holding him back but never bothered to look round and it was not until the child began to scream that Sir Watkin was checked in his wild career.

Sir Watkin.

Corbet also got involved with a lengthy correspondence with the North Staffordshire hunt committee about the Doddington coverts, which had long been a bone of contention. The N.Staffs. was under new management and Corbet wanted to make sure that that bit of the old Woore country was only to be drawn by permission of the Cheshire. 'Between ourselves, they prefer pheasants at home and foxes on their friends,' he complained and was all for referring the matter to Boodle's. Broomlands and Hankelow were also being disputed and he wrote to the new Master, Lord Shrewsbury, to protect the Cheshire's rights.

The Cheshire Hunt Secretary had also corresponded with George Wilbraham about coverts he owned at Betchton, which Corbet declined to draw. As he wanted them drawn, the owner had written out of courtesy before offering them to the adjacent hunt.

Now Handley Gorse at Tattenhall was under fire and Sir Watkin loosed off the first salvo. He had just resigned from the Tarporley Hunt Club and had been unanimously elected an Honorary Member.

WYNNSTAY, RHUABON
DEAR CORBET,   Nov.26 [1871]
I see you meet next Saturday at Tattenhall. Is it to draw Sandbach's new covert? I have allways [*sic*] considered it in my country. The late Mr Leche allways met at Handley & drew Mr Sandbach's coverts. I have not drawn them often as they have been so hollow it was not worth while but I have allways considered them in my country . . .

yours sincerely
W W WYNN

[†] In his subaltern days he had sported silk and carried the Wynnstay red and green to victory more than once. His trainer was William Scott.

Sam Sandbach of Cherry Hill, Malpas.

DALE FORD, NORTHWICH
Nov 27/71

DEAR SIR WATKIN,

The meet on Saturday was fixed expressly for Handley covert which is within the Cheshire Hunt limits & has been drawn by the Cheshire hounds during my mastership as also during that of Lord Grosvenor, Arthur Mainwaring & White, without dispute. I see you meet at Carden on Friday next & in case you have any intention of then drawing Handley covert I must now enter my protest.

We have done very little of late & only had four good things since we commenced.

Yours very truly
H.REGᴰ CORBET

P.S. Since writing the above I have seen Mr Shakerley and he tells me Sir Harry Mainwaring always drew Handley Gorse and that he, Mr Shakerley, always drew that covert. This will take us back at least 32 years during which time each consecutive master has drawn the covert in question.

HRC

He immediately forwarded the correspondence to Warburton:

Sir Watkin's encroachments upon the Cheshire hunt are becoming of so serious a nature that unless the hunt quietly submit to a repetition of the late Doddington case a special meeting should be at once called to remonstrate with Sir Watkin and come to a proper understanding with him as to what is his country and what is not, for should he continue

his present course a very large part of the Cheshire's hunt country must soon become neutral between the two hunts.

For some years Sir Watkin has taken it upon himself to draw the Quoisley Meres to which I understand he has no right. Then again he lays claim to a considerable portion of Combermere and regularly draws not only that portion but very frequently the whole of the covers in Combermere Park. Boodle's committee should be avoided if possible, for unfortunately it is in a great measure composed of M.F.H.'s who have formed their country much in the same manner as Sir Watkin now endeavours to enlarge his.

He wasted no time in getting corroboration from Sir Harry's son and wrote again next day to Sir Watkin, who, it must be remembered, had been entitled to wear his green collar since 1841.

I have this morning received a letter from Sir Harry Mainwaring in which he says Handley Gorse was made for his father when Master of the Cheshire Hounds about the year 1819 [and that it and Huxley are the two oldest coverts in Cheshire] and that he, the present Sir Harry, frequently saw it drawn by the Cheshire up to 1857. This together with what I told you in my letter of yesterday shows pretty clearly that Handley covert has been drawn by the Cheshire over fifty years and up to the present time as I drew it myself last season.

Back came Wynn's riposte:

I do not think the evidence of Sir H.Mainwaring conclusive as in the year 1819 during the time Sir R.Puleston had no hounds, the Cheshire hounds came occasionally to Hampton Post kennels for a week to hunt that side of Sir R.Puleston's country but in 1829 on Sir R.Puleston again keeping Hounds they discontinued that practise [*sic*].

I have occasionally drawn the Handley Coverts but as they were not preserved they were not worth going out of the way to draw. I do not think I shall be down that side of the country to-morrow as I hear Aldersey is shooting the Gorse to-day & several of Leche's Coverts have not been drawn this year so I shall have to go there.

followed by:

Since writing to you yesterday I have looked over the Papers which were collected when I had a dispute with Rowland Hill. I find that Sir R.Puleston's hounds on Wed. 9th Feb., 1825 met at Han[d]ley Green besides Tues. Mar.26th Chowley and several times at various other places [nearby]. I find also Mr Leche's hounds meeting at Han[d]ley but I have only one year's fixtures so I spoke to Westminster to-day he suggested a reference so I drew the other way today I hope you will do so to-morrow as I think adopting his advice the wisest plan for both parties... not a good day, foxes bad, not having been cub-hunted.

Sir Watkin for ever!'

Corbet sent on the reply to the Hunt Secretary:

MY DEAR WARBURTON,

I enclose another letter from Sir Watkin. I must now wash my hands of the affair. I will hunt the Cheshire country and give information where I see encroachments but the Hunt must fight the battles, as these affairs almost always occur with my personal friends and with whom I wish to keep on terms of friendship.

DEAR SIR WATKIN,

I received your letter on Saturday morning and was not a little surprised at your request that I should not draw one of the Cheshire coverts which has been drawn by them for over 50 years without dispute until you raised one last week... I was glad to hear you refrained on Friday from encroaching on the Cheshire country. As I have only undertaken to <u>hunt</u> the Cheshire country and not to fight its battles please in any future correspondence on this subject address yourself to Mr Warburton at Arley.

In another letter to Rowland, he added:

Mr Sandbach [(215)], the owner of Handley Gorse told me yesterday that his mother could not understand what Sir Watkin meant by claiming Handley as she always understood it to belong to the Cheshire. Mr Sandbach has the head of a fox found in that covert and killed at Ashton

Hayes in Mr Shakerley's time by the Cheshire.[*]

Chowley, which is referred to in Sir W's letter, is in his country according to the Hunt Map. I do not think we dispute this, but because Sir R.Puleston met at Handley Green where in all probability he had no right to meet, is no earthly reason or clue that he drew Handley Gorse. I can answer for it if Sir Watkin draws coverts of ours that he has no claim to. These Welchmen seemed as indifferent of encroachment in former days as they are now.

I have met at Adderley many times since I had the Cheshire but of course that gives us no rights to the Adderley country. I am collecting some evidence which I will forward to you. I have drawn Handley Gorse twice prior to yesterday in the last six years. Lord Richard drew it in his brother's time. Mr Hayes recollects Capt.White & Sir Harry always drawing it.

And writing again the same day (December 4th):

I enclose a letter just received from the Welsh Baronet. I hope you will ignore Boodles *in toto* after the disgraceful

---

* Handley was drawn from the meet at The Black Dog in those days, but no such run is mentioned in Shakerley's diary, though there was 'a very good day' from Duddon Heath with 25 mins. at best pace, 'Sir Richard, Maiden and W.Tollemache in first place' from Huxley to The Willingtons followed by a slow hunt to ground at Ashton Hayes.

JENKINSON [Tomkinson] *(to M.F.H. who dislikes being bothered)* *"What do you think of this horse?"* *(No answer)* *"Bred him myself you know!"*
M.F.H. [CORBET] *(looking at horse out of corner of eye)* *"Umph! I thought you couldn't have been such a damned fool as to have bought him!", from a water-colour dated 1890 by "J.C.H."*

decision they gave against us in 1870 [concerning the N.Staffs.' claim for Doddington], added to their refusal to reopen the case when I had evidence laid before them that all the grounds on which they based their decision were false. I think we should be careful how we submit anything to their tender mercy. Of course Sir Watkin will dispute anything for the simple reason he has everything to gain and nothing to lose in the matter.

P.S. The only thing Sir W puts forward in evidence of his claim is that Sir R.Puleston met at Hanley Green. Now in Sir Watkin's other letters he spells our covert as it should be Handley. I enquired when at Handley the other day where the Green was. No one knew, nor is it marked on either the ordnance map or on the old inch & half scale map of Cheshire, but there is a Hanley, Hanley Park near Norbury by Cholmondeley.[*] It is as well to bear this in

* Now also Handley, it was Hanley on the 1831 Ordnance Map. It was originally a stick covert and the spinney there is known as Handley Sticks. Stickheaps are specially constructed 'fox castles' of large logs about nine feet square and packed on the outside and piled up with thorns and hedgeclippings to make them weatherproof. Shutters fixed to the exits and entrances facilitate stopping and a stickheap is drawn by poking a long pole downwards and rattling it.

mind though Sir W has as much right to the latter as he has to the former.

Sir Watkin had written:

I am extremely astonished after my letter to you on Friday stating that Lord Westminster had proposed a reference & that I refrained from drawing Handley Covert on that day you should have drawn it yesterday. I shall take steps to have the case brought before the Stewards of Boodles.

and then sent two strongly worded letters to Rowland, stating his intention to go before Boodle's.

Whether or not Mr Sandbach's mask was a Handley fox, and in all probability it was, further evidence was produced of another splendid run from Handley Gorse on Christmas Eve, 1843, an account of which in *The Sporting Magazine* was sent to Mr Corbet. The gallant fox had gone off to Bolesworth, through the park and grounds and away for Broxton and over the Bickerton Hills to Cholmondeley. The pack ran into him after he had passed Peckforton Moss and made his point for Ridley Hall. The report concluded:

"The Pride of Cheshire," Lord Delamere, rode throughout close to the hounds, and was up at the who-whoop, which was not the case with many who aspire to fame.

While all this was going on, disaster had struck. The hounds had gone down with rabies once again. In his entry for December 16th Rawson wrote: 'Heard of dumb madness having made its appearance in the kennels, & of the loss of 9 couple of hounds in consequence '. There seems to have been no let up of hunting as a result. In fact for Appleton on December 30th he noted for the first time: 'Corbet hunted the hounds.'

And then on January 15th after what had started as a fairly happy day from Norley with hounds being stopped 'as it was getting dark':

> It was the mixed pack that was out & it was destroyed on getting home in consequence of the reappearance of dumb madness.

On December 10th the Master, staying at Hartford Grange, had written a long letter to Rowland Warburton:

> I am in the greatest distress and it is no longer possible for me to hide the fact that we have again got Hydrophobia in the kennels amongst one of the three packs.
>
> A young hound (puppy) was attacked in August and was destroyed before, as we hoped, any mischief was done. All went well until about six weeks back when another showed symptoms and was destroyed, together with one or two known to have been bitten... I now see no hope of saving any of the mixed pack. Most unfortunately the finest of the Bitches are amongst them . . . I had to destroy a couple yesterday, one mad, the other bitten. The same thing has occurred to-day.
>
> Do you wish to call a meeting or will you on your own responsibility give me instructions to destroy the lot at once. It most undoubtedly ought to be done. The other two packs I trust I may keep right. I shall of course have to knock off one day a week . . .

The Secretary recommended some anti-hydrophobia and Regie (both he and his son preferred this spelling) replied that he had 'sent over for the jar and will certainly give it a trial'. Matters were not helped when Jones broke his ribs, but at least it gave Corbet the excuse he had wanted to carry the horn.

At the end of January the Subscribers met at the Weaver Navigation Office, Northwich, and authorized the Master not to exceed £1,000 for 12 couple of working hounds. Twenty-seven couple had either died or been destroyed, one third of the entire pack. For the next few months Corbet was writing on heavily black-edged writing paper (there had been no apparent loss in his

family) and by March he reported that he had bought the Bitch pack belonging to Lord Poltimore, who had just given up hunting the Cattistock country he had founded. He bought the entire pack for 1,700 gns. and drafted on the ones he did not want. Those he kept cost the Subscribers £62 per couple.

But hunting continued and Harry Mainwaring, surprisingly not the enthusiastic preserver of foxes his father had been, noted in his List of Meets that on February 19th there had been 'a capital run from Rudheath thro' Peover to Capesthorne.' This is how Harry Rawson described the day after hounds met at Peover:

> On arriving at the meet it was announced that a fox had that morning been caught in a trap! Everybody was glad to hear the news, because no one believed in the existence of any specimen whatever of the genus vulpus about the place. A fox, even with three legs, was therefore an agreeable surprise. The fates were more propitious later in the day, when a wild animal was found at Rudheath and lost at Capesthorne . . . 1 hr. 5 mins., first 40 mins. very good.

On March 30 Rawson had 'a very fine run from Hurleston', 'a hot and oppressive day which ended in a thunderstorm', but failed to witness the astonishing feat of the recently married James Tomkinson, who gave a somewhat different account:

> We had a wonderful run from Hurleston, a very fast ring nearly to Haughton and back to the Hurleston Reservoir, and thence past Poole Hill's Gorse, Calveley, Oulton Adjets, and to ground at Cassia! I rode "Ulster" and was well carried. Seven horses died, the country being awfully deep and the weather hot.
>
> At Hurleston Reservoir, being shut in at the Canal, I jumped the narrow lock, in which a boat lay at the time, my horse copping on and off the flat top of it. Several others followed me to the indignation of an old woman living inside it!

Rawson gave the time as 1 hr. 24 mins. One of the horses that died was his, the pulmonary veins of its diaphragm having been ruptured.

A water-colour at Willington commemorates the feat. It is entitled THE TOMKINSON TOUCH Little wonder Jimmie got his green collar the following November, after his father's death at the end of August. His elder brother, Willie, one of Tarporley's finest baritones, had died two years previously. James had first hunted after he had come down from Oxford, aged 22, in 1862.

It then got put about that Corbet was going to hunt six days a week. Old Geoffrey Shakerley was upset and vehemently opposed and Hugh Westminster wrote from

THE TOMKINSON TOUCH. *From a water-colour in the possession of C.R. Tomkinson, Esq.*

Cliveden worried about the reaction of the farmers, who

must have something to say on the subject, considering that now the field consists of non-county men speaking generally, and they cannot altogether approve of Liverpool and Manchester riding over the county except "in moderation" – my idea of "moderation" is the old fashion of 4 days a week. I should be glad as far as I am concerned to see the old order of things established without a bye day if you will. But I suppose it is settled and there nothing to be done.

That was in March, 1872, but it was not until October that the Master, who was going to carry the horn two days a week, wrote to explain:

I do not know how the report has gone abroad that I intend hunting 6 days a week. My intention is to do what I have always done since I took the hounds, viz to advertise 5 days and have a bye day in either the forest or Peckforton (which are full of foxes) once a week. In hunting a five day a week

country one is obliged to keep as many hounds as will do 6. I have therefore always found it necessary to have a bye day up to Xmas as I can show you by the journals.

At the A.G.M. in April the new Secretary, in an effort to reduce the size of the fields and the consequent damage, proposed that Mr Corbet no longer advertised the fixtures and that the cards sent to the Members be marked private. But the decision was reversed at the next meeting in November with Piers the sole dissenter. At that same meeting Lord Combermere's proposal that it be open for anyone to subscribe to hounds was met with a direct negative.

In July, 1872 Corbet reported a further outbreak of rabies, though everything was being done to contain it. It had broken out in one of the bitch packs in March, but after three months' isolation, it had broken out again and three of the Poltimore hounds were affected. The Master had a further scare when he received the following letter at the beginning of August:

FOREST KENNELS

FRIDAY

MR CORBET

SIR

There is one of the young dog hounds gone mad since I wrote to you yesterday. I dont think he done any harm as we had him out the day before. This is a mistry as he has never been with any of the others neither in the kennel nor out & it is quite a diferent madnefs from the other. He is raging mad now.

Your obedient Servant

JOHN JONES

With Piers's approval he called a meeting 'to consider the best course to pursue in regard to the terrible disaster which has befallen the hounds.' A sensible resolution was made to remove all the old woodwork from the hound benches and generally make the place more hygienic. Nothing more was heard and the Master went off to Banffshire for his holiday.

He was away until the middle of October. It had been a bad cub-hunting season with $23\frac{1}{2}$ brace killed, according to Mr Rawson who also recorded Corbet having the Poltimore pack out 4 times with a run each day, but not having once killed their fox. It was not until November 15th at Tabley that they tasted blood for the first time, their victim having been dug out.

Thereafter it was abysmal with scant days of any note and the ground very heavy, until January when there was 'a week of wonderfully good hunting runs, including an extraordinary $4\frac{1}{4}$ hrs. from Petty Pool to the Old Pale, back *via* Abbot's Moss to Petty Pool, where he turned back to Oak Mere, thence to Norley, Crowton and Weaverham to the outskirts of Hartford, where not surprisingly he was lost at dark.'

That was Reginald Corbet's Presidential Year. Although a disappointing Season was to follow, at least he must have had a rousing reception when he won the

Hester Cotton gives Alice Tollemache a lead.

Tarporley Hunt Stakes, a Hunter Steeplechase that year, with his brown horse, Cotton. He had chosen the Hon.Hester Cotton, one of the most accomplished and dashing lady riders in the county, as his Lady Patroness.

> *"Few ladies so gallant – if any,*
> *Did Cheshire e'er send to the chase;*
> *Each dingle for her has a cranny,*
> *Each river a fordable place;*
> *She knows the best line from each covert,*
> *She knows where to stand for a start,*
> *And long may she live to ride over*
> *The country she loves in her heart!"*

R.E.E.W.

(As plagiarized by the Rev. W.G. Armitstead from the lines written about old Wilbraham Tollemache.)

In November Rowland Warburton had resigned as Secretary to the Cheshire Hunt; though perhaps retired is a more appropriate word. After all he had to cope with, many a lesser man would have handed over the task long since. In his case it was the failure of his eyesight that

Piers, who succeeded Rowland Egerton Warburton as Secretary of the Cheshire, father and son completing some 67 years service.

The Hon. Hester Cotton, later Lady Alexander Paget. Her son, Charles, succeeded as 6th Marquess of Anglesey.

made him do so. He had held office for 35 years and it gave him immense pleasure when his son was elected to take his place.

In his memoranda he recorded that before Sir Harry Mainwaring's retirement in 1837 no accounts of the subscriptions and no minutes of the meetings had been kept. George Cornwall Legh, who had been acting as Treasurer for some years, and himself had then become Joint Secretaries and Treasurers until the former resigned in 1849. Harry Brooke had stood in for Rowland when he was abroad from 1848 to 1850. The Laureate waited a year before resigning from Tarporley and was elected an Honorary Member.

Piers recounts his last day of the 1872/73 season. From The Three Greyhounds they had ended up just opposite Somerford:

> The fox ran us out of scent, so home – horse very tired. I suppose Sir C.Shakerley will kill this fox if he crosses the river. What a curse a fellow like that is to the hunting country. Rode home with Cole, R.Grosvenor and Arthur Smith-Barry. Feeling very sad that the fun is all over till next year. Hunted 52 times.

Rawson rated it a poor day and was with hounds again for the final day at Hurleston next morning, when there were 'four hundred fellows out.' After a couple of runs they had a long, slow hunting run and ended up in the neighbourhood of Audlem:

> Many men in grief during the day. Cecil Trafford, Ld Cole & Corbet in the canal. Ld R.Grosvenor got a fall and had his lip cut through and many teeth loosened. So ends the season and a very indifferent one it has been. If it had not been for a few redeeming runs in Jany it w^d have been very bad indeed.

He was out 124 times.

* * *

THE HUNT WAS GOING THROUGH A BAD SPELL with its public relations, mainly owing to the steps both the Master and the Subscribers to Hounds themselves were taking to reduce the fields in the interests of the farmers more than anyone, however inconvenient the hordes of outsiders may have been to themselves. And so far as the Press was concerned, it was the Tarporley Hunt Club that got the blame. Collectively, of course, it was nothing to do with the Club, but individually the Subscribers were almost exclusively Green Collars, hence the censure which appeared at the beginning of the 1873/74 Season in *The Chester Chronicle*:

The Members of the Tarporley Hunt Club have taken a highly unpopular step in passing a rule that for three months no announcement of their "meets" shall appear in the papers. The object... is avowedly that of keeping down the fields . . . ; the complaint of late years being that they were overrun with people from the towns, who did not help the respectability of the hunt, and embarrassed the green collars a good deal in their sport.

We regret if the small society having its headquarters at The Swan, at Tarporley, have suffered from the rudeness of plebeians who have presumed to join their ranks in the field. They are not very particular about careering over other people's land, but the world at large ought to be extremely careful about intruding upon their pastimes. It does not strike them, perhaps, that if fox-hunting is in itself so healthful and enjoyable, they ought not to be so niggardly in the way they allow others to participate in the amusement; or that, having the charge of supporting what is boasted to be a fine old English instition, it becomes them to do it in something like an open English spirit. Let us suppose all the other masters of hounds in the country doing the same thing: how the sport would at once sink from the place it now holds in the regard of the people into the unwelcome indulgence of a few small if privileged coteries!

But the fact is this new regulation will bring all the odium of affected exclusiveness upon the hunt without accomplishing the end in view. Men from Birkenhead and Liverpool and anywhere else, who keep hunters and are determined to use them, will still learn the whereabouts of the meets by "tipping " keepers and others, while the farmers, as a writer in *The Courant* properly puts it, find themselves utterly unable to take the precautions necessary to keep their stock out of harm's way, because they possess no such information.

The step, there is no doubt, is one in the wrong direction. It will help to popularize SIR WATKIN'S meets, and all the others accesssible from this county, while the glories of the famous old Cheshire will be quietly shelved. As to the same writer's indignation at some newspaper publishing the appointments last Saturday "in defiance of the wishes of the Hunt," it is mere moonshine. The hunt do not care for the public, so the public cannot be expected to regard their wishes in the least.

Someone against 'the fence-breaking rabble' added:

"The Secret Hunting Association" musters just as strong in numbers as the Cheshire Hunt ever did and the damage done to farmers is as great as ever before, while foot people throng the cover's side and head the fox with more unabated and savage delight than ever they did heretofore.

If that was not enough, at the Opening Meet 'the talk of the day,' Rawson wrote, 'was about a row there had been the night before at Dale Ford in which Corbet had fired at and wounded a man.' It was in fact around midnight on the Saturday, after he and his household had retired to bed, that they had been disturbed by a souling party of nine men and boys, who refused to leave until they were given 'a drop of good beer', having rung the bell for a good fifteen minutes.

It was All Hallow's Eve and it was evident they had all been drinking at the Blue Cap. Having first sung 'Gentlemen of England' and then just embarked on 'Now pray we for our country' by way of an encore, Squire Corbet and his staff rushed out at them, the former striking to the ground the first man he saw. He afterwards said he had been threatened by some sacked stable hands and thought they had come to seek revenge. He had his gun in his hand and his butler was brandishing a sword. Other domestics, including Lord Cole's valet, were armed with stout canes. According to the newspaper account the party received 'more whacks halfpence' and not satisfied with that Mr C. chased after two of the men towards the high road. Seeing no chance of overtaking them, he called on them to stop or he would shoot at them. As they did not do so, he fired and one of the men, John Tomlinson, a farm labourer, received a score of pellets in the calves of his legs.

An anonymous wit later set the incident to verse (*See Book Two, Part Two*):

> *A single glass of ale apiece*
> *We looked for, for our carol,*
> *Instead of that he gave us all*
> *The contents of a barrel.*

In fact they were rounded up and taken to the mess room where they were detained for two hours, while a groom was sent for the local constable, who proved to be out. Corbet took their names and allowed them to go, but said later he was not aware of Tomlinson's injuries until the Monday, when he immediately sent Lord Delamere's agent to pay him £25 by way of compensation and a promise to pay his doctor's bill. Mrs Corbet went round to his home at Marton to take him provisions. Tomlinson had signed a paper agreeing to withold prosecution, but by then it was in the hands of the police.

On the Wednesday, Tarporley Race-day, Corbet appeared before his fellow magistrates, including Lord Combermere, at a special session of the Peace and received a summons, no evidence being taken at that stage. He was released on bail, with Dick Grosvenor, who used an old cottage nearby as a hunting box and lived mostly at Dale Ford, as surety. The Master then went off to ride in the Tarporley Hunt Stakes, which he won for the second year running. 'Public feeling runs very high,'

ran *The Chronicle* report, 'and it is clear that Mr Corbet was no favourite with the spectators at Tarporley Races.'

It was on the Saturday that the case was heard at the new Court House at Oakmere. Mr G.F.Wilbraham (149) was in the chair. The much-respected Cheshire surgeon, Mr George Okell of Over Hall, to whom Tomlinson had gone in a gig on the Sunday, was one of the witnesses called.

PROSECUTING COUNSEL: Can you give the bench any idea as to when he may recover his strength and get rid of the shots?
WITNESS: The shots may remain in the leg. For ever? – Yes.
THE CHAIRMAN: I believe shots don't do much harm?
WITNESS: No, a bullet may remain in a man's brain.
THE CHAIRMAN: I have a shot in my finger.
COUNSEL, cross-examining: It is not customary to take them out? – It would be bad surgery to do so.

The hearing went on for seven and a half hours. The case was to go before a jury and Mr Corbet was admitted to bail, totalling £400. He was duly brought to trial on November 26th at the Knutsford Sessions, presided over by Sir Harry Mainwaring, on three counts, unlawful malicious wounding, causing grievous bodily harm and common assault. A witness stated Corbet had in fact shouted: 'Run! Run! or I'll shoot,' adding 'I'd rather run than be shot.' (Laughter.)

George Wilbraham of Delamere Lodge, November 1st, 1876.

After twenty minutes the jury gave the verdict of 'Guilty of common assault' and the Master of the Cheshire Hounds was fined £100 'and that he should further enter into recognisance himself of £500, with two sureties of £250 each [Lord R.Grosvenor and Capt. E. Wynne Griffith] to be of good behaviour to all Her Majesty's subjects for 12 months.'

It had not been his fortnight, despite the winning ride. Two days later, on his way to the meet at Twemlows, he got an upset driving across a field and had a narrow escape. The only minor support was an angry letter in the paper, deploring the ritualism of Mumming Parties, which had been encouraged by the parish magazine, *Tarporley Review*, and stating that such customs should be discouraged as they were half pagan, half papal.

Later he withdrew his resignation, which he had made for the usual financial reasons, in case it was misconstrued 'by all the outer world who know nothing' and

'To the manner born,' from a cartoon of H. Reginald Corbet by SPY *in* Vanity Fair.

'would at once be put down to this unfortunate case of shooting'.

That season a significant change happened in January, according to Harry Rawson's journal. Its pages are full of references to the presence, a profusion even, of ladies in the hunting field. But it seems there was a little more to it than that as some of the following extracts show:

Jan. 26. . . . Lord Cole [yet to get his green collar] mounted Miss Reynolds. Nearly ridden over by a lady. Heard at night that the horse ridden by Miss Royds on Saturday died from the effects of a fall.
Jan. 27. . . . C.W. appeared in most gorgeous array. He was got up quite regardless of expense & was the observed of all observers.
Jan. 31. Rookery. A beautiful hunting morning & a large field out. Did not go into the breakfast. . . . A good many ladies out, Mrs Littledale, Miss Cotton, Miss Bibby, Mrs Tomkinson, Miss G.Morris, the last well waited upon as usual, and The Female Fiend.
Feb. 11. Twemlows. . . . Sundry casualties during the day. Saw a young Brocklehurst overhead in Peover brook. Came upon Trotter a prisoner. His horse was on its back in a field with its legs in the air & with Trotter's legs under it. Saw him released by someone rolling the horse over. Heard of another man who was, or pretended to be, stunned. Perhaps he wanted a drink. A fair sprinkling of ladies out who all comported themselves as ladies sh[d] do.
Feb. 17. Vale Royal. As regards the chase, a shocking bad day, but very pleasant inasmuch as there were many of the "Merry Wives" of Hartford out, who were all as pleasant as ever, to wit Mrs Marshall, Mrs Littledale, Mrs Corbet, Mrs Villiers &c &c. Mrs Villiers was mounted by Corbet and looked and rode very well . . .
Feb. 20. Cholmondeley. . . . Not a very large field out, but a g[t] many carriages present at the meet, to wit Tollemache's, Kennedy's, Earle's, Hall's &c &c. Sundry horsewomen out too. Miss Cotton, two Miss Davenports, Miss Warren, but not Miss M. [Morris].

and so on, until

Feb. 24. Tarporley. . . . The great flirtation w[h] seemed on the wane yesterday [when no names were mentioned in the diary], carried on as vigorously as ever to-day. Everyone talking of it. A very large field out, but few ladies. Only two, Mrs Beatty & Miss Dunn got falls. The responsibility of looking after womankind in the hunting field must be appalling –appalling enough to bring down a fellow's grey hairs with sorrow to the grave. Miss G.M. hung by the pommel of her saddle for the third time this season.

On the 26th he did not go to Wrenbury as his horse was coughing and he missed the run of the season, in which 'Miss Cotton rode gallantly throughout' and the

The Pastor and his flock': the Rev. J.R.Armitstead of Cranage Hall with Mrs Bolton Littledale, Miss May Royds and Mrs Marshall (on Chirk).

estimates of which varied from 20 to 30 miles. But at Oulton next day

> . . . A good many ladies out – Mesdames Beatty, Villiers, & Lady Cole, Misses Royds, Warren &c. Lady Cole got a fall. She was riding a mare of Coupland's [of Rushton Bank]. Royds of Brereton also got a fall and was said to be considerably hurt about the head. Miss Morris riding J.S.B.'s grey mare.
>
> The flirtation seemingly less active than usual. When Lady Cole got her fall she was rescued by C.Way! Ld Cole great on the occasion. "Thank you, thank you, &c &c. Can't you let her go!"
>
> Feb. 28. High Leigh. A day fine as regards the weather, but beautiful in nothing else. A very large and disagreeable field out – nearly all, both men and women, strangers. High Leigh produced a good fox but owing to want of scent nothing but a slow hunting run of 30 mins. followed the find. The remainder of the day spent about Arley. Home much depressed & wishing that Fate would never take me to High Leigh again. The only fun of the day was watching the mob ride and seeing how, when their horses jumped, the tailors did not remain. The only remarkable feature – the hat in which Mrs Lyon appeared. It <u>was</u> a hat – a sweet pretty thing entirely.
>
> Mar. 3. Hargrave Green. Another disappointing day... Few ladies out. One or two from Chester, strangers, two of the Duke's daughters[*] & Mrs Beatty were the only ones.

From Wilkesley on March 5, when most people had gone to the Grand Military Steeplechases at Rugby, H.R. was rewarded with a very pleasant 40 mins. into the N. Staffs. country to a point between Woore and Whitmore. Hester Cotton had a fall, 'but picked herself up again & was none the worse.' Next day at Appleton he was out with an eye for the ladies and again on the Saturday from Tabley where there were no ladies, but 'a very large field of Manchester riders'.

> Mar. 9. Calveley. All the merry wives & merry maidens of my acquaintance put in an appearance at the meet. Most of them had a glass of Kennedy's curaçao w^h the coldness of the day made almost a necessity . . .

A few days' snow and frost set in, but on Friday at Church Minshull:

> . . . Misses Cotton, Morris, Court and Mary & May Royds out. Mrs Marshall also. Except Mr Way no one afforded the least matter worthy of record. He (W.) received the Master's displeasure by damaging fences unnecessarily & amused the field by falling off occasionally without the least necessity for so doing. On being remonstrated with he announced himself a late Captain in 16th Lancers & complained of having been unfairly treated since he settled in Cheshire.[†]

Harry had eleven more days before the last day at Peckforton on March 28, and yet more grief to report:.

> Mar. 21. . . . On going away from the gorse & immediately after fording the river, C.Trafford got a heavy fall owing to his horse having put his foot in a drain. When he got up, he looked like an Irishman that had been "kilt entirely" in a row. His nose was cut, his eyes were blackened, his face was covered in mud and his hat – well his hat looked the very thing with which to give a scarecrow a handsome finish.
>
> Mr Chas.Way also came to grief. He rode fiercely at a brook. Instead of jumping, his horse stopped dead short & Mr Way, having a wash bowl seat, went head foremost into the water & may be there to this day for anything known to the contrary. Nobody seemed inclined to help him out – indeed everybody thought a bottomless brook the proper place for the man. The field consisted of upwards of 200 horsemen.

But he was a hard man to please.

> Mar. 25. Wilkesley. Scent as bad as ever & sport as bad too. A Kent's Rough fox & another from Walkmill were both unaccounted for, neither having given a run to speak of. The Wrenbury misery is now over for the season which is something to be thankful for. So far never remember a March in which good runs were so few and far between as they have been this year. Except for the gallop from

---

* Their father had been created a Duke the previous Friday. They were Lady Elizabeth ('Lilah'), who was Lady Patroness the next season and married the Marquess of Ormonde before the end of it, and Lady Beatrice Grosvenor, aged fifteen, two years younger. When the Duke married his second wife, he became Beatrice's brother-in-law, she by then having married the 3rd Lord Chesham.

† A diligent search of the Army List has failed to find any officer called C.Way, nor can the 16th/5th Queen's Royal Lancers find any mention of him in any rank.

Calveley on the 9th & those on the 5th and 6th have had nothing at all worth going out for.

On Grand National Day Rawson discloses his weakness for the ladies:

Would not go but stayed at home to see if any ladies would call. Mrs Villiers & Lady Cole came as I was beginning to feel very cross & my tea muffin boiled to rags. The ladies were as charming & agreeable as usual and I only regretted that they had come to say goodbye.
"How happy could I be with either
Were t'other fair charmer away." [*]

The last day was, however, 'a pretty good one considering the dryness of the weather. Plenty of foxes, too'. Several were found on the hills, one in Ridley (hounds whipped off as it was a heavy vixen), one from Spurstow, which took them to Wardle and a Hurleston fox which also ran to Haughton Hall and Wardle and thence by Bunbury and Peckforton Wood back to the Hills. He names the usual crowd of ladies.

. . . Ms Corbet and Villiers both came to grief. The first got a fall, lost her hat & all her hair came down. She wasn't hurt but her appearance for the moment was not improved. The second galloped into a ditch & came out with a scratched face, a bloody nose, a slightly blackened eye, a shake & a fright. She was taken to Calveley & the Kennedys, like good Samaritans, poured oil into her wounds & sent her home in their carriage. So much for lovely women hunting. Saw both ladies on the following day & found both as well as could be expected.

So ends the season of 1873/74. There have been better & there have been worse. It may perhaps fairly be called a moderately good one.

From Oct.17 to Mar.28 Corbet hunted the hounds 40 times and killed 22 foxes. Jones hunted hounds 75 times and killed 34, *viz*:

	CORBET	JONES
By digging	4	4
bolting	2	1
chopping	6	6
Handsomely	9	21
do (3 legs)	1	–
Lame & in traps	–	2

* * *

* This verse from *The Beggar's Opera* by John Gay (1685-1732) continues:
But while ye thus tease together,
To neither a word will I say.

Before long Piers was in receipt of terse letters from dissatisfied Masters of Fox-hounds, landowners and subscribers, in the same way his father had had to cope with all those years. Before the next season was out, the Squire of Peover was upset because his coverts had been pointedly avoided. 'It should be decided whether the coverts are to be hunted for the future, or to be given up', he demanded. In this instance Corbet had the backing of the Subscribers. In nine years he had only found three foxes there and a letter was sent off to 'young' Sir Harry expressing the hope that 'with a change of keepers, the country would be hunted both to his satisfaction and that of the Hunt.'

And then from Norton Priory, an estate of 4,788 acres[†]: 'I cannot help thinking that the members of the Cheshire Hunt have hitherto refrained from expressing to me that they consider my estate & the immediate neighbourhood not worth hunting, but their conduct on Friday convinced me that neither they nor the Master of the Hounds wish to hunt here . . .' wrote Sir Richard Brooke. He was no longer going to preserve foxes and, as he put in his letter, he had said at Tarporley that he had long felt 'that railroads, canals & delectable wire fences must be making hunting in its true sense impossible.'

Apparently when the proper meet had been fixed for Norton Priory, the vast majority had gone off with Corbet and another pack to hunt at Oulton, leaving Jones and a whipper-in to go to Norton. He resigned from the Club forthwith. He subsequently wrote to Piers that he had been mistaken and accepted an apology on behalf of the Hunt. It transpired that due to recent frost the Master felt Oulton in need of attention; furthermore he had a letter from Boodle's to read to the Subscribers' Meeting that it was normal practice with many hunts to have two packs out on one day. But nevertheless come Tarporley Week in November, Sir Richard chose to resign.

Also Corbet had complained because Payne had gone through the stone lodge at Combermere to draw Robert Cotton's coverts. Sir Watkin pointed out that the Wellington Covert was the hunt boundary on the estate,

† The acreages of the principal Cheshire estates at this time were:
Peckforton: 25,380, Cholmondeley: 16,842, Eaton: 15,001, Doddington: 13,830 (as much again and more in Staffs.), Crewe: 10,148, Capesthorne: 9,259, Tatton: 8,876, Oulton: 8,840, Dunham Massey: 8,612, Combermere: 8,310, Bostock: 7,500, Arley: 7,029, Tabley: 6,195, Arderne: 6,191, Somerford: 5,978, Vale Royal: 5,611, Alderley: 5,011, Norton: 4,788, Wilbraham: 4,300, Withington: 3,702, Mere: 3,535, Bolesworth: 3,376, Dorfold: 3,348, Darnhall (*c.*1900): 3,319, Marbury (N): 3,124, Aldersey: 2,300, Rode: 2,032, Peover: 1,898, Astle: 1,526, Willington: 966.

Jamie Tomkinson out hunting.

but his huntsman had not drawn beyond the county boundary, which coincided with the hunt's.

However the 1874/75 season produced no spectacular sport according to Harry Rawson's diary.[1] Corbet, who, it seems, had rather more falls than usual, hunted hounds 30 times, killing 9 brace, whereas his huntsman carried the horn on 63 occasions, accounting for 18 brace. Henry Tollemache (204) was one of the green-collared thrusters and from Tattenhall Station charged a railway gate and had a nasty-looking fall, but that season the Master no longer had to cope with the over-enthusiasm of one of his younger fellow Tarporley Members. 'A *poet*, as well as a *prophet* is, it would appear,' concluded a gossip paragraph in *Land and Water*, 'often

James Tomkinson, Esq. of Willington.

"without honour in his own country," for hath not Warburton sung, and in vain:

The fox takes precedence of all from the covert,
The horse is an animal purposely bred,
After the pack to be ridden, not over,
Good hounds were not reared to be knocked on the head!

We earnestly commend these lines to our friend from the County Palatine.'

According to the article the gentleman in question, 'bearing an old Cheshire name' had deserted the 'Chester on and off step' in favour of the 'Leicestershire clearing all'. He claimed that this 'customer from the Land of Cheeses' had but one intent, 'the *personal* capture of the fox . . . unassisted by the hounds'.

A cutting in Harry's diary reveals the culprit as none other than Jas. Tomkinson, who was now living in London, employed by Matheson & Co. in Lombard Street. Jimmie and Effie, the former Miss Palmer, each had a horse stabled at Rugby and occasionally hunted with the Atherstone and Pytchley. His mother, twenty-four years younger than Colonel William, lived in London, but sometimes went to Leamington Spa for health reasons where they would visit her. For four seasons they took lodgings at Melton. After Christmas

[1] There is no record of Harry Rawson ever having dined as a guest at Tarporley. However, on the day of the Opening Meet he concludes:
  Dined at Oakmere. Large gathering. Smash of crockery and extinguishment of gas *the* feature of the evening.

Tomkinson would hunt on the Saturday and Monday, going to London for business Tuesday to Thursday.

James thought the world of his mother, who was a great beauty. Indeed her father, Thomas Tarleton, Jnr. had been considered one of the handsomest men in the county when he was at Bolesworth. She was of the old school and carried refinement and delicacy to an extreme, for instance, always speaking of 'nether garments' rather than trousers.

James Tomkinson retired from business in 1879 and settled at Willington, buying a partnership in a bank in Chester. After several attempts, it was not until 1900 that he got into parliament.* As a landowner in Conservative and Convivial Cheshire he had two besetting sins. Not only was he an advanced Radical, he was also an avid teetotaller. But out hunting he had undaunted pluck. In Leicestershire, as a young man, his style of riding and fondness for stiff timber and forbidding obstacles got him named 'Tommy Jumpkinson' the first week he was there and the epithet followed him to parliamentary circles. Rawson's diary often referred to various disasters he had out hunting, for instance:

Dec.31st 1885. Tarporley. . . . a good deal of grief. Amongst the victims was Jas. Tomkinson. He got a fall at a small fence near Stapleford & was struck on the head by his horse. He had to be sent home on wheels and seemed to be much hurt. Nov.2nd 1886. Ox Heys Farm. . . . The universally beloved Mr Tomkinson's horse reared in a road & threw its rider.

But he retained his reputation as a goer to the end, dying as he did from a fall in a Point-to-Point at the age of 70. Sir William Eden wrote[†]:

Mr Tomkinson met with a good end. I remember many a time riding by his side in Cheshire. He was very hard. You could not beat him unless he fell, which was often. He was too old for the game. It is better to accept one's liabilities of old age and pot bellies when they come . . .

---

* He was an ardent supporter of the Daylight Savings Bill, which was for some time bitterly opposed.

† See Chapter XI. Sir William, the father of the 1st Earl of Avon, once finished second at Tarporley in borrowed boots and breeches, the intended jockey for his horse, the Hon.George Lambton, having been taken ill at the last moment.

'The merciful man is merciful to the beast.' James Tomkinson.

XV

Puffles and The Imperial Huntress

BUT FOR THE MISGUIDED INTERVENTION OF THE NEWLY-CREATED Lord Tollemache of Helmingham, another Smith-Barry would have had his name in red in the Hunt Room. At the end of February, 1877 the Subscribers received a proposal from their Manager, whose father had died the previous month. Mr Corbet was no longer going to be able to devote the time required to look after a six-days-a-week hunting establishment and he suggested running the whole thing jointly with Mr J.S.Barry. In effect, he would only hunt the South two days from Adderley and the rest would be hunted four days from the Kennels at Sandiway with Mr Barry in command. No increase in the guarantee would be entailed.

At the meeting, with Lord Combermere now chairman of the Subscribers, Mr Corbet accepted the railway line from Crewe to Beeston station as the boundary and left it in the hands of those present as to whether he should be refunded for any of the additional hounds he had bought. He then left the room. Meanwhile Captain Park Yates's name had been proposed instead of Smith-Barry.

> Ld. de Tabley [(145)] rose and whilst expressing his high appreciation of Mr Park Yates as a sportsman & a gentleman, said he considered that the name of Smith-Barry had a higher claim to the consideration of the Subscribers than that of Park Yates.
>
> Mr James Smith-Barry then stated to the meeting that he declined to undertake the Mastership of the North.

Smith-Barry, so Piers recorded in the Cheshire Hunt Minute Book, came to this decision after seeing a letter from Lord Tollemache to Mr Corbet stating that he would allow no one to draw his coverts who was not a landowner in Cheshire. 'So Lord Tollemache, who has not hunted for thirty years and does not subscribe a penny to the Hounds, gave his judgement of who should be Master against over 40 other landowners in Cheshire,' added the Secretary.

At this time a heart complaint prevented seventy-seven-year-old Geoffrey Shakerley from attending the meets in his 'four-wheeler little carriage'. He mentions his condition in a correspondence he was having with a woman in Liverpool, rather intriguingly signing himself 'your well wisher' and sending regular bi-monthly

James Smith-Barry.

219

payments of £5. (He would send half a note and the other half when he heard it had been safely received.) However, he still took a keen interest in hunt affairs and seconded by Piers, opposed the division and wanted the country hunted 'as heretofore, by one Master hunting from the present kennels, not less than 4 days per week'. But a counter proposal to accept Corbet's suggestion was carried, de Tabley, Littledale, Heath and Marshall being the only other dissentients.

This time nothing was heard on the subject from Farmer Dobbin.

The arrangements were all confirmed the following October, but meanwhile the Gorse Covert Committee had difficulties. Some of Lord Tollemache's tenants were

Arthur Smith-Barry.

claiming compensation for damage to grassland and their landlord had been brought into the dispute, mainly due to the disparity of the valuations given by his agent with that of the valuer called in by the Committee, the members of which were concerned about such claims being entertained and encouraged by landlords. The Hunt had already been paying reasonable claims for poultry losses for many years.

PECKFORTON
TARPORLEY

DEAR PIERS WARBURTON

On my arrival yesterday afternoon I found your note. I know not into whose head the idea entered of farmers valuing their own losses, it certainly was not into mine . . .

The hounds with three large fields crossed one of the farms, on which £1,000 had been expended in bonedust, four times in one day, over the other three times in one day. Can I with propriety call upon a tenant to spend hundreds of pounds in bone manure if his land is likely to be ridden over perhaps 2 or 3 times in one day without guaranteeing him compensation in case of serious injury?

. . . I am anxious as anyone to keep up the hunting in Cheshire by making it popular, instead of its becoming an insupportable nuisance. I believe the comparatively few tenants who are seriously injured might receive a fair compensation at no great cost to the hunt...,

y^{rs} very sincerely

Tollemache of Helmingham

Piers promptly sent him a repayment of £18 for the compensation the tenants had already received from the estate and his lordship passed it straight on to the Chester Infirmary.

During the time Corbet had the whole country, the best cub-hunting season was in 1875 and what Rawson called 'a tolerably good season' followed. There were no blank days and he assessed 35 good days, 28 moderate days and 52 bad ones. The best was on January 18th when a fox from 'Wharton' was run to ground at Abbot's Moss, not far from the Kennels. The meet had been at Tattenhall and the run lasted upwards of 2 hrs., *via* Stapleford, Clotton and Huxley and on to Ash Wood, skirting the Willingtons and back to Clotton before going over the steeplechase course and on to High Billinge and Cotebrook before making for Abbot's Moss. Rawson left in disgust when he heard spades called for. His day, however, was complete when 'two ladies came to tea & made themselves exceedingly pleasant'.

At the opening meet at Sandiway Head that season, he noted:

There was the usual large field & the materials there were of the usual mixed quality. More carriages and vehicles of the low sort were at the rendezvous than ever & more noisy foot people too.

When hounds met at Tattenhall on the Wednesday he commented:

Some of the men looked all the worse for their previous night's jollification at The Swan.

The Master was laid up for a time and Jones took his place. On a day from Highwayside in December, after a good 1 hr. 15 mins. from Calveley, there was a difference of opinion as to what the next draw should be. Darnhall was on Jones's written instructions, so thither they went, resulting in a catastrophe. Rawson continues:

Of a brace of foxes found in the Willow Bed one was chopped, the other gave a good hunting run ending in the Forest without blood. When near Booth Lane Smithy poor Arthur Barry got a fall at a boggy brook & his horse either rolled over him or struck him in the back. The result was that the poor fellow's spine was injured. A shutter was procured & he was carried to Williamson's farm. By & by the White Hall dog cart . . . was converted into a sort of ambulance by taking out the seats and filling the vehicle with straw. The victim was carefully transferred into this from the shutter & sent off to Marbury.

As if fate had not been cruel enough for one day, it had in store for the wounded man another trial, *viz.* the death of a valuable horse on which he had mounted [a friend]. The animal was fatally injured in the last run & died almost immediately.

This was the accident that put an end to Arthur Smith-Barry's hunting career.

When Corbet gave up the North in 1877 after ten seasons, he had had according to Rawson, 300 good days, 225 moderate and 574 bad out of 1,099 days sport.

So the country was divided and remained so for the next thirty seasons, with Corbet controlling his allotted South from newly-built kennels at Adderley up to 1901, when his son took over. He had a succession of Kennel Huntsmen, who whipped-in for him, Jimmy McBride, who had been with the Quorn, was one and afterwards he had a man called Littleworth, a good painstaking hunt servant, whom Corbet frequently and unjustly told he was rightly named. Charles Littleworth was with him for over twelve years and only left owing to a bad fall.

It was only a popular notion that the country was divided, for the whole remained under the control of the Subscribers. It was solely a matter of managerial convenience. Strictly speaking the Cheshire continued

John Jones, Huntsman, 1869-1895.

to be kennelled at Sandiway, though it became known as the North Pack, whereas Mr Corbet was Master of the South Cheshire. He started off by taking 25 couple. And Edmund Park Yates of Ince Hall, known affectionately as 'Puffles', continued in charge at Sandiway up to the time of his death from a fall out hunting in 1896. He took Sandiway Lodge as his hunting box. Jones remained as his huntsman.

The Captain was considered a good man in kennels. He favoured a large hound, standing fully 25". Soon he was being successful at Peterborough, chiefly with his bitches. Panic, Tidings, Trivial, Prudence and Passion were all winners. The Cheshire stock was to throw back to these for many generations. Puffles tended to be a bit idle about his desk work and always relied on Mrs P.-Y. to do it for him. 'She's my Chancellor of the Exchequor,' he once wrote to P.E.W.

Jones at this time was at his best and, although heavy, he was well-mounted and always with hounds. Like his previous Master, he had a great knowledge of 'foxcraft'and the way the pack hunted was a credit to him after the depletions from dumbmadness and with the best bitches being taken off to Adderley. Finally his and the Captain's efforts were justly rewarded at Peterborough.

It was said of the South in the *Sporting Gazette & Agricultural Journal* of 1879 that although the country is of small extent, . . . a blank day is unknown, notwithstanding that most earths are stopped at least once a week. There is very little plough. The fences are generally small, but trappy; the land very holding, though carrying good scent. The pack are remarkably quick and handy, and show most excellent sport.

As can well be imagined from the shooting incident of 1873, Corbet had a matchless vocabulary when it came to venting his spleen on a transgressor. But one much quoted story, told of many an M.F.H., had its origin at his expense. Corbet's hounds could make nothing more of their fox after a lengthy run and the Master was reduced to asking an elderly and very deaf rustic if he had 'seen him'. After a great deal of cross-examination, the old fellow admitted to seeing a fox cross the road and go through the hedge. Having made every possibly cast, Corbet returned for reassurance. Was the man quite sure he had seen the fox and how long ago was it? His face must have gone the colour of his coat when he got the reply: 'The day before yesterday, Mister!'

At all events, when Regie Corbet retired from his management of the entire country, a testmonial, limited to a maximum subscription of £5, raised over £1,000. He was presented with a large collection of silver plate

Two good friends, Combermere and Poole.

at the Grosvenor Hotel, Chester, and two hundred or more sat down to a banquet afterwards.

In the corner of a field at Brereton Park Farm, Huxley a stone monument is inscribed 'John Radcliffe died crossing this field with the Cheshire Hounds, 7th March 1879', but no further details are known.

A year or two previously there was a big affair of the heart going on and from which the covert at Combermere got its name – 'Mrs Poole's Riding Wood.' The wife of the future Secretary of the Tarporley Hunt Club, Isabel, eloped with Robert Cotton (211) to Paris and eventually they were married in 1879 after a double divorce, but not before two children had been born and with but a month to spare before the arrival of the legitimate heir in tail mail. The eldest boy, Cecil, was settled with a ranch in British Columbia and his sister, Madeleine, married and left Cheshire. Robert had no issue by his first wife, Charlotte. An unfortunate aspect of this was that his father, Lord Combermere, and Cudworth Poole were at one time inseparable.

The sport in 1879/80 was indifferent, mainly due to the cold winter, and the next season little better. Towards the end of it the Empress of Austria was to arrive at Combermere, though not even in the Cheshire Hunt minute book is there any mention of her first visit in February.

The entry for Tarporley Week that season in Rawson's diary reads:

Heard that sundry members of the Tarporley Club distinguished themselves during the week by the exuberance of their conviviality, also that the club could not agree as to who should be appointed to the vacancy caused by H. Brooke's retirement . . .

Cudworth Poole.

Apparently the candidates included Lord Petersham, the future 8th Earl of Harrington, who was serving in the Cheshire Yeomanry, of which he was to become Honorary Colonel, and Charles Thornycroft. The former never got his green collar; the latter had to wait two years.

* * *

IT WAS IN 1876 AT THE AGE OF THIRTY-EIGHT that the Empress Elisabeth first came to England to hunt, thirty-two years before she was fatally stabbed by an assassin as she boarded a steamer at Geneva. Her visit was at the instigation of her younger sister, Madi, the exiled Queen of the Two Sicilies, who was every bit as accomplished in the saddle. Their father was Duke Maximilian in Bavaria, 'The Good Duke Max'. Madi had been staying for a season or two near Althorp and had suggested Easton Neston as a suitable establishment for her sister to install her entourage and enjoy the

The Imperial Huntress.

sport the Shires had to offer. Sisi had been longing to escape from the Austrian Court and her husband, Franz Josef, gave her the chance she had been seeking ever since she had discovered the joys of hunting in Hungary.

There at Gödöllö, the Royal estate near Budapest, she had first experienced the chase. But it was not always on private land and she hated being the centre of attention of the crowds that gathered. She took to using a leather fan, hung at her saddlebow, to shield herself from the inquisitive stares, well-meaning and admiring though they were. She was one of the first royal personages to attract the *paparazzi*. But the season was short and there was scarcely ever a long run or anything much to jump to test her stud of English-bred hunters.

First the Prince of Wales on a visit to the Vienna Exhibition of 1873 fired her desire to sample Leicester-shire for herself, as only an enthusiastic fox-hunting man can do. The next summer she visited the Isle of Wight incognita as Frau Gräfin Hohenembs, for the stuffy Austrian courtiers and her husband disapproved of foreign tours. Her excuse then was a course of sea-bathing for her youngest daughter. There, for the first time, she met Queen Victoria, who drove over from Osborne; but she shunned her proffered hospitality.

She went up to London, rode in the Row with the Ambassador, and inspected the horses on offer at Tattersalls and later those at Melton, but, mindful of the Emperor's pocket for once, she did not buy and went to stay at Belvoir Castle as a guest of the Duke of Rutland. Before returning to the Isle of Wight, she had a day's cub-hunting. They did not do much, but she was excited by the thud of her horse's hooves on English turf.

At last, early in 1876 with nothing of state importance to prevent her departure, the Empress Sisi with her extensive suite took up residence at Easton Neston, near Towcester. She had leased it from Sir Thomas George Fermor-Hesketh, the 6th baronet and bachelor son of Sir T.G. Hesketh (171), whose wife, Lady Arabella Fermor, had inherited the place from her brother, the last Earl of Pomfret. At the time the family were still very much committed to their Lancashire properties, including Rufford New Hall. Young Sir Thomas was delicate and died at the end of May that year. He was not even present when the inaugural meeting of the Duke of Grafton's Hunt Steeple Chases was held in the park at Towcester in the Empress's honour, a race meeting she herself had suggested.

The very next Monday after her arrival she was out with the Grafton and drove over to Althorp next day for luncheon with Earl Spencer, who arranged to bring out his Pytchley hounds on a bye-day for her on the Wednesday. He at once arranged for Captain 'Bay' Middle-ton[*] of the 12th Lancers, aged 30, to act as her pilot. Although a bye-day, the gentlemen wore scarlet and Bay, in his smart new-fangled high-buttoned cutaway coat, was presented to his royal and lovely charge in the great hall at Althorp.

Captain 'Bay' Middleton.

It was to become an almost permanent relationship and all the time he led her, never once did he spare her; though on occasions when he fell, which were not infrequent, she was perfectly capable of taking her own line.

---

* He was so named after the 1836 Derby winner. Captain W.G.Middleton had been A.D.C. to Lord Spencer when he was Lord Lieutenant of Ireland and, as well as being a brilliant man to hounds, was one of the leading Gentlemen Riders of his day, once winning fourteen consecutive races on one of his horses.

On the visit to Easton Neston one of the greatest moments was when the Empress presented him with her Hohenembs Cup at Towcester Steeplechases amid prolonged cheering.

She acquired a copy of *Hobson's Fox-hunting Atlas for England* and in pencil round the margin of the Northamptonshire page she wrote the dates she hunted from March 7th to 31st, the meets and the horses she rode. For instance:

Castle Thorpe 8 March	Althorp Castle 9 March
Tipperary Lad, Mary Anne	Merry Andrew, Goldney
Mr Lowndes 14 March	Bicester Hounds 18 March
Asteroth	Asteroth

She was out 13 times, thrice with the Bicester. She took the book back to Austria with her, but made no subsequent annotations. It has her tiny book label (XI 22b).

Cold though she may have been to Bay at her first greeting, at the end of the season she invited him to join her at Gödöllő for the opening of the coming season there. Both knew the stakes were unobtainable in the game they were to play, and both stuck rigidly to the strictest rules throughout. Bay also stayed at the Schönbrunn Palace in Vienna, and whilst there, slipped away during a rather grand evening to visit the ladies of the town. He forgot to take any money with him and discovered in the early hours his clothes had been removed as surety. Wrapped in a blanket, he had to march back through streets and creep past the Palace guard to his bed – empty, unlike the one he had just left.(This is as told to the author by the present Lord Langford. In *The Sporting Empress* Welcome gives a more elaborate version, relating it to Gödöllő 20 miles from Budapest, where he ended up at the police station.

The Empress returned to England next year and took up her residence at Cottesbrooke, also in Northamptonshire, from December to February. This time there was no question of being incognita. Nothing like as grand as Easton Neston, Cottesbrooke Park was a Palladian mansion administered by the Commissioners in Lunacy, as Sir James Langham, the current baronet, was insane. On arrival she went immediately to inspect the stables and give Middleton her approval of the hunters he had bought for her. She put her hand on his arm and said: 'Remember, I do not mind the falls, but I will not scratch my face.' So well had Bay schooled them, that she went through the season without a fall.

A year later she arrived in Ireland to hunt from Summerhill with the Ward, Meath and Kildare Hounds. She leased the place from a crony of Spencer and Middleton, Lord 'Paddy' Langford, who hunted from Melton and seldom used his Irish seat. She was again supposed to be travelling as Countess von Hohenembs, but word got about and she received a tumultuous red

carpet welcome to 'Royal Meath'. Her entire suite numbered forty-six persons and her expenditure was £400 a day. But she usually dined frugally alone and refused to accept hospitality from the Viceroy or the Lord Mayor of Dublin.

Almost everywhere she went, she was to be greeted with triumphal arches. Her relations with Buckingham Palace were already strained, and now all the more so, since it had got back to Queen Victoria that Her Imperial and Catholic Majesty, who had installed a private Catholic chapel at Summerhill, had even taken refreshment at a Catholic seminary. One day she had quite innocently accepted hospitality from the President when the Ward Union's carted stag took refuge in the grounds. She was wet through at the time and Dr Walsh, later to be Archbishop of Dublin, wrapped her in his priest's cloak and produced the College's best wine for her party.

Later that season, on the way home from hunting with the Ward Union, she and Bay even 'larked' over the Irish Grand National course at Fairyhouse, then run over banks, including the famous Ballyhack double. She boasted at dinner that she did not think them anything like as formidable as some she had met out hunting. News over her private telegraph of a national disaster at home cut short her visit, but so free and radiantly happy had she been in Ireland, that for the St.Patrick's Day meet she had even worn a sprig of shamrock in the breast of her *matclasse* habit, which had gold buttons bearing the Imperial cipher. Little wonder she was determined to return to her beloved Erin in her thinly disguised anonymity for another season's sport, despite all sorts of political complications, all of which she chose happily to ignore. But the gay Irish atmosphere and Captain Middleton's companionship apart, the visit proved to be not so much fun as her first. In spite of this and the worsening political situation, she still longed to return and to hunt once again with Middleton, who, as it happened, had fractured his skull in a crashing fall against the park railings in a race at Towcester.

In 1880 *The Sporting Life* published these lines:

> *The Queen of the Chase!*
> *The Queen! Yes the Empress!*
> *Look, look, how she flies,*
> *With a hand that ne'er fails*
> *And a pluck that ne'er dies.*
> *The best man in England can't lead her – he's down!*
> *"Bay" Middleton's back is done beautifully brown.*
> > *Hark horn and hark halloa!*
> > *Cram on for a place!*
> > *He must ride who would follow*
> > *The Queen of the Chase!*

They were first chanted as she entered the long dining room at Summerhill. Bay's horses had been letting him down, but he could always take a joke against himself* For when her pilot was otherwise engaged, Elisabeth had taken to carrying a supply of Viennese lace handkerchiefs, which she would drop as a keepsake for anyone opening a gate or assisting her.

Having left her horses at Summerhill, Sisi yearned to return to Ireland for a third season. There was even talk of Kilkenny Castle being put at her disposal. But when this was forbidden by her husband, she sought a new hunting centre, as she was loath to go back to the Pytchley. Fate then took a hand in the matter. Herr Linger, her Hungarian private secretary, who acted as Comptroller of her Household on her visits abroad, had apparently once been employed as a cook at Wynnstay† His ambition and thrift had got him where he was, and the Irish visit falling through, he wrote to Sir Watkin to ask his advice, in the hope that his former employer would suggest a suitable residence.

* * *

BY JANUARY, 1881 THERE WAS AN AIR OF EXPECTANCY in Cheshire hunting circles at the prospect of having such a graceful and attractive Royal visitor in their midst. Corbet had sent a plea to Piers to act 'as soon as possible and before the Empress of Austria arrives'. 'I am quite unable to cope with the unruly blackguards who pest the hunting field and are the cause of so much serious damage to the farmers,' he wrote. At the ensuing meeting he put forward a resolution, adopted from the North

Colonel Sir Wellington Henry Cotton, 2nd Viscount Combermere of Bhurtpore.

Warwickshire Hunt, to introduce a minimum for the Covert Fund subscribers. Except landowners and tenant farmers, anybody else would pay a capping fee of 10/- each hunting day. In future all subscribers of over £20, whether landowners or not, were to be considered Members of the Hunt and 'allowed to wear the 𝕮𝕳 button on their coats'.

By chance Wattie's old friend and fellow officer was staying at Wynnstay Hall when Herr Linger's letter arrived, and, as it happened, after Christmas he was just off to Antigua on a visit with Lady Combermere to inspect the Halladay estates his father had bought from John Tollemache (124). So the whole thing was virtually fixed up over the breakfast table. It was certainly going to be to the Cheshire Chairman's advantage. It was not the first time Royalty had stayed at Combermere. King William III 'lay for the night' there on his way to Ireland and the Battle of the Boyne, his visit commemorated in the Abbey by 'the Orange Room'.

The Empress was to take Combermere Abbey from mid-February to the end of March, the rent being finally agreed at £600 per month. In the meantime extensive improvements and alterations were necessary. The

---

* Staying in the Shires for a Christmas house party, Bay once objected to a fellow guest persisting in wearing his dress-coat after everyone else had changed into smoking jackets to play pool after the ladies had retired. 'Look, here, old chap,' he warned the offender, 'if you come down in a swallow-tail to-morrow, I'm blest if I don't rip it up.' Sure enough the tail-coat appeared as usual and true to his word, as the fellow was making a shot, Bay ripped it clean up the back. 'No harm done, old cock,' snorted the bounder. 'This is *your* coat. If you trot upstairs, you'll find mine on my bed.'

He himself was also an inveterate practical joker and a bit of a 'bear-fighter'. He would bet a lady that he could hide so effectually in her bedroom that she could never find him. She searched high and low, inspecting the bed, testing the floor and every nook and cranny. She was more puzzled still when she heard him cry: 'Cuckoo! I see you!' All was revealed when he wriggled out of the bolster.

† Carl Linger had been Adjutant Court Comptroller since 1875 and became a Knight of the Order of Franz Josef in 1875. He died in 1911. He may possibly in his youth have been employed by Gunter & Co. and worked for a time at Wynnstay, but there is no substantiation of this story.

Gothic windows in her apartment were doubled and the doors were heightened. The house was wired with electric bells and a hot water apparatus was installed by Smith of Whitchurch.

The dressing room next to the Royal bedroom was fitted up as a gymnasium. Sisi had always been fanatical about keeping fit and liked to exercise on wall-bars and trapezes wherever she went. There had to be a special room for all her clothes and a waiting room for those in attendance. Her entire retinue was to number eighty persons. There were twenty-five grooms in the stables.

Among others were her Chamberlain, H.E. Baron Nopcsa and Countess Festetics who acted as her lady-in-waiting as well as Dr Langyi, her personal physician, not to mention a host of servants. Prince Rudi Liechtenstein came along for the hunting. He had the breakfast room as his bedroom. In the ever-hospitable Robert Salusbury Cotton (8)'s day it had been known as the 'deadhouse', where carousing guests, stupified with an excess of wine, were littered on straw to be carried away by footmen.

Browns of Chester supplied furniture and carpets. Lord Combermere's collection of pictures remained *in situ* including the grand picture of the Battle of Bhurtpore and another by Sir Thomas Lawrence of the

1st Viscount at Salamanca, as well as many of the old warrior's Indian trophies, armour, weapons, shields and colours, not to mention a Hindoo idol and a 128 *lb.* elephant tusk, believed to be the largest ever brought to England.*

In addition telegraph wires were laid from Whitchurch and a telephone line put in the housekeeper's room from Wrenbury Station, where a private waiting room for the Empress was constructed on the L.N.W.R. down side and a new siding made for the use of railway horseboxes for her and her party. Sadly the little lonely waiting room was demolished by British Rail in 1967.

The tranquillity of the place with its expanse of water near the house was ideal. Its restful panelled upstairs library, with all the quarterings of the Cotton arms round the coving of the plastered ceiling, a room, which was once the refectory for the XII Century Cistercian monastery, was used by the Empress as a chapel. Above all, its secluded rolling parkland and its woodland were to suit her admirably. The bill to the Emperor's privy purse for everything, including all the improvements to Combermere Abbey, was £10,000. Herr Linger arrived three days early to supervise the finishing touches.

The departure from Vienna had been on the Monday.

The Empress and her pilot, from a sketch by Jno. Sturgess in The Illustrated Sporting and Dramatic News, *19th March, 1881.*

Captain Middleton gives the Empress a lead, from a sketch by W.C.S. in The Whitehall Review. l. to r. *Mr Corbet, Mr H. Tollemache, Mr W. Tollemache, Sir W.W. Wynn, Capt. Park Yates, Lord Rocksavage, H.I.M. the Empress of Austria, Prince R. Liechstenstein, Lord Combermere, Captain Middleton and Lady Rocksavage.*

After a short stay with the King and Queen of the Belgians, again travelling as Countess Hohenembs, she had continued across the Channel and, according to the meticulous *Chronicle* reporter, arrived at 'about seven minutes to six' on the Wednesday evening, straight from Dover, where she had lunched at the Lord Warden Hotel. On arrival at the little Cheshire station there was a large crowd of villagers to greet her, as there had been when her train stopped at Nantwich. 'Her single saloon was 115 ft. from the engine and 157 ft. from the rear' to minimize damage in the event of an accident.

To her delight she was met at Wrenbury Station by Captain Middleton, fully recovered from his fall. The train had come from Euston with the top-hatted Crewe Stationmaster himself on board to see all was well for the last part of the journey. She immediately asked after her horses.

Wearing a black velvet travelling jacket, trimmed with sable, the Empress and her lady-in-waiting then seated themselves in a brougham, drawn by 'two spirited brown horses'. Mr Wycherley, the landlord of the Salamanca, had provided a dozen carriages and traps and the procession set off for the cheerful lights of Combermere where the avenue was lit up.

The previous week Major Rivers Bulkeley had already taken some of her horses out hunting at Tattenhall.

Charles Rivers Bulkeley, who lived near Combermere at Oak Cottage, had, like Park Yates, served in the Indian Mutiny. He was an officer of the Oxfordshire Militia and eventually went on to command the Oxford Light Infantry in South Africa. He had originally served in the Life Guards when he became a firm friend of Sir Watkin, moving to Cheshire at his instigation.[†] He had formerly been Clerk of the Course at Ascot. Much the Empress's

---

[*] There was also a portrait, dated 1568, of Catherine de Burgh, who buried six husbands. Coming back from the funeral of the last, a proposal of marriage was made to her. She expressed her regret, but alas, she had accepted another on the way to the interment.

[†] In May 1884 he was dining with Wattie at his house in St. James's Square, when he heard an explosion. He rushed to the door and suffered severe blast when a second bomb went off, blowing it in. The first had been at the Junior Carlton Club and a second bundle of dynamite had been intended for the Intelligence Dept. of the War Office next door. In Sir Watkin's case the outrage did him no good at all. He was already in poor health and he died a year later. The Major was just recovering from a nasty fall he had just had on the flat, when his horse put his foot in a drain, and what with that and the blast he was kept out of the saddle for two years. But it did not stop him from living to the age of 96. By then, he used to inspect his farm from a pony and trap. He was breaking in a new pony and, to make it handy, he drove it round a field, weaving in and out of the haycocks. Unfortunately one wheel hit a cock, upsetting the trap. He was thrown out and broke his neck.

own age, he was married to the daughter of Mr Davenport of Maer. With the help of Frank Cotton he had bought and schooled some fresh horses for the Royal visitor, all in Cheshire or the Wynnstay country.

At the time the Empress was due, both packs had been showing good sport, so it augured well. There were over a dozen hunters for her, under the charge of Edward MacDonald, her Stud Groom, and Tom Healy, the rough-rider, and including four Austrian horses the two had been schooling in Ireland before bringing the string over. Eight others, belonging to Prince Rudi Liechtenstein, Master of the Imperial Horse and a constant member of her suite, filled the stable yard at Combermere. There was no room for Middleton's horses, which were quartered down the road at Burleydam. Another of her acolytes was young Count Charles Kinsky, by then attached to the Austro-Hungarian Embassy. A dashing rider, who had hero-worshipped Bay ever since he first met him at Gödöllö Castle, he had been with the Empress at Cottesbrooke and got leave to join her in Cheshire. He was put up at Whitchurch, with his horses at the Salamanca Inn, Wrenbury.

In Cheshire as in Ireland, the Empress usually wore a close-fitting blue cloth habit, the collar and cuffs trimmed with Astrakhan, 'unless it threatened wet, and then she was encased in white waterproof'. When she first came to England she brought sixteen habits and more were ordered from London. Like others before them, the Cheshire ladies were slightly shocked that she did not wear a petticoat, but preferred next to her skin a special garment of chamois leather, into which she was sewn.

It was always a lengthy business getting ready on a hunting morning and she had kept many a Master waiting. At Combermere, a Whitchurch tailor, called Mr James, would be in attendance to sew the skirt of her habit to the tight-fitting bodice to prevent the slightest crease or wrinkle round her eighteen-inch waist. Her long auburn tresses were plaited up under her tall silk hat and her appearance has been described as the ultimate of femininity. She liked to wear two pairs of silk gloves, usually under a third pair of tan-coloured leather, trimmed with fur, and to carry a long gold-mounted cutting whip.

But before her dresser helped her into her clothes, she underwent a complicated toilette. 'Her facial preparation was made up of cold cream camphor and borax. There was also a strawberry ointment made from the juice of wild berries mixed with vaseline and preserved with salicylic acid,' it is disclosed in *The Sporting Empress*, such cosmetic preparations having been made up by specialists under her personal supervision. And

if her skin had been exposed to the sun for any time at all a mask of honey, carefully purified, or potcheese as a variant, was applied to her face and left there for at least two hours. A hair shampoo was made up of a mixture which combined pressed onions, cognac and Peru balsam. For massage another special lotion comprising ox-gall, alcohol and glycerine was used. During the hunting season or if she was riding every day this was varied by yet another special receipt of her own known as her 'muscle water'. She was convinced that this relaxed all body tensions and so proud of it was she that barrels of this strange love potion were actually shipped to England for the personal use of Captain Middleton.

So fanatical was the Empress about her complexion, that she had even been known to have 'the gladiator's bath' of oil brought almost to boiling point and mixed with water as hot as she could stand. It had originated in Corfu, but intrigued though her sister was by Sisi's cosmetic aids, the Queen of Naples refused this one. 'I am neither a sardine nor an old leather saddle to be preserved in oil,' she told her.

However, at Combermere tanks of sea water were brought by rail and road from the Welsh coast to provide Her Majesty with hot sea-water baths, as well as Lake Vyrnwy drinking water. Her bath maid was Ethel Slater, aged only 11, who later became nurse to the Crossley family and remained in their employment when Sir Kenneth bought Combermere after the Great War.

Usually a bowl of chicken, beef and game broth of her own concoction was all she had before setting out. At the end of the day when she may have been offered to take tea, she often relished instead a glass of beer. By the time she was at Combermere, fearful of putting on weight or acquiring unsightly wrinkles, she was on a much stricter diet. At one time her riding weight had been a mere 8st.7lb., including her cumbersome side-saddle. Her masks of raw veal and crushed strawberries were failing to iron out the tiny lines about her mouth and eyes. Live turtles were brought to the kitchens, and these supplemented her diet of raw meat juice and oranges, to which she restricted herself whenever she tipped the scales a few ounces more than her liking.

All the while she took an immense pride in her physical fitness. On non-hunting days she would personally school horse after horse almost to exhaustion, returning to the stables time after time, quite unfatigued, to bring out another and work it to her satisfaction. The dapper Tom Healy had now been promoted to 'Rider in Attendance' – 'My Tom' she called him – and he it was who lifted her onto the saddle, first removing his hat and placing it safely to one side. On visits further afield, a carriage would go on ahead with her dresser, Frau von

H.I.M The Empress of Austria, from a painting by C. de Grimm for Vanity Fair.

were Nihilist, Sweetheart, Patience, Prudence, Sunflower, and Quicksilver. Apparently she was not satisfied with the new ones MacDonald had produced.

Her insistence on only Tom riding her horses was sometimes the cause of annoyance. On a day with Lord Stafford's Hounds soon after her arrival and after a long run there was no sign of her second horseman, even after Captain Middleton had scoured the countryside. They met him on the way home, too late to be of any use. The second groom always had to ride another horse and lead H.M.'s second mount and coming to some big fences it was impossible to get both over, so he had to go back a long way and round by the road.

Her Majesty's first appearance in the Cheshire hunting field was from a meet at Adderley Hall the day after her arrival. As she alighted from her carriage and pair. Corbet was presented by Bay Middleton and she immediately mounted one of her chesnuts, which, repeatedly tossing its head, seemed to know its royal mistress. But there were no more than thirty present and there followed a nice little hunt of 1 hr. 20 mins. *via* Wilkesley, Ash House and back to the lake at Combermere. The scent failed after the fox had swam the mere, and he was given up.

The very next day she was at Cholmondeley, met by Lord and Lady Rocksavage and a few close friends, including Lord Cole, and mounted her favourite Hard Times privately in the Castle forecourt; while down below an eager field with smiling faces waited as Mr Corbet threw his bitches in to hunt through the laurels. It was a fair but cloudy morning and the overnight wind had dried up the ground. The Special Correspondent of *The Chester Chronicle* described the Empress as 'the finest horsewoman in Europe':

> She is tall, a brunette in complexion, with a figure that is simply divine; lithe as a willow, and her every movement, as she guides her horse with consummate skill, is graceful in the extreme. She wears a silk hat, dark habit, tight-fitting, which shows all the graceful outlines of her lovely form. She carries a switch whip in her hand, and I hear a fan that she has to shield her from the intrusive stare of the vulgar gaze, but today I did not even see it.

After a scurry up to Bulkeley and back with Middleton and his Royal charge in the van, hounds were taken off to Quoisley where another fox exercised the three-hundred strong field for 1 hr. 40 mins. before surrendering his brush just in front of Marbury Hall. Not many were there at the end and even the Empress lost her place for a time, when Bay's horse slipped on a bank and fell back into a ditch.

Feyfalik, and a footman with her carefully packed hunting clothes and other accoutrements, which included Her Majesty's gold chamber pot, bearing the Imperial arms and usually conveyed round the lanes in a special carriage as a convenience for herself and the ladies of her suite. At local meets a young lad called Jimmy Sudden would go with the second horsemen, proudly in charge of the royal sandwich case, strapped to his pony's saddle.

On Sundays after Mass, usually celebrated by a priest from Nantwich, Father Derry, she would have a schooling session in the park, jumping fences which Healy had erected for her. This once gave rise to a report in the local press that she had had a drag hunt on the Sabbath, but it was quickly scotched by Herr Linger. Apart from 'endearing epithets' in her soft musical voice, she would reward her mounts with slices of apple or turnip, which she carried wrapped in tissue paper. Her favourites in Cheshire were Hard Times, Mercury, Chatterbox, The Doctor, Domino, Bay and Cameo. Among the others

On the Saturday she graced the Wynnstay field at Macefen on a crisp bright morning and hounds were soon on a good line heading for Cholmondeley with the Empress sailing along with just Tom Healy in attendance, the Captain having again dropped behind. She spent much of the day chatting with Lord Combermere's daughter, Hester, who had married 'Dandy' Paget (228) the previous August. Her husband acquired his soubriquet owing to his immaculate turn-out, no matter what sport was on the *tapis*. When he travelled by train, he invariably went 1st Class, his valet 2nd and his wife and the children 3rd. It was probably on his spouse's insistence as, in spite of being a director of the company, he was not well off, being a younger son.

'Dandy' (228)

Following an afternoon Mass on Sunday, the Empress's entire stud was paraded for her inspection in the stableyard, before she had a gallop in the park with Prince Rudi, Bay and Charles Rivers Bulkeley, followed by a ride in the surrounding countryside.

There was no hunting on Monday. Next day Mr Corbet took his hounds to Wrenbury, where the Royal party was supposed to meet him. They arrived late and missed him altogether. On the Wednesday she had a day at Woore with the North Staffordshire Hounds, again on Hard Times. It was a hot sunny day and her fan was much in use. There was a long slow hunt of 2 hrs. over big fences.

An article in *The Whitehall Review* mentions that Captain Middleton had been staying near Ash and was training his steeplechasers on Mr Bourne's farm. The Ash Grand National Hunt Meeting took place on Thursday, February 24th attended by the Empress, who viewed the proceedings with Prince Liechtenstein from a commanding hill. To the delight of the crowd she had ridden elegantly over a few of the fences on her way from the paddock to her vantage point, acknowledging the cheers that rang out with a graceful little nod of her head. She had donated £200 to the organizers through Charles Bulkeley, acting as Clerk of the Course. The Starter was Lord Combermere, back from the West Indies, and living in his little house at Bunbury. (He continued to

lease the Abbey after the Empress had gone, this time to the Grosvenor family for many years.)

The Cheshire race, in which Willie Hall Walker had a ride, was won by Arthur Brocklehurst on a horse of Captain Beatty's and in the North Stafford Hunt Chase Lord Stafford's nomination was just beaten by Mr Regie Corbet, Jnr. After anxiously watching Bay, who had broken a stirrup-leather going over the third fence in the last race, his only ride, she could not resist it and jumped in behind the runners over the last two fences. Bay got beat a length by an unnamed three-year-old filly at long odds; *The Whitehall* claimed a more exciting neck! But what the writer could not have known was that the winner was a future Aintree heroine. Bay advised Kinsky to buy it, which he did a year later and in 1883, on Zoedone, he became the first foreign rider to win the Grand National, with a tremendous 'View Holloa!' from Bay as they jumped the last. Kinsky and Middleton were the greatest of friends and one of the former's favourite reminiscences was about the terrific 'bear fight' at the Café Royal a year or two later, when Bay took on a score of opponents on his stag night. The Count's admiration for Bay was as his *beau-ideal* of a first-rate rider to hounds. 'Though his was rather a military seat,' he once wrote, 'it was not in the least stiff – on the contrary very elastic; and I don't think I ever saw a man in more perfect unison with his horse than he was... Her Majesty, who always addressed him as "Bay", had a great private regard for him as a faithful and always cheery and amusing friend.'

Friday saw her with Mr John Leche (173) and Sir Watkin at Carden. She arrived shortly after 10, but frost

Count Charles Kinsky on Zoedone.

Sir W.W.Wynn's Hounds meet at Carden on Thursday, February 24th, 1881. The Empress comes out of the Hall with some biscuits for the horses after an hour's delay. From an oil painting by Elizabeth Scrivener.

caused a delay and she stayed in the house until midday when she took some biscuits out to her horse before mounting. Off they went to draw The Royals.

On Saturday she was out again with the Wynnstay at Cloverley Hall, next door to Shavington. Ill-health had been keeping 'The Prince in Wales' out of the saddle, but on this occasion Sir Watkin himself was out to show her the right line. The *Whitehall* reported:

> . . . Her Majesty had a splendid run at Cloverley; leading throughout. The Empress won her first brush after a hard race with Lady Rocksavage in the middle of a fearful hailstorm.

With both Bulkeley and Middleton close by, she and Hard Times had led the field over the Ash Steeplechase course and hounds ran into their fox just short of the Cheshire's Square Covert at Burleydam. The Major whipped off the hounds at once to preserve the brush, which Payne deftly removed with his coiled lash, and the Master was soon on the scene to order the award.

She beamed with pleasure when Charles Payne handed the brush to her. Inevitably someone set it to verse:

WITH THE WYNNSTAY

A welcome to the Kaiserinn, who rides so straight and well,
No other lady in the Hunt from her may bear the bell.
From Austria's old imperial halls she comes to English land,
And not a rider in the field has lighter bridle hand,
So gallantly she races on through all the livelong day;
And who would shirk the fences when an Empress leads the way?
The meet was fixed for Cloverley – the hounds were Watkin
    Wynn's,
An old dog-fox was quickly found, and 'Yoicks'! away he spins,
Past Ightfield on to Hall, he ran for Wilkesley like the wind;
But there upon the course at Ash the hounds were close behind.
Heads up they ran, before them fled the fleet fox for his life;
In sooth it was a 'crowded hour' of not inglorious strife.
So fared me with the Wynnstay Hunt, and ever in the van,
Though Middleton and Bulkeley rode as English sportsmen can,
Upon her grand old horse Hard Times, the Empress sailed away;
The dark blue habit shone for us an oriflamme that day.
She topped the fence, she flew the brook–now sound the fox's
    knell,
And doff the cap, and hand the brush the Empress wins so well.

The hailstorm then caused everyone to gallop to Mr Bourne's farmyard for shelter and Her Majesty was congratulated on all sides. There was a delay of some 15 mins. and many began to drift away as there was no other Wynnstay covert near enough to draw. The Empress scarcely had time to change on to her second horse, Butterduck, when farmworkers sheltering in a ditch gave a resonant hollao. The clattering of the horses on the farmyard had caused a fox to sneak away along the headrows and soon the dog pack was on its scent as the field gave chase in a snowstorm. He eventually saved his brush at Cloverley Wood, after passing Shavington and making for Styche. For all one knows, the Empress may have jumped 'the Squire Trap'.

For some reason best known to himself the London columnist had continued:

> I cannot describe how the Empress regrets more and more every day that the trouble prevented her from going to Ireland. She finds the fences here small and far between; and when she does come across a thumping one she always turns her head in sheer contempt for it. This amuses the field.

She may have made scant pretence at her disdain for the Cheshire fences, but it was Sir Watkin Williams-Wynn, himself, who said she looked like an angel and rode like the devil. Her best horses, 'Cameo, in particular, always a tricky ride in a trappy country, disliked Cheshire almost as much as she did herself', wrote one of her biographers. Besides Hard Times, Quicksilver, Sunflower and the one called Butterduck turned out to be the best rides. Most of them had been brought over from Summerhill. She had twenty-two days out of a possible twenty-eight, two of which were lost through snow. Bay piloted her on each, except for two when he was away racing and the Major stood in for him.

In spite of its correspondent's forthright comment *The Whitehall* published yet another version of *The Queen of the Chase* with some additional verses in honour of her Cheshire visit:

> *Now, o'er the big pastures she's sailing away;*
> *You may go as you please, you'll not catch her to-day;*
> *For, if you should try it, you'll find to your pain*
> *"Hard Times" still before you and "coming again".*
> *Hark, horn! &c.*

Augustus, Puffles and Moses.

Oh, Corbet, Rocksavage, your crests you must bow;
Dread lords of the Cheshire, where, where are you now?
A woman can beat you, and if 'tis a sin,
You must bear it, and like your own Cheshire cats, grin.
    Hark, horn! &c.

Oh, often and long may the Empress be here,
To brighten the shadows of old Combermere!
Let the "Leaguers" take heed of WHITEHALL'S *true report –*
That England won't stand any spoiling of sport!
    Hark, horn! &c.

The Empress had a dinner party on Sunday the 27th. Snow had been falling all day.

On the Monday, while the snow dispersed, Elisabeth had a quiet day inspecting her horses, sacked an Irish groom or two, and went for a quiet trot in the afternoon. But frost and more snow prevented any hunting on Tuesday, when hounds were supposed to have been at Wrenbury. Conditions at Combermere did not prevent her taking the opportunity to do some schooling.

Thick snow looked like making Wednesday another day of forced abstention, but the thaw set in and at two o'clock Corbet set off from a meet at Brown Hall, Wrenbury, going towards Combermere, where Rudi, Charles Kinsky and Bay were ready with the Empress for whatever sport could be had. A fox gave them an exciting run of 30 mins. before eluding his pursuers. The small field of thirty or forty was soon off again and this time scent ran out before they reached Whitchurch Station. Hounds were taken to try again at Wirswall, but it being 4 o'clock, the Empress decided on home and to the delight of the local populace rode back through the town, allowing Healy to dismount for a moment at the Victoria Hotel.

Edmund Park Yates had been hoping to welcome her at Calveley on the Thursday, but the Imperial visitor did not arrive in the special train. She had considered it too cold to venture out and instead went in the afternoon to the Victoria Hotel to meet her niece, Countess Larisch, who had arrived with her husband from London. They had brought horses with them to join the Royal hunting party. Meanwhile Prince Rudi, Bay and the Major had moderately good sport with Captain Puffles.

Again frustrated on the Friday, a private bye-day was arranged overnight for Ridley Toll Bar, where the Master of the North Cheshire was with Corbet's select field of about fifty, invited to join in the sport laid on overnight for the party from Combermere. The Empress arrived in a brougham with Count Georg Larisch and Bay was just behind in a polo cart, having ridden a winner at Sandown the previous day. There was no shortage of foxes and they had a twisting, turning sort of a day,

running first to Haughton and then back all along the foot of the Peckforton Hills. The quarry was lost after 1 hr. 30 mins. with the Imperial Huntress in the first flight throughout.

Harry Rawson's first mention of Empress Elisabeth's visit was

> Feb. 26 Saighton.
> The Empress being expected there was a vast crowd at the meet. In consequence of the howling and screaming of this multitude, two foxes were chopped in the Eaton plantation. A third, however, got away and gave a smart scurry to Royalty where it was lost. Yates then trotted off to Handley where there was a find, but the animal was a vixen, so hounds were whipped off. The day ended with a good gallop from Crow's Nest to Cote Brook, which had a bloodless end.

But that was the day the Royal visitor had decided to go to Sir Watkin's meet at Cloverley.

At last it was Captain Yates's turn on Monday, March 7th at The Three Greyhounds and a train was waiting overnight at Wrenbury to take the party to Holmes Chapel at an early hour. Sadly it was a most disappointing day. Word had got out and the lanes were thronged with people of every description on foot and on horseback and in carriages and traps. At least the sun shone, as she wended her way, escorted by Bay and Rudi, constantly inclining her head as hats were doffed. But to the Master's chagrin, covert after covert was drawn blank and there was not a trace of scent. To make matters worse there came a dreadful thunderstorm, followed by a continuous downpour, but the faithful Feyfalik was waiting with a change of clothes when Sisi got back to the train at 4 o'clock.

> 'Left at three o'clock,' wrote Harry Rawson, 'up to which time there had not been a find. This was the more disappointing for the Master, as the Empress was out for the first time with the North pack. Her Imperial Majesty rides one bit better a horsewoman than many of the Cheshire dames and damsels, who follow, & is not as good looking as some of the latter.'

It was a warm day with thunder showers at intervals. After other coverts were drawn in vain, 'Yates scored his first blank day'.

Sisi missed a good run from Dunham on March 9th when there was a small field out. Lady Alexander Paget excelled herself on 'this most enjoyable day'. Riding a strange horse, she 'took a line of her own & was at the tail of the hounds during all the fast part of the 1st run'.

That day a train from Crewe with no less than forty-five horse boxes steamed into Wrenbury Station for Mr

Corbet's meet, conveying contingents from Lancashire, Staffordshire and Shropshire. The Empress, wearing a dark brown tweed habit, joined the cavalcade at Oakwood on the way to draw Broomhall. This time there was a burning scent and a regular stampede as the fox had gone away from the far side of the Gorse. Making for Hatherton and then Aston, and back towards Broomhall before being headed for Broomlands and on towards Audlem. Hounds ran into their fox with the field spread-eagled. But the Empress, Winifred Rocksavage, known to her close friends as Tiger, and Henry Tollemache were all up in the last 10 mins. They then all hacked three miles back to Broomhall and on to the Wrenbury coverts, which were all blank.

Meanwhile it had been extensively reported that Her Majesty was to be the guest for a short time of Mr and Mrs Wilbraham Tollemache, Henry's parents, at Dorfold Hall, where the James I Room had been refurbished for her.

Next day there was a choice of going to Norton-in-Hales with the Marquess of Stafford or to Carden again with Sir Watkin, both equidistant. She chose the latter, preferring his country. After the first draw was blank, hounds were put on to the line of the fox, which had been seen sneaking away from a plot of gorse half-a-mile away and were soon on good terms, running for Langton before wheeling for Broxton and completing the circle back to Carden. She had plenty of stiffish fences to jump.

When she got home, much to the disappointment of the landlord of The Swan when word reached him, she altered her plan to join the North Cheshire at Tarporley Town End next morning and ordered her train for Whitchurch to take her for a day as a guest of Sir Vincent Corbet and the North Shropshire at Shawbury. They had a good little run from Acton Reynold to Hawkstone, but not much else to please her.

When Empress Elisabeth did not turn up on Friday, March 11th at The Rookery, Baron von Schröder's place, for a day with Mr Corbet's South Cheshire pack, the Baron and Marie, his wife, were much disappointed, as were the workers from the Nantwich boot factories who took the day off to clog up the lanes, hoping for a glimpse of her. Word soon came that she had chosen at the last moment to go in her private train to hunt with Sir Watkin's hounds at Baschurch, rather than face the eager throng. By then Paddy Langford had also arrived and joined the party.

Rawson reported the Worleston meet:

A most unsatisfactory sort of day by all accounts. A line of carriages extending for a mile, crowds of people on foot & inumerable horsemen out. The sport consisted in running

a fox from Poole into the town of Crewe. Some wag suggested that the animal was probably making its way back to London.

She was out again on the Saturday with the Wynnstay locally at Iscoyd, reported *The Illustrated Sporting and Dramatic News*,

... the élite and sporting gentry of the neighbourhood were there, the crowd of yesterday were conspicuous by their absence. I think Her Majesty could have no complaint of being made uncomfortable. Although the fan was used very freely, I think it was more from habit or to shield [her] from the sun. I cannot say myself it looks becoming; perhaps in Austria it might be considered the correct thing.

As the deer browsed in the park, Mr Godsal provided a hearty breakfast for those of his guests who had ridden from afar. Many had to shake out their waterproofs before setting out, for there had been heavy rain. These garments were usually rolled up in a narrow valise strapped to the saddle. But the sun soon began to shine on the large assemblage outside. Sir Watkin was in-disposed and the Empress, on Quicksilver, asked Payne about him and when hounds moved off she followed immediately, with Captain Middleton just ahead. Hounds eventually lost a Macefen fox to ground by Grindley Brook and she was close behind them all the way. Not so the Countess of Rocksavage, whose favourite chesnut got stuck in a gully on the drop side of the first big rasper, she herself soon lightly on her feet. Her Majesty enjoyed a second run on Shamrock.

On Sunday evening she received a wire informing her of the Emperor of Russia's assassination and instantly telegraphed her husband in case she should be needed to return at once to Vienna. But no such command was received and the Imperial train went to Holmes Chapel next morning. But they waited at the station while an engine was sent back to Wrenbury to pick up the mail, just in case. No word came and she ordered the horses to be unboxed and they rode off to join Captain Park Yates at Jodrell Hall for her second day with him, but not a fox was found all day. Her presence was the topic of much chit-chat among those who thought she should have stayed at home.

As Harry Rawson put it: 'That she should have been out at all, was a matter of surprise to some.'

The Empress was dressed in mourning when she arrived at Wilkesley next day. This time it was Mr Corbet's turn to apologise when not a covert yielded a fox. On Wednesday she drove in the brougham to Doddington, where the recently engaged Mr Broughton was on the steps to receive her before a great crowd in

Lord Combermere and his daughter, Lady Alexander Paget, follow the Empress and Bay Middleton.

front of the hall, which had not been occupied for fifteen years. Before mounting Sunflower she had some refreshment in the oak-wainscoted dining room, Henry Tollemache, the Rocksavages, Baron von Schröder and Lord Combermere among the familiar faces present. Not surprisingly, with all the crowd, the home coverts were blank but they later hacked off back to Combermere, satisfied after a run of 35 mins. from a wood two miles away.

All Cheshire seemed to converge down the coach avenue leading to Oulton Park on the Thursday morning, and by 11 o'clock 400 horsemen and women had congregated on the sward in front of the great Vanbrugh mansion. The Royal train was delayed owing to the derailment of another engine between Winsford and Hartford and she still had a six-mile hack through Whitegate and Little Budworth to the meet. To avoid further delay getting through the crowded park, Major Bulkeley escorted her up the back drive to be greeted by Sir Philip, who found time to show her over the Hall before taking slight refreshment. With him were the Corbets, Captain Park Yates and Lady Charlotte Barry, Lord Cole's sister.

The Pleasure Grounds and Hazelhurst were un-tenanted, but a brace went away from Darley Gorse, as if for Darnhall. Puffles was hunting hounds and unfortunately chose the one which made for Marton when they divided, about five good fences later. They ran for 25 mins. to Abbot's Moss and the Forest, before a keeper told them she was a vixen heavily laden. Hounds were whipped off at once, but not before there had been many falls and a lot of hats crushed or scratched by branches overhead. The Master then took them across country to Calveley, trying some small coverts on the way. A ploughman reported the other travelling fox, whose scent was picked up, and they ran to Wardle and then back to Page's Wood in the Oulton country, which enabled the Captain to provide some good sport for his Royal guest at last and Hard Times allowed not a soul to head her on the tail of the pack.

On Saturday, with Sir Watkin confined to bed with a cold, Payne provided a really busy day from Cloverley, eventually ending up at Burleydam – a run of 1 hr. 40 mins. and the distance no less than 17 miles with but three checks. Snow fell heavily all over Cheshire on the Monday, but, indefatigable, she joined Sir Vincent Corbet for a meet at Hawkstone, where she found Lord Spencer was staying with Lord Hill; the latter, a martyr to rheumatism, was riding to hounds for the first time for many years. Hounds were put into the rhododendron beds and a fox was found, just as a terrible snowstorm started, accompanied by a hurricane. Taking shelter for a while, they tried again with the field diminished to an intrepid twenty. But down came the snow again and everyone made for home. Lord Spencer went back with Sisi to Combermere.

Corbet was determined to hunt on the Tuesday, despite the snow and sent a whipper-in to the Abbey to let them know he was at Wrenbury with the hounds and that hunting was just possible. The Empress for once did not care to risk the venture, but Lords Combermere and Spencer, Middleton, Bulkeley and Rudi Liechtenstein presented themselves as well as Captain and Mrs Beattie who had been to lunch. It was reported that the party had a 'most exciting 45 mins. run'. The snow had been 4 ins. thick that morning.

A misty rain fell next day and by noon the snow was dispersed, but the Combermere party had decided on Woore for a final day with Lord Stafford and arrived at Woore Hall in broughams for a light lunch. Hounds had no sooner been lifted into a spinney half-a-mile away, when the heavens opened and everyone clambered for their overcoats. The Empress herself donned her smart white cloth waterproof,

which fitted her as wonderfully as her habits, [reported *The Chronicle*]. It would have been well for half the ladies present if they had brought a like garment... The field took up a position to the windward side of the spinney, while Captain Middleton brought the Empress round the corner to get into some kind of shelter. Hardly had the pack been thrown in when a fox broke away right between the Empress and Captain Middleton, going up wind . . .

 . . . everyone took his horse by the head and faced the storm. The fox ran at a rattling pace for Doddington, the hounds not being three fields behind, running up wind with heads up and sterns down, followed closely by the Empress, who took some very stiff posts and rails in her flight.

 . . . of those who rode up late, many were stained with the trade-mark that mother earth always afflicts her sons with. . . The run lasted about 30 mins., the first half of which was run at a clinking pace dead against a blinding storm of rain. The country was simply flooded and the shower of clods and dirt sent up by the foremost riders' horses into the faces of those that followed covered them with a layer hardly distinguishable from those who had been down; in fact when the field drew up, each presented more the appearance of a London mud-cart man than the spic and span-clad sportsmen that hied to the meet in the morning.

Elisabeth did not wait to see any other coverts drawn and rode off home to Combermere.

Next morning, March 24th, she went by train to Tattenhall, where Captain Park Yates had to cope with a very large crowd. Unfortunately she went straight to Handley, thinking it would be the first draw. Owing to the presence of a litter of cubs, it had been decided not to draw it and the field was kept waiting nearly an hour until Park Yates trotted off by himself to fetch 'the great Lady'. Crow's Nest was drawn and after a while a fox broke in the direction of Beeston Castle, before wheeling towards Peckforton Gap and was eventually lost on Bickley Hill. Two hours were spent trying to find a fox round Peckforton and Beeston. It was a cold day and the Captain decided to trot on to Huxley for a final draw, but it was blank.

Rawson wrote in his diary:

Left Jones going to try Huxley. A large & rough field out. The incident of the day was that a young dame was ridden over. The culprit was one of the Empress's suite!

Next day Bay accompanied her in the train from Wrenbury to Edgehill station, where Lord Sefton put a brougham at her disposal to convey them to Aintree for the Grand National. There, a lot of friends from Ireland, as well as Paddy Langford, joined her party and the rest of the suite. They were all on the winner, Woodbrooke, trained by Henry Linde, the Curragh trainer, his second in succession.* It was a wet and windy day with the race run in a heavy storm.

The Empress of Austria left for London on the Monday and visited the Queen at Windsor before going on to Paris.

So far as Cheshire society was concerned, she restricted her formal calls to Wynnstay, the Rocksavages at Cholmondeley and to Eaton, where she was enchanted by the tour of the Stud the recently bereaved Duke gave her. 'She stood in mute admiration for many minutes at the splendid mares and beautiful foals.' Sir Philip, who was to die that April, and Lady Grey-Egerton, who was a Legh, gave a dinner party for her at Oulton.

The Cheshire ladies invited her to their houses the first year, but she only used to ask the men in return. They did not bother to ask her when she came again the next year.

---

* Linde's Grand National winner the previous Spring had been the 5 y.o. mare, Empress, named by him in Elisabeth's honour. She and Bay had gone round his stables a few weeks beforehand. The apple of her then owner-trainer's eye was lying down and refused to rise in the Royal presence. Fortunately Sisi had one of her lace handkerchiefs to hand to smother her laughter as the great horsemaster, noted for his rough tongue, kicked the poor creature in the ribs and shouted: 'Get up, you bitch!'

On March, 26th the Empress missed what Rawson described as 'the severest day of the season, but by no means the most enjoyable'. The meet was at Appleton.

Proceedings commenced with a bagman which broke its neck by jumping down a steep place into a road and which smelt villainously of aniseed. Then whilst trotting off to draw again there was a holloa. Jones took his hounds to it & a run lasting 2 hrs. 30 mins. ensued. Points: the Hill Cliff, Walton Hall, Rose Wood, Hatton, Newton, Grimsditch, Whitley, Grimsditch again, Cobbler, Stretton Heath, nearly to High Legh, then Grappenhall, Appleton, Hill Cliff & Walton Hall again, & Rose Wood to the neighbourhood of Daresbury where the fox was lost.

The last day was April 2nd – 'not a bad season on the whole,' thought Rawson, ' a better one than 1879/80. The features were the bad weather, the great gale of January 18th, the loss of hounds by drowning, by being killed on the railway, and the visit of the Empress.'

* * *

THE FOLLOWING SEASON Rawson was plagued with gout. By the end of it there had been six stoppages for frost and snow in the North and the South only twice with not a single blank day. Yates had three. Rawson summed it up as

A remarkable season in every way. Sport good throughout & weather equally so. Accidents unusually numerous, Mrs Littledale, Reiss, Hy Tomkinson, self, &c &c all victims . . . Self came to grief on Feb. 20th [after being off for a week or two with gout] & was not able to hunt afterwards. On the 14th October, 1881 one of the greatest gales ever remembered occurred. It extended all over the country and did an immense amount of damage . . . Although neither pack had a great run, both had innumerable runs above the average. There was hardly a day after which fellows went home disgusted.

Despite the gale, hounds were out cub-hunting at Calveley next morning – a cold disagreeable showery day, 'no scent, no sport & not many foxes', but they killed one in covert at Tilstone. At Arley in November Mrs Littledale had had to be carried off the field on a gate. After the High Legh earths were found to be unstopped, he commented 'that in consequence of the late affray & the threatened vengeance of the poachers on the keepers, the latter had been afraid to go out at night'. Some armed salt miners had had a set-to with Colonel Legh's keepers, who gave them as good, if not better than they got. The culprits were sent down for 18 months hard labour. It

seems the field was 'very rough' that day too. 'Monkey' Hornby broke his collar bone, but the most dramatic accident was when Henry Tomkinson's horse bolted with him at Combermere and crashed into some iron railings. The steed was much cut and the rider broke several ribs.

On the second visit the Empress of Austria left Calais on February 4th and arrived at Combermere at 6 o'clock the same evening, when she learnt to her consternation that Captain Middleton had become engaged. (The lady he married, Miss Charlotte Baird, sister of the Master of the Cottesmore and kinswoman of the reprobate 'Squire', 'Mr Abington' Baird of Bedford Lodge, Newmarket, brought with her £20,000 a year.) Major Rivers Bulkeley took his place and few were better qualified for the task. He had already been supervising her stud of hunters. 'Very "slippy" must hounds have gone away to leave him behind,' was *Baily's* appraisal, though Moreton Frewen described him as being rather a stooping square-shouldered rider and not particularly fashionable to look at on a horse. But that did not stop him being a competent steeplechase rider, once winning the first four races at Bangor-on-Dee and having a crashing fall on the hot favourite in the last. In his younger days he rode as 'Mr Charles'.[†]

Col. Rivers Bulkeley, CB, *from* "The Throne & Country" *cartoon.*

What is more, Major Rivers Bulkeley would have known the country much better than Middleton, especially the Wynnstay, as he had often acted as field master for his old friend, Wattie.

At the ivy-clad Abbey Sisi had the same small bedroom looking out on the mere and its teeming wild fowl, but the thrill of the chase was just beginning to pall and this was to be her last season in the hunting field, except for a few days at Chantilly, just after she left, and in Hungary. The Major was no substitute for the Captain

† In 1953 for sentimental reasons his grandson, Brigadier T.F.R. Bulkeley, entered his good hunter-chaser for the Empress of Elisabeth Steeplechase at Towcester and won with ease.

so far as she was concerned. As John Welcome wrote in *The Sporting Empress*:

> . . . Apart altogether from the sport and success [Bay] brought her, in her intensely feminine way she loved the domination he exerted over her when they hunted together. The shouts of where and when to go, the uninhibited language when she disobeyed, redeemed always by his infectious laugh, were things to be treasured and preserved.[*]

She was out on the Monday after her arrival. But unlike Middleton, Rivers Bulkeley could not bring himself to give his orders direct to Her Majesty, but would address them almost comically to the groom in attendance upsides. 'Ride on here, Tom,' he would call or 'Take a pull at this one, Tom,' he would shout to the amusement of the Cheshire field. Elisabeth herself did not see the funny side.

Her first outing was with Sir Watkin, but he had enough by two o'clock and took his hounds home. Not so the Empress; she had some lunch, mounted a fresh horse and had an exhilarating spin with the drag-hounds in the vicinity of the Abbey. But perhaps she had done too much for she did not go with the others to Marbury next day and stayed indoors. There was plenty of sport and two foxes were killed.

Her Majesty joined a big field at Doddington on Wednesday, but nothing was done until the afternoon when they ran in a circle round Adderley, Audlem, Hankelow and back to Doddington. On Friday the meet was at Cholmondeley Castle with the usual large field and crowd of onlookers, who were not disappointed. Also out was a party from Eaton, including two future Masters of the Queen's Buckhounds, Lord Ribblesdale and Compton Cavendish with his wife, Lady Beatrice, and her brother Lord Arthur Grosvenor. Also there were Sir Thomas Hesketh and his sister. They had a fast 20 mins. to the Peckforton Hills, came back to draw the Mosses and then on towards Combermere without success. Rawson described it as a very bad day, but was not out.

In lovely warm weather the Empress thoroughly enjoyed herself with Sir Watkin's hounds, hacking the dozen or so miles to the Saturday meet at Sarn bridge in Flintshire. A busy day followed with a nice steady run of 45 mins. and another past Chorlton Hall and Cherry Hill, where Captain Beatty was then living for a time, his ten-year-old son, the future Admiral of the Fleet, often out on his pony. It was 4 o'clock when Her Majesty set off to ride back to Combermere.

Bay.

On the Monday she went to Prees with the North Shropshire Hounds.[†] She again hacked on with Charles Kinsky, Rudi and the Major to The Twemlows for what was described as 'a rather tame day'. She had chosen to wear a grey habit with a demure Russian-style felt hat. But for her it was far better than was realized. As they joined the mounted field, a figure came forward removing his black silk hat. Her face lit up as she saw it was Bay. It may not have been much of a day, but *she* enjoyed it. They had an hour's easy canter home for tea. Next day Corbet brought his hounds to Burleydam. The Major tactfully withdrew and away they went with the South Cheshires on a fast 55 mins. to Wrenbury. Rawson's laconic report was merely:

> Feb.14. Burleydam. Weather very fine. But an indifferent day by all accounts.

The local paper nevertheless reported that 'Her Majesty enjoyed the day's sport thoroughly'. So the tongues began to wag and a society paper made out the Cheshire ladies held her reputation to be exaggerated. 'Why, she cannot go without a pilot *and I can*,' one of them is supposed to have told the gossip writer.

On a day she was out with the North Cheshire, everybody had held hard as hounds had checked in the next field. Just at that moment one of the wild Manchester brigade came crashing past and jumped the fence straight on to one of the best bitches, killing her outright. Captain Park Yates was in charge and was so taken aback, he jumped the fence after him and in his

---

* Elisabeth of Austria's romance with Bay Middleton is said to have inspired Whyte-Melville's Hunting Song, '*A Day's ride, a Life's romance*'. *See* Book Two, Part Two.

† Two places in Shropshire commemorate her visit, Side-saddle Lake at Hodnot, where her girth broke, and, down the road from Shavington,New Stirrup Lane, now New-street Lane.

booming voice in full earshot of everyone, including the Empress, and using a flood of language which would have made Lord Willoughby de Broke's vocabulary mere basic English, he told the scoundrel precisely what he thought of him. As related to the author one night at Tarporley by the Master's great-nephew, Humphrey Griffith (299), Puffles finally rounded on him and roared: 'Go home at once, Sir! And if I had my way, I would have you publicly buggered by six Irish navvies.'

Elisabeth, of course, was quite unperturbed. Had she not once heard Willoughby de Broke himself castigate Bay for arriving an hour late 'and riding over hounds all day'? By using her fan, she had no need to keep a straight face. Puffles wrote an abject letter of apology and received a most gracious reply to the effect that she was in total sympathy with everything he had said to the wretched man.

It might be mentioned here that by no means all the riders out from the cities were in the habit of over-riding hounds. The majority would have regarded themselves as privileged participants. One such at this time was a

Captain E. W. Park Yates, M.F.H.

young Gibraltarian student from Owen's College, Pablo Larios, his happiest English memories being his days with the Cheshire Hounds, an experience he valued greatly. Two or three seasons later he was the first civilian Whipper-in to the Garrison Fox-hounds back home. In 1910 he married the Marquésa de Marzales and was for forty-six years Master of the Royal Calpe Hounds.

Whilst there was certainly no romance, so far as her new pilot was concerned, the Empress had a great respect for all Charles Rivers Bulkeley did to make her visits to Cheshire run smoothly. His quiet confidence in the hunting field may not have inspired her the same way that Bay had done, but she did invite him, too, one Christmas to Gödöllö. Of any *contretemps* Her Majesty may have had with either of her pilots, many were likely to have been in the deep mud of the notorious Cheshire gateways, had either of them chosen such a 'convenient' short-cut in preference to leaping a low hedge-plashed bank and ditch alongside.

Captain Middleton was criticised in Cheshire as being too reckless. 'Too bold of course he could not be, but he seemed at times to forget how precious a life he was responsible for,' wrote the Rev.W.G.Armitstead, the Editor of Frank Massey's *Portrait Sketches of Cheshire Hunting Men (1850 to 1890)*. Colonel Rivers Bulkeley he found faultless as a pilot, with 'prudence, good sense and courage' his virtues.

Elisabeth once made a surprise visit to Oak Cottage on a day there was no hunting. The Major was out and she asked the groom to show her the horses. There was one box which was shut and the man explained that this mare was extremely dangerous and on C.R.B.'s express orders only he and the Major himself were allowed near her. Proud of her way with animals Her Majesty found this challenge impossible to resist and insisted on going inside. In a trice she was pinned in a corner, the mare's teeth bared. Prompt action by the stable staff rescued her from a savaging, but neither them nor the Empress from the wrath of Rivers Bulkeley on his return, fully realizing all the dreadful implications. Next day she turned all her charm and sweetness on him as she apologized profusely to all concerned. 'You were right and I was wrong,' and there the matter ended.

In 1882 at long last proper steps were taken to try to curb the size of the fields. There had been so much reckless damage perpetrated for years by many who neither resided in the country nor contributed to the costs, 'vast crowd of roughs' as Harry Rawson called them. The non-advertising of the fixtures had never had the desired effect.

The Master of the North was laid up with a bronchial attack and missed a few days. A mask at Sandy Brow

Mrs Park Yates.

shows he missed a goodish 1 hr. 10 mins. on February 4th from Whitley, through Arley to Marbury and a kill in the open somewhere between Pickmere and Tabley.

Harry Rawson was out at Minshull Village on Thursday, February 16th, 1882:

> Trotted to Aston and drew it blank. On leaving the place, however, a bagman was turned down & killed at Minshull, in Balshaw's Wood. Jones had not got far on his way to Cholmondeston before the hounds were again on a line. This also was supposed to be a bagman, a brace of foxes having been dug out the day before!!! This disreputable work over, the pack were trotted off to Calveley, where they found immediately & had a sharp run lasting about half an hour & ending where it began, viz at the Gorse. Wettenhall Wood and its surroundings, the Darnhall Dingles & Park Wood were then drawn blank. Being wet through & very cold, left for home at this stage of the performance. The Empress was out with a very decided look of paint about her face.

He made scarcely another mention of her.

The Imperial train had gone to Worleston, and thence on to Calveley to pick the party up at the end of the day. There was plenty of time for her to change there after a wet day, as they had to wait for the down Irish mail to pass. The signalman's day was made when he spotted the hunted fox lying in the grass nearby, dead beat, and was able to report that on regaining his wind he had retired to a neighbouring coppice.

A fox from Baddiley Gorse on Shrove Tuesday ran a sharp 7-mile ring for 27 mins., but the Empress found herself outside the circle and for once was not in her accustomed place. It was steeplechase pace all the way with a kill in the open and the Hon. Mrs Bunbury took the honours. On Ash Wednesday there was no hunting.

Those who mustered at Oulton Park on Thursday in anticipation of the Empress honouring the North Cheshire were disappointed, for she had gone to Tunstall with the North Staffordshire. She arrived late, wearing an exquisitely fitting blue stockinette habit, led an exciting gallop for nearly an hour, changed on to a fresh horse and cantered home ten miles across country, reaching Combermere at 5 p.m. (Rawson did not go to Oulton but sent a friend on one of his horses and reported a typically good Oulton day – Budworth Pool to Tilstone, a gallop from Cocked Hat to Darnhall and round back to Oulton by Oulton Lowe, finishing with a third run from Blakeden to ground at Tilstone Fearnall.)

Elisabeth joined the field at Brindley Lea on Friday when the day was saved by a Poole Hall fox, which gave them a good run. Next day she went by carriage to meet her horses at Edge Green for a day with Sir Watkin. It was a raw, wet day with no sport. The Empress and her suite went off at a rapid pace and had lunch at the Red Lion at Malpas, where the brougham was waiting for her.

The Wynnstay hounds made it up on Monday and gave her a grand run from a meet at Carden Park. From Carden Cliff a gallant fox ran past the Hooks and on to Edge Park and up the hill to Overton Scar before swinging back on a different route to Carden where he was lost by the lodge gates. It was 1 hr. 40 mins. over rough and heavy country. It rained incessantly and Her Majesty was well pleased to have been in a leading position throughout and went in to tell Mr Leche all about it.

She was out to the last on Tuesday from Wilkesley in a Nor'easter, on the move the whole time. A Shavington fox gave a short run, but the Walkmill and the Combermere coverts were all blank, until a brace was found in Mr Poole's Gorse next door. One of these took them best pace in a ringing hunt, ending up at The Heald at Wrenbury.

Sisi had intended to have a last day with Lord Stafford on Wednesday and her horses had been sent on overnight to Adderley, but Her Majesty sent word to the meet that she was indisposed for sport that day. But that did not stop her walking the five miles into Whitchurch and back in the afternoon.

Her last day and the last of the season turned out to be the worst day of all. Sir Watkin, who was in much better health, had arranged a special meet four miles south of Whitchurch at The Green Dragon and everybody had come from all directions 'to hunt with Sir Watkin to-day'. What few foxes there were, hounds could do nothing with them and all the promising coverts were blank, such as Peel's Gorse later on and not even Mr Godsal could come to the rescue with a fox at Iscoyd.

She left for Vienna on Monday. Her farewell gift to Lord Combermere was a gold snuffbox with her cipher set in diamonds. On the day of her departure Bay came to say good-bye. She was to meet Queen Victoria at Windsor that afternoon, but she refused to be hurried to catch her train. The indoor staff were lined up in the hall and MacDonald and Healy were on the drive with the outside staff. Eventually, the parting made, Middleton came down from the private apartments. The carriages were brought to the portico, but there was still no sign of Her Majesty. Then everyone looked up as, in a black travelling costume and sealskin jacket trimmed with fur, she swept down the staircase, looking every inch an Empress. She paused with a word for each servant and a piece of jewellery for the butler and housekeeper, before being driven in her carriage to the little wayside station.

As would be expected, to see her off there was a large crowd, controlled by six policemen in full dress. Mrs Corbet presented her with a bouquet and she graciously bowed to all around her, giving them her lovely smile. It seems she forgot no-one. Mr Humphries, the Crewe Stationmaster, who had made all the arrangements for her special trains, was given diamond shirt-studs and cuff-links. (The previous year he had got a diamond cluster ring.) Her final word was that all her horses should be sold by Tattersalls at Rugby.

In January, 1881, before her arrival, the Club's Poet Laureate composed *Cheshire's Welcome* in her honour – the last of his Hunting Songs. He was already blind. Sadly her visits did not coincide with Tarporley Week, so there was never a chance for her courtiers, Rudi Liechtenstein, Charles Kinsky or even Bay Middleton, to dine with the Club. In fact Major Bulkeley had been a guest of Cudworth Poole in 1880. But it would be nice to think that their host, Wellington Combermere, had found time to show them, and perhaps even the Empress herself, the Presidents' Boards in the old room, where, as Rowland Warburton would have had it, the Royal Huntress would have found a loving welcome.

In 1892, six years before the Empress met her fate, Bay Middleton died in a fall

at the House of Commons Point-to-Point Meeting at Kineton and was buried in full hunting costume. He had just lost the ring she had given him.

* * *

THE ADVENT OF THE EMPRESS had not exactly helped to check the size of the Cheshire fields, and despite the efforts of 'the Authorities' as Harry Rawson called them, things were little better in this respect. It was a matter constantly taxing the Subscribers, but they did not seem to be able to get to grips with it. Somebody even suggested issuing tickets and having two mounted policemen to check them. During the next season Rawson often complained of 'the great rabble', 'immense field of roughs' and, at Peover, 'the carriages a g^t nuisance'. On the odd occasion he did report the crowd as 'well-behaved', to give them their due. The large cavalcades which Captain Park Yates had to marshall stretched along the country lanes for a mile or more.

There had also been another spate of mischievous letters to the local Press, which only served to undermine the relationships with the non-hunting farmers.

In September '82 some hounds had been poisoned at Cranage, $2\frac{1}{2}$ couple having to be destroyed. After Christmas there were several instances of hounds not being sent to meets due to adverse weather.

Jany. 26th. Worleston. Wind W. Blowing a gale. In consequence of the wind the Hounds did not appear!!!! A hundred people were disappointed for the sake of one man & perhaps a few of his satellites – confusion to all fine weather sportsmen!

A Meet at Thornycroft Hall, Siddington.

Ld A. Paget was bucked off.' Dandy's practice on such occasions was to scramble to his feet shouting 'Ware hole! Ware hole', hoping to disguise the fact he had cut a voluntary. In 1885/6, it was reported he 'stood on his head with the Wynnstay and was rendered unconscious'. His brother Lord Berkeley Paget also hunted with the Cheshire at this time and got badly kicked; it seems he was prone to accidents in the hunting field. 'Berkeley Paget again in grief,' wrote Rawson in 1888. 'He fell at the Blakeden brook & was struck on the head by his horse & a good deal cut.' Only two days previously he was run into by a pony cart driven by a woman and his horse impaled. He lived at Blakemere, Sandiway, near the Kennels.

Later there had been flooding in the meadows, and 'several duckings' and Sir Watkin's hounds had not been out. Corbet had changed a meet from Marbury to Wrenbury

> as he of Combermere and he of Marbury had given him notice to discontinue hunting over their lands as long as the wet weather lasts! What next?

On February 15th a fox from Handley was killed on Tarporley Racecourse after an hour's run,

> Yates did not draw again. Hounds home by 2 o'clock. The fact was that an intimation had been read both from him of Peckforton and him of Eaton Hall to the effect that in the present state of the ground more consideration was due to farmers. No doubt he of Adderley had inspired the great men with his own motives.

In March 'a dozen or so of men who had gone to Brindley Lea turned up at Sandiway at two o'clock owing to the fact that Corbet had sent word that it was not fit to hunt!! Subscribers to hounds are truly a long suffering & an abject lot. The sixth time the South have been stopped by frost,' grumbled Harry Rawson.

Notable casualties this season included Mrs Corbet with a dislocated shoulder from being 'upset' with Lady Charlotte Barry, and John Jones broke his collar bone on February 22nd, after which Park Yates hunted hounds himself. Rawson liked to record such incidents, for instance that from the Kennels on March 3rd 'Mrs Beatty got a fall and Miss E.Fuller did not "remain" when her horse swerved in the middle of a field, also that

The diarist was kept at home by an attack of gout in the hand on April 2nd, the last day of the season, which he summed up as follows:

> It began very badly and ended as badly. In the interval, however, there were a few moderately good gallops, but neither pack had "the" run of the season.

On the subject of visitors, he was even more forthright with his entry for November 3rd, 1883:

> Weather fine, everything else foul. The features of the day were innumerable carriages, crowds of howling foot people & the number of apparent tailors on horseback. Foxes at Marbury [Great Budworth]. At the last named place the mob caught one, cut off its brush & turned it loose! At Arley was a fox in a trap! Left Jones in pursuit. A very bad scent.

1883/84 he described as 'a remarkably good season & an extraordinary mild one.' He was out 95 times in all. There were only four

Edward Townshend of Wincham.

(1) Meet of the Cheshire at Saighton Grange, Dec 6th 1883.

From Miss S. Turner of Aldford's Hunting Notes with the Cheshire and Sir W.W.Wynn's Hounds.

blank days and hounds were only stopped twice by frost. But the feature of the next season, rather better than average, according to the Rawson journal was the number of accidents.

In a lighthearted vein, on January 29th at Oulton,

after the great Tarporley ball had taken place the night before there was a large field out and many strangers. Everyone got up in his best. Mr Coupland and Billy Baldwin especially so. The fates however had decided that both should come to grief. He of Cotebrook was bucked off in the Park and the Lion Hunter was seen early in the day at the bottom of a deep & dirty ditch & was not seen again.

And then, on a day at Cranage, by far the most serious:

Feb. 9th. . . . In the first scurry which was fast and lasted about 10 mins. Edward Townsend came to grief. He was upset by wire & landed on his head and was taken home in Mrs Rushton's carriage in a state of insensibility. Supposed to be a state of concussion of the brain. Another misdeed of the day was that Miss Rushton got into a brook...

Feb.10th. A fine hunting day. Heard that Townsend, besides concussion, had several ribs broken & that a broken rib had lacerated the lungs. The late Sir Robert Peel died after a fall from his horse, from a similar injury.[*] Corbet had a good day.

Feb.23rd. Poor Townsend died . . .

Feb. 26th. No hunting owing to the fact of its being poor Townsend's funeral.

As a result of this tragedy the Cheshire Hunt Wire Fund was instituted, though not without a certain amount of opposition to Captain Park Yates's original proposal to set it up to supply farmers with rails.

The following year there was an unusual run, by modern comparison, from the quarry at Ashton Hayes over a great deal of country. It lasted 3 hrs. on a day hounds met at The Abbey Arms, now a notoriously dangerous crossroads. The route was to Tarvin, Barrow, Manley and Peel Hall and thence back through the Delamere Forest to the Abbey Arms and on to Abbot's Moss and Kennel Wood to go to ground in Petty Pool. But there were few good runs compared to the unusual number of foxes killed. The North pack killed $56\frac{1}{2}$ brace and were stopped by frost 32 times. 'Heard that Yates had a fall on Feb.25th & hurt himself. Knee crushed,' wrote Harry, himself all too often off with gout and influenza, but nevertheless faithfully recording the doings of both packs, albeit sometimes sarcasticly about Corbet – 'A

* At the age of 72 the former Prime Minister fell from his horse when it grew restive as he was riding up Constitution Hill.

John Jones and the North Cheshire Hounds, 1883 by H. Hardy Simpson.

cold, moist, disagreeable morning with rain and snow occasionally – just the day to please the man who is hunting hounds at Stapeley.' What many did not know was that Regie Corbet, like all good Masters of Hounds, was constantly sending presents of game to the South Cheshire tenant farmers, especially during long frosts.

Lord 'Rock' succeeded his grandfather to the family estates in 1884 and at this time he and the Marchioness were seldom missing from the field. 'Foxes are as thick as blackberries round the Castle and the vale surrounding it,' it was reported. On the huge Cholmondeley Estate, both round the Castle and on the Rocksavage land near Frodsham, no wire was allowed on any account. Hounds were seldom at Rocksavage but it was not allowed there just in case they came. About this time it was possible to ride virtually from Tarporley to Whitchurch crossing only three estates with not a strand to be found.

Lord Cholmondeley, who was an efficient and well-liked field master, well capable of controlling the enormous fields, occasionally went to Badminton and to Melton to hunt as well. Winifred Cholmondeley herself had a superb seat. Jumping a six-barred gate at Haughton one day, an old farmer standing near was

overheard to say: 'There goes a beautiful wench o'er the gate, there was no daylight between her and the saddle.' She was one of the first Cheshire ladies to don scarlet and leathers, complete with her green collar.

In Season 1886/87 there were still massive fields occasionally – four hundred at Oulton in March. The week before there were 'the usual roughs from Manchester and Warrington out and,' Rawson went on, 'the usual bad High Leigh doings. A little to & fro running with two foxes, both of which got to ground… Corbet said to have killed 6 foxes yesterday!' Hounds did not throw off on the last day of a 'very moderate season' on April 12th from the Kennels until 1.30, following a Subscribers' Meeting, after which Puffles had asked everybody back to lunch at Sandiway Lodge.

Jones was still huntsman and had been joined by his son, Harry, as 2nd Whipper-in to replace Harry Reynolds, who had gone to hunt the Roman Fox-hounds.* Jack Goddard, who came to the Forest Kennels in 1875, was still turning the hounds and although both the Master and his Huntsman were growing older and heavier, the pack was still composed of real good hunting material. They would cast themselves and hit off the line, even if Jones was not quite as quick as he had been.

Captain Edmund Park Yates and John Jones had a complete understanding and affection for each other. They looked upon the horse purely as a medium for seeing the hounds at work, the latter probably not even knowing what he was riding once hounds found. Above all they had a keen sense of humour and saw the funny side of everything.

Some years later Jones had the greatest difficulty in keeping a straight face on the arrival at the meet for the first time of Mr Alfred Mond, who had quite rightly decided to take some recreation from his hard work in his chemical industry with Mr Brunner. All honour to him, the eventual creator of Imperial Chemical Industries decided he would like to go hunting. He arrived clad in somewhat odd nether garments, bright green waistcoat and a brown velvet coat. His hat was not fashionable and he did not seem much at home in the saddle. A member of the field went up to greet the Huntsman, and finding him looking serious, asked what was the matter. 'Well, Captain, they say "God made man in his own image." Do you really think he is anything like that?'

The future Lord Melchett, thanks to his boundless enthusiasm, went from strength to strength and whatever his attire and his ability as a horseman, he and his old hireling, Blue Peter, used to jump more and bigger fences than most people. His son became a Joint Master of the Tedworth.

Harry Rawson was to die at the end of April, 1888, but he kept up his journal to the end, including his usual meticulous notes about the weather conditions. He himself was out very little and he reckoned the season 'the worst for many years'. The last time he went to a meet was at the nearby Blue Cap on March 31st, but

could not ride owing to his gout. 'Let Rance see a covert or two drawn;' this would be one of Tom's sons, probably his groom at the time. He had been out at Twemlow in January when 'Young Bolton Littledale [not yet a Green Collar] also made an incident. He and his horse parted on meeting a traction engine near Shipbrooke & went home separately'. That day a fox was found in Cranage Willows with a collar on. 'What next?'

It was a fortnight later at Shipbrooke that Colonel William F. Cody, 'Buffalo Bill' himself, had a day with the Cheshire Hounds. The weather was fine and warm and there was not a great deal of sport. Rawson was there too: 'Appearance of Buffalo Bill, who called the hounds dogs, talked of them not barking enough when running their fox & was all over his horse when the animal jumped.'

Buffalo Bill, from a sketch by George A. Fothergill.

'The finest figure of a man that ever sat a steed', as Cody was billed, had come out from Manchester where at the Castle Irwell racecourse at Salford he was winding up his tour of England with his Wild West Show.

* * *

SHOWING EXTRAORDINARY INSENSITIVITY Regie Corbet thought fit in a circular to all the gorse covert fund subscribers to draw attention to 'some very curious figures compiled by the *Sheffield Telegraph*'. He felt they showed who were the friends of the farmer and were well worth extensive quotation. They were as follows:

---

* Founded in 1836 by the 6th Earl of Chesterfield, who had wintered in Italy for the sake of his wife's tuberculosis. Run by a committee of Italian noblemen, it was their tradition to have an English or Irish huntsman and it was customary for only English to be spoken in the hunting field. They rode over the *Campagna Romana* and some very stiff timber, with a man bringing up the rear with an axe and saw in his saddle bag for the benefit of those who failed to get over. It was not unknown for both horse and rider to disappear suddenly into the catacombs beneath the surface.

When Reynolds returned after nine seasons he took over the forty-odd boxes at Blue Cap Cottage, eventually expanding to the Station Hotel at Hartford and employing forty-two strappers, two foremen and two blacksmiths with over 200 horses, either at livery or for hire. He eventually handed over to his son, Willy, while a younger son, Reg, started a career in hunt service by riding 2nd horse at the Forest Kennels. From 1921-24 young Willy hunted the private pack of harriers at Eaton for the Duchess of Westminster, Bend Or's second wife.

On one occasion the Reynolds took no fewer than seventy-nine hunters in a special train for a meet at Wrenbury. Willy continued in business until 1945 and ran a large remount centre at Hartford during both wars, sending out over 3,000 horses from Hartford in the Great War.

	PER ACRE		
Average rental of land in the United Kingdom	£1	16	5½
Average charged by owners of over 5,000 acres		13	2½
Average charged by owners of 1,000 to 5,000 acres		17	3½
Average charged by owners of 100 to 1,000 acres	1	13	11½
Average charged by owners of under 1 acre	192	12	7½
Average charged by landlords in Lower House		17	1¾
Average charged by landlords in Upper House		15	11½
Average rental charged by members of present Liberal Cabinet		2	6
Average rental charged by members of late Tory Cabinet		12	0¾
Average rental charged by Mr Gladstone		2 6	2
Average rental charged by Lord Beaconsfield	1	9	8¾

From the above figures we learn that (1) large estate owners, who are generally Tories, charge the least; (2) small landowners, who are generally Liberals, charge the most; and (3) that the upper orders charge less than the lower orders.

Needless to say it brought forth an outraged editorial in *The Chronicle*, to which it was inevitably leaked. An indignant farmer wrote:

Mr Corbet evidently thinks himself not only the Master of the hounds but of the farmers also. Many of us have no objection to the hounds crossing our land when they hunt there. Rough-riders and green young Irish horses crashing through our fences and across our crops or dashing like madmen through our sheep and cattle is quite sufficient without telling us that Tory landlords are better than Liberals. Find me two Tory landlords who are better than Lord Crewe or G.F.Wilbraham.

The Master had to send a letter of apology to all concerned. He had been in gross contravention of the Tarporley Hunt Club's non-political constitution.

Thirty-one farmers, with any number of names which could have been added, had they thought necessary, wrote to the Subscribers in October, 1887, complaining about the numbers and suggesting that the hunting season could be curtailed. They were all for the Members of the Hunt themselves, but in principle objected to non-ratepayers, 'whose horses are not even kept in the county . . . chiefly men unaccustomed to country life [who] do much damage to clover roots, young wheat & fences.' Piers called a meeting for Tarporley Week and wrote to acknowledge it and 'the friendly spirit' in which it was written.

The farmers were informed that the Hunt would do all it could to meet their views and minimize the damage, to which end a a deputation was invited to meet a committee which had been appointed. This included

Viscount Combermere, Sir P.Grey-Egerton, and Messrs. Tomkinson, Poole, Kay and Piers Egerton Warburton, himself, who duly waited at the Grosvenor Hotel, Chester, but nobody turned up.

Meanwhile it had been resolved

No.1.   That hunting should cease on March 31st with no bye-days after that date.

No.2.   That all hay, straw and corn be purchased direct from farmers in the county.

No.3.   All grooms to keep to the roads as much as possible and be strictly under the orders of the Kennel 2nd horsemen.

The meeting was re-convened and this time a deputation did turn up. A strong grumble about the quantity of grooms and others coming out cub-hunting was added to the substance of their complaints and for good measure one farmer said that he had once had a heifer that galloped for three miles with hounds and might have been injured but wasn't.

Sir Philip told them about the resolutions and also that they had gone very carefully into the question of gentlemen who kept their horses out of the county. The investigation had shown that out of 150 horses belonging to gentlemen living outside the limits of the hunt all but 16 were kept in Cheshire and that, notwithstanding reports to the contrary, gentlemen who hunted, almost without exception, bought their hay and corn from the farmers. He added that nine out of ten men who came out, did, in one way or another subscribe to the support of hunting.

Agents were to be appointed to whom gentlemen requiring fodder could apply and the deputation withdrew after thanking the Committee and expressing their approval.

At their Meeting in 1889 the Tarporley Hunt Club made it a condition of their Horse Show that 'any farmer having wire of a dangerous nature in his fences during the hunting season' would be disqualified from competing.

Corbet put forward another scheme in 1890 to reduce the crowds. One idea was for any person not entitled to the T.H.C. or C.H. buttons to wear a non-transferable badge 'on his shooting coat'. This, together with ten other suggestions laid before the Subscribers on a printed notice, did not get the support he hoped for. Not even his idea of the Covert Fund subscribers hunting in a scarlet or black coat having a special C.F. (for 'Covert Fund') button, met with the approval of the Subscribers, who with some notable exceptions were still all Cheshire landowners. However no card was to be issued to anyone until his subscription had been paid and a list of the

Wellington Cotton, 2nd Viscount Combermere, from an oil painting by H. G. Herkomer.

Covert Fund Subscribers was to be printed and sent to each Subscriber to the Hounds. There were 227 names on the first list. At that time there were 59 Subscribers to the Hounds.

Even though the large fields were coming out in the North, it seems that it was Corbet rather than Park Yates who had been getting all the letters from landowners and so had taken the initiative. In the meantime he had got his agent to send a most forcibly-worded letter to all his tenants forbidding the use of wire on his estate during the hunting season. One of the Master's chief grumbles was the amount paid by the majority of those on the Covert Fund list. As he wrote to Piers*: 'No country in England can run a hunt with so paltry a subscription, £10 as here'. In fairness some paid a good deal more, for instance the young Earl of Dudley, who had come to live at The Bollings, Malpas, sent £100. Later he leased Cholmondeley Castle for a while.

There was some correspondence at this time between Hughie Peel's younger brother, Herbert, who had taken Calveley Hall, with the Secretary to the Subscribers. By special arrangement he had been hunting the Peckforton Hills with his own pack, as Lord Rocksavage had done previously, and wrote to tell Piers he would have to give up. He had found it too expensive. 'The farmers offered to find part of the money, but I thought it very unadvisable to start a Farmers' Hunt,' he wrote, after he had been rattling the hill foxes with the blessing of both Masters. He did in fact manage to carry on for another season or two. Charlie Garnett whipped-in for him and occasionally the Duke invited him over to Eaton. He had a notable hunt when a fox from Duck Wood swam the Dee, raced along to Tattenhall Road Station, thence to Bolesworth and was lost behind Rawhead.

Lady Meg Grosvenor, a fearless lady across country with a firm seat and wonderful hands, saw the run better than anyone. Both she and her husband, Prince Alexander of Teck, known as Dolly, much enjoyed their hunting in Cheshire. The Duke's youngest daughter by his first marriage, she was petite and graceful with undaunted nerve. She was always mounted superbly from Eaton on horses well above her weight and usually over-corned by Naylor, the old stud groom. She had that great knack of dropping into her place, galloping to the front and taking her own line. Their elder daughter, Mary, married 'Master', the 10th Duke of Beaufort.

In 1897 a Mr John Pennefather took these hounds on with an amateur huntsman, C.J. Paget of Stoke Cottage.

---

* The earliest typewritten letter among the documents of the Cheshire Hunt Archive is one from H.R. Corbet to Piers Egerton Warburton dated November 7th, 1891.

By then the former was living at Calveley Hall. It caused considerable friction with Sir Watkin, who disapproved of them, especially when they strayed onto the neutral country. When Pennefather was not in Cheshire he was with the North Herefordshire, of which he was Master, 1901-03, with Walter Morgan as his huntsman.

At the end of the 1890/91 Season Park Yates wanted to resign but Lord Enniskillen, in the chair at the Subscribers' Meeting at The Swan in Tarporley Week, was able to announce 'amidst general cheering' that he was to continue for at least two more seasons. During his mastership he had become very keen in the kennel, favouring a large hound, fully 25", and as mentioned was having considerable success with his bitches at Peterborough.

Meanwhile, in March, Cudworth Poole had called the Members of the Tarporley Hunt Club to the Crewe Arms Hotel next to Crewe Station for a Special Meeting, at which it was resolved 'that Lord Combermere be requested to "sit" for his portrait to be hung in the "Club Room" at Tarporley'. The Club devoted up to £250 for the purpose. At their Meeting in November it was announced that Herman G. Herkomer (b.1863) had been chosen and was authorized to exhibit it at Burlington House. Only the previous year Lord Combermere had given the chandelier for the Hunt Room. Second perhaps only to Rowland Egerton Warburton, he was one of the most enthusiastic Members ever, since he joined almost fifty years before, the

> *At Tarporley glorious*
> *Always uproarious*
> *Combermere Abbey young man*

One of the foremost judges of horse and hound of his day, as well as a great fly fisherman, he was always full of energy and 'go'. His Wynnstay neighbours at Cherry Hill had loved him just as much as all his host of friends in Cheshire, the county that was so dear to him. He still came out hunting in his latter seasons, seeing a deal of the sport on sturdy 15hh cobs. He must have missed the days he lived in style at the Abbey with a stable full of hunters and his accomplished daughter to ride them for him. He always fancied himself as a horse coper, who in those days had to have a licence. At one time 'Viscount Combermere, Dealer in Horses' was painted over the stable arch.

It seems that his kind heart and his sense of duty as a landlord brought about his change of circumstance, though he never lost his cheery and kindly disposition when he moved from the great house to a small house at Bunbury. He had spent all his money on his estate rebuilding farms and cottages and draining the land. The trouble was he never increased the rents according to the money he spent. Only the love and esteem for him went up.

It was a profound shock to all when they learnt of his accident, coming back from a sitting at Herkomer's studio one dark winter evening. A hansom cab came suddenly on him from behind a cart. The cab horse struck into his leg and he ruptured all the muscles above the knees as he tried to spring forward to get out of the way.

A few days later he wrote cheerfully to say he was making progress and had already 'taken a canter on crutches', but the lack of his usual exercise upset his heart and on December 1st, 1891 he had only been ill half-an-hour at his rooms in St.James's Place when he died from a clot of blood. One of those at the funeral at Wrenbury was Hughie Peel of Bryn-y-Pys, the future owner of dual Grand National winner, Poethlyn, and firm friend of Brian Egerton and many other Tarporley men. He had been born in a hansom cab.

On the day of the funeral a photographer happened to have made an appointment to take some pictures of the interior of the Abbey for the new tenant. In the library it was necessary to have an exposure of half-an-hour or more. When the plate was developed and printed, a distinct bearded figure was seen to be seated in the chair, with one elbow resting on an arm. The ghostly figure was missing an arm and a leg, the very limbs injured in the accident which caused his death. The photograph is in the possession of the present viscount. *See* page 79.

'Make up into a smart one that.' Lord Combermere, in his horsecoping days, and Jack White.

XVI

Quæsitiana Tertius

THE WATERLOO CUP was won in 1880 by the **Earl of Haddington (202)** and in 1912 by **E.L.Townshend (246)**. Another very keen coursing man was the **Earl of Enniskillen (218)**, whose nomination ran up in the WATERLOO PURSE of 1923.

* * *

LORD CREWE (244) HUNTED WHENEVER he could in Cheshire and also in Ireland when he was Viceroy, but afterwards concentrated on the turf and acquired some brood mares for the paddocks he had laid out at Crewe. John Porter trained a few winners for him at Kingsclere. He was appointed Senior Steward of the Jockey Club in 1899. At the time Tod Sloan had arrived from America with his 'monkey-up-a-stick' style of race-riding, but unfortunately got in the hands of some undesirable characters. Going out to dine with Leopold de Rothschild on the evening after the 1900 Cambridgeshire, in which Sloan had finished second on a French outsider, the Senior Steward gave Captain Machell a lift. This well-known racing manager and personality, probably forgetting whom he was with, mentioned that Sloan had told him he had stood to win £40,000 had he won. Crewe made no reply but had the American jockey brought before him next day and told him he need never apply for a licence again. After this he remained a power behind the scenes right up to the time of his death.

On visits to Cheshire he delighted in shooting parties and entertained King George V. In true Crewe tradition the fare for the picnics would be sent up from Fortnum & Mason and served by liveried staff, usually at Town House, Barthomley. He would sometimes get the famous Rosa Lewis of The Cavendish Hotel to see to the arrangements, as she had for his Ministerial banquet in 1908. One of her earliest employers was the then **Major Wm.Hall Walker (268)** for whom she cooked at Gateacre Grange and on his stalking visits to Scotland. Rosa considered him one of the best-looking men she had ever seen. ('But I couldn't be in love with Walker,' she once told her husband; 'I couldn't be one of a hundred! I couldn't be in a syndicate!')

In his old age the Earl of Crewe spent much of his time with his brother-in-law, Lord Rosebery, at Mentmore, where in his younger days he had dined out on the terrace in the full moon. At the time he was courting the former Prime Minister's daughter, whom he married as his second wife.

* * *

DURING AN EDWARDIAN CHRISTMAS PARTY at Eaton **Lord Cholmondeley (222)** came over for dinner and boasted about his new burglar alarms, fitted to every window of the Castle. After brandy, cigars and a game of billiards, the Marquess was given sufficient time to get back home and to bed before the members of the Eaton house party, led by their host, drove over to Cholmondeley. They had no difficulty in prising open a window, removing the Southdown Cup, a racing trophy Rock himself had won on a horse appropriately called Screech Owl, and all his Lordship's best cigars. Next morning the butler reported the burglary. There was consternation all round, as detectives arrived from Chester. As soon as Bend Or heard that the Chief Constable himself had been sent for, he decided to own up. Many national newspapers were unwittingly hoaxed and produced streamer headlines. The cup was returned but by then the cigars had been smoked. 'It was a very festive season,' as Lord Cholmondeley said when he forgave the burglars.

These included two of Bend Or's greatest friends, the Grenfell twins Francis and Rivy. The former, serving in the 9th Queen's Royal Lancers, was one of first officers to gain a Victoria Cross in the Great War. They were both killed within a year of hostilities being declared and Bend Or's mother had trees planted at Saighton in their memory.

* * *

ON THE OUTBREAK OF WAR IN 1914 the **Duke of Westminster (248)** had been earmarked by Kitchener for a Home Front job. This did not suit him at all as he had enjoyed his South African war. He had been the first British officer to fly the Union Jack over Pretoria and had relished the cigar which had been left by a well-wisher for such a person. In August, 1914 his yacht happened to be in the Solent – it was just after Cowes Week – so he slipped aboard and sailed for France after dark, installing himself in the Hotel de l'Univers in Arras. On arrival he discovered that a squadron of the 9th Lancers commanded by his close friend, Captain Francis Grenfell, had been ordered to attack. Typically he joined in, discovered Grenfell badly wounded and motored him off in a hail of bullets to a hospital run by some nuns. The story got exaggerated by the Press, but there were plenty who regarded his action as worthy of a V.C. All he got was a reprimand from Kitchener for disobeying orders.

It was soon afterwards he put up his idea of forming an Armoured Car Force to his good friend, Winston Churchill, then First Lord of the Admiralty, and together they had gone by destroyer to discuss it with Field-Marshal Sir John French. When they did not get his blessing, the two friends had sublimely gone ahead. In fact they were to see each other constantly towards the end of the war, Bend Or often accompanying Winston on visits to the front, giving him lunch at the Ritz to meet important contacts and the Duke sometimes acting as a confidential go-between at home and abroad.

The Duke was gazetted a Lieut.-Commander, RNVR, the primary purpose of the armoured cars at that time being to protect Naval airfields. Before long he was reported as roaming the shell-pocked fields of Belgium driven by George Powell, his chauffeur from Eaton, in his own Rolls-Royce tourer with a Hotchkiss mounted where the back seat should have been, harrying the Germans like a crusader.

By the Spring of 1916 the Duke was in action in the Western Desert with his Light Armoured Car Brigade, this time as a Major in the Cheshire Yeomanry. He had hand-picked his crews, one of the star drivers appropriately called S.C.Rolls. Another was Willie Griggs, the jockey, and of course George Powell. What they all had in common was unlimited keenness, inspired by His Grace's own boundless enthusiasm.

The prototypes of the armoured cars had been built entirely at the Duke's own expense and to his own specifications by Rolls-Royce. He had even tested them in an exercise against the Cheshire Yeomanry. In his *Steel Chariots in the Desert, the story of an armoured car driver with the Duke of Westminster in Libya and T.E.Lawrence in Arabia*, Sam Rolls, who later kept a garage at Nottingham, gives some idea of the discomfort in Bend Or's private war:

> The full crew . . . consisted of a driver and two gunners, but as the confined space made it almost impossible for three men to be usefully employed at one time, only two men were carried usually in each vehicle. The driver acted as assistant gunner, making shift as best he could to feed the cartridge-belt into the gun breech with one hand, while managing the steering wheel with the other. Only short men could stand upright in the cylinder; and tall men, who had to half double themselves up, took up very much more room and were always cramped and uncomfortable... Even small men had to crouch when firing the Maxim or a rifle. Most of our fellows were short, and the great height of the Duke of Westminster no doubt added a trial to his pains and fatigues, such as the rest of us were spared.

Two of their favourite cars were called Blast and Bulldog. They weighed four tons and could touch 70 m.p.h. on hard level sand.

The Duke had already been in action in an old-style cavalry attack on the Turks, riding in his open car at the head of his squadron of Light Armoured Cars. They took a lot of prisoners and brought them back to the garrison at Sollum Bay on the Libyan coast. There they were all paraded 'with tremendous palaver', as Lieut.Jack Leslie, Bend Or's close friend and 2 i/c put it, to be inspected and praised by Major-General W.E.Peyton, GOC Western desert. The next day word reached them that the British prisoners from HMS *Tara*, torpedoed four months earlier by a German submarine, were now in a fort at Bir Hakkim, some 120 miles away to the West. The Germans had handed them over to Ahmed es Senussi, who had moved them continuously, refusing all offers for their release and had now held them in a state of starvation for weeks on end in his desert fastness.

Bend Or wasted no time and set off at 3 a.m. to drive through the night. Not many hours after sunrise the troopers' sweat-stiffened shirts chaffed them raw and progress was slow for the convoy of some forty-two vehicles, including ambulances, through soft sand strewn with boulders. He had nine armoured cars, and three Fords mounted with Maxims as additional escort, and led the way in his own Rolls.

Petrol was running low and all but the Duke were beginning to show anxiety. It was 3 p.m. when the Major seized his glasses as two small pimples appeared on the skyline. These were the wells of Bir Hakkim. Speed was essential on the last run in to prevent the Arabs from shooting their captives. The armoured cars formed line ahead at full throttle and Willie Griggs claimed that he won by a short bonnet. In no time Bend Or and his crews were surrounded by the eighty-nine surviving British sailors, clad in old burnouses, rice sacks and tattered remains of naval uniform, living skeletons all.

It was then that some of the troops in the heat of the moment mistakenly gave chase after the fleeing Arabs and all but a handful were mown down with ruthless machine gun fire. The Duke had been greeting the naval Captain and asking about their treatment when this happened and they dashed to the well mound to try to recall the men, but all in vain. The nine caring Senussi guards were lying dead on the desert scrub, most of their women and children beside them. The gaolers had been sharing what little food they had and in fact had shown kindness to the starving sailors, who now ravenously devoured what bully beef was available, trying to rip open the tins with their teeth.

The Duke boarded the fastest car and raced back to report to headquarters, driven by Powell. It was Rolls who led the convoy home in Blast. The G.O.C., Western Desert was there next day to tell them all he had awarded Major the Duke of Westminster with an immediate D.S.O. and rather rashly announced he was recommending him for the Victoria Cross. George Powell rightly earned a D.C.M. and for the rest of his life talked about the day 'when me and Duke received the D.S.O.'

Jack Leslie was awarded the Military Cross for his part in these actions. He had been in the front line with his regiment, the XII Royal Lancers, since 1914. He once wrote: 'I got my men out, fixed bayonets, gave a View Halloa, and charged. The hunting noises fairly set the men off.' His daughter, Lavinia, married the **Marquess of Cholmondeley (312)**.

Bend Or received the thanks of everyone for his action. The King of Egypt sent him the Gold Medal of Mohamed Ali, the first time an officer had ever been so invested and a letter in French '...c'est un des faîtes d'Armes le plus glorieux.' The Lords of the Admiralty and the War Council were both highly complimentary and even Kitchener grudgingly admitted the action 'had been well managed and boldly led.' The retiring G.O.C.-in-C., Egypt, General Sir John Maxwell, sent his 'hearty

congratulations on the truly magnificent performance of your motor cars' and the Grand Senussi's standard. But he never got his V.C.

It was Maxwell who conferred the D.S.O., in accordance with his powers, and forwarded to the Secretary of State Peyton's recommendation for the supreme award for valour. The latter wrote to Westminster that he

> . . . was more disgusted that I can express that the award of the V.C. had been refused. The Mi[ly] Sec[ty]. told me that the system was that every recommendation was considered by a committee of three senior generals & their views together with the original recommendation was then submitted through the S o S to the King.
>
> All were agreed that in ordinary times there would have been no doubt that you would have got it but that the very large number of gallant actions in France that had to go unrewarded militated against favourable consideration elsewhere. I cannot see this as a fair argument & I do not mean to let the matter drop at this. I cannot think of a more well-earned cross than yours should be . . .
>
> . . . I know you don't care a damn for honors as honors but this is a special case & it is due to yourself, your officers & men & to your family records . . .

He had an appointment to see Lord Kitchener and he hoped he could get at Lord Stamfordham, the King's Private Secretary, whom he knew slightly. When he wrote again three weeks later on May 1st, Sir John Maxwell had already had official notification from the Military Secretary that

> . . . the act . . . does not come up to the very high standard which has been reached in this War . . .

Peyton's letter read:

> . . . Lord K. told me you could not get it because you were in command!!!!!! & my recommendation could not be accepted as I was not present!!! The King said the standard set in France was so high that it was difficult.

He wrote again the next week, still determined not to take no for an answer, but it was all in vain. 'Winston Churchill was probably right when he said that it was only because he was a Duke that Bend Or was denied the V.C.,' George Ridley wrote in his biography.

During the 1st World War 488 V.C.'s were gazetted up to Armistice Day for deeds in France and Belgium out of a total of 598, 17.9% being for other theatres of war. In 1914 7.3% were awarded elsewhere; 1915, 35.7%, 1916, 23.5%, 1917, 18.6% and 1918, 7.1%. Arguably an award for the Duke of Westminster would have increased the 1916 percentage by less than 1% and overall by only 0.1%. What is not known is the number rejected.

* * *

KNOWN AS TOLLY TO HIS FRIENDS, Lord Tollemache's relaxations were croquet and bridge. **Bentley Tollemache (254)** also had a passion for fast cars. He was unfortunately convinced that the best way to negotiate a crossroads, no matter in which direction he was travelling, was to put his hand firmly on the horn and his foot on the accelerator pedal.

He also enjoyed his golf at Delamere Forest and to get there had to go over the Fishpool and the Abbeys Arms crossings, both notoriously dangerous. The police became anxious for the safety of other road users, quite apart from that of his lordship, and set a trap one morning at his accustomed time. Sure enough the peer raced over the Abbey Arms crossroads and roared off on his way to play golf, oblivious to frantic waving and shouting from the Inspector and his Sergeant. Riding furiously on his bicycle the latter managed to catch up, just as Tolly was driving from the first tee, to tell him he would be summoned.

In due course he appeared at Oakmere Courthouse before the Chairman of the Bench, **Major Hugh Wilbraham (237)**. The Inspector gave his evidence, followed by the Sergeant who made the mistake of adding: 'And what's more your Worship, the car was going that fast, it blew me 'elmet off!' 'Don't believe it,' growled old Wobbles, 'case dismissed!'

Lord T. was driving through Eaton one day and nearly ran into a herd of cows. The farmer's wife shouted abuse at him. 'You're almost as bad as the bluidy mon, Lord Tollymash!' she cried.

As a bridge player Lord Tollemache was somewhat intolerant and reduced many a lady partner to tears and he was on occasion volcanic to the extent of inflicting physical violence by taking her head in his hands and banging it on the table if she played a wrong card.

He was the author of *The Key to Slam Bidding* and said to be 'of fine perception and a very keen analyst'. Always a gambler, he once advocated a card evaluation system by making the Ace valued £1, the Queen 10/-, etc., so that even a wretched Yarborough would be worth thirteen bob. The popular Tollemache Cup is played as a county championship for teams of eight.

* * *

IT WAS A HOT DAY when Lord Tollemache came before the bench and after a while, as the other cases were

Major Hugh Wilbraham.

brought before him, Major Wilbraham dozed off. His portliness prevented him from getting his stomach under the steering wheel of his car, hence the name his friends affectionately gave him. He was long overdue for retirement, but efforts to get him to do so had been in vain. The Clerk nudged him and said: 'The verdict, Your Worship, the verdict.' Wobbles came too with a start. 'Fined five pounds,' he declared. 'We must put a stop to this furious driving.' The only trouble was that by then the case he was hearing concerned a young woman who was trying to get a paternity order.

* * *

'WHITE MISCHIEF AND THE ANGEL OF DEATH'
A PLAYLET IN TWO ACTS

ACT I SCENE I.   A road junction some miles outside Nairobi in the early hours of January 24th, 1941. The body of the Earl of Erroll, Hereditary High Constable of Scotland and incorrigible philanderer, is discovered on the floor of his Buick with a bullet through his head. The headlights are still blazing.

ACT I Scene II.   Nairobi Gaol. **Sir Delves Broughton, (266)**, the 11th baronet, known to all as Jock, is sleeping in a cell awaiting trial for the murder, having been arrested at his home at Karen on March 10th.

ACT I Scene III.   Prosse's Restaurant and Bar at Haifa, Palestine the following Sunday, where officers of the Cheshire Yeomanry have arrived from Acre for their Sunday lunch, including **Dick Verdin (310), Philip Lever (313), Charles Brocklehurst (327)**, and **Michael Higgin (337)**. As the others study the menu, the first-named is reading the Sunday edition of *The Palestine Post*, which the bell-ringing paperboy has just brought round. The others continue their conversation when suddenly they are interrupted:

Dick Verdin (a budding barrister): Good God! Jock's been charged with murder. I must go to Nairobi to defend him.

ACT II Scene I.   Nairobi Central Court, the trial begins on May 26th and the verdict is delivered on July 1st. Imperturbable, urbane, almost insouciant and certainly aristocratic, Broughton gives testimony for twenty hours, when his turn comes. His Counsel in the event is Harry Morris, KC, who has demanded a fee of £5,000, agreed by the accused's wife, Diana. Dick Verdin did not get leave of absence to participate as a junior. Morris, later known as 'the Genius of the Defence', relies mainly on ballistics to prove his client's innocence, and leaves for Johannesburg before the jury returns at 9-15 p.m. after 3 hrs. 25 mins. Sir Delves Broughton describes the moment in a letter to a friend in England:

Broughton, writing: The Foreman, in a very clear voice said, 'Not Guilty' and a loud sob of relief came from all over the court and a good deal of clapping. One could almost feel the Angel of Death, who had been hovering over me, flying out of that court disgruntled.

ACT II Scene II.   In Iraq, near Baghdad, over a year later, and shortly after his father's suicide at the Adelphi Hotel, Liverpool on December 5th, 1942 by giving himself fourteen injections of Medinal some two days earlier, **Captain Sir Evelyn Delves Broughton, Bart., (320)** R.A.S.C., who was by then serving with the Polish Army,

opens his mail and finds a bill for £5,000 for his father's defence, sent on by his step-mother, Diana, whom he had never liked.

* * *

COLONEL WILLIAM HALL WALKER **(268)** had the distinction of making the principal speech at the York Gimcrack Club four times, three years running from 1905 and again in 1909. It would have been five, but for one of his two runners in the 1908 Gimcrack Stakes being beaten $\frac{3}{4}$ length. Among the improvements to the racing and breeding industries he advocated were greater Government support and in effect the Nationalization of racing, greater encouragement for National Hunt racing and the re-introduction of Hunter Chases, and the retention of the best stallions for the best breeding stock. He warned about the possible effects of glanders and influenza, unless drastic steps were taken by the Board of Agriculture and deplored the rule which, until 1929, meant that nominations were void on death.

The first and last Lord Wavertree, from a drawing by John Stringer Sergeant.

In 1893 he claimed the British record of 120 stags in 40 days. He used a Fraser double-ejector 450 express and six stags fell on one day at Fasnakyle, and on another, accompanied only by a mongrel terrier, in one stalk five to five bullets in five seconds – the first lying down, the second getting up, the third and fourth right and left, and the fifth at the moment when it paused, at 250 yards, to look back. This astonishing feat is well documented and is quoted in *The Badminton Magazine*.

At Harrow he was champion at fencing and singlestick and took part in the Royal Military Tournament in 1884, reaching the fencing final.

* * *

BRIGADIER-GENERAL H.A. TOMKINSON (271), affectionately called Mouse, was Racing Manager to King George V in succession to Captain F.H. Fetherstonhaugh. He used to wager half-a-crown annually with Sir Philip Hunloke, the Sailing Master of His Majesty's yacht *Britannia*, as to whether the King's horses or his yacht gave him the more victories.

* * *

WHEN SERVING with the 9th Lancers, **The Earl of Rocksavage (279)** won the Open Polo Championship of America in 1910 with his team, The Freebooters, which included Bend Or's friends, the Grenfell twins. Young Rock had a handicap of eight. He set a fashion with his immaculate polo shirts and the cut of his breeches and dress clothes and such innovations as the pleated trousers with a highly polished waistbelt, which he favoured for tennis.

Three years later he married his bride, Sybil, eleven years his junior and the daughter of a Sassoon and a Rothschild. She was the leading débutante of the previous season. And, as a curly haired Adonis, Rock was considered the handsomest man in England. After an engagement of only a few weeks, they were married quietly at a registry office near Buckingham Palace Road without any of the pageantry that a marriage solemnized in a fashionable London church would have involved. Plenty of pageantry was to follow in his capacity as Lord Great Chamberlain.

* * *

MAURICE, THE 4TH AND LAST **Lord Egerton of Tatton (280)** was a bachelor. He had a passion for big game hunting and spent much of his life in Africa. As a young man, when his family thought he was lost, he was found living with a tribe in the Gobi Desert. He shot his last tiger and tigress in India at the age of eighty-one. His museum of specimens is on display at Tatton. He was a pioneer motorist and in 1900 owned the first car in Cheshire, a Benz, registration number M 1. He later took to flying and obtained his pilot's certificate in 1910. He was at one time associated with the Wright brothers' trials. In 1940 he gave land in Kenya for what became Egerton College, a memorial to Lord Delamere. On his death in 1958 Tatton Park was bequeathed to the National Trust.

* * *

Brigadier-General Sir William Bromley-Davenport (235), from a portrait in oils by Sir Oswald Birley, 1942. He was a bachelor and, when he died in 1949, had been a Member for 63 years and three months, longer than anyone else in the Tarporley Hunts Club, but see page 59. He was 23 when he was elected and served the county as its Lord Lieutenant from 1920.

XVII

More 'Bright Green-Collar'd Young Men'

A CRYPTIC NOTE in Lady Mordaunt's diary for April 3rd, 1869, a little mark and the words '280 days from June 27th', meant that Viscount Cole, implicated in a highly publicized Divorce case, was also irrefutably the father of her daughter, as Sir Charles had not been with her that summer day and Lowry Cole had. The little girl was to become the chatelaine of Longleat and mother of the 6th Marquess of Bath. It was not the last time Coly got into such a scrape and probably not the first. *Vanity Fair*, that most perceptible mirror of Victorian personalities, featured him in the 'Men of the Day' series:

> Lord Cole is one of the pretty, joyous young men who are popular models in their own set of London Society. Blessed with good looks, even temper and a determination to make the best of this world, he became a Rifleman at twenty, and being soon found to be an exquisite dancer, he pursued a successful social and military career of three years duration. Having, however, discovered the charms of domestic felicity, he early retired upon his laurels. He made a brilliant marriage and unmade a famous one and now at two and thirty he is still a favourite partner at any ball he may please to honour, until time shall make him an hereditary legislator.

He had married in July, 1869 and succeeded his father – Sir Philip Egerton's great friend – in the Earldom of Enniskillen in 1886. Long before then he had established his happy hunting grounds in Cheshire where he was

> *A great Viscount young man*
> *A jolly and stout young man;*
> *A galloping, following,*
> *Bucketing, holloa'ing,*
> *Bright green-collared young man.*

He occasionally hunted with Sir Watkin's Hounds too.

The first time he dined at Tarporley was as a guest of Dick Grosvenor in 1875. He was elected a Member the following year.

Although he did not have any horses in training, he liked his racing and would stay at Newmarket with the Duke of Portland at St. Agnes's Cottage, a little house in the High Street. Lord Rocksavage and Lord Berkeley Paget were often among the guests who made up the party, taking their hacks on the heath to see the work and returning to devour a breakfast of prawns and Newmarket sausages. One of the Duke's horses once won a race by the shortest of short heads and before the number went in the frame, Enniskillen announced in a loud voice: 'By Jove, old chap, if you've won I'll knock your hat off, or somebody else's!' By the time the number went up, there was quite a row of people standing around with their hats in their hands, quite expecting the excitable Irishman to carry out his threat.

It was in 1880 that the Duke had sent his horses to Cheshire and stayed with his friend Lord Cole at Cassia Lodge to hunt with 'dear old Puffles' as well as with Regie Corbet, whose figure on horseback and turn-out he much

'Good looks,' from a caricature by SPY *in Vanity Fair.*

admired. Once Corbet pulled up sharp to let him take precedence at a fence during a fast gallop. Afterwards he thanked the Master for his courtesy. 'I don't know what you mean by kindness and civility,' replied Regie, 'I thought there was wire in it and that you might as well break your neck as I mine. The Duke had even heard Corbet once swear at the Duke of Westminster, who often came out in his old age. 'Oh, Reginald! I thought you might have let *me* off, an old Master of the Cheshire Hounds, too!'

Despite his youthful peccadilloes, in 1891 Lord Enniskillen was privately invested as a Knight Companion of St. Patrick in the throne room at Dublin Castle. In Cheshire he now usually acted as Chairman of the Subscribers to Hounds and it was largely due to his influence and to Piers Warburton's that Captain Park Yates was persuaded to continue in the Mastership of the North. At the end of the 1892/93 Season Mr Corbet also announced he would resign unless he had more money. A long correspondence ensued between the two Masters and Piers, with Mrs P.Y., who looked after the money side for her husband, also joining in with her say. The Captain was notoriously idle, except for anything to do with sport, and relied heavily on his efficient wife to look after his business affairs. She herself was a proficient horsewoman and hunted regularly. She was devoted to the hounds, but being shortsighted was not a hard rider. And she was an accomplished hostess.

The Duke of Westminster's eldest surviving son, Lord Arthur Grosvenor at the age of 32, had also expressed a willingness to take on the North, subject to some help from his father, who rather enigmatically told him it would take a lot of consideration. 'So there it is,' wrote Arthur from Grosvenor House, 'a rather curious position not knowing what to do.'

Lord Arthur wanted to be Master.

But that question was soon answered:

> . . . My father says that I had better <u>not</u> undertake the North, but if Corbet gives up I may take his country two days a week. I had set my heart on the North, but as it is not for me to speak, thus it remains.

In the end it was happily resolved. The Hunt was in

funds and Puffles got an extra £400 and Regie, only four years younger incidentally, £300. But as it happened the promised contribution of £500 from the Covert Fund was not forthcoming and they had to be paid in delayed instalments. A notice was sent out stating that £10 was no longer adequate as a minimum and relying on the generosity of ladies and gentlemen hunting with the Cheshire Hounds. A petition, signed by over eighty farmers was also received stating that they were 'strongly in favour of Mr Corbet continuing as Master'. They added: 'Mr Corbet has always done all he could to prevent wanton damage and has considered us in every way.' Much of the credit must go to Walter Starkey, the Marbury agent and for years *fidus achates* to Squire Cudworth Poole. He was now acting as Hon. Secretary of the South.

Lord Cholmondeley, unable to come to the meeting, had also vehemently hoped Corbet would continue.

In the North, Gilbert Greenall's brother-in-law, Cyril Greenall, was taking a great interest and was a member of the Gorse Committee, which ran the Covert Fund, under the chairmanship of Christopher Kay (216) and of which Sir Gilbert had previously been Secretary. Writing from Walton Hall, he sent some bills to the Treasurer, Charles Reynolds of Frodsham:

Sir Gilbert Greenall, Bart., from a painting by Sir Oswald Birley.

> . . . I am disgusted with the people round here – more especially at Dutton and Antrobus – they shoot the foxes and then send poultry bills in.

Though the family had built a capacious hunting box at Tilstone House in 1886, Gilbert Greenall himself, given his green collar on succeeding to the baronetcy, was hunting more and more with the Fitzwilliam, but Mr Fitzwilliam had died and he moved on to the Belvoir. The Duke of Rutland, a close friend of the old Sir Gilbert, was getting past it as Master. Lord Granby did not hunt and Lord Edward Manners, who acted as field master, was in failing health. And so, to the Cheshire's great loss, the seeds were sown for what proved to be the Greenalls' long association with the Belvoir; Gilbert's mastership running from 1896 to 1912, Cyril's from 1915 to 1918 and Toby, the former's son, as Joint from 1934 to 1947. By the time there was a vacancy in Cheshire, it was a *fait accompli*. And Gilbert Greenall went on to run the Belvoir in a style of which his ducal predecessors would have been proud. He supplied leathers for the hunt servants and employed a man whose sole task was to clean them.*

Most of all, Gilbert Greenall was a great agriculturist and was readily able to talk to his farmers on common ground. On arrival he recognized the responsibilities of maintaining such a classic kennel as the Belvoir and has gone down in history as a superb hound breeder according to the fashion of the day.

But Sir Gilbert and his family were by no means divorced from their Cheshire interests, not to mention the Warrington Brewery of which he was an active Chairman. In 1914 he organized a scheme to improve the hedges and fences of Cheshire, circulating an instructional leaflet to encourage farmers and landowners to plant hedges and lay them in the correct way. To aid this there was a competition for the best kept fences, ditches and gates. First prize that year went to Samuel Sherwin, Jnr. of Iddenshall Grange. In later years Sir Gilbert also used to judge the puppies on the flags at Sandiway.

It was during the late '80s and '90s that Lee Townshend (246) started a custom, which he called 'Bachelor's Ordinaries'. Each would take it in turn to give a dinner party for the rest, usually on a Saturday – Brian Egerton at Oulton, Hughie Delamere at Vale Royal, very often Lee Townshend himself at Wincham before he got married and moved to Gorstage, Bo Littledale at Sandiway, Massey at Poole, Griffith at Tiresford, *etc*. No ladies were allowed and only the occasional married man as a special compliment. Unless you were lucky enough to be a guest in the house, it was a long drive home after these cheery affairs, following a hard day's hunting and some mild gambling after dinner.

On January 23rd, 1895 Corbet's hounds had a remarkable run from a meet at Cholmondeley, as recorded by Walter Starkey:

Bo, sometimes spelt Beau.

. . . We then went to Barmere & just as hounds were being put into Bickley Wood, a fox jumped up out of a pithole and leaving Barmere on the right, ran past Handley Park covert & on over Norbury, past the Rye Bank Farm, over Wrenbury Frith, & leaving the Yeld on the left, ran on over Wrenbury Hall Park up to Woodcott Hill. There we had a check caused by the flooded brook. Hitting the line off again, we ran on past Sandford Bridge into & through Court's Gorse & from there ran on *via* Barnett's Brook, Walkmill Covert, Burleydam, Ash Wood, Ash Village, leaving the Brown Moss on our left, ran up to Edgeley, where hounds were stopped in the dark. Time up to Court's Gorse 50 mins. & up to Edgely 1hr. 45 mins.

He described it as 'a good hunting run', but did not estimate the distance. A frost then set in and they did not hunt again until March 2nd. Owing to frost January 23rd had been the first day since December 28th.

In April, 1895 Yates put the idea into Regie Corbet, Jnr.'s head to take over the whole Cheshire country if he and his father resigned. 'It would be of immense interest to me, & I should work hard to show sport and please my supporters,' disclosed young Regie to his friend the Hunt Secretary. But on reflection he wrote again in a long thoughtful letter from his Leicestershire home:

. . . I agree with you most thoroughly in what you say as to hunting 6 days a week from one Kennel, so much so that

---

* Sir Gilbert was not offered the Belvoir Mastership until March and there was no suitable house available; so he built Woolsthorpe with stabling for seventy horses, a circular school and all the other buildings and cottages necessary for such an establishment. No time was wasted with bricks coming smoking from the kilns and the horses were in by November 1st. There was even a small range of boxes built over a stream for the benifit of horses with dubious legs.

nothing would induce me to undertake such a task. Hunt Servants can't stand it, to say nothing of the Master.

Nevertheless under the present system he deplored the Wrenbury country being over-hunted by his father – 'In these days of Agricultural depression the farmers can't stand large fields so often crossing their land, their fences suffer so much. Only this season I saw the South on three consecutive hunting days in the same field' – and he referred to the meeting of farmers at Nantwich, which had been widely reported three weeks before. He thought the old regime of four days a week and a bye-day might well be best and he expressed a willingness to be considered under those terms. He did not think the subscriptions would diminish, in fact it would suit the 'trainers' hunting with the South pack, who now found themselves constantly drawing away from the railway for home.

No new ideas emerged from the Nantwich Farmers' Club meeting. It was the same old story. They did not mind the Green Collars going over their land, nor those who were resident. It was the visiting hordes to which they objected. They came out by train, enjoyed their day's hunting and were off again 'without asking anyone to have even a glass of beer,' grumbled one farmer. It seemed the hunt authorities were taking insufficient steps to curtail 'these trespassers'. Strong views were expressed about the removal of barbed wire during the hunting season and gates being left open for cattle to stray.

It was to be a long time before somebody thought of building hunt jumps and introducing a roster of gate-shutters.

John Jones, who was just about to start his twenty-seventh season as huntsman at the Forest Kennels, died very suddenly after coming back from hound exercise on July 3rd, aged 63. He felt a pain in his chest and 'expired from a ruptured blood vessel in his heart'. He was the longest serving Huntsman in the Cheshire's history. The Captain was utterly overcome at the funeral of his servant and friend.

At the Subscribers meeting in October it was announced that Captain Park Yates at very short notice had engaged a man called Boore and had temporarily

John Goddard.

given him permission to occupy the old Committee Room next to the Huntsman's Cottage, which was too small for his family. As the room was too small for their meetings anyway, the Secretary's suggestion to add it on to the cottage was adopted. Jack Boore had been Whipper-in and Kennel Huntsman with Lord Willoughby de Broke in Warwickshire, but although he was good in kennel and a nice enough fellow, he turned out to be a very indifferent huntsman.

In addition, the faithful Jack Goddard had left after twenty years' service as 1st Whipper-in.[†] Like Tom Rance, he had never wanted to take over as Huntsman. He was a brilliant horseman and had a wonderful voice, but, to Captain Park Yates's astonishment and disgust, for some extraordinary reason the Subscribers decided to turn down his proposal for a testimonial. However a subscription limited to 5/- was readily raised towards a tombstone for the late huntsman's grave at Whitegate. £52 was collected.

But the Master did not leave matters there, he organized a testmonial himself for Goddard and, no doubt mainly due to his own generosity, he was later able to make a presentation of a substantial cheque. In paying tribute to his former servant he recalled the happy days he had had in his youth in Leicestershire with some of Goddard's relatives.

But worse was to follow. On Monday, March 9th hounds met at Jodrell and the Master had driven to the covertside accompanied by Lord Enniskillen. Park Yates mounted what was afterwards described as a capable hunter – a mare usually ridden by one of the whippers-in – and, after a run, hounds found a fresh fox at Pogmere. Many jumped the hedge, but Enniskillen asked him to follow him along the road towards Brereton. As Puffles passed him at speed, Enniskillen shouted: 'Can you stop her?' 'Oh yes,' came the reply. 'Well pull up then! The hounds are crossing the road.' As he did so, his right foot slipped from the stirrup, and losing his

† A coloured engraving of J.C. Goddard was made and a copy hangs beside one of Jones in the passage outside the Hunt Room together with others of Captain Park Yates, Lord Enniskillen, H.R. Corbet, W.R. Court and Lord Wavertree. They were formerly at the Cheshire Kennels.

'Scent to View at Spurstow Lower Hall', from an oil painting by Archibald Mackinnon, 1903, probably made from a photograph of the premises dated 1890, when it had been farmed by the Dutton family, father and son for 150 years.

balance, fell on his back, his head pounding onto the road. He was taken on a hurdle to Brereton Rectory and never regained consciousness.

There Enniskillen spent an anxious night with his old friend and wrote next day to Piers:

> Poor dear Yates lost his stirrup galloping along the road close here & got the most awful fall and is suffering from suffusion of blood to the Brain. He has been & still is quite unconscious & is in the most critical state. We have [Dr] Moreton here & two nurses & a specialist, Jones of Manchester, came today. He says that 48 hrs. will tell us all – if no worse, then he has hope . . .

He died at 4.50 a.m. on the Wednesday. The inquest was held at The Rectory the same morning – 'death due to concussion of the brain.' Coly to Piers:

> I go to Sandiway tomorrow Broken Hearted. I am writing you this line to ask if any notice should be sent out on Friday as to the Hounds. Mrs Yates of course can do nothing & she

would like to hear what you think ought to be done. The funeral is to be at Ince on Monday . . .

> P.S. The dear old man looks so quiet and peacable. not a wrinkle in his face & so young.

Warburton wired back to meet him at 4 p.m. the next afternoon.

One of the first to write was the Duke, the same day:

> I suppose that owing to the lamentable death of poor Park Yates, the question of further hunting this season will arise . . . my opinion must incline me to believe that a discontinuance might not be unadvisable – the season has been open throughout... We hear that Enniskillen would be likely to take the hounds if offered.

Clearly the poor Secretary was going to have to face up to another extensive correspondence, requiring the utmost tact, about a new master or even masters.

However, first he must stand by Clementine in her grief and decide what was to be done. He called a meeting of Subscribers for the 17th. Corbet wrote on the 14th:

> No one is more grieved at poor dear Yates's death than Anne & myself. She was constantly at Sandiway and spent many an evening with him in his little den smoking, whilst others played cards elsewhere. Yet Anne feels as strongly as I do that a Subscription pack of hounds cannot stop hunting. This is not a matter of personal feeling . . .

And he took the strong view that hunting should continue, both packs being subscription packs. 'Of course no person is compelled to hunt whose feelings are against it.' (Two days after his neighbour, Mr Lonsdale, the Master of the North Shropshire, died the next year, Corbet was to change his meet from Adderley to Burleydam. And when the Duke died at Christmastide, 1899, he made the mistake of not cancelling hunting for a whole week, especially as it got frosted off anyway. 'We might have had the credit of doing the right thing and this to the cost of no one,' he wrote to Piers. When the Queen died in January, 1901, hunting was stopped until after the funeral.)

Piers had hunting stopped until after the funeral at Ince. The hunt servants were in uniform. By a coincidence Jones's tombstone was erected the same day his master was laid to rest. At the Subscribers' Meeting it was carried unanimously that the North should not hunt again that season. A letter of condolence was sent to Mrs Park Yates 'expressing the great sorrow we all feel at the loss of the most popular Master that ever managed the Cheshire Hounds'.

Corbet had already sent out cards to the Covert Fund Members, but it was also carried that the South pack should stop too and the Point-to-Point was cancelled.

Two people put forward their names to take on the North, Mr W. Court, who had been a Member of Tarporley since 1889, and the young squire of Oulton, Sir Philip Grey-Egerton, aged 32, who wrote to the Hon. Sec. formally to say that he had been considering the taking-over of the Mastership, stating that he could not do it without a guarantee of £3,400:

> I am aware that this is an increase, but even then it is money out of pocket, & in these days when a master has to be so tied down & has so much to do I do not see that he should be called upon to put his hand deeply [inserted] in his pocket to supply sport for those people who do not contribute anything towards the hounds who in this country are very many.

At the Subscribers' Meeting on April 14th the Hon. Secretary was instructed to accept Sir Philip's offer, but to state they were unable to guarantee the sum beyond one year. Two days later Brian replied from the Royal Hotel, Aldershot, stating he could not accept without a firm guarantee and thanking the Committee for having considered his proposal. Court had withdrawn. There was to be another meeting on April 25th, at which George Dixon was in the chair.

Meanwhile Piers had heard from Hughie Delamere (240), writing from Vale Royal, where Coly, his future father-in-law, was a frequent guest:

> DEAR COLONEL,
> I believe Lord Enniskillen would take the hounds if he were asked. I have heard this from one or two people who ought to know. Would it not be well to ask him; as at present if Brian Egerton falls through you have no alternative but Court and that would be very unpopular . . .
> . . . several people say that Lᵈ E would make such a much better master than Brian and I think so myself. Besides, Brian being master would mean that we should have more Corbet influence in the country and after the other day that hardly seems desirable . . . [Brian and Corbet Junior were first cousins and the latter had been born at Oulton].

He went on to make it abundantly clear that Brian was dismally lacking in experience on all counts, his sole asset being his popularity with everybody. And he foresaw that Mosley Leigh would be permanently in charge.

> P.S. Why on earth doesn't Mr Corbet resign and then the whole country could be settled at once.

The Duke of Westminster held the same view. 'It is unfortunate that Mr Corbet does not resign now, but he does not always do the right thing at the right time, but sometimes, as we know, the reverse,' he had written in another letter to Warburton.

The Chairman had also written, '. . . Cole will be an infinitely better Master than Brian Egerton.

Lord Enniskillen, writing from the Turf Club in London, was hesitant to put himself 'in opposition to Brian', but in view of the financial difficulty, offered to take the hounds for £3,000 *per annum*.

> . . . People in Cheshire have been so kind to me all my life that it will be a great pleasure to me to try & make them some little returns & am willing, if you will all forgive my shortcomings, to have a try.

He was readily accepted – 'such acceptance not to prejudice the sum now paid to Mr Corbet'.

His Lordship said long afterwards that if he had known how expensive it was going to be, he would never have taken the hounds on. However, he always liked a decent bit of cattle in his stable, so at the time he set about getting his horses from one of Ireland's best dealers, John Daly of Liffey Bank, Dublin. In his memoirs Ned Griffith, whom Coly had taken with him, reported the following exchange:

"Daly, do you know what I call a good hunter? It is a horse that will help you when opening gates, let you blow your horn or crack your whip without noticing it, gallop down the road or on the flat like a Derby winner, and let you make water off his back without moving."

"A very good description of a horse, M'Lord, and to be sure won't I be doing my best to be suiting you?"

During his term of office Lord Enniskillen conscientiously attended the Masters of Fox-hounds Association meetings and put forward a proposal which meant that the National Hunt Committee could punish fraud and corrupt practices at Point-to-Point Meetings, not hitherto in its power.

Lord Cole.

On April 25th, 1896 a proposal was also accepted that 'A Hunt Committee be appointed to advise on the management of the Hunt (outside the duties of the Masters.) . . .' These were the first twelve to be elected:

MARQUESS OF CHOLMONDELEY
LORD ARTHUR GROSVENOR
SIR PHILIP GREY-EGERTON, BT.
MR P.EGERTON WARBURTON
COL. FRANCE-HAYHURST
MR C.REYNOLDS
EARL OF CREWE
MR G.DIXON
MR W.R.COURT
MR S.SANDBACH
MR JAMES TOMKINSON
MR JOHN BIRKETT

A fortnight before the Meeting Piers had written to Corbet explaining financial difficulties, due to the Covert Fund falling off. But Corbet was not going to accept any such notice from the Hunt at such a late date and so far as he was concerned his contract was to remain the same.

It was not quite the end of the matter. Poor Brian Egerton had been very hurt to receive a telegram from Piers in reply to his wire enquiring how the meeting had gone: ENNISKILLEN HAS TAKEN THE HOUNDS. In October he wrote a long letter to the Club's President, Baron von Schröder, the merchant banker, asking for leave of absence from Tarporley Week and explaining the whole saga from his point of view. He did not feel he had been properly treated and did not relish the idea of attending the Tarporley Week Subscribers' Meeting.

Wishing the Baron 'a cheery Tarporley' and asking

him to make his letter public, he added:

. . . I feel this treatment not only discourteous but unbusinesslike & causes me to remove my name from the Committee & prevents me from writing to the Subscribers thanking them for their kindness in having endeavoured to meet my proposals.

He sent a copy to Warburton, who had evidently written to him as a result of hearing that he was hurt by Enniskillen's appointment. Happily in the end Brian attended both Tarporley and the first Committee Meeting the next May. And Piers Egerton Warburton withdrew his resignation as Hunt Secretary.

Once it had been realized Boore was the wrong man, he had been given notice by Captain Park Yates. At the April Meeting the new Master was authorized to part with him and offer him £200 compensation for short notice; but there had been some sort of misunderstanding and he stayed on to serve Lord Enniskillen for his first season before going on to hunt Lord Rothschild's Stag-hounds. Lord Enniskillen replaced him in 1897 with Frederick Gosden, with whom he established a good rapport. He had been with the Wexford and could rank with the best of his profession. He had perfect control over his hounds and was adept at casting them forward. He certainly showed plenty of sport.

The story is told of the day when Lord E. called for his flask from his 2nd Horseman, Billy Hammond, after a spanking run, only to find it empty. Gosden, his huntsman, was normally always allowed to finish off the contents on the way home. On this particular day, after a frustrating hour or two in Delamere Forest, Gosden had called up Hammond and downed the lot. Finding all his whisky gone when it came to his turn, the Master turned to his Huntsman with more than a touch of tetchiness, and said: 'Damn it, Gosden, you've drunk the lot.

Fred Gosden

You know I always keep you a drop.' 'Beg pardon, m'lord,' replied the Huntsman, 'I had to take out your share before I could get to mine!'*

It was not so much that at times Gosden took a little bit more than was good for him – 'I drinks because I likes it' was always his answer – but that he had a mind of his own and tended to be quick tempered. Captain Ap

Griffith of Tiresford had occasion to remonstrate with him for being rude to some of the field, pointing out his duty to be civil and please the people who hunted. After thanking him for telling him his faults, Gosden had a ready reply, to which there was no answer:

> Well, Sir, I pleases them as pleases me, and if I doesn't please them as doesn't please me, well then I pleases meself.

At all events there was some first class sport in Enniskillen's day, much of it due to Gosden and his ability to get away quickly. He left Cheshire to go to the Meynell for four seasons and was later in Ireland hunting some Stag-hounds in East Antrim. He remained in hunt service for the rest of his life and was Kennel Huntsman to Mr Selby Lowndes at the East Kent, 1915-18.

At the November Meeting Corbet had strong words with Warburton as he said the latter had given him an order to hunt the Peckforton Hills and not a request. It was agreed that in future both packs should do so.

In the meantime a memorial fund was set up for the late Master and suggestions for its use varied from a Village Room at Ince to a new fox covert and to the Sandiway Church Building Fund. £503 was raised and spent mainly on a large portrait in oils of Puffles by Leslie Ward (aka SPY, 1851-1922) for Mrs Park Yates and two stained glass windows at Ince Church. When Sandiway Church came to be built, Miss Mainwaring raised a further fund from the ladies of the hunt and this paid for the West Window as another memorial to the Captain.

In a warm-hearted gesture Clementine Park Yates had a copy of the portrait made by Harrison Dutton and presented it to the Club for the Hunt Room. She was a

Captain E.W.Park Yates, Manager of the North Cheshire Hounds, 1877-1896, from portrait in oils by J.F.Harrison Dutton after Sir Leslie Ward.

lady of immense dignity and enjoyed forty years of widowhood, living in style at Ince.

The Committee was at pains to co-operate with the Nantwich Farmers' Club, particularly with regard to the purchase of forage. Landowners were circulated to encourage them to make arrangements for the removal of wire from growing fences during the hunting season. The two Masters also sent out a plea for 2nd Horsemen not to ride over the country but to follow the Masters' 2nd Horsemen. It was about eight years later that the

---

* Lionel Edwards's version of this story refers to 'a veritable magnum flask', but the silver stoppered flask itself, together with the Earl's coronetted sandwich case, is in the possession of the author and holds but 8 fluid ounces.

FOUR OIL PAINTINGS BY GEORGE GOODWIN KILBOURNE (1839-1924)

The Meet at Calveley Hall.

Breaking Cover.

Full Cry, making for Peckforton Hills.

The Kill at Peckforton.

Sir Philip Grey-Egerton, 12th Baronet of Oulton and for 39 years Secretary to the Club.

practice of 2nd horsemen wearing a stirrup leather over the shoulder, if not in livery, was requested. But the main trouble was still the crowds and for some extraordinary reason the Subscribers seemed loath to impose a proper system of capping on the visitors, except on occasions for those who were guests of Subscribers.

It was about this time that the Covert Fund was merged with the Subscribers' Income Fund for administrative purposes. There were by now some ninety gentlemen who were 'Subscribers to Hounds', in effect Members of the Cheshire Hunt. The Hunt Committee also made a proper arrangement, which evidently had not been previously in force, for the senior green collar subscriber out to act as Field Master for the day in the absence of the Master, failing his nomination.

At the end of his third season Lord Enniskillen found he required more money and as Mr Corbet was obliged to mount a huntsman, he, too, asked for more. Fortunately the Subscribers were able to concede to their requests, but a proposal for the South Cheshire to increase its country on the Crewe side by Col. Egerton Warburton did not find a seconder, Mr Bolton Littledale refusing to allow Mr Corbet to draw his coverts there.

At Tarporley at the beginning of what proved to be the last season for each of the Masters, glasses were doubtless raised to the Members away in South Africa, Lord A.Grosvenor, Bromley-Davenport and Mosley Leigh with the Imperial Yeomanry, and the new Duke of Westminster, due back in England from the Cape that week, who was elected. He had already sent word through his agent for the fixture cards to be forwarded to Saighton Grange and his intention to continue the subscription of £200 to the Cheshire Hounds.

Corbet Senior had not been well enough to attend. Sending on his list of hounds to Piers, he reported, writing from Cotebrook: 'I have just met a young fellow returning from hunting. He tells me that the Vale is a Parrot Cage of wire. We have seen the best of it. It is becoming far too dangerous an amusement.'

Corbet's sense of humour is seldom apparent in his letters, but when Lord Enniskillen consulted him on the advisability of sending out a notice to landowners and farmers about the increasing use of wire in the fences with a view to getting them to remove it during the hunting season, he was all in favour; but he could not resist adding to Enniskillen, who was noted for making considerable use of the roads when hunting:

I have not noticed that the wire you mention has ever been put across the high roads, so I don't imagine it can therefore interfere with you much, old fellow!

How amused old Regie would have been, had he lived to see the set of four oil paintings by G.D.Giles the Newmarket artist, commissioned in 1904 by Corbet Junior! In one, the huge field is setting off behind the hounds in full cry from Calveley Gorse. All except for one unmistakably moustached figure, determinedly thrusting his way to the back to get to the nearest road.

But in fairness Lord Enniskillen did his best. He once called out to a man called Cooke, standing in a muddy gateway at Baddiley: 'Here, my man, will you please give

The Earl of Enniskillen, M.F.H.

me a handful of that dung to put on my saddle. It is a bit slippery to-day and I want to stick on!'

Enniskillen kept up with his Cheshire friendships to the last and never lost his enthusiasm. He delighted in acting as starter at the Point-to-Points and was especially pleased to be asked to judge at the Puppy Show, which he did on numerous occasions after giving up the hounds. He rejoiced in the farmers' lunches and as a raconteur he was high in the handicap.

In January, 1898 James Tomkinson had written a petition which was sent to the Squire of Adderley:

> WE, the undersigned, being Subscribers to, and followers of, the South Cheshire Hounds, desire to place on record our appreciation of MR CORBET'S long and invaluable services to the Cheshire Hunt, and our gratitude to him for the excellent sport with which he has provided us, as Master and Huntsman, for a period little short of the third part of a Century.
>
> We further desire to express our unabated confidence in him in both these capacities, and our earnest hope that he may long be spared, in health and strength, to occupy the position which he still fills with such credit to himself and satisfaction to his friends and supporters.

By now Corbet was making arrangements for his son to take over the South Pack. He had been hunting the hounds for him since 1899 and had as 1st Whipper-in and Kennel Huntsman Alfred Earp, who had been seventeen seasons under Tom Firr at the Quorn. 'It is rather a wrench after thirty-four years of what has given me the greatest pleasure,' wrote the Master to Piers on New Year's Eve, tendering his resignation. And hearing of this, Enniskillen felt it sensible to write in at the same time. For some undisclosed reason Lord Cholmondeley, suffering badly from gout, did not approve of Corbet Junior and let it be known that 'for the sake of Fox-hunting' he was not to have his support. He was staying with Algy Burnaby and his wife Sybil, Hughie Delamere's sister, at Baggrave Hall in Leicestershire at the time. It may have been because he did not think he was any good as a huntsman, or possibly some private reason not disclosed.

As for Lord Cholmondeley himself, then in his mid-forties, 'trying' though some may have found him, he was one of the greatest supporters of fox-hunting at a time the sport was adjusting to the XX Century. Not a strand of wire was to be found on his vast estate. It should be emphasized that he was an acknowledged horseman with a great understanding of fox-hunting and, indeed, he was one of the best field masters the county ever had. There was one occasion about this time when, from a meet at Bulkeley X-rds., hounds had run a fox to the hills from

Reginald Corbet, Esq., M.F.H.

Ridley. On arrival at the Copper Mines one of Sir Philip's Bickerton keepers, standing nearby, called out: 'Dog fox, M'lord!' 'How do you know?' shouted Lord Rock over his shoulder as he trotted past. 'I saw his balls as he scaled yonder wall, M'lord.'

Back in Cheshire at the Subscribers' Meeting, the day after Queen Victoria died, his proposal to resume hunting the whole country six days a week from the Forest Kennels was beaten by Lord Shrewsbury's counter proposal to continue as before by 18 votes to 14. In turn Lord Cholmondeley added a rider to Shrewsbury's further proposal that Corbet Junior should succeed his father. This was that a professional huntsman should be engaged and new Kennels built at Ridley, but his amendment was not accepted.

Tributes had already been paid to H.R.C. 'for the admirable way in which he had hunted this country for so many years, and the capital sport which he has always shown during that time' and the Secretary was instructed to write to the Earl of Enniskillen 'thanking him for his past services and to express a hope that we should still

H.Reginald Corbet, M.F.H. from a portrait in oils by William Carter.

he was one of the best amateur huntsmen of his day and had a marvellously quick eye to hounds. Like all good huntsmen he lost no time in getting away on the fox's back. And when he was not hunting hounds himself, he kept rigid control of his field and invariably went first so that he knew what his hounds were doing. Nobody ever dared get in *his* way or over-ride *his* hounds. Raymond Carew said of him that 'he knew the run of almost every fox in the country, that he hunted his hounds either with unlimited patience or the utmost dash, just as occasion required.' And there was no question that as a horseman he was unrivalled.

He used to ride all his horses in very long-cheeked double bridles, often with their head tied down with a short standing martingale. They all jumped faultlessly and never refused. When he had his sales from the Kennels people like Lord Richard Grosvenor, R.C. Naylor and Baskervyle Glegg vied with many others to buy them.

Like most strong men he had his opponents, but he was a born leader and ruled with both a velvet glove and an iron fist where necessary. When he used his caustic tongue, he always meant to apologize, even if he never got round to it.

Hubert Wilson, whose home was The Hermitage, Holmes Chapel and was currently Master of the Ledbury Hounds, which he had taken over on the sudden death of his brother two seasons earlier, had been put forward for the North. Both he and R.Corbet, Jnr. were called into the room and duly accepted the Masterships, the former with 'a salary of £3,200' and the latter £1,600.

have the pleasure of his cheery company in the field.'

A fund was opened for a retirement present to Mr Corbet, but soon after, he became ill and died before his portrait could be given to him. The chosen artist was William Carter (1863-1939), brother of Howard Carter, the Egyptologist, and there were sufficient funds for him to make a copy for the Hunt Room. Mrs Corbet received the original. It was in 1926 that Regie's widow presented the Club with a mahogany cheese cradle, which Lord Combermere had given to her many years before.

Reginald Corbet Senior may have had his critics, but

Unfortunately Lord Cholmondeley took offence. Enniskillen wrote to Piers that he had been to see him but threw no further light on the matter. However, Rock made his views quite clear to the Secretary:

> ... As to Regie Corbet <u>why</u> are you to <u>keep</u> him? He is not a Cheshire man, by that I mean he owns no land in Cheshire, or if so only a very few acres. He has never subscribed one penny to the Hunt & he has never taken any trouble to try to take wire down or in any way be of service to the hunt. When [he] acted as Master for his father he was absolutely useless and the field paid no attention to him. As a Huntsman I think him very moderate, therefore I say let him go.

At Tarporley, the next November, Brian Egerton, now the Club Secretary, read out a letter he had received from Lord Cholmondeley, resigning his Membership. The Club elected the new Manager in his place. The father of the Hunt, Earl Egerton of Tatton, dined that year after many years absence and the young Duke drank his quæsitum, as well as Hubert Wilson. Another small ceremony took place with an exchange of presents between the new Master of the North and his predecessor. By a coincidence they gave each other a silver 'hunting horn' cigar lighter.

Captain Hubert Wilson, Master of the North Cheshire, 1901-07.

It was seven years before the Marquess was re-elected and he did not attend again except for the wartime Business Meeting at the Crewe Arms Hotel in 1915.

His letter of resignation was not preserved, but in his note to Piers Warburton confirming his disapprobation, he wrote:

> ... I am afraid you will think I am an awful nuisance and also perhaps think that I ought not to go against the meeting... I also think it is a very wrong thing that a landowner's vote is not better than anybody else's vote that only pays £25 a year.

Nevertheless the Cholmondeley coverts were drawn by the South pack the next season, but he forfeited his own hunting in Cheshire for the time being. Evidently everything was put right, for by 1904 he was again having his say at Subscribers' Meetings, though of course he came off the Hunt Committee. Whatever young Corbet's failings were in the Marquess's eyes, Starkey's diary records ample days over the next few seasons when good sport was had, although he put down the 1903/04 Season as the worst he ever remembered.

However it was during this season that G.D.Giles came up to stay at Adderley and to paint both hunts. He did four oils in all:

March 17th, from Duddon Heath:
    THE CHESHIRE – BEESTON BROOK. CLOTTON TO THE HILLS
March 18th, from Combermere Abbey:
    THE SOUTH CHESHIRE – IN COMBERMERE PARK
March 23rd, from OULTON PARK:
    THE CHESHIRE – A MEET AT OULTON and
    THE CHESHIRE – HOLLOA AWAY FROM CALVELEY

For details of the personalities depicted see the captions to the illustrations. There was a really busy day from Duddon Heath, not finishing until 5 p.m. and with two good runs.

There was certainly a good day from Combermere when Regie was back in the saddle after a short illness. This is what Walter Starkey wrote in the official diary:

> Went straight to the Big Wood, found a fox in the young larches & ran out by Newhall, past Court's Gorse over the Brook leaving Hall-a-Coole on the left down to Coole Lane where the fox turned short left-handed, past Devil's Nest up Sandford Bridge, & crossing the brook short of Woodcott Hill, ran through Aston Coppice & on over the Royals through Hewitt's Moss & back into Combermere Big Wood where "a" fox was killed on the Island. Time 1 hr.10 mins. Did not find in Brankelow Moss [or Poole's Gorse] so went on to Marley Moss where we found a good fox & and had one of the best runs I have seen for years of 2 hrs. 20 mins. & as Hounds ran about 20 miles. Leaving

THREE OIL PAINTINGS
BY MAJOR GODFREY DOUGLAS GILES (1857-1923)

ABOVE: *THE CHESHIRE – BEESTON BROOK: CLOTTON TO THE HILLS*
The meet was at Duddon Heath with Mr H.M.Wilson in charge. The field included Lords Shrewsbury, Ingestre, & Linlithgow, Capt. & Mrs Higson, Mrs Park Yates, Mr & Mrs Littledale and Miss Littledale, Maj. Mosley Leigh and Messrs Geo. Barbour, A. Knowles, W.Massey, Lee Townshend, A.Brocklehurst, J.Fergusson, W.R.Court and V.Hermon. There is no key.

Above right: *THE CHESHIRE – A MEET AT OULTON*
There is no key, but Fred Champion, Huntsman, and Frank Freeman, 1st Whipper In, lead off with the hounds, followed by the Master, Mr H.M.Wilson. In the centre is the ex-Master, Lord Enniskillen, with Mr Reginald Corbet in hunting cap behind; riding on the former's left is the Hunt Secretary, Col. Piers Egerton Warburton. The Duke of Westminster is on the dappled grey with the Duchess beside him. The figure with the bicycle is 'Running Tom'.

Sir Philip Grey-Egerton, Bt., the host, stands in the doorway of the Hall.

Marley Moss we ran over Marbury Hayes & Wrenbury Frith & past Norbury Meres into Cholmondeley, round & out of Cholmondeley, over Wrenbury Frith into Wrenbury Mosses & on to Baddiley, Sound Heath, Edleston, Dorfold, Tally Ho Covert back past Baddiley Gorse & killed him between Baddiley Gorse and Swanley Covert, at 5-30 p.m. a great hound run.

From Oulton the following Wednesday, with Hubert Wilson in charge again and many visitors who were staying in Cheshire for the Grand National, there was a fast 25 mins. from Philo to Hill's Gorse and later a

Right:: *THE CHESHIRE – HOLLOA AWAY FROM CALVELEY*
Mr Hubert Wilson, Master of the Cheshire, in cap, is being pressed by his field which had run from Philo. In the distance the 1st Whipper In, Frank Freeman, can be seen holloaing. The only other identifiable figure is the Earl of Enniskillen, the moustached gentleman determinedly making his way to the back of the field and the nearest lane. Mr Corbet, Master of the South Cheshire, with whom the artist had been staying, had suggested this detail to poke fun at his father's old friend.

'capital hunt' of 45 mins. Jimmy Tinsley (288), who kept the diary for the Cheshire, missed the former. Hounds did not draw Calveley that day, so the artist has probably taken a certain amount of licence with 'Holloa Away from Calveley' during the run to Hill's Gorse.

Prominent in the foreground of 'A Meet at Oulton' is Running Tom. For decades well into the 1930's he was a

Running Tom.

great character of the Cheshire hunting scene. He was a chimney sweep, one Thomas Kelsall from Sandbach, and was a familiar figure in an old hunt servant's coat, breeches and hunting cap with a handy stirrup leather across his shoulder. In his latter years he would be mounted on a lady's bicycle.

Tom would leap from his machine and run like a hare to be in at the kill. Ned Griffith recalled:

> . . . Whatever his age by his teeth he had the legs of a boy. No matter where hounds were, there was Tom, clad in his old red coat and cap with a hunting whip instead of a stick which one would have thought more useful in running – tobacco juice streaming down his chin.

He made quite a handsome living by being at the right place at the right time to open a gate or hold a horse. Indeed he kept a mistress in Sandbach. More often than not he would return to the Kennels to sleep in the barn, having amply quenched his thirst from the beer barrel kept there. He was also known to economize on his butcher's bills by cadging some choice cuts of horseflesh from the knacker shed.

Back in 1901 before the beginning of Hubert Wilson's first season, his attention was drawn to the wanton cutting of wire fences by some irre-sponsible followers. It became the practice for wirecutters to be carried solely by one of the hunt servants. But better still, two years later the Wire Fund organization was properly set up and during the 1903/04 Season a total of 79,088 yards (nearly 45 miles!) of wire was taken down. The total cost for removal and refixing at the end of the season came to £124 6s 5d. The following season the total length was an astonishing 254,623 yards, 246,143 in 1905/06.

In the Letter Book there is one about some cubs from Sir Philip's secretary addressed to Mr Wilson:

> I am in receipt of yours of yesterday. I am glad to say the cubs are getting stronger. I am sorry Mr Stock [He lived at White Hall, near to Oulton] does not approve of my having moved them. If we had not moved them, all except two would have been dead. By some means or other the earth got flooded & the poor little beggars were an awful mess, two lying practically dead & the others starving. We took 2 of them home and put them by the fire and fed them on whisky & milk and then in the afternoon as the vixen had not been near them, and they could not lie in the bed of the earth & one was nearly dead, I had them all brought home. We have only lost one and the others are getting stronger every day. I will put them back with pleasure if you like, but I think it would be a mistake. Perhaps you will let me hear what you think.

In those days, incidentally, the cub-hunting meets were at 5 a.m., 4-30 a.m. even at Delamere Post Office on August 19th, 1905.

Hubert Wilson was to do much to level out the pack. Jack Boore had introduced a wiry Warwickshire type which ill-matched Jones's hounds of substance. The Cheshire-bred hounds that took leading honours at Peterborough in the course of the next thirty years were a tribute to him. The new Master chose five outstanding lines: *Belvoir* Fallible and Weatherguage, *Croome* Rambler, *Milton* Solomon and *Grove* Harkaway. By the end of the 1910/11 Season, out of 80 couple at the Forest Kennels, some 65 couple had these five crosses in their pedigrees.

The Master brought his huntsman, Tom Cubberley, with him from the Ledbury, but he never really made the grade as the carrier of the horn and suffered from poor health. He was replaced in 1903 by Fred Champion, who was to stay with the Cheshire until 1911.[*] Turning hounds for Cubberley his second season and one season for Champion was none other than Frank Freeman, an Irishman by birth, who became, arguably, the most brilliant huntsman of all time. He was to go on to hunt the Bedale for two seasons before he went to the Pytchley, where he stayed until 1931. In January, his first season in Cheshire, he broke his thigh, and, like Maiden with his affliction, it caused him a great deal of pain for most of his career. This was most probably the reason few who worked under him found it a pleasure. Once asked how a new whipper-in was shaping, he declared: 'He won't never be any use. Do you know I caught him whistling in kennel yesterday when *I hadn't caught my fox!*' (G.D.Armour used the story for a *Punch* cartoon.) The Tarporley Hunt Club possesses a crayon sketch of him done from life at Market Harborough in 1921 by Cecil

Frank Freeman, from life at Market Harborough, a crayon sketch by Cecil Aldin.

Aldin. It was presented by Sir John Dixon (281) in 1964.

There was much concern after the accident as to whether he would be fit enough in time for the next season and for that reason Captain Wilson passed him over and had engaged Champion, who had seven seasons' experience as Huntsman with the Galway Blazers and the Kildare. Frank spent the Summer in the hands of a London bone-setter and the Master need not have worried. His over-cautiousness turned out to be a big mistake, for, quite unconsciously, whenever young Frank carried the horn, he outshone the new huntsman, competent though he was.

Unfortunately a certain Mr Herbert Gill, who used to come out from Manchester, moved to Darlington and persuaded the new Master of the Bedale to engage Freeman as huntsman. The news of his outstanding success there can hardly have been the cause of Wilson's ultimate resignation, but just the same the Green Collars were extremely displeased at missing the chance of having such a brilliant man for years to come at Sandiway, especially as they had been betrayed by one of the Manchester brigade.

The first season under the new regimes was reported

* His nephew, Bob Champion, Jnr., whipped-in for Mr Peter Russell Allen when he hunted the North Cheshire, 1934-36. He was the father of Bob Champion, who won the 1981 Grand National on Aldaniti.

† His great grandfather, Joseph Leigh of Oak Hill, Liverpool, bought Belmont. His grandmother was a Mosley, daughter of the second baronet and granddaughter of the Oswald Mosley who bought Bolesworth from John Crewe (2).

as 'moderate'in the North, where there were only a few good runs, including an excellent 35 mins. from High Legh, but a poor scenting season generally and both were badly affected by foxes with mange, the only effective cure for which was to have the earths permanently stopped.

Throughout his mastership Hubert Wilson could rely on Colonel Mosley Leigh (245) to help out as field master when required. In 1907 he went to Ireland to hunt hounds there for five seasons. On his return Old Mo still lived for his hunting and continued long afterwards at an advanced age. On one occasion hounds finished at the Verdin Arms at Minshull Verdin, a good 17 miles from Great Budworth. 'Would you like a lift back to Belmont?' somebody asked him. 'No thanks,' the old boy replied, 'I shall enjoy the ride home.' He had an immense zest for life and was always immaculate, whether on horseback or the dance floor or at a Horse Show in his grey bowler. He seldom went to bed sober.†

Col. O.Mosley Leigh.

Next season hounds ran from Astle to Hale, where they had not been for years and all in all sport improved, though mange was still prevalent. But by the next season it was checked and for the 1905/06 Season it was practically extinct. Sport was better than it had been for some time, thanks to the removal of the wire.

In February, 1905, in what was generally considered to be a good season despite lack of scent, Hubert Wilson

FROM A PRINT OF AN OIL PAINTING
BY MAJOR GODFREY DOUGLAS GILES (1857-1923)

THE SOUTH CHESHIRE – IN COMBERMERE PARK

KEY as given on the back of the original oil painting formerly in the possession of the Corbet family.

left to right:
1.   *1st Whipper In (Albert Earp)*
2.   *Reginald Corbet, Master and Huntsman of Adderley Hall*
3.   *John Bellyse Baker, late of Highfields, Audlem*
4.   *Cibel [sic] Corbet of Adderley*
5.   *Lord Gerald Grosvenor*
6.   *James Gordon Houghton of Gardenhurst, Tarporley*
7.   *2nd Whipper In (Edwin Tyrell)*
9.   *Earl of Shrewsbury*
10. *Duchess of Westminster*
13. *Arthur Brocklehurst of Nantwich*

left to right (upper row):
8.   *Frederick Voller Grange of 'The Hollows'*
11. *Albert Neilson Hornby of Parkfields, Nantwich*
12. *William Brown of Nantwich*
14. *Lady Helen Grosvenor*
15. *Marquis of Cholmondeley*

NOTES:
Sybil Corbet, the Master's daughter, was born in 1892.

Lord Gerald Grosvenor, 7th son of the 1st Duke of Westminster, lived at Ash Grange, Whitchurch.

The Duchess of Westminster was Constance [Shelagh] Cornwallis-West.

Lady Helen Grosvenor was the 1st Duke's 6th & youngest daughter, born in 1888. She later married Brig.-General Lord Henry Seymour.

caused some consternation by putting in his resignation. He found the call on his time too great to do it properly and it was impossible for him to forego his other commitments. As well as his business in Manchester and the Yeomanry, he had ambitions to stand for the Knutsford Division. Fortunately he was prevailed upon

to continue. Piers Egerton Warburton resigned as Secretary and was replaced by Major Hugh Wilbraham (237).

At long last proper steps had been taken to levy a cap of £5 for strangers. There was a minimum subscription to the Covert Fund of £15 'which should be increased when it is intended to hunt regularly more than one day a week.' Already motor cars were becoming a nuisance and it was carried unanimously that they 'be requested not to follow hounds after they have moved off from the meet to draw'. It was of little effect, any more than a request made in 1907 to the Automobile Club & Association asking for its influence to put an end to the practice.

During the 1905/06 Season Regie Corbet nearly lost his life. Hounds had met at the Farmers' Arms, Ravensmoor on January 19th and ran a fox from Hurleston, through Acton down to The Rookery at Worleston. They turned for the Pool Brook which was flooded and a couple and a half got carried over the flood-gate into a whirlpool. The Master jumped in to save them and was himself carried away by the torrent. He sank twice before being rescued by a thirty-six-year-old Nantwich horse dealer called Wm.Brown, who went in holding on to a whip thong and was able to get him to the side. His conduct was reported to the Royal Humane Society by Lord Shrewsbury and he was given a 'Testimonial on Parchment', the sixth grade of the Society's awards. Lord Gerald Grosvenor*assisted Fred Earp in rescuing and resuscitating the hounds. Mean-while the main body had run on a ring back to Hurleston where they were stopped by the Field after two hours, when they realized the Master and his whipper-in were missing. Subsequently on that near calamitous day and with Regie none the worse and attired in borrowed clothes, there was a fast hunt from Wardle to Bunbury before hounds were stopped at dusk travelling on another wide ring back to Hurleston.

It was never an easy task for Hunt Secretaries to get everyone to pay their dues. Although shortfalls have very often been more than compensated for by the generosity of other individuals, times have not changed. Hugh Wilbraham preserved this particular correspondence:

Jan. 10th, 1906

CHESHIRE HUNT COVERT FUND

Dear Sir,

In reference to your letter & circular of the 8th inst. my subscription of £15 is intended to cover my wife's hunting & my own with the South Cheshire Hounds. We never go with the North & we don't have second horses out.

Our average would be in an <u>open</u> season about twenty days each. This season I have had ten and my wife six. My

son in the Field Artillery when at home on leave for about six weeks hunted a few times... In proportion to what other subscribers pay, who with their families hunt three or four days a week with both packs, my subscription appears to me quite sufficient. It would be a different thing if money was required, but I understand there is always a balance to the good . . .

Estate Office, Delamere House
11th Jan.

Dear Sir,

I beg to acknowledge receipt of your letter... I can only come to the conclusion that the minimum of £15 is inadequate in your case and I hope you will see your way to increase it. All cases of inadequate subscriptions brought to my attention are dealt with and my request in almost all cases is complied with. I may inform you that there is not a large surplus over every year, although a balance has to be kept to meet expenses . . .

Estate Office, Delamere House
25th Jan.

I am sorry not to have heard from you in response to my letter . . . Your subscription was brought to my notice by several influential members of the hunt and since hearing from you I have consulted several members of the Hunt Committee who all agree that your subscription should be increased . . .

I hope you will see your way to increase your subscription and so avoid my having to bring the matter officially to the notice of the Hunt Committee.

Jan. 26th.

. . . I am sorry you have written to me a threatening letter on this matter. I never submit to threats. If you had left the matter in my hands and at the end of the season I had found I had hunted oftener than my subscription justified I would have sent you a further one.

I have only been out eleven times and my wife six, three or four of which she was mounted by a friend (a subscriber) living in Cheshire. No one with any sense of fairness can call my subscription at the present time inadequate. I consider the way you have treated me offensive and unjust taking into consideration the amount of hunting other subscribers are allowed to get without undue interference. Your system of espionage also makes matters unpleasant. I have subscribed eighteen years and never before had the least un-pleasantness.

Estate Office, Delamere House
2nd Feb.

Your letter of 26th will be laid before the Hunt Committee at their next meeting. Meanwhile as you appear unwilling to comply with the rules of the Hunt the weekly card of fixtures will no longer be forwarded to you, a course I regret having to adopt.

---

*Lord Gerald had revived the Royal Agricultural College Beagles in 1900. 'Billy' Brown had a son who became a sergeant in the Cheshire Yeomanry and eventually head lad to Gordon Johnson Houghton.

Feb.6th

. . . You have no right to take such a step as stopping my card, having accepted my subscription for the season. As far as the card goes it is of no consequence except that it is an undeserved insult on your part. I have sent you particulars of my hunting with the South Cheshire Hounds in former letters but I may add that since Dec. 22nd I have hunted twice with these hounds & my wife once & that it is extremely improbable that I shall hunt with any pack of hounds again this season. The way you have acted in this matter seems to me extraordinary & greatly wanting in courtesy from one gentleman to another.

Colonel George Dixon, the Chairman, approved Hugh's stand and Walter Starkey's report had given him every reason to take it. Even the Master, who had nothing to do with it, was brought in before the row died down, accused as the instigator. 'I have told him that if I did say that I continuously saw him & his wife out hunting, I was quite ready to repeat the statement,' Regie wrote to Hugh a month later.

Meanwhile the wife joined the fray, reiterating much of what her husband had already written. 'Nobody regrets more than we do that there has been unpleasantness, but I feel sure it has been caused by wrong information,' she added. A final salvo from the miscreant, who came from outside the county, was sent on Feb.27th:

My wife has handed me your letter of the 17th. It does not appear to occur to you that the only way to settle what you call 'an unfortunate disagreement' is to send us a full apology for the extremely unjust way we have been treated, also an apology should come from the person who gave you false information as to our hunting. Nothing else will satisfy us. I may say it is the first time in my life I have been treated as if I was not a gentleman.

It was in Hugh Wilbraham's day that an Agreement was drawn up for the Cheshire Hunt to enjoy the Sporting Rights of Delamere Forest, some 2,000 acres of Crown property for a yearly rent of £50.

But far weightier matters were going to tax the new Secretary and the Hunt Committee from now on. In October, 1905 Hubert Wilson had written to say there was a feeling in the country that the Cheshire Hounds should be united once more, but that he was willing to carry on until it was resolved. The Duke of Westminster, in South Africa, was anxious for his views to be known to the Committee. They were relayed by his private secretary:

"Owing to misunderstandings which have existed, and still continue to exist, between the Master and the largest landowner in the South Cheshire country, it is impossible for the former to carry on any longer. I would therefore suggest that Lord Cholmondeley be asked to take over the whole country; that a professional huntsman should hunt the hounds 4 days and Lord C two days a week. This appears to me to be the only way out of the difficulty. If Regie Corbet thinks of retiring I can only add how much I shall regret it, as he has got together a grand pack of hounds and has shown us great sport."

Colonel Wilford Lloyd added:

So you will see that the pith of his opinion is that it is impossible to hunt a country if you are not on friendly terms with the largest landowner.

A year later Lord Cholmondeley suggested an exchange of country between the North and South packs as a way out of the problem. Henry Tollemache's proposal was carried:

That the Subscribers whilst gratefully acknowledging Lord Cholmondeley's kindness in supporting hunting on his property, do not feel justified in acceding to [his] suggestions, which they consider would be practically impossible to carry out and moreover would be contrary to the wishes of landowners farmers and subscribers who are quite satisfied with the present arrangement.

A Subscribers' Meeting was called for January 29th, 1907. The Duke wrote to say he did not want to take the hounds as, amongst other reasons, he was most probably going to be in Uganda all the following Winter. 'I rather think from what I hear that Linlithgow if approached would very likely take them on, & we could'ent [*sic*] possibly do better than him, in my opinion,' he added. He wrote again next day with further thoughts:

As I wrote some two years ago, saying that in such an unsatisfactory state and without any prospect of this being put straight under existing circumstances, [I suggest] that the Marquess of Cholmondeley should be offered the whole country. It is not here necessary for me to enter into his qualifications for this post, as they go without saying.

No one will be sorrier than I shall be if it is found necessary for my friend R.Corbet to give up the South Cheshire, but I do not see any other way out of the difficulty. His country is small and without the use of the coverts on the Cholmondeley Estate, it would make hunting a farce. So I suggest that Lord Cholmondeley be formally asked to take over the country.

Lord Cholmondeley wrote to say that he had intended to express his views, but had been advised by Henry Tollemache not to 'as he says I shall upset the whole county'.

I shall do nothing at present but stay at home when my coverts are drawn. Henry Tollemache tells me that Mr Corbet does everything that is right & is very popular with all the subscribers etc., this I doubt very much from what I hear. Am so sorry for having given you all this trouble for nothing. You can tell Dixon what I am doing if you wish to.

Both these letters were read out at the Meeting and Hubert Wilson's final letter of resignation was accepted. A consultation committee was appointed to advise the Subscribers and a further meeting convened.

Referring to Lord 'Rock', Regie wrote to Hugh, who had apprised him of the proceedings:

> . . . The man is impossible & unreasonable without any cause except jealousy. He cannot bear seeing me with the hounds. He tries to rule everybody with his overbearing manner & I cannot tell you how delighted I am that the meeting would not give way to him.
>
> Those who know him say it is far better to say nothing & leave him alone. When I was put on to hunt the hounds he was furious & said he ought to have been consulted, & that he should not allow the hounds to draw his coverts, but nothing came of it. This may also end in smoke. Should he do anything against hunting, I am sure, considering that he has no just cause, he would be very severely tackled by the Duke of Beaufort, his friend Lord Lonsdale[*] and others.

Before the next meeting Lord C. had also sent a letter to Colonel Dixon:

> Since seeing the Committee on Saturday I have carefully thought over my case before writing you this letter.
>
> In view of Lord Tollemache's action in 1877, I consider that I have a perfect right to say who shall draw my coverts.
>
> But seeing that it may make a great deal of ill feeling between landowners which is the last thing I want to do, I now write to say that I wish my own grievances on this Hunting question placed on one side, and will withdraw my words saying that Mr Corbet should not draw my coverts next season. And therefore I now place my coverts at the disposal of the Cheshire Hunt, should they wish them hunted in the same manner that they have been during the last six years.
>
> I take this course having a very strong feeling that in these days, if landowners do not pull together, it may be a bad thing not only for Fox-hunting but also for the county.

And he concluded with a further apology for the trouble he had caused. Meanwhile Henry Tollemache had got up a petition from the farmers for Corbet to continue and presented it at the meeting, at which a motion was carried by 13 votes to 7, with only owners of 500 acres and over voting 'for the present arrangement to continue so far as the South Pack is concerned'.

Lord Linlithgow, who as Lord Hopetoun, had long

enjoyed hunting in Cheshire, expressed the meeting's appreciation of Lord Cholmondeley's action in placing his coverts at their disposal and 'the kindly and sportsmanlike feeling which he has shown in the matter'. It was Lord Crewe who proposed the Mastership of the North be offered to his Lordship with a re-arrangement of the boundaries to suit him, more or less as the Duke had previously suggested. There was then an exchange of telegrams and this was the reply from Mayfair to Wilbraham at the Crewe Arms:

THANKS BUT PREFER NOT TO TAKE THE HOUNDS CHOLMONDELEY

A letter, written from the Turf Club, followed thanking them for the compliment. It had never really been his intention to take the hounds, 'although I did once say to you that if the country were made into one and you were stranded . . . I would see what I could have done.' But what now irked him was the petition and he asked for a copy.

> I consider it a most uncalled for and unsportsmanlike action to take. I do not know where they got all the names from, but I can tell you that my gardener was one who was asked to sign it. That being the case probably half the signatures were not those of farmers.
>
> I think it is one of the worst things that could have been done in the interest of Fox-hunting. And if I had known that this canvassing was going on, I should not have written to Dixon as I did at the last meeting.

It transpired that of the 326 signatures on the main petition many were those of small occupiers, who, as Henry Tollemache confessed, might more properly be described as cottagers. But he was adamant there was nothing 'bogus' about it.

So once again the Committee found themselves facing a difficulty and the next meeting was arranged for February 18th. Would a Grosvenor come to the rescue? 'If it would really help you in the difficulty of finding a Master for the Cheshire Hounds,' Bend Or wrote to Wilbraham from Grosvenor House on February 11th, 'I am prepared to come forward as such...' And he stipulated that it would be six days a week from the Forest Kennels with the country united. 'Of course all

---

* It was Lord Lonsdale who eventually took advantage of the situation when he became Master of the Cottesmore in 1907, by spending 1,800 gns. at Rugby on 15½ couple of the Corbet-owned bitches and 4 couple of whelps, including 250 gns. for Hecuba and Warcry, and 230 gns. for Virtue and Truelove. A compliment was paid to Regie Corbet when he was asked to judge at Peterborough in 1910.

A Meet at Willington Hall, 1905.

A Meet in Tarporley High Street.

this may not fit in with the views of subscribers & others, but if you are really in difficulties . . . I am ready to take over . . .'

At the meeting the previous resolution for the South Pack to continue was rescinded by 12 votes to 5 and the landowners of 500 acres or more carried another by 14 votes to 6 to hunt the whole country as one. The Duke's offer was then accepted unanimously and Major Wilbraham had the unpleasant task of advising R.Corbet accordingly. There was a fourth resolution conveying the regrets of the Cheshire Landowners and Subscribers for the severance of the long connection with his family and recording their 'high appreciation of the long and valued services . . . in the interests of sport.'

But it was never going to be as simple as that. All the farmers in the South were then up in arms about the shabby way young Mr Corbet had been treated, having had his Mastership rescinded. The whole sorry matter was to be fully aired in the Press. Mr Henry Tollemache, who had recently retired from Parliament and no longer hunted, addressed a large gathering of farmers at Audlem Public Hall, which ended 'with ringing cheers for Mr Corbet, mingled with hunting cries and the sounding of a horn' in support of their resolution that it was in the best interests of the farmers for hunting to continue under his Mastership.

A fortnight later a similar discussion took place at the Nantwich Farmers' Club, who wanted the continuance of the good relations they had built up. There was anxiety that less horses would be kept in the area and less money spent with the farming community.

On March 2nd a small deputation of farmers from the South called upon the Duke of Westminster, who had the Hunt Secretary in attendance. After expressing their disapproval of the cavalier way Mr Corbet had been dismissed, the Duke treated them with great civility, but explained to them he had been put into the position he was in by the Subscribers and it was entirely up to the

Subscribers to alter it if they wished in the light of the subsequent reaction. Later he wrote to Wilbraham:

> . . . My only reason was a belief that by taking the hounds I might assist the Committee out of a difficult situation. If in their opinion my offer will not assist them, my only reason for making it disappears, & with it my offer. But, if they still think it will assist them my offer stands – it is for the Committee & no one else to decide whether my offer will, or will not, assist the only purpose for which I made it.

On March 10th covert owners and landowners of South Cheshire were invited to Dorfold to discuss the matter. There was a strong feeling that something should be done. A deputation subsequently met the Hunt Committee, who to their intense indignation refused to call an official meeting of the Subscribers.

In April Henry Tollemache took it upon himself to arrange a meeting of subscribers at the Crewe Arms Hotel to consider the situation, before which Hugh Wilbraham, issued a disclaimer that it was of a private character and nothing to do with the Cheshire Hunt. For all that, quite a few influential members attended, including the Chairman, Linlithgow, Baron Schröder, Colonel Bulkeley, and Messrs Glegg, Littledale, Behrens and inevitably Walter Starkey and A.N.Hornby who had both done so much for the South pack. (In a red ink entry in the journal, the former referred to the 'great "Roo" in the county' and did not hunt at all the next season.) The Press were invited. It was a prolonged affair and ended with threats to deny the Hunt their right to draw many of the coverts. Tollemache had typed letters prepared and a few were signed and sent in to the Hon.Sec., even one from the absentee Lord Kilmorey, who could not have fully understood the circumstances.

The Secretary sent a summary of the situation to all the landowners and sought their individual views. Seventeen were in favour of the *status quo*, seven wanted to go to arbitration with the M.F.H.Committee, three

were doubtful, two neutral and Sam Sandbach, who owned Handley Gorse, did not know.

The Chairman of Wilson's Brewery had never skimped anything while he was Master of Cheshire and calculated that he had spent a good £10,000 a year over his guarantee. He even had his hunt servants' livery tailored by Sandon of Savile Row. But it could not go on indefinitely.

At the end of Hubert Wilson's final season as Master a huge field turned out at Whatcroft Hall for their last day with him and as a tribute to their respect of all he had done. One particular attribute of Hubert Wilson was his kindness in giving his whippers-in a chance to hunt hounds and the high commendations he gave them when they sought promotion. Besides Frank Freeman (Pytchley), there were Will Tongue (Oakley and Braes of Derwent), Frank Bishop (Hurworth and Lord Eglinton's), George Walters (Tynedale and Duke of Beaufort's) and Ted Tyrell (Tynedale), besides Walter Wilson, who went to the Quorn from 1918 to 1929. Another Cheshire whipper-in, Jack Molyneux (1908-11), used to write under the *nom de plume* Why Not. Charlie Johnson, who was 2nd and then 1st Whipper-in during the 1930s, went on for a long career as a huntsman to the Bicester and Warden Hill. In more recent times Teanby (Fitzwilliam), Jim Webster (Belvoir), David Anker (Sinnington), Ron Stouph (Cheshire Forest) and, only this season, Paul Bellamy (Oakley) are among those who have gone on from Sandiway to carry the horn with distinction elsewhere. The Cheshire may be called the 'Funker's Paradise' by its detractors, but it has certainly been the nursery of some good huntsmen.

'Sabretache'(the pseudonym of A.S. Barrow) wrote in *Shires and Provinces* (1926):

It requires a good horseman to go well in this country, and I myself consider it a far more difficult country to ride over than any in Leicestershire.

There was yet another heavily attended meeting of the Nantwich Farmers' Club with Mr Tollemache supported by Mr James Tomkinson. Henry Tollemache even stated at one stage that the Duke had once threatened that if the one pack plan was not adopted, he would warn hounds off his property and start a pack of his own. The affair became very tedious and repetitive and dragged on into June. The Hunt Committee stood their ground. Mr Corbet gracefully handed over the hounds on May 1st, Lord Cholmondeley got his solicitors to issue a disclaimer, and the Duke behaved with great dignity. He wrote an open letter to Henry Tollemache in connection with the proceedings of the meeting at Nantwich and quoted a speaker there:

. . . "Foxes will run as well for one Master as for another"; therefore, for the sake of sport, I would now ask that this distressful controversy may end, and that the present arrangements for carrying on the Hunt may be accorded by all concerned that goodwill and fair-play, which are so essential for the welfare of sport and the continued success of fox-hunting in our county.

There was little wonder Henry Tollemache resigned from the Tarporley Hunt Club. However, all was forgiven in 1925 when, as a former Secretary of the Club, he was elected an Honorary Member and he received a great welcome when he dined at The Swan the next year at the age of eighty.

F. Champion (Huntsman, 1903–1911) on Tally Ho, from a coloured engraving after Alfred G. Haigh.

XVIII

Hunting in Style - Peace and War

BORN IN THE COTTESMORE COUNTRY in 1882, Joe Wright, the son of a blacksmith, spent his school-days playing truant to follow the Shire packs on foot and learning to ride at eleven. He rode from six o'clock in the morning to six o'clock in the evening through the summer holidays and then got a job with a horse dealer for six seasons. His next job was riding second horse for Lady Angela Forbes at Manton in Rutland and became well-accustomed to hunting six days a week.

By the time he was appointed 2nd Horseman to the 1st Whipper-in at the Cheshire Kennels in 1907, before being promoted to 3rd Whipper-in the next season, he had gained ample experience working for the Duke of Sutherland at Trentham, Colonel Gordon Colman of the Surrey Union and back at the Cottesmore under Arthur Thatcher. He was with the Duke of Westminster all the time he was Master. Towards the end of his life he recorded his memories under the title *Some Hunting Days* and this is what he said of the Duke and his first stay at Sandiway:

He was absolutely the finest gentleman that ever walked. I mean it was a great pleasure for anybody to ever serve such a gentleman as him. We hunted six days a week, occasionally two packs a day twice a week. Several years we started hunting the last week in July or the first week in August.

Of course there were no vans in those days. We used to hack to Cholmondeley five mornings in succession, sixteen mile away and be there by five o'clock and leaving kennels at Sandiway at half past two in the morning. On the sixth morning we would go to Astle Hall which was another sixteen miles away and all done by road. One year, 1908, I remember hounds killing 164 brace of foxes and the following year we killed 146 brace, but . . . there were 110 killed in the cub-hunting.

We hunted up to April, as many as three horses a day in the wet weather, we had sixty horses at the kennels and thirty men to do them – no one was allowed to do any more

than two horses – a Stud groom[Lawrence] and a foreman, and up at the kennels there was the huntsman, the first, second and third whippers-in, first, second and third kennelmen and the Huntsman's second horseman – all kept at the kennels. There was another man kept, with two Stallions, Rydal Head and Johnny Morgan, for the use of the farmers; another man, who fetched the knackers in, had two more horses and there was a man to keep the place tidy. [There was also a terrier man.]

The Duke used to join us at the meets and he kept his horses at Eaton Hall. He wouldn't allow you to ride a bad one, wouldn't allow that. They were the most marvellous horses for anybody to put their leg over. I did four years with him and then in 1911 he took me to France, you see, hunting wild boar.

For Joe's experiences with the Duke's Boar-hounds, *see* Appendix J.

The Duke, who was born at Saighton Grange, had his first day with hounds as a small boy at Carden. He lost his hat early on and his pony scampered across the Cheshire countryside with him, his flaxen curls shining in the autumnal sunshine. As Lord Belgrave, he was at Eton, before joining the Royal Horse Guards and going off to South Africa. Soon after his marriage, he and the Duchess hunted for a time in Leicestershire, but they preferred Cheshire. For one thing they hardly ever dined out there, most of the men being too tired after their hard day.

At the age of twenty-eight and with a son and heir, he was now ready, like his grandfather before him, to take on the Mastership of the Cheshire, uniting it as one. It was natural for him to do it in style. However he was at Court during Tarporley Week and so Captain Wilson deputized for him at the Blue Cap and the other meets. The former Master also advised the Duke on the breeding of hounds throughout his mastership.

On November 9th Bend Or's uncle, Lord Chesham,

Captain Wilson at Ox Heys, 1907.

was killed out hunting with the Pytchley, which necessitated a further absence.

For Friday, November 29th he arranged a meet at Eaton.[*] The golden gates were opened and hounds met in the quadrangle, beside G.F.Watts's huge bronze statue of Hugh Lupus. The Eccleston schoolchildren, at the Duchess's invitation, were all ranged beneath the clock tower. The ill-fated Earl Grosvenor, Hugh aged three, was there with his elder sister, Lady Ursula, sitting in an open break. The meet was in honour of the young King of Spain, Alfonso XIII, and there were fully six hundred in the mounted field. (They were counted through a gateway.) He himself, wearing 'full hunting costume',[†] was on the Duke's chestnut, Skylark and 'laughed his happy way in the company of the Duchess as hounds came flying like phantoms to Champion's horn', as Cuthbert Bradley put it.

A fox was found by the Iron Bridge and ran a ring round the drives and then with several on foot, hounds pushed one across the Aldford road towards the Beechin. It was a good stout one and it gave His Catholic Majesty the experience of a lifetime as it led the field for Newbolt before swinging back and over the brook past Aldersey Hall. Scent was strong and hounds raced past

Bolesworth and Broxton Old Hall before marking to ground at Duckington, making a 6-mile point after a good 60 mins.

A Handley Gorse fox crossed the railway into Bolesworth Park, but the promise of another good run ended in a stick heap at Tattenhall. The rest of the day was spent with a fox from Hatton Spinney. A fresh fox jumped up when they got to Hatton Heath and was killed, with the original pilot crossing the main railway line before being lost by the canal at Waverton.

In the King's suite was the Duque de Alba, the Marqués de Villalobar, the Marqués de Torrecilla and Lord Herschell, acting as his Lord-in-Waiting.

The Chester Chronicle account read:

> The King of Spain rode close to hounds throughout the day being accompanied by the Duchess of Westminster. H.M. proved himself a splendid horseman and his skill was admired even by the keenest followers of the hounds. He had three horses at his disposal, and took his own line and freely mixed with the field. He talked with several and one

---

[*] From 1943 to 1946 Waterhouse's grand gothic edifice housed H.M.S. BRITANNIA, the Royal Naval College, evacuated from Dartmouth, after which the War Department took the place over as the Eaton Hall Officer Cadet School, except for the large private wing, where the Duke remained in residence, when in Cheshire, up to the time of his death in 1953. Until the polo ground was used, the Passing-Out Parade was at one time in the quadrangle with the officer cadets lined up in front of the gates and the huge mounted statue of the 1st Earl of Chester between them and the spectators sitting in front of the hall and to either side. On one occasion, some officer cadets stole out during the night, bored two holes in the giant horse and in the lower one was inserted a cork, attached to a longish piece of string. They then filled the horse with water.

Next morning as he marched on parade one of them succeeded in tugging out the cork and the horse staled throughout the entire parade.

[†] With King Edward VII he had been Joint Patron, since the previous year, of the Royal Calpe Hounds, Gibraltar's Garrison Fox-hounds, founded in 1812 and which hunted in Spain and whose Members wore a blue velvet collar on their red coat. (See *Hounds are Home* by the author.)

gentleman remarked that His Majesty "spoke English like a native."

At one stage a man crossed him at a fence and nearly put him down. His ejaculation in Spanish was more vulgar than polite and to his dismay the man pulled up and humbly apologised in fluent Spanish. He had just come from the Argentine.

Cuthbert Bradley celebrated the King's visit with a painting, putting Hubert Wilson and the Duchess in the foreground and the Duke giving Alfonso a lead. Champion is shown, too, and prominent is Colonel W.

Opposite, bottom left; *The King of Spain at Eaton: hounds move off.*

Opposite, bottom right: *The King of Spain,* right, *moves off with the Duchess of Westminster,* centre *and Captain Wilson.*

Left: *The Field leaves through the Golden Gates.*

Above: *King Alfonso XIII after a run with the Cheshire.*

Fred Champion   The Duke of Westminster, M.F.H.   H.M. The King of Spain on "Skylark"   Colonel W. Hall Walker, M.P.
     Mr. Hubert M. Wilson, ex-M.F.H.   The Duchess of Westminster
THE CHESHIRE BY EATON HALL

1. *His Majesty and the Countess Grosvenor (on left) at the meet.*
2. *The King inspecting the pack.*
3. *Mr. Herbert Wilson, the deputy-Master.*
4. *Lady Ursula Grosvenor, the Duke's daughter.*
5. *The starting place for the shooting, showing the Duke's private railway train just arrived with party.*
6. *Hounds arriving through the Eaton gates.*
7. *Hounds reaching Eaton Hall, where his Majesty inspected them, and afterwards left with the party to shoot the Chester beat.*
8. *The Royal party outside Eaton Hall.*

HIS MAJESTY'S VISIT TO THE DUKE AND DUCHESS OF WESTMINSTER.—A MEET OF THE CHESHIRE F.H. AT EATON HALL, &c.

A page from the Sporting & Dramatic News, December 25th, 1909.

Hall Walker. The Earl of Shaftesbury, Bend Or's brother-in-law, suffered a broken collar bone when he was thrown heavily from his horse near Broxton. He was picked up in a wagonette, containing Lady Grosvenor, Lady Desborough, and the Countess of Mar and Kellie, as well as his wife.

The King was back in time for tea, shot with the Duke next day and returned to London on Sunday after attending Mass in Chester. The Duke had his own polo ground at Eaton and the King of Spain and the elegant and dashing Jimmy Alba were among his closest polo-playing friends. The latter was hardly ever absent from the Eaton Polo Weeks, but in the course of time paid rather too much attention to his hostess, Shelagh, for Benny's liking.

There were very few moderate days during the Duke's first season, during which hounds hunted 71 times, killing $120\frac{1}{2}$ brace and running to ground $52\frac{1}{2}$, with twelve days stopped by frost and fog. Hounds were out six days a week with Ted Tyrell relieving Champion by carrying

The Duke of Westminster

the horn in the South. It was said to be the best season's sport for a great number of years. Tyrell was to become a popular huntsman of the Tynedale for sixteen seasons.

Two years later, on December 16th, the King of England honoured the Master of the Cheshire Hounds with his presence at a meet at Eaton, when staying with him for some shooting. There had been a big shoot the previous day, with the party being conveyed to the coverts by the private railway and with lunch in a special marquee, lined in Royal blue and white drapery. There was a bag of 1,450 pheasants and ironically two of the guns were Jimmy Alba and George Keppel. The latter's wife, Alice, the King's mistress, was also in the party. After inspecting the hounds the King went shooting again when they had moved off, returned to the Hall for lunch and resumed sport afterwards until dusk. Meanwhile there was a good hunt from Eaton to the Beechin and back and then, out of the Snipe Bog, hounds ran 'nicely to Carden and lost'. They came back to draw Handley and killed at Aldersey. Bend Or had handed over command to Hubert Wilson in time to return to lunch with the King.

No Hunt could have wished for a more munificent Master than the Duke in every way, but after four seasons

he felt his commitments, both social and otherwise, prevented him from running it how he wanted. In January, 1911 he sent in his resignation, at the same time offering to hunt a portion of the country for two days, should the Subscribers so wish. Accepting his resignation, the Committee hoped he would continue for one more season, in view of the difficulty of arranging a new mastership at such short notice. At the same time everyone was keen for the country not to be split up again.

Lord Shrewsbury went off immediately to discuss the situation with Bend Or and returned promptly to announce that he was unable to reconsider his decision. The Committee then advertised for a Master.

They did not have to wait long. In February the Hon.Sec. reported that no replies had been received, but that Mr Court and Captain Higson were willing to hunt the country 6 days a week as joint masters at a subscription of £5,200 and their offer was readily accepted. Both had been hunting in Cheshire since they were children, the former from the age of eight, the latter from seven. Both were polo players and Higson had played for his regiment, the IV Hussars, for seven seasons. He retired from the Army in 1893, when he succeeded his father to Oakmere Hall. Court played with the London clubs, Ranelagh, Roehampton and Hurlingham, as well as Rugby. His father had been a popular and most successful rider at Tarporley Races and the chief instigator of the Club's Stallion scheme.

Needless to say it had not been quite so straightforward. Champion, who had poor health, had a bad fall at Wrenbury the previous season, breaking three ribs, and the sport had deteriorated, although there were big fields out. A lot of subscribers wanted the huntsman to go, but it had been realized that the Duke would resign if he was asked to change his servants. Hubert Wilson had suggested to Wilbraham that Champion be quietly persuaded to resign of his own accord. It was as well the Duke pre-empted the situation. Evidently both Cholmondeley and Sir Joseph Laycock had been at him to get rid of Champion and it seems the reason for

Captain Hubert Wilson, Master of the North Cheshire, 1901-07.

W. Roylance Court, Esq., M.F.H.

Captain Wm. Higson, M.F.H.

his resignation was as much his loyalty to his huntsman as anything. He nevertheless assured his continued support. The Duke took Champion to France with him when Joe Wright returned to England in 1913. Champion died in a London hospital in 1917.

It was highly appropriate that the Duke won a race at the Point-to-Point on his estate at Waverton his last season. With regard to the 'horrible crowds' out, the Wynnstay was experiencing similar problems and Sir Watkin Williams-Wynn sent a circular letter to all concerned stating that those not resident in his country were no longer welcome.

Court and Higson engaged Edwin Short from the Puckeridge and they remained in office until 1915. Short hunted hounds four days a week and Walter Wilson, the 1st Whipper-in, who had been with the Bicester, the other two. In 1911/12 Sir Gilbert Greenall, the President of the Tarporley Hunt Club, was out all week with Lady Greenall and his Lady Patroness, Miss Corbet, and things went well under the new regime with

large crowds. But the Masters were aggravated by the increasing number of car followers.

The 1912/13 Season was very wet. There were 48 days cub-hunting and 116 regular and plenty of good sport was shown. The Duchess of Teck was badly cut when she was struck in the face by a bough of a tree.

Some good sport was shown and one particular travelling fox was picked up at Squire Starkey's Gorse from a Marbury meet on March 1st, 1912. Hounds ran him for 50 glorious minutes over some of the best Cheshire country, covering 7 miles. He took them to the hills by Peckforton Gap; there the pack got on to a fresh fox and ran him to Bolesworth.

The hills were alive with foxes the following December when hounds met at Peckforton Gap. The pack split into three, one fox making for Little Rawhead Farm where it turned aside in front of its pursuers and picked up a hen. Such incidents are sceptically received, but there were plenty who witnessed this one, including Lord Arthur Grosvenor.

The Club's 150th anniversary fell in 1912, but it was not until the next year that the President, Lord Crewe, suggested a Club Ball to commemorate it.

It was a magnificent affair and took place at Oulton on January 13th, 1914.* Four hundred people attended with many guests from outside the county. The grand hall with its lofty dome and Corinthian pilasters was converted into a ballroom, with banks of pointsettias and ferns in every alcove and crevice. Its black and white marble floor was covered with parquetry. Monsieur Frederick Casano's orchestra played through the night and later supper was served in the dining room with twelve tables bedecked with scarlet carnations. Sir Philip thoughtfully provided a smoke-room and his study was used as a bridge room. In the corner was a big black bear with a rare Indian necklace encircling its neck and an uplifted paw serving as an electric light holder. Outside, in a large marquee food and refreshments were provided for the chauffeurs, coachmen and estate workers.

It was the last big celebration to be held in the great house, for twelve years later it was to be gutted by fire with such terrible loss of life. Sir Philip, who was in Paris, rushed home. At the time the house was let to a Manchester steel manufacturer called Frank Cooper. However, all the Tarporley plate was kept there in the strong room. It was fortunately found to be unscathed, together with the Club records.

The President also held a Summer Ball in 1914 at Crewe Hall.

When war was declared, it was decided to continue as best they could and the policy was to have the country well 'cubbed', killing as many foxes as possible. This was also the M.F.H.A.'s suggestion, which met with Government approval, 'the intention being to prevent a large body of men being thrown out of employment, and also to keep the organization of the various hunts intact'. In fact the main reason for killing foxes was to alleviate the Poultry question and the Duke of Beaufort, President of the M.F.H.A., was worried that not every hunt would continue, thus jeopardising all the others. The Board of Agriculture had received many complaints about poultry losses, and they regarded the loss of food as significant. The matter had been raised in Parliament and there was a very live threat that legislation would be brought in for the compulsory destruction of Foxes. That must surely stand as further proof that fox-hunting conserves the species.

As time went on, the Government decreed that the number of hounds in Great Britain should be reduced

Little Lord Grosvenor, known to the family as Hugh, attends a meet at Saighton just before his tragic death, in February, 1909, following an operation for acute appendicitis. He is with his grandmother, Lady Sibell Wyndham, the former Countess Grosvenor.

from 7,000 to 3,000 couple and that no oatmeal should be used, the hounds to be fed on damaged rice and maize instead.

Over 10,000 hunting men and 15,000 horses were called to the colours. In Cheshire, subscribers on military service were to retain their membership on payment of half subscription, though this did not apply if their families continued to hunt in their absence. Colonel Hall Walker advanced £1,000 to enable the Hunt to carry on. Hounds were out four days a week. Not surprisingly the Mastership was offered to him when the Joint Masters resigned. The Tarporley Hunt Club then donated £300 to the hunt.

There were no dinners or meetings during the war, except for a Business Meeting at the Crewe Arms in November, 1915, when seven new Members were elected, including the new Manager, Colonel W. Hall Walker, proposed by Sir Philip and seconded by Lord Cholmondeley. There being no President, the Meeting was chaired by Sir Edward Cotton-Jodrell, though others of the fifteen present were senior to him, including Enniskillen. Colonel Walker had recently been in France, visiting his

Col. Cotton-Jodrell

---

* The invitations and Dance Cards were ordered from Harrods.

THREE WATER-COLOURS BY CECIL ALDIN (1870-1935) FROM HIS SERIES TWELVE HUNTING COUNTRIES.

Away for Tattenhall.

regiment. Fourteen of those present dined at The Swan that evening, charged to Club funds at £1 a head.

This was the year that Mr W.H.Cooke had given the Club Calvert's water-colour version of his large canvas of the Cheshire Hunt, 1839. Other matters discussed included the postponement of the idea to change the button to one with the crest on. As well as the donation

to the Hunt, they gave £100 to the Cheshire Branch of the British Red Cross Society.

Considering it was war-time, the 1915/16 Season was highly successful. With the good fortune to have a wealthy man as Master, Short and his staff were well-mounted and they killed 130 brace in 150 days. There were still 20 couple of dog hounds and 60 couple of

Away from Bath Wood. l. to r. *E.Short (huntsman), Col. O. Mosley Leigh, Mr Roylance Court and Mr A.N.Hornby.*

Away from Peckforton Wood.

bitches in kennel, but it was all credit to the huntsman that he kept 15 to 18 couple in the field six days a week on a war-time diet. The Master found forty horses in Leicestershire at an average cost of 200 gns. These, supplemented by some of his thoroughbreds, and turned out as well as war rations would permit, enabled the staff to do the job well. Most were stabled at Sandy Brow. Nor was the breeding of hounds neglected; *Cheshire* Sergeant '14 had the distinction of siring two Peterborough winners. And none other than septuagenarian the Rev. Cecil Legard, one of the all-time best judges of a fox-hound, came to Hall Walker's first Puppy Show.

Unfortunately the Colonel missed one of the best runs of the season at the end of January from The Three Greyhounds. Owing to an accident he was confined to his bed at Sandy Brow. Found at Drakelow at 3 p.m., the fox headed for Marshall's Gorse but bearing right, crossed the Holmes Chapel road near the Duke of Portland public house and ran straight through Holford Moss. He then crossed the Plumley-Peover road and, leaving Plumley Station on the left, he made for Toft and by Bexton Hall to the Cheshire Lines Railway two fields from Knutsford. There had been but one slight check in a ploughed field by the Duke of Portland. Short now cast his hounds, recovered the line and continued along the railwayside into Knutsford, killing the quarry close to the station. Only four were with them, including the Master's brother-in-law and predecessor, Mr Roylance Court.

During his mastership Col. Walker had often to be absent on parliamentary and military duties. On such occasions Court and Lord Cholmondeley were the principal field masters, and sometimes Higson or Poole.

Hounds were out on 145 days. Hunting was stopped 11 days. They killed 83½ brace cub-hunting and 51½ in 103 regular days. Despite the war, the organization was just the same and even the Earthstoppers' pay-outs were held as usual, one at the Blue Cap on May 2nd and the other the next morning at the Star Inn, Acton. In later years the Abbey Arms was a popular venue for this function when clay pigeon shooting would be part of the entertainment. After this first season, hunting was reduced to four days a week. The tally of foxes was especially creditable as no other Hunt killed more, though all were above average.

Members of the Armed Forces on leave were always welcomed. One such was Siegfried Sassoon, who managed to snatch a few days with the Cheshire when stationed near Liverpool. After a day in 1917, his diary reads:

. . . I was readily given leave off Saturday morning duties, since an officer who wanted to go out hunting was rightly regarded as an upholder of pre-war regimental traditions.... On such Saturdays I would get up in the dark with joyful alacrity . . . I was escaping from everything associated with the uniform I wore and eyed my brown Maxwell boots affectionately. . . . My consolations included a heavy fall over timber which I ought to have more sense than to tackle, since my hireling was a moderate though willing performer. Anyhow the contrast between Litherland Camp and the

Colonel W. Hall Walker on Buttercup with Cheshire Sergeant '14.

Cheshire Saturday country was like the difference between War and Peace – especially when – at the end of a good day – I jogged a few miles homeward with the hounds, conversing with the cheery huntsman in my best pre-war style.

Another important justification for the continuance of hunting was put forward to the M.F.H.A. in 1917 by the Cheshire Manager. It was for the betterment of Light Horse Breeding, as hunting was a great inducement to farmers to breed horses. The point he was making was that without hunting a farmer would only get £40 to £50, whereas a good hunter could fetch £150 to £200.

It was a pet theme of Colonel Hall Walker and, as the Member for Widnes, he had already addressed the House of Commons on the subject more than once.* Indeed the same year he took on the Cheshire Hounds he had made the generous offer to give all his bloodstock at his Tully Stud to the Government, thus founding the National Stud with the Nation buying the property at Tully and Russley Park in Wiltshire at their own valuation. His original idea was to keep up, directly and indirectly, the standard of horses required for the army. At first the Board of Agriculture demurred, but on the eve of the entire stud of 6 stallions, 43 brood mares, 10 two-year-olds and 19 yearlings coming under the hammer at Tattersalls, the Government changed its mind and

accepted the gift, which also included many fine paintings by Seymour, Sartorius, Wootton and Stubbs, which had been at Tully. Some of these were ultimately presented to the Jockey Club. In 1918 Colonel Hall Walker – he became Lord Wavertree (of Delamere) in October, 1919 – bought the Horsley Hall estate at Gresford. In January he informed Major Wilbraham that he was unlikely to continue, owing to the uncertain prolongation of the War, and he confirmed his resignation in March:

> . . . In the Kennels you will find as fine a working pack of fresh young hounds as we have ever seen, although reduced in numbers by government compulsion and we are happy to possess four young stallion hounds of exceptional merit. . . . I have not the exact number of foxes killed and moved in these three seasons, but the total is over a thousand.
>
> Taking up my residence in a neighbouring county, necessitates my retirement as your Master, but I shall always look back with pleasure to my association with the Cheshire Hunt in that capacity, while hoping to continue as one of its supporters for many years to come.

Horsley was a capacious mansion and Lord Wavertree created exquisite gardens there. The Wynnstay Hunt Ball was held there on several occasions during his lifetime.

Lord Wavertee was given a silver statuette of himself on The Yeoman with the stallion hound *Cheshire Sergeant '14* at his side. It was a curious coincidence that the day Major Charlie Tomkinson, the Chairman, made the presentation at a children's Fancy Dress ball in the theatre at Horsley in 1923, was the sixtieth anniversary of the day the recipient was blooded with the Cheshire Hounds as a boy of six at Darnhall Hall, where his father was temporarily residing.

Short also left in 1918 to go to the Bramham Moor and received a silver salver and £300 in War Certificates from the Hunt followers. Peter Farrelly came from the Bramham Moor to take his place with Joe Wright back in Cheshire as 1st Whipper-in. Prior to his eight seasons at the Bramham Moor, Farrelly had succeeded Frank Freeman at the Bedale.

A decision had been

B.D. Poole.

---

* Another matter he brought up in Parliament as long ago as 1901 was the prevalence of young boys smoking. He suggested to the Chancellor of the Exchequer to impose a tax on cigarette tobacco.

Col. William Hall Walker, M.P. on Buttercup, from an oil painting by Lynwood Palmer, 1910. The green collar was added on his election to the Tarporley Hunt Club. The huge canvas, now at Croxteth Park, was loaned by the Walker Art Gallery for the Bicentenary Ball and hung in the supper room at Arley.

taken in March for the management of the hounds the ensuing 1918/19 Season to be in the hands of a committee, consisting of Bryan Poole, Hugh Wilbraham and William Higson. Their average age was 57. Finances were not good and the immediate post-war policy of the M.F.H. Association was for any increase in hunting to be done slowly and quietly.

The next season, although there was a worry about finance, things got back to normal. Wire had become prevalent again and Major Cyril Dewhurst, the new Hunt Secretary, appealed for its removal and it was also necessary for him to warn against riding over seeds, jumping in and out of roads when hounds were running slowly and there was a gate handy, and not to gallop through cattle. There had earlier been a request for motorists not to follow hounds. An important innovation

was the acquisition of a motorized hound van, the gift of the Duke of Westminster. Jimmy Tinsley, who had been whipping-in to Short for several seasons as an amateur, was then appointed Master; and in 1920 the Point-to-Point was resumed at Saighton, preceded by the Farmers' Lunch.

There were three Tinsley brothers, James, Frank and Hugh (commonly called Jack), and the Cheshire Hunt owed much to them in that era for what they did by way of organizing the Hunt affairs. Frank was Secretary of the Point-to-Point for some years and lived with his brother at Bunbury Heath. Jack lived at the Kennels and ran everything there, including the Earthstopping and the Puppy Show; he used to follow hounds on a bicycle, wearing a grey bowler. He often ran miles with the terriers and was fresh as a daisy at the end of the day.

(There was a fourth brother who farmed in Hereford-shire.) In the off season Jimmy spent much of his time badger digging and more often than not was accompanied by his close friend, Mrs Clara Littledale, the wife of Bo.(241).* Whenever he wanted her, he would go outside his door and blow his hunting horn, which could be heard at Bunbury House the other side of the village, if the wind was blowing in the right direction.

During his three seasons James Tinsley had a wonderful record of good runs. He had accepted the responsibility at a difficult time and successfully made the transition from war to peacetime conditions, especially studying the interests of the covert owners, improving the earthstopping and looking after the farmers. When James Tinsley retired as Master, he was given an illuminated address framed in gilt and signed by fifty farmers. In his old age Jimmy was a familiar figure riding his old cob through the village of Bunbury, invariably wearing a tattered covert coat and a grey bowler hat. Later on – he was 92 when he died and had only just given up driving his ancient motor car – he sometimes got lost and it became necessary for his housekeeper to accompany him on a bicycle.

* * *

JOE WRIGHT WAS PROMOTED TO HUNTSMAN and who better than he to describe what hunting was like in Cheshire after the Great War?

After spending but two years in France with the Duke's boar-hounds, he pined for England, but had great difficulty in getting away and in the end he had to get Sir Joseph Laycock and others to persuade Bend Or to release him. He worked for the former for a time before going to whip-in for the American Master of the Cottesmore and then Lord Lonsdale. Having whipped-in to Farrelly for a season, he was to remain as Huntsman for a further nineteen seasons, three with Mr Tinsley and sixteen with Mr Walter Midwood, who succeeded him. The following is a transcript from the taped interview a

Joe Wright,
Huntsman of the
Cheshire Hounds,
1920-1936.

few years before Joe died and the incidents he recalled are not necessarily in chronological order:

After the First War the fields were nowhere near as big as in the Duke's time. Still they were pretty big and we had some hard riding people out with us. You remember Albert Hornby, I dare say, and Colonel Tomkinson and Lady Ursula Filmer-Sankey and Fred Hassall and the Moseleys. They were all pretty hard riding people. The fields were pretty big up till I finished and then the last war came. The cream of Cheshire were killed in the first Great War, Sir Philip Grey-Egerton's two sons and many others. And when the Second War came, a lot more got killed. But now I don't know half the people out.

I had the pleasure of breaking the hounds in when I first

Jimmy – He goes
like the devil, not
just in the queue.

---

*Their son, Lieut.-Col. Ronnie Littledale, would have been elected a green collar after the Second World War, had he not been killed when his jeep was blown up by a landmine in Normandy in September, 1944. He had insisted on taking his battalion of the 60th out there after his return from Colditz, from which he was one of the few ever to have escaped successfully two years earlier. He went out through the kitchen with Major Pat Reid and two others. Of the Brtitish contingent there were only eleven successful escapees in all.

Before he was taken to Colditz, Littledale had been in Poland, looked after by the Polish underground after escaping from the reprisal fort at Posen. He was eventually passed on to Bulgaria and had five months of freedom before being handed back to the Germans.

came, although I was only a Whipper-in. Going after a hare is so natural to hounds that we spent so much time with them, perhaps three or four times a week and we would go amongst the hares and if a hare jumped up, the hounds were told not to go after it. For a start it is no use shouting and balling and crashing about the woods. You get very excited, but ever after, for sixteen years after, I had them broken as I wanted, you see, and you could stake your life that they would never hunt a hare.

But you have got to devote the whole of the summer to breaking in hounds. It's no use going out on a bicycle for a month or two and thinking that you can do it in five minutes. It takes a long, long time. You have got to be well in with all the farmers and get out early in the morning and just wander about amongst the hares. And as soon as they do attempt to go after 'em, you speak to them and they soon get used to it. And when you start cub-hunting you start to hunt, not to keep on checking them and cracking the whip and shouting at them. You never allow the hounds to be hit after you have started hunting, not even the first morning. You might get a young one to look at a hare but he wouldn't go, especially if you said "Now then! Now then!" and just mentioned his name.

Once Peter Farrelly called my attention and said: "Joe, that is what I call a steady pack of hounds." There were three young ones that just lifted their heads up and looked at the hares and then down again and was hunting the fox. They was like that the whole time.

I remember once going from Crow's Nest to Waverton and over the canal. As we crossed over between Waverton and Waverton covert, the Duke's keeper came on the canal bridge and started shouting: "You're hunting a hare and my boy's going to stop them." Well, we went on

Pat Moseley

Lady Ursula

and had to stop them; we crossed the canal and then came back again over it and I says: "Come on, we are the wrong side to hesitate." So we got on the towpath and we went to the Egg Bridge and crossed, and then got them on the line and away they went. We never had the sign of a hare and eventually we killed a fox. It was practically ten minutes before anyone came up. They was the other side of the canal, you understand, they'd got so far to go. We just got round in time to get the line off and they absolutely flew. Mr Tinsley said: "We've never seen anything. We have just been tracking all the way." And I said: "You heard how it started – that was the Duke's keeper. I hope you will say something to him." And he said: "You leave that to me."

So the first time he saw him he said: "We never killed that 'hare'." And the Keeper says: "I am very sorry." "Sorry? You ought to be ashamed of yourself!" Mr Tinsley says, "It's not a pack of harriers or a pack of beagles. It's a pack of fox-hounds. We don't hunt hares. What would you do, if you were to ask Joe to come out shooting one day and he told you how to do your work, though he didn't understand it. You don't understand his work." "I am sorry," he says, "never as long as I live do I interfere again." "I shouldn't think so," said Mr Tinsley. "These hounds hunt foxes, not hares." And we did – you can stake your life on that.

The three seasons with Mr Tinsley as Master were probably the best I had in Cheshire, because he was such a fine field master. He gave me every chance. We had some marvellous sport every day we went out.

We couldn't go wrong. You see, I have been a terrible man all my life for feeling things – for instinct. I couldn't explain to anybody how this came about. I would go on as long as six weeks and never make a mistake.

I remember the Cheshire country when there was no wire at all in the Duke of Westminster's time. Fifty-two years ago there was no such thing as wire. You got some grand hunts in those days – nothing to stop you. We always had a good pack of hounds with a real big drive, one of the best driving packs in England.

Once we found a brushless fox close to the Castle grounds at Cholmondeley and His Lordship said: "Stick to him, Joe. He's a stranger." He went across the park and across the

Malpas road and outside Bickley Moss to Wrenbury. Definitely that fox was a stranger, because he went right round Wrenbury, all round the Chorley country, Bath Wood, Ridley – never touched a covert –and we brought him back and killed him within ten yards of where we found him at Cholmondeley. And we examined this fox and he never had had a brush in his life. There wasn't even a scar there. Prince Henry was out – the Duke of Gloucester, as he is now. And I said: "I am sorry I couldn't bring you the brush, your Royal 'ighness, as he hasn't got one. Would you like the mask?" And he said he'd would love it. So he has the mask.[*]

Walter Morgan [Huntsman to Sir W. W. Wynn since 1907] told the Master, sometime after, that he had hunted this particular fox two years previous. He was definitely a stranger to Cheshire, because he never touched a covert after leaving Cholmondeley and he went over the loveliest country in the World. It was a forty-five minute run. And I remember Lord Cholmondeley[†] was on one side of me and Prince Henry on the other. He used to ride very well to hounds in those days. The last road we jumped in, the Whitchurch road, he slipped off and I caught his horse. And while he got on, Lord Roden said: "That's the stuff, Joe. That's the stuff to give 'em."

We once had an extraordinary hunt from Wrenbury to Willett Hill to ground, seven-mile point, forty-five minutes, and we had a good hunt from Radmore Green to Ashbrook Towers, sixteen-mile point, the longest I ever knew in this country. Once in France we had a forty-kilometre point, as I told you.

One National day, we had a hunt from Hall o'Coole to the hills and that's a 10-mile point. We killed our fox at the foot of the hills. And we had one from Bache House to Duckington Woods in Sir Watkin's country, 10-mile point. Bache House was where a fox went up into a tree and poor old Fortitude went up into the tree after him and made a grab at him. She got hold of his brush and there the fox hung and all the hounds waited underneath. She stuck on for nearly ten minutes before she loosed him and it dropped right in amongst the hounds. Poor old Fortitude, she was the finest bitch we ever had. I hunted her for five seasons.

There is a place in this country I used to hunt near Mere Moss. Nowadays, ever since I finished, they probably send as many as five people along. I sent one only and that was Jack Hewitt [1st Whipper-in, 1921-29]. He had a particular place that he used to stand. He was only one field from the Chester road. It is extraordinary fine country over this road and when a fox went away, he would watch them sit in the fence till there'd be a break in the traffic and then they'd run over. And then he holloaed. And then I have gone over, and we have had a good hunt. But he never holloaed until after the fox was gone over and if he holloaed before, and this fox had bumped into a bit of traffic, the fox would have come back and there's nobody living who would ever have got him

'With the Green Collars', the Cheshire near Beeston. 1914, by Lionel Edwards, presented to the Club in 1928 by Mrs Robert Barbour.

A check with the Cheshire near Wrenbury. Hounds pick up the line across the canal, from a water-colour by F. A. Stewart. Members depicted include Mrs Wilbraham, Mrs Poole, Col. Mosley Leigh, Mr Starkey and Joe Wright, huntsman.

away again. They say that I was the only one that ever did get 'em away. I have no doubt I did, because we had this particular method, you see, me and Jack Hewitt. As Lord Lonsdale says: "There's always too many people go on. One will see as much as six."

The best day I ever had in my life in any country was the day we had a 9-mile point to Overton Scar. And we came back to Sooty Wood and we found the fox and we hunted this fox for an hour and thirty minutes and got him stone cold. He went into the bush and the hounds wasn't six yards behind him when he went in. And another fox went away the other side and the Whipper-in on the other side of the field holloaed it away. I says: "You are wrong." "He is very wet and dirty," he says. I says: "Yes, there will be a lot of foxes wet and dirty, but this one isn't ours. Ours was stone cold, when he went in there." Mr Tinsley said: "I am finished, my horse is done." And the Whipper-in said: "My horse is done." So I said to the Whipper-in: "You've got me in a good mess, haven't you?" Our fox never come out of that bush, but the hounds kept on, going and going on and I fell through eight fences. Then I see Lady Ursula coming up with her fresh horse and she said: "Joe, get on my horse." I said: "No, m' Lady, I'm not going to spoil your pleasure. You go on." "No, you get on!" And she made me get on and for three quarters of an hour I never saw another living soul

that was hunting. They had all ridden their horses to a standstill. The first one I saw was Fred Robinson [his 2nd Whipper-in] on the Whitchurch road with a horse called The Boy. And he was leading this horse down the road and I says: "Fred, do you think you can stop them?" "I'll have a try," he says, and then he got on his horse and he tried fourteen times to stop the hounds. And finally he stopped them all but a bitch called Fortune and she wouldn't be stopped and she went on to Handley. I picked up my tired horse at Saighton and came home. I could hardly get a walk out of him. It was very late when we got home, ten o'clock at night, but that was the best hunt I ever remember in Cheshire. We was going for three solid hours without a single check.

Once, when we had the foot and mouth,[‡] we went from Saighton Cross over the Whitchurch road to Broxton Police Station. It was an area affected with foot and mouth and all the policemen came out on their motor bicycles and motor cars running up one road and down another, telling us to stop hounds. "I am trying my hardest to stop them," I said and a few years afterwards I was in Chester and I saw one of these policemen. "Hey," he said, "you are just the man I want to see. You remember me chasing you on the motor bike, when you crossed over into the foot and mouth area? Was you really trying to stop them?" I said: "I was not! I never reckoned to stop them. The biggest job is getting them to go!" "Well," he said, "I thought as much!"

We had a wonderful dog hound called Dexter in Mr Tinsley's time. He was a *Heythrop* hound by Darter. He was an extraordinary hound. Walter Wilson [Quorn huntsman] said that we would get as fine day hunting with Dexter and Darter as any other hounds. And when he went to the Quorn, he said: "I'm having some of these hounds." And he once had thirty couple in the kennel by these two particular dogs. And we had a dog of Dexter's, walked with Mr Pitton of Darnhall, a most marvellous dog. I once showed him to Mr. Tinsley and said: "Now you will see these hounds swinging back this way, directly." We was coming on the railway. "And when the fox has gone up this

---

* Whether or not he ever had the mask mounted is not known, but there is no trace of it at Barnwell Manor. Whilst on his visit to Cheshire, Prince Henry went over to Sandy Brow and rode a school under the tuition of the author's father, 'Jock' Fergusson.

† This same Season Lord 'Rock' had a bad fall out hunting in the Mosses at Cholmondeley. His horse struck a tree root and his Lordship was badly concussed and suffered a broken thigh when his mount rolled on him. About a fortnight later he got a clot of blood on the lungs and died from heart failure.

‡ Both the Cheshire and Sir Watkin's countries were badly affected by foot and mouth in the 1923/24 Season. They got through the cub-hunting but the Cheshire only had one regular day's hunting.

Jimmy Tinsley, M.F.H.

side of the fence, you will see the first dog that touches the line, it will be Demon. Take particular notice of him. He is the best driving dog you shall see as long as you live." And this dog came through the fence there and touched the line and he says: "I have never seen one like that." I says: "No, and neither will you, he is one of the best dogs that ever lived."

One day Mr. Tinsley said: "Where can we find a fox?" I says: "We can try Wettenhall. It's a big wild place and the bigger the place the wilder the fox. You don't want to go. Stop this side." And he kept the field together and Demon found this fox and this farmer, Mr Pitton, stood there with five or six more and he says to them: "You'll hear Joe shout out: 'Good old Demon!' because he is the hound that will find him." And Demon did and I shouted: "Good old Demon!" and away we went and Mr Midwood was helping the field and we went closeby and they took him to Beeston Station and it wasn't far. It didn't last long, only a matter of eleven minutes, but they absolutely flew, when they had sight of him. There was a train that just pulled in to the station from Chester, and the fox jumped up at the carriage window, which was closed, and he dropped back on the platform and the hounds had him.

Many, many a time we would take those bitches out and have four hunts a day and kill each fox. I remember a man coming out from the Pytchley and he said: "Well, Huntsman, I'm from the Pytchley." And I says: "I thought you was, by your white colour." "Yes," he says, "we have got a pack of bitches we boasted about." This was in Frank

Freeman's time. He said: "But you've got the best pack of bitches in England, though, the best pack of bitches in the World. If I hadn't seen them, I wouldn't have believed it. The funny part about it is, you have had four real good hunts and killed each fox and never touched them." I said: "We don't as a rule, Sir. We only specialize in one thing in Cheshire and that's getting away on his back and leaving it to them." "Yes," he said. "I've never seen hounds come out of a covert like that in my life. They come out of the covert like peas out of a pod!"

But those bitches were absolutely marvellous... the two packs of bitches that I hunted for sixteen years averaged a hundred brace a year, not counting what the dog hounds did. We had a wonderful fine pack of dog hounds that old Jack Hewitt hunted. Wonderful fellow, Jack was, you know, one of the finest fellows that ever walked. He could hunt hounds beautifully. He would come home and say: "Well, Master, we've hunted a brace of foxes and we have killed them both" or "We've found two brace and we have run a brace to ground and we have killed a brace." And he has gone as long as six or seven weeks and accounted for every fox that he has hunted and I consider that something, don't you?

Lord Arthur Grosvenor once said: "We didn't get much scent in this country." But we used to get some sport whether we had scent or whether we didn't, because we have got a very fine pack of hounds and we used to get a very good start, you understand. And there might be only enough scent for two or three couple, but we have had some good hunts in spite of that. They went out to hunt and to hunt alone, and they never was checked in any way, because you knew they weren't going to hunt any hares.

They was broken from deer also in those days and we had two parks, you see, with deer, Cholmondeley and Oulton. And once, when we was hunting at Cholmondeley, Jack Hewitt holloaed a fox away for Wrenbury and he said: "Master, since I holloaed that fox away there, there are eight deer gone and they have gone on exactly the same line." "Never mind, Jack," I said, "Just watch 'em." And we went on for eight fields on exactly the same line. "Watch that deer," I said, and they turned right-handed. "Now," I said, " you will see something you have never seen in your life before. You will see those hounds won't turn when the deer turns. And they didn't. They went straight on. They took this fox all the way round the Wrenbury and Chorley country and we killed him at Bath Wood. Extraordinary good hunting.

But now there is no deer to break them on in Cheshire. They was all destroyed and the fact there is very few rabbits now, makes no difference to the hunting or to the foxes. Around these farms you generally get some offal, a few dead lambs, calves and such like, which are chucked out and foxes collect them up and eat them. Foxes is in very good condition, there is no doubt about that. They get plenty of food and I don't think there is quite so many of them in Cheshire, mark you, as there was at one time.

A meet at Marbury, from a sketch by F.A.Stewart.

I remember once Mr. Tinsley started cub-hunting very early in Delamere Forest and we spent three weeks at it for a start. It was a bit sickening for hounds and for everybody else. It was a bit too much, but I've seen some good old 'uns at Delamere Forest. One never left the Forest till he went to die and he went out to a village called Kelsall and they killed him there. He had a big black patch on his near side and I remember him very well.

They also used to take hounds to Combermere and stay a week. Joe Wright was a great one for staying out late and had some of his best hunts as dusk was falling, especially when he had the bitches out. He found they had more stamina.

Mr Tinsley used to say many a time: "We'll go home!" and I used to say: "I hope you're not going home yet, Sir." And he would say: "I've never seen anybody like you, Joe. You are never satisfied. If you think we can have a hunt, we will but it will soon be dark." I says: "Well, we can go home then, Sir. We can't hunt in the dark, but we can go home in the dark."

XIX

Quæsitiana Quartus

THE THREE OLDEST BARONIES OF ENGLAND, still extant, are de Ros (AD1264), Mowbray (1285) and Segrave (1295). Summoned to parliament at Shrewsbury as barons by writ in 1299, among others, were John de Clinton, Robert de Clifford and Sir Henry de Grey, of Codnor. In 1496 the barony of Grey of Codnor went into abeyance on the death of the 7th Baron, whose three sons were illegitimate, although he had been twice married. Both his wives were widows, the first being a Duchess of Norfolk.

In 1926 the Select Committee of the House of Lords decided that, once their recommendation became law, no claim would be considered, for any peerage which had been dormant or in abeyance for more than one hundred years. **Charles Cornwall-Legh (286)** was advised by the College of Arms that he had an interest in three, the Norman baronies of Bassett of Sapcote in Leicestershire, which dated from 1371, and Mortimer of Richard's Castle in Shropshire, also from 1299, as well as Grey of Codnor (pronounced 'Cudner'). Having decided to go for 'Grey', sixty-three years later and after the lawyers and heralds had received innumerable 'refreshers', his son **Legh (296)** took his rightful seat in the House of Lords.

The Select Committee of Privileges had been duly satisfied that the family had proved their descent, document by document, birth and marriage certificates included, all the way from the 7th Baron's Aunt Lucy, one of the 4th Baron's three daughters, each of whom had had an equal share to the abeyant title. Twelve coheirs were found and after all reasonable steps had been taken to trace the others, the Committee of the House of Lords considered any possible counter-claim could be discounted. The claim to the three baronies had come to the Legh family through the marriage in 1731 of George Legh to the heiress of Francis Cornwall,

sixteenth and last feudal Baron of Burford (not a peerage title).

The 4th Baron Grey of Codnor, a former Admiral of the Fleet, incidentally, had been 107th on the roll of the Knights of the Garter, taking the place of Sir Henry Percy (better known as Harry Hotspur), Earl of Northumberland. His father had been in the Crécy expedition and joined Edward III at the Siege of Calais, but it was a kinsman, Lord Grey of Rotherfield, who was a founder Knight of the Order in 1348.

However, on investigation at the Herald's College, it became clear that it is necessary to prove that an ancestor was not only summoned by writ, but also sat in a particular parliament and took the oath, for the barony to have been established. In the case of the 4th, 5th, 6th and 7th Lord Greys this was possible, but prior to 1397 it seems it is impossible to prove that a peer sat in Parliament and in any case there was good authority for stating the Parliament of 1333, for one, was not a peerage Parliament. This means that the 4th Lord Grey of Codnor is now considered to be the first baron and Legh is shown in the reference books as the 5th.

* * *

A LADY once asked **Toby Daresbury (300)** what he did with his old hunting clothes. 'Quite simple,' he replied, 'I fold them up carefully, put them on the chair beside my bed and put them on again next morning.'

* * *

IT WAS REALLY A STOLEN PAT OF BUTTER at Malvern during the First World War that saved the life of **Sir Walter Bromley-Davenport (311)**. A bully used to reach across the dining table and pinch butter off a new-boy who had been sent it by his father. He did it once too often. The victim cracked him hard on the knuckles with a large spoon. 'I'll meet you in the gym tomorrow morning and bring your boxing things,' snarled the bully and young Walter Bromley-Davenport decided to go along to see fair play. To his amazement the bigger boy was pasted all over the gym and Walter lost no time in asking for a boxing lesson from the victorious new boy. In 1922 Walter became the Army Boxing Champion when serving with the Grenadier Guards.

A year or two before his retirement Sir Walter was chatting to the visitors in the gardens at Capesthorne when a man pushed his way in front of him. 'Are you Lord Bromley-Davenport? You should not have a title,' he said in a most menacing way before producing a knife with a nine-inch blade. He then stabbed him with a vicious uppercut to the stomach. As Sir Walter fell to the ground his would-be assasin was sat on by his brother and son who were fortunately at hand. The knife had stopped a mere one eighth of an inch short of a fatal puncture to the heart. And all thanks to an instinctive 'stop-punch' to his attacker's upper arm, a boxer's trick learnt all those years ago from the new boy at Malvern. It was said that his being mistaken for a peer of the realm helped his recovery.

Once during the War when he arrived in the black-out at Crewe Station, returning from leave, he and his fellow officers and men found the train completely packed and not a seat to be had. He resourcefully marched up and down calling in his stentorian tones: "All change to Platform Four." As everybody scurried across, he and a large contingent of his 5th Cheshire Battalion were able to entrain in comfort.

On one occasion, when Government Whip, he was on guard at a House of Commons exit to discourage Tory M.P.s from slipping away in case of another vote. A figure stole past him, totally ignoring his polite advice. An infuriated Walter gave the retreating figure a hefty kick, accompanied with some choice reminders about loyalty to the Party. Unfortunately the gentleman was the Belgian Ambassador and His Excellency's formal complaint to the Foreign Secretary brought to an end that phase of the over-zealous Walter's career.

His constituency enjoyed one of the largest majorities in the country, but Walter regarded every vote as his own personal property and was once very put out to discover some of his local Young Conservatives had gone off to canvas elsewhere. 'They should be helping me in my marginal seat,' he complained vociferously.

The Right Hon. David Howell was at Capesthorne during the 1964 Tory leadership crisis when several of the Party Grandees were guests of Sir Walter for the Blackpool Conference. He recalled to the author:

> Walter had more political influence than he himself pretended. Coming down to breakfast one morning I was electrified to hear them discussing who they thought would win. After a few minutes Walter said he thought the winner would be Scobie Breasley. It turned out they were discussing not the Tory leadership but the Jockeys' championship. All the same Walter told me later that day that he thought Alec Douglas-Home was the right man to lead us and he proved, of course, to be correct.

* * *

H UGH ROCKSAVAGE (312) was serving with the 1st Royal Dragoons when he won his Military Cross at El Alamein. As he wrote in his book *A Day's March Nearer Home*, his troop was 'brewing up' columns of transport and anything that came their way as they fanned out across the desert, no longer cooped up among the minefields. 'Operating behind the enemy lines just South of Fuka on November 3rd, 1942, the Earl of Rocksavage discovered an infantry position protecting the enemy line of supplies,' read his citation. With only two cars in his troop he captured six A/Tk guns, fifteen 20 mm Breda guns and machine guns, took many prisoners and destroyed much transport.

> . . . During this operation his troop was under a concentrated attack [from a dug-in position] by six C.R. 42's . . . but owing to his dash and complete disregard for personal safety he completed the destruction of all guns and vehicles before withdrawing to a new area. During this harassing operation... his initiative and behaviour in the face of the enemy have largely contributed to the success gained.

He was one of the most brilliant Armoured Car Troop Leaders to survive the North African War, with but two brief leaves in Cairo to recharge his own batteries. The Royals went triumphantly on to Sicily, Italy and finally from Caen to Nijmegen in July, 1944. He was then posted as the Collective Training Instructor of the H.A.C. Squadron (the armoured car squadron) of the 100th (Sandhurst) O.C.T.U., Royal Armoured Corps. There, the author was privileged to come under his charismatic spell and it is little wonder that we hung on his every word and his tales of 'swanning about' and going 'like bats out of hell' across the Desert.

The Royals had plenty of adventures with their horses in Palestine and Syria, before the sad day they gave them up to become a crack Armoured Car Regiment in the Western Desert. Military historians would do well to study Hugh's memoirs, privately printed in 1947. They

Hugh, 6th Marquess of Cholmondeley, Lord Great Chamberlain, from a portrait in oils by John Ward, RA.

are a most poignant day-to-day account of the life of a cavalry subaltern and evoke it all so accurately.

> . . . I shall always remember that first day, as we sat in the heat, everything quiet except for the hum of the wireless and the buzz of flies. Looking at the other cars, I could see their commanders sitting on the top, watching the flanks . . .
>
> . . . There is no doubt that if one has got to fight, the desert is the ideal place. It is really like a vast football ground, and the wire is the halfway line. We had Rommell up in our penalty area once or twice, but thanks to some nippy goal-work by Monty, he never scored.
>
> . . . Shaving was very painful in this weather, but we did it daily, usually inside the car out of the wind... During the hot weather one never got really dirty, as one wore very few clothes and the dust could be sponged off quite easily. But in the winter one kept one's clothes on for weeks on end and that meant the dirt was well rubbed into the skin. One just longed for a good soak in a hot bath.
>
> . . . The other car joined me and we started disarming them of their automatics and horrid little red grenades. There were about ten officers, including a colonel and two majors. There was also an awful-looking padre fellow with a dirty dog collar round his bare throat. He kept moaning away about the wounded and crying with righteous indignation until we told him to pipe down.
>
> . . . My gun was all right this time, and we got off five

good rounds that kicked up big dust fountains right among them. The other cars were firing everything they had and it was soon plain that we had stopped them good and proper... Two chaps held up a huge red flag with a *Swastika* on it. I suppose they thought we were Germans and had mistaken them.

The future Lord Great Chamberlain of England took his book title from Winston Churchill's speech on February 3rd, 1943 to the 8th Army in Tripoli: 'In the words of the old hymn, you have "nightly pitched your moving tents a day's march nearer home".'

* * *

AFTER THE BATTLE OF EL ALAMEIN General Alexander told **Major (temporary Lieutenant-Colonel) Gerald Hugh Grosvenor (316, army number 36661)** that he had awarded him an immediate D.S.O. This was the citation:

> On 28th October 1942 about 869295 near El Alamein, the 9th Lancers were facing West and North about Pt.30. A German tank attack developed against the infantry from the West in the neighbourhood of Pt.30. Lieut.-Col. Grosvenor by the quick handling of his regiment stopped this attack which threatened the Royal Sussex then holding a salient and inflicted heavy casualties on the German tanks. On the 3rd November 1942 by the expert handling of his regiment he managed to knock out practically all the A/T weapons on his front about 861297 which enabled the whole brigade to advance the following day. During the period 24th October to 4th November the 9th Lancers knocked out 71 German tanks, with very small loss to themselves.
>
> This feat was entirely due to the untiring energy of the C.O. who constantly visited individual tanks and encouraged his crews, who were constantly under very heavy shell fire.
>
> His example was an inspiration to the whole regiment.

On October 28th he himself, with his Adjutant, had ventured forward in his tank. Mindful of his responsibility of his Colonel's safety ('and possibly his own' as the regimental historian put it) the latter had just suggested they had gone far enough when the vehicle shuddered all over from a direct hit. Luckily they were able to beat a hasty retreat, as the 50mm shell had gone through a road wheel and lodged in the gearbox casing.

They were still under heavy fire the next week when the Divisonal Commander came up front. Pointing to an absolute inferno of shot and shell, he told him: 'There's the gap I want you go through.' 'I don't call that much of gap!' was the Colonel's brief reply, but through they went and after a terrific tank battle at Aqqarir, the Africa Corps broke and ran.

When it was over, on November 5th they all just flopped down to sleep and the first thing they saw when they opened their eyes was a German soldier standing over Colonel Gerald. Then a quavering voice said in English: 'I've been trying to surrender for the three hours.' A sleepy voice replied: 'Shut up and sit down.'

* * *

MAJOR **D.P.G.MOSELEY (318)** won the Liverpool Fox-hunters' Steeplechase in 1928. Appropriately one of the hymns at his funeral in 1986 was *Lord of the Dance*, for no Cheshire Hunt Ball had ever been complete without him performing his spectacular standing somersault to a roll of drums after an evening spent energetically on the dance floor. He was able to perform this feat when well over sixty.

* * *

ONE RARE AWARD gained under unusual circumstances by a subsequent Member of the Club, **Colonel Geoffrey Churton (328)**, was a Commander-in-Chief's Certificate of Commendation. At the time the Cheshire Yeomanry had just given up their horses and were waiting (in vain as it happened) to be mechanized in Syria. A telephone message was received one morning that the black Algerian soldiers of the 22^{ieme} Compagne Nord Africaine Frontier Force had just mutinied and their Free French officers had fled. Their C.O. had visited the Yeomanry the day before and made them aware that trouble was brewing. Geoffrey, as Regimental Intelligence Officer, was despatched to their camp on a motorcycle and sidecar, driven by another officer, both wearing boots and breeches.

On arrival he offered his services as mediator to the Colonel of the Free French Fusilier Marines, who had already been called in and had been under fire from the mutineers. There was a great deal of shouting in a foreign tongue and he boldly marched in where no French officer would have dared to tread. In a short while Lieutenant Churton sat down with the senior black N.C.O.s to try to resolve the matter, though none of them could understand a word he was saying, nor he them. It transpired very simply that they had no food and had received no pay for some time. Fortunately at that moment two aeroplanes flew overhead, and the gallant Englishman pointed out that they were under close scrutiny and were liable to be bombed. He gave them a promise and returned later with a truck-load of rations,

but no pay. By then they had calmed down. No more shots were fired and in due course the junior French officers returned and the Yeomanry R.I.O. got the credit for quelling the mutiny.

* * *

JUST BEFORE THE BATTLE OF ARNHEM in September 1944 the 4th/7th Dragoon Guards were leading the 50th Division in the wake of the Guards Armoured Division heading for Brussels. In the course of the 'Great Swan' **Captain P.G.Verdin (349)**, was commanding the Regiment's A Echelon, parked in a wood with the rest of the Brigade Echelons peacefully having 'a brew' and cooking breakfast, when suddenly they were set upon by a force of German paratroopers, intent to destroy a nearby bridge. This was the action, as he recounted it, in which Philip won his Military Cross. (He had lost his eye in a training accident in 1942.)

> I was standing by [the SSM's] truck when [a trooper] shouted: 'There's a Jerry!' and let fly with his rifle. Next moment a whistle blew and bullets flew from all directions. I saw one lorry go up in flames, and then another. There seemed no point in trying to fight a battle with ammunition and petrol lorries all round, so I shouted to the drivers to get their lorries out as best they could. The Germans were so close now that I fired my revolver at them. I found [the RSM] and we made for the gin palace but it wouldn't start and bullets were whistling all round, so it had to be abandoned to its fate, plus the RSM's kit. [He] and I then collected all the men we could find with their weapons, took up position in a ditch and fired back with Brens and rifles.'

* * *

LADY DARESBURY'S LAST BRUSH

THE AUTHOR IS INDEBTED TO **Philip Hunter**, Honorary Member under Rule XV since 1956 and Master for twenty-nine years of the Cheshire Forest Hounds (1947-76), for this personal memoir of Frances, Lady Daresbury, the widow of **Lord Daresbury (242)**. She died in December, 1953.

Philip recalled that she insisted her parrot was to come to him on her death. It used to greet her in the morning with: 'Good Morning, you silly old bitch! Whoo-op!!' and he was granted the same privilege when on her land, though he would only whisper the greeting.

> It was one day during her last illness, [P.G.H. recalled], that we found a fox in Owl's Nest, one of her best coverts and always a sure find, but unfortunately now within yards of a

Lady Daresbury.

motorway. We ran this fox locally and finally through Rose Wood, across the park at Walton Hall and killed it on the lawn right in front of her main windows.

I galloped round to the front of the house just as the butler came running out, saying: "For God's sake, sir, get your hounds away, her Ladyship is at her worst and sinking fast." I jumped off and abandoning my horse, I ran on to the lawn blowing for my Kennel Huntsman, Will Welbourne, and then for my two whippers-in as I ran.

All the while there was a terrific hullabaloo going on and, from what appeared to be from the skies behind me, I kept hearing a very strong and musical "Whoo-whoop", repeated continuously. I looked up and there was Lady Daresbury, leaning through a bedroom window whooping away at the top of her voice, whilst a young and hefty female nurse was clawing at her to get her back to bed, quite without avail.

Her last words were "Thank God and you Master, you've put new life into me – come in and have a drink!" She obviously was not going to consider inviting the field in as well, so I had to refuse and offered her the mask or the brush and she chose the brush. My horse came up to me at that moment across the beautifully mown lawn on its own, so I jogged off with bared head with three of my staff to draw again.

My Kennel Huntsman, who had been in hunt service all his life and knew every butler in the county, said: "I had better take the brush into her Ladyship, hadn't I, sir?" I said: "Right", and out of the corner of my eye saw Welbourne going off into the house with the butler. Some hours later he rejoined us, looking very happy, but a little sheepish. On my enquiring why he had been so long, he replied: "I couldn't get away, sir." This was partly true, as his horse with empty saddle had joined us two hours earlier.

Not long afterwards we had a special 9 o'clock meet at Belmont Hall, had a very good morning and in our hunting clothes, covered in mud, we went straight on to her funeral at St.John's, Walton. Those of the field who could not get into the crowded church, waited outside to pay their last respects.

Philip Hunter with the Cheshire Forest pack at The Cock, Great Budworth.

XX

Carry on Hunting

IT WAS IN 1923 THAT THE MASTERSHIP was taken over by Walter Midwood, who was then living at Calveley Hall. He remained in office fifteen seasons. But in 1931 it was decided to split the country once again with the North being taken off his hands by Major B.W.Heaton, who had come to live at White Hall, Little Budworth, where he kept the hounds during his mastership. It was not reunited until 1944 and from 1946 onwards the North country has been loaned by the Cheshire to the Cheshire Forest, of which Major Heaton had for a time been Master, Huntsman and Secretary.* It was a private pack owned by the Master, who had Will Welbourne as his K.H. & 1st Whipper-in. In 1931 Ben Heaton handed over the Forest hounds and what was then the Forest country to Peter Russell Allen, who also hunted hounds himself. In 1947 that great fox-hunter and well-loved personality, Philip Hunter, took on the Cheshire Forest pack and remained in charge for twenty-nine seasons. More often than not he hunted hounds himself. His sons, Peter and John, later joined him in the Mastership. Welbourne was with him from 1950 to 1957 as Kennel Huntsman.

Whilst Major Heaton had the North an incident rated a mention under 'Unusual Happenings' in *Baily's*

Hunting Directory. Lady Daresbury had arranged a special day at Walton Hall for her Pony Club:

> Among the most interested spectators were a leash of foxes up in a tree who were spotted just as hounds were moving off to draw. All that was necessary was a crack of the whip to make one of the trio decide to trust to his legs, which he did to such good purpose that he ran hounds out of scent after leading them and the youngsters a merry dance for the space of 45 mins.

Walter Midwood was a prosperous Liverpool cotton merchant and in his youth had been a leading amateur rider in the Far East and at one time champion jockey at Hong Kong and Shanghai. No doubt he used to enjoy the sport the Shanghai Hunt Club had to offer with a great variety of quarry. Besides the fox and an occasional deer or badger, they used to hunt otter and chase wild cat, hare and coon dog. When in Cheshire he was known as a successful point-to-point rider, at sixteen stone often giving away twenty-eight pounds to his rivals. At his weight he was a fine man to hounds. He kept some good steeple-

Walter Midwood, M.F.H.

chasers in training with Frank Hartigan at Weyhill in Hampshire and Shaun Goilin's Grand National victory as 2nd favourite at 100-8 in 1930 did much to endear him to the Cheshire farmers.

One brilliant run was in March, 1926 when hounds

---

* The hunt was formerly Captain W.H.Ockleston's. He lived at Mouldsworth where he kennelled his hounds at the Station Hotel. His country was six miles square, loaned by the Cheshire Hunt. This was what had formerly been hunted by Mr Pennefather for several seasons up to 1902. Ockleston could not blow his horn and used a reeded one. He ran the little hunt in a happy-go-lucky way until 1928, when his resignation was demanded by his Committee because he had been rude to a lady landowner.

In 1947 the Cheshire Forest also took over the country hunted by the Wirral Fox-hounds, formerly Harriers. Before 1868 it was hunted by Sir William Stanley's Hounds and from then until 1937 by the Wirral Harriers.

Mr Walter Midwood with his huntsman, Joe Wright.

made an 8-mile point from Highwayside, quite 10 miles of country in 40 mins. Robert Barbour (262) was one of but two to swim the flooded Weaver, only to get badly wired up on the other side. It was on the outskirts of Doddington Park that scent suddenly vanished with the dead-beaten fox only a field ahead of hounds in the North Staffordshire country.

Four years later hounds had a fox in front of them for 14 miles. Again they were stopped in the dark after a circuit incorporating Hurleston, Ridley, Peckforton and back to Haughton, Wardle and Radmore Green.

Mr Midwood spared no expense at the Kennels and kept as fine a pack as ever, with Colonel Hubert Wilson advising on the breeding. The horses were taken to the meets in a trailer, towed by a Rolls with a liveried chauffeur and another uniformed chauffeur drove the hound van, though by then the latter vehicle was known to have been overtaken by bicycles going uphill. He had as 'Master of the Horse' George Goswell, a famed steeplechase jockey, who had once gone through the card at Haydock Park and rode his share of winners at Tarporley. Joe Wright again:

We had to breed an enormous lot of puppies, nearly seventy or seventy-five couple of pups every year. There were only two months left for people to get their holidays, April and May. We were short-handed. We all had those pups to look

after and the young hounds to break-in long before Christmas. There were 125 couple in the kennels.

You would get your good seasons and bad seasons and we lost as many as 20 or 30 couple of pups in a season with distemper, pneumonia and that. But, you know, all the time I was at the kennels there were no inoculations.

Major Heaton said one day: "Joe, what is the most puppies you have ever sent to walk?" "Well," I said, "I just can't tell you for sure, but something like 70 couple." "Seventy couple? Never!" "Oh, yes, we did!", I said. "Well," he said, "I have had a job to get 15 out this time." I went home to have a look at the record and do you know, 70 couple was the smallest number of couple I ever sent out to walk the whole time I was Huntsman. The most I sent out was 85 couple. For several years I sent out 80 couple. I always said there was a cure for distemper. I'll tell you for why. Once we had about 24 or 26 couple of hounds in hospital. Some were isolated and ready to go back into the kennels, but there were about 6 couple with the worst distemper that anybody has ever seen in their lives.

I was feeding them with eggs and milk and I went to them one night at about 7 o'clock. I had an oil lamp and it got on fire. Then the hospital got on fire. I rushed over to the good ones and we got them out quick. Then I went over to where the bad ones were and as soon as I opened the door the flames and smoke met me, but I went in, got the hounds out and slung them across the asphalt yard. We'd got them all bagged up with cotton wool. The bags were all on fire. I ripped those bags off and thought: "Oh well, that's finished them." But I just saw one open its mouth, would you believe it? I said: "Carry them over there, dead or alive, and put them to bed with the others."

I never had any sleep that night, but do you know the next morning every hound was up? "For goodness sake," I said, "break some food up and we'll feed them. And every hound went in and fed and then we doctored them up. One was minus a ear, some had scars on their ribs and all sorts of places. We put them right and never lost one. Now it was the fumes that had killed that germ, isn't that funny?

Now you will hear people say that when an animal with young dies, the moment they die, the young are dead too. Now, I once had a very valuable bitch and I was up one night pretty late with her and I was frightened to death that something might happen. The next morning at 6 o'clock she was dead. She was not only dead, she was cold and stiff. How long she had been dead, I don't know, but I took her out and felt under her and took fourteen live puppies from her. I could have saved every one of them, but I went out straightaway with the hounds and was out all day and never told Mrs Wright to give them a drop of milk. We could not find any fosters, so we decided to give them milk and we saved one, Forger . . .

Joe liked the North country. This is what he said about it:

The North Cheshire is a lovely country. We have had some very fine hunts there. You remember me telling you about

In full cry from Bath Wood, from a water-colour by F. A. Stewart. l. to r. *W.H.Midwood, MFH, Major C.W.Tomkinson, Sir Thos. Royden, Mr Anthony Dewhurst, Mrs Phyllis Tomkinson and Joe Wright.*

having a hunt from Mere Moss, where Jack used to go on alone. Well, we hunted a fox all around there by Cobbler's and right round the Mere country back to Mere Moss. We made a second circle round, and eventually took him over the road again and killed him. We had an hour and forty-five minutes, one of the loveliest hunts you'd ever seen.

I remember another real good hunt when I'm afraid the biggest part of them got left. We went to Shacklers by the Racecourse Common and the Shooting Box and what you call the Rudheath, great big woods.

I remember being there once after the hunt ball, and Mr. Midwood says: "Let's get away from this place, skim it over." And I says: "Skim it over, Sir? By gum, this is where you'll find a good fox." He says: "Damn you and your big woods! You're all for big places." I says: "The bigger the place, the wilder the fox! And as we were going on, I said to Arthur Redfern [1st Whipper-in]: "We'll get a good hunt from here today, Arthur." . . . So when we got to the Shacklers covert, I said: "You come with me, Arthur. It won't matter if anybody sees this fox or whether they don't. We'll hunt him away." And we hunted him away and we had about an hour and ten minutes, but unfortunately I had asked the Master to keep in touch. And I said: "Keep touching the horn as I am going through. But he didn't and he got left and there was only twenty-one people left with us. I couldn't help it. They went over the loveliest bit of country you'd ever seen, not a strand of wire anywhere.

In 1929 Jack Hewitt left. He was Joe's great friend and 1st Whipper-in and had been replaced by Arthur Redfern. who was eventually to succeed him as Huntsman. During his first period at Sandiway he hunted the dog hounds in the North. That same season Joe Wright, Jnr. was taken on as 3rd Whipper-in. The Master had a bad fall that season and wanted to give up the hounds, but was persuaded to carry on. Jimmy Tinsley sometimes deputized for him.

On occasions the Master got in the habit of getting a lift in a car from covert to covert, rather like his younger son, Eric, whom *Tough Skin* also rather unkindly accused of being 'too tired to shiver when he's cold'. One day Walter dwelt a little too long enjoying the refreshments in the Rolls when they arrived at Handley, where Hamilton Carter had cantered on to go on point at the far end. He got there just in time to see a strong dog fox slipping away. He holloaed at once and Joe wasted no time getting his hounds on the line and away they went, the field and all except the Master, for a splendid run into the Wynnstay country. Back at Calveley, Joe was summoned to the presence and got 'a right ticking off'.

In 1931 when Major Heaton had been given the North to be hunted two days a week for £2,000, an offer had been made by Lord Daresbury and Sir Keith Nuttall to hunt the South Country. The latter had come to live at Overdale, Sandiway, while the Mersey Tunnel was being constructed by his family firm. However, Walter Midwood was prevailed upon to continue and it was his offer that was finally accepted. He was to receive £4,500 to hunt it four days. There was no animosity and Sir

The Cheshire Hounds at Bolesworth Castle.

Joe Wright.

Keith offered £1,000 towards the Season's expenses. This was the year of National Economy when the Tarporley Hunt Club gave up their dinners.

It was during Joe Wright's last season, 1935/36, that he had the misfortune to lose an ear. Drawing along the canal by Simpson's Rough at Tiverton he jumped an iron hurdle in a bit of bullfinch and his horse came down with him and severed it. Leslie Bragg, the local Veterinary Surgeon who was never far behind out hunting, was quick on the scene and took him off to Dr 'Bobs' Okell to stitch it on again, though in time it gradually withered.

Besides Lord Royden, still going well, and others already mentioned, no history of this time in Cheshire would be complete without

Joe Wright with Running Tom at Burleydam, 1936.

mention of Chris. Sparrow, who later lived at Higginsfield. If ever there was an enthusiastically mad rider to hounds, it was he, and he continued long into his old age after the Second World War. Of the ladies none was bolder or more graceful than Phyllis Tomkinson. Other female worthies were the formidable Clara Littledale, Pauline Boumphrey and Helen Greenwood and also Miss Foden of the motor works family. 'The kittens' who rated a mention in *Cheshire Cats and Cheshire Cheeses* included Molly Moseley, Marmie Spiegelberg, Molly Glegg, Rose and Angie Clegg, (two sisters married to two brothers), and Joan and Betty Adshead.

In 1936 the time had come for Walter Midwood to retire and a huge garden party was held at Calveley Hall attended by all the farmers and their wives, some 1,500 people in all. There had been an appeal by a committee, of which the leading lights were Mr John Barnett of Brindley and Miss Philippa Ethelstone of Whitchurch, one of the most dedicated hunt supporters of all time. After tea, on a showery summer afternoon, they gave the Master a large silver tray engraved with a map of the Cheshire country, as well as an illuminated album with all their names. Mrs Midwood received two silver-

Ben Heaton.

tried to bar his way through a gate. It emerged that he had just taken over the farm from his father. As Charlie Johnson recounted to the author:

> I saw a young lad place his bicycle in front of the 1st Whip (F. Pavitt) and then rush forward to get in front of the Huntsman and he fell over the bicycle just in front of me. He picked up his bicycle and threw it in the hedge and then ran forward to the gate.

Lord Daresbury.

mounted photograph frames and Joe Wright a handsome gold watch and chain and a cheque. There was a silver afternoon tea set and tray for Mrs Wright. Eulogy after eulogy was showered upon them – 'the most popular mastership of all time'.

A closing speech was made to thank the host and hostess and the farmer making it added that it had been a pleasure to go to the meets 'and Mr Midwood had always met them with a smile.' Happily he had overlooked an unfortunate incident which had occurred

There was then a scuffle as the farmer tried to prevent Joe Wright from opening the gate, striking him in the face with his fist and as he dragged the huntsman's whip from him, the butt end swung round and hit him on the head. Who struck the first blow was later disputed, but Joe Wright ended up on the ground, his face streaming with blood, the young man intent to do serious injury, 'striking wildly in all directions' and catching Pavitt one. Charlie Johnson was ordered by the Master to go to defend him. Further blows were exchanged, Charlie 'accidentally' striking the young man with his whip. 'You

Peter Russell Allen, M.F.H.

John Smith-Maxwell.

on a January day three seasons earlier. Hounds were being taken down the bridle path, which crosses the railway on the way from Waverton Gorse, to draw Hatton Spinney, a route the Hunt had been accustomed to take for many years, when the huntsman was confronted by the farmer's son in a white smock. He

From a cartoon by "Mac", Sporting & Dramatic News. l. to r. Top: *Maj. Alan Casey, M.F.H., Capt. John Smith-Maxwell, Maj. & Mrs Chas. Tomkinson, Gen. Sir Henry Jackson, James Tinsley, George Spiegelberg, Sir Delves Broughton, Bt., Lady Ursula Filmer-Sankey, Capt. H.V.Herman;* Middle: *The Hon. Mrs Alan Casey, Maj. Gilbert Cotton, G.B.Radcliffe, John Barnett, Capt. Richard Barbour, Mrs. Carter, Miss Eliza Barbour, Miss Noël Winterbottom, W.H.Midwood;* Bottom: *Maj. Jackie Ashton, Tony Dewhurst, Miss Betsann Dewhurst, Joe Wright, Arthur Redfern, Col. Hubert Wilson, D.P.G.Moseley, Mrs Melancy Chambers, Chips Chambers.*

Brian Grey-Egerton, who died in July, 1937, having been Hon. Secretary to the Tarporley Hunt Club since 1897.

have no right to assault my servants,' cried the Master and he and the field moved up towards the farm and through another gate.

It was not the end of the matter, for they all ended up in court at Broxton with the County Court Judge presiding and none other than David Maxwell Fyfe – he took silk the following year and later became the Lord High Chancellor and 1st and last Earl of Kilmuir – acting for the defend-

ants, Mr Midwood and his hunt servants. It was an hour before the case was called and many members of the Hunt Committee were in court, including Major Tomkinson, Sir John Dixon and Captain John Smith-Maxwell. Also there was Mrs Melancy Chambers, whose husband was the instructing solicitor. She was for many years as fearless a side-saddle rider as ever graced a Busvine* in Cheshire, and despite various afflictions hunting well into her late middle-age after the Second World War. Colonel Hubert Wilson was normally Chairman of the Bench and so could not preside. In the meantime it was an unlucky day for the lorry drivers and motorists, who received some fairly draconian sentences for their minor offences. The future Recorder of Birkenhead, Mr Elsden, acting for the Plaintiff, then announced to the Judge that they had been able to reach an amicable settlement and the summonses and cross summonses were all withdrawn.

After such an event, isolated though it was, it seems surprising that *The Chester Chronicle* reporter at the Calveley garden party was able to preface his account by writing, perhaps just a little sycophantically:

> Rarely has such a large gathering of farmers been seen in Cheshire, and rarely has the Hunt stood in such happy relation to the general life of the Cheshire countryside.

It must be added that when the individual farmer concerned was visited by the Master and Hunt Secretary over thirty years later to make amends, he at last gave permission for just the hounds and hunt staff to cross his land, though the wound was most certainly still there.

The new Master for the 1936/37 Season, with a guarantee of £3,500, was Major 'Tim' Casey, formerly of the Royals, who took up residence at Cassia Lodge, Whitegate. He had previously hunted Lord Harrington's Hounds. He engaged Tom Peaker, who had been with the Worcestershire, as his Kennel Huntsman. The Committee had chosen him in preference to Captain Maurice Kingscote, the recently resigned Master of the V.W.H. (Cricklade). This was much to the displeasure of Lord Cholmondeley, who was the latter's cousin. When Peaker hunted hounds he was far too slow, nor did the new Master suit the Cheshire field.

There was a notable hunt on January 2nd, 1937, after a meet at White Hall. Hounds divided hunting two foxes from Blakeden. Those with Peaker had a good run to the Church Minshull area, where Tom had a fall. The others, hunted by Charlie Johnson, now the 1st Whipper-in, ran for 3 hrs. to Aston's Gorse with only twelve of the field finishing, including the hosts, Ben and Mary Heaton, and Chubb Paterson, who just arrived as hounds were being blown away from Blakeden, having been working at the family tannery in Birkenhead early that morning. Also at the end were G.B.Radcliffe of Tarvin and his rough-rider, Freda Sutton, as well as Chubb's father, John.[†] Charlie Johnson came to the end of his fourth horse, having made two points, one of 6 miles and one of 5 in the deepest going ever remembered. Billy Filmer-Sankey then took over the horn. It was 18 miles as hounds ran. Captain Smith-Maxwell made it 22 in his report for *Horse and Hound* . As for 'G.B.', he would hunt six days a week and preach in the chapel on Sunday. He was virtually blind in his late eighties, long before he ceased to hunt.

Eighteen years later Smith-Maxwell returned for a day with the Cheshire Hounds as *The Field* correspondent and recalled the happiest hunting days of his life spent with them, when as the dedicated secretary of the Wire Fund, he 'had known every covert, keeper, earthstopper, every field, hunting latch, landowner, farmer-occupier and smallholder'. He concluded his article, just like Nimrod over a century earlier, with a comment on the country:

> From a riding point of view, parts of it could not be more difficult. It appears so small at first sight, but, in reality, it takes more getting over, day in and day out, than any county in England I know. There are those funny small fences, on the top of little banks, with those death trap poached ditches to every fence. I have seen the "cut-me-down-thrusters" from the Shires, before the war, set sail from Oulton heading for Calveley. Though beautifully mounted they met their Waterloo within three fields.

Casey's mastership only lasted two seasons and he resigned when the Committee, still under the Chairmanship of Major C.W. Tomkinson with Sir John Dixon as Honorary Secretary, decided against his request to bring back Walter Midwood as a Joint Master. Instead they appointed Richard Barbour (294) of Bolesworth and 'Bill' Clegg of Gatesheath Hall. With war pending, it was a brave undertaking. They took it in turns to be field master, the latter always elegant in a cutaway.

War broke out just before their second season and as in the

'Bill' Clegg, M.F.H.

Great War the policy of the Ministry of Agriculture and Fisheries was for hunting to continue on a reduced scale to minimize poultry losses and without recourse to giving County War Agricultural Executive Committees powers for compulsory fox destruction. This was again relayed to Hunts by the M.F.H.A., whose Committee wanted them all to discontinue normal hunting during

---

[*] Mr Busvine of Hanover Square had the reputation of being the best habit maker. His establishment closed a few years after the Second World War.

[†] The two horses he rode that day became his son's chargers in the Syrian campaign with the Cheshire Yeomanry and one of the ones Chubb rode also went to the Middle East with his brother-in-law, Maurice Mitchell. "B" Squadron, commanded by Major Richard Johnson Houghton with Captain Dick Verdin as his 2 i/c, had occasion, during a rapid advance to draw their swords against a Spahi patrol, who declined to meet their charge.

Captain Barbour and Mr J. N. Clegg with the Lady Patroness, Miss Susan Tatton, at the Opening Meet at Ox Heys.

the war emergency, to cut down their establishments and do nothing that would be an affront to public opinion and seriously affect the popularity of fox-hunting. The strict instruction, as the National Poultry Council had been informed, was for Masters of Fox-hounds to control the fox population and pay particular attention to any complaints of damage by foxes that may be reported to them.

The Cheshire Hunt owes a large debt of gratitude to Bill Clegg and especially his mother, Mrs Laura Clegg of Abbey Wood, Delamere, for their support during the difficult wartime days, but it was really Ben Heaton, when his Home Guard duties permitted, who saw the Cheshire Hounds through the war; and of course the faithful Arthur Redfern, ably assisted by G.B.Radcliffe as his amateur whipper-in. That great hunting couple Jimmy Tinsley and Clara Littledale, surrounded by terriers, were constantly out on bicycles and were never far away when needed. Richard Barbour gave up in 1940 and was away on active service with the Cheshire Yeomanry. Bill Clegg stayed on in the Mastership, jointly with Colonel Ben, and participated so far as his military duties allowed and would be out as Field Master whenever he could get leave. In his absence Rose would

Ben Heaton of White Hall, Little Budworth, Master of the Cheshire Forest Hounds, 1928–31 and the Cheshire Hounds, 1940-49, from a portrait in oils by Will C.Penn.

occasionally take charge. They hunted the country two days a week with a bitch pack of some 30 couple.

Only one dog hound was kept – Governor, which Redfern had brought with him from the Middleton, by Ikey Bell's *S. & W. Wilts.* Godfrey '28. In 1942 they had a long and strenuous hunt, again from White Hall, and had to hack back from somewhere near to Nantwich, arriving in the black-out after 10 p.m. They were all so exhausted that Governor was allowed to bed down with the bitches. His two litters which resulted were the best Colonel Ben ever remembered having.

Nearly five decades have passed since the war, throughout which, under various masterships, the Cheshire Hounds have continued to show good sport. In 1946 John Paterson joined Ben Heaton in control of the whole country before the North was loaned to Philip Hunter and his Cheshire Forest Hounds. For the post-war masterships see Appendix C. But mention must be made of the successful period that Richard Tomkinson was at the helm, owing partly to his horsemanship of which his forebears would have been proud, but mostly to his relationships with the Cheshire farmers. He was a brilliant field master and his 'politeness' in dealing with transgressors into clover root would have brought a blush even to the countenance of Captain White.

His retirement, mainly due to an unfortunate injury which curtailed his riding ability, really saw the end of an era. His was virtually the last Mastership of any duration to receive a guarantee from the Hunt Committee. After Pat Moseley's two seasons and Michael Higgin's one as Joint Masters with Mrs Naomi Rae, from then on, all expenses at the Kennels and all the ancillary costs, which normally came out of the Master or Masters' pockets were, with a few possible exceptions, paid entirely out of Hunt funds. Some with M.F.H. after their names were even known to have received expenses.

Richard Tomkinson had Dermot Kelly of the Meynell to advise him on hound breeding and it was from him that he acquired the services of an exceptional huntsman, who was to stay on for twenty-five years under no less than fifteen

Richard Tomkinson.

a fox in front of his hounds, the whole field thrilled by the melodies from his horn.

With their host, Lord Cholmondeley, riding to hounds for the first time since his election to the Tarporley Hunt Club, there was a great gathering of Cheshire sportsmen and sportswomen on foot, including Anne, Duchess of Westminster. The Senior Joint Master, Sir John Barlow, passed on a message of goodwill from the Prince of Wales, who has enjoyed many a day with Johnnie as his pilot. Virtually the entire country had been stopped and a good wedge of the Wynnstay country as well, ready for whatever magic this remarkable fox-hunter could conjure.

A fox, found in Coronation, was holloaed away from Nevill's Wood and made left-handed for Croxton Green, crossed the main road and, leaving Chesterton to the right, was pulled down just short of Bath Wood. A chorus of earsplitting holloas from all those hunt servants straightaway heralded another fox on foot and hounds

The Duke and the makers of the Vice-President's chair, Mark Boddington and Adrian Foote of Silver Lining Workshops. It is in walnut with inlays on the legs and a flying fox on each side rail. On the back is a Grosvenor and Cheshire wheatsheaf in laminated pear wood, in the centre of which is the Club's Swan Badge and garter in repoussé silver. It is also decorated in three places with a gilt Westminster portcullis. There is a small silver plaque, engraved with the Ducal coronet and monogram and the date of the gift. The manufacturers' hall-mark trademark is on the bottom rail.

mastership, after succeeding the loyal Leslie Moss. In addition a new draft of 'white' hounds was acquired, though the old Bluecap strain is still represented.

Regarding his Huntsman's prowess, here is a description of the Invitation Day given for Johnny O'Shea shortly before his retirement after a quarter of a century as Huntsman. It was published in *Horse and Hound* with photographs by Jim Meads.

JOHNNIE O'SHEA'S INVITATION DAY AT CHOLMONDELEY

No less than fourteen hunt servants, besides his own three Whippers-in, and an elegant field of one hundred and twenty turned out to support Johnnie O'Shea, when he brought the Cheshire Hounds to Cholmondeley Castle for his Invitation Day on 5th February, 1991. Even his wife, Ann O'Shea herself, was in the mounted field, the first time for thirty-two years. Visitors from all over the British Isles came to honour him before his forthcoming retirement after twenty-five seasons carrying the horn. Owing to the frost, the prospects of high quality sport were not as promising as one would have hoped for such an occasion. However, all those who took the risk were rewarded with a real connoisseur's day with Johnnie at his best, dancing on ahead across the Cheshire pastureland, almost the whole time with

THE GREEN COLLARS AT THE SWAN, November 1992.

hunted him to ground at Haughton. Drawing over Highash, hounds picked up an outlier, who led the way back across by Cook's Pit and over Chorley Brook to be killed close to the Beeston Lodge at Cholmondeley.

Here a brace was spotted up a tree. One was rolled over after three fields with the entire cavalcade close at heal. The intrepid Roy Morris, the Cheshire Beagles' Amateur Huntsman, had been close-up on foot all day. After changing horses, hounds found at Dowse Green and away they went again to Bath Wood before losing what little scent there was. While hounds were drawing Peckforton Wood, a fox was seen across the plough on the other side of the road. In fact it was the only plough the visitors had seen all day, a day on which Sir John had led his field over spectacular fly fences galore. But this fox was not persevered with and hounds were taken back to Cholmondeley to end what, as everybody agreed later over a glass or two of tea at Bulkeley Grange, was a memorable day.

The Cheshire subscribers were delighted to welcome O'Shea's successor, Stuart Coley, for whom the day doubtless proved to be a valuable experience and confidence booster before assuming Johnnie's mantle next season.

GAMECOCK

In recent seasons there has been more and more the tiresome presence of the hunt saboteurs. It is to be hoped that they will soon desist and realize that, but for fox-hunting the survival of the fox itself, if that be their principal object, would be in dire jeopardy. Perhaps the main threat to the national sport of the countryside of Great Britain will come from neither them nor our legislators, but from the Channel Tunnel and the invasion, despite all the assured precautions, of rabid European foxes.

Still distant the day, yet in ages to come,
When the gorse is uprooted, the fox–hound is dumb...

KEY: THE GREEN COLLARS AT THE SWAN, November 1992.

1. Major P.G.Verdin, MC, (President) 2. Capt. J.G. Fergusson, (Hon. Secretary) 3. *Viscount Leverhulme, KG, TD. 4. R.C.Roundell 5. H.D.Wilbraham 6. Sir Richard Baker Wilbraham, Bt. 7. R.D.C.Brooke 8. D.M.Stern 9. Hon. Michael Flower 10. R.C.Mosley Leigh 11. W.A.Bromley-Davenport 12. Hon. Richard Cornwall-Legh 13. S.P.Dewhurst, (Vice-President) 14. Major W.R.Paton-Smith 15. R.J.McAlpine 16. G.B.Barlow 17. S.Z. de Ferranti 18. M.E.S.Higgin, TD 19. *Col. G.V.Churton, MBE., MC, TD 20. Lord Tollemache 21. E.G.M.Leycester-Roxby 22. P.J.M.Boddington 23. Sir John Barlow, Bt., MFH 24. E.M.W.Griffith, CBE 25. P.J.P.Hunter, MFH 26. *Lord Grey of Codnor, CBE, AE (Hon. Member) 27. *A.D.Paterson, TD 28. R.J.Posnett 29. W.H.Midwood 30. Randle Brooks 31. A.W.A.Spiegelberg, TD 32. *Major P. Egerton-Warburton 33. R.A.Gilchrist.

Absent: *C. R. Tomkinson, *Sir Evelyn Delves Broughton, Bt., M.G.Moseley, DFC Duke of Westminster, Q.H.Crewe, Hon. Peter Greenall, MFH, A.G.Barbour and the Marquess of Cholmondeley.

* Those present in 1962.

Meanwhile the Tarporley Hunt Club continues to flourish, albeit as a dining club. The 225th Anniversary was commemorated by a limited edition green enamel box with the Club's badge in gold. The Lady Manager herself, Mrs Pauline Windsor, has so far found time to provide the catering. In 1990 the Duke of Westminster (347) commissioned a modern ceremonial chair for the Vice-President's use to complement Wilkinson's 18th century Great Chair, used by the President and Rogers' heavily carved mahogany chair, given in 1862 by the Duke's great grandfather.

As this book was being prepared for publication and less than three months before the Club was to hold its 244th Meeting at The Swan, the owners decided to sell it privately. But fortunately this was not before the Committee were able to negotiate a 999-year Lease for the use of the Hunt Room in Tarporley Week as well as encapsulating all the rights and privileges it has so long been able to enjoy. The Secretary and Ricky Roundell, as Trustees for Club, breathed a sigh of relief as, perhaps a shade ironically, the deed was signed by them and sealed with the Greenalls Group new hunting horn logo on the Twelfth of August.

Before the 1992 Business Meeting the Members were photographed for an article in *The Field* to commemorate the thirtieth anniversary of Cuneo's Bicentenary portrait.

The sport they began may we still carry on,
And we forty good fellows, who meet at The Swan,
To the green collar stick, tho' our breeches be gone.

Part Two

Appendices

Appendix A

MEMBERS OF THE TARPORLEY HUNT CLUB
(Founded 14th November 1762)

The rank, title and address of each Member are given as for their year of election.

▻— Sometime Manager of the Cheshire Fox-Hounds.   ◁— Honorary Secretary of the Club.
* A Member with a brother also a Member concurrently.   † A son elected during his father's Membership.

ORIGINAL		PRESIDENT	LADY PATRONESS
1.	Rev. Obadiah Lane of Longton, Staffs., later of Chester. b.1733; m.sis.14; Honorary Member, Oct.1779; d.1780.	Nov.1762	Miss Townsend (of Hem, Denbigh)
2. ◁—	John Crewe of Bolesworth Castle, s.of Rev. Dr. Joseph Crewe, D.D., Rector of Astbury. b.1740; Secretary, 1762–1786; H.S.1771; d.1786.	Nov.1764 & Feb.1784	Miss Anne Maria Barnston (of Chester) Miss Frances(Fanny) Brooke,2nd sis.41
3. ◁—	Hon. Booth Grey of Wincham Hall, Budworth Magna, 2nd s.of 4th Earl of Stamford. b.1740; Deputy Secretary, 1762; M.P.(Leicester 1768–74); m.eld.sis.44; r.c.1790; H.S.1796; d.1802.	Feb.1763 & Oct.1779	Miss Elizabeth Falkner Miss Johnson
4.	Sir Henry ('Harry') Mainwaring, 4th and last Bart., of Peover Hall. b.1726; H.S.1772; Maj., R.Chester Regt. of Militia; Grandmaster, Order of Merit, 1788; r.1793; d.unm.1797.	Feb.1765 & Feb.1780	Miss Ann Warburton, sis.35 Lady Henrietta Grey (Harriet), e.dau.25
5.	* George Wilbraham, eld.s.of Roger Wilbraham of Townsend House, Nantwich, living at The Grange, Weaverham before building Delamere Lodge. b.1741; H.S.1773; M.P.(Bodmin 1789–90); r.1802; d.1813.	Feb.1770	Miss Eleanor Holdford (of Davenham), m.29
6.	Rev. Edward Emily of West Clamdon, Surrey. b.1739; Honorary Member, Feb.1764; Vicar of Chesham, 1767; Rector of Wilden, Beds, 1779–81; Dean of Derry, 1781–83, Vicar of Gillingham and Motcombe, Dorset, 1783–92; Preb. of Salisbury, 1784–92; d.1792.	—	
7.	Richard Walthall of Wistaston Hall, Nantwich, 2nd s.of Peter Walthall. b.1733; d.unm.1766.	—	
8.	Robert Salusbury Cotton of Combermere Abbey, Dodcott cum Wilkesley eld.s.of Sir Lynch Salusbury Cotton, 4th Bart. Later for a time of Llewenny Hall, Denbigh and also of Berkeley Sq. b.1739; suc.as 5th Bart., 1775; M.P.(Cheshire 1780–96); F.R.S.; r.c.1794; d.1809.	Nov.1763	Miss Penelope Leche, au.139

9.	* Roger Wilbraham, 3rd s.of Roger Wilbraham, later of Swaffam, Norfolk and Stratton St., W.1 and also Twickenham. b.1743; r.*c*.1797; M.P.(Helston 1786–90 & Bodmin 1790–96); F.R.S., F.S.A.; d.unm.1829.	Jan.1776	Miss Elizabeth Croxton, sis.36

ELECTED BY BALLOT

10. 14thNov.1762	* Commander the Hon. Richard ('Dick') Barry, R.N.(Retd.), of Marbury Hall, Great Budworth, 2nd s.of Lieut.-Gen. the 4th Earl of Barrymore. b.c.1719; H.S.1762; M.P.(Wigan 1747–61); r.Feb.1780; *d.s.p.s.*1787.	Feb.1766	Miss As[s]h[e]ton (of Ashley) sis.27 [*prob.*] sis.27
11. 14th Nov.1762	* Hon. Arthur Barry of Fota Island, Co Cork, 3rd s.of 4th Earl of Barrymore. b.*c*.1722; d.unm.1770.	Nov.1765	Miss Anne Baldwin, (of Hoole) mo.83
12. 14th Nov.1762	Thomas Cholmondeley of Vale Royal. b.1726; M.P.(Cheshire 1756–58); Knight of the Belt, Nov.1772; r.Feb.1774; d.1779.	Nov.1770	Miss Mary Brooke, e.dau.33
13. Feb.1763	Sir Peter Byrne Leicester, 4th Bart., of Tabley House, s.of Sir John Byrne, 3rd Bart. of Timogue, Ireland. b.1732; assumed matronymic of Leicester, 1744; H.S.1760; d.1770.	Feb.1764	Miss Anne Susannah Warburton (of Winnington)
14. Feb.1763	John Crewe of Crewe Hall, later 1st Baron CREWE OF CREWE, cos.of John Crewe (2). b.1742; H.S.1764; M.P.(Staffordshire 1765–68 & Cheshire 1768–1802); r.1800; d.1829.	Nov.1766	Miss Kitty Barry, yr.dau.17
15. Feb.1763	Sir John Thomas Stanley, 6th Bart., of Alderley Park. b.1735; Gentleman of the Privy Chamber, 1761; Clerk of the Cheque to the Yeomen of the Guard; r.Nov.1765; d.1807.	–	
16. Feb.1763	Richard Whitworth of Batchacre Grange, Salop. b.1734; H.S.(Staffs.)1758; M.P.(Stafford 1768–80); Honorary Member, Nov.1779; d.1811.	Feb.1769	Miss Smith
17. Nov.1763	* Hon. John ('Jack') Smith-Barry of Belmont Hall, 4th s.of 4th Earl of Barrymore and yst.br.of Richard (10*) and Arthur Barry (11*). b.1725; H.S.1765; Master (Mr Smith-Barry's); d.1784.	Feb.1767 & Feb.1779	Miss Baker Miss Dobb
18. Feb.1764	George Heron of Daresbury Hall. b.1700; m.au.of 41 & 60; d.1780.	Nov.1767	Miss Frances (Fanny) Stapleton, m.8
19. Nov.1764	Sir Richard Grosvenor, 7th Bart., 1st Baron GROSVENOR OF EATON, later 1st Viscount BELGRAVE and 1st Earl GROSVENOR, of Eaton Hall, Eccleston. b.1731; Master (Grosvenor Hunt); M.P.(Chester 1754–61); r.Nov.1769; F.R.S.; Jockey Club; Won Derby Sks., 1790 (Rhadamanthus), 1792 (John Bull), 1794 (Daedalus); d.1802.	–	
20. Nov.1765	John Arden, Junior of Utkinton Hall and later also of Ashley Hall and Pepper Hall, Northallerton, eld.s.of John Arderne of Harden. b.1742; H.S.1790; r.1800; d.unm.1823.	Feb.1768	Miss Ann Barry, e.dau.17

21. Nov.1765	Lord Archibald Hamilton, later 9th Duke of Hamilton and 6th Duke of Brandon, of Ashton Hall, Lancs. b.1740; M.P.(Lancashire 1768–72); e.u.r.Nov.1770; H.M.L.L. (Lanarkshire)1799–1802; d.1819.	Oct.1768	Miss Bell Turton
22. Nov.1766	Charles Townley of Towneley Hall, Whalley, Lancs. and later of 7, Park St., Mayfair. b.1737; r.Nov.1774; d.unm.1805.	Nov.1769	Lady Almena Carpenter
23. Nov.1767	Sir Watkin Williams-Wynn, 4th Bart., of Wynnstay Hall, also 18, St.James's Sq. b.1748; e.u.r.Nov.1769; M.P.(Salop.1772–74 & Denbighshire 1774–89); H.M.L.L.(Merioneth)1775–89; dau.m.55; d.1789.	–	
24. ▷—• † Nov.1769	James Hugh Smith-Barry of Marbury Hall and Ruloe, eld.s.of John Smith-Barry (17) and nep.of Richard (10) & Arthur Barry(11). b.1746; Master (Mr.Smith-Barry Jnr's); r.Feb.1780; H.S.1795; *d.s.p.l.*1801.	Jan.1771	Miss Byron
25. Nov.1769	(George) Harry Grey, Colonel Lord Grey of Groby of Little Aston Hall, Staffs., later 5th Earl of Stamford, lst Baron DELAMER OF DUNHAM MASSEY and 1st Earl of WARRINGTON (Second Creations), also of Enville Hall, Staffs. and Dunham Massey Hall. b.1737; Page of Honour, 1761; M.P.(Staffordshire 1761–68); F.S.A.; H.M.L.L.1783–1819; Master (Enville Hounds) c.1765/92; Col., R.Chester Regt. of Militia; r.*c.*1794; d.1819.	Nov.1771 & Nov.1773	Miss Norbury Miss Harriott Warburton, yr.sis.35
26. Nov.1770	Rev. Dr Sir Thomas Delves Broughton, 6th Bart. of Broughton Hall, Staffs., later of Doddington Hall. b.1745; LL.D.; Assumed surname of Broughton in *lieu* of Broughton-Delves, 1766; H.S.(Staffs.)1772; r.Oct.1779; Rector of Cheadle, Cheshire, 1794–1807; Lt.-Col., Vol.Infantry; eld.dau.m.60, 3rd dau.m.68; d.1813.	Feb.1772	Miss Mary Darby
27. Nov.1770	Thomas ('Tom') Assheton, Junior of Ashley Hall, Cheshire, Brymbo, Denbighshire and Vaynol Hall, Co. Caernarvon, and later Tidworth, Hants., eld.s.of Thomas Assheton of Ashley. b.1752; assumed (with his father) additional surname of Smith in 1774; M.P.(Caernarvonshire 1774–80); Comptroller, Denbighshire & Ruthin Hunt, 1775; r.Nov.1782; Honorary Member, Nov.1782; H.S.(Caern.)1783; M.P.(Andover 1797–1821); H.M.L.L.(Caern.) 1822–28; d.1828.	Nov.1774	Miss Harriet Smith, [*prob.*] cousin
28. Nov.1770	† (Peter) Kyffyn Heron of Moor Hall, 2nd s.of George Heron (18) of Daresbury Hall. b.1752; H.S.1777; r.*c.*1796; d.1801.	Feb.1774 & Nov.1785	Miss Emma Warburton, m.36
29. Nov.1770	Thomas Highlord Ravenscroft of Davenham Lodge. d.m.a.1795.	Feb.1775 & Feb.1785	Miss Wright Miss Jane (Jenny) Brooke, yst.sis.41
30. Nov.1771	John Needham, Colonel the 10th Viscount Kilmorey, late Coldstream Regt. of Foot Guards, of Shavington Hall. b.1710; Grenadier Coy.Comdr., 2nd Ft.Gds., 1738–48; r.Feb.1774; d.1791.	Nov.1772 & Feb.1773	Miss Fanny Alcock (of Runcorn) Miss Alcock

31. Nov.1771	Rev. Stephen Glynne, later 7th Bart., of Broadlane Hall, Hawarden, s.of Sir Stephen Glynne, 6th Bart. b.1744; d.1780.	Nov.1775	Miss Harriott Warburton, (2nd term)
32 Nov.1774	† Hon. Robert Needham, later 11th Viscount Kilmorey, of Shavington Hall, 2nd s.of Lord Kilmorey (30). b.1746; m.dau.8, sis.78; r.*c.*1796; d.1818.	Feb.1777	Miss Wade
33. Nov.1774	* Richard Brooke of Norton Priory, later 5th Bart. b.1753; H.S.,1787; d.1795.	Nov.1777	Miss Hulton
34. Nov.1774	* Thomas ('Tom') Brooke of Church Minshull Hall and also Hefferston Grange, Weaverham, 2nd s.of Sir Richard Brooke, 4th Bart. and br.of Richard Brooke (33*). b.1754; M.P.(Newton 1786–1807); Capt., Ches.Supp.Militia, 1797; r.1801; H.S.1810; d.1820.	Nov.1778	Miss Bover
35. ▷══ Nov.1775	Sir Peter Warburton, Bart., o.s.of Sir Peter Warburton, 4th Bart. of Warburton and Arley, of Arley Hall, 5th and last Bart. b.1754; m.sis.52; H.S.1782; Lt.-Col., R.Chester Regt. of Militia; d.1813.	Nov.1776 & Feb.1783	Miss Delia Maude Miss Mary Mainwaring, sis.44
36. Nov.1775	James Croxton of Norley Bank. b.1751; m.sis.35; dau., mo.of 125; r.Feb.1784; d.1792.	Feb.1778	Miss Sophia Heron, eld.sis.28
37. Oct.1779	Davies Davenport of Capesthorne Hall. b.1757; H.S.1783; Maj., Ches.suppl.Militia, 1797; Lt.-Col., Macclesfield Foresters, 1803; M.P.(Cheshire 1806–30); r.1819; d.1837.	Nov.1780	Miss Catherine Leicester, o.dau.13
38. ▷══ *† Oct.1779	Rev. George Heron, Rector of Lymm with Warburton, 1776–1832,and also of Grappenhall, 1786–88, e.s.of George Heron (18) and br.of P.K.Heron (28*). b.1749; r.1816; d.1832.	Feb.1781	Miss Lydia Parker, sis.52 & mo.150
39. Oct.1779	Rev. Offley Crewe, Rector of Barthomley, 1777–1782, eld.s.of Rev.Dr. Randulph Crewe, Rector of Warmincham, and cos.of John (2) and John Crewe (14). b.1751; m.dau.27; Rector of Astbury 1782–1820; r.*c.*1796; d.1836.	Nov.1781	Miss Elizabeth Mainwaring, eld.sis.44, m.3
40. Nov.1780	William Egerton of Tatton Park, s.of William Tatton of Wythenshawe Hall. b.1749; H.S.1778; assumed matronymic of Egerton, 1780; m.2ndly, dau.45; M.P.(Hindon 1784–90, Newcastle-under-Lyme 1792–1802 & Cheshire 1802–06); d.1806.	Nov.1782	Miss Francesca (Fanny) Brooke, yst.sis.33
41. Nov.1780	Jonas Langford Brooke of Mere Hall, eld.s.of Peter Brooke of Mere Hall. b.1758; d.unm.1784.	Feb.1782	Miss Fanny Bootle, dau.45
42. Nov.1780	Sir William Stanley, 6th Bart., of Hooton Hall. b.1753; m.nie.22; *d.s.p.* 1792.	Nov.1784	Miss Mary Cunliffe
43. Nov.1781	Sir Thomas Egerton, 7th Bart., M.P. of Heaton House, Lancs., later 1st Baron GREY DE WILTON, 1st Viscount GREY DE WILTON and 1st Earl of WILTON. b. 1749; M.P.(Lancs.1772–84); Lt.-Col., R.Lancs.Regt.Vol.Fencibles; Col., Heaton Corps, Vol.Artillery; r.*a.*1799; H.S.(Lancs.)1804; *d.s.p.m.s.*1814.	Nov.1783	Miss Hester Cholmondeley, eld.dau.12

44. Nov.1782   James Mainwaring of Bromborough Manor and Avignon, France   –
                    (*prob.* 1784–91). b.1757; sis.m.3; r.*a.* 1799; d.1827.

45.   Richard Wilbraham Bootle, M.P. of Rode Hall and Lathom House,   –
                    3rd s.of Randle Wilbraham of Rode Hall, the u.of George (5)
                    and Roger Wilbraham (9) and yr.br.of their father. b.1725;
                    M.P.(Chester 1761–90); assumed wife's surname in addition
                    under will of her uncle; Elected Honorary Member, Nov.1782;
                    dau.m.40; d.1796.

46. Feb.1784   Colonel Henry Hervey-Aston, 12th Foot, of Aston Hall.   1789
                    b.1761; d.1798 in East Indies in command.

47. Nov.1784   Domville Poole of Dane Bank, Lymme, e.s.of Rev. Domville   Feb.1786
                    Halstead. b.1761; assumed surname of Poole in *lieu* of
                    Halstead, 1782; H.S.1794; d.1795.

48. Nov.1784   John Bower Jodrell of Henbury Hall and later also of Taxal   Nov.1786
                    Lodge, e.br.of Foster Bower. b.1746; m.Frances Jodrell of
                    Yeardsley Hall and assumed surname of Jodrell, 1775; ;
                    H.S.1775; d.1796.

49. 1786   Thomas Tarleton of Aigberth Hall, Lancs., later of Bolesworth   1788   Miss Elizabeth
                    Castle, Tattenhall. b.1753; r.1811; d.1820.   Egerton, eld.sis
                                                                                             53 & 76, m.69

50. 1788   Sir John Fleming Leicester, 5th Bart., of Tabley House,   1791
                    later 1st Baron DE TABLEY, 4th.surv.s.of Sir Peter Byrne
                    Leicester, Bart. (13). b.1762; M.P.(Yarmouth, Isle of Wight
                    1791–96, Heytesbury, Wilts.1796–1802 & Stockbridge, Hants.
                    1807); Lt.Col., Ches.Militia, 1784–96; Col., Ches.Vol.Cav.,
                    1797; Col., Commdt.,Ches.Yeo., 1803–20; r.1803; H.S.1804;
                    d.1827.

51. 1788   † (George) Harry Grey, Lord Grey of Groby of Enville Hall,   1790   Miss Forester
                    Staffs., later 6th Earl of Stamford & 2nd Earl of Warrington,
                    eld.s.of Lord Stamford (25). b.1765; Page of Honour to H.M.
                    George III; M.P.(Aldeburgh 1790–96 & St.Germans 1796–02);
                    Col., R.Cheshire Militia; H.M.L.L.1819–45;
                    Chamberlain & V.-Adm.Ches.(1829–45); r.1832; d.1845.

52. 1788   Thomas Parker of Astle Hall. b.1766; Col., Ches. Militia;   1793   Miss Briggs
                    m.dau.12; r.1829; d.1840.

53. 1788   John Egerton, eld.s.of Philip Egerton of Oulton Park, later   1795   Miss Emma Wilbraham,
                    Sir John Grey-Egerton, 8th Bart. b.1766; M.P.(Chester   dau.5
                    1807–18); H.S.1793; Capt., Delamere Foresters, 1803;
                    Maj., R.Chester Vols., 1807; r.1824; d.1825.

54. 1788 ⟨⟨⟩⟩— * (Henry) Augustus Leicester of Ashton Hayes, 5th surv.s.of Sir   1794   Miss Sophia Cotton,
                    Peter Byrne Leicester, Bart.(13) and br.of Sir John Leicester   dau.8, m.81
                    (50*). b.1765; Secretary 1790–1808; Capt., Ches.Vol.Cav.,
                    1797; Lt.-Col., Ches.Yeo; r.1811; d.1816.

55. 1788   Thomas ('Tom') Cholmondeley of Vale Royal, also Carlton   1792   Miss Williamson
                    House Terrace, later 1st Baron DELAMERE, eld.s.of Thomas
                    Cholmondeley (12). b.1767; m.dau.23; H.S.1792; Lt.-Col.,

90th Foot; Lt.-Col., 4th Foot, 1799–1800; Capt.Commdt., Delamere Foresters, 1803; Lt.-Col. Commdt., 2nd Ches.Yeo.; M.P.(Cheshire 1796–1812); r.1839; d.1855.

56. 1788	Charles Watkin John Buckworth of Somerford Hall. b.1767; assumed matronymic of Shakerley, 1790; H.S.1791; Capt., Ches. Vol.Cav., 1797; r.1802; d.1834.	1798	Miss Frances Egerton, 4th sis 53 & 76, m.67
57. 1788	Captain Thomas ('Tom') Grosvenor, Jnr., Grenadier Guards, nep.of Lord Grosvenor (19) of Grosvenor House, Walthamstow, Essex, for a time of Brooksby, Leics. and afterwards of Stocken Hall, Rutland and Mount Ararat, Richmond, Surrey. b.1764; Ensign, 3rd Guards, 1779; Col., 1799; Brig.-Gen., 1800; Maj.-Gen., 1802; Lieut.-Gen., 1808; Gordon Riots; Flanders; Holland; Helder; Ackmaar; Cadiz; Copenhagen; Walcheren Expedition; Col., 97th Queen's German Foot, 1807; Col., 65th Foot, 1814; m.2ndly, dau.5; r.1817; General, 1819; A.D.C. to Prince Regent; M.P.(Chester 1795–1826 & Stockbridge, Hants, 1826–30); Jockey Club; Field-Marshal, 1846; d.1851.	–	
58. 1788	Thomas Crewe Dod of Edge Hall. b.1754; Lt.-Col., Ches.Vol. Cav., 1797; r.1816; d.1827.	1799	Miss Jane Tarleton, eld.dau.47
59. 1788	John Ashton of Hefferston Grange, Weaverham, gr.nep.of Philip Henry Warburton. b.1765; Lt.-Col., Ches.Yeo.; d.1814.	1797	Lady Sophia Grey, 4th dau.25, m.cos.85
60. 1790	Thomas Langford Brooke of Mere Hall, yr.br.of Jonas Langford Brooke (41).b.1769; H.S.[1797]; m.dau.26 & sis.69 & 74; Maj.,Ches.Vol.Cav., 1797; Lt.-Col., Ches.Yeo., 1803–12; r.1813; d.1815.	1796	Miss Essex Cholmondeley, 2nd dau.12
61. 1792	Colonel Peter Patten, s.of Thomas Patten of Bank Hall, Warrington and later Bold Hall, Prescot. b.1764; m.sis.52; M.P.(Newton 1797–1806, Lancaster 1807–12 & Malmesbury 1813–18); assumed additional surname of Bold, 1813; Maj., Loyal Ches.Vols; Lt.-Col., Lancs.Vol.Cav.; Col., R.Lancs. Militia; d.1819.	1802	Miss Sybella Egerton, yst.sis.53 & 76, m.s.45
62. 1792	*Charles Leicester of Stanthorne Hall, Middlewich, 6th surv.s.of Sir Peter Byrne Leicester, Bart.(13) and br.of Sir John (50*) and Augustus Leicester(54*). b.1766; m.1stly, 3rd sis.53 & 76; Capt., Ches.Yeo.; r.1802; d.1815.	1800	Miss Russell
63. 1794	George John Legh, D.C.L. of High Legh Hall (East Hall), eld.s of Henry Cornwall Legh. b.1769; m.au.171; H.S.1805; d.1832.	1804	Miss Eliza Susanna Tarleton, yst.dau.49
64. 1794	†Major John Crewe, Junior, 125th Foot, later General the 2nd Baron Crewe of Crewe of Crewe Hall, s.of Lord Crewe (14†). b.1772; Lieut., 77th Regt.of Ft.,1787; Major, 103rd Regt., 126th Regt. and 134th Ft.(Lewes's); 2nd R.Chester Militia; r.1801; Maj.-Gen., 1808, Lieut.-Gen., 1813, Gen., 1830, ret.1831; d. at his Château in Liége, 1835.	–	

65. 1795	†William Tatton of Wythenshawe Hall, eld.s.of William Egerton (40) of Tatton. b.1774; M.P. (Beverley 1796–99); Capt., Ches.Supp.Militia, 1797; d.unm. *v.p.* 1799.	—	

66. 1796   *Charles Cholmondeley of Overleigh Lodge, Chester, later of   1803   Miss Elizabeth Emma
Heath House, Knutsford, 3rd s.of Thomas Cholmondeley (12) of   Crewe, dau.14
Vale Royal and br.of Lord Delamere (55). b.1770; Capt.Lt.,
Ches.Vol.Cav, 1797; Secretary, 1808–1839; r.1840; d.1846.

67. 1796   †Thomas Tarleton, Jnr., 1st Royal Dragoons, of Bolesworth   1805   Miss Charlotte Dod,
Castle, later Capt., 26th Dragoons, eld.s.of Thomas Tarleton   eld.dau.58
(49). b.1776; A.D.C. to u., C.in-C., Portugal, 1799; Trs.,
12th Light Dragoons, 1802; h.p. Cor., 1808; m.4th sis.53 & 76;
r.1820; d.1836.

68. 1796   Trafford Trafford of Oughtrington Hall, 2nd s.of John Leigh.   —
b.1770; assumed matronymic in pursuance of uncle's will,
1791; m.sis.69; Col., Ches. Militia; r.1802; d.1859.

69. 1796   Lieutenant-Colonel John Delves Broughton, 100th Foot, of   1801   Miss Mary Anne
Broughton Hall, later 7th Bart. of Doddington Hall, 2nd s.of   Tarleton,
Sir Thomas Broughton (26) and ultimately of Bank Farm,   3rd dau.49
Kingston-on-Thames. b.1769; m.eld.sis.53 & 76; Ensign,
100th Foot, 1785, Lieut-Col., 1794, Col., 1800;
Maj.-Gen., 1808; r.1812; Lieut.-Gen., 1818, Gen., 1830;
d.s.p. 1847.

70. 1797   Sir Thomas Mostyn, 6th and last Bart., of Mostyn Hall,   —
Flintshire. b.1776; H.S.(Carnarvon) 1798 (Merioneth)1799;
Master (Sir Thos.Mostyn's Woore Country);
M.P.(Flintshire 1796–97 & 1799–1831);
Master (Bicester 1800–1829); Lt.-Col.Commdt.,
Flintshire Fus., 1803; r.1813; d.unm.1831.

71. 1797   George Brooke of Haughton Hall, Salop., formerly   —
George Brooke Brigges Townshend, o.s.of George
Salisbury Townshend of Chester. b.1802; assumed surname of
Brooke only in 1797; r.1802; H.S.(Salop.)1811; d.unm.1847.

72. 1798   *John Leigh, Junior, of Oughtrington Hall,   —
e.br.of Trafford Trafford (68*). b.1768; d.unm.1800.

73. 1799   Francis Bower ('Frank') Jodrell of Henbury Hall,   —
s.of John Bower Jodrell (48). b.1776; *Détenu* at Dijon,
*c.*1802; r.1812; H.S.1813; res.Lausanne, Switzerland,
1816–26; d.1829.

74. 1799   *Rev. Henry Delves Broughton, later 8th Bart. of Doddington Hall.   —
Incumbent of Broughton and later of Haslington, 3rd s.of
Sir Thomas Broughton (26) and br.of General
Sir John Delves Broughton, Bart.(69*). b.1777; Rector of
Cheadle, Cheshire, 1807–29; r.1817; d.1851.

75. 1799   Humphrey Trafford, eld.s.of John Trafford of Trafford Park,   —
Whalley Range, formerly of Croston Hall, Preston.
b.1776; d.unm.1801.

76. 1799   *Rev. Philip Egerton of Oulton Park, 2nd s.of Philip Egerton   1807
and br.of John Egerton (53*), later
Rev.Sir Philip Grey-Egerton, 9th Bart. b.1767; Rector of Malpas,
Higher Moiety (1804–29) & of Tarporley (1816–29);
Chaplain to the Club, 1799; r.1816; d.1851.

77. 1799   †George Wilbraham, Junior, 56, Upper Seymour St., London and   1813   Miss Aston,
Delamere Lodge, 2nd s.of George Wilbraham (5). b.1779;   *prob.* Harriet,
Lieut., Ches.Militia; Lieut., 4th King's Own Regt.;   dau.46
N.Holland; *Détenu* in Paris, 1802–06; r.1815; F.R.S.;
M.P.(Stockbridge 1826–31, Chester 1831–32 & Cheshire South
1833–41); H.S.1844; d.1852.

78. 1800   Colonel Stapleton Cotton, 25th Light Dragoons, of Combermere   –
Abbey, formerly of Llewenny Hall, Denbigh and ultimately
of Colchester House, Clifton, Glos., later General
Sir Stapleton Stapleton-Cotton, 6th Bart., 1st Baron
COMBERMERE and afterwards Field-Marshal 1st Viscount
COMBERMERE OF BHURTPORE, G.C.B., G.C.H., K.S.I., P.C.,
2nd s.of Sir Robert Cotton (8). b.1773; 2nd Lt., 23rd Royal
Welch Fusilers, 1790; Capt., 6th Dragoon Guards, 1793;
Maj., 59th Foot, 1794; Lt.-Col., 25th Light Dragoons, 1794;
Lt.-Col., 16th Dragoons, 1800; Maj.-Gen., 1805;
Lieut.-Gen., 1812; Col., 20th Dragoons, 1813–18; Col,
3rd Dragoons, 1821–29; Gen., 1825; M.P.(Newark 1806–14);
Governor of Barbados and C.-in-C., Leeward Islands, 1817–20;
Governor of Sheerness, 1821–52; C.-in-C., Ireland, 1822–25;
C.-in-C., East Indies, 1825; Flanders (Premont, Cateau);
Cape of Good Hope, Malavelley; Seringapatam; Peninsular:
Lincelles, The Douro, Talavera, Torres Vedras, Busaco,
Villa Garcia, Llerena, Castrajon, Fuentes d'Onor, Cuidad Rodrigo,
Salamanca; El Bodon; South of France: The Pyrennes, Orthes,
Toulouse; Bhurtphore. K.B., 1812; Knight Grand Cross of the
Order of the Tower and Sword (Portugal); Knight Grand Cross
of the Order of St.Ferdinand (Spain); Knight Grand Cross of the
Order of Charles III (Spain); assumed surname of Stapleton
before Cotton, 1827; r.1836; Col., 1st Life Guards and Gold
Stick, 1852–65; Field-Marshal, 1855; Constable of the Tower of
London & H.M.L.L. (Tower Hamlets) 1852–65; d.1865.

79. 1800   Edwin Corbet of Darnhall Hall and later Tilstone Lodge.   1809   Miss Harriett
b.1779; m.au.of 170; dau.m.173; r.1818; d.1858.   Catherine Davenport,
                                                                       dau.37

80. 1801   Thomas Case of Thingwall Hall and Ince Hall, Lancs.   –
b.1777; r. 1805; d.1845; g-dau.m.219.

81. 1801   Henry Mainwaring ('Harry') Mainwaring, later 1st Bart.   1808
(second creation) of Peover Hall, later of Marbury Cottage,
Marbury cum Quoisley, s.of Thomas Wetenhall, who assumed
surname of Mainwaring on inheriting the property from his
uterine half- brother, Sir Henry Mainwaring, Bart.(4). b.1782;
m.yst.dau.8; H.S.1806; Capt., Ches.Yeo.; r.1837;
Honorary Member, 1837; d.1860.

82. 1801	Edwin Venables Townshend of Wincham Hall, cos.of George Brooke (71). b.1774; Lt.-Col., Ches.Yeo.; Peterloo, 1819; r.1821; d.1845.	1806	Miss Emma Grey, nie.3 & 25, g-dau.152, m.95
83. 1801	Colonel Peter Heron of Moor Hall, Daresbury, 90th Foot, o.s.of Peter Kyffyn Heron (28). b.1770; Ensign, 11th Foot, 1790; Capt., 90th Foot, 1794; Capt., Commdt., Norton Yeomanry, 1804–07; M.P.(Newton 1806–14); Maj.-Gen., 1808; r.1809; Sicily, (Staff) 1811–12; Lt.-Gen., 1813, Gen.1830; d.1849.	–	
84. 1802	†Wilbraham Egerton of Tatton Park, 2nd s.of William Egerton (40). b.1781; H.S.[1808]; M.P.(Cheshire 1812–31); Capt., R.Ches.Militia, 1803; Lt.-Col., Macclesfield Regt., 1809; Capt., Ches.Yeo., 1819, Lt.-Col., 1831, Commdt., 1835; r.1847; d.1856.	1812	Miss Frances Brooke, dau.34, sis.111
85. 1802	Booth Grey of Ashton Hayes, o.s.of Hon. Booth Grey (3). b.1783; H.S.1811; m.cos.,dau.25; r.1819; d.1850.	1814	Miss Anne Blackburne, au.170; m.79
86. 1803	(John) Thomas Stanley of Alderley Park, later 7th Bart. and 1st Baron STANLEY OF ALDERLEY, s.of Sir Thomas Stanley, Bart.(15). b.1766; F.R.S., F.S.A.; M.P.(Wootton Basset 1790–96); Maj., R. Cheshire Militia; Gentleman of the Bedchamber, 1796–1816; H.S.(Anglesey)1809; r.1823; H.S.1831; d.1850.	–	
87. 1803	Sir Stephen Richard Glynne, 8th Bart. of Broadlane Hall (later - known as Hawarden House, becoming Hawarden Castle in 1809), s.of Sir Stephen Glynne, Bart. (31). b.1780; H.S. (Co.Flint)1802; r.1808; d.1815.	–	
88. 1803	Sir Watkin ('Bubble') Williams-Wynn, 5th Bart., M.P. of Wynnstay, s.of Sir Watkin Williams-Wynn, Bart.(23). b.1772; H.M.L.L. (Denbigh & Merioneth); M.P.(Beaumaris 1794–96 & Denbigh 1796–1840); Col., Ancient British Dragoons, 1794–1800; Denbigh Militia, 1797, Irish Rebellion, 1798; Lt.-Col., Commdt., 3rd Bn., Militia (France), 1814; Col., Denbigh Yeoman Cav.; Welsh Militia A.D.C.; Master (Sir W.W.-Wynn's); President, Soc. of Ancient Britons; r.1835; d.1840.	1811	Miss Anna Wilbraham, dau.5; m.57
89. 1803	Thomas Joseph ('Tom') Trafford of Trafford Park, later Sir Thomas de Trafford, 1st Bart., s.of John Trafford and yr.br. of Humphrey Trafford (75). b.1778; Maj., Manchester & Salford Yeo.Cav.; Peterloo 1819; r.1821; Master of Own Harriers; H.S.(Lancs.)1834; altered orthography of surname, 1841; d.1852.	1818	
90. 1805	Rev. William Wickham Drake, Rector of Malpas (Lower Moiety), 1802–1832 & of Harthill, 1816–32. b. 1778; m.dau.49, sis.67; r.1822; d.1832.	1810	Miss Ann Dod, 3rd dau.58
91. 1806	Sir Richard ('Dicky') Brooke, 6th Bart. of Norton Priory, also Hope Hall, Flint and occasionally Hefferston Grange, s.of Sir Richard Brooke, Bart.(33). b.1785; H.S.(Co.Flint)1815; H.S.1817; r.1863; Honorary Member,1863; d.1865.	1815	Miss Mary Earle

92. 1806	Francis Richard Price of Bryn-y-Pys. b.1786; m.1stly, e.sis.106; H.S.(Co.Flint)1810; r.on marriage, 1827; H.S.(Co.Denbigh)1834; d.1853.	1817	Hon. Henrietta Grey, g-dau.51
93. 1806	* Rev. William Cotton, 3rd s.of Sir Robert Cotton, Bart. (8) and br.of Maj.-Gen. Stapleton Cotton (78*). b.*c.*1774; Vicar of Audlem, 1802–35; r.1817; d.1853.	–	
94. 1806	John Baskervyle ('Johnnie') Glegg of Gayton Hall and Old Withington Hall. b.1784; m.yr.sis.106; H.S.1814; d.1865.	1816	Miss Harriet Brooke, yr.dau.34,sis.111, m.106
95. 1806	*Thomas William Tatton of Wythenshawe Hall, 3rd s.of William Egerton (40), br.of Wilbraham Egerton (84*) and gs.of Richard Bootle-Wilbraham (45). b.1783; resumed surname of Tatton, 1806; m.nie.25; H.S.1809; d.1827.	1819	Lady Charlotte Grey, eld.dau.51
96. 1809	Domville Halsted Cudworth Poole, of Marbury Hall, Marbury--cum Quoisley, eld.s.of Domville Poole (47). b.1787; r.1833; d.1869.	1820	Miss Harriet Brooke e.dau.71
97. 1809	Edward Tomkinson of Dorfold Hall, Acton, eld.s.of Henry Tomkinson. b.1773; d.unm.1819.	–	
98. 1811	*Rev. James ('Jemmy') Tomkinson of Dorfold Hall, 2nd s.of Henry -Tomkinson. b.1786; Vicar of Acton and Rector of Davenham, 1820; r.1838; d.1841.	–	
99. 1811	*Captain Thomas Brooke, Grenadier Guards, of Norton Priory, later of Hefferston Grange, 2nd s.of Sir Richard Brooke (33). b.*c.*1786; Peninsular: Corunna, Nivelle, Nive; Col., 1837; r.1864; d.1870.	1821	Lady Maria Grey, 2nd dau.51. Appointed but died before the meeting.
100. 1812	Rev. Rowland Alleyne Hill, Rector of St. Mary on the Hill, Chester, 1803–1819, gs.of Sir Rowland Hill, 1st Bart. of Hawkstone, Salop. b.1776; vacated by rule, 1823; d.1844.	–	
101. 1812	Captain William Wilbraham, R.N., 3rd s.of George Wilbraham (5). b.1781; r.1817; d.1824.	–	
102. 1813	Lieutenant.-Colonel Joseph Francis Buckworth, of Wootton, Beds., yr.br.of Charles Watkin John Shakerley (56) of Somerford Hall. b.1770; Ches. Militia; r.1816; d.1846.	–	
103. 1813	Henry Charles Hervey-Aston of Aston Hall, s.of Colonel Henry Hervey-Aston (46). b.1792; H.S.1818; d.at Genoa, 1821.	–	
104. 1813	Peter Langford Brooke of Mere Hall, later of Mere New Hall, eld.s.of Thomas Langford Brooke (60). b.1793; Capt., Ches. Yeo., H.S.1824; r.1831; drowned skating,1840.	1822	Lady Jane Grey, yst.dau.51
105. 1815	*Rev. Dr John Edward Tarleton, D.C.L., LL.D., 3rd s.of Thomas Tarleton (49) by then of Bolesworth Castle and br.of Thos.Tarleton (67*). b.1783; r.1823; Rector of Chelsfield, Kent; d.1849.	–	

106. 1815	(Robert) Townley Parker of Cuerden Hall, Preston, Lancs. and of Astley Hall, Lancs., o.s.of Thomas Townley Parker. b.1793; m.yst.dau.34; H.S.(Lancs.)1817; r.1828; M.P.(Preston 1837–41 & 1852–57); d.1879.	1823	Miss Mary Legh, dau.63; cos.170
107. 1816	Thomas (aka 'T.L.') Legh of Lyme Hall, eld.n.s.of Thomas Peter Legh of Lyme Park, Haydock Lodge and Golborne Park. b.1792; D.C.L., LL.D., F.R.S., F.S.A.; M.P.(Newton, 1814–32); Civ.A,D,C. to C.-in-C., Forces on the Continent, Quatre Bras, Waterloo; Capt., Ches.Yeo.; r.1836; d.1857.	1824	Miss Sophia Francis Mainwaring, eld.dau.81
108. 1816	Lawrence Armitstead of Cranage Hall and The Hermitage, Holmes Chapel. b.1791; H.S.1829; r.1835; d.1874.	1825	Miss Hester Mainwaring, 2nd dau.81
109. 1816	James France France of Bostock Hall, s.of Thomas Hayhurst who assumed his uncle's surname of France in *lieu* of Hayhurst, 1796. b.1793; H.S.1820; r.1836; d.unm.1869.	1826	Miss Maria Stanley, sis.129
110. 1817	* Lieutenant-Colonel Henry Tarleton, 60th Foot, 4th s.of Thomas Tarleton (49) of Bolesworth Castle and br.of Thos.(67*) and Dr.J.E.Tarleton (105*). b.1787; Major, 7th Ft., 1814; Peninsular; h.p.,1817; r.1823; d.1829.	–	
111. 1817	Henry ('Harry') Brooke of The Grange, Weaverham, later of Ashbrook Hall, Church Minshull and also Forest Hill, s.of Thomas Brooke (34) of Church Minshull. b.1798; Capt., Ches.Yeo.; Secretary, 1847–1865; H.S.1848; Honorary Member, 1880; d.1884.	1827	
112. 1817	Charles ('Charlie') Wicksted of Betley Hall, Staffs. and Baddiley Hall, later of Shakenhurst, Bewdley, s.of George Tallet. b.1796; assumed his matronymic, 1814; H.S.1822; Master (Mr.Wicksted's, Woore Country, 1825/36); r.1842; re-elected without fine & appointed Honorary Member, 1850; d.1870.	1828	Miss Mary Anne Elizabeth Egerton, eld.dau.76
113. 1817	Major Clement Swetenham, 16th Light Dragoons, of Somerford Booths, eld.s.of Roger Comberbach who had assumed matronymic. b.1787; Capt., 1807, 16th Light Dragoons; Peninsular War: Busaco, Fuentes d'Onor, Salamanca, Vittoria; Quatre Bras, Waterloo; r.1831; d.1852.	1829	Miss Emma Elizabeth Warburton, eld.sis.125
114. 1818	Richard Grosvenor, Viscount Belgrave, M.P. of Eaton Hall, gs.of Lord Grosvenor (19) and of Lord Wilton (43), Earl Grosvenor, 1831 and later 2nd Marquess of Westminster, K.G., P.C., 9th Bart., residing also at Halkyn Castle, Flint and Motcombe House, Shaftesbury. b.1795; M.P.(Chester 1818–30, Cheshire 1830–32 & Cheshire South 1832–35); Capt., R.Flints. Militia; Maj., Flints.Yeo.; r.1842; H.M.L.L.1845–68; Lord Steward of the Household, 1850–52; d.1869.	1830	Miss Harriot Brooke, 2nd dau.91
115. 1818	Thomas Hibbert, Junior, of Birtles Hall, gs.of Robert Hibbert of Marple. b.1788; m.dau.66; Lt., Ches.Yeo; r.1827; H.S.1839; d.1879.	–	

116. 1819	Charles Stanley-Massey-Stanley, 4th s.of Sir Thomas Stanley, 7th Bart. and gs.of Sir William Stanley (42), of Hooton Hall. b.1787; r.1829.	–	
117. 1819	John Smith-Barry of Fota Island, Co. Cork and Marbury Hall, e.n.s.of James Hugh Smith-Barry (24). b.1793; H.S.1819; m.2ndly 2nd dau.83; d.1837.	1831	Miss Mary Anne Elizabeth Egerton, (2nd term)
118. 1819	John Hosken Harper of Davenham Hall. b.1786; assumed wife's surname in *lieu* of Hosken; r.1823; d.1831.	–	
119. 1820	(Thomas) Henry Hesketh, Jnr. of Rufford New Hall, Lancs., later 4th Bart. of Rufford Old Hall, s.of Sir Thomas Dalrymple Hesketh, 3rd Bt. of Rufford Old Hall. b.1799; r,1839; d.1843.	1832	Miss Georgiana Cholmondeley, 2nd dau.66
120. 1822	† (George) Harry Grey, Lord Grey of Groby of Dunham Massey Hall and Enville, Staffs, e.s.of 6th Earl of Stamford (51) b.1802 Lieut.-Col., Commdt., Ches.Yeo., 1827; *d.v.p.*1835.	1833	Miss Anna Maria Emma Cholmondeley, 4th dau.66
121. 1823	Vice-Admiral John Richard Delap Tollemache of Tilstone Lodge, Tilstone Fearnall, s.of John Delap Halliday of The Leasowes, Salop. and gs. & co-heir of 4th Earl of Dysart. b.1772; Captain, R.N., Napoleonic Wars, Toulon; Mediterranean; Rear Admiral of the Blue, 1819; assumed matronymic of Tollemache, 1821; r.1834; d.1837.	–	
122. 1823	Edmund William Antrobus of Antrobus Hall, s.of John Antrobus of Eaton Hall, Congleton. b.1792; suc.u. as 2nd Bart., ; 1826 r.1856; d.1870.	1834	Miss Susan Mary Glegg, eld.dau.94
123. 1823 ⊳━o	Charles Ingram ('Jack') Ford of Abbeyfield, Sandbach. b.1797; r.1854; Honorary Member, 1854; d.1862.	1835	Miss Katharine Mainwaring, 4th dau.81
124. 1823	†John Jervis Tollemache of Tilstone Lodge, afterwards of Peckforton Castle and Helmingham Hall, Suffolk, and later 1st Baron TOLLEMACHE OF HELMINGHAM, eld.s.of Vice-Admiral John Tollemache (121). b.1805; assumed surname of Tollemache in *lieu* of Halliday; r.1834; H.S.1840; M.P.(S.Cheshire 1841–68 & W.Cheshire 1868–72); d.1890.	–	
125. 1825	Rowland Eyles Egerton Warburton of Arley Hall, at one time residing at Norley Bank, eld.s.of Rev. Rowland Egerton Warburton, 7th s.of Philip Egerton of Oulton, nep. of Sir John (53) and Rev. Sir Philip Grey-Egerton (76) and gr.nep. of Sir Peter Warburton (35) and gs.of James Croxton (36). b.1804; assumed additional surname of Warburton, 1813; m.eld.dau.91; Capt., Ches.Yeo.; H.S.1833; r.1873; Honorary Member, 1873; d.1891.	1838	Miss Georgiana Kaye, sis.216 [*prob.*]
126. 1826	* (Gibbs) Crawfurd Antrobus, of Eaton Hall, Congleton, yr.br. of Sir Edmund Antrobus, 2nd Bart. (122*). b.1793; Sec., Legation, U.S.A., 1816, Turin. 1823, Two Sicilies, 1824–26; Capt., Ches.Yeo.; H.S.1834; M.P.(Aldborough 1820–26, Plympton Erle, 1826–32); r.1858; d.1861.	1837	

127. 1827 ⬅️— James Walthall Hammond of Wistaston Hall, gr.nep. of Richard   1836   Miss Susan Fanny
Walthall (7). b.1805; Secretary (*prob.*), 1840–46;   Glegg, 3rd.dau.94
r.1846; d.unm.1854.

128. 1827   (Charles) George Walmseley of Bolesworth Castle. b.1799;   —
H.S.1830; r.1838.

129. 1828   William Thomas Stanley-Massey-Stanley of Puddington Hall and   —
Melton Mowbray, later Sir William Stanley, 10th Bart., nep.of
Charles Stanley (117). b.1806; Master (Sir W.M.Stanley's);
r.1835; M.P.(Pontefract 1837–41); H.S.1845; Jockey Club;
d.unm.1863.

130. 1829   Philip de Malpas Egerton of Oulton Park, later Sir Philip   1839   Miss Emma Legh,
de Malpas Grey-Egerton, 10th Bart., eld.s.of Rev. Sir Philip   sister-in-law,
Grey-Egerton, Bart. (76). b.1806; m.dau.63; Lt.Col.,   6th dau.63
Ches.Yeo.; F.R.S., F.G.S.; M.P.(Chester 1830–32,
S.Cheshire 1835–68 & W.Cheshire 1868–81); Antiquary,
Royal Academy, 1876; d.1881.

131. 1829   John William Jodrell of Henbury Hall, later res.Sheerwater,   —
Hants.; eld.s.of Frank Jodrell (73). b.1808; Lieut., Grenadier
Guards 1830–31; r.1842; d.unm.(*felo per se*)1858.

132. 1829   † William Tatton Egerton of Mere Hall and afterwards Tatton   1840   Miss Clare Brooke,
Park, later 1st Baron EGERTON OF TATTON,   5th.dau.91
eld.s.of Wilbraham Egerton (84). b.1806; Maj., Ches.Yeo.;
M.P.(Lymington 1830–31 & N.Cheshire 1832–58);
H.M.L.L.1868–83; r.1871; Honorary Member, 1871; d.1883.

133. 1829   * Major William ('Willie') Tomkinson, 16th Light Dragoons of   —
Dorfold Hall and later The Willingtons, 4th s.of Henry
Tomkinson of Dorfold Hall and br.of Edward (97) and
Rev. James Tomkinson (98*). b.1790; Cornet, 1807,
Capt., 1812; Peninsular: A.D.C. to G.O.C., Cavalry (78),
1812, Busaco, Fuentes d'Onor, Salamanca, Vittoria; Quatre Bras,
Waterloo; m.5th dau.67; Master of Own Harriers; Maj.,
24th Dragoons, 1819; h.-p., 1821; Lt.-Col., 1837; r.1839; d.1872.

134. 1829   (John) Wilson Patten of Bank Hall, Warrington and Light Oaks,   —
Stafford, later 1st and last Baron WINMARLEIGH, P.C. of
Winmarleigh House, Garstang, nep.of Peter Patten-Bold (61).
b.1802; m.cos., dau.61; M.P.(Lancashire 1830–31 & N.Lancashire
1832–74); r.1833; Col., R.Lancs.Militia, (Gibraltar,1854);
Militia A.D.C.; Chancellor of Duchy of Lancaster, 1866–68;
Chief Sec. for Ireland; *d.s.p.m.s.*1892.

135. 1829   Captain William Owen Stanley, Grenadier Guards, of Penrhôs,   —
Anglesey and of Alderley, twin s.of Sir Thomas Stanley,
Bart. (86). b.1802; r.on marriage, 1832; M.P.(Anglesey 1837–47,
Chester 1850–57 & Beaumaris 1857–74); H.M.L.L.(Anglesey);
d.1884.

136. 1830   * Rowland Errington of Puddington Hall and later of Sandhoe,   —
               Northumberland and Red Rice, Hants, yr.br.of
               Sir William Stanley, Bart.(129*). b.1809; assumed sole surname
               of Errington, 1820; r.1835; Master (Quorn, 1835/38); suc.as
               11th.Bart., 1863; *d.s.p.m.* 1875.

137. 1832   (George) Cornwall Legh of High Legh Hall, eld.s.of George   1841   Miss Charlotte Lucy
               Legh (63). b.1804; H.S.1838; M.P.(N.Cheshire 1841–68 &   Beatrix Egerton,
               Mid.Cheshire 1868–73); Col., R.Ches.Militia; r.1869; d.1877.   o.surv.dau.84

138. 1832 ▷━ Geoffrey Joseph ('Geof') Shakerley of Whatcroft Hall and later   1842
               of Belmont Hall, 2nd s.of Charles Watkin John Shakerley (56).
               b.1800; d.1878.

139. 1832   John Hurleston Leche of Carden Park. b.1805; H.S.1832;   —
               Master (Mr Leche's); d.1844.

140. 1833   Captain Baskervyle ('Birkenhead') Glegg, 12th Royal Lancers,   —
               of Backford Hall. b.1806; d.unm.1843.

141. 1833   Henry Dixon, 15th Hussars, of Astle Hall, eld.s.of Colonel   —
               John Dixon of Gledhow Hall, Yorks. and nep.of Thomas Parker
               (52). b.1794; d.1838.

142. 1833   * Captain Francis Charles ('Frank') Jodrell, Grenadier Guards, of   —
               Yeardsley and Taxal, res.London and later Hyéres, France;
               3rd s.of Francis Bower-Jodrell (73) and br.of John Jodrell
               (131*). b.1812; Lieut., 87th Regt., 1831–2; Grenadier Guards,
               1832–41; r.(Ru.XI)1835; *d.s.p.l.* 1868.

143. 1834   * Right Hon. Lord Robert ('Bob') Grosvenor, P.C., later 1st Baron   1844
               EBURY OF EBURY MANOR, of Moor Park, Herts.,
               3rd s.of 1st Marquess of Westminster and br.of Lord Belgrave
               (114*). b.1801; M.P.(Shaftesbury 1822–26, Chester 1826–47 &
               Middlesex 1847–57); r.1846; Comptroller of the Household,
               1830–34; Groom of the Stole to the Prince Consort, 1840–41;
               Treasurer of the Household, 1846–47; d.1893.

144. 1834   Humphrey Trafford of Trafford Park, late 1st Royal Dragoons,   1843
               later 2nd Bart., s.of Sir Thomas de Trafford, Bart. (89). b.1808;
               Capt., Ches.Yeo.; Master of Own Harriers; H.S.(Lancashire)1861;
               r.1883; d.1886.

145. 1835   Sir George Warren, 6th Bart., 2nd Baron de Tabley,   1846
               of Tabley House, e.s.of Lord de Tabley (50). b.1811; assumed
               surname of Warren, 1832; m.2ndly, wid.147; Lt.-Col., Ches.Yeo.;
               Lord-in-Waiting, 1853–58 & 1859–66; Treasurer of the
               Household, 1868–72; P.C., 1869; r.1869; d.1887.

146. 1835   Hon. Hungerford Crewe, later 3rd and last Baron Crewe of   —
               Crewe, of Crewe Hall, o.s.of Lord Crewe (65). b.1812; r.1838;
               F.R.S., F.S.A.; d.unm.1894.

147. 1836 ▷━ †James Hugh Smith-Barry, Jnr. of Marbury Hall, eld.s.of   1845
               John Smith-Barry (117). b.1816; H.S.1846; H.S. (Co. Cork);
               d.1856.

148. 1837   Thomas William ('Tom') Tatton of Wythenshawe Hall, o.s.of   1847
              Thomas William Tatton (95). b.1816; m.eld.dau.106;
              Capt. 11th Dragoon Gds.; Capt.(unatt.) 1st Dragoon Gds.; Capt.
              Ches.Yeo.; H.S.1849; r.1850; d.1885.

149. 1838   George Fortescue Wilbraham, Jnr., of Delamere Lodge, eld.s.of   1849
              George Wilbraham (77). b.1815; H.S.1858; d.unm.1885.

150. 1838 ▷——▪ Lieutenant-Colonel John Dixon, 1st Royal Dragoons,   1848
              of Astle Hall, 2nd s.of Colonel John Dixon of Gledhow Hall,
              Yorks. and br.of Henry Dixon (141). b.1799; m.6th dau.95;
              H.S.1843; r.1859; d.1873.

151. 1839   † Richard Brooke, lst Life Guards, of Norton Priory, later 7th   1863   Miss Cecely Louisa
              Bart., eld.s.of Sir Richard Brooke (91). b.1814; Lieut.,   Egerton,
              1st Life Guards, 1832–41; Capt., Ches.Yeo.; Lieut.-Col.,   yr.dau.130
              R.Cheshire Militia; H.S.1870; m.2ndly, g.dau.81; r.1875; d.1888.

152. 1839   Ralph Gerard Leycester of Toft Hall, Knutsford. b.1817; Capt.,   –
              Ches.Yeo.; H.S.1847; fined on marriage & r.1840; d.1851.

153. 1840   Captain Henry Hayhurst France, 6th Dragoons Guards, of   1850
              Ystyn-Colwyn House, Montgomery, 3rd s.of Thomas Hayhurst
              of Bostock Hall and br.of James France (109). b.1806; d.1875.

154. 1840   John Upton Gaskell of Ingersley Hall, Rainow. b.1804;   –
              r.1853; d.1883.

155. 1841   Sir Watkin ('Watty') Williams-Wynn, 6th Bart., M.P., 1st Life   1851
              Guards of Wynnstay Hall, e.s.of Sir Watkin Williams-Wynn,
              Bart.(88). b.1820; Cor., 1st Life Guards, 1839, Lieut., 1842–43;
              M.P.(Denbigh 1841–85); Capt., Denbighshire Rifle Vols.;
              Lt.-Col., Montgomeryshire Yeo.; Militia A.D.C.; Jockey Club;
              Master (Sir W.W.-Wynn's); r.1870; Honorary Member, 1870;
              *d.s.p.m.*1885.

156. 1841   William Roylance Court of Newton Manor House, Middlewich.   1852
              b.1812; Lt., Ches.Yeo.; Lt.-Col., Denbighshire R.V.C.; d.1881.

157. 1842   Hon.Wellington Henry ('Cheese') Stapleton-Cotton, 1st Life   1855
              Guards, later 2nd Viscount Combermere and 7th Bart., of
              Combermere Abbey, later of North Lodge, Bunbury and at one time
              Cherry Hill, Malpas, s.of Lord Combermere (78). b.1820 at
              Barbados; Cor., 7th Hussars; Canada, Pampean's Rebellion;
              Lieut., 1st Life Guards, 1841, Capt., 1846, Major, 1850,
              Lieut.-Col., 1857, Col., 1861, ret., 1866; M.P. (Carrickfergus
              1847–59); Sec. to Master Gen. of Ordnance, 1852; Master
              (Wynnstay 1858/59); d.1891, as a result of being run down by a
              hansom cab.

158. 1842   Commander Thomas John Langford-Brooke, R.N. of   1853
              Mere New Hall, nep.of Peter Langford Brooke (104) and s.of
              Thomas Langford Brooke (161). b.1820; d.1864.

159. 1842   Captain John ('Jack', also 'Leicestershire' or 'Black') White, of Park Hall, Hayfield near Stockport and Dale Ford, Sandiway. b.1790; Capt., Derbyshire Yeo.Cav.(N.High Peak Troop), 1819; r.1865; d.1866.   –

160. 1842   Thomas Bache Booth of Twemlow Hall, later of Pen-y-Bryn, Llangollen. b.1815; r.1865.   1854

161. 1843   Thomas Langford Brooke of Mere New Hall, 2nd s.of Thomas Langford Brooke (60), br.of Peter Langford Brooke (104) and f.of Commander Thomas Langford Brooke (158†) b.1794; Capt., Ches.Yeo.; d.1848.   –

162. 1843   Captain the Hon. Robert ('Bobby') Needham, 12th Royal Lancers, 2nd s.of 2nd Earl of Kilmorey and gr.nep.of Lord Kilmorey (32). b.1816; Maj., 1847; r.1847; d.1899.   –

163. 1844   Francis Elcocke ('Frank') Massey of Poole Hall and later also of Carrickfergus, Co.Antrim. b.1822; Capt., R.Ches.Militia; H.S.(Co.Antrim)1875; d.1897.   1856

164. 1844   John Sidebottom of Harewood Lodge, Mottram-in-Longdendale. b.1793; r.(Ru.XI)1863; d.unm.1865.   1857

165. 1845   Thomas Townley Townley-Parker of Cuerden Hall, Preston and Astley Hall, Chorley, eld.s.of Robert Townley-Parker (106). b.1822; m.nie.170; r.1850; d.1906.   –

166. 1845   Thomas Lyon of Appleton Hall. b.1823; Capt., Ches.Yeo.; r.1852; d.1855.   –

167. 1845   William Worthington of The Brockhurst, Leftwich, also of Newton Park, Staffs. b.1799; Lt., Ches.Yeo.; r.1859; d.1871.   1858

168. 1846   Sir John Gerard, 12th Bart. of Wintle Hall, Lancs. and New Hall, later of Lower Grove House, Roehampton. b.1804; Col., 3rd.R.Lancs. Militia; r.1850; *d.s.p.* 1854.   –

169. 1846   Captain Harry Heron of Manley Hall, e.s.of General Peter Heron (83). b.1809; Ensign 9th (E.Norfolk) Regt., 1827; Capt., 1835–38; Master of Own Harriers; r.1856; d.1874.   –

170. 1846   Captain (John) Ireland Blackburne, Jnr., 5th Dragoon Guards, of Hale Hall, Lancs. b.1817; r.1846 (on election); Col., S.Lancs. Militia; M.P. (S.W.Lancashire 1875–85); d.1893.

171. 1847   Sir Thomas George Hesketh, 5th Bart. of Rufford New Hall, Lancs., later of Easton Neston, Northants, o.s,of Sir Thomas Hesketh, Bart. (119). b.1825; H.S.(Lancs.)1848; Col., Lancs. Militia; Lt.-Col., Lancs.Rifle Vols.; M.P.(Preston 1862–72); assumed additional surname of Fermor, 1867; r.1869; d.1872.   1859

172. 1847   Cornet John Wilson Fox, 12th Prince of Wales's Own Lancers, of Statham Lodge,Lymm. b.*c.*1825; Capt., 1850; Capt., Ches.Yeo.; r.1871.   1860   Lady Theodora Grosvenor, 9th dau.114

173. 1847	John Hurleston ('Jack') Leche of Carden Park and Stretton Hall, eld.s.of John Leche (139). b.1827; m.1stly, dau.79; Cornet, Ches.Yeo.; Capt., R. Ches. Militia; H.S.1853; r.1868; d.1903.	1861	Miss Annie Shakerley, 5th dau.138
174. 1848 ▷—	Hugh Lupus Grosvenor, Earl Grosvenor, M.P. of Eaton Hall and Stack Lodge, Sutherland, and later for a time Calveley Hall (Ten), later 3rd Marquess of Westminster, 10th Bart., and in 1874 created Duke of WESTMINSTER, K.G., P.C., A.D.C., eld. surv.s.of Lord Westminster (114). Later also residing at Grosvenor House, Cliveden House, Berks., Halkyn Castle and Lochmore Lodge, Sutherland. b.1825; M.P. (Chester 1847–69); Master of the Horse, 1880–85; Hon.Col., Queen's Westminster Rifle Vol.; Hon.Col., Ches.Yeo.; Yeo.A.D.C., 1881; H.M.L.L. 1883–99 & (Co.London)1889–99; Jockey Club; Leading Owner, Jockey Club Rules, 1886, 1899 & other years; Won Derby Sks., 1880 (Bend Or), 1882 (Shotover), 1886 (Ormonde), 1899 (Flying Fox); d.1899.	1862	Lady Gertrude Talbot, 3rd dau.190
175. 1848	(George) Harry Grey, 7th Earl of Stamford and 3rd and last Earl of Warrington, of Dunham Massey Hall, Enville Hall and Bradgate Park, Leics., occasionally residing at Newmarket, o.s.of Lord Grey of Groby (120). b.1827; Capt., Ches.Yeo.; Col., Lancs.Rifle Volunteers; Master (Albrighton 1848/49, 1855/56, & Quorn 1856–63); Jockey Club; National Hunt Committee; r.1869; *d.s.p.*1883.	—	
176. 1848	* (John) Randolphus de Trafford of Croston Hall, Preston, Lancs., 3rd s.of Sir Thomas de Trafford, Bart. (89) and br.of Humphrey (144*), Cecil (187) and Augustus de Trafford (192). b.1820; r.1852; d.1883.	—	
177. 1850	Captain the Hon. Thomas Grenville Cholmondeley, 43rd Regt., of Abbot's Moss, 2nd s.of Lord Delamere (55). b.1818; Lt.-Col., R.Cheshire Militia; Hon.Col., 3rd Bn., Cheshire Regt.; d.1883.	1864	Hon. Elizabeth Egerton, eld.dau.131
178. 1851	Richard Christopher Naylor of Hooton Hall and also later of Kelmarsh Hall, Northants., s.of John Naylor of Hartford Hill. b.1814; H.S.1856; r.1861; Won Derby Sks., 1863 (Macaroni); Master (Pytchley 1872–74); d.1899.	—	
179. 1852	Colonel the Hon. James Yorke Scarlett, 5th Dragoon Guards, of Bank Hall, Burnley, yr.s.of 1st Baron Abinger. b.1799; Cornet, 18th Hussars, 1818; Maj, 5th Dragoon Guards, 1830; M.P.(Guildford 1836–41); Eastern Campaign, 1854/55, Brig.-Gen., Heavy Cavalry Brigade, Maj.-Gen., 1854, Alma, Balaklava, Inkerman, Tchernaya, Siege and Capture of Sebastopol; K.C.B., 1855, Sardinian and Turkish Medals; Cdr., *Légion d'Honneur* (France); Knt. of the Medjidie (Turkey); Adjutant-General, 1860; G.O.C.-in-C., Aldershot, 1865; Gen., G.C.B.,1869; *d.s.p.* 1871.	1865	Miss Gertrude Lascelles, 2nd dau.181
180. 1852	Charles John Mare, M.P. of Broomlands, Nantwich and Orchard Yard, Blackwall, n.s.of M.Mare of Hatherton Hall, Nantwich. b.1815, M.P.(Plymouth 1852–53); r.1857; d.1898.	—	

181. 1853   Hon. Arthur Lascelles of Norley Bank, 5th s.of 2nd Earl of Harewood. b.1807; m.4th dau.91; Maj., Ches.Yeo.; r.1874; d.1880.   1866   Hon. Catharine Leicester-Warren, eld.dau.145

182. 1853   Arthur Henry Davenport, 1st Life Guards, of Capesthorne Hall, gs.of Davies Davenport (37). b.1832; Capt., Ches.Yeo.; H.S.1859; d.unm.1867.   –

183. 1854   Thomas ('Tom') Aldersey of Aldersey Hall and Spurstow Hall. b.1832; H.S.1862; Capt., Ches.Militia; r.1875; d.1899.   1867   Hon. Margaret Leicester-Warren, 4th dau.145

184. 1856   Charles George Cholmondeley of Cholmondeley Castle and Kirklington Park, Oxford and later Malpas Lodge, Torquay, eld.s. of Lord William Henry Cholmondeley later 3rd Marquess of Cholmondeley. b.1829; Capt., Ches.Yeo., late R. Cheshire Militia; *d.v.p.*1869.   1868   Miss Amy Lascelles, 5th dau.181

185. 1856   Lieutenant (Thomas) Henry Lyon, R.N. of Appleton Hall, 2nd br.of Thomas Lyon ((166). b.1825; m.1stly, 3rd dau.134; Capt., Ches.Militia; H.S.1867; r.1876; d.1914.   1873   Miss Mabel Dorothy Brooke, 2nd dau.151

186. 1857   †Hon. Wilbraham Egerton of Rostherne Manor and Tatton Park, later 2nd Baron Egerton of Tatton and 1st and last Viscount SALFORD and Earl EGERTON OF TATTON, P.C., K.G.St.John, eld.s. of Lord Egerton of Tatton (132†). b.1832; M.P.(N.Cheshire 1858–68 & Mid.Cheshire 1868–83); Lt., Ches.Yeo., 1851, Hon.Maj., 1881; H.M.L.L.1900–06; *d.s.p.m.* 1909.   1869   Miss Jessie Dixon, 3rd dau.150

187. 1857   *(Charles) Cecil de Trafford of Hartford Manor, 4th s.of Sir Thomas de Trafford, Bart.(89). and br.of Sir Humphrey (144*), John (176) and Augustus de Trafford (192). b.1821; Cor., Ches.Yeo.; Secretary, 1870–1878; d.unm.1878.   1870   Miss Beatrice Sarah Cholmondeley, eld. dau.177, m.s.115

188. 1858   William John Legh of Lyme Park, later 1st Baron NEWTON, nep.of Thomas Legh (107). b.1828; Capt., 21st Fusiliers; Eastern Campaign: Inkerman; M.P.(S.Lancashire 1859–65 & E.Lancashire 1868–85); Lt.-Col., Lancs.Hussars; d.1898.   1871   Miss Cecely Egerton yr.dau.130 (2nd Term)

189. 1859   Henry Reginald ('Regie') Corbet of Adderley Hall and later for a time of Sandiford Lodge, Delamere and then Dale Ford, s.of Richard Corbet, 2nd s.of Sir Andrew Corbet, 1st Bart. of Moreton Corbet. b.1832; Master (Adderley Harriers, 1849); m.e.dau.130; H.S.(Salop.)1892; d.1902.   1872   Hon. Hester Cotton, yr.dau.157; m.228

190. 1860   (Henry) John (aka The English Pope) Chetwynd-Talbot, Rear-Admiral the 18th Earl of Shrewsbury and Waterford and 3rd Earl Talbot of Alton Towers and Ingestre Hall, Staffs. b.1803; M.P.(Hertford 1830–31, Armagh 1831, Dublin 1831–32 & S.Staffordshire 1837–49); Lord-in-Waiting, 1852; Hereditary High Steward of Ireland; Capt., Hon. Corps of Gentlemen-at-Arms, 1858–59; Vice-Admiral, 1861; Admiral, (ret.list) 1865; Navarino; C.B.; P.C.; Naval A.D.C.; Lt.-Col., Staffs.Militia; Knt. of St.Louis and Knt. of St.Anne, 2nd class, (Russia), Knt. of the Redeemer (Greece); d.1868.   –

191. 1861	†Captain Philip le Belward Egerton, later Sir Philip le B. Grey-Egerton, 11th Bart. of Oulton Park, e.s.of Sir Philip Grey-Egerton, Bart.(130). b.1833; 2nd Bn. Rifle Bde., 1852–55, Capt., 1855; Eastern Campaign, medal and clasps, Alma, Sebastopol; Coldstream Regt. of Foot Guards, 1857–61; Maj., R.Cheshire Militia; Hon.Col., 4th Bn., Ches.Regt.; d.1891.	1875	Lady Elizabeth Grosvenor, eld.dau.174
192. 1863	*Captain Augustus Henry ('Gus') de Trafford, 1st Royal Dragoons, of Hartford Manor and later also Haselour Hall, Tamworth, Staffs., 5th s.of Sir Thomas de Trafford, Bart.(89) and br.of Sir Humphrey (144*), John (176) and Cecil de Trafford (187*). b.1823; r.1876; d.1895.	1874	Miss Ruth Lascelles, 7th dau.181
193. 1863	Colonel Charles Hosken France-Hayhurst of Bostock Hall, nep.of James France (109) and gs.of John Hosken Harper (118). b.1832; Capt., 77th Regt.; m.1stly, sis.205, 2ndly sis.231; Secretary, 1865–1870; Lt.-Col., Cmdg. & Hon.Col., 3rd Bn., Cheshire.Regt.; Lt.-Col., R.Cheshire Militia; H.S.1879; d.1914.	1876	Miss Essex Cholmondeley, dau.177, m.217
194. 1864	†Piers Egerton Warburton of The Dene, Northwich and later Arley Hall, o.s.of Rowland Eyles Egerton Warburton (125). b.1839; Col., Ches.Yeo.; Comd.9th Yeo.Bde.; M.P.(Mid. Cheshire 1876–85); r.1912; d.1914.	1877	Miss Dulcibella Legh, e.dau.188
195. 1865	William ('Willie') Tomkinson, Junior of Doddlespool Hall, Betley, eld.s.of Lieutenant-Colonel William Tomkinson (133) and gr.s.of of Thomas Tarleton, Jnr. (67). b.1839; Capt., Ches. Militia; *d.s.p.* 1870.	–	
196. 1865	(John) Bolton Littledale, s.of Thomas Littledale of West Derby, of Sandiway Bank, Hartford. b.*c.*1818; d.1889.	1878	Hon. Hester Cotton, (2nd Term)
197. 1865	*Lord Richard de Aquila ('Dick') Grosvenor, M.P., of Saighton Grange, later 1st Baron STALBRIDGE, P.C., F.R.G.S., of Motcombe House, Shaftesbury, and afterwards Stalbridge Park, Dorset, 4th s.of Lord Westminster (114) and br.of Lord Grosvenor (174*). b.1837; M.P.(Flintshire 1861–86); Vice-Chamberlain of the Household, 1872–1874; Patronage Secretary to the Treasury and Liberal Chief Whip, 1880–85; Hon.Col., Dorset Yeo.; r.1894; d.1912.	1879	Hon. Sybil Cholmondeley, gr.dau.55 & sis.240
198. 1866	Captain Edmund Waldegrave ('Puffles') Park Yates of Ince Hall and later also Sandiway Lodge. b.1836; Cornet, 3rd Dragoon Guards, Indian Mutiny: Siege of Delhi; assumed additional surname of Yates, 1857; Capt., lst Royal Dragoons; Lieut., Lancs.Hussars; Chairman, M.F.H.A., 1891; d.as a result of an accident in the hunting field, 1896.	1880	Miss (Susannah) Maud Mainwaring, 3rd.g-dau.81
199. 1867	(Thomas) William Langford Brooke of Mere New Hall, Royal Horse Guards, o.s.of Commander Thomas John Langford Brooke, R.N.(158). b.1843; Capt., Ches.Yeo.; d.unm.1872.	–	
200. 1868	Arthur Hugh Smith-Barry, M.P. of Marbury Hall, 20, Hill St., Mayfair and Fota Island, later 1st and last Baron BARRYMORE, P.C., e.s.of James Hugh Smith-Barry (147). b.1843; Lt., Ches. Yeo.; M.P.(Co.Cork 1867–74 & S.Huntingdonshire 1886–1900); H.S.1883; H.S.(Co.Cork)1886; *d.s.p.m.*1925.	1881	Miss Emma Sophia Mainwaring, eld.g-dau.81

201. 1868   †Captain Geoffrey Joseph Shakerley, Junior, of Belmont Hall and   1882   Miss Blanche Helen
             Butterton Hall, Staffs., later Pimley Manor, Salop. and   Antrobus,
             afterwards Grove House, Warwick, s.of Geoffrey Shakerley (138).   g–dau.126
             b.1832; Captain, Royal Artillery; Crimean War; Lieut.-Colonel;
             r.1904; d.1913.

202. 1869   George Baillie-Hamilton-Arden, Lieutenant-Colonel Lord   1884
             Binning, late Royal Horse Guards, of Eaton Banks, Tarporley
             (afterwards Arderne Hall), later 11th Earl of Haddington,
             K.T., A.D.C. of Tyninghame House, East Lothian and
             Mellerstain, Kelso. b.1827; m.nie.20; assumed additional
             surname of Arden, 1858; H.S.1871; Hon.Col., Lothian &
             Border Horse, T.D.; H.M.L.L. (Haddington) 1876–1917;
             Yeo.A.D.C.(to 3 monarchs); V.-L.; Brig.-Gen., Queen's
             Bodyguard for Scotland (Royal Company of Archers);
             Member (292), Royal Caledonian Hunt Club (1858–91);
             Joint M.F.H.(Berwickshire 1876–86); d.1917.

203. 1869   James Hugh Smith-Barry of Louth, of Marbury Hall when in   1885
             Cheshire, and later of Stowell Park, Wilts. and also of Fota
             Island, yr.s.of James Hugh Smith-Barry (147) and yr.br.of
             Arthur Smith-Barry (200). b.1845; Ensign, 1st (Grenadier)
             Regt. of Foot Guards., 1865–69; Capt., R.Cheshire Militia;
             H.S.(Co.Louth)1870; m.sis.218; r.1896; d.1927.

204. 1869 ⬦➤ Henry James Tollemache of Dorfold Hall, gs.of Rev.James   1883
             Tomkinson (98). b.1846; Secretary, 1879–1887; M.P.
             (W.Cheshire 1881–85 & Eddisbury 1885–1906); r.1907;
             Maj., Ches.Yeo.; Honorary Member, 1925; d.1939.

205. 1869 ⬦➤ Cudworth Halsted Poole of Marbury Hall, Marbury cum   1886
             Quoisley, nep.of Domville Poole (96). b.1847; H.S.1880;
             Secretary, 1887–1897; *d.s.p.m.*1906.

206. 1870   Charles John Chetwynd-Talbot, late 1st Life Guards, of Ingestre   –
             Hall, Stafford and Shavington Hall, Crewe, 19th Earl of
             Shrewsbury and Waterford and 4th Earl Talbot, eld.s.of Lord
             Shrewsbury (190). b.1830; Hereditary High Steward of Ireland;
             M.P.(Stafford 1857–59, N.Staffordshire 1859–65 & Stamford
             1868); P.C.; Maj., Staffs.Yeo.; Capt., Hon.Corps of Gentlemen-
             at-Arms; Jt.Master (N.Staffs., 1869–71); d.1877.

207. 1870   William Bromley Davenport of Capesthorne Hall and Baginton   –
             Hall, Coventry, o.s.of Rev. Walter Davenport Bromley of
             Wootton Hall, Staffs., who had assumed the additional surname
             of Bromley, and gs.of Davies Davenport (37). b.1821; Crimean
             War, att. Coldstream Guards; Lt.-Col., Staffs.Yeo.; M.P.(N.
             Warwickshire 1864–84); authorized to discontinue surname of
             Davenport before that of Bromley and to take the surname of
             Davenport in addition to and after that of Bromley; d.1884.

208. 1870   Thomas Horatio Marshall of Hartford Beach, later of   –
             Bryn-y-Coed, Bangor. b.1833; Lt., Ches.Yeo.; Lt.-Col.,
             Ches. Regt., Col., 3rd Vol.Bn., Cheshire Regt.; V.D.;
             r.1882; C.B.; Knt.Bach., 1906; d.1920.

209. 1872   James ('Jim', 'Jimmie' or 'Jamie') Tomkinson of Halkin St.,   1887
             S.W.1, later of Willington Hall and also Brunswick House,
             Cromer, 2nd s.of Lieut.-Colonel William Tomkinson (133) and
             br.of William Tomkinson (195). b.1840; Maj., Ches.Yeo.; H.S.
             1887; M.P.(Crewe 1900–10); P.C., 1909; d.from fall in House of
             Commons Ch., 1910.

210. 1872   Captain Edward Townshend of Wincham Hall, late 5th Foot, gs.   –
             of Edward Venables Townshend (82). b.1835; Lt., Ches.Yeo.;
             d.from fall over wire, 1885.

211. 1872   †Hon. Robert Wellington Stapleton-Cotton, later 3rd Viscount   –
             Combermere and 8th Bart., one-time of Combermere Abbey
             and of Chaseley House, Rugeley, e.s.of Lord Combermere (157).
             b.1845; Cor., Ches.Yeo.; Lt., Salop.Yeo.; r.1882; m.2ndly, div.
             w.of 205; d.1898.

212. 1873   John ('Johnnie') Baskervyle-Glegg of Old Withington Hall, gs.of   –
             John Baskervyle Glegg (94). b.1844; H.S.1876; d.1877.

213. 1874   Major George Dixon, late 25th King's Own Borderers, later 1st   1888
             Bart. of Astle Hall, eld.s.of Lieut.-Col. John Dixon(150).
             b.1842; Fenian Raid, 1866, Canadian Medal; H.S.1881; V–L.;
             m.wid.212; Col., Ches.Rifle Vol.Regt.; d.1924.

214. 1875   Captain Egerton ('Eggie') Leigh of West Hall, High Leigh,   1889
             Jodrell Hall and Twemlow Hall, later resident in London.
             b.1843; Cor., 1862, Capt., 1st Royal Dragoons; A.D.C. to G.O.C.,
             Cav.Bde. at The Curragh; Hon. Lt.-Col., Ches. Militia; H.S.1882;
             r.1924; d.1928.

215. 1875   Samuel Henry ('Sam') Sandbach of Broxton Old Hall, later of   1890
             Cherry Hill, Malpas. b.1846; Lt., Ches.Yeo.; r.1912; d.1927.

216. 1876   Christopher Kay of Davenham Hall and later Ravenscroft Hall,   1891
             and formerly of Winsford Lodge, Middlewich. b.1823; Maj.
             Ches.Yeo.; H.S.1891; d.1897.

217. 1876   Thomas Egerton Tatton of Wythenshawe Hall, eld.s.of Thomas   –
             William Tatton (148). b.1846; m.dau.177; r.1884; d.1924.

218. 1876 ▷═ Lowry Egerton ('Coly') Cole, Viscount Cole, later 4th Earl of   1892   Miss Mildred
             Enniskillen, K.P., of Florence Court, Co.Fermanagh,   Henrietta
             also of Cassia Lodge, Whitegate, Heyesmere, Hartford and   Cholmondeley,
             Pettypool Hall, Sandiway (Ten.) and Cuddington Grange for a   5th dau.177, m.246
             time. b.1845; Lieut., Rifle Bde., 1865–68; H.S.(Co.Fermanagh)
             1870; M.P.(Enniskillen 1880–85); Hon.Col., 4th Bn., Royal
             Inniskilling Fusiliers; Steward, Turf Club (The Curragh),
             1896–1921; National Hunt Committee; r.1920; d.1924.

219. 1877   Lieutenant-Colonel Henry Martin Cornwall Legh, Grenadier   1893
             Guards, of High Legh Hall, nep.of George Cornwall Legh (137).
             b.1839; H.S.1884; m.5th g-dau.80; d.1904.

220. 1878 ▷━━○ † Reginald ('Regie') Corbet, Jnr. of Adderley Hall and The Pool   1894
Farm, Adderley, also for a time Grangewood House,
Ashby-de-ia-Zouch, eld.s.of Reginald Corbet (189†).
b.1857; Maj., Salop.Yeo.; Col., 1st Vol.Bn., Shrops.L.I.;
r.1923; d.1945.

221. 1878   William Gilbert Baskervyle-Glegg of Old Withington Hall,   –
yr.br.of John Baskervyle-Glegg (212). b.1849; d.1882.

222. 1879   George Henry Hugh ('Rock') Cholmondeley, Earl of   1895
Rocksavage of Cholmondeley Castle, later 4th Marquess of
Cholmondeley, o.s.of Charles Cholmondeley (184). Afterwards
also of Houghton Hall, Norfolk and some time of Wroughton
House, Swindon, Wilts. b.1858; Sub-Lieut., R.Cheshire
Militia; 2nd Lt., Ches.Yeo.; Lord Great Chamberlain of England
1901–10; P.C.; National Hunt Committee; High Goal Polo Player;
M.H.(Lord Rocksavage's 1883–85); National Hunt Committee;
r.1901; re-elected 1908; d.following a hunting accident, 1923.

223. 1879   Sir Philip Tatton ('Harry') Mainwaring, 4th Bart. of Peover   –
Hall, gs.of Sir Henry Mainwaring, Bart.(81) and also of Thomas
William Tatton (95). b.1838; r.1889; d.1906.

224. 1881   Baron William Henry von Schröder of The Rookery, Worleston,   1896
and also of Attadale, by Isle of Skye, 3rd s.of Baron John
Henry von Schröder of Holstein, Mecklenburg and Hamburg.
b.1841; Master of Harriers; H.S.1888; d.1912.

225. 1881   Captain Edward Thomas Davenant ('Jack') Cotton, late   1897
Royal Horse Artillery, of Reaseheath Hall, also sometimes
res. at Shallcross Manor, Taxal, s.of Right Rev.Dr.George
Edward Lynch Cotton and gr.nep. of Thomas Jodrell
Phillips-Jodrell, cos. & heir of Frank Jodrell (73), and also
of Edward (97), Rev.James (98) and Lieut.-Col. William
Tomkinson (133), and descended from 3rd br.of Sir Robert
Cotton (8). b.1847; Lieut., Royal Artillery, 1868; Hon. Secretary,
Calpe Hunt, Gibraltar, 1870; M.P.(Wirral 1885–1900);
Col., 2nd Ches. R.E.(Railway Vol.), 1888–1908; assumed
additional surname of Jodrell, 1890; C.B.; Col., D.A.D., T.A.,
War Office, 1906–12; K.C.B., 1912; d.1917.

226. 1881   † Lord Arthur (Hugh) Grosvenor of Broxton Lower Hall,   1898   Lady Constance
2nd s.of Duke of Westminster (174†). b.1860; Capt.,   Sibell Grosvenor,
Ches.Yeo.; Maj., 21st Coy., Imp.Yeo., S.Africa, Queen's Medal   niece, g.-dau.174
(clasp); Lt.-Col., Ches.Yeo., 1905, Hon.Col., 1910; Lt.Col.,
Cheshire Vol.Regt.; T.D.; d.1929.

227. 1882   Hon. Lyonel Plantagenet ('Tolly') Tollemache of Peckforton   –
Castle, gs.of Lord Tollemache (122). b.1860; r.1889; *d.v.p.*1902.

228. 1882   Lord Alexander Victor ('Dandy') Paget of The Oaklands, Bunbury,   –
3rd s.of 2nd Marquess of Anglesey. b.1839; m.yr.dau.157;
Hon.Lt., Royal Naval Artillery Volunteers (Liverpool Brigade);
d.1896.

229. 1882 | Charles Edward Thornycroft of Ollerton Lodge, Knutsford, later of Thornycroft Hall, Siddington. b.1849; Lt., R.Ches. Militia; Sub.Lt.,Ches.Yeo.; r.1908; d.1927. | 1899 | Miss Dorothy Lynch Cotton-Jodrell, dau.225

230. 1883 | Humphrey Francis de Trafford, later 3rd Bart., of Trafford Park and Hill Crest, Market Harborough, eld.s.of Sir Humphrey de Trafford (144). b.1862; Maj. & Hon.Col., Lancs.Hussars; r.1926; d.1929. | 1900 | Miss Jenyns (Davenham)

231. 1884 | (William) Otho (Nicholson) Shaw of Sand Hey, Hoylake and Bishopswood, Herefordshire and later of Wyastone Leys, Monmouth, formerly of Arrowe Park, Birkenhead. b.1846; F.R.G.S.; Maj., Ches.Yeo.; r.1904; d.1910. | 1901 | Miss Elizabeth Helen France-Hayhurst, niece, dau.193

232. 1884 | *Captain the Hon. Alan de Tatton Egerton, M.P. of Rostherne Manor and Taplow Cottage, Bucks., 3rd s.of Lord Egerton of Tatton (131) and br.of Lord Egerton of Tatton (186*), later 3rd Baron Egerton of Tatton of Tatton Park. b.1845; Capt., Rifle Bde; Maj., Ches.Yeo.; M.P.(Mid.Cheshire 1883–85 & Knutsford 1885–1906); V.-L.; d.1920. | 1902 | Miss Dorothy Egerton-Warburton, eld.dau.194

233. 1884 | Delves Louis Broughton, later 10th Bart., of Doddington Hall, e.s.of Sir Henry Delves Broughton, 9th Bart. and gs.of Rev. Sir Henry Broughton (74). b.1857; Lieut., N.Staffordshire Regt.; d.1914. | 1903 | Miss Olive Harriett Cotton-Jodrell, 2nd dau.225, m.nep.211

234. 1885 | Captain John Kennedy, of Brookside, Sandbach and Kirkland, Dumfriesshire. b.1839; Cor., later Capt. 4th Hussars; Capt. 5th Dragoon Guards; Capt.,Ches. Yeo.; Lt.-Col., Ches. (Railway) R.E.Vol.; r.1890; m.4thly, nie.108; d.*p*.1914. | –

235. 1885 | William Bromley-Davenport of Capesthorne Hall and Wootton Hall, Derbyshire, also 1, Belgrave Pl., S.W., later Sir William Bromley-Davenport, K.C.B., C.M.G, C.B.E., D.S.O., T.D., eld.s.of William Bromley Davenport (207). b.1862; Corinthian XI: Maj., Staffs.Yeo.; Lt.-Col., Commd. 4th Bn., Imp.Yeo., S.Africa, D.S.O., des., Queen's Medal (5 clasps); Lt.-Col., Staffs. Yeo., later Hon. Col.; M.P.(Macclesfield 1886–1906); Hon. Lt.-Col., Financial Sec., War Office, 1903–5; Financial Member of Army Council, 1904–5; 1914/18, Brig.-Gen., 22nd Mounted Inf. Brigade, Egypt; Asst.Dir., Labour, France, 1917; Italian Expeditionary Force, 1917–18; Order of Crown (Italy); Croix de Guerre (Belgium); Legion of Honour (France); C.M.G., 1918, C.B.E.(Mil.), 1919, C.B.(Civ.) 1922, K.C.B.(Civ.), 1924; H.M.L.L.1920–49; Hon. Air/Cdre, 610 Sqn., R. Aux. A.F.; d.unm.1949. | 1905 | Lady Lettice Legh, eld.sis.284, m.1stly 255 & 2ndly 292

236. 1889 | †Captain (Philip Henry) Brian Egerton, late Cheshire Regt., later Sir Philip Grey-Egerton, 12th Bart. of Oulton Park, also 12, Berkeley Sq., 2nd s.of Sir Philip Grey-Egerton, Bart. (191).b.1864; Maj., Ches.Yeo.; Secretary,1897–1937; *d.s.p.m.s.*1937. | 1906 | Lady Cecely Arden-Baillie-Hamilton, 4th dau.202 & sis.273

237. 1889 Captain Hugh Edward ('Wobbles') Wilbraham, late 82nd Regt. & 1904 Miss Barbara
E. Lancs. Regt., of Massey's Lodge, Oakmere and later Delamere Elizabeth
Lodge. which became known as Delamere House, gs.of George Tomkinson,
Wilbraham (77). b.1857; later Major, Vol.Bn., Cheshire Regt.; dau.209
M.B.E.(Civ.); O.B.E.(Mil.); d.1930.

238. 1889 ▷━━ William Roylance Court of Newton Manor House, Middlewich, 1907 Lady Lettice
eld.s.of William Roylance Court (156). b.1852; m.sis.268, Cholmondeley,
dau.m.272; Maj., Ches.Yeo.; d.1917. dau.222

239. 1890 *Colonel Henry Tomkinson, 1st Royal Dragoons, for a time of 1908 Miss Joyce
Doddlespool Hall, later of Wynlatan House, Exeter and finally Tomkinson,
The Pole, Ide, 3rd s.of Lieutenant-Colonel William Tomkinson niece, dau.209
(133) and br.of James Tomkinson (209*). b.1842; Ensign,
61st (S.Glos.) Regt., later Capt. & Adjutant, 1861–77,
Bermuda and Canada, Red River Expedition; Bde.Major,
The Curragh, D.A.A.& Q.M.G., Trs., 1st R.Dragoons 1877,
commd, 1891–1896; d.1915.

240. 1891 Hugh ('Hughie') Cholmondeley, Captain the 3rd Baron Delamere, –
late Cheshire Regt., of Vale Royal and later Soysambu, Elementeita,
British East Africa, gs.of Lord Delamere (55). b.1870; Capt.,
Ches.Yeo.; m.1stly, dau.218; Member, Legislative Council,
Kenya Colony; K.C.M.G.; d.1931.

241. 1892 John Bolton ('Bo') Littledale of Sandiway House and later 1909 Miss Vere May
Brookdale, afterwards called Bunbury House, e.s.of Bolton Wilbraham,
Littledale (196). b.1868; Oxford XI (Football); eld.dau.237
1914/18, Capt., R.A.S.C.; d.1942.

242. 1894 Sir Gilbert Greenall, 2nd Bart., afterwards 1st BARON 1911 Miss Sybil Corbet,
DARESBURY, C.V.O., LL.D., of Walton Hall, Warrington dau.220, (2nd Term)
and later of Woolsthorpe, by Belvoir and also Mount Coote,
Co.Limerick. b.1867; Lt., Ches.Yeo.; m.nie.198, au.299;
H.S.1907; Officer of the Order of the Crown (Belgium);
M.F.H. (Belvoir 1896–1912); President, Royal Agricultural
Society, 1910 & 1930; d.1938.

243. 1894 Charles Henry John ('Charlie') Chetwynd-Talbot, 20th Earl of 1910 Miss Corbet,
Shrewsbury and Waterford, 5th Earl Talbot of Ingestre Hall, (1stTerm)
Alton Towers and Shavington Hall, Crewe, o.s.of Lord
Shrewsbury (206). b.1860; Hereditary High Steward of Ireland;
Sub.-Lt., Staffs.Yeo.; Hon.Maj., Royal Welch Fusiliers;
K.C.V.O.; 1914/18, Maj., Remount Depot; d.1921.

244. 1896 Right Hon. Robert Offley Ashburton ('Bob') Crewe-Milnes, 1913 Miss Judith Mimi
2nd Baron Houghton, 1st Earl of CREWE, P.C. of Madeley Poole, dau.257,
Manor, Staffs., Crewe Hall, Crewe House, Curzon St., W., (2nd Term)
Fryston Hall, Ferrybridge and latterly West Horsley Place,
Leatherhead and as a guest at Mentmore, later 1st Earl of
MADELEY and 1st Marquess of CREWE, K.G., P.C.,
nep.of Lord Crewe (146). b.1858; Lt., Yorks.Dragoons; Col.,
Co.London Vol.Regt.; F.S.A.; Lord-in-Waiting, 1886;
Viceroy of Ireland, 1892–95; Lord President of the Council,
1905–08 & 1915–16; Secretary of State for the Colonies,
1908–10; Lord Privy Seal, 1908–11 & 1912–15; Secretary of

State for India, 1910–15; President, Board of Education, 1916;
H.M. Ambassador to French Republic, 1922–28; Sec. of State for
War, 1931; H.M.L.L.(London) 1912–44; Royal Victorian Chain,
1912; Grand Cross, *Légion d'Honneur* (France); Order of White
Eagle, lst class (Serbia); assumed additional surname of Crewe,
1894; Jockey Club, 1895; *d.s.p.m.s.*1944.

245. 1896	Oswald ('Mo') Mosley Leigh of Belmont Hall, for a time of Cassia Lodge and also later Hartford House, at one time giving his address as The Bachelors' Club and in his latter years residing occasionally at The Swan Hotel. b.1864; Capt., Ches. Regt.; Capt., Ches.Yeo; Capt., 22nd Coy., Imp. Yeo., South Africa, Queen's Medal (3 clasps), King's Medal (2 clasps); Maj., Hon. Lt.-Col., Ches.Yeo.; Master & Huntsman (Earl Fitzwilliam's and Island 1907/08, Wexford 1908/12); 1914/18, Lieut.-Col., W. Kent Yeo., Commd. Royal E. Kent Mounted Rifles, 1915; T.D.; d.1949.	1912	Miss Poole, (1st Term)
246. 1897	Captain (Edward) Lee Townshend, late Cheshire Regt., of Gorstage Hall, o.s.of Edward Townshend (210). b.1868; Lt., Ches.Yeo.; m.dau.177; d.1914.	–	
247 1899	Lieutenant-Colonel Henry Lewis Brooke ('Harry') Langford-Brooke of Mere New Hall, nep.of Thomas Langford-Brooke (158). b.1842; Capt., 60th Rifles; assumed surnames of Langford-Brooke in *lieu* of White, 1874; Maj., Hon.Lt-Col., Cameron Highlanders; d.1907.	–	
248 1900	Sir Hugh Richard Arthur ('Bend Or' or 'Benny') Grosvenor, 2nd Duke of Westminster, 11th Bart., Royal Horse Guards, of Eaton Hall, Halkyn Castle and Grosvenor House, also of Lochmore Lodge,later residing at Bourdon House, Davies St. and also Fortwilliam House, Co. Waterford, gs.of Duke of Westminster (174). b.1879; 2nd Lt., Ches.Yeo., 1898, att. 15th King's Hussars (when styled Viscount Belgrave); Lt., Royal Horse Guards; A.D.C. to High Commissioner of S. Africa and Governor of Cape of Good Hope, 1898–99; S.Africa, A.D.C. to C.-in-C., 1899–1900, des., Queen's Medal (5 clasps); G.C.V.O., 1907; Master of Own Boar-Hounds, (Mimizan & Saint-Saëns, France, 1911/14 & *c.*1928–39); 1914/18, Maj., Ches. Yeo., Extra A.D.C. to C.-in-C., Overseas Forces, T./Cdr., R.N.V.R., Commd. Armoured Motor Cars, France, Ypres, des., and N.Africa, des., D.S.O.; P.A., Controller, Mechnical Dept., Min. of Munitions, 1917; Hon.Col., Ches.Yeo., 1917–46; Hon.Col., 16th Bn., Co.London Regt.; Order of Isabel the Catholic, 1st class, (Spain); Cdr., *Légion d'Honneur* (France); Gold Medal of Mohamed Aly (Egypt); H.M.L.L.1906–20; Jockey Club, 1903; National Hunt Committee, 1901; *d.s.p.m.s.*1953.	–	
249. 1901	Captain Hubert Malcolm Wilson of The Hermitage, Holmes Chapel and later Barmere, Bickley (Ten.). b.1860; M.F.H.(Ledbury 1899–1901); Lt.-Col., Ches.Yeo.; 1914/18, Egypt, des., O.B.E. (Mil.), *Cavaliere, Ordine Militare di Savoia* & Asiago Plateau Medal (Italy); r.1915; re-elected 1919; r.1936; d.1939.	1935	Miss Elizabeth Barbour, dau.262, m.2ndly 307

250. 1902   Captain William Francis Elcocke ('Billy') Massey, late W.Yorks.   1920   Miss Barbara
Regt., of Heathfield, Hatherton, Higginsfield, Cholmondeley   Francesca
and afterwards Nether House, Market Harborough, o.s.of Frank   Wilbraham,
Massey (163). b.1873; Lt., Ches.Yeo.; Lt., 22nd Coy., Imp.Yeo.,   dau.237
S.Africa, Queen's Medal; 1939/45, Maj.; r.1955.

251. 1904   John ('Johnnie') Baskervyle-Glegg of Wistaston Hall, Nantwich,   1919   Miss Barbara de
also Withington Hall and Gayton Hall, Neston, o.s.of John   Knoop, dau.269
Baskervyle-Glegg (212). b.1876; 2nd Lt., Ches.Yeo.;
1914/18, Lieut., Montgomeryshire Yeo.; r.1920; d.1954.

252. 1904   Lieutenant-Colonel Hugh Cecil Cholmondeley, C.B., of Abbot's   –
Moss Hall and of Edstaston, Wem, Salop., eld.s.of Thomas
Cholmondeley (177). b.1852; Rifle Brigade, Afghan, 1878–79,
(medal & clasp); Col., London Rifle Brigade, 1890–1901;
cmdd City Imp.Vol.(Mounted Inf.), S.Africa, des (2),
Queen's Medal, (6 clasps); 1914/18, Brigadier-General, cmdg.
173rd Inf.Bde., Staff Officer, Volunteer Services, Western Cmd.,
C.B.E.; M.F.H.(N.Shropshire 1920–1925); r.1920; d.1941.

253. 1905   (George) Littleton Dewhurst of Beechwood, Lymm and   –
Aberuchill Castle, Perthshire, eld.s.of George Bakewell
Dewhurst of Oughtrington Park. b.1863; H.S.1904; d.1907.

254. 1907   Captain Bentley Lyonel John ('Tolly') Tollemache, 3rd Baron   1921   Lady Ursula
Tollemache, late Cheshire Regt. & K.O.S.B., of Peckforton   Grosvenor, dau.248
Castle, Helmingham Hall and later South Cliff, Eastbourne,
eld.s.of Lyonel Tollemache (227). b.1883; S.Africa (2 clasps);
1914/18, Temp.Lt.-Cdr., R.N.V.R.; Pres., National Bridge
Assoc.; *d.s.p.m.*1955.

255. 1907   †Captain John Egerton-Warburton, Scots Guards, of   R.o.H.
Arley Hall, e.s.of Piers Egerton Warburton (194†). b.1883;
2nd Lt., Ches.Yeo.; 1914/18, Capt. & Adj., R.Fus.
(City of London Bn.); m.eld.sis.283; d.of wounds, *s.p.m.*1915.

256. 1907   Lieutenant-Colonel Hubert Cornwall Legh of High   1922   Miss Margaret Alice
Legh Hall and Chyknell, Bridgnorth, gs.of George John Legh   Leicester-Warren,
(63). b.1858; Maj., King's Royal Rifle Corps; Lt.-Col., City of   dau.267
London Regt, (Reserve of Officers); *d.s.p.*1926.

257. 1907   Bryan Davies Poole of Marbury Hall, Marbury cum Quoisley,   1923   Miss Barbara
eld.s.of Colonel Bryan George Davies-Cooke of Colomendy,   Grosvenor,
and nep.of Cudworth Poole (205). b.1861; assumed surname   2nd dau.226
of Poole in *lieu* of Cooke, 1907; Capt., Denbigh & Merioneth
Militia; d.1930.

258. 1908   †Captain Frederick Charles France-Hayhurst, late Royal Welch   R.o.H.
Fusiliers, of Bostock Hall, eld.s.of Charles Hosken
France- Hayhurst (193). b.1872; 1914/18, France,
Lieutenant-Colonel Royal Welsh Fusiliers, killed in action, 1915.

259. 1909   Robert Henry Grenville ('Peter') Tatton of Wythenshawe Hall,   1924   Miss (Alice)
later of Rodesyde, Chelford, Carden Bank, Tilston, Roundstone,   Kathleen Mary
Connemara, Wigmore, Walmer, Kent, Salterswell House,   Dixon, g-dau.150

Tarporley and Wynbunbury Cliffe, Cheshire, o.s.of Thomas
Tatton (217). b.1883; Lt., Ox. & Bucks.L.I.,(Vol.); 1914/18,
Capt., att. Connaught Rangers; H.S.1936; d.1962.

| 260. 1910 | Charles William ('Charlie') Tomkinson of Willington Hall, eld.s.of James Tomkinson (209). b.1877; Maj., Ches.Yeo., 1914/18, Maj., Ches.Yeo., Egypt, France; H.S.1927; V.-L.; d.1939. | 1925 | Miss Olivia Dewhurst, e.dau.277 |

261. 1912 ▷━ Captain William ('Will' or 'Willie') Higson, late 4th Hussars, of Oakmere Hall and afterwards Burton Lazars Hall, Melton Mowbray. b.1863; 1914/18: Col.; d.1945.

1926   Miss (Elizabeth Ann) Betsann Dewhurst, yr.dau.277

262. 1912   Major Robert Barbour of Bankhead, Broxton, later of Bolesworth Castle. b.1876; Lt, Ches.Yeo.; Lt., 21st Coy., Imp. Yeo., S.Africa, Queen's Medal; Maj., Ches. Yeo.; 1914/18; H.S.1925; killed out riding on his estate by his runaway horse, 1928.

1927   Miss Bryony Johnson

263. 1912   Captain (Richard) Norman (Harrison) Verdin of Stoke Hall, Nantwich, formerly of Darnhall Hall and later Garnstone Castle, Herefordshire. b.1877; m.sis.262; Capt., later Lt.-Col., Ches.Yeo.; 1914/18; H.S.1933; d.1956.

1928   Miss Molly Baskervyle-Glegg, dau.251

264. 1915 ◁═━ Captain Geoffrey Egerton-Warburton, late Cheshire Regt., of Grafton Hall, Malpas, formerly of Sandicroft, Gt.Budworth, yr.s.of Piers Egerton Warburton (194). b.1888; Lt., Ches.Yeo.; 1914/18, Maj., Machine Gun Corps, Egypt, des., D.S.O., France; Lt.-Col., Ches Yeo., 1920, T.D.; Hon.Col., Ches.Yeo., 1951; Secretary, 1937–1961; V.-L., 1940; d.1961.

1929   Miss Rachel Verdin, dau.263

265. 1915   Captain William Hosken France-Hayhurst of Bostock Hall, formerly of Davenham Hall, 2nd s.of Charles France-Hayhurst (193). b.1873; 2nd Lt.,Yorks.Dragoons; Capt., Ches.Yeo.; H.S.1929; d.1947.

1930   Miss Baskervyle-Glegg, (2nd Term)

266. 1915   Captain Sir (Henry John) Delves ('Jock') Broughton, 11th Bart. of Doddington Hall, Broughton Hall, Staffs. and 6, Hill St., Mayfair, eld.s.of Sir Louis Broughton (233). b.1883; Lt., N. Staffs. Regt.; 1914/18, Maj., Irish Guards; H.S.(Staffs.)1921; *d.felo per se* 1941.

1931‡
&
1932   Miss Susan Dorothy Ramsden-Jodrell, g.-dau.225

267. 1915   Captain Cuthbert Leicester-Warrren, London Regt., of Tabley House and later Davenport House, Bridgnorth, gs.of Lord de Tabley (145) and 2nd s.of Sir Baldwin Leighton, 8th Bart. b.1877; assumed surnames of Leicester-Warren in *lieu* of patronymic, 1899; 1914/18, 2nd Lt., Ches.Yeo., later Maj., R.A.S.C., M.T.(V.); H.S.1921; r.1938; d.1954.

1933   Miss Betty Catherine Tatton, dau.259

268. 1915 ▷━ Colonel William Hall ('Willie') Walker, T.D., M.P., M.F.H., later 1st and last Baron WAVERTREE, K.G.St.J., of Sandy Brow, Delamere, Sussex Lodge, Regent's Park and Tully House, Kildare and later also of Horsley Hall, Marford, 3rd s.of Sir Andrew Barclay Walker, lst Bart. of Gateacre Grange,

–

‡ *No Presidential Dinner owing to the general demand for National Economy.*

Childwall. b.1856; Col., Lancs. R.F.A., Special Res.,1876–1906;
Hon.Col., King's Liverpool Regt., 1894; Lancs. R.F.A. &
W.Lancs.Div., R.E., 1914/18; M.P.(Widnes 1900–19); Leading
Rider, Pony & Polo Racing Rules, 1888, 1889; Leading Owner,
Jockey Club Rules, 1905, 1907; Won Grand National
Hcp. Ch,, 1896 (The Soarer); Breeder/Owner, winner of The
Derby Sks, 1909 (Minoru, leased to King Edward VII);
Founder and Donor, National Stud, 1916; Turf Club
(The Curragh), 1901; Jockey Club, 1919; sis.m.238, nie.m.272;
*d.s.p.m.l.*1933.

269.	1915	Captain (John Julius) Jersey de Knoop of Calveley Hall (Ten.), fomerly of Cuddington Grange, Sandiway, s.of Baron de Knoop of 31, Rutland Gate, S.W.1. b.1876; Oxford VIII, 1896–97; Maj., Ches.Yeo.; 1914/18, Lt.-Col., Imp. Camel Corps,; killed in action, 1916.	R.o.H.	
270.	1915	Lieutenant-Colonel Charles Lyon, R.A., of Appleton Hall, later of Egerton Terrace, S.W.3., nep.of Thomas Lyon (185). b.1865; Maj., Royal Artillery, ret.1908; 1914/18, Royal Field Artillery, des.; H.S.1924; d.1944.	1934	Miss Priscilla Egerton-Warburton, yr.dau.255, m. 2ndly, eld.s.of 284
271.	1919	*Lieutenant-Colonel Henry Archdale ('Mouse') Tomkinson, D.S.O., 1st Royal Dragoons, later of Sefton Cottage, Newmarket, 3rd s. of James Tomkinson (209) and br.of Charles Tomkinson (260*). b.1881; S.Africa, Queen's Medal (5 clasps); 1914/18, Commd. 10th Hussars, D.S.O. & bar; Commd., lst Royal Dragoons, 1919–23; Brig.-Gen., Commd.3rd Meerut Cavalry Brigade, 1924–27; International Polo Player (*v.*America, 1914 & 1921); Manager H.M.'s Racing & Breeding Studs, 1932–37; National Hunt Committee; d.1937.	1936	Miss Rosamund Broughton, dau.266
272.	1919	Lieutenant-Colonel Douglas Hervey Talbot, 17th Lancers, of Aston Hall. gr.gs.of Henry Hervey-Aston (103) and gr.gr. nep.of Lord Shrewsbury (190). b.1882; S.Africa, Queen's Medal (3 claps); m.dau.238; 1914/18, des., D.S.O., M.C.; d.1927.	–	
273.	1919	Captain the Hon. Henry Robert Baillie-Hamilton Arden of Arderne Hall, 3rd s.of Lord Haddington (202). b.1862; assumed additional and final surname of Arden, 1918; Capt., Coldstream Guards; d.unm.1949.	1937	Miss Rosamund Barbour, yr.dau.262
274.	1919	Hon. Sir Arthur Lyulph Stanley, K.C.M.G., later 5th Baron Stanley of Alderley, 5th Baron Sheffield, 4th Baron Eddisbury and 11th Bart., of Alderley Park and later Penrhôs, Anglesey, gr.gs.of Lord Stanley of Alderley (86). b.1875; S.Africa, Capt., R.Anglesey R.E.Militia; Capt., Ches. Yeo.; M.P.(Eddisbury 1906–10); P.P.S., Postmaster-General; H.S.(Anglesey)1913; Governor of Victoria, 1914–20; Hon.Col., 29th Inf.Regt., Commonwealth Force; d.1931.	–	
275.	1920	Sir Richard Christopher ('Chris') Brooke, 9th Bart. of Norton, Priory, later of The Elms, Abberley, Strathmore, Killiney, and afterwards Oaklands, St.Saviour, Jersey, gs.of Sir Richard Brooke (151). b.1888; Lt., Ches.Yeo.; Lt., Scots Guards; 1914/18; H.S.(Worcs.)1931; d.1981.	1938	Miss Susan Tatton yst.dau.259

276. 1920   Roger Grey, 10th and last Earl of Stamford of Dunham Massey   –
     Hall. Rejected his election. b.1896; 2nd Lt., Territorial
     Force Res.; Hon. Attaché, British Legation, Berne, 1918–19;
     P.P.S., Sec. of State for India, 1922; d.unm.1976.

277. 1921   Major Cyril Dewhurst of Tilstone Lodge (Ten.), and later of   §
     Overdale, Sandiway yr.br.of George Littleton Dewhurst (253). b.1873;
     Maj., Lancs. Hussars; 1914/18, Commd. 15th Bn., W.Yorks.
     Regt.; d.1941.

278. 1921   William Prinsep Langford-Brooke of Mere (Old) Hall, yst.br.of   –
     Lieutenant-Colonel Henry Langford-Brooke (247). b.1857;
     assumed surnames of Langford-Brooke in *lieu* of White, 1908;
     d.1927.

279. 1923   George Horatio Charles ('Rock') Cholmondeley, 5th Marquess of 1946   Miss Diana
     Cholmondeley of Cholmondeley Castle, Houghton Hall, Norfolk   Tomkinson,
     and 12, Kensington Palace Gdns., e.s.of Lord Cholmondeley   e.dau.260
     (222). b.1883; Capt., 9th Queen's Royal Lancers; International
     Polo Player; S. Africa, Queen's Medal (3 clasps); A.D.C. to Viceroy of
     India, 1910–13; 1914/18, Capt., R.A.F,; Maj., 1920; 1939/45,
     A.R.P. Warden, London; Lord Great Chamberlain of England
     1936–37 & 1952–66; G.C.V.O., 1953; d.1966.

280. 1923   Maurice Egerton, 4th and last Baron Egerton of Tatton, of   –
     Tatton Park, Rostherne Manor and Ngata Farm (Egerton Castle),
     Njoro, Kenya, 3rd s.of Lord Egerton of Tatton (232). b.1874;
     Capt., Ches.Yeo.; 1914/18, Maj., Ches.Yeo, Lt.-Comdr.,
     R.N.V.R.; r.1953; d.unm.1958.

281. 1924   Sir John ('Johnnie') Dixon, 2nd Bart. of Astle Hall, o.s.of 1948‖ Miss Anne Heaton,
     Sir George Dixon (213). b.1886; d.1976.   dau.302

282. 1924   Captain Ralph Aldersey of Crooke Aldersey and also for a time 1949   Miss Josephine
     Stubton, Lincs., gs.of Thomas Aldersey (183). b.1890; 1914/18,   Clegg, nie.333
     Capt., Cheshire Regt., des; r.1956; d.1972.

283. 1925   Colonel Robert Raymond Smith-Barry A.F.C. of Fota House,   –
     also Hamerton, Hunts. and Marbury Hall, later of Conock Manor,
     Wilts., s.of James Smith-Barry (203). b.1886; 1914/18, Col.,
     R.F.C., Order of Leopold, (Belgium); r.1932; 1939/45, Air
     Transport Auxiliary; *d.s.p.*1948.

284. 1926   Captain the Hon. Richard William Davenport Legh of Lyme   –
     Park, later 3rd Baron Newton, gs.of Lord Newton (183). b.1888;
     Capt., Lancs.Hussars; 1914/18, des.; Hon. Attachè, Vienna and
     Constantinople; Hon.Col., Cheshire Regt., (T.A.), 1939–1950;
     T.D.; r.1950; d.1960.

285. 1926   Walter Henry Midwood, M.F.H. of Calveley Hall and Syre   –
     Lodge, Sutherland. b.1865; Won Grand National Hcp.
     Ch., 1927 (Shaun Goilin); d.1942.

§ 1939–1945 *No Presidents due to the War. Major Cyril Dewhurst thereby missed his Presidential Year. His name and arms are painted on the Presidents' Board accordingly.*
‖ *In 1947 there was no Presidential Dinner owing to the demand for General Economy.*

286. 1927   Charles Henry George Cornwall Legh of High Legh Hall, cos.of   –
Colonel Hubert Cornwall Legh (256). b.1876; assumed
surnames of Cornwall Legh in *lieu* of Walker, 1926; d.1934.

287. 1927   Sir Thomas ('Tom') Royden, 2nd Bart., C.H. of Frankby Hall,   –
Rake Hall and Tillypronie, Aberdeenshire and afterwards
Brockwood Park, Hants, later 1st and last Baron ROYDEN.
b.1871; H.S.1917; M.P.(Bootle 1918–22); Cdr.,*Légion d'Honneur*
(France); Cdr., Order of St.Maurice and St. Lazarus (Italy);
Star of Afghaur (Afganistan); d.1950.

288. 1928 ▷—   James ('Jimmy') Tinsley of The Manor House, Bunbury, formerly   –
of Daresbury Hall (Ten.). b.1865; d.unm.1957.

289. 1929   Captain Robert Arthur ('Robin') Grosvenor, M.C., 4, Chester Sq.   –
S.W.1., later of Sunrising House, Banbury, Oxon., o.s.of Lord
Arthur Grosvenor (226). b.1895; 1914/18, 2nd Lt., Ches.Yeo.,
Fl.Lt., R.A.F., des., M.C. & bar; Capt., Queen's Bays; d.1953.

290. 1930   Captain George Hugh de Vernon Wilbraham of Delamere House,   1950   Miss Jennifer
later of Delamere Manor and Sweet Briar Hall, Oakmere, e.s.of   Barlow, dau.305
Major Hugh Wilbraham (237). b.1890; E.African Mounted Rifles,
1913–1915; 2nd.Lt., Ches.Yeo., 1910 & Capt., 1915–16;
King's African Rifles (Kenya), 1916–19; 1914/18; *d.s.p.*1962.

291. 1931   Ronald Prinsep ('Ronnie') Langford-Brooke of Mere Hall,   1951   Miss Avril
s.of William Langford-Brooke (278). b.1906;   Dunkerley, niece
Maj., Ches.Yeo.; 1939/45, Ches.Yeo., Middle East, N.W.Europe,
T.D.; Col., Ches.Yeo., 1949; H.S.1966; d.1980.

292. 1931   Lieutenant-Colonel John Dallas Waters, D.S.O., late Royal   1952   Miss Rosemary
Fusiliers, 9 Berkeley Sq., W.1. and of Arley Hall and afterwards   Cornwall-Legh,
Ormersfield Farm, Basingstoke. b.1889; 1914/18, D.S.O., des.(4);   eld.dau.296
m.sis.284, wid.255.; Registrar, Privy Council, 1940–54; C.B.,
1936; K.C.S.G. with star; d.1967.

293. 1932   Thomas Pitt Hamilton ('Tom') Cholmondeley, 4th Baron   1953   Miss Virginia
Delamere of Vale Royal and later The Hall, Six Mile Bottom,   (Ginny) Wrigley
Newmarket and Soysambu, Kenya Colony, o.s. of Lord
Delamere (240). b.1900; Lt., later Capt., Welsh Guards;
m.3rdly, wid.266.; d.1979.

294. 1932 ▷—   (George) Richard Barbour of Bolesworth Castle, e.s.of Major   –
Robert Barbour. b.1911; Lt., Ches.Yeo., att. 17th/21st Lancers,
Egypt, 1931; Capt., Ches.Yeo.; A.D.C. to Governor of Victoria,
1933–36; 1939/45, Maj. Ches.Yeo., Middle East, T.D.; r.1957;
d.1989.

295. 1933   Colonel Thomas Marshall ('Tom') Brooks, M.C. of Stoke Hall,   1954   Miss Sheelagh Ronan
Nantwich and later Portal, Tarporley. b.1893; 1914/18, Capt.,
Ches,Yeo, M.C., *Croix de Guerre avec palme*, (France),;
Col., Ches.Yeo., T.D.; d.1968.

296. 1935   (Charles) Legh (Shuldham) Cornwall-Legh of High Legh Hall,   1955   Miss Jill Moseley,
later of High Legh House, e.s.of Henry Cornwall Legh (286).   e.dau.318; m.361
b.1903; assumed surnames of Cornwall–Legh in *lieu* of Walker,

1926; H.S.1939; 1939/45, Sqn.Ldr., A.A.F. & R.A.F.; A.E.; O.B.E., 1971, C.B.E., 1977; r.1985; Honorary Member, 1985; suc.as 5th Baron GREY OF CODNOR, on termination of the abeyance, 1989.

297. 1936	Captain Richard Domville ('Dick') Poole, Rifle Brigade, c/o Marbury Hall, Marbury cum Quoisley, from 1944 c/o Boodle's Club and later of The Mill, West Hendred, Berks., s.of Bryan Davies Poole (257). b.1900; India; Palestine; Maj., 1938; 1939/45, Middle East; Lieut.-Col., Rifle Bde.; d.unm.1979.	1956	Miss Julia Warton, step-dau.303
298. 1937	Philip Reginald le Belward Egerton of Oulton Park House and afterwards Stafford House, Dorset, later Sir Philip Grey Egerton, 14th Bart., gr.gs.of Sir Philip Grey-Egerton (76). b.1885; Lt., K.S.L.I.; Hon.Col., 521st Light A.-A.Regt., R.A. (T.A.); Order of the Nile, 4th class, (Egypt); H.S.1941; d.1962.	1957	Miss Jacqueline Lyon-Gandy
299. 1937	Humphrey Wynne Griffith of Garthmeilio, Denbighshire, gr.nep. of Captain Edmund Park Yates (198). b.1904; 1939/45, Maj., Royal Artillery, M.B.E.; d.1985.	1958	Miss Meriel Buxton, step-dau.307
300. 1938	Sir Edward ('Toby') Greenall, 2nd Baron Daresbury, 3rd Bart., M.F.H. of Waltham Hall, Melton Mowbray and afterwards Clonshire House and later Alta Villa, Co.Limerick, 2nd s.of Lord Daresbury (242). b.1902; Lt., Life Guards, Capt., 1939/45; Joint Master (Belvoir 1934–47); Master/Joint Master and Huntsman (Co.Limerick 1947–82); d.1990.	–	
301. 1938	John Leighton Byrne Leicester-Warren of Tabley House, s.of Major Cuthbert Leicester-Warren (267).b.1907; Capt., Ches.Yeo.; 1939/45, Maj., Ches Yeo.,T.D.; Lt.-Col., Ches.Yeo.; H.S.1965; V.-L., 1968–1974; d.unm.1975.	1959	Miss Patricia ('Trish') Moseley, yr.dau.318
302. 1945 ▷	Colonel Benjamin William ('Ben') Heaton, M.C., M.F.H. of White Hall, Little Budworth. b.1886; Lt., Duke of Lancaster's Own Yeo.; 1914/18 des., M.C.; Col., Res.; 1939/45, Sector 38 Comdr., Home Guard; H.S.1947; M.H.(Pendle Forest 1917–27); M.F.H.(Cheshire Forest 1928–31); d.1964.	1961	Miss Amanda (Mandy) Moseley, dau.342; gr.g-dau.238
303. 1945	Garry Hardy Rigby, O.B.E. of Poole Hall, later of The Farm, Lydart, Monmouthshire. b.1885; 1939/45, Maj., H.A.C. & R.F.A.; d.1965.	1960	Miss Carolyn Naylor, g-dau.178
304. 1945	Desmond Llowarch Edward Flower, 10th Viscount Ashbrook of Arley Hall. b.1905; m.e.dau.255; Maj., R.A.(T.A.); 1939/45, M.B.E.(Mil.), 1945; V.-L.1961–67; Member of Council, Duchy of Lancaster; K.C.V.O., 1977; r.1981.	1962	Miss Mary-Anne Naylor, g.-dau.178
305. 1945	Sir John Denman ('Jack') Barlow, 2nd Bart., M.P. of Bradwall Manor, Sandbach. b.1898; M.P.(Eddisbury 1945–50 & Middleton & Prestwich 1951–66); d.1986.	1963	Miss Dinah Carnegie, gr.-dau.266
306. 1945	Christopher Foulis Roundell, C.B.E. of Dorfold Hall and later 53, Ashley Gardens, London, S.W.1., gr.nep.of Henry Tollemache (204). b.1876; S.Africa, 2nd Lt., Coldstream Guards, Queen's Medal (clasp); O.B.E., 1918; C.B.E., 1920; O.St.J.; Chief of Staff,	–	

Civil Commissioners Dept.; Cdr., Order of the Crown (Belgium); Officer, Order of the White Eagle (Serbia); Officer, Order of the Crown (Italy); *Médaille de la Reconnaissance* (France); r.1951; d.1959.

307. 1945   Major Alexander Ludovic ('Sandy') Grant of Marbury Hall, Marbury cum Quoisley. b.1901; Lovat Scouts, 1920–1940; T.D.; H.S.1956; d.1986.   1964   Miss Anne Toler

308. 1945   Major John Anthony ('Tony') Dewhurst of Stoke Hall (Ten.) and later Barmere House, Bickley (Ten.), eld.s.of Major Cyril Dewhurst (277). b.1899; Capt., Royal Scots Greys, 1914/18; Maj., Cheshire Regt. & R.Northumberland Fus. 1939/45, Italy; Col., S.Lancs. Regt.(T.A.); T.D.; k.in car accident, 1978.   1965   Miss Carolin Mary Grant, e.dau.307 & g.-dau.262

309. 1948   Colonel (George) Noah Heath, C.B.E., D.S.O. of The Grey House, Macclesfield. b.1881; Col., 125th Lancs. Fusiliers, Inf.Bde.(T.A.); 1914/18, Gallipoli, Egypt, Palestine, Syria, des., D.S.O. & bar; 1939/45, C.B.E.(Mil), 1944; d.1967.   1966   Miss Julia Cornwall-Legh, yr.dau.296

310. 1948   †Major Richard Bertram ('Dick') Verdin of Stoke Hall, later Lieutenant-Colonel Sir Richard Verdin, eld.s.of Colonel Norman Verdin (264). b.1912; 2nd Lt., Ches.Yeo., 1931; 1939/45, Maj., Ches.Yeo., Middle East, N.W.Europe, T.D.; Lt.-Col., Ches.Yeo.; O.B.E.(Mil.)1954; Knt.Bach., 1962; Secretary, 1961–1976; d.1978.   1967   Miss Gemma Dewhurst, dau.308

311. 1949   Lieutenant-Colonel Walter Henry Bromley-Davenport, M.P., of Capesthorne Hall, nep.of Brig.-Gen. Sir William Bromley-Davenport (235). b.1903; 2nd Lt., later Captain, Grenadier Guards; Army Boxing (Welter Weight) Champion, 1926; Lt.-Col., Cheshire Regt., 1939/45; T.D.; M.P.(Knutsford 1945–70); Conservative Whip, 1948–51; Knt.Bach., 1961; d.1989.   1968   Miss Gemma Dewhurst¶

312. 1949   †(George) Hugh Cholmondeley, Earl of Rocksavage, late Major, Grenadier Guards, later 6th Marquess of Cholmondeley of Cholmondeley Castle and Houghton Hall, Norfolk, e.s.of Lord Cholmondeley (279). b.1919; Capt., 1st Royal Dragoons, 1939/45, Middle East, N.Africa (El Alamein, M.C.), Italy, N.W.Europe; Lord Great Chamberlain of England, 1966–90; G.C.V.O., 1977; National Order of Merit (France); Order of Merit (Federal Republic of Germany); Order of Civil Merit (Spain); d.1990   1969   Lady Rose Cholmondeley, eld.daughter

313. 1949   Sir Philip William Bryce Lever, 3rd Viscount Leverhulme, 3rd.Bart., of Thornton Manor, Thornton Hough. b.1915; 2nd Lt., Ches.Yeo., 1938; 1939/45, Maj., Ches.Yeo., Middle East, N.W. Europe, T.D.; Hon.Col., Ches.Yeo., 1971–79; Hon.Col.Queen's Own Yeo., 1979–81; Hon.Air/Cdre., R.Aux. A.F.; H.M.L.L.1949–90; K.G., 1988; K.G.St.J.; Steward, National Hunt Committee, 1965–68; Senior Steward, Jockey Club, 1973–76.   1970   Miss Vanda Mary Paterson, dau.323

¶ *Appointed for 2nd Term since there was no hunting in 1967, owing to Foot and Mouth Disease, the first outbreak in Cheshire occurring on the eve of the Opening Meet at Ox Heys Farm.*

314. 1950 ▷— John Craig Paterson of Oaklands, Bunbury. b.1881; —
d.in the hunting field, 1955.

315. 1951 ▷— (Charles) Richard Tomkinson of Willington Hall, o.s.of 1971 Miss Penny Moseley,
Major Charles Tomkinson (260). b.1929; Constable, later 2nd dau.342
Chief Superintendent and Commandant, Cheshire Special
Constabulary.

316. 1953 ▷— Colonel Gerald Hugh Grosvenor, late 9th Lancers, later 4th Duke —
of Westminster, 13th Bart.,of Saighton Grange, gs.of Duke of
Westminster (174). b.1907; 2nd Lieut., 9th Queen's Royal
Lancers, 1926, Egypt, India; Capt., 1939; 1939/45, Capt.
Sherwood Rangers, Middle East, Bde.Maj., 22nd Armoured
Bde; Lt.-Col., 9th Lancers, Sep., 1942 – Apr., 1944,
N.Africa (El Alamein, D.S.O.), Lt.-Col., 22nd Dragoons,
Apr. 1944 to July N.W.Europe, wounded; Hon.Col., 9th/12th
Royal Lancers, 1961–67; Hon.Col., Ches.Yeo.; H.S.1959;
Exon, Queen's Bodyguard of the Yeomen of the Guard,
1952–64; P.C., 1964; Lord Steward of the Household, 1964–67;
Jockey Club; Pres., R.Soc. of St.George; *d.s.p.*1967.

317. 1953 Randle John Baker Wilbraham of Rode Hall, later Sir Randle 1972 Lady Leonora
Baker Wilbraham, 7th Bart., gr.gr.gr.gs.of Richard Wilbraham Grosvenor,
Bootle (45). b.1906; 1939/45, Sqn.Ldr., R.Aux.A.F.; e.dau.335
H.S.1953; d.1980.

318. 1953 ▷— Major David Patrick Grange ('Pat') Moseley of Dorfold Cottage. 1973 Miss Jennifer Rae,
b.1907; Master, (Cambridge University Drag-Hounds, 1927/28); later step.dau
1939/45, Maj., Cheshire Regt.; d.1986. 343

319. 1954 ▷— Colonel William Moncrieff ('Billy') Carr of Oldfield Browe, —
Dunham Massey. b.1886; Lt.-Col., 55 W.Lancs.Div.R.E.(T.A.);
1914/18, France, N.Russia; Hon.Col., 107th Field Engineer Regt.
(T.A.); O.B.E.,(Mil.) 1934; C.B.E.(Civil) 1950; T.D.; d.in the
hunting field, 1957.

320. 1955 Major Sir Evelyn Delves Broughton, 12th Bart. of Doddington 1974 Lady Jane
Park and later Kensington Square, London, W.8, o.s.of Major Grosvenor,
Sir Henry Delves Broughton (266). b.1915; 1939/45, Lt., yr.dau.335
Irish Guards, Maj., R.A.S.C., Middle East; m.1stly, e.dau.293,
d.1993.

321. 1955 Lieutenant-Colonel John Baskervyle-Glegg of Withington Hall —
and Chelsea, London,S.W.3., s.of John Baskervyle-Glegg (251).
b.1904; Lt., Royal Scots Greys; Spec.Emp. China Comd.,
1929–33; 1939/45, Lt.-Col., Anglo-French Mil.Mission, Russia,
1939; Mil.Mission to French N.Africa, 1939–40; G.S.O.I, W/O.,
1943; V.Chm., S.S.A.F.A.; d.1973.

322. 1955 John Edward Hamilton Tollemache, Major the 4th Baron —
Tollemache late Coldstream Guards, of Helmingham Hall
and Home Farm, Beeston, gr.gs.of Lord Tollemache (122).
b.1910; 1939/45, M.C., B.E.F., Dunkirk, N.W.Europe; d.1975.

323. 1956   Alfred Dobell ('Chubb') Paterson of Oaklands, Bunbury, o.s.of John Paterson (314). b.1913; 2nd Lt., Ches.Yeo., 1937; 1939/45, Capt., Ches.Yeo., Middle East, N.W. Europe, T.D.   1975   Miss Camilla Ziani de Ferranti, e.dau.343

324. 1957   Major Sir (Arthur) Harold Bibby, of Tilstone Lodge, later Sir Harold Bibby, 1st.Bart. b.1889; Maj., R.F.A. (T.A.), 1914/18, D.S.O., des.; H.S.1934; Knt.Bach., 1956; d.1986.   1976   Miss Elizabeth Gilchrist, dau.346

325. 1957   Lieutenant-Colonel Ronald Henry Antrobus, late Royal Artillery, of Eaton Hall, Congleton, gs.of Gibbs Antrobus (126). b.1891; Royal Artillery Special Reserve, 1910–13; R.A., 1913–44; 1914/18, M.C.; 1939/45; H.S.1960; r.1979; d.1980.   1977   Miss Susan Freeth

326. 1957   Lieutenant-Colonel Ronald Whitehead Whineray of Spurstow Hall. b.1899; Royal Artillery (T.A.); 1939/45; T.D.; d.1974.   –

327. 1957   Lieutenant-Colonel Charles Douglas Fergusson Phillips-Brocklehurst of Hare Hill, Macclesfield. b.1904; Joint Master (Oxford University Drag-Hounds, 1925/26); 2nd Lt., Ches.Yeo., 1923; 1939/45, Lt., Ches.Yeo., Middle East, N.Africa (El Alamein), Lt.-Col., G.S.O.I, Albania, 1944; H.S.1957; d.unm. 1977.   –

328. 1957   Lieutenant-Colonel Geoffrey Vardon Churton of The Cottage, Bunbury, later of The White House, Bunbury and afterwards of Manley Cottage. b.1913; Joint M.H.(Royal Rock Beagles, 1937–47); Lt., Ches.Yeo., 1935; 1939/45, Capt., Ches.Yeo., Maj., 11th Hussars, Palestine, Greece, Syria, N.Africa (El Alamein, M.B.E.(Mil.), M.C., des.), G.II (Air), Western Desert and later8th Army, A.D.C. to G.O.C. 7th Armd.Div. and later G.O.C. 30 Corps, Italy (Salerno), N.W.Europe, T.D. (3 bars); Col., Ches.Yeo.; Col., 2 i/c 22 Armd.Bde., R.A.C.; H.S.1964; m.2ndly, wid.346.   1978   Miss Sally Churton, daughter

329. 1961   Captain Peter Egerton-Warburton, late Coldstream Guards, of Grafton Hall, Malpas and afterwards Mulberry House, Hants., o.s.of Colonel Geoffrey Egerton-Warburton (264). b.1933; Maj., Ches.Yeo.   1979   Miss Lucy Clegg, g.-dau.333

330. 1962   Captain Ralph Venables ('Sim') Wilbraham of Brook House, Cuddington, yr.s.of Major Hugh Wilbraham (237). b.1894; 1914/18, Capt., Ches.Yeo., Palestine, M.C.; 1939/45, Capt., Auxiliary Military Pioneer Corps, N.W.Europe; P.o.W., Germany, 1940–1945; Red Cross Vol. Service Medal; d.1983.   1980   Miss Nicola Hawke

331. 1962   Charles Wilbraham Roundell of Dorfold Hall, afterwards of Terling, Essex, s.of Christopher Roundell (306). b.1912; Maj., 72 S/L Regt., R.A., 1939/45; r.1972.   –

332. 1962   Geoffrey Carter Dean of Haughton Hall. b.1900; Lt., R.N.V.R., 1917–1928; *d.s.p.*1987.   1981   Miss Isabel Henrietta Dean, niece

333. 1965   Gavin Hamilton Clegg of Poole Hall. b.1901; 1939/45, Capt., G.S. Corps., Billeting Officer, Western Cmd.; d.1988.   –

334. 1965		Francis Edward Frederick ('Frank') Spiegelberg of Cotebrook House. b.1900; 1939/45, R. Observer Corps; d.1979.	–	
335. 1967		Sir Robert George ('Pud') Grosvenor, 5th Duke of Westminster, 14th Bart., of Eaton and Ely Lodge, Enniskillen, yr.br.of Duke of Westminster (316). b.1910; Maj., City of London Yeo.; Lt.-Col., R.A., 1939/45, Middle East, N.Africa (El Alamein, Mareth Line, Wadi Akarit); Lt.-Col., N.Irish Horse; T.D.; H.S. (Co.Fermanagh) 1952; M.P.(Fermanagh and S.Tyrone 1955–64); P.P.S., Sec. of State, Foreign Affairs, 1957–59; Senator, N.Ireland, 1964–67; Joint M.H. (Fermanagh Harriers) 1959–62; K.G.St.John; Knt.Cdr., Commandery of Ards (Order of St.John); d.1979.	–	
336. 1967		Ralph Midwood of Rookery Hall, Worleston and Syre Lodge, Sutherland, formerly for a time of Daleford, Sandiway, e.s.of Walter Midwood (285). b.1896; 1914/18, Capt. Montgomeryshire Yeo.; 1939/45, Bn.Comdr., Ches.Home Guard; d.1970.	–	
337. 1967		Michael Earle Sinclair Higgin of Sandymere, Delamere and afterwards Old Quarry, Sherborne, Dorset. b.1920; 2nd Lt., Ches.Yeo., 1938; 1939/45, Capt., Ches.Yeo., Middle East, N.W.Europe, T.D.	1982	Miss Sofia Mary Rae, later step-dau.343
338. 1970		Edward George Maude ('Teddy') Leycester-Roxby of Yew Tree Farm formerly of Toft Hall. b.1913; assumed additional surname of Leycester, 1957.	1983	Miss Vanessa Caroline Brown, grand-daughter
339. 1972		Captain (John) Gordon Fergusson of Sandy Brow, Delamere. b.1925; 1939/45, 2nd Lt., 27th Lancers, attached 6th Airborne Armoured Recce Regt., R.A.C.; Palestine, 1945–47; 12th Royal Lancers, 1946–50; A.D.C. to Governor & C.-in.-C., Gibraltar, 1948–50; Secretary, 1976–	1984	Miss Samantha Victoria Hunter, grand-daughter
340. 1972		†John Kemp Barlow of Bulkeley Grange, e.s.of Sir John Barlow (305), later Sir John Barlow, 3rd Bart. b.1934; Joint Master,(Cambridge University Drag-Hounds, 1955/56); H.S.1979; Steward of the Jockey Club, 1988–90.	1985	Miss Victoria Hanbury-Williams
341. 1973		Richard Charles ('Ricky') Roundell of Dorfold Hall, e.s.of Charles Roundell (331). b.1944; H.S.1984.	1986	Miss Louisa Jane Egerton-Warburton, dau.329
342. 1974		* Michael Grange ('Micky') Moseley of Booth Bank House, Millington, yr.br.of Major D.P.G.Moseley (318*). b.1914; 1939/45, P.O., R.A.F., Coastal Cmd., D.F.C.	1987	Miss Kate Wilkins, great-niece, dau.318
343. 1974		Sebastian Basil Joseph Ziani de Ferranti of Kerfield House, Knutsford, later of Henbury Hall. b.1927; Lt., 4th/7th Royal Dragoon Guards; Palestine, 1946–47; Capt., Ches.Yeo., 1951; H.S.1988; Fellow Univ of Manchester Inst. of Science and Technology, D.Sc., Salford Univ.	1988	Miss Francesca Ziani de Ferranti, daughter
344. 1975		Robert Clunie Cunningham of Guerdon Cottage, Beeston, formerly of Forest Hill. b.1913; 1939/45, Capt., Cheshire Regt.; d.in the hunting field from a fall, 1984.	–	

345. 1975	Timothy John Edward ('Tim') Tollemache, 5th Baron Tollemache of Helmingham Hall, Suffolk, eld.s.of Lord Tollemache, (322). b.1939; Lieut., Coldstream Guards, Kenya, Persian Gulf, Zanzibar, Kuwait, 1959–61.	1989	Hon. Selina Tollemache daughter
346. 1977	Commander (Richard) Ian Gilchrist, R.N.R., of Manley Cottage. b.1922; 1939/45, Lt.-Cdr., R.N.R., V.R.D.(& bar); Cdr., Fleet Air Arm, R.N.V.R., M.B.E.; H.S.1981; d.1985.	–	
347. 1977	†Gerald Cavendish Grosvenor, Earl Grosvenor, of Ely Lodge, Enniskillen, later of Eaton and Abbeystead, Lancaster, 6th Duke of Westminster, 15th Bart., o.s.of Duke of Westminster (335). b.1951; Lieut.-Col., Queen's Own Yeo.; K.J. St.J.; F.R.S.A.; LL.D. (Univ. of Keele and Westminster College, Foulton, Missouri, U.S.A.); D.Litt., Manchester Metropolitan Univ.	1990	Miss Alice Baker Wilbraham, dau.354
348. 1978	Simon Peter Dewhurst of Sicily Oak, Cholmondeley, e.s.of Colonel Anthony Dewhurst (308). b.1947.	1991	Miss Gemma October Hunter, god-dau., dau.363
349. 1979	Major Philip George Verdin of The Buttas, Canon Pyon, Herefordshire, yst.s.of Col. Norman Verdin (263) and br.of Sir Richard Verdin (310). b.1917; Maj., 4th/7th Royal Dragoon Guards, 1939/45, N.W.Europe, M.C., des.; H.S.(Herefordshire)1966.	1992	Miss Sarah Josephine Daly
350. 1979 ▷—	(Philip) John (McLean) Boddington of Baddiley Corner, Ravensmoor. b.1921; 1939/1945, Capt., Royal Artillery, N.Africa, Italy; Lt., 1947, later Maj., Ches.Yeo.	1993	Miss Sarah Boddington, daughter
351. 1979	David Bethune Lindesay-Bethune, Viscount Garnock, late Scots Guards, later 15th Earl of Lindsay, of Combermere Abbey. b.1926; Member, Queen's Bodyguard for Scotland (Royal Company of Archers); O.St.J.; d.1989.	–	
352. 1979	Quentin Hugh Crewe of Netherset Hey, Madeley and later Le Grand Banc, Oppedette, France, gs.of Lord Crewe (244). b.1926; assumed matronymic in *lieu* of Dodds, 1945. r.1992.	–	
353. 1979	Richard Chandos Mosley Leigh, M.F.H. of Belmont Hall, o.s.of Captain (Oswald Edward Stanley) 'Tweets' Mosley Leigh and gs.of Col. Oswald Mosley Leigh (245). b.1940; Joint M.F.H. (Cheshire Forest, 1973–82).		

His Royal Highness Prince Charles Philip Arthur George Mountbatten-Windsor,
K.G., K.T., G.M.B., P.C., A.K., Q.S.O., A.D.C.,
Prince of Wales and Earl of Chester, Duke of Cornwall and Rothesay,

JAN.
1980

Earl of Carrick, Baron of Renfrew, Lord of the Isles and Great Steward of Scotland
consented to become Patron.

ELECTED BY BALLOT

| 354. 1980 | Sir Richard Baker Wilbraham, 8th Bart. of Rode Hall, o.s.of Sir Randle Baker Wilbraham (317). b.1934; Lieut, Welsh Guards; H.S.1991. | | |

355. 1980   Anthony William Assheton ('Bill') Spiegelberg of Oulton Park
       House (Ten.), eld.s.of Frank Spiegelberg (334). b.1936;
       2nd Lt., 5th Royal Inniskilling Dragoon Guards; Maj.,
       Ches.Yeo; Maj., 80 (Ches.Yeo.) Signal Sqn.; Maj., Queen's
       Own Yeo.; Hon. Col.Ches.Yeo. Sqn. (Queen's Own Yeo.), T.D.

356. 1981   (Robert) John Posnett of Tiresford, Tarporley, nep.of Geoffrey
       Dean (332), later of Haughton Hall. b.1929; H.S.1982.

357. 1981   Hon. Michael Llowarch Warburton Flower of The Old
       Parsonage, Arley Green, e.s.of Lord Ashbrook (304). b.1935;
       Lieut., Grenadier Guards; V.-L., 1990.

358. 1982   (Richard) David (Christopher) Brooke of The Manor House,
       Cholderton, Wilts., gs.of Sir Richard Brooke (276). b.1938;
       Lieut., Scots Guards.

359. 1983   Hugh Dudley Wilbraham of The Gage, Little Berkamstead,
       Herts., o.s.of Captain R.V.Wilbraham (330) and gr.gr.gr.gr.gs.
       of George Wilbraham (5). b.1929; Lt., W. Yorks. Regt.; Lt.,
       Ches.Yeo.

360. 1983   Peter Gilbert Greenall of Hall Lane Farm, Daresbury, eld.gs.of
       Lord Daresbury (300). b.1953; H.S.1992; Leading Amateur
       Rider, National Hunt Rules, 1975/76 and 1976/77; Won
       Point-to-Point Championship, 1982, 1985, 1986; Joint
       M.F.H.(Sir W.W.Wynn's 1991–).

361. 1985   (Edward) Michael (Wynne) Griffith of Greenfields,
       Trefnant, e.s. of Humphrey Griffith (299). b.1933;
       Lieut., Royal Welch Fusiliers; m.e.dau.318; H.S.
       (Denbighshire)1969; V.-L.(Clwyd), 1986; C.B.E., 1986.

362. 1985   Richard Henry Cornwall-Legh of Dairy Farm, High Legh,
       o.s.of Legh Cornwall-Legh, later Lord Grey of Codnor
       (296). b.1936; Royal Navy; Suez, 1956; Captain, British
       Ski Team, 1960/61; H.S.1993.

363. 1985   Peter James Pierrepont Hunter, M.F.H. of Keeper's Cottage,
       Oulton (Ten.), e.s.of Philip Gore Hunter, formerly of Littleton
       Old Hall. b.1943; Joint M.F.H.(Cheshire Forest, 1973–82 &
       N.Staffordshire, 1970–72); M.F.H.(Cheshire Forest, 1982–).

364. 1986   Robert James ('Bobby') McAlpine of Tilstone Lodge. b.1932;
       Jockey Club.

365. 1986   David Maurice Stern of Brassey Green Hall. b.1932; H.S.1990.

366. 1986   Randle Brooks of Peover Hall. b.1941.

367. 1987   * George Bradwall Barlow of Robin's Cob, Henbury, later of
       Bradwall Manor, yr.s.of Sir John Barlow (305) and br.of Sir
       John Barlow (340*). b.1938.

368. 1987   Major William Richard ('Bill') Paton-Smith, late Queen's Royal
             Irish Hussars, of Marbury Hall, Marbury cum Quoisley. b.1941;
             A.D.C. to G.O.C. Berlin (British Sector), 1964–1966; m.e.dau.307.

369. 1987   Richard Anthony ('Ricky') Gilchrist of Manley Cottage, later of
             The Lodge, Willington (Ten.), o.s. of Commander Ian Gilchrist
             (346). b.1951; Joint Master, (Cambridge University Drag-Hounds,
             1972/73).

ELECTED BY POSTAL VOTE

370. 1990   William Arthur ('Bill') Bromley-Davenport of The Kennels,
             Capesthorne and Capesthorne Hall, o.s. of Sir Walter
             Bromley-Davenport (311). b.1935; Lieut., Grenadier Guards;
             Hon.Col., 3rd Bn.Cheshire Regt.; H.S.1983; H.M.L.L.1990–

371. 1990   Anthony George Barbour of Bolesworth Castle, ad.s.of Richard
             Barbour (294). b.1938; assumed surname of Barbour *in lieu* of
             Weston Saunders, 1945; H.S.1987.

372. 1990   William Henry Midwood of Broomy Bank, Malpas, yr.s. of
             Ralph Midwood (336). b.1953.

373. 1990   David George Philip Cholmondeley, 7th Marquess of
             Cholmondeley of Houghton Hall, Norfolk and Cholmondeley
             Castle, o.s. of Lord Cholmondeley (312). b.1960; Lord Great
             Chamberlain of England, 1990–

ELECTED BY BALLOT

374. 1993   Michael Anthony Tudor Trevor-Barnston of Crewe Place,
             Farndon. b. 1943; 2nd Lieut., 1st Bn., 22nd (Cheshire) Regt.,
             Northern Ireland, 1961. Assumed additional surname of
             Barnston, 1990.

Appendix B

TARPORLEY HUNT CLUB
LIST OF HONORARY SECRETARIES
&
MEMBERS OF THE COMMITTEE

Secretaries to the Club

1762–1786	JOHN CREWE (2)
Deputy	HON. BOOTH GREY (3) (1762–1786)
1786–1801	*No record*
1801–1808	HENRY LEICESTER (54)
1808–1839	CHARLES CHOLMONDELEY (66)
1840–1846	JAMES HAMMOND (127) *[prob.]*
1847–1865	HENRY BROOKE (111)
1865–1870	CHARLES FRANCE-HAYHURST (193)
1870–1878	CECIL de TRAFFORD (187)
1878–1887	HENRY TOLLEMACHE (204)
1887–1897	CUDWORTH POOLE (205)
1897–1936	SIR PHILIP GREY-EGERTON, Bart. (236)
1937–1961	GEOFFREY EGERTON-WARBURTON (264)
Acting–	C.L.S.CORNWALL-LEGH (296) (1960–1961)
1961–1976	SIR RICHARD VERDIN (310)
1976–	GORDON FERGUSSON (339)

Members of the Committee

NB: *Resignation (from the Club) – resignation (from the Committee)*

1808 –	Sir Harry Mainwaring (81)	Rev.Wm. Drake (90)	CHARLES CHOLMONDELEY (66)
1822 –	do.	Henry Hesketh (119) on Resignation of 90	do.
1837 –	Geoffrey Shakerley (138) on Resignation of 81	do.	do.
1839 –	do.	JAMES HAMMOND (127) on Resignation of 119	do.
1840 –	do.	do.	Charles Ford (123) on Resignation of 66
1846 –	do.	HENRY BROOKE (111) on Resignation of 127	do.
1854 –	do.	do.	John Dixon (150) on Resignation of 123
1859 –	do.	do.	Hon.W. H. Stapleton-Cotton (157) on Resignation of 150
1865 –	Hon. Thomas Cholmondeley (177) on resignation of 138	CHAS. FRANCE-HAYHURST (193) on resignation of 111	do.
1870 –	do.	CECIL de TRAFFORD (187) on resignation of 193	do.
1878 –	do.	HENRY TOLLEMACHE (204) on death of 187	do.
1883 –	Sir Philip Grey-Egerton, Bt.(191) on death of 177	do.	do.

1887 – CUDWORTH POOLE (205)	do.	do.
on resignation of 191		
1892 – do.	do.	P. Egerton Warburton (194)
		on death of 157
1898 – SIR PHILIP GREY-EGERTON, Bt.(236)	do.	do.
on resignation of 205		
1899 – do.	Henry Legh (219)	do.
	on resignation of 204	
1904 – do.	Henry Tomkinson (239)	do.
	on death of 219	
1912 – do.	do.	Sir E. T. D. Cotton-Jodrell (225)
		on Resignation of 194
1915 – do.	J. B. Littledale (241)	do.
	on death of 239	
1919 – do.	do.	Major Hugh Wilbraham (237)
		on death of 225
1930 – do.	do.	Bryan Davies Poole (257)
		on death of 237
1931 – do.	do.	Wm. France-Hayhurst (265)
		on death of 257
1937 – G. EGERTON-WARBURTON (264)	do.	
on death of 236		do.
1944 – do.	Philip Egerton (298)	do.
	on the death of 241	
1945 – do.	do.	Sir John Dixon, Bt. (281)
		on resignation of 265
1956 – do.	Legh Cornwall-Legh (296)	do.
	on resignation of 298	
1961 – R. B. VERDIN (310)	do.	do.
on death of 264		
1969 – do.	do.	J. A. Dewhurst (308)
		on resignation of 281
1975 – do. J. G. FERGUSSON (339)	do.	do.
on alteration of Rule IV, to have four elected members and the President		
1978 – R. C. Roundell (341)	do.	R. P. Langford-Brooke (291)
on death of 310		on death of 308
1980 – do.	do.	Lord Cholmondeley (312)
		on death of 291
1986 – do.	Hugh Wilbraham (359)	do.
	on Resignation of 296	
1990 – do.	do.	Lord Leverhulme (313)
		on death of 312

Charles France

The Author

Cecil de Trafford

Appendix C

MANAGERS OF THE CHESHIRE HOUNDS
AND
EX OFFICIO SUPERNUMERARY MEMBERS AND HONORARY
MEMBERS UNDER RULE XV
OF
THE TARPORLEY HUNT CLUB

		ELECTED	
*c.*1745–1784	The Hon. John Smith-Barry (Own Hounds).	Nov.1763	(17)
1784–1794	Sir Peter Warburton, Bart.–Subscription Pack formed, but no details kept.	Nov.1775	(35)
1794–1810	Sir Peter Warburton, Bart.–Assisted financially by Sir Richard Brooke, Bart.(33) followed by his son (91) William Egerton (40) and Thomas Brooke (34).		
1810–1818	The Rev. George Heron.	Nov.1779	(38)
1818–1837	Sir Harry Mainwaring, Bart.	1801	(83)
1837–1839	G. J. Shakerley, Esq	1832	(138)
1839–1840	J. H. Smith-Barry, Esq., Joint with Lieut.-Col. J. Dixon.	1836	(147)
1840–1841	J. H. Smith-Barry, Esq.	1838	(150)
1841–1842	C. I. Ford, Esq.	1823	(124)
1842–1855	Captain J. White.	1842	(159)
1855–1858	Captain Arthur Mainwaring, late 66th Foot, of Oakmere Lodge, 4th and yst.s.of Sir Harry Mainwaring (81). b.1815; d.1876.	Not elected	
1858–1866	Earl Grosvenor.	1848	(174)
1866–1877	H. R. Corbet, Esq., Amateur Huntsman.	1859	(189)
1877–1901	H. R. Corbet, Esq. (South Cheshire Hounds)		
1877–1896	Captain E. W. Park Yates. (North Cheshire Hounds)	1866	(198)
1896–1901	The Earl of Enniskillen. (North Cheshire Hounds)	1876	(218)
1901–1907	R. Corbet, Esq. Amateur Huntsman. (South Cheshire Hounds)	1878	(220)
1901–1907	H. M. Wilson, Esq. (North Cheshire Hounds)	1901	(249)
1907–1911	The Duke of Westminster.	1900	(248)

RULE XV   In 1911 the following resolution was made:

ANY PERSON APPOINTED MASTER OR JOINT MASTER OF THE CHESHIRE HOUNDS AND NOT BEING
A MEMBER OF THE TARPORLEY HUNT CLUB, MAY BE INVITED TO BECOME AN *EX OFFICIO*
SUPERNUMARY MEMBER OF THE CLUB DURING HIS TERM OF OFFICE ONLY. DURING SUCH
PERIOD HE MAY WEAR THE CLUB UNIFORM AND BUTTON, BUT HE SHALL NOT ATTEND THE BUSINESS
MEETINGS OF THE CLUB NOR SHALL HE BE CALLED UPON TO PAY ANY SUBSCRIPTION THERETO.
DURING THE HUNT WEEK IN NOVEMBER HE SHALL BE A CLUB GUEST. NOTHING IN THE ABOVE,
HOWEVER, SHALL PREVENT HIM FROM BEING ELECTED TO FILL A VACANCY IN THE ROLL OF MEMBERS,
IF QUALIFIED UNDER RULE V.

In 1923 the following words were added:

AND ANY SUCH PERSON AT THE TERMINATION OF HIS MASTERSHIP MAY BE INVITED TO BECOME
AN HONORARY MEMBER OF THECLUB SO LONG AS HE CONTINUES TO RESIDE AND HUNT IN THE
CHESHIRE COUNTRY.

		Ex Officio SUPERNUMERARY MEMBER	HONORARY MEMBER (RULE XV)	
1911–1915	W. Roylance Court, Esq., Joint with			1889 (238)
	Captain W. Higson.	1911		1912 (261)
1915–1918	Col. W. Hall Walker, T.D., M.P.			1915 (268)
1918–1919	Cheshire Hunt Committee.			
1919–1923	James Tinsley, Esq.	1919	1923	1928 (288)
1923–1931	W. H. Midwood, Esq.	1923		1926 (285)
1931–1936	W. H. Midwood, Esq. (South Cheshire Hounds)			
1931–1934	Major B. W. Heaton, M.C., Amateur Huntsman (North Cheshire Hounds)	1931	1934	1945 (302)
1934–1944	Peter L. (aka 'The Bolster') Russell Allen., Esq., Amateur Huntsman (North Cheshire Hounds), of Davenham Hall. b.1899; d.1983.	1934	–	Left Cheshire
1944–1946	Col. G. N. Heath, C.B.E., Joint with	1944	1946	1948 (309)
	Col. W. M. Carr, C.B.E., T.D., (North Cheshire Hounds)	1944	1946	1954 (319)
1936–1938	Major Alan Stuart ('Tim') Casey, Amateur Huntsman (South Cheshire Hounds), late Royal Dragoons, of Cassia Lodge, Whitegate. Joint-Master of the Earl of Harrington's Hounds, 1934-1936. 1939/45, Lt.-Col.	1936	1938	Left Cheshire
1938–1940	Captain G. R. Barbour, (South Cheshire Hounds)			1932 (294)
	Joint with Joseph Neville ('Bill') Clegg, Esq. of Gatesheath Hall, later Captain, Cheshire Regt. b.1905; d.1990.	1938	–	Left Cheshire
1940–1945	Col. B. W. Heaton, Joint with Captain J. N. Clegg. (South Cheshire Hounds)			
1945–1946	Col. B. W. Heaton. (South Cheshire Hounds)			
1946–1949	Col. B. W. Heaton, Joint with J. C. Paterson, Esq.	1946	1949	1950 (314)
1949–1952	Lt.-Col. J. A. Dewhurst.			1945 (308)
1952–1954	Lt.-Col. J. A. Dewhurst, Joint with			
	R. F. ('Dick') Haworth, Esq. of Woodrough, Sandiway.	1952	Declined	
1954–1956	Philip Gore Hunter, Esq. of Littleton Old Hall. Amateur Huntsman. Master and Huntsman, Cheshire Forest Hounds, 1947-1976, Joint Master 1973-1976, and Joint-Master, North Staffordshire Hounds, 1970-1972. b.1913; later of Portal, Tarporley and afterwards Carden Cliff.	1954	1956	
1956–1957	P. G. Hunter, Esq., Joint with			
	The Earl of Rocksavage			1949 (312)
1957–1959	The Earl of Rocksavage, Joint with			
	Col. G. H. Grosvenor and			1953 (316)
	The Viscount Leverhulme.			1949 (313)
1959–1962	Lord Leverhulme and Col. G. H. Grosvenor, Joint with			
	Lady Leverhulme (*née* Miss Margaret Ann Moon).	1960	1962	d.1973

Kind Hearts and Coronets, 1958, from a caricature by Noël Dewhurst.

In 1962 RULE XV was altered to read:

ANY PERSON APPOINTED MASTER OR JOINT MASTER OF THE CHESHIRE HOUNDS, NOT BEING A MEMBER OF THE TARPORLEY HUNT CLUB, MAY BE INVITED TO BECOME AN *EX OFFICIO* SUPERNUMERARY MEMBER OF THE CLUB DURING HIS OR HER TERM OF OFFICE ONLY, AND ANY SUCH PERSONS AT THE TERMINATION OF THEIR MASTERSHIPS MAY BE INVITED TO BECOME HONORARY MEMBERS OF THE CLUB SO LONG AS THEY CONTINUE TO RESIDE AND HUNT IN THE CHESHIRE COUNTRY. LADIES ELECTED UNDER THIS RULE WILL BE EXCUSED FROM WEARING THE HUNT UNIFORM AS SET OUT IN RULES II AND III EXCEPT FOR A GREEN COLLAR ON THEIR HUNTING COATS AND WILL NOT BE ELIGIBLE TO ATTEND THE HUNT DINNERS

1962–1963	Lord Leverhulme and the Duke of Westminster, Joint with			
	C. R. Tomkinson, Esq.		1951	(315)
1963–1970	C. R. Tomkinson, Esq.			
1970–1971	C. R. Tomkinson, Esq., Joint with			
	Mrs J. E. K. Rae (née Miss Naomi Pattinson).	1970	1975	
1971–1972	C. R. Tomkinson, Esq. and Mrs Keith Rae, Joint with			
	Mrs C. R. ('Moppy') Tomkinson			
	(*née* Miss Margaret Isabella Salmon).	1971/72	Not Invited	
1972–1974	Mrs Keith Rae, Joint with			
	Major D. P. G. Moseley.		1953	(318)
1974–1975	Mrs Keith Rae, Joint with		1967	(337)
	M. E. S. Higgin, Esq.		1967	(337)
1975–1976	C. R. Tomkinson, Esq.			
1976–1977	C. R. Tomkinson, Esq., Joint with			
	Joseph Heler, Esq. of The Laurels, Hatherton.	1976	1981	
1977–1981	Joseph ('Joe') Heler, Esq. b.1927			
	Lieut.-Col. Peter Ben Sayce, T.D., late Royal	1980	Nov.1984	
	Artillery, of Eagle Cottage, Bunbury, as			
	Hon. Secretary of the Cheshire Hunt since 1974.			
	b.1915.			
1981–1982	J. K. Barlow, Esq., Joint with		1972	(340)
	P. J. M. Boddington, Esq.		1979	(350)
1982–1985	P. J. M. Boddington, Esq., Joint with			
	John Sutton Warrington, Esq. of Oscroft House.	1982/85	–	
	b.1944. and			
	John Geoffrey ('Geoff')Cooke, Esq. of Brereton	1982	1988	
	Park Farm. b.1944.			

1985–1987	P. J. M. Boddington, Esq., and J. G. Cooke, Esq., Joint with	
	Michael John Dixon, Esq. of Wilson House,	1985/88
	Grange-over-Sands, Lancs.	
1987–1988	Sir John Barlow, Bart., J. G. Cooke, Esq. and	
	M. J. Dixon, Esq.Joint with Guy D. Ross-Lowe, Esq	1987/90
	of Hetherson. Green Farm, Cholmondeley	
1988–1989	Sir John Barlow Bart. and G. D. Ross-Lowe, Esq., Joint with	
	J. S. Warrington, Esq. of Broom Butts, Tarporley.	1988
1989–1990	Sir John Barlow, Bart., G. D. Ross-Lowe, Esq. and	
	J. S. Warrington, Esq., Joint with	
	Mrs R. F. Windsor (*née* Miss Pauline Margaret	1989
	Bancroft) of Philo House, Rushton.	
1990–1991	Sir John Barlow, Bart., J. S. Warrington, Esq. and	
	Mrs R. F. Windsor.	
1991–1993	Sir John Barlow Bart. and Mrs R. F. Windsor.	
1993–	Sir John Barlow Bart. and Mrs R. F. Windsor, Joint with	
	Robin Stanley Williams, Esq. of Brook House,	1993
	Radmore Green, Haughton. b.1957.	
	David Harold Woolley, Esq. of Lane End Farm,	1993
	Brereton Park, Huxley. b.1957.	

The Modern Managers.

Appendix D

HUNTSMEN OF THE CHESHIRE HOUNDS

1763–1778	Thomas Cooper	1895–1897	John Boore
1784–?	Richard Bratt	1897–1901	Frederick Gosden
1801–1803	Philip Payne	1901–1903	Tom Cubberley
1803–1810	Leech	1903–1911	Fred Champion
1810–1820	William Gaff	1911–1919	Edwin Short
1820–1823	John Jones	1910–1920	Peter Farrelly
1823–1832	Will Head	1920–1936	Joe Wright
1832–1844	Joe Maiden	1936–1937	Tom Peaker
1844–1854	William Markwell	1937–1953	Arthur Redfern
1854–1856	George Whitemore	1953–1957	Ted Rafton (K.H.)
1856–1860	David Edwards	1957–1963	Jim Stanley, M.M.
1860–1862	Henry Nason	1963–1966	Leslie Moss
1862–1869	Peter Collison	1966–1991	Johnnie O'Shea
1869–1895	John Jones	1991–	Stuart Coley

Appendix E

MEETS AND COVERTS OF THE CHESHIRE HUNT

(The figures refer to the letterpress on the endpapers. Those in small capitals are still in fashion, with slightly changed locations in brackets. [C.F.] indicates Cheshire Forest Hunt.)

1. Dunham Massey. Dunham New Park, Brick-kiln Nursery Wood, Whiteoaks Wood, Headsman's Covert, Pitstead.
2. HighLegh. Big Wood, Moss Strip, Bolt's Spinney, Moss Oaks, Hey's Wood, Jones's Covert, The Oaks, Ditchield's Covert Peter's Covert, Park Covert, Cherry Lane Willows.
2a. Rostherne Manor. Harper's Bank Wood, Rostherne Banks, Wood Bongs, Twiss's Wood, Hancock Banks, Ryecroft Covert.
3. Appleton Hall. Appleton Firs, Hillcliffe Quarry, Witherwing Dingle, Ford's Rough, The Gorse, Birchel's Gorse, Grappenhall Willows, Sink Moss.
4. Norton Priory. Windmill Hill, Acton's Wood, Sandymoor Wood, Haddock's Wood.
5. Aston Hall. Beckett's Wood, Mare Clough Wood, Whittle's Corner, Chapel Wood, Bird's Wood, Bank Rough, Reservoir Wood, Longacre, Baker's Hollow, Stretche's Gorse, Dutton Dingles, Murchishaw Wood.
6. Daresbury. Row's Wood, Mort's Wood, Keckwick Hill, Daresbury's Firs, Daresbury Depth, Slaughter's Rough, Crow's Nest.
   CHETWODE ARMS, LOWER WHITLEY [C.F.]. Dutton Dene, Dutton Hollows, Sevenacre, Dodswood, Whitley Gorse, Reedbeds, Sandholes, Claypits, Merryfall.
7. Stretton. Grappenhall, Pewterspear Gorse, Appleton Park, Firs Gorse, Hull Wood Denna, Bog Rough, Row's Wood, Daresbury Firs, Newton Gorse, Owl's Nest, Whitley Gorse.
8. Arley Hall, MOSS END, ARLEY [C.F.]. Big Wood, The Belts, Willowbed Wood, Aldehedge Wood.
9. Mere Hall. Mere Moss, Clemhanger, Tabley, Holdford.
10. Tatton Park. Willow Slips, Dairy Wood, Saddle-back Plantations, Yew Wood, Lodge Plantation, Croft's Wood, Ward Plantation, Fishpond Coverts, Half Plantation, The Birken, Rostherne Willows.
11. Castle Mill, Ringway.
12. Norbury Booths.
12a. Booth's Obelisk. Ollerton, Victoria Wood, Holford Moss, Tabley, Lower Peover Gorse, Drakelow.
13. TOFT HALL [C.F.]. The Oak Wood, Plantation, Garden, Victoria, The Island, Dams Head, Spring Wood, Lamb's Wood, Windmill Wood.

WHITE BARN FARM, OVER ALDERLEY [C.F.].
CHAIN & GATE, NORTH RODE [C.F.]. Cock's Moss, Blackwood, Titnock, Marton Heath, Pallotti, Simpson's.
14. Tabley House. Belt Wood, Willowbed Wood, Botany Bay Wood, School Wood, Dog Kennel Wood, Round Wood, Rinks Wood, Royd Wood, Black Clump.
15. BOSTOCK HALL. Pennel's Wood, Fiddle Clump, Oak Wood, The Willow-beds, Earls Wood, Holford Moss, Hulme Mill, Bull's Wood.
16. BELMONT [C.F.]. Quebec, The Island, The Dene, Ladies' Wood, Cogshall, Marbury Mere, Dog kennel, Clay Pits, Barker's Hayes.
   PICKMERE COUNTRY CLUB [C.F.]. Pickmere, Pickmere Bottom, Blackwood, Folly, Deakin's Yard, Smoker, Leonard's, Round Wood.
17. Marbury Hall. Kennel Wood, Gunners.
18. Dutton Hall Farm. Whitley, Grimsditch Moss Willows, Owl's Nest, Newton Gorse, Morts.
19. Crewood Hall.
20. Mickledale. Mickledale, Alvanley Cliffe, Manley Quarry, Fox Hill, Symmond's Hill, Royalty Banks. Black Lake.
21. Ince Hall.
22. DUNHAM O'THE HILL (WHEATSHEAF INN) [C.F.]. Dunham Hill, Blackwood, Rose Wood, Rose Wood Valley, The Cliffe, Ravelstone, Manley Old Hall, Scramble track, Claim Valley, Commonside, Towers Lane Valley, Willowbeds, Barnhouse.
22a. Horn's Mill. Dunham Gorse, Dunham Willows, Barnhouse, Barrowmore, Gowy, Hill's Gorse.
23. ALVANLEY [C.F.]. Royalty, Claim Valley, Newton Firs.
24. Norley Hall.
25. Delamere House. Delamere Willows, Heath's Willows, Littledale's Gorse.
26. SANDIWAY HEAD (BLUE CAP INN) [C.F.]. Littledale's Gorse, Willowbeds, The Moss, The Riddings, Hunt's Hill, Railway Embankment, Chapel Wood, Ruloe.
   THE KENNELS. Barry's Wood, Pettypool, Abbot's Moss.
27. VALE ROYAL (WHITEGATE BEECHES). Sherratt's Rough, Churchill Wood, Papermill, Sixe's Bottom, Catsclough.
28. Shipbrook Bridge. Target Wood, Marshall's Gorse, Whatcroft, Drakelow.

29. THREE GREYHOUNDS [C.F.]. Yarnshaw Pitholes, Marshall's Gorse, Nook Gorse, Drakelow, Ravenscroft, Whatcroft.

30. PEOVER HALL [C.F.]. Big Wood, Eel Cage, Blackwood, White Gate.

31. ASTLE HALL (MIDDLE GATE) [C.F.]. Sir John's Bottom, Galey, Barnshaw, Bomish, Hazel Wood, Fox Wood, Pheasantry, Shooting Box, Goostery Bongs, Snelson.

32. Jodrell Hall. Gailey Piece, Jodrell, Withington Gorse, Taylor's Piece, Pigeon House, Strawberry Wood, Blackwood, Goostrey.
 HENBURY HALL [C.F.]. Big Wood, Cock Wood, Smithy Wood, Hollin's Wood, Whirley, Birtles.
 CAPESTHORNE HALL [C.F.]. Capesthorne Coverts, Siddington Bottom, Mere Moss, George's Wood.

33. WITHINGTON HALL (BLACK SWAN, LOWER WITHINGTON) [C.F.]. Porter's, Strawberry, Dooley's Grigg, Welltrough, Gleade's Moss, Pigeon House Clough, Jodrell, Bowshott.

33a. Bomish Wood.

34. Twemlow Hall. Pigeon House Clough, Bomish Wood, Hermitage Willows.

35. Holmes Chapel (HERMITAGE X-RDS.) [C.F.]. Hermitage Willows, Rudheath Gaily, Goostrey Bongs, Taylor's Piece, Shakerley's Wood, Warrington Common.

35a. Saltersford Bridge.

36. BRERETON GREEN (LEG'S O'MAN, SMALLWOOD) [C.F.]. Bechton, New Planting, Smallwood, Brookhouse Moss, Moss End.
 BRADWALL MANOR [C.F.]. Garden, Bradwall Wood, Union, The Marshes, Palm Wood, Sproston.
 NEWBOLD AST BURY [C.F.]. Brereton Moss, Bagmere, Mow Cop.

37. MANOR HOUSE, MIDDLEWICH. Old Gorse, New Gorse, Ockleston.

37a. Kinderton Guide Post. Sproston, Kinderton New Covert, Manor. Nook Gate, Shakerley's Wood, Unicorn.

38. ABBEY ARMS (FISHPOOL INN OR CABBAGE HALL). Abbey Wood, Blackbank, Fishpool, Oak Mere, Hogshead Wood, Relick's Moss, Tirley Hollow, Primrose Hill.
 EDDISBURY LODGE, DELAMERE FOREST [C.F.]. Woodside, Brickfield, Blackwood, Manley Knoll, Hatchmere Wood.

39. ASHTON HEYES. (GOSHAWK, MOULDSWOTH) [C.F.]. Horton Hall, Millwood, Sand Quarry, Brickfield, Rookery, Chapel Brook, Fishpond, Manley Rookery, Chapel Wood, Barnhouse, Wright's Gorse, Beckett's Wood, Ashwood, Longley Wood, Rookery, Spy Hill.

40. Kelsall Toll Bar. Phills Gorse, Waterworks, The Slack, Primrose Hill.

41. WILLINGTON HALL. Willington Wood, Willington Big Wood, Willington Mill, Dickinson's Rough, Jones's Wood, Bentley Wood, Ox Pasture, Ash Wood, High Barn, Duddon Mill, Primrose Hill.

42. Tarvin.

42a. Barrowmore. Barrowmore Gorse, Barnhouse, Manley Quarry.

43. DUDDON HEATH. Stapleford, Hoofield, Huxley Gorse, Iddinshall Rough, Simpson's Rough, Waterless, Sheaf, Frog Lane.

43a. Stapleford Mill.

44. FOX & BARREL (ALVANLEY ARMS). Tom's Hole, Mill Covert, Oulton Common, Eaton Hill, The Maddings.

45. OULTON PARK. (EGERTON ARMS). Pleasure Grounds, Hazelhurst, Darley Gorse, The Adjuncts, Cocked Hat, Hunt's Hill, Old Lane, Oulton Lowe, Little Budworth Pool.

45a. Wheatsheaf, Over. Hollowbacks Dingle, Rookery Pipe.

46. Darnhall Knobs. Darnhall Dingles

47. OX HEYS FARM. Page's Wood, Philo, Tilstone, Tilstone Moss.

48. Hargreave Green. Waverton, Cotton, Eaton Drives, Handley.

48a. Black Dog, Waverton. Waverton Gorse, Cotton, Waterless,

49. SAIGHTON. Saighton Gorse, Sooty Field, Penlington's Wood, Common Wood, Horse Pasture, Platt's Rough, Eaton Drives.

50. TATTENHALL STATION (ALDERSEY ARMS). Crow's Nest, Brickyards, Brockholes, Gatesheath, Handley Gorse, Millbank.

51. Tarporley Town End. Ash Wood, Ox Pasture.

52. Bolesworth Castle. Stable Bank, Coal Pits, The Kopje, Harthill Park, Harthill Coombs, Coach Drive, Iron Gate Plantation, Oak Plantation. Barnhill Wood, Goschen Spinney, Park Wood, Millbank.

53. BEESTON CASTLE (BEESTON SMITHY). Peckforton Mere, Willis's Wood, Gregory's Wood, Pennsylvania, Peckforton Wood.

54. Peckforton Lodge. COPPER MINES. Rawhead, Peckforton Gap.

55. Four Lane Ends.

56. HIGHWAYSIDE. Wardle, Radmore, Bache House, Verona.

57. CALVELEY HALL (GATES). Calveley Old Gorse, New Gorse, Hill's Gorse, Woodlands, Wettenhall Big Wood, Wettenhall Pipe.

58. Nantwich.

59. CHURCH MINSHILL. Aston's Gorse, Poolefield, Oaker's Brook, Ashbrooke Towers, Whitby's, Owen's Wood, Trelfa's Wood, Paradise, Tall Trees, Cholmondeston, Lawyers, Little Beech, Sandholes, Spoil Banks, Black Knight.

60. BRADFIELD GREEN. Red Hall Wood, Aquaduct, Picken's, Burnt Gorse and formerly Crewe Willows and Groby Manor.

61. WARMINGHAM. Tetton, Warmingham, Rookery,

62. Crewe Hall. Crewe Park, Bradeley, Foxholme, Groby.

63.   Wistaston Hall.
64.   WORLESTON GRANGE.
64a. THE ROOKERY.
65.   POOLE HALL. Eel's Gorse, Poole Gorse.
66.   Hurleston. Verona.
67.   RAVENSMOOR WINDMILL. Long Plantation, Admiral, Tally Ho, Bull's Wood, Baddiley Gorse, Cook's Pit.
68.   RIDLEY TOLL BAR. (BULKELEY GRANGE). Ridley Bache, Ridley Moss, Chesterton, Ridley, The Breeches, Bath Wood, Roseground, Peckforton Wood, Peckforton Moss.
69.   CHOLMONDELEY CASTLE. Nevill's Wood, Coronation, Garden Covert, Bret's Mere, Cholmondeley Mosses, Bickley Pipe, Bar Mere, Handley Sticks, Cholmondeley Meres, Chorley Sandholes.
69a. MARBURY HALL. Big Mere, Marbury, Quoisley, Oss Mere, Little Mere, Marley Moss, Poole Hook, Poole Gorse, Hewitt's Moss, Adamley Pool, Peel's Gorse.
70.   WRENBURY. Wrenbury Moss, Black Firs, The Heald, Starkey's Gorse, Canal Bank, Baddiley, Swanley.
70a. SOUND HEATH. Court's Gorse, Rockey Hole, Walkmill, Hall o'Coole
71.   Broomhall. Broomhall, Devil's Nest, Stick, Acton's Gorse.
72.   Broomlands.
73.   HANKELOW HALL. Hankelow Moss, Long Hill.

74.   WILKESLEY. Wilkesley, Kent's Rough.
75.   BURLEYDAM. Square, Combermere Big Wood, the Empress's Covert, Brankelow Moss, Mrs Poole's Riding Wood, Long Walk, Stonebridge Wood.

ADDITIONAL OR ALTERNATE MEETS INCLUDE:

CHESHIRE (*FORMER*).– Adderley Station; Alsager Heath; Barr Bridge; Bartington Heath; Booth Lane Smithy; Bruera Stapleford; Bucklow Hill; Bunbury Heath; Davenport Hall; Hartford Bridge; Holford Toll Bar; Hoo Green; Mere; Mickle Trafford; Ollerton; Peckforton Gap; Rocksavage; Saltersford Bridge; The Smoker; Stamford Bridge; Swettenham Village; Sutton Pinfold; Tarvin Village; Walgherton Lodge; Weaver Hall; Weston Green; Whatcroft.
(*RECENT*).– The Parkes, Audlem; Brindley Lea; Bulkeley X-Rds.; The Pheasant, Burwardsley; Plough Inn, Christleton; Cholmondeley Arms; Red Lion, Eaton; Glen Royal (Children's Meet); Hatton Hall; Haughton Hall; Hetherson Green; Red Hall, Leighton; Rowton Hall Hotel; Swan Inn, Marbury; Tiverton Smithy; Boot & Slipper, Wettenhall.
CHESHIRE FOREST.– Cock o'Budworth; Hare & Hounds, Crowton; Grimsditch Mill; Two-Lane-End, Lach Dennis; Manley Cottage; Higher Mutlow Fm., Marton; Tiger's Head, Norley; The Dog Inn, Over Peover; Bells o'Peover; Manor Farm, Snelson (Children's Meet).

Oulton Lowe

Appendix F

TARPORLEY JUMPS

THE HORSE SHOW was inaugurated as a special event to celebrate the Centenary and took place during the Races, which at that date were always on the Wednesday of the Hunt Week. Prizes were given for the following classes:

1. Best 4 y.o. Colt, for hunting purposes. £25. (Won by Mr R.N.Pervival of Tetton Hall, Middlewich.)
2. Best Cart Mare. £10. (Won by Mr Wm.Whitlow of Lymm.)
3. Best pair of Cart Mares or Horses. £15. (Won by Mrs Martha Austin of Little Budworth.)

The judges were Colonel Cotton and Captain White.

The Show proved so successful that it was made an annual event, being held simultaneously with the Races on Lord Shrewsbury's land at Cotebrook. When Tarporley Races became a Spring Steeplechase fixture, the Show continued to be held on the Wednesday afternoon of Hunt Week and except for the War years it continued to be held until 1953, on the racecourse or later in Portal or Arderne Park and sometimes in the field opposite Salterswell House.

In 1881 what was then called 'the Annual Leaping Competition' was introduced. The Show was for several years held in Daine's field at the back of the Swan Hotel stables. There was a luncheon tent for the Cheshire farmers and Sir Philip Grey-Egerton used to have a tent to entertain the ladies. It came to be known as 'Tarporley Jumps' and the classes were advertised in the local papers. Though there were always prizes for Shire Horses, Mares, Foals and Yearlings and other Show classes, the jumping became very much of a feature. And there was always free beer and a free lunch for the farmers at the Club's expense.

Sir Gilbert Greenall (242), later Lord Daresbury, always took a keen interest in Tarporley Week, despite his commitments with the Belvoir and invariably supplied all the show jumps, for which the Club would annually propose a hearty vote of thanks.

The most famous showjumper ever to take part was Nizefella and his 1952 Helsinki Olympics Gold Medal winning rider, Wilf White of Malpas, who joined a select band of sportsmen and women elected Honorary Members of the Cheshire Hunt. Nizefella's presence at any show in those days ensured a high attendance, if only to witness his famous 'kick-back' as he cleared the jumps.

In accordance with the Rule of 1799 for Hunt Uniform to be worn by Members on the racecourse, the same tradition always applied to the Show, whether or not it was held in Hunt Week.

A George IV silver gilt two handled campana-urn by Robert Garrard was used as a Challenge Cup for the Best Ridden Hunter from 1924 onwards, won by:

1924 W.H.Midwood's Wilkinstown
1925 W.H.Midwood's Wilkinstown
1926 G.B.Radcliffe's Huntsman
1927 W.H.Midwood's Wilkinstown
1928 Miss Diana Russell Allen's Trespasser
1929 Miss Diana Russell Allen's Swallow
1930 Mrs Melancy Chambers's Honour Bright
1931 Miss Diana Russell Allen's Dungannon
1932 W.H.Midwood's Golden Dawn
1933 W.J.Straiton's Ribblesdale
1935 Lady Mary Grosvenor's Deputy
1937 Lady Ursula Filmer-Sankey's Carverdoon
1938 D.P.G.Moseley's Robot
1946 G.B.Radcliffe's Bruce
1948 G.B.Radcliffe's Tiny
1950 G.B.Radcliffe's Remember Limerick
1951 R.L.Matson's Cinders
1952 R.F.Haworth's Second Thoughts
1953 R.L.Matson's Owt for Nowt

Bob Matson surrendered it when Chubb Paterson dined with him some 24 years later and it now adorns the dining table.

Silver-gilt Wine Cooler by R.Garrard, 1822, used as permanent Challenge Cup for the Tarporley Horse Show, 1924 to 1953.

Appendix G

HUNT CLUB STALLION

by Geoffrey Egerton-Warburton (1950)

FOR TWENTY-THREE YEARS, 1888 to 1911, the Club kept one or more stallions for the use of Farmers living within the limits of the Cheshire Hunt. Members subscribed for nominations, each Member being allowed three £1 and one £3.

In 1887 **Michael Angelo** was bought for £70. He was sold in 1893 for £30.

Mares served: 1888-90, no record, '91 50, '92 49

In 1889 **Lord Maldon** was bought for £75. He was sold in 1894 for £14.

Mares served: 1890, no record, '91 71, '92 54, '93 45, '94 29

In 1893 **Fenrother** was bought for £110 and sold in 1897 for £125.

Mares served: 1893 46, '94 45, '95 35, '96 40, '97 23

In 1895 **Innisfall** was bought for £300, of which £100 was given by the Steeplechase Committee.

Mares served: 1895 56, '96 43, '97 71, '98 53, '99 60, 1900 4

In 1900, owing to the sudden death of **Innisfall**, the loan of **The Dale** was offered by Mr Hubert Wilson and was gratefully accepted.

Mares served: 1900: 23, '01 49, '02 32

Graduate was also used in 1900, serving 7 mares.

In 1901 **Stapeley** was lent by Mr Arthur Knowles, serving 35 mares, but did not find favour with the farmers.

In 1901 **Johnny Morgan** was presented to the Club by the Duke of Portland with the stipulation 'that he should not pass out of their hands, except to be returned to Welbeck or placed under the sod'.

Mares served: 1902 24, '03, 31, '04 42, '05 44, '06 51, '07 42

After 1907 the Horses used were kept at The Kennels and appear to have been the property of the Cheshire Hunt, but nominations were still subscribed for by Members of the Club and £78 per annum for livery was paid by the Club.

Cherry Ripe –mares served: 1908 27, '09 31
Rydal Head – mares served: 1908 17
Tankard – mares served: 1910 17
Prince Hubert – mares served: 1910 22, '11 38
St.Aidan – mares served: 1911 26

After 1911 the Club gave up the practice of keeping a Stallion in view of the fact that, from that date onwards, a Premium Horse was supplied for the use of Farmers by the Cheshire County Council. The Club has since always been represented on the Light Horse Breeding Committee of the County Council and the Club was for many years a subscriber to the Shire Horse Society.

*

NOTE: Covering certificates were sent and a specially printed and an indexed book was kept for the Mares 'Served' by the Tarporley Hunt Club Stallions showing a record of the progeny.

Appendix H

RECIPES

THE TARPORLEY HUNT CLUB BLACK PUDDING:

Ingredients
7 kg (14 lb) groats
3.5 kg (7 lb) leaf or back fat
2 kg (4 lb) fine oatmeal
1 kg (2 lb) rusk
1 kg (2 lb) onions
4.8 litres (1 gal.) pigs' blood
50 g (2 oz) bergice (dry antiseptic)
Bullock runners or hog casings

Seasoning
340 g (12 oz) salt
170 g (6 oz) white pepper
2 kg (4 lb) ground coriander
1.5 kg (3 lb) ground pimento
1 kg (2 lb) ground caraway seed
170 g (6 oz) of this
seasoning will flavour
7 kg (14 lb) Black Pudding mixture.

Method: Put the groats loosely into a bag and tie. Boil until they are well swollen and thoroughly cooked. Empty into a large tub, add seasonings, rusk and onions and mix well while still hot. Add the back fat cut into 1 cm (1/2 in) cubes. This can be softened slightly to facilitate filling. Now add the blood and stiffen with oatmeal. Fill the bullock runners in wide hog casings, allowing about four pieces of fat to each pudding. Tie up firmly and boil gently for 20 mins. To obtain a rich black colour, add 30 g (1 oz) of *mancu* to every 36 litres (8 gal.) of water while boiling.

This recipe for black puddings, as supplied for generations by V.Millward & Sons of Tarporley, was given pride of place in the section on Black Puddings in The Book of the Sausage *by Antony and Araminta Hippesley Cox (Pan Books, 1978). It is the seasoning which distinguishes one black pudding from another.*

*

MULLED ALE FOR THE LOVING CUPS AND TOASTED CHEESE:

6 bottles of Old Chester
1.5 tablespoons of demerara sugar
large pinch of ground cloves
    do.   *do.*   *ginger*
    do.   *do.*   *grated nutmeg*

Bring almost to the boil and add 1.5 measures of Brandy and more sugar to taste.
A Whatcroft recipe dated 1856 for 'Ale Cup', found loose in Mr Shakerley's diary, recommended that it should be put on the toasted bread which should be allowed to stand for an hour before use.

Appendix J

SOME HUNTING DAYS

by Joseph Wright

WITH THE DUKE'S HOUNDS IN FRANCE

IN 1911 I WENT TO SOUTH WEST FRANCE near Arcachon for the wild boar hunting and took 26 couple of dog hounds from the Cheshire kennels and the horses from Eaton Hall. His Grace bought 22 couple from Mr Wroughton of the Woodland Pytchley. The new joint masters Mr Higson and Mr Roylance Court seemed to fancy the bitches so they told the Duke if he could let them have the bitches, they would let him have the dog hounds. So he took the dog hounds out to France. Everybody clacked on saying I was ruining myself and all that, but I said that His Grace is the finest Gentleman in the whole wide world and I would not disappoint him.

But the experiences I had going out there. We went on board from St. Catherine's Docks to Bordeaux and through the streets – all young hounds, or practically all young ones, in couples. We were round mules legs and donkey carts and all sorts of blooming things – you didn't see such a job in your life – till we got them on the train.

It was pitch dark when we arrived at Mimizan and a fellow met me there with a horse and a hurricane lantern. "Going to let the hounds out, of course," this fellow hollers, and off down the bloomin' road went these hounds after a bit of freedom.

They'd got a place ready for us. You've never seen such a place – it was wire netting only a yard and half high. We put these hounds in and stopped with them a bit. It was all right while I was there, but as soon as I went away to the Hotel de France for some food, they followed me up the road. So I took them back and tried again. And they followed me back again. So I said: "Somebody go and get me some food and I shall stop with them till you come back."

About ten o'clock I was very tired and I thought, "Well, they are quieter now – just sneak away if you can". But when I got to the hotel they came up the street in full cry. So I took them

back again and stopped until pretty late. But at one o'clock in the morning, well, there they were playing up Old Harry outside the hotel and I had to take them all back again. I got them settled down and then I went back to the hotel again, but there they all was outside the next morning when I got up and came down. So after that I just slept outside with those hounds and never had a roof over my head for six weeks. They were all right while I was there but they wouldn't settle down till we got the new kennels and it was impossible for them to get out. Funny thing, isn't it?

His Grace had a big Chalet built over there on his estate. It has been burnt down since and when he first started, he used to ask his friends to come out to France. He probably had ten or eight at a time and they would stay for a month and then perhaps he would ask another party out.[*] We went hunting every day. Sunday was a big day with us.

We started in October and went on till April when it got too hot. We had got all the exercising to do. At times we used to start at two o'clock in the morning so as to get finished by about eight because it was so hot. The first year I was out there, it was a very hot summer and we would get it 110 degrees in the shade – very, very hot . . .

When we first started hunting we lost the hounds eight times – straight off the reel. And those horses – they couldn't keep up with the hounds. The hounds absolutely left them on eight days – I am ashamed to say, really – we came home without a single hound. They had gone on hunting. So His Grace says: "Well, we want them a bit different to this next year, Joe". I said: "Yes, Your Grace, you leave it to me. I'll take charge of all the horses and that." And so we started exercising very early. I had a very fast horse and I used to walk, walk, walk him for nearly six weeks. Then after that we started trotting three mornings a week and walking three. Then eventually we started cantering three mornings a week and trotting three. We used to go down from Mimizan plage to St.Miriam plage at a canter for 17 kilometres, have a rum and coffee and then canter back again to Mimizan plage and then walk the 4 kilometres through the forest back to the kennels.

Now them horses was as fit as you would ever see in your life. You would never see one sweat. Once we took some horses

[*] One of the regular guests was Winston Churchill, with whom Bend Or had first had a day's hunting near Capetown, during the Boer War.

sixty kilometres, hunted the next day, brought them back again the next and hunted the next. Nobody will know what a horse can really do when he is really fit.

LIMIERS, TRACKING THE BOAR AND HUNTING.

I WAS THE FIRST HUNTSMAN to go out with His Grace. A man named Rawlinson [Mr.A.C.Rawlinson had been Master [had been out there for three seasons, but he hadn't killed a boar in all that time and we wouldn't have done, I quite agree, unless we had had these lymerers [as Joe pronounced *les limiers*, so called from the French word for spy or detective]. They're the fellows who get up to the boar while they're asleep. It is no use thinking you're going to do any good, unless you get up to the Boar while he's sleeping. They'll go – terrific the pace they can go, you know.

We killed our first boar after about six mornings out. Mind you, you don't kill them half so quick as foxes. I suppose we killed about 30 or 35 in a season. The boar is a thing you have got to follow about. You don't find them like hunting foxes, you know. You really can't do without what they call lymerers to rambush these pigs.

People laugh at you and they say: "A pig?" A pig, yes. But it can go as fit as a fiddle. It goes probably anything from six to eight miles every night of its life. Talk about fight. There is no animal that fights like a wild boar. They call them the kings of the forest and it is perfectly true. You couldn't explain to anybody really how they do fight.

The lymerers would track them the day before. You have to get on the boar asleep, because if they hear you, they'll get on the move and there is no possible chance of catching them. Before you start out, the lymerer would tell you what he thought the best place was to meet, because he had been out the day before rambushing a pig or trying to. We had three of these fellows. They lived in little houses in the village and they were marvellous fellows, no doubt about it.

One would go out to the North, another one South and another East. They'd go single-handed. They had a French dog called a *brache* which had a long cord on. It could track these boars after 24 hours by scent. These lymerers would go to what they call a *coupe*. This *coupe* was a kilometre square where the trees had been felled and left wild for five or six years. The boars used to go in there and these lymerers would track them in and go right around this kilometre square to see that no tracks were leading out of it. And, if there were none going away, to make definite sure they would come back to where they traced the boar in and the *brache* would go in. It was held on a cord all the time to check it, you see. And when it got within fifteen or twenty yards of the boar, up would go its head, (sniff sniff) like that, and it would pull the lymerer in; so he'd probably *see* the boar and tell you practically the weight of it. The boar was asleep, you see.

The next evening, when the lymerer came home, he'd say "If you meet at such and such a place, the boar probably won't be far from that." But there is no guarantee of course how far you would be away and sometimes we would have five or six

kilometres to go after we had met the lymerer and sometimes only a couple of kilometres. We used to take him a fresh horse, mind you. He had been out since day break and he would come out hunting with us. He would tell us he had had a 'très bon rambush' and he was absolutely certain of this, you could see.

He would take us up to the boar and the boar would give just one grunt and off! And then you have got 30 minutes at the very best with the boar probably two kilometres in front of you. He couldn't go so fast after that because he had bested himself, you understand. But he would go on until he would say: "Oh I have had enough of this!" and then he would stand and you could see him perhaps a quarter of a mile in front of you on a rise, waiting for you. And when you are anything within twenty yards, he charges. Terrible things, you know! Once he charged me from behind when I was on my feet. I have never jumped so high in my life. I jumped up to the branches of a tree because he went under. Oh yes, it was a very exciting time.

We used to destroy them as quick as we could, because their hides are that thick a bullet wouldn't penetrate twelve yards away. You can only kill him in the joint of the neck and the back of the shoulder. It's the only place and it's a bit of a blood and thunder business. They won't step out of the road for no one. They would even shift a mule and a cart - anything – out of the road. We had one fellow ripped up very bad. He stood on the track where the boar was going when we was hunting him and the boar ripped him up and oh, I don't know how many stitches he had, but he was bad for about twenty-two weeks.

But it was very rare that sort of thing happened. You could stand by the track within a yard as long as you stood still, but if you started, the boar would step out on the track to have a go at you. One went for me one day – I thought he was quite a small boar. We never used to shoot them. We used to stick them with a big knife that we carried in a socket on the side of the saddle and I fell into a bog up to me armpits and it turned out to be a huge one. I egged the hounds on and they hung onto his ears and other parts of him, till I could get up to stick him. But if he had got loose, I would have been no more.

The best boar that we ever got up to only had one tusk and it was seven and three quarter inches long. It killed a couple of hounds, Havelock and Dalesman, and ripped up four couple and a half. It also ripped up a horse, but I got this horse bound, stitched him up, and got him home. He was none the worse for it eventually. I had to put as many as thirty or forty stitches in some of the hounds. The next day we went out and another four hounds were ripped up. But if hounds get ripped up once they never get ripped up again, not unless they bump into a tree or a bit of thick stuff. The boar's never still a second. Talk about charge! They charge every minute, and they give a grunt every time they charge. If they catch anything its all up with it. They rip the innards clean out, but it is the finest sight you have ever seen to see the hounds after they have got used to boar hunting. They make a complete circle with the boar in the centre and he is charging, all the while charging. But as he charges, those hounds fall back while others close in. And there is this circle of hounds going to and fro. Oh, beautiful to see!

The boar go a terrific pace. If you have a very fast thirty minutes with them, you can rely on them being your boar, but it may be a long time – maybe two hours – before you get them. They're terrible things for water. They'll make for it and swim until they are freshened up again. They never stop until they're absolutely beat. Now that boar in my parlour: we ran two and a half hours with him before we killed him. But the one in the other room, that was the biggest hunt we ever had to kill – five hours and twenty minutes, forty kilometre point. There was nobody else at the finish but me. He knocked me flying three times. He was just charging me the fourth time when I shot him. As I said you can only shoot 'em in the joint of the neck and the shoulder. We used colt revolvers with ordinary gunstocks to get a better aim.

Well, then we had to stop out for the night in a little place about two kilometres away. The French are a very excitable race of people and they wanted to have a bit of a jollification. I said "Yes!", so this was arranged for eight o'clock and the kids went off on their bicycles shouting "M'sieur Joe arrivay! M'sieur Joe arrivay!" and fetched everybody to the village and they got magic lanterns and everything all decorated round a little café yard and they fetched the boar out and weighed him; he weighed 300 pounds. We skinned him and let the hounds feed on the carcass later. I brought the head home and the Duke had it set up for me, as you see.

Well, everybody was invited into this little café. There was about 60 or 70 people there and we had a six-course dinner with champagne, and played cards till 4 o'clock in the morning. I thought "Well I don't know! I don't know I'm sure who's

going to foot the bill? Not me!" But do you know, the landlord wouldn't take anything. He was so pleased to see us there and said he hoped we'd come the following week. They all wanted to know what time I was leaving for home. I said: " 9 o'clock." And they all came to see me off and had a farewell drink and on the way home we saw a little boar about the size of a hound, crossing the riding. We ran thirty minutes with him and killed him and the hounds ate him. We went on another two kilometres and another one crossed. We did not catch him, the horse was that tired and I stopped the hounds, all but two couple.

Three days after, when we was going out, me and His Grace, I said: "Would you believe it? Look! There's Petulant, Flagman and Painter all coming down the ride." They was so full up with food that I said: "We can't take these. We shall have to leave them with the Guard of the Forest." So we left them with the Guard of the Forest and went on hunting. After we had been hunting some considerable time, we came across a local fellow, who gave us the history about these hounds. They'd killed a boar quite close to him and he had been trying for three days to get some of it. The French are very keen about boars' meat, you know. He told us the hounds would go away for water one or two at a time, leaving the others on guard. When the first lot came back, the others would go for water. They never left the carcass, but cleaned the whole thing up before they went home. He tried for two or three days to get at the carcass, but he never got any. All that was left was the bone.*

HUNTING WITH OTHER PACKS – THE PAU AND GRIFFON HOUNDS.

WE USED TO HUNT with the Pau Hounds, too, when Mr.[F.H.] Prince was Master. They are all for hunting foxes, sometimes in the forest near the Pyrenees. We wore scarlet, same as here, and brown breeches. The French mostly wore blue with a lot of facing on the collars and cuffs. Different hunts wore different colours. His Grace wore scarlet and an ordinary hunting cap, same as he does in this country.

There was an enormous lot of packs out there, fox-hounds, stag-hounds and boar-hounds. Not many were pure English. In fact the only pure English were the Pau Hounds. All the others were crossed. There were some Americans, two packs of French and Americans crossed, crossed English and all sort of things. Once we all went to a large six day exhibition at Bordeaux with twenty couple of hounds. There were about

---

* When the author visited him at his home, Ridley Bank, Cuddington, shortly before he died in 1962, Joe Wright told him that those hounds could scent anything for miles around and once they went there was no stopping them. Joe was returning to kennels one evening with two stragglers when they suddenly gave tongue and away they went. He knew there were no boar about and was puzzled as to their quarry. Fortunately his keen eye spotted the figure of a man walking along the skyline a good mile distant. He got up in the nick of time to whip them off. It was a poacher with a rabbit in his pocket.

thirty different packs there – I was surprised really. They came from all over France. We paraded our hounds in the afternoon and won first prize for the best conditioned lot. We also won first prize for the dog named Weatherguage, which was walked at Weaverham [where Bluecap was as a puppy.] He was first champion of the whole lot and we won about £26. It was quite an exciting time.

Sometimes we took our hounds to hunt with Monsieur de Perron's hounds at Arcachon. That was a pack of griffons. They are like Welsh hounds, all long coated, not very big. We would travel to a meet perhaps 60 kilometres away one day, stay the night, hunt the next day and come back the next. At the meet one pack would stand twenty yards away from the other and these Frenchmen had horns that went round them, you know. But we stuck to the English hunting horns.

Before we met, one of these lymerers had probably rambushed the pig and if so he would be very excited and he could probably tell you the weight of it by its tracks. Very clever people, these lymerers. They wouldn't come right to the meet, but they would turn the bells of their horns towards you and blow to give you a signal and then the Master of the Griffon Hounds would blow his horn and give the lymerer a call. Then the lymerer would blow again we would all listen to hear exactly what had happened. And he wouldn't half rattle his blooming horn. Then the Master would tell us, as soon as he knew, that the lymerer had got a 'très bon rambush' and then we would all jump on our horses and go cantering off and when we got up to this lymerer, they would pull chocolate out, and little bottles of wine and all sorts of things. Make a terrible fuss of him. Then away we'd all go after the boar and hope we'd get him.

Once we started after a boar and eventually killed it with all our hounds there, twenty-two couple, but the nineteen couple of Griffon Hounds – they were nearly ten minutes before they came up. You could hear those hounds hunting, though we killed the boar a good ten minutes before. Whether there was anything in the feeding, I don't know. We used oatmeal, they used maize, ground maize.

I remember Lady Arthur Grosvenor, who used to come out quite a lot and hunt with us. She had a caravan and used to camp in the forest. One day we had the Griffon hounds out with us, and we went round the lake for about an hour and a half before the boar left and she said: "Well, Joe, if you can find a man that that sound doesn't appeal to, I'd be very much

surprised. I have never heard anything like it in my life," she said. "Like bells from heaven, I shall never forget it till my dying day." It was a beautiful cry, too. They were very heavy-noted hounds, you see. And with our hounds packed together it was one of those things you could not explain. A lovely cry it was, and going round and round and round this lake before the boar got away.

*

ONCE WE WENT TO LUE, 22km away, to stay the night. We hunted the next day. Then we visited General Sir Joseph Laycock's house with the Duke and hunted over the border onto the Biarritz main line. To get over the line, all you had to do was cut one strand of wire and we hunted round and round a long time, till it was getting late. His Grace says: "Joe, I think we had better stop." Of course I went to stop hounds and fell in a ditch. There is no jumping out there, you see, only ditches and you didn't find them till you fell in them. Well I fell into this one. And I could hear the Duke and Sir Joseph coming up. And the Duke says here's Joe, you see, here, and they pulled the horse off me and got me out and I went on and stopped hounds.

"Now then, Joe, which way?" says the Duke. "We shall have to go this way, Your Grace," I says. We should hit off the Labouheyre-Bordeaux main road. Now we had a little dog hound called Palafox with us. He'd had distemper and he wasn't very fit and quite a young dog. It was only his second time out hunting. I said: "Come on, Palafox!" and he lay on the ground. "I think he will come, Your Grace" I said so we went on and got onto the main road after about 4 km. "Now which way?" says the Duke. "Lets go right-handed," said I. "It should lead to Labouheyre." However, we went about a kilometre and found a post which said 16 km from Labouheyre – that was 64 km from home. "Now then," says the Duke, "What must we do?" I said "You and Sir Joseph canter on as quickly as you can to Labouheyre and telephone for your car to pick you up and I shall stay the night in Labouheyre and you can bring me some clothing for me and food for the horses and hounds. It'll be all right." So this is what they did.

The next day I started off home and when I got home, I said to the kennelman: "We've lost Palafox." He said: "You've not, you know. He was here this morning at six o'clock when I came

to the kennels." Now that little dog had travelled all that way. I sent another dog hound, Hanover, 140 mile away by train, it was sixty mile from the kennels as the crow flies. The next morning when I came to the kennels, Hanover was there. "Well I never," I said, "would you believe it? You got back all right." And I sent him off again and back he came again. "Hanover, you'll never go away from here," I said, and he didn't go no more.

Now with regards to horses you had to use your brains a bit and watch where the sun sunk so as to know where to steer for home, because you were twisting and turning and going about in the forest. Altogether it was hundreds of miles long, this forest and you couldn't tell where you were. The French Government owned it but the Duke bought a part of it. Oh, it was the most lovely forest with great big wild ridings fifteen yards wide, all fine silvery sand, kept raked in case of fire. You had to ride in between the trees, but after they had thinned them out, ready for cultivation, they were quite wide apart, six or seven yards perhaps.

There was the Guard of the Forest who knew his trees just like a shepherd knows his sheep.

Now there were dozens and dozens of people that spent nights in the forest before I went, but I never did. I never had a night there. I just left it to the horse and he'd take me miles and miles. Many a night it's been eleven o'clock when I got home. The forest was dense-like, the trees met above and you couldn't see nothing; but the horse would take you up little trackways and over railways up and down dale and he'd never let you catch your leg. You had to leave yourself entirely to him, but if you was clever and thought: "No, I am sure you're wrong. Come this way!" you were done for. You'd got the horse lost as well. Now, if you take a horse miles away for three days and ride him round about, he'll take you home if you leave it to him. Absolutely marvellous what those horses will do. Nobody will ever know unless they go through the kind of experience that I had, and what sense horses and hounds have got.

FISHING – CROSSING RIVERS – AMPHIBIOUS BOARS.

THAT PART OF FRANCE south of Bordeaux is very quiet. They speak a patois language. You don't get very good French till you come to Bordeaux, but those Frenchmen can make you understand anything and you can make them understand. I was very, very fond of them. I don't like to hear anybody run the French down.

Its all right for fishing, too, down there. We used to go deep-sea fishing in the Bay of Biscay and find all sorts of fish. Sometimes when we were walking out with the hounds at Mimizan plage, we would take a line, a big cord about fifty yards long, and put about a dozen hooks on it and sling it out to the sea. Then we would walk on down the coast and when we came back we would get a basketful of fish. Nearly every hook had something.

Now that river I spoke of – it ran right through the forest into the sea and the sea-fish used to come up it. There was a

big lake about seven miles by five in the forest. It was only two or three miles from the sea and when the tide was going back, this river flowed very fast, very, very fast. You couldn't bottom the water. You would spin round like a top until you found a little place where you could catch hold...

I remember once, when we were coming to the river, His Grace said to Pat Nicholls, the big polo player: "Now look out! We're coming to the river and you'll be overturned. You'd better wait." Mr. Nicholls said: "If Joe is going to cross, I'm going too." "We're crossing the river, Joe," he said, "aren't we?" "Yes, going over," I said. "Right," he says, "I am coming with you." And the Duke of Sutherland said he was coming too.

Well the Duke of Sutherland went so far, and then his horse went down and couldn't bottom the river. Pat Nicholls, he lost his horse the first time down but he stuck to it and swam out with it. Eventually I got out all right, but the Duke of Sutherland lost his horse the first time he went down. And when he got his horse out, there was no stirrup irons or leathers on. So I had to direct him the way to go home.

When we'd picked a place where His Grace thought he would cast, now, there's I in a whirlpool with everybody shouting "Get out!" "I can't get out!," I said. I was spinning around like a top in the water, you see. Eventually I did get out but it was a terrible place. Since I left, His Grace has had a lot of bridges put over the river, but there were no bridges in my day. Sometimes the boar would swim up and down the river and you wouldn't not see a ripple. I remember once, we had a real good hour with a boar, which went into one of these huge lakes in the forest. The Duke waded in and shot, oh, twelve times at the boar. But each time he shot, the boar just ducked his head, as if to say: "Thank you!". I persuaded His Grace to go out in the boat, while I hid to see if the boar would come out of the lake. Well he did come out and we had another hour with him, before we killed him and that particular day I'd got a folding spear which Pat Nicholls wanted to try. He put this spear in position and had a go at the boar. But the boar quickly upset him and his horse. It then upset another man and his horse. But His Grace shot it and when they skinned it, the spear, which Pat Nicholls had a go with, hadn't even got through the hide. It is so thick, you know. As I said, you can't possibly kill them except in the joint of the neck and the shoulder.

The boar can swim for miles and miles and the hounds can't

do that, you see. After I came back to England, they lost a lot of hounds by drowning. Just didn't get there in time to stop them. Aye, they were some good experiences out there. I wouldn't have missed them for anything else on earth.

NOTE:

During the inter-war years the Duke of Westminster took his boar-hounds to Normandy to hunt from a rented establishment at St. Saëns. The kennels were at Château d'Hirondelle. With him there, as 1st Whipper-in, was William Jull, previously at the Pytchley and afterwards war-time kennelman at the Forest Kennels at Sandiway, where he remained so long that the tiled wall by the coppers are still scarred to this day at the place he kicked them with his clogs as he leant over to ladle out the porridge and the cooked flesh.

The Prince of Wales was often a visitor and always insisted on Jull being his valet during his stay – he never found his boots and shoes better polished. Like Joe, Jull became adept at washing the wounds, in a nearby stream, of any hounds that had become casualties, sometimes having to put their entrails back in and stitch them up on the spot. Being so fit and tough, they would still be able to return to kennels on their own feet. And, like Joe, Will got his own share of wounds, once being gored in the face so badly that his eye-socket was down by his mouth. Miraculously his sight was not impared. He was then rushed off to the London Clinique and became an early and successful 'guinea-pig' for the man who was destined to become the eminent plastic surgeon for the Royal Air Force, Sir Archibald McIndoe.

The Huntsman was Tom Hawtin, who had come to the Duke from the Blankney in 1919 and Kenny, the 2nd Whipper-in, had been with the Suffolk. J. Wentworth Day visited to former on his 94th birthday, living in Westminster Cottage, his grace and favour home near Mimizan in the Landes, and still enjoying Bend Or's cigars. They and Jull were with the hounds when War was declared and it was their painful duty to shoot no less than 90 couple before getting safely back to England, where Will, incidentally an addicted snuff-taker (in preference to Woodbines, pipe-smoking or chewing tobacco), wore his old blue beret for the rest of his days. The print, from which this illustration is taken, was formerly in his possession.

THE ST. SAËNS HUNT, 1936.

From the oil painting by André Marchand in the possession of the Duke of Westminster and photographed from a print now belonging to the Hon. Mrs Jonathan Forbes.
l. to r. (mounted): *T. H. Hawtin, Huntsman, Wm. Jull, 1st Whipper-in, Col. Crémière, Col. R. E. ('Poss') Myddelton, the Duke of Westminster, Capt. St. G. ('Sainty') Clowes, Col. C. F. Hunter, J. Kenny, 2nd Whipper-in.* In foreground: *Germain Dufourg, Limier.*

Appendix K

WINNERS OF THE RICHMOND CUP FOR THE TARPORLEY HUNT CLUB OPEN STEEPLECHASE AT THE CHESHIRE HUNT POINT-TO-POINT.

1959 Mrs W.B.Higgin's Tell Tale*
1960 H.V.Willis's Lady Emm
1961 R.M.Peacock's Barney
1962 Mrs M.Langford-Brooke's Kyleakin
1963 Mrs G.V.Churton's Come to Good*
1964 T.Nicholas's Clodhopper
1965 H.S.Tate's All Aboard II
1966 G.J.Forward's Question Lad
1967 J.M.Spurrier's Head Lad
1968 Foot & Mouth Disease
1969 J.K.Barlow's Hinch*
1970 K.P.Owen Good Lad
1971 J.M.Spurrier Hilton Gravelle
1972 Mrs A.B.Garton's Gladeyes
1973 T.A.Garton's Jaydix
1974 J.Lilley's Colonian Queen
1975 J.Lilley's Colonian Queen
1976 R.H.Salmon's Hidden Treasure

1977 J.Froggatt's Ridware Fox
1978 E.V.Oliver's Bor Da III
1979 K.R.Owen's Moya's Star
1980 E.S.Oliver's Bor Da III
1981 A.C.R.Stubbs's Patronage
1982 R.K.Aston's Bor Da III
1983 Meeting Abannoned
1984 D.F.Dippie's Sentimental Me
1985 A.D.W.Griffith's Brief Barnie
1986 Meeting Abandonned
1987 H.J.K. Edwards's Kenstone
1988 F.J.Dilworth's Sunday School
1989 F.J.Dilworth's Sunday School
1990 F.J.Dilworth's Sunday School
1991 Mrs E.M.W.Griffith's Bryn Glas*
1992 Messrs. C.Coxen & J.W.M.Barlow's Oakley House*
1993 J.A.Griffiths's Equity Player

* Horses whose owners were connected with Members of the Tarporley Hunt Club.

The Richmond Cup.

Abbreviations

a.	...	*ante*	*d. felo per se*	...	committed suicide
A.D.C.	...	Aide-de-camp	Dir.	...	Director
A.E.	...	Air Efficiency Award	div.	...	divorced
A.K.	...	Knight, Order of Australia	*d.s.p*	...	*decessit sine prole* (died without issue).
aka	...	also known as	*d.s.p.l.*	...	*decessit sine prole legitima*
A.R.A.	...	Associate of the Royal Academy			(died without lawful issue)
Assoc.	...	Association	*d.s.p.m.*	...	*decessit sine prole mascula*
att.	...	attached			(died without male issue)
au.	...	aunt	*d.s.p.m.s.*	...	*decessit sine prole superstite*
					(died without surviving male issue)
b.	...	born	*d.m.a.*	...	died middle-aged
Bart. or Bt.	...	Baronet	*d.unm.*	...	died unmarried
br.	...	brother	*d.v.p.*	...	*decessit vita patris*
Brig.	...	Brigadier			(died in the lifetime of his father)
c.	...	*circa*	e.	...	elder
C.B.	...	Companion of the Order of the Bath	eld.	...	eldest
		(Civil Division)	e.u.r.	...	expelled under Rule of 4th Meeting
C.B. (Mil.)	...	Companion of the Order of the Bath			
		(Military Division)	f.	...	father
C.B.E.	...	Commander the Order of the British	F.B.A.	...	Fellow of the British Academy
		Empire	F.G.S.	...	Fellow of the Geological Society
C.H.	...	Member of the Order of Companions of	F.R.G.S.	...	Fellow of the Royal Geographical Society
		Honour	F.R.S.	...	Fellow of the Royal Society
C.M.G.	...	Companion of the Order of St. Michael and	F.S.A.	...	Fellow of the Society of Antiquaries
		St. George	Fl.Lt.	...	Flight Lieutenant
C.St.John	...	Commander of the Order of St. John of			
		Jerusalem	G.C.B.	...	Knight Grand Cross of the Order of the
C.V.O.	...	Commander of the Royal Victorian Order			Bath (Civil Division)
Capt.	...	Captain	G.C.B.	...	Knight Grand Cross of the
Cav.	...	Cavalry	(Mil.)		Order of the Bath (Military Division)
Cdr.	...	Commander	G.C.H.	...	Knight Grand Cross of the Order of the
cf.	...	*confer* (compare)			Hanovarian Order
Ch.	...	Steeplechase	G.C.V.O	...	Knight Grand Cross of the Order of the
Chm.	...	Chairman			Royal Victorian Order
C.-in-C.	...	Commander-in-Chief	G.M.B.	...	Great Master and First or Principal Knight
Col.	...	Colonel			Grand Cross of the Most Honourable
Comdg.	...	Commanding			Order of the Bath
Commd.	...	Commanded	g-dau.	...	grand-daughter
Commdt.	...	Commandant	Gen.	...	General
Cor.	...	Cornet	gr.	...	great
cos.	...	cousin	gs.	...	grandson
d.	...	died	Hcp.	...	Handicap
D.C.L.	...	Doctor of Civil Law	hh	...	hands high
D.C.M.	...	Distinguished Conduct Medal	h.-p.	...	half-pay
D.D.	...	Doctor of Divinity	H.C.M.	...	His Catholic Majesty
D.F.C.	...	Distinguished Flying Cross	H.I.M.	...	His or Her Imperial Majesty
D.Litt.	...	Doctor of Letters	H.M.	...	His or Her Majesty
D.Sc.	...	Doctor of Science	H.M.L.L.	...	Lord Lieutenant, (of the City and County
D.S.O.	...	Companion of the Distinguished Service			of Chester except where stated otherwise)
		Order	H.R.H.	...	His or Her Royal Highness
dau.	...	daughter	H.S.	...	High Sheriff, (Cheshire except where stated
des.	...	mentioned in despatches			otherwise)

H.S.H.	. . .	His Serene Highness
Hon.	. . .	Honourable/Honorary
Imp.	. . .	Imperial
Inf.	. . .	Infantry
Jt.	. . .	Joint
k.	. . .	killed
K.B.	. . .	Knight of the Order of the Bath (pre 1816), subsequently Knight Grand Cross
K.B.E.	. . .	Knight Commander of the Order of the British Empire
K.C.B. (Mil.)	. . .	Knight Commander of the Order of the Bath (Military Division)
K.C.M.G.	. . .	Knight Commander of the Order of St. Michael and St. George
K.C.S.G.	. . .	Knight Commander of the Order of St. Gregory
K.C.V.O.	. . .	Knight Commander of the Royal Victorian Order
K.G.	. . .	Knight Companion of the Order of the Garter
K.G. St. J.	. . .	Knight of Grace of the Order of St. John of Jerusalem
K.J. St. J.	. . .	Knight of Justice of the Order of St. John of Jerusalem
(K.H.)	. . .	Kennel Huntsman
K.P.	. . .	Knight of the Order of the St. Patrick
K.T.	. . .	Knight of the Order of the Thistle
Knt. Bach. or Kt.	. . .	Knight Bachelor
Lieut. or Lt.	. . .	Lieutenant
Lt.-Col.	. . .	Lieutenant-Colonel
LL.D.	. . .	Doctor of Laws
m.	. . .	married
M.B.E.	. . .	Member of the Order of the British Empire
M.C.	. . .	Military Cross
M.F.H.	. . .	Master of Fox-Hounds
M.F.H.A.	. . .	Master of Fox-Hounds Association
M.H.	. . .	Master of Hounds or Harriers
M.M.	. . .	Military Medal
M.P.	. . .	Member of Parliament
Maj.	. . .	Major
mo.	. . .	mother
N.C.O.	. . .	Non-Commissioned Officer
n.s.	. . .	natural son
nep.	. . .	nephew
nie.	. . .	niece
o.	. . .	only

O.B.E.	. . .	Officer of the Order of the British Empire
O.St.J.	. . .	Officer of the Order of St. John of Jerusalem
p.	. . .	*post*
P.C.	. . .	Privy Counsellor
prob.	. . .	*probabiliter* (probably)
P.O.	. . .	Pilot Officer
Pres.	. . .	President
Q.S.O.	. . .	Queens Service Order (New Zealand)
R.	. . .	Royal
r.	. . .	resigned
R.A.	. . .	Royal Academician/Royal Artillery
R.A.C.	. . .	Royal Armoured Corps
R.A.F.	. . .	Royal Air Force
R.A.S.C.	. . .	Royal Army Service Corps
R.F.A.	. . .	Royal Field Artillery
R.N.R.	. . .	Royal Naval Reserve
R.N.V.R.	. . .	Royal Naval Volunteer Reserve
R.o.H.	. . .	Roll of Honour (President Board)
Regt.	. . .	Regiment
Res.	. . .	Reserve
res.	. . .	resided
ret.	. . .	retired
Rev.	. . .	Reverend
s.	. . .	son
sic.	. . .	thus, so, in this way
sis.	. . .	sister
Sqn.Ldr.	. . .	Squadron Leader
Sks.	. . .	Stakes
suc.	. . .	succeeded
surv.	. . .	surviving
T./	. . .	Temporary
T.A.	. . .	Territorial Army
Ten.	. . .	Tenant
trs.	. . .	transferred
u.	. . .	uncle
Univ.	. . .	University
v.	. . .	versus
V.C.	. . .	Victoria Cross
V.-L.	. . .	Vice-Lord Lieutenant of Cheshire
Vol.	. . .	Volunteer(s)
w.	. . .	wife
wid.	. . .	widow
W/O	. . .	War Office
Yeo.	. . .	Yeomanry or Imperial Yeomanry
yr.	. . .	younger
yst.	. . .	youngest

Glossary of Hunting Terms

This is not intended to be a comprehensive list, but to include most of those mentioned in this book. See also *The Language of Sport* by C.E.Hare (Country Life, 1939).

At fault:	When hounds check, they are said to be at fault.
Bag fox, bagman:	Any fox which is turned out especially for hounds to hunt. A practice which has been TOTALLY FORBIDDEN for very many years.
Bob-tailed:	A fox without a brush.
Bolt:	To bolt a fox is to force it out of a drain or earth.
Brace of foxes:	Two foxes. Plural – brace.
Break up:	Hounds break up their fox when they eat its carcase.
Brush:	The fox's tail.
Bullfinch:	A thick, high and uncut hedge, which cannot be jumped over, but a determined horseman and bold horse will jump through it.
Burst:	The first part of a run.
Cast:	The effort by the pack, or by the Huntsman with his pack, to recover the scent after a check.
Charley:	A slang term for a fox; origin: Charles James Fox.
Check:	Hounds check when they stop running and temporarily lose the fox's scent.
Chop:	Hounds are said to chop a fox when they kill one asleep, or surprise one before it gets away.
Couple:	Two fox-hounds. Plural – couple.
Course:	To run a fox 'in view' without heed to scent.
Covert:	Any woodland (unless very big) or place that might hold a fox.
Cub:	A young fox – becomes a fox on November 1st.
Dog fox:	A male fox.
Draft:	Hounds which have been brought into or sent out of the kennel.
Drag:	An artificial line of 'scent' made by a strong-smelling substance. (Some Drag Hunts, with a zoo in the vicinity, have found bears' urine ideal, laid down in advance at strategic places on the line by a horseman carrying a mop soaked with the liquid, no easy task as he has to jump the intervening fences with a bottle in his pocket.)
Draw:	A covert is drawn by the hounds when the Huntsman puts them in it. The draw for the day is the country the Master intends to hunt. A hound is drawn when the Huntsman takes one away from the rest of the pack.
Earth:	A fox's underground home. His billet is his excreta.
Earthstopper:	The earthstopper of a covert is sent a 'night stop' if his covert is to be drawn the next day and a 'morning stop' if hounds are likely to run to his covert, thus stopping the foxes in so that they cannot be hunted that day.
Enter:	Teaching young hounds to hunt a fox is to enter them.
Field:	The mounted men and women following the hounds.
Fox-hunter:	A fox-hunter has two legs. *See* Hunter
Gone to ground:	When a fox has got into an earth or drain.
Headed:	A fox which turns away from its original line is said to have been headed.
Hounds:	Generic term for a pack of any type of hunting dog – beagle and harrier, which hunt hares, fox-hounds, otter-hounds *etc.*, or even Bassett hounds, which hunt 'clean-boot', *i.e.* human scent. It does not need the definite article.
Hunter:	A hunter has four legs. *See* Fox-hunter.
Huntsman:	The person who hunts hounds and carries the horn. He is also in charge of the Kennels. 'To carry the horn' is to hunt hounds. The members of the field are hunt followers, members of the hunt or subscribers to hounds. *See* Fox-hunter.
Kennel huntsman:	The man in charge of hounds in the kennels for an Amateur Huntsman.
Leash:	Three foxes.

Leathers:	White leather breeches, notoriously difficult to clean.
Mark:	Hounds are marking to ground when they gather round and bay outside an earth or drain where a fox has gone to ground.
Mask:	The fox's head.
Meet:	The place designated for hounds to meet the Master. 'A Lawn Meet' is at a private house, where refreshments ('stirrup cups') are provided for the Field.
Music:	The cry of hounds.
Oxer:	Thorn fence with a guard rail.
Pad groom:	A lightweight second horseman who would fit a pad by a surcingle with stirrups and girth attached, over the saddle, usually a side-saddle, to protect it and save the trouble of changing saddles for his master or mistress.
Poached:	Ground on the take-off side of fence, badly cut up by horses' hooves.
Point:	The distance of a run, measured as the crow flies. The actual distance is described as 'as hounds ran'.
Pudding:	The meal porridge as fed to hounds.
Rasper:	Any big fence.
Rate:	To reprove or scold a hound is to rate it.
Ride:	A path through a covert.
Riot:	Any animal, other than a fox, hunted by hounds. The rates are 'Ware (pronounced war) hare' (for rabbits and hares), 'Ware wing' (birds) and 'Ware haunch' (deer) or simply 'Ware riot'.
Scut:	The hare's tail.
Shires:	The Shire packs are the Belvoir, Cottesmore, Quorn, Pytchley and Fernie, covering parts of Leicestershire, Rutland and Northants, as opposed to the Provinces which are any hunting country in England, Scotland and Wales, except for the Midlands and Shires.
Skirt:	A hound which does not follow the true line is a 'skirter'.
Soil:	When a stag has been hard hunted, he takes to swimming in river or lake and is said 'to take soil'.
Stern:	A hound's tail.
Tally-ho!:	A hunting cry made when the fox has been viewed. The word is supposedly of Chinese origin, though some attribute it to the French.
Thruster:	A rider who thrusts himself forward in the field and tends to get too close to hounds.
Timber:	Posts and rails.
Tongue:	Cry of hounds which 'throw tongue' when they speak to a line.
View:	The sight of a fox.
View Halloa, or Holloa:	The scream given when one has viewed a fox.
Vixen:	A female fox.
Walk:	Hound puppies are sent out 'to walk' when they are looked after on farms or by private individuals during their early months, culminating in the annual Puppy Judging at the Kennels, colloquially known as 'The Puppy Show'.
Whipper-in:	Turns hounds to the huntsman out hunting and generally assists with the kennel work. It is incorrect to refer to a whipper-in as ' a whip', which is a driving term for one who drives a horse or horses in harness. A hunting whip, composed of a crop with a crooked handle and a keeper with thong and lash attached, is the correct accoutrement for all who ride to hounds, only to be cracked in exceptional circumstances.

Book Two

Part One

The Hunting Songs
of
Rowland Egerton Warburton

Rowland Eyles Egerton Warburton, Poet Laureate of the Tarporley Hunt Club.

Bibliography

There have previously been Ten Editions, and other books of poetry, published as follows:

Poems – Chester, 1833 (Foolscap 8vo., pp30 – Written at Orleans, 1822, sold at the bazaar, 1833, for benefit of Chester Infirmary.

Hunting Songs, Ballads, &c. (First Edition) – Chester, 1834 (Demy 8vo., pp 47, col.frontis., 11 lithographs & 9 tailpieces by W.Crane)

Hunting Songs and Ballads (Second Edition) – London, 1846 (Super Royal 8vo., pp 152, 16 l.d.)

Three Hunting Songs – Chester, 1855 (Oblong 12mo., pp 16, 4 engrav. by Hablôt K. Browne – "Phiz")

Four New Songs – 1859 (Fcp.8vo. pp 16)

Miscellaneous Verses and Sonnets – 1859 (Fcp., 8vo., pp 76)

Hunting Songs and Miscellaneous Verses (Third Edition) – London and Manchester, 1859 (Fcp 8vo., pp 224, no illus.)

Hunting Songs and Miscellaneous Verses (Fourth Edition) – London and Manchester, 1860 (Fcp.8vo., pp 254, no illus.)

Epigrams & Humorous Verses by *Rambling Richard* – London, 1867 (Crown 8vo, pp 74)

Hunting Songs (Fifth Edition) – London, 1873 (Fcp.8vo., pp 224, frontis.)

Hunting Songs (Sixth Edition) – London, 1877 (Fcp.8vo., pp 240, no illus.)

Poems, Epigrams and Sonnets – 1877 (Cr.8vo., pp 152)

Songs & Verses on Sporting Subjects – London,1879 (Fcp.8vo., pp35)

Arley in Idleness – 1879 (Privately printed, vellum bnd, ltd.25, pp 225 and abridged paper bound edition, pp 22)

Twenty–Two Sonnets – London, 1883 (Fcp 4to., pp 26, illustrated)

Hunting Songs (Seventh Edition) – London, 1883 (Fcp.8vo., pp 248)

Counsel for Cottagers and A Looking Glass for Landlords – London, 1887 (Fcp.4to., pp 36)

Hunting Songs (Eighth Edition) – London, 1887 (Fcp.8vo.)
   do. – reprinted 1892

Hunting Songs (Ninth Edition) – Liverpool, 1912 (Cr.4to., ltd.375, pp.280, 29 pl., memoir by Sir Herbert Maxwell, Bt.)

Hunting Songs (Tenth Edition) – London, 1925 (Cr.4to., pp 128, 8 mtd.col.pl.by Lionel Edwards.);

together with various songsheets and broadsides published individually.

The introductions to the Fifth, Sixth, Seventh, Eighth and Ninth Editions, bound in scarlet and green, include a short account of the Tarporley Hunt Club from 1762 to 1869, with extracts from its proceedings.

This, the **Eleventh Edition**, with a few exceptions, contains only Rowland Egerton Warburton's Hunting Songs and Verses connected with Cheshire, selected and annotated by Gordon Fergusson who re–dedicates them to their author's family.

A Memoir of R.E.Egerton Warburton

by

Gordon Fergusson

ROWLAND EGERTON WARBURTON must surely have been the Cheshire Victorian squire personified – friendly, sympathetic and sensitive, a veritable *beau-ideal*. At the same time he was firmly convinced of the God-ordained nature of the social hierarchy and took a benign, though no less autocratic, attitude to the responsibilities which had been thrust upon him. He was a man of extreme and genuine piety. His friend Bishop Wilberforce said of him that he was equally at home in the hunting field and the parish church. He had ridden to hounds ever since he was a jacket–clad boy on a pony.

In his *Counsel for Cottagers*, consisting of over a hundred rhyming couplets, he took Genesis III. 19. for his text:

> *By sweat thy bread thou here shalt earn,*
> *Till thou again to dust return.*

Although very well travelled, his home at Arley meant everything to him, as witnessed by these lines from *A Looking-Glass for Landlords*:

> *To sunnier clime let those who need it roam,*
> *No spot so happy as an English home;*
> *The summer flowers in radiant beauty clad,*

> *The social mirth that maketh winter glad,*
> *The Christmas chimes from village bell–tower ringing,*
> *Once more glad tidings to the faithful bringing,*
> *The group close clustered round the blazing fire,*
> *The child, the mother, and the grey grandsire.*

There followed some sound advice:

> *Talk not to bishops of the last week's run,*
> *Nor drag the bookworm from his favourite shelf*
> *To some dull pamphlet written by yourself;*
> *To some your house, to some your pictures show,*
> *Welcome when coming, speed them when they go . . .*

and especially

> *. . . The gun must ever to the horn give way,*
> *Disband your beaters till the following day . . .*

Choral matins was sung daily in the Arley Chapel, which Rowland had had rebuilt by Salvin, and with his beloved wife, Mary, by his side, he was never missing from his pew – on hunting mornings attired in scarlet and buckskins.

When the time came to make his will he prefaced it by expressing a 'desire that everyone whom I have offended will forgive me, as I heartily forgive all the world.'

The Poet Squire of Arley had an output of great versatility and for such a pious man he had an extremely impish sense of humour, which time and again is reflected in his songs.

He had quaint fingerposts put up around his estate, carved with verses for those who passed that way. These are some examples:

> Trespassers this notice heed,
> Onward you may not proceed
> Unless to Arley Hall you speed.

and

> No cartway, save on sufferance, here.
> For horse and foot the road is clear
> To Lymm, High Legh, Hoo Green and Mere.

And this was on the road leading to Arley Hall from the highway between High Legh and Northwich:

> This road forbidden is to all,
> Unless they wend their way to call
> At Mill or Green or Arley Hall.

There are also inscriptions on a house in the Northwich road, near Great Budworth:

> Take thy calling thankfullie,
> Love thy neighbor neighborlie
> Shun the path o béggarie

and over the door in the porch of the George & Dragon Inn at Great Budworth on a slate tablet, engraved with his monogram:

> As St. George in armed array
> Doth the fiery dragon slay
> So may'st thou, with might no less
> Slay the dragon Drunkenness.

In his book of epigrams he even included an Irish joke:

> *"Pat! buy a trunk? Sure for what?" he replied,*
> *"Why to carry your clothes," said the dealer, "inside."*
> *"Bedad! now a mighty queer notion is that,*
> *Would you have me go naked entirely?" said Pat.*

Many of his poems, legends and sonnets he wrote to record his experiences on the Continent, which he and his family visited on several occasions. But he was essentially a home lover and only ventured to the Metropolis when duty called. One such occasion was during the religious riots at Pimlico in 1850–51. The Squire of Arley was there night after night with an ardent band of laymen, protecting the worshippers from the violence of the mob.

Like many before and after, he liked nothing better

Rowland Egerton Warburton.

than his annual pilgrimage to The Swan for Tarporley Week. And there, in his time more than ever, the rafters really rang after dinner to his rollicking hunting songs in what, in those days, was the dingy old club room. In his youthful prime and in his old age he delighted in his title of Laureate of the Tarporley Hunt Club. His output never faltered and never failed in originality. He was never short on humour and always free from cant.

> *Good fun how rare it is!*
> *I know not where it is,*
> *Save at The Swan!*

His cousin, Cecely Egerton, once wrote to ask him to compose a poetical round robin to persuade Hugh, the 2nd Lord Delamere to restore the old swinging sign 'Hark to Blue Cap', which had been removed. A year or two later Rowland heard from Vale Royal:

> . . . I know nothing will please you more than to hear that we have unearthed the old sign from a back room in the house & Bluecap now "floats the wanton air" in his old place at Sandiway Head, & I hope will inaugurate a new era of prosperity for the old inn. I dined with the tenants to-day after the rent-receiving & you would have been edified. I gave the toast of fox-hunting, which was responded to by one of the tenants getting up and reciting one of your hunting songs, without a stop or a hesitation, from beginning to end; who shall say that a prophet is not honoured in his own country?
>
> Ever sincerely, DELAMERE

Rowland's marriage lasted fifty years and was blessed with a son and two daughters, Mary Alice and Mary after their mother, the sister of his good friend Richard Brooke of Norton. His courtship had lasted two years. They used to go on 'Riding Parties' and one day, when he was getting quite warm in his advances, her horse stumbled. She noted in her diary:

> Mr Warburton said he would go "quite white" if she did it again.

and in 1831 Miss Brooke wrote:

> I am to be married to Mr Warburton! The very last person I have thought would have got so soon into this scrape.

To celebrate their Golden Wedding he gave his beloved Mary a gold bracelet with a gold locket containing a leaf for each of their five happy decades together. They were inscribed with the chief domestic events:

INSCRIPTION ON GOLDEN WEDDING BRACELET,
APRIL 7TH, 1881.

> *Each of ten the eldest born,*
> *Wedded on an April morn*
> *Fifty summers pass'd and gone,*
> *Golden decades every one,*
> *Joined by God in holy love,*
> *Blest with blessings from above,*
> *Unto Him our thanks we pay*
> *On our Golden Wedding day.*

Mary's present to him was a gold whistle, inscribed:

> *As the bird on greenwood tree*
> *Whistles, whistle thou to me,*
> *Whistle and where e'er she be*
> *She will come who loveth thee.*

The happiness she radiated was to last but a fortnight more. Mary's death in 1881 was to make Arley a doubly darkened home for Rowland. He had contracted glaucoma in 1874 and, despite visits to a specialist in Germany, he was as blind as Milton within a year. He had a new verse engraved on the whistle:

> *As the lark on soaring wings*
> *At the gate of heaven sings,*
> *Let thy voice from earth uprise*
> *Till it reach me in the skies,*
> *Prayer in Paradise for thee.*
> *Shall my loving answer be.*

From George A. Fothergill's Sketch Book.

He bore it all with fortitude and patience and his other faculties remained undiminished, almost to the end of his life. And happy was the listener who heard him talk of the palmy days and of every 'good fellow' in Cheshire, with whom he had been intimate, Tom Cholmondeley, the 1st Lord Delamere in particular. He deemed old Geoffrey Shakerley and Long John Dixon the two most lovable men that ever got into a saddle and Wilbraham Tollemache and Jack White the two best men, in his opinion, that ever crossed Cheshire.

He got a life-long friend, an aged gardener called Peter Burgess, to lead him about the grounds by a leather strap attached to his belt and he rejoiced in touching his favourite trees. But old Burgess could not give him enough exercise, so he had a Furlong Walk made with a wire stretched along the terrace and a bell at each end to tell him when to turn back. After Mary's death, his younger daughter, Mary Ussher, came to nurse him and moved in to Arley with her husband and children. There was also a loyal lady to read to him daily and keep him abreast of everything. On occasion he would get angry with himself and impose a penance. This took the form of breaking stones for road repair, just like a common criminal, stone blind though he was. The large stone slab he used for the purpose is by a window at the S.E. corner of the Hall.

But the excellence of his verse was sustained, the rhythm and content as compelling as ever. Some of his best work was produced in his declining years. *The Mare and her Master* and *Farewell to Tarporley* both first published in *Baily's Magazine* in 1871, are prime examples and as late as 1881 he wrote *Cheshire's Welcome* to the Imperial Huntress, when she came to Combermere.

Major G. J. Whyte-Melville was his great contemporary sporting lyrist and, William Bromley-Davenport apart, his chief compeer. There has been much argument about whose songs were superior, but some of the best judges have given the laurels to Rowland, who paid his own poetic tribute to the former,

Above: *R.E.E.W. in his old age.* Above right: *R.E.E.W. and the faithful Peter Burgess with his leading strap, c. 1890.*

the author of *A Rum One to Follow, A Bad One to Beat*, when he was killed from a fall in the Vale of the White Horse in December, 1878.

He himself died in 1891. The day of his funeral was stormy, but the clouds rolled away and the sun came out as the cortége passed on its way along the Cheshire lanes to the family vault at the church of St Mary and All Saints, Great Budworth. Every blind was drawn.

These then are the songs he gave for all lovers of the Chase to enjoy. They are for sportsmen of every age and in every age.

Health to the old, to the young recreation;
All for enjoyment the hunting field seek.

Let's all drink a bumper to that!

The Woore Country

NOW summer's dull season is over,
　　Once more we behold the glad pack;
And Wicksted appears at the covert,
　　Once more on old Mercury's back;
And Wells in the saddle is seated,
　　Though with scarce a whole bone in his skin;
His cheer by the echo repeated,
　　'Loo in! little dearies! 'Loo in!

How eagerly forward they rush,
　　In a moment how widely they spread;
Have at him there, Hotspur! hush! hush!
　　'Tis a find or I'll forfeit my head;
Fast flies the Fox away – faster
　　The hounds from the covert are freed;
The horn to the mouth of the master,
　　The spur to the flank of his steed.

May the names now recorded in metre
　　While hunting endureth survive;
From Tunstall comes one they call Peter,
　　And three from the Styche they call Clive.
There's Hammond from Wistaston bringing
　　All the news of the neighbouring shire;
Fitzherbert renowned for his singing,
　　And Dorfold's invincible Squire.

Few sportsman so gallant if any,
　　Did Woore ever send to the chase;
Each dingle for him has a cranny,
　　Each river a fordable place;
He knows the best line from each covert,
　　He knows where to stand for a start,
And long may he live to ride over
　　The country he loves in his heart.

There's Henry the purple-clad Vicar,
　　So earnestly plying the steel;
Conductor conducting him quicker,
　　Each prick from the spur at his heel.
Were my life to depend on a wager,
　　I know not which brother I'd back:
The Vicar, the Squire or the Major,
　　The Purple, the Pink or the Black.

On a light thoroughbred there's a bruiser,
　　Intent upon taking a lead;
The name of the man is John Crewe, sir,
　　And Ajax the name of the steed;
There's Aqualate's Baronet, Boughey,
　　Whose eye still on Wicksted is cast;
Should the fox run till midnight, I know he
　　Will stick by his friend to the last.

Ford, if well mounted, – how cheery
  To ride by his side in a run;
Whether midnight or Morn, never weary
  Of revel and frolic and fun.
When they lay this good fellow the tomb in,
  He shall not be mocked with a bust.
But the favourite evergreen blooming
  Shall spring and o'ershadow his dust.

With Chorister, Concord and Chorus,
  Now Chantress commences her song,
Now Bellman goes jingling before us,
  And Sinbad is sailing along;
Old Wells closely after them cramming,
  His soul quite absorbed in the fun,
Continues unconsciously damning
  Their dear little hearts as they run.

His voice by the horsemen unheeded
  At whom he ne'er ceases to swear,
Should the pace by a check be impeded
  Then Charlie trots up in despair;
"Friends, gentlemen, fox-hunters, pray now,
  Hold hard, let 'em make their own cast,
Oh! shame, if for lack of fair play now,
  Hard run they should lose him at last."

'Tis but for a moment we tarry,
  Away! they have hit it anew;
And we know by the head they now carry,
  Ere long they will have him in view
See! Soldier prepared for the brunt,
  Hark! Champion's challenge I hear;
While Victory leads them in front,
  And Havock pursues in the rear.

More eager for blood at each stroke,
  See Vengeance and Vulpicide rush;
Poor Reynard he thinks it no joke,
  Hearing Joker so close at his brush.
When ended, half mad with the scurry,
  Charlie flings on the saddle his rein;
First dances then shouts, "Worry! worry!"
  Then shouts and then dances again.

1830 - All Editions, 1 to 10.

NOTE: *The Woore Country* was written in 1830 as a tribute to Charles Wicksted who hunted this country between 1825 and 1836 from his kennels at Betley. R.E.E.W. commented:

> It was ever Mr Wicksted's chief delight to know that his hounds had afforded a good day's sport to his friends, though no one enjoyed a run more keenly, or described one with more enthusiasm than himself.

This Hunting Song was composed in reply to *The Cheshire Hunt* written by Wicksted himself. (*See* Cheshire Miscellany, and also Book One, Chapter VIII for an explanation of the fifth verse, which is about the Tomkinson brothers.) This was the first Hunting Song in the first and subsequent additions. There were originally thirteen verses and its author made many alterations. For instance these lines were the original version of the second half of the first verse:

> *He calls them each to him in turns*
>   *Admiring the shape of each limb*
> *And joyfully lashing their sterns,*
>   *They acknowledge their fondness of him.*

The same applies to almost all of his major songs and ballads, but the present editor feels it would be tedious, apart from a few exceptions, to give every version. This is from the Ninth Edition.

This was another verse the poet-squire of Arley wrote in praise of Wicksted:

> *A fig for your Leicestershire swells*
>   *While Wicksted such sport can ensure;*
> *Long life to that varmint old Wells!*
>   *Success to the country of Woore!*
> *Let statesmen in politics parley,*
>   *Let heroes go fight for renown,*
> *While I've health to go hunting with Charley*
>   *I envy no monarch his crown.*

Quæsitum Meritis

A CLUB *of good fellows we meet once a year,*
When the leaves of the forest are yellow and sear;
By the motto that shines on each glass, it is shown,
We pledge in our cups the deserving alone;
Our glass a quæsitum, ourselves Cheshire men,
May we fill it and drink it again and again.

We hold in abhorrence all vulpicide knaves,
With their gins, and their traps, and their velveteen slaves;
They may feed their fat pheasants, their foxes destroy,
And mar the prime sport they themselves can't enjoy;
But such sportsmen as these we good fellows condemn,
And I vow we'll ne'er drink a quæsitum to them.

That man of his wine is unworthy indeed,
Who grudges to mount a poor fellow in need;
Who keeps for nought else, save to purge 'em with balls,
Like a dog in a manger, his nags in their stalls;
Such niggards as these we good fellows condemn,
And I vow we'll ne'er drink a quæsitum to them.

Some riders there are, who, too jealous of place,
Will fling back a gate in their next neighbour's face;
Some never pull up when a friend gets a fall,
Some ride over friends, hounds, horses and all;
Such riders as these we good fellows condemn,
And I vow we'll ne'er drink a quæsitum to them.

For coffee-house gossip some hunters come out,
Of all matters prating, save that they're about;
From scandal and cards they to politics roam,
They ride forty miles, head the Fox, and go home!
Such sportsmen as these we good fellows condemn,
And I vow we'll ne'er drink a quæsitum to them.

Since one Fox on foot more diversion will bring
Than twice twenty thousand cock pheasants on wing,
The man we all honour, whate'er be his rank,
Whose heart heaves a sigh when his gorse is drawn blank.
Quæsitum! Quæsitum! fill up to the brim,
We'll drink, if we die for't, a bumper to him.

O ! give me that man to whom nought comes amiss,
One horse or another, that country or this;
Through falls and bad starts who undauntedly still
Rides up to this motto: "Be with 'em I will."
Quæsitum! Quæsitum! fill up to the brim,
We'll drink if we die for't, a bumper to him.

O! give me that man who can ride through a run,
Nor engross to himself all the glory when done;
Who calls not each horse that o'ertakes him a "screw,"
Who loves a run best when a friend sees it too!
Quæsitum! Quæsitum! fill up to the brim,
We'll drink, if we die for't, a bumper to him.

'Some never pull up when a friend gets a fall.'

O! give me that man who himself goes the pace,
And whose table is free to all friends of the chase;
Should a spirit so choice in this wide world be seen,
He rides, you may swear, in a collar of green;
Quæsitum! Quæsitum! fill up to the brim,
We'll drink if we die for't, a bumper to him.

1832 (In all editions, unchanged.)

REEW's own note reads: 'A quæsitum is the name given to the drinking glass occasionally used at the Tarporley Hunt Meeting, and on which the above quotation from Horace is inscribed.' This is on one side and on the other, also with oak branches is: 'Success to the Tarporley Hunt.'

NOTES: A bumper is a glass of wine, filled to the brim. One of REEW's epigrams, *The Little I Drink*, reads as follows:

"My Lord, pray excuse the remonstrance I make
To the bumpers which still after dinner you take;
You appear what you told me just now to forget,
That the little you did drink you drank when you eat."
"As you say, 'twas the little *I spoke of before,*
The great deal *I drink is when dinner is o'er."*

But he did not disclose with which peer of the realm, temporal or spiritual, he was conversing.

Egerton Leigh (214) included Quæsitum Meritis in his *Ballads and Legends of Cheshire*, 1867, with a footnote that he had 'heard and old Cheshire sportsman assert vehemently that he would sooner have written the above song than the "Annals" of Tacitus'.

This song has recently been set to music by Karen Myers for the repertoire of the White Hart Singers. (*Harmonius Companions, Vol. I, Perkunus Press, USA, 1993*).

Carving and Gilding

'You see,' said our host, as we entered his doors,
'I have just furnished my house à la Louis Quatorze.'
'Then I wish,' said a guest, 'when you ask us to eat
You would furnish your board à la Louis Dixhuit;
The eye can it feast when the stomach is starving?
Pray less of your gilding and more of your carving.'

3rd Edition.

Old Oulton Lowe

I

BAD LUCK to the country! the clock had struck two,
We had found ne'er a Fox in the gorses we drew;
When each felt a thrill at the sound, "Tally-ho!"
Once more a view hollo from old Oulton Lowe!

II

Away like a whirlwind towards Calveley Hall,
For the first thirty minutes Pug laugh'd at us all;
Our nags cur'd of kicking, ourselves of conceit
Ere the laugh was with us, we were most of us beat.

III

The Willington mare, when she started so fast,
Ah! we little thought then that the race was her last;
Accurst be the stake that was stain'd with her blood;
But why cry for spilt milk? – may the next be as good!

IV

'Twas a sight for us all, worth a million, I swear,
To see the Black Squire how he rode the black mare;
The meed that he merits, the Muse shall bestow,
First, foremost, and fleetest from old Oulton Lowe!

V

How Delamere went, it were useless to tell,
To say he was out, is to say he went well;
A rider so skilful ne'er buckled on spur
To rule a rash horse, or to make a screw stir.

VI

The odds are in fighting that Britain beats France;
In the chase, as in war, we must all take our chance.
Little Ireland kept up, like his namesake the nation,
By dint of "coercion" and great "agitation."

VII

Cheer'd on by the Maiden who rides like a man,
Now Victor and Bedford are seen in the van;
He screech'd with delight as he wip'd his hot brow,
"Their bristles are up! Sir! they're hard at him now."

VIII

In the pride of his heart, then the Manager cried,
"Come on little Rowley boy; why don't you ride?"
How he chuckled to see the long tail in distress,
As he gave her the go-by on bonny brown Bess.

IX

The Baron from Hanover hollow'd' "Whoo-hoop,"
While he thought on the Lion that eat him half up;
Well pleas'd to have balk'd the wild beast of his dinner,
He was up in his stirrups, and rode like a winner.

X

Oh! where 'mid the many found wanting in speed,
Oh! where and oh! where was the Wistaston steed?
Dead beat! still his rider so lick'd him and prick'd him,
He thought (well he might) 'twas the Devil that kick'd him.

XI

The Cestrian chesnut show'd symptoms of blood,
For it flow'd from his nose ere he came to the wood.
Where now is Dolgosh? Where the racer from Da'enham?
Such fast ones as these! what mishap has o'er ta'en 'em?

XII

Two gentlemen met, both unhors'd in a lane,
(Fox-hunting on foot is but a labour in vain,)
"Have you seen a brown horse?" "No, indeed, Sir, but pray,
In the course of your ramble have you seen a grey?"

XIII

As a London coal-heaver might pick up a peer,
Whom he found in the street, with his head rather queer,
So Dobbin was loosed from his work at the plough,
To assist a proud hunter, stuck fast in a slough.

XIV

I advocate "movement" when shewn in a horse,
But I love in my heart a "conservative" gorse.
Long life to Sir Philip! we'll drink ere we go,
Old times! and old Cheshire! and old Oulton Lowe!

1833 - All editions.

NOTES: Oulton Lowe was at the time a gorse covert belonging to Sir Philip Egerton, 'formerly in great repute, but which of late years had never held a fox. The run mentioned in the song took place on the 16th of February, 1832.'

Major Tomkinson's mare was staked during the run and died the next day. The Black Squire was his brother, the Rev. James Tomkinson. It was a Mr Brittain of Chester, who took on Mr France of Bostock Hall with young Ireland Blackburne of Hale, close behind; (*See* verse VI).

Little Rowley is of course the Poet himself and the only change he made to this, his first version, was to transpose the first two lines of Verse VII and to take out the reference to a lion in the verse about the Baron from Hanover. This was Baron Osten 'long distinguished in the English service' who had a miraculous escape from a tiger in the East Indies, the following couplets no doubt being the cause of Rowland's mistake:

By the king of the forest, out hunting one day,
The Baron was captur'd and carried away;
The king in his turn by the hunt was beset,
Or the Baron *had been but a* Baron-eat.

Badly mauled though he was, the jokes in the clubs of St.James's, which this former member of the German Legion much frequented, ascribed his escape to the beast finding him lean, dry and too bitter.

Of the other horses mentioned the Wistaston steed referred to Mr Hammond's mount, the Cestrian chesnut was Sir Philip's, Dollgosh Mr Ford's and the Racer belonged to the James Tomkinson, the Black Squire's son, who lived at Davenham Cottage.

One of the gentlemen in the lane, according to an annotated edition in the editor's possession, was the Rev.W.H.Egerton. Sir Philip's 4th son, from 1846 the Rector of Whitchurch, an appointment once held by his distant kinsman, the 8th Earl of Bridgwater (*see* Addenda). His 2nd son became the 13th Baronet, the Rev. Sir Brooke de Malpas Grey-Egerton, who died in 1945 aged 100.

'Fox-hunting on foot is but a labour in vain.'

The Old Brown Forest

1.
BROWN Forest of Mara! whose bounds were of yore
From Kellsborough's Castle outstretch'd to the shore;
Our fields and our hamlets afforested then,
That thy beasts might have covert – unhouse'd were our men.

2.
Our King the first William, Hugh Lupus our Earl,
Then poaching I ween was no sport for a churl:
A noose for his neck who a snare should contrive,
Who skinn'd a dead buck was himself flay'd alive!

3.
Our Normandy nobles right dearly, I trow,
They loved in the forest to bend the yew bow:
The Knight doff'd his armour, the Abbot his hood,
To wind the blythe horn in the merry green wood.

(2nd couplet altered, 6th Ed.)

3a.
They wound their "recheat" and their "mort" on the horn,
And they laugh'd the rude chase of the Saxon to scorn.

4.
In the right of his bugle and greyhounds to seize
Waif, pannage, agistment and windfallen trees,
His knaves through our forest Ralph Kingsley dispersed,
Bow-bearer in Chief to Earl Randle the first.

5.
This horn the Grand Forester wore at his side
Whene'er his liege lord chose a hunting to ride:
By Sir Ralph and his heir for a century blown,
It passed from his lips to the mouth of a Done.

6.
Oh! then the proud falcon, unloosed from the glove,
Like her master below, play'd the tyrant above;
While faintly, more faintly, were heard in the sky,
The silver-toned bells as she darted on high.

7.
Then roused from sweet slumber, the ladie high-born,
Her palfrey would mount at the sound of the horn;
Her palfrey uptoss'd his rich trappings in air,
And neigh'd with delight such a burden to bear.

8.
Versed in all woodcraft and proud of her skill,
Her charms in the forest seem'd lovelier still;
The Abbot rode forth from the abbey so fair,
Nor loved the sport less when a bright eye was there.

9.
Thou Palatine prophet! whose fame I revere,
(Woe to the bard who speaks ill of a seer)
Forewarn'd of thy fate as our legends report,
Thou wert born in a forest and clemm'd in a court.

10.
Now goading thine oxen, now urging amain
Fierce monarchs to battle on Bosworth's red plain:
'A foot with two heels, and a hand with three thumbs!'
Good luck to the land when this prodigy comes!

11.
'Steeds shall by hundreds seek masters in vain,
Till under their bellies the girths rot in twain';
'Twill need little skill to interpret this dream,
When o'er the brown forest we travel by steam!

12.
Here hunted the Scot whom too wise to show fight,
No war save the war of the woods could excite;
His learning, they say, did his valour surpass,
Though a hero when armed with a couteau de chasse.

13.
Ah! then came the days when to England's disgrace,
A King was her quarry, and warfare her chase;
Old Noll for their huntsman! a puritan pack!
With psalms on their tongues – but with blood in their track.

14.
Then Charlie our King was restor'd to his own,
And again the blythe horn in the forest was blown;
Steeds from the desert then cross'd the blue wave,
To contend on our turf for the prizes he gave.

15.
Ere Bluecap and Wanton taught fox-hounds to skurry,
With music in plenty – Oh! where was the hurry?
When each nag wore a crupper, each Squire a pigtail;
When our toast, the brown forest, was drank in brown ale.

(This stanza subsequently omitted.)
16.
The days that came next were the days of strong port,
A toil then was hunting, and drinking a sport:
Beneath the red bumpers at midnight they reel'd,
And day-break beheld them again in the field.

17.
As they crossed the Old Pale with a wild fox in view,
'Ware hole!' was a caution then heeded by few:
Oppos'd by no cops, by no fences confined,
O'er whinbush and heather they swept like the wind.

18.

Behold! in the soil of our forest once more,
The sapling takes root as in ages of yore;
The oak of old England with branches outspread,
The pine tree above them uprearing its head.

19.

Where, 'twixt the whalebone the widow sat down,
Who forsook the Black forest to dwell in the brown;
There, where the flock on sweet herbage once fed,
The blackcock takes wing, and the fox-cub is bred.

20.

This timber the storms of the ocean shall weather,
And sail o'er the waves as we sailed o'er the heather;
Each plant of the forest, when launched from the stocks,
May it run down a foeman as we do a fox!

All editions.

NOTES:

THE DELAMERE HORN. Delamere Forest was originally the Forests of Mara, stretching roughly from the Mersey to what became the Borough of Vale Royal, and Mondrem beyond, in the direction of Nantwich. Randle I, the third Palatinate Earl of Chester from AD1120-1128, granted the Master-Forestership to Ranulph de Kyngselegh in sergeantry by tenure of a horn and Cheshire tradition required the holder of this office to attend with the horn and two white greyhounds whenever the Earl was disposed to hunt in the forest.

The Chief Forestership passed to the Dones and Sir John Done was knighted at Utkinton Hall in 1617 by James I after a day's hunting when he stayed at Vale Royal. It then became vested in the Crewe family, the

Ardernes, the Baillie-Hamiltons and finally the O'Briens, passing with the spindle when there was no male heir.

By the Act of Parliament for the enclosure of Delamere Forest in 1812, one moiety of the whole was retained by the Crown as a nursery for timber. (Verse 18.)

Robert Nixon.

THE CHESHIRE PROPHET. At the time of Edward IV, Robert Nixon was born at Bark House, Whitegate, near the Cistercian Abbey of Vale Royal (founded and so named by Edward I in 1277), but no entry of his birth or baptism has been found and it is likely the name derived from a contraction of 'Old Nick's son'. A second version refers him to the time of James I, but most scholars, including REEW find the latter date palpably false, as many of the supposed prophecies were to be fulfilled at an antecedent period. See also *Cheshire Gleanings* edited by Egerton Leigh (214). Lysons (*Magna Britannia*, 1810) considered 'the story as very suspicious, if not wholly legendary'.

This simple-minded ploughboy is supposed to have been taken to Hampton Court on foretelling in Cheshire the result of the Battle of Bosworth. As predicted by himself, he starved to death in a closet where he had been locked in and forgotten when the officer in charge of him was summoned away.

Besides a miller named Peter to be born with two heels and a boy with three thumbs, his prophecies included:

A crow shall sit at the top of the Headless Cross,
  In the forest so grey,
And drink of the nobles' gentle blood so free,
Twenty hundred horses shall want masters,
Till their girths rot under their bellies.

(The Headless Cross is close by the gallops and polo ground on the Sandy Brow estate and the same legend about it is also mentioned by Merlin de Rymer and other prophets as a sort of English Armageddon.)

Of Vale Royal he predicted:

When the harrow cleaves this lea
Yon house a raven's nest shall be.

At the Dissolution the Abbot's name was Harrow and Henry VIII bestowed the place on Sir Thos. Holcroft, whose crest was a raven. And again:

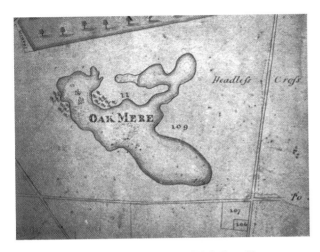

When an eagle shall sit on the top of Vale Royal house,
Then shall an heir be borne, who shall live to see
great troubles in England.

Sure enough when Charles Cholmondeley, the father of Thomas (12), was born, an eagle remained in the vicinity for three days.

Peckforton mill shall be removed to Luddington hill,
And three days blood shall turn Noginshire mill.
But beware of a chance to the lord of Oulton,
Lest he should be hanged at his own door.

Sir John Crewe moved a windmill to Luddington Hill, and apparently there was one Squire of Oulton who was killed by a fall from his horse, at his own gate, having caught his neck in a branch of a tree as he was returning from hunting.

THE OLD WOMAN OF DELAMERE FOREST. In the summer of 1815 a mysterious stranger came on foot to Vale Royal, bearing a letter she had addressed to Thomas Cholmondeley's wife, Elizabeth, the daughter of Sir Watkin Williams-Wynn. 'Most Honerth, Highborn Lady, My Lady Thumley' it began, and the writer went on to seek permission to remain awhile at Oakmere. She spoke good English with a pronounced German accent. Already the local gossip had made her a heroine in disguise, and in time the fables even had it her appearance concealed Napoléon himself.

It transpired she was Anna Maria Hollingsworth, the fifty-year- old daughter of a Lutheran clergyman and the widow of a soldier in the 22nd Regt., killed at the Battle of Bergen op Zoom. She had lately arrived in England, having been able to obtain a small pension and to apprentice her son to a carpenter in Hanover. With her daughter and all her worldly goods in a donkey cart, which had given them shelter, and followed by two goats to provide them with milk, she had been seeking a solitary spot where she might live in tranquillity and without expense. Disillusioned by being treated as vagabonds, she had decided to make her way to Liverpool, hopefully to gain passage to America.

Delamere Forest, still unenclosed, was on her route and the spot on the Iron Age settlement at Oak Mere where stood two whale ribs proved ideal. Many years before, Mr Philip Egerton of Oulton had placed the whale bones there when he leased the mere from Thomas Cholmondeley's father 'in consideration of his friendship and 5/- *p.a.*'. She had only intended to rest a day or two and wash her clothes in the mere, but with 'Madame' Cholmondeley's blessing she was to remain there for fourteen years.

Between these ribs, sheltered by a few Scotch firs, she formed a rude dwelling, using her cart and making a wall of sods and a roof of boughs. The donkey died and his hide served to make the roof more weathertight. They tended their little garden and the daughter went to Tarporley Market to sell eggs, from the fowls given them by friendly neighbours. As time went by, she improved her home with a door and a small casement and decorated the interior with flowers, ferns, stones and from Frances Williams-Wynn's (Lady Delamere's sister) description, written in 1834, considerable ingenuity. She became an object of much curiosity, almost a tourist attraction of the day. She was provided with a dog and two pistols for security.

Her daughter went into service in London in 1820 and she stayed on by herself until going to a Dutch Almshouse in Bishopsgate St., as late as July, 1829. The two sisters visited her there in London in June, 1832, finding her in very poor health. In her room she had a model of her little hut in Delamere Forest.

Anna Maria Hollingsworth, commonly called THE OLD WOMAN OF DELAMERE FOREST.

'Scorning the weather, Sir'.

Tarporley Hunt, 1833

WHEN *without verdure the woods in November are,*
Then to our collars their green is transferred;
Racing and chasing the sports of each member are,
Come then to Tarporley booted and spurred:
Holding together, Sir,
Scorning the weather, Sir,
Like the good leather, Sir,
Which we put on:
Quæsitum Meritis!
Good fun how rare it is!
I know not where it is,
Save at The Swan.

Lo! there's a Maiden whose sweet disposition is
Bent, like Diana's of old, on the chase;
Joy to that sportsman whose horse in condition is
Able and willing to go the best pace:
Racers are sweating now,
Owners are fretting now,
Stable boys betting now,
France! ten to one:
Quæsitum Meritis, &c.

Lo! where the forest turf covers gentility,
Foremost with glory and hindmost with mud;
Now let the President prove his ability,
Umpire of speed, whether cocktail or blood:
Go-by and Adelaide.
Though they were saddled,
Led forth and straddled,
Judge there was none!
Quæsitum meritis, &c.

How with due praise shall I sing the Palatinate,
Ably with Presidents filling our chair;
The Greys and the Leghs, and the Brookes that have sat in it,
Toasting our bumpers and drinking their share?
Each Squire and each Lord, Sir,
That meets at our board, Sir,
Were I to record, Sir,
I ne'er should have done:
Quæsitum meritis, &c.

"Sume superbiam quæsitam meritis,"
Shades of Sir Peter and Barry look down;
Long may we good fellows, now a days rarities,
Live to make merry in Tarporley town!
Fox preservation,
Throughout the whole nation,
Affords recreation,
Then pledge it each man:
Quæsitum meritis!
Good fun how rare it is!
I know not where it is,
Save at The Swan.

All editions.

NOTES: Mr France of Bostock was 'odds-on' having won The Tarporley Hunt Stakes for many years in succession.

In his article on the Tarporley Hunt Club in the January, 1914 issue of *Baily's Magazine*, G. T. Burrows recommended that this be hummed to the tune of *Father O'Flynn* when 'the sentiment of the song will sink deeper into your soul'.

On the New Kennel,

about to be erected on Delamere Forest. May, 1834.

WE *gaze with a feeling of pride on St. Paul's,*
And Westminster's Abbey our glory recalls;
A pile which reminds us of England's bright days,
The nation herself should assist us to raise.
> *Derry down, down, down derry down.*

Great names in the Abbey are graven in stone,
Our kennel records them in good flesh and bone;
A Bedford, *a* Gloster, *to life we restore,*
And Nelson *with* Victory *couple once more.*
> *Derry down, &c.*

Were the laws of the kennel the laws of the land,
The shillelagh should drop from the Irishman's hand;
Any journeymen tailors, on "striking" intent,
Should stick to their stitching like hounds to a scent.
> *Derry down, &c.*

Ye gods! in that house were our discipline known,
Where they snarl at the altar and growl at the throne,
A lash for the back of that hound who runs riot!
One cut and O'Connell should keep his tongue quiet.
> *Derry down, &c.*

Oh! grant ye reformers, who rule o'er us all,
That our kennels may stand though our colleges fall;
Our pack from long trial we know to be good,
Grey-hounds admitted might ruin the blood.
> *Derry down, &c.*

Fond parents may dote on their pride of thirteen,
Switch'd into Latin and breech'd in nankeen!
A puppy just enter'd a language can speak
More sweetly sonorous than Homer's own greek.
> *Derry down, &c.*

Oh clothe me in scarlet! a spur on each heel!
And guardsmen may case their whole bodies in steel;
Lancers in battle with lancers may tilt,
Mine be the warfare unsullied with guilt.
> *Derry down, &c.*

Gilpin! uproot me the laurels I scorn,
And plant me ten acres of gorse and blackthorn;
Though the shape of the covert to zig-zag incline,
May the fox that we find there describe a straight line!
> *Derry down, &c.*

Be mine the oak parlour, old fashion'd and neat,
Where round the free board fellow fox-hunters meet;
Each chorus we sing, from their kennel hard by,
The pack within hearing shall join in the cry.
> *Derry down, &c.*

All editions.

NOTES: Bedford '26, Gloster '22 (Mr Osbaldeston's Wonder), Nelson '29 (Duke of Beaufort's Piper - Mr Chadwick's Novelty) and Victory '28 were all hounds in the kennel.

It was William Somervile, MFH, the poet-sportsman of the XVIII Century [1677-1742], who described the chase as 'the sport of kings, the image of war, without its guilt.' In 1843 Surtees added that it had 'only five and twenty per cent of its danger.'

A Mr Gilpin was the author of *Practical Hints on Landscape Gardening*, in which, according to REEW, he justly censures the practice of disfiguring the wild scenery of a park or a natural wood by the introduction of exotics.

The Irish chorus is presumably an allusion to the builder's workforce. REEW deleted it from the later editions.

The Little Red Rover

THE grey morn is flinging
   Its mist o'er the lake;
The skylark is singing
   "Merry hunters awake;"
Home to the covert
   Deserted by night,
The little Red Rover
   Is bending his flight.

Resounds the glad hollo;
   The pack scents the prey;
Man and horse follow;
   Away, Hark, away!
Away! never fearing,
   Ne'er slacken your pace:
What music so cheering
   As that of the chase.

The Rover still speeding,
   Still distant from home,
Spurr'd flanks are bleeding,
   And covered with foam;
Fleet limbs extended,
   Roan, chesnut or grey,
The burst, ere 'tis ended,
   Shall try them to-day.

Well known is yon covert,
   And crag hanging o'er;
The little Red Rover
   Shall reach it no more!
The foremost hounds near him,
   His strength 'gins to droop;
In pieces they tear him,
   Whoo-hoop! Whoo-who-Whoop!

All Editions.

NOTE: "Could words more stirringly describe the hope and promise of joy, the vitality, the buoyant exhilaration of a hunting morning?" – Whyte-Melville paying his tribute to REEW in *Riding Recollections*.

Riding to Hounds

WHEN jealous horsemen, jostling side by side,
The pack unheeded, at each other ride,
More glorious still the loftier fences deem,
And face the brook where widest flows the stream;
One breathless steed, when spurs no more avail,
Rolls o'er the cop, and hitches on a rail;
One floundering lies – to watery ditch consigned,
While laughing schoolboy leaves them both behind,
Pricks on his pony 'till the brush be won,
And bears away the honours of the run.
Thus when two dogs in furious combat close,
The bone forgotten whence the strife arose;
Some village cur secures the prize unseen,
And while the mastiffs battle, picks it clean.

All Editions.

The Fox and the Brambles;
A FABLE

INTENT on keeping corn and cheese up,
Though farmers cannot study Æsop,
Their intellects no doubt are able
To comprehend a modern fable.

Before the pack for many a mile
A fox had sped in gallant style;
But gasping with fatigue at last
The clamorous hounds approach'd him fast.
Though painful now the toilsome race,
With draggled brush and stealthy pace
Still onwards for his life he flies –
He nears the wood – before him lies
A tangled mass or thorn and bramble;
In vain beneath he tries to scramble,
So springing, heedless of his skin,
With desperate bounds he leaps within.
The prickly thicket o'er him closes;
To him it seemed a bed of roses,
As there he lay and heard around
The baying of the baffled hound.
Within that bush, his fears allayed,
He many a sage reflection made.
"'Tis true, whene'er I stir," he cried,
"The brambles wound my bleeding side,
"But he who seeks may seek in vain
"For perfect bliss; then why complain?
"Since mingled in one current flow
"Good and evil, joy and woe:
"Oh! let me still with patience bear
"The evil, for the good that's there.
"Howe'er unpleasant this retreat,
"Yet every bitter has its sweet;
"The brambles pierce my skin no doubt,
"The hounds had torn my entrails out."

Attend ye farmers to the tale,
And when while ye mend ye broken rail,
Reflect with pleasure on a sport
That lures your landlord from the court,
To dwell and spend his rents among
The country folk from whom they sprung.
And should his steed with trampling feet
Be urged across your tender wheat,
That steed, perchance, by you was bred,
And your's the corn on which he's fed.
Ah! then, restrain your rising ire,
Nor rashly damn the Hunting Squire.

All editions.

Another of REEW's fables was 'The Fox and the Pheasant', published in the 5th, 6th, 7th, 8th and 9th editions.

In addition to the foregoing REEW's 1st Edition also included the following:

The Ever-Blooming Evergreen.

This originally had three verses, the second being the most appropriate:

'ERE the adventurers nicknamed Plantagenet,
  Buckled the helm on, their foes to dismay,
They pluck'd a broom sprig which they wore as a badge in it,
  Meaning thereby they would sweep them away.
Long the genista shall flourish in story,
  Green as the laurels their chivalry won;
As the broom-sprig excited those heroes to glory,
  May the gorse-plant encourage our foxes to run.

The Spectre Stag,
(A Legend of the Rhine).

The Raven and the Rooks,
(A Fable).

as well as:

The Dead Hunter

HIS sire from the desert, his dam from the north,
The pride of my stable, stept gallantly forth,
One slip in his stride as the scurry he led,
And my steed, ere his rivals o'ertook him, lay dead.

Poor steed! shall thy limbs on the hunting field lie,
That his beak in thy carcass the raven may dye?
Is it thine the sad doom of thy race to fulfil,
Thy flesh to the cauldron, thy bones to the mill?

Ah! no. – I beheld thee a foal yet unshod,
Now race round the paddock, now roll on the sod;
Where first thy young hoof the green herbage impress'd,
There, the shoes on thy feet, will I lay thee to rest!

All Editions.

and

Inscription on a Garden Seat
Formed from the Bones of an Old Racer.

STILL tho' bereft of speed,
Compell'd to carry weight;
Alas! unhappy steed,
Death cannot change thy fate.

Upon the turf still ridden,
Denied a grave below,
Thy weary bones forbidden
The rest that they bestow.

All Editions.

NOTE: The sketch of this seat was made in 1833 in the garden of General Francis Moore at Hampton Court.

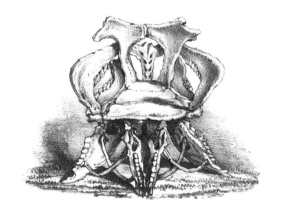

THIS, THE 2nd Edition, had 106 Subscribers listed and he dedicated it to Lord John Manners, MP, later the 7th Duke of Rutland.

Lord John Manners was the Leader of the Young England Party and had been campaigning for the introduction of Bank Holidays. REEW's letter of dedication sympathized with his aims and agreed that the Sports of the Country Gentleman were not to be enjoyed in forgetfulness of the recreations of the Poor.

Cheshire Chivalry

On December 23rd, 1837, the Cheshire Hounds found a fox in the plantation adjoining Tilstone Lodge. Running directly to the house, he baffled for a time all further pursuit by leaping through a window-pane into the dairy. When captured, he was turned out at Wardle Gorse, and after an unusually quick burst, in the course of which he crossed two canals, was killed at Cholmondeston.

I

Unpunish'd shall Reynard our dairies attack,
　His fate unrecorded in song?
Ah! no; when the captive was loosed from a sack,
There was not, fair milkmaid, a hound in the pack,
　But was bent on avenging thy wrong.

II

Would that those who imagine all chivalry o'er,
　Had encounter'd our gallant array;
Ne'er a hundred such knights, e'en in ages of yore,
Took the field in the cause of one damsel before,
　As were seen in the saddle that day.

III

Their high-mettled courage no dangers appal,
　So keen was the ardour display'd;
Some lose a frail stirrup, some flounder, some fall,
Some gallantly stem the deep waters and all
　For the sake of the pretty milkmaid.

IV

For thirty fast minutes Pug fled from his foes,
　Nor a moment for breathing allow'd;
When at Cholm'ston the skurry was brought to a close,
The nags that had followed him needed repose,
　As their panting and sobbing avow'd.

V

There, stretch'd on the greensward, lay Geoffry the
　stout,
　His heels were upturned to the sky,
From each boot flow'd a stream, as it were from a
　spout,
Away stole the fox ere one half had run out,
　And away with fresh vigour we fly!

VI

Once more to the water, though harrass'd and beat,
　The fox with a struggle swam through;
Though the churn that he tainted shall never be sweet,
His heart's-blood ere long shall our vengeance
　complete,
　And the caitiff his villainy rue,

VII

Stout Geoffry declared he would witness the kill
　Should he swim in the saddle till dark;
Six horsemen undauntedly follow'd home still,
Till the fate that awaited the steed of Sir Phil
　Put an end to this merry mud lark.

VIII

Back, back, the bold Baronet roll'd from the shore,
　Immers'd overhead in the wave;
The Tories 'gan think that the game was all o'er,
For their member was missing a minute or more
　Ere he rose from his watery grave.

IX

Quoth Tollemache, more eager than all to make sail
　(A soul that abhorreth restraint),
"Good doctor," quoth he, "since thy remedies fail,
Since blister, nor bleeding, nor pillbox avail,
　Cold bathing may suit my complaint."

X

When Williams past o'er, at the burden they bore
* The waters all trembled with awe;*
For the heaving canal, when it wash'd him ashore,
Ne'er had felt such a swell on its surface before,
* As the swell from the Leamington Spa.*

XI

Harry Brooke, as a bird o'er the billow would skim,
* Must have flown to the furthermost brink;*
For the moisture had reach'd neither garment nor limb,
There was not a speck the boot polish to dim,
* Nor a mudstain to tarnish the pink.*

XII

The fox looking back, saw them fathom the tide,
* But was doom'd ere they cross'd it to die;*
Who-whoop may sound sweeter by far on that side,
But, thinks I to myself, I've a twenty-mile ride,
* And as yet my good leather is dry.*

XIII

Life-guardsman! why hang down in sorrow thy head?
* Could our pack such a fast one outstrip?*
Looking down at the ditch where his mare lay for dead,
"Pray, which way to Aston," he mournfully said,
* And uptwisted the hair of his lip.*

XIV

Though of milk and of water I've made a long tale,
* When a livelier liquor's display'd,*
I've a toast that will suit either claret or ale,
Good sport to the Kennel! Success to the Pail!
* And a health to the pretty Milkmaid!*

1837. 2nd and subsequent Editions.

NOTES: Verse X: Henry Williams was the son of the Peninsular veteran, Major-General Sir Edmund Williams of Leamington and was commonly known as 'Swell Williams'. Verse XIII: Captain Henry Hervey-Aston, not mentioned in Ormerod's pedigree of the family, was then serving in the 1st Life Guards. On January 1st, 1838 Joseph Maiden was given a silver fox's mask stirrup cup (hall-marked 1806) by Arthur Wellington Hervey-Aston, who was the son of Henry Hervey-Aston (103).

'May Fox-hunting flourish ten thousand years more' is engraved round the rim.

Arthur Harvey-Aston was only 23 when he died the following year and his father, who had married the daughter of a Spanish grandee, had died at Genoa at the age of 29. In addition to Sir Willoughby Aston (*see* Chapter I), there was an Aston ancestor, Sir Arthur, one-time Governor of Oxford and who had commanded a regiment of dragoons at Edgehill. In 1655 he was captured defending a garrison at Tredagh in Ireland and had his brains beaten out with his own wooden leg.

Maiden's silver stirrup cup.

On the Picture of the Cheshire Hunt
PAINTED BY H. CALVERT IN 1840

I

WHEN our Kennel a coal-hole envelop'd in smoke,
Blood and bone shall give way to hot water and coke;
Make and shape, pace and pedigree, held as a jest,
All then power of the Stud in a copper comprest;

II

The green collar faded, good fellowship's o'er,
Sir PETER and BARRY remember'd no more,
From her Tarporley perch the poor Swan shall drop down,
And her death-note be heard through the desolate town,

III

Then GEOFFRY! bequeath them thy journal, to show
How prime was the sport which our children forego;
Let posterity learn, in the reign of Queen Vic,
How the horse and his rider could still do the trick.

IV

In colours unfading let CALVERT design
A field not unworthy a sport so divine;
For when JOE was their Huntsman, and TOM
their First Whip,
Who then could the chosen of Cheshire outstrip?

V

Let the Laureate, ere yet he be laid on the shelf,
Say how dearly he lov'd the diversion himself;
How his Muse o'er the field made each season a cast,
Gave a cheer to the foremost and rated the last.

VI

All the glories of Belvoir let DELAMERE tell,
And how Leicestershire griev'd when he bade them farewell;
Tell how oft with the Quorn he had liv'd through a burst
When the few were selected, the many dispers'd.

VII

With so graceful a seat, and spirits so gay,
Let them learn from SIR RICHARD, erect on his grey,
How the best of all cures for a pain in the back
Is to sit on the pigskin and follow the pack.

VIII

Let WICKSTED describe and futurity learn
All the points of a hound, from the nose to the stern;
He whose joy 'tis to dance, without fiddle or pipe,
To the tune of Who-whoop with a fox in his gripe.

IX

CHARLEY CHOLMONDELEY, made known how, in
Wellesley's campaign
When the mail arriv'd loaded with laurels from Spain,
How cheers through the club-room were heard to resound,
While, upfill'd to the brim, the Quæsitum went round.

X

By the annals of Fame let our children be taught
How the Willington Colonel with WELLINGTON fought;
Who at Huxley the field as at Waterloo led,
Nor e'er thought of retreat till at length he got wed.

XI

Let CORNWALL declare, though a long absentee,
With what pain and what grief he deserted High Legh;
How he car'd not to prance on the Corso at Rome,
While such sport Winterbottom afforded at home.

XII

Say, GLEGG, how the chace requir'd judgement and skill,
How to coax a tir'd horse over valley and hill;
How his shoes should be shap'd – how to nurse him when sick –
And when out how to spare him by making a nick.

XIII

Say, Dorfold's black Squire, how, when trundling ahead,
Ever close to your side clung the Colonel in red;
He who, charge what he would, never came to a hitch,
A fence or a Frenchmen, it matter'd not which.

XIV

The rules of hard riding let TOLLEMACHE impart,
How to lean o'er he pommel and dash at the start;
Emerging at once from a crowd in suspense,
How in safety he rides who is first at the fence.

XV

How with caution 'tis pleasanter far to advance
Let them learn from de TABLEY, TOM TATTON, and FRANCE;
Who void of ambition still follow the chace,
Nor think that all sport is dependent on pace.

XVI

Let ENTWISTLE, BLACKBURNE and TRAFFORD disown
Those Lancashire flats, where the sport was unknown;
Releas'd from St. Stephen's let PATTEN declare
How fox-hunting solac'd a senator's care.

XVII

Twin managers! tell them, SMITH-BARRY from Cork,
And DIXON, who studied the science at York,
Though we boast but one neck to our Tarporley Swan,
Two heads in the kennel are better than one.

XVIII

Then FORD, should the march of improvement proceed
Till each gorse bush be burnt as a profitless weed,
May thy sons from destruction one specimen save,
And revere the green plant that o'ershadows thy grave.

XIX

Let the bones of the steed which SIR PHILIP bestrode
'Mid the fossils at Oulton be carefully stow'd;
For the animal soon, whether hunter or war-horse,
Will be rare in the land as an Ichthyosaurus.

XX

Say, PHILIP the little, how sons would aspire
To rival the fame of a fox-hunting sire,
How aptly they learnt, when their study was pace,
How early developed the love of the chace!

XXI

Still distant the day, yet in ages to come,
When the gorse is uprooted, the fox-hound is dumb,
May verse make immortal the deeds of the field,
And the shape of each steed be on *canvas* reveal'd.

XXII

Let the pencil be dipt in the hues of the chace,
Contentment and health be portray'd in each face;
Let the foreground display the select of the pack,
And Chester's green vale be outstretch'd in the back!

XXIII

When the time-honour'd race of our gentry shall end,
The poor no protector, the farmer no friend,
They shall here view the face of an old Tatton Squire,
And regret the past sport that enlivened our Shire.

XXIV

They shall say, when this canvas the pastime recalls,
Such, once, were the gentry that dwelt in our halls!
Such, once, in our land were the noble, the brave,
They were loved in their lives, they were wept in their grave.

2nd and later editions.

NOTES: This was published in Manchester as a Cr.4to leaflet, entitled *THE CHESHIRE HUNT*, with the key for the prints engraved by Charles G. Lewis. The Common Prints cost 3 gns., Lettered Proofs, 5 gns. and First Class Proofs, before the Letters (*sic*), 7 gns. There were twenty-five verses, largely as above. Only seven stanzas were put in the 2nd (1846) Edition of HUNTING SONGS, but in subsequent editions, all but five were put in. Verse XV formerly read:

Say, GROSVENOR, DE TABLEY, (the fox well away)
BROOKE, TATTON, FRANCE, HAMMOND and
                              WORTHINGTON, say,
Ambition extinguished, and envy supprest,
How sweet in a skurry to ride all abreast!

However REEW adapted it from an earlier song, published as a broadside and called *A Good Merry Gallop for Me!* with 18 verses, half of which he did not change. Overleaf is the original version:

A Good Merry Gallop for Me!

I

His purse daily pick'd by some new fangled scheme,
Oh! the brain of John Bull is quite addled with steam;
But the Queen of our Isle is a Queen, be it known,
Who can sit on the saddle, as well as the throne.
CHORUS:
Sing Ballinimona Oro,
  A good merry gallop for me!

II

Make and shape, pace and pedigree, held as a jest,
All the power of the stud in a copper comprest,
Our kennel a coal hole, envelop'd in smoke,
Blood and bone shall give way to hot water and coke.

III

Let Geoffrey then hand down his journal, to show
How prime was that sport, which our children forego;
Let posterity learn – in the reign of Queen Vic,
How the horse and the rider could still do the trick.

IV

All the glories of Belvoir let Delamere tell,
And Leicestershire wept, when she bade them farwell;
How oft with the Quorn, he surviv'd a quick burst,
When the few were selected, the many dispers'd.

V

Say Glegg! how the chase required judgement and skill,
How to coax a tir'd horse over valley and hill;
How his shoe should be shap'd, how to nurse him when sick,
And when out, how to spare him, by making a nick.

VI

From Legh let them learn, that far dearer to him,
Than the groves of the south, were the dingles of Lymn;
How he car'd not to prance on the Corso at Rome,
Such sport Winterbottom afforded at home.

VII

By the annals of Fame shall our children be taught
How the Willington Colonel with Wellington fought;
Who at Huxley the field, as at Waterloo led;
Nor e'er thought of retreat, till at length he got wed.

VIII

To his grandsons at Norton, Sir Richard shall show,
How our aches we forget, when a hunting we go;
How a ride o'er the vale cures a lumber attack,
Oh! there's nought like the pigskin for pains in the back.

IX

The descendants of Wicksted from Charlie shall learn
All the points of a hound, from the nose to the stern;
How he caper'd and danc'd without fiddle or pipe,
To the tune of whoop, with a fox in his gripe.

X

'Mid the mammoths at Oulton, a skeleton stow'd,
Shall be shown as the steed a Sir Philip once rode;
Who for the sake of a fox, would with water contend,
As through fire he would pass, for the sake of a friend.

XI

When, as rarities greater, the tower they equip,
Not with buckler and blade, but with saddle and whip;
That the folk may then stare at our fox-hunting suits,
Let Royd send his breeches, and Tollemache his boots.

XII

Let the curious then in antiquity's lore,
O'er the stag-hunting records at Somerford pore;
Where "the merrie conceite" of a clown in a cart,
Baulk'd the mob of their haunch, and the hounds of their start.

XIII

Let Leche in his hall, so old fashion'd and quaint,
On some durable panel a steeplechase paint;
While a gap in each fence shall remain as a mark,
To show what their ancestors meant by a "lark".

XIV

How the bookshelves at Bostock, the world shall astound,
When a treatise on training the racer is found;
With but one at a time, in the stable, at most,
That one still a winner, when brought to the post!

XV

Then Ford! should the march of improvement proceed,
Till each gorse bush be burnt as a profitless weed,
May thy sons from destruction one specimen save,
And revere the green plant that o'er shadows's thy grave.

XVI

Then spectres of coachmen shall haunt Aston Hall,
And drag-chains loud clanking its inmates appal;
Once portly and plump, but alas! like the team,
The coachmen all died of starvation and steam.

XVII

Then, the last of the green collars faded away,
Sir Peter shall crumble, and Barry decay;
From her Tarporley perch the poor Swan shall drop down,
And her dying whoop shall be heard o'er the town.

XVIII

But still distant that day, – then as yet why repine?
Oh! drown the sad thought in a bumper of wine;
Our horse still fresh, and our gorse-covers green,
Fox-hunting shall flourish while Vic [Liz] is our Queen.

The Breeches

WHEN I mention the breeches, I feel no remorse,
For the ladies all know 'tis an evergreen gorse;
They are not of leather, they are not of plush,
But expressly cut out for Joe Maiden to brush.

Though my Muse, making known inexpressible things,
And wearing the breeches, exultingly sings;
I should need the nine Muses to praise him enough
Who order'd these breeches and gave us the stuff.

Good luck to the 'prentice by whom they were made!
His shears were a ploughshare, his needle a spade;
May each landlord a pair to this pattern bespeak,
The breeches that lasted us three days a week!

The fox is away and Squire Royds made it known,
Setting straightway to work at a pace of his own;
Past him sped Tollemache, as instant in flight
As a star when 'tis shot through the azure of night.

They who witness'd the pack as it skirted the Spa.
By the head they then carried the struggle foresaw;
At their heels a white horse with his head in the air,
But his rein it was loose, and his saddle was bare.

May Peel, near the Breeches at starting o'erthrown,
Where he left the impression in mud of his own;
When next he thinks fit this white horse to bestraddle,
See less of the Breeches and more of the saddle.

From Spurstow we pointed towards Bunbury Church,
Some rounding that covert, were left in the lurch;
By Hurleston we hurried, nor e'er tighten'd rein,
Till check'd for one moment in Baddiley lane.

They who rode the first skurry were fortunate men,
They may ne'er live to ride such a fast one again;
Oh! it thrills me with joy to record in this lay,
How the best blood of Cheshire was foremost all day.

When we pass'd the old gorse and the meadows beneath,
When, across the canal, we approached Aston Heath,
There were riders who took to the water like rats,
There were steeds without horsemen, and men without hats.

How many came down to the Edleston brook,
How many came down, not to leap – but to look;
The steeds that stood still with a stitch in their side,
Will remember the day when the breeches were tried.

The pack, pressing onwards, still merrily went,
Till at Dorfold they needed no longer a scent;
Man and maid rushing forth stood aloft on the wall,
And there raised a view hollo that shook the old hall.

Too weak for the open, too hot for the drain,
He cross's and cross'd back over Ran'moor in vain;
When he reach'd the Bull's wood he lay down in despair,
And we bellow'd whó-whoop, as they worried him there.

Puss in boots is a fable to children well known,
The dog in a doublet at Sandon is shewn,
Henceforth when a landlord good liquor can boast,
Let the Fox and the Breeches be hung on his post,

From Vulpicide villains our foxes secure,
May these evergreen breeches till doomsday endure!
Go! all ye good squires, if my ditty should please,
Go clothe your bare acres in breeches like these.

1841. 2nd and all later editions.

REEW's NOTE: This covert [which lies midway between Bath Wood (Spa Plantation) and Woodhey Hall to the South], pre-eminent above all the gorses in the county for the sport it has shown, belongs to John Tollemache, Esq.[, but the Tollemache in the Song is Wilbraham Tollemache of Dorfold.]

A sheet for this hunting song is one of the few still among the Club's papers; it contains three additional verses, which came after the third stanza above, the last being:

The fox thought at first he was fated to lose
In the breeches his life, like a rogue in his shoes;
Go! doff your red coats ye who coverts surround,
But where'er there are breeches, there tailors are found.

Inscription on the Handle of a Fox's Brush, mounted and presented by REEW to Wilbraham Tollemache, Esq., February 20, 1841, [following the run described in *The Breeches*]

WE found our fox at Brindley; thrice that week
The gorse was drawn, and thrice with like success.
For nigh two hours, o'er many a mile of grass,
We chas'd him thence to Dorfold, where he died.
Tollemache! in admiration of thy skill'd
And gallant riding to the pack that day,
To thee I yield the Brush, esteem not thou
The trophy less thus proffer'd by a friend.

To Wilbraham Tollemache Esq.
on his presenting REEW with a Hunting Cap.

BRING forth my best steed, that can gallop apace,
For arm'd cap-à-pie *I'm away to the chase;*
Now thanks to thee Tollemache, fresh ardour I feel,
A friend's cap on head and my own spur on heel,
At each fence will I slap,
Scorning gateway and gap,
And pick up a feather to wear in my cap!

Oh, who save thyself shall presume to o'erspread
With a mudstain, the cap that now covers my head?
No disgrace in the dirt that is flung from thy heel,
Nor a splash, save from thee, shall the velvet reveal;
If well the caps sits,
Ods bridles and bits!
If I don't beat the Beaverites all into fits.

Old wiseheads, complacently smoothing the brim,
May jeer at my velvet and call it a whim,
They may think in a cap little wisdom there dwells,
They may say he who wears it should wear it with bells;
But when Broadbrim lies flat,
I will answer him pat,
Oh! who but a crackskull would ride in a hat?

Old Hats, now both beaver and silk we hold cheap,
Ye wide-awakes, now ye may all go to sleep!
Now a fall is not felt when capsized in a run,
Oh! to ride in a cap is right capital fun;
Though it make, as you say,
All the hair fall way,
Like Cæsar we'll cover the baldness with bay.

2nd Edition.

NOTE: Tall hats were at one time made of beaver fur and the fashion for silk was set in Leicestershire after Sir Robert Peel had removed the duty from that commodity.

In 1911 Cuthbert Bradley, describing a meet at Saighton, noticed that the green collars were wearing 'low-crowned silk hats'.

The Gallant Ship "The Swan"
Written for and sung by J. H. Smith-Barry,
the President of the Tarporley Hunt Meeting, 1845.

Now riding safe at anchor, idly floats the Columbine,
And the perils of the Ocean in November I resign;
With other Messmates round me, merry comrades every one,
To-night I take command, boys, of the gallant ship The Swan,

Chorus.
Then up, boys! up for action, with a hearty three times three,
What tars are half so jolly as the tars of Tarporley?

'Tis true, though strange, this gallant ship in water cannot swim,
A sea of rosy wine, boys, is the sea she loves to skim;
The billows of that red sea in bumpers toss'd about,
Our spirits rising higher as the tide is running out!

Chorus.

Still swinging at her moorings, with a cable round her neck,
Though long as summer lasteth all deserted is her deck,
She scuds before the breezes of November fast and free,
Oh! ne'er may she be stranded in the straits of Tarporley,

Chorus

By adverse gale or hurricane her sails are never rent,
Her canvas swells with laughter, and her freight is merriment;
The lightning on her deck, boys, is the lightning flash of wit,
Loud cheers in thunder rolling till her very timbers split!

Chorus.

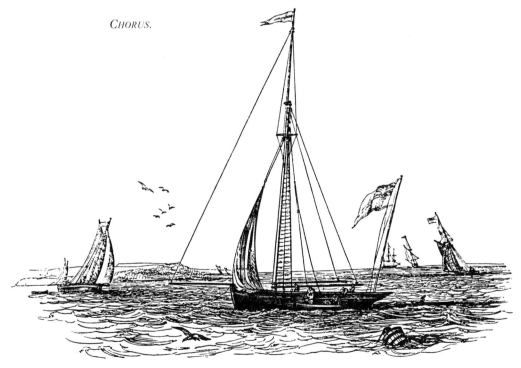

We need not Archimedes with his screw on board The Swan,
The screw that draws the cork, boys, is the screw that drives us on,
And should we be becalm'd, boys, while giving chase to care,
When the brimming bowl is heated we have steam in plenty there,

CHORUS.

No rocks have we to split on, no foes have we to fight,
No dangers to alarm us, while we keep the reckoning right;
We fling the gold about, boys, though we never heave the lead,
And long as we can raise the wind our course is straight ahead,

CHORUS.

The index of our compass is the bottle that we trowl,
To the chair again revolving like the needle to the pole;
The motto on our glasses is to us a fixéd star,
We know while we can see it, boys, exactly where we are.

CHORUS

One smile boys for our sweethearts, for our wives one fond adieu,
One bumper for our comrades who are absent from our crew;
Oh! never while we've health, boys, may we quit this gallant ship,
But every year, together here, enjoy this pleasure trip.

CHORUS.

Behind me stands my ancestor, Sir Peter stands before,
Two pilots who have weather'd many a stormy night of yore;
So may our sons and grandsons, when we are dead and gone,
Spend many a merry night boys in the cabin of The Swan.

CHORUS

Then up, boys! up for action, with a hearty three times three,
What tars are half so jolly are the tars of Tarporley?

1845. 2nd and later editions.

NOTE: James Smith-Barry sang his song every year and became a star turn with everyone joining heartily in the chorus. A generation later his son Arthur, later Lord Barrymore, maintained the tradition with *Troll, troll the bonnie brown bowl.*

Smith-Barry was the owner of Columbine which he converted from a cutter to a yawl, preferring cruising to racing. Both he and his father, John Smith-Barry (117), were Members of the Royal Yacht Squadron at Cowes.

Other members of the Club to have flown the white ensign are: R.C.Naylor (178), who won the Queen's Cup at Cowes in 1848, Baron Wm. von Schröder (224), 2nd Duke of Westminster (248), Lord Wavertree (268), Lord Royden (287), Col. R.P.Langford-Brooke (291), 5th Duke of Westminster (335), Cdr. R.I.Gilchrist (346) and R.A.Gilchrist (369).

A Cheshire Song to an Irish Tune

IF black instead of scarlet
  Be the cloth that we must don,
It shall be the garb of mourning
  For a pastime that is gone!
When, spurs pluck'd off from every heel,
  At coverts do we meet.
Then fast or slow, we all must go
  A hunting on our feet!

When laws can check the autumn leaves
  From falling as they die,
When fences in November
  Are as blind as in July,
We then will strip our collars off;
  But till that day be seen,
We Cheshire men we'll stick till then
  To wearing of the Green.

These two verses are from lines written for *Baily's Magazine* and dedicated to Mr J.H.Smith-Barry.

Song

STAGS in the forest lie, hares in the valley-o!
  Web-footed otters are speared in the lochs;
Beasts of the chase that are not worth a Tally-ho!
  All are surpass'd by the gorse-covert fox!
    Fishing though pleasant,
    I sing not at present,
    Nor shooting the Pheasant,
      Nor fighting the Cocks;
    Song shall declare a away
    How to drive care away,
    Pain and despair away,
      Hunting the Fox!

Bulls in gay Seville are led forth to slaughter, nor
  Dames, in high rapture, the spectacle shocks;
Brighter in Britain the charms of each daughter, nor
  Dreads the bright charmer to follow the fox.
    Spain may delight in
  A sport so exciting;
    Whilst 'stead of bullfighting
      We fatten the ox;
    Song shall declare a way, &c.

Hunters of Chamois surmount the acclivity,
  Bounding o'er torrents and scaling the rocks;
Horns on the mountain the prize of activity,
  Ours in the valley the brush of a fox!
    While him who thinks fit, sir,
    To follow the Switzer
    To bottomless pits, sir,
      An avalanche knocks;
    Song shall declare a way, &c.

England's green pastures are grazed in security,
  Thanks to the Saxon who cared for our flocks!
He who reserving the sport for futurity,
  Sweeping our wolves away left us the fox.
    When joviality
    Chases formality,
    When hospitality
      Cellars unlocks;
    Song shall declare a way,
    How to drive care away,
    Pain and despair away,
      Hunting the fox.

2nd Edition. (The third verse was omitted in later editions.)

The Second Edition (1846) also included the following additional hunting songs, *etc*:

The Tantivy Trot, (1834).

HERE'S *to the old ones of four-in-hand fame,*
Harrison, Peyton, and Ward, Sir!
Here's to the fast ones that after them came,
Ford and the Lancashire Lord, Sir!
Let the steam pot
Hiss till it's hot,
Give me the speed of the Tantivy Trot.

Here's to the team, Sir, all harness'd to start,
Brilliant in Brummagem leather;
Here's to the waggoner, skill'd in the art
Coupling the cattle together.
Let the steam pot &c.

Here's to the dear little damsels within,
Here's to the swells on the top, Sir!
Here's to the music in three feet of tin,
And here's to the tapering crop, Sir!
Let the steam pot &c.

Here's to the shape that is shown the near side
Here's to the blood on the off, Sir!
Limbs with no check to their freedom of stride,
Wind without whistle or cough, Sir!
Let the steam pot &c.

Here's to the arm that can hold them when gone,
Still to the gallop inclin'd, Sir!
Heads in the front with no bearing-reins on,
Tails with no cruppers behind, Sir!
Let the steam pot &c.

Here's to the dragsman I've dragged into song,
Salisbury, Mountain and Co., Sir!
Here's to the Cracknell who cracks them along
Five twenty-fives at a go, Sir!
Let the steam pot &c.

Here's to MacAdam, the Mac of all Macs,
Here's to the road we ne'er tire on;
Let me but roll o'er the granite he cracks,
Ride ye who like it on iron.
Let the steam pot
Hiss till it's hot,
Give me the speed of the Tantivy Trot.

NOTE:

This was written in 1834 at the request of Charles Ford (123) for Cracknall, the coachman of the Birmingham Tantivy, who once drove it at a sitting 125 miles (5 x 25m. stages!). Cracknall's achievement was by no means a record. Captain John Bastard, a distant relative of the editor, often drove the "Exeter Telegraph" the 200-odd miles to Piccadilly without surrendering the reins.

Of the names mentioned, the Lancashire Lord was the Earl of Sefton, the others being celebrated whips, both amateur and professional. Supremely evocative of the spirit of the day, it was always a favourite of 'the brazen-throated young sportsmen of the Bullingdon Club' at Oxford and was sung to the air, 'Here's to the maiden of bashful fifteen'.

Hawkstone Bow-Meeting, (1835)
The Ball and the Battue, (1837).
The Sawyer, (1844).
Tarwood - A run with the Heythrop, (1845)

(A song, which runs to 224 lines and no chorus, it describes a run on Christmas Eve, 1845 with a sixteen miles point of 1 hr. 42 mins. after an extremely stout and intrepid fox when Lord Redesdale was Master. Jem Hill was the Huntsman. Considered by many to be one of REEW's best works. Mr Whippy, the London saddler, won the brush.)

as well as:

The Earth Stopper.

Terror of henroosts! now from hollow sandearth,
Safely at nightfall, round the quiet farmstead,
Reynard on tiptoe, meditating plunder,
            Warily prowleth.

Rouse thee! Earth stopper! rouse thee from thy slumber!
Get thee thy worsted hose and winter coat on,
While the good housewife, crawling from her blanket,
            Lights thee thy lantern.

Clad for thy midnight silent occupation,
Mount thy old doghorse, spade upon thy shoulder,
Wiry hair'd Vixen, whereso'er thou wendest,
            Ready to follow.

Though the chill rain drops, driven by the north wind,
Pelt thy old jacket, soaking through and through thee,
Though thy worn hackney, blind and broken winded,
            Hobble on three legs;

Finish thy night-work well, or woe betide thee!
If on the morrow irritated Huntsman,
Back'd by a hundred followers in scarlet,
            Find the earths open!

A Recollection
A Sonnet

I WELL remember in my youthful day,
When first of love I felt the inward smart,
How one fair morning, eager all to start,
My fellow hunters chided my delay.
I followed listless, for with tyrant sway
That secret grief oppress'd my aching heart,
Till fond Hope whisper'd, ere this day depart
Thy lov'd one thou shalt see – Away! away!
The chace began, I shar'd its maddening glee,
And rode amid the foremost in that run,
Whose end, far distant, Love had well foretold,
Her dwelling lay betwixt my home and me;
We met, still lingering ere it sunk, the sun
O'erspread her blushes with a veil of gold.

5th and subsequent editions.

"Importation of Vermin"

"A steamship arrived yesterday from Boulogne with a cage of live foxes, consigned to order." – *Daily News*, February 1st, 1848, at which time there was much talk of the possibility of a French invasion.

"IMPORTED vermin:" – say, thou scribbler, when
Those fiercer vermin on our coast alight,
Who bark with drumstick and with bayonet bite,
As daily threat thy brethren of the pen;
When England summons her true-hearted men
(Whether invader to the chace invite
With foes or foxes, putting both to flight),
Say, of these twain which best will serve her then.

The joyous hunter, he who cheers the pack,
His fleet steed urging over vale and hill,
Who shuns no hardship and who knows no fear,

Or he, who bending o'er the desk his back,
In gas-lit office drives the flippant quill,
And talks of "vermin imports" with a sneer?

1848. 5th, 6th and 9th Editions.

NOTE: REEW clearly upheld the maxim of the Hunting Field being a School for Soldiering. A Cheshire Hunt Subscription rule that 'Officers of H.M.Services on full pay, and their wives, who are residing within the registered boundaries . . . or who are attached to any regular or Territorial Unit with Headquarters or Drill Hall in Cheshire will be entitled to hunt at half the rates . . .' was not rescinded until the 1960s, and then not without protest, Colonel Gerald Grosvenor, Major Pat Moseley and Gordon Fergusson among those who opposed the motion at the Hunt Meeting.

Farmer Dobbin

A DAY WI' THE CHESHUR FOX DUGS

"OUD mon, it's welly milkin toim, where ever 'ast 'ee bin?
Thear's slutch upo' thoi coat, oi see, and blood upo' thoi chin;"
"Oiv bin to see the gentlefolk o' Cheshur roid a run;
Owd wench! oiv been a hunting, an 'oiv seen some rattling fun.

"Th' owd mare was i' the smithy when the huntsman hove in view,
Black Bill agate o' fettling ['ammering] the last nail in her shoe;
The cuvver laid so wheam loik, an' so jovial foin the day,
Says I, 'Owd mare, we'll tak' a fling and see 'em go away.'

"When up, and oi'd got shut ov aw the hackney pads and traps,
'Orse dealers an 'orse jockey lads, and such loik swaggering chaps,
Then what a power o' gentlefolk did I set oies upon!
A reining in their hunters, blood 'orses every one!

"They'd aw got bookskin leathers on, a-fitten 'em so toight,
As roind and plump as turmits be, and just about as whoit;
Their spurs wor maid o' siller, an' their buttons maid o' brass,
Their coats wor red as carrots an' their collurs green as grass.

"A varmint looking gemman on a woiry tit I seed.
An' another close besoid 'im, sitting noble on his steed;
They ca' them both owd codgers, but as fresh as paint they look,
John Glegg, Esquoir, o' Withington, an' bowd Sir Richard Brooke.

"I seed Squoir Geffrey Shakerley, the best 'un o' that breed,
His smoiling feace tould plainly how the sport wi' him agreed:
I seed the 'Arl ov Grosvenor, a loikly lad to roid,
I seed a soight worth aw the rest, his farencly young broid.

"Zur Umferry de Trafford an' the Squoir ov Arley Haw,
His pocket full o' rigmarole, a-rhoiming on 'em aw;
Two Members for the Cointy, both aloik ca'd Egerton; –
Squoir Henry Brooke and Tummus Brooke, they'd aw green collars on.

"Eh! what a mon be Dixon John, ov Astle Haw, Esquoir,
You wudna foind, and measure him, his marrow in the shoir;
Squoir Wilbraham o' the Forest, who deloighteth i' the sport,
An' noicely clad, the Capesthorne lad, Squoir Arthur Davenport.

"The Honerable Lazzles, who from forrin parts be cum,
An' a chip of owd Lord Delamere, the Honerable Tum;
Squoir Fox an' Booth an' Worthington, Squire Massey and Squoir Harne,
An' many more big sportsmen, but their neames I didna larn.

"I seed that great commander in the saddle, Captain Whoit,
An' the pack as thrung'd about him was indeed a gradely soight;
The dugs look'd foin as satin, an' himsel look'd 'ard as nails,
An he giv the swells a caution not to roid upo' their tails.

"Says he, 'Yung men o' Monchester an' Livverpoo, cum near,
Oiv just a word, a warning word, to whisper in your ear,
When startin' from the cuvver soid, ye see bowd Reynard burst,
We canna 'ave no 'unting if the gemmem go it furst,'

"Tom Rance has got a single oie, wurth many another's two,
He held his cap abuv his yed to show he'd had a view;
Tom's voice was loik th'owd raven's when he skroik'd out 'Tally-ho!'
For when the fox had seen Tom's feace he thoght it toim to go.

"Ey moy! a pratty jingle then went ringin' through the skoy,
Furst Victory, then Villager began the merry croy,
Then every maith was open from the oud'un to the pup,
An' aw the pack together took the swellin' chorus up.

"Eh moy! a pratty skouver then was kick'd up in the vale,
They skim'd across the running brook, they topp'd the post an rail,
They didna stop for razzur cop, but play'd at touch an' go,
An them as miss'd a footin there, lay doubled up below.

"I seed the 'ounds a-crossing Farmer Flareup's boundary loin,
Whose daughter plays the peany and drinks whoit sherry wine,
Gowd rings upon her finger and silk stockings on her feet;
Says I 'It won't do him no harm to roid across his wheat.'

A sketch by Piers Egerton Warburton, which could well be Farmer Dobbin having another day out.

"So, toightly houdin on by th' yed, I hits th'owd mare a whop,
Hoo plumps into the middle o' the wheatfield neck an' crop;
And when hoo floinder'd out on it I catch'd another spin,
An', missis, that's the cagion o' the blood upo' my chin.

"I never oss'd another lep, but kep the lane, an then
In twenty minutes' toim about they turn'd toart me agen;
The fox was foinly daggled, an the tits aw out o' breath,
When they kilt him in the open, an' owd Dobbin seed the death.

"Loik dangling of a babby, then the Huntsman hove him up,
The dugs a-baying roind him, while the gemman croid 'Whoo-hup!'
As doesome cawves lick fleetings out o' th' piggin in the shed,
They worried every inch of him, aw but his tail an yed.

"Now, missis, sin the markets be a-doing moderate well,
Oiv welly maid my moind up just to buoy a nag mysel;
For to keep a farmer's spirits up 'gen things be getting low,
Theer's nothing loik Fox-huntin' and a rattling 'Tally-ho!'"

1853. 3rd and all later editions.

NOTE: It is interesting that REEW subsequently omitted the reference to Arthur Henry Davenport (182) in verse VIII, the last two lines of which he changed to:

Squire Wilbraham o' the Forest, death and danger he defoies,
When his coat be toightly button'd up, and shut be both his oies.

Sadly Arthur Davenport fell from grace with many of his friends, owing to alcoholic overindulgence, though why REEW chose to tease George Wilbraham in this way must have been a private joke. It was said that the bachelor squire of Capesthorne and former Lifeguardsman over-stepped the mark at a ball and caused great offence.

Then on September 28th, 1861 Arthur and a friend were devilling bones in the upstairs library at Capesthorne and went to bed without seeing that the fire was properly extinguished. A footman raised the alarm, but the centre portion of the hall was completely gutted. Thanks to the direction of the wind, the two wings were saved.

Arthur Davenport was the President Elect for 1867 and his name was duly printed on the Notices, but he died before the meeting.

The foreign parts, whence came 'the Honerable Lazzles', were the Yorkshire domains of the Earls of Harewood.

Cheshire Jumpers.

I ASKED in much amazement, as I took my morning ride,
"What means this monster meeting, that collects at
    Highwayside?
Who are ye? and what strange event this gathering crowd
    excites?
Are ye scarlet men from Babylon, or mounted Mormonites?"

A bearded man on horseback answered blandly with a smile, –
"Good Sir, no Canters are we, though we canter many a
    mile;
Nor will you find a Ranter here amongst our merry crew,
Though if you seek a Roarer, there may chance be one or two.

"With Shakers and with Quakers no connection, Sir, have
    we;
We are not Plymouth Brothers, Cheshire Jumpers though we
    be;
'Tis mine between two champions bold to judge, if judge I can,
And settle which, o'er hedge and ditch, will prove the better
    man.

Mark well these two conditions, he who falls upon the field,
Or he whose horse refuses twice, the victory must yield."
As thus he spake he strok'd his beard, and bade the champions
    go;
His beard was black as charcoal, but their faces white as snow.

The ladies wave their kerchiefs as the rival jumpers start,
A smile of such encouragement might nerve the faintest heart;
The crowd that follow's after with good wishes cheer'd them
    on,
Some cried, "Stick to it, Thomas!" others shouted, "Go it,
    John!"

Awake to competition and alive to any game,
From Manchester and Liverpool the speculators came;
They calculated nicely every chance of loss or gain;
Some stak'd cash on cotton, some preferr'd the sugar cane.

Bold Thomas took precedence, as a proper man to lead,
And straightway at a hedgerow cop he drove his gallant steed;
He's off – he's on – he's over – is bold Thomas in his seat?
Yes, the rider's in his saddle, and the horse is on his feet!

Make way for John! the Leicester Don! John clear'd it far
    and wide,
And scornfully he smil'd on it when landed t'other side;
The prelude thus accomplished without loss of life or limb,
John's backers, much embolden'd, offer two to one on him.

Now John led off; the choice again was fix'd upon a cop,
A rotten ditch in front of it, a rail upon the top;
While shouts of "Bono Johnny!" to the echoing hills are sent,
He wink'd his eye, and at it, and right over it he went.

Hold him lightly, Thomas, lightly, give him freedom ere he
    bound,
Why shape your course, with so much force, to run yourself
    aground?
Thus against a Russian rampart goes a British cannon ball:
Were Thomas at Sebastopol, how speedily 'twould fall!

Would you gain that proud pre-eminence on which your rival
    stands,
Upraise your voice, uprouse your horse, but slacken both
    your hands;
'Tis vain, 'tis vain, his steed again stands planted in the ditch,
The game is o'er, he tries no more, who makes a second hitch.

Thus, unlike the wars of Lancaster and York, in days of yore,
The Chester strife with Leicester unexpectedly was o'er;
We else had learnt which method best insures us from a fall,
The Chester on-and-off step, or the Leicester, clearing all?

Whether breeches white, or breeches brown, the more adhesive
    be,
And which the more effective spur, Champagne or Eau-de
    vie?
These alas! and other problems which their progress had
    reveal'd,
Remain unsettled questions for the future hunting field.

One lesson learn, young ladies all, who came to see the show,
Remember, in the race of life, once only to say "No";
This moral, for your warning, to my ditty I attach,
May ye ne'er by two refusals altogether lose a match!

1854. 3rd and subsequent Editions.

REEW'S NOTE: This strange match, so hastily arranged
and so quickly decided, took place on the Friday of
Tarporley Hunt Week, 1854. The competitors were
Thomas Langford Brook, of Mere, Esq. and John
Sidebottom, of Harewood, Esq. Davenport Bromley,
Esq. was Umpire.

NOTE: Peter Brooke of Mere (1723-1783) had married
the heiress of Jonas Langford of Antigua, so the family
still owned sugar plantations. Mr Sidebottom was in
cotton.

Tarporley Hunt Song

THE Eagle won Jupiter's favour,
  The Sparrow to Venus was dear,
The Owl of Minerva, though graver,
  We want not its gravity here;
The Swallow flies fast but remember
  The Swallow with Summer is gone;
What bird it there left in November
  To rival the Tarporley Swan?

Though scarlet in colour our clothing,
  Our collars through green in their hue,
The red cap of liberty loathing,
  Each man is at heart a True Blue;
Through life 'tis our sworn resolution,
  To stick to the pigskin and throne;
We are all for a good constitution,
  Each man taking care of his own.

Though the Sailor, who rides on the ocean,
  With cheers, may encounter the foe;
Wind and steam, what are they to horse motion?
  Sea cheers, to a land Tally-ho?
The canvas, the screw, and the paddle
  The speed of a thoroughbred lack,
When fast in the fox-hunting saddle
  We gallop astern of the pack.

Quæsitum, that standard of merit,
  Where each his true level may know,
Checks pride in the haughty of spirit,
  Emboldens the timid and slow;
The liquor that sparkles before us,
  The dumb when they drink it can speak,
While the deaf in the roar of our chorus
  A cure for their malady seeks.

Forget not that other Red Jacket,
  Turn'd up with green laurel and bay!
The tri-colour'd banners that back it!
  The might of their mingled array!
Forget not the deeds that unite 'em
  As comrades, though rivals in fame;
But fill to the brim the quæsitum
  Which Friendship and Chivalry claim.

1855. 3rd and subsequent Editions.

A Remonstrance on Lord Stanley's Suggestion that the Session of Parliament should be held during the Winter Months.

Joy! when November bids our sport begin,
  When ringing echoes through the vale resound,
  When light of heart we to the saddle bound,
And health and pleasure from the pastime win.
These must I barter for the Senate's din?
  Forego the music of the tuneful hound
  For midnight rant in adverse clamour drown'd?
Lay by the whip to be myself whipp'd in?
Debaters! listen, while the Chace propounds
  Her precepts – words too many work delay;
Your babblers draft, as we our tonguey hounds;
Rate without mercy those who riot run;
  Let those speak only who have ought to say,
Speak to the point, and stop when they have done.

1855. 5th, 6th and 9th Editions

NOTE: The Foreign Secretary and future 15th Earl of Derby had just written an inordinately long-winded letter to *The Times* under the heading THE SESSION AND THE SEASON to propose that the House should sit for six weeks from November 1st. Whilst conceding that those 'whose love of sport leads them to prefer a winter recess, and who must either sacrifice their favourite pursuits or neglect their public duties,' two months would thus be gained and Parliament could be prorogued in June instead of August, when 'the blunders which escape the vigilance of parliament are perpetrated' and 'the attractions of our brief summer have driven away... all except some 70 or 80 members.'

We are all of us Tailors in Turn

I WILL *sing you a song of a fox-hunting bout,*
They shall tell their own tale who to-day were thrown out;
For the fastest as well as the slowest of men,
Snobs or top-sawyers, alike now and then,
　　　　　We are all of us tailors in turn.

Says one, 'From the covert I ne'er got away,
Old Quidnunc sat quoting The Times *on his grey,*
How Lord Derby was wrong and Lord Aberdeen right.,
And the hounds, ere he finished, were clean out of sight.'
　　　　　We are all of us tailors in turn.

Says one, 'When we started o'er fallow and grass,
I was close at the tail of the hounds, but alas!
We came down to a drain in that black-bottom'd fen,
O had I but been on my brook-jumper, then!' –
　　　　　We are all of us tailors in turn.

'Dismounting,' says one, 'at a gate that was fast,
The crowd, pushing through, knocked me down as it pass'd;
My horse seized the moment to take his own fling,
Who'll again do, out hunting, a good-natured thing!'
　　　　　We are all of us tailors in turn.

'Down the lane went I merrily sailing along,
Till I found,' says another, 'my course was all wrong;
I thought that his line toward the breeding-earth lay,
But he went, I've heard since, just the opposite way.'
　　　　　We are all of us tailors in turn.

From the wine-cup o'er night some were sorry and sick,
Some skirted, some cran'd, and some rode for a nick;
Like whales in the water some floundered about,
Thrown off and thrown in, they were also thrown out.
　　　　　We are all of us tailors in turn.

'You will find in the field, a whole ton of lost shoes.' –
A credulous blacksmith, believing the news,
Thought his fortune were made if he walked o'er the ground; –
He lost a day's work, but he ne'er a shoe found!
　　　　　We are all of us tailors in turn.

What deeds would one hero have done on his grey,
Who was nowhere at all on his chesnut to-day!
All join in the laugh when a braggart is beat,
And that jest is lov'd best which is aimed at conceit.
　　　　　We are all of us tailors in turn.

Good fellows there are, unpretending and a slow,
Who can ne'er be thrown out, for they ne'er mean to go;
But when the run's over, these often timers tell
The story far better than they who went well.
　　　　　We are all of us tailors in turn.

How trifling a cause will oft lose us a run!
From the find to the finish how few see the fun!
A mischance, it is call'd, when we come to a halt;
I ne'er heard of one who confess'd it a fault,
　　　　　We are all of us tailors in turn.

1855 in Three Hunting Songs

'We are all of us tailors in turn', from an etching by Hablôt K. Browne ('Phiz').

Hard-riding Dick

FROM the cradle his name has been "Hard-riding Dick,"
Since the time when cock-horse he bestradled a stick;
Since the time when, unbreech'd, without saddle or rein,
He kick'd the old donkey along the green lane.

Dick, wasting no time o'er the classical page,
Spent his youth in the stable without any wage;
The life of poor Dick, when he entered his teens,
Was to sleep in the hay-loft and breakfast on beans.

Promoted at length, Dick's adventures began: –
A stripling on foot, but when mounted a man;
Capp'd, booted, and spurr'd, his young soul was on fire,
The day he was dubb'd "Second Whip" to the Squire.

See, how Dick, like a dart, shoots a-head of the pack;
How he stops, turns and twists, rates, and rattles them back!
The laggard exciting, controlling the rash,
He can comb down a hair with the point of his lash.

O! show me that country which Dick cannot cross –
Be it open or wood, be it upland or moss,
Through the fog or the sunshine, the calm or the squall,
By day-light or star-light, or no light at all!

Like a swallow can Dick o'er the water-flood skim,
And Dick, like a duck, in the saddle can swim;
Up the steep mountain-side like a cat he can crawl,
He can squeeze like a mouse through a hole in the wall!

He can tame the wild young one, inspirit the old,
The restive, the runaway, handle and hold;
Sharp steel or soft-souder, which e'er does the trick,
It makes little matter to Hard-riding Dick.

Bid the chief from the Desert bring hither his mare,
To ride o'er the plain against Dick if he dare;
Bring Cossack or Mexican,, Spaniard or Gaul,
There's a Dick in our village will ride round them all!

A whip is Dick's sceptre, a saddle Dick's throne,
And a horse is the kingdom he rules as his own;
While grasping ambition encircles the earth,
The dominions of Dick are enclosed in a girth.

Three ribs hath he broken, two legs and one arm,
But there hangs, it is said, round his neck a life-charm;
Still long odds are offer'd that Dick, when he drops,
Will die, as he lived, in his breeches and tops.

1855 in Three Hunting Songs – all three in
subsequent editions.

'Hard riding Dick', from an etching by 'Phiz'.

A Word ere we Start

BOYS, to the hunting field! though 'tis November,
  The wind's in the South; – but a word ere we start. –
Though keenly excited, I bid you remember
  That hunting's a science, and riding an art.

The order of march and the due regulation
  That guide us in warfare, we need in the chace –
Huntsman and Whip, each his own proper station,
  Horse, hound and fox, each his own proper place.

The fox takes precedence of all from the covert;
  The horse is an animal purposely bred
After *the pack to be ridden, not* over –
  Good hounds are not rear'd to be knocked on the head.

Strong be your tackle, and carefully fitted,
  Breastplate and bridle, girth, stirrup and chain;
You will not need two arms, if the mouth be well bitted,
  One hand lightly used will suffice on the rein.

Buckskin's the only wear fit for the saddle;
  Hats for Hyde Park, but a cap for the chace;
In tops of black leather let fishermen paddle,
  The calves of a fox-hunter white ones encase.

If your horse be well bred and in blooming condition,
  Both up to the country and up to your weight,
  O, then give the reins to your youthful ambition,
Sit down in your saddle and keep his head straight!

Pastime for princes! – prime sport of our nation!
  Strength in their sinew and bloom in their cheek;
Health to the old, to the young recreation;
  All for enjoyment the hunting field seek.

Eager and emulous only, not spiteful; –
  Grudging no friend, though ourselves he may beat;
Just enough danger to make sport delightful!
  Toil just sufficient to make slumber sweet!

1855 in Three Hunting Songs – all three in subsequent editions.

'A Word ere we start', from an etching by 'Phiz'.

Count Warnoff

When the war with our Muscovite foemen was o'er,
Then the Offs and the Koffs came to visit our shore;
Their hard and stern features your heart would appall,
But the face of Count Warnoff was sternest of all;
    A terrible man was Count Warnoff!
      As cold as the snow
      That envelops Moscow
    Was the heart of this horrid Count Warnoff!

Woe! woe! to the sport of the fox-hunting Squire
When the Count set his foot in this peaceable shire!
So clean his own hands, his own morals so strict,
A hole in each Redcoat he presently prick'd;
    Such a virtuous man was Count Warnoff!
      Without speck of dirt
      You must ride with clean skirt
    If the wrath you'd avert of Count Warnoff!

The Count could not tolerate foible or folly,
He never made love, and he never got jolly;
He vow'd that fox-hunting he'd have at no price
Unless horses and men were alike free from vice;
    Such a virtuous man was Count Warnoff!
      We must all be good boys
      Or farewell to the joys
    Of the chase, if we nettle Count Warnoff!

Low whisper'd the huntsman (lest mischief befall him)
"I don't like the look of that Count What-d'ye-call-'im?"
Tom winked his blind eye as he lifted his cap,
"He's a rum 'un, sir, ain't 'e, that Muscovy chap?"
    Such a terrible bugbear was Warnoff!
      Not a brush, nor a pad
      In the shire could be had,
    Such a terrible bugbear was Warnoff!

He lock'd all the gates, and he wir'd all the gaps,
And the woods were all planted with spikes and steel traps;
No more the earth-stoppers were dragg'd their warm bedsoff,
The nags in the stable stood eating their heads off;
    Such a terrible man was Count Warnoff!
      Little children grew pale
      As the nurse told the tale
    Of this terrible ogre, Count Warnoff!

Cheer up, my good fellows, Count Warnoff is gone!
Gone back to the banks of the Volga and Don;
He may warn us, and welcome, from off his own snow,
From the land where no fox-hunter wishes to go;
    But to bother the pack
      May he never come back
    To this peaceable county, Count Warnoff!

1857. First published in *FOUR NEW SONGS*, (1859), which include *Thompson's trip to Epsom.*, 12 verses, as well as the *Le Gros Veneur* and *A Railway Accident with the Cheshire*, all of which are in the 4th and subsequent Editions.

Highwayside
A CHESHIRE "FIXTURE" WITHOUT A "DIFFICULTY"

Rare luck for the Cheshire, warn'd out from the field,
That the Highway such endless diversion can yield;
That the Huntsman can still with no coverts to draw,
Blow his horn on the road without breaking the law.

'Twixt highways and byeways still ringing the change,
From gravel and sand to McAdam they range;
When quite on the pavé *their gallop restrain,*
And jog-trot down a hard Cheshire lane.

Steeds good in dirt, let the featherweights urge
Slapdash through mud that encumbers the verge,
Let heavy ones follow the track of the 'bus,
Shouting, Ibis in medio tutissimus.

They may jump on and off o'er the broken stone heap,
In triangular fenders fine timber to leap,
The towing path too may afford them a run
Just to keep the game going and vary the fun.

No alarm the most timid old gentleman feels,
Babes may perambulate, hunting on wheels;
Dyspepsy and gout the amusement may share,
So go it, ye cripples! and take a Bath chair.

The use of the milestone, now coaching is done,
Is to measure exactly the length of a run;
While each tap on the road they alternately try,
Till Tom sees two doubles with only one eye.

With such sport has this mud-larking lately supplied 'em,
The Huntsman has call'd his crack horse Rodum-Sidum,
Who dares say these hounds have had nothing to do,
Highwayside for their fixture the whole season through?

1858. 5th and subsequent editions.

NOTE: A slightly different version of the above was originally published in *Bell's Life. See* Book One, Chapter XII.

In March, 1858 at the end of Captain Mainwaring's last season the ever patient Secretary of the Cheshire Hunt, REEW himself, had managed to retain his sense of humour against all odds and produced *"CHESHIRE SWEEPS, a new Nigger Song to the tune of 'Dance Boatman Dance'"*. The incident on which it was based was evidently on a day some chimneysweeps joined in the hunt along the Cheshire roads:

Cheshire Sweeps

HUNTING *time is well nigh done,*
Never again will you see such fun;
Twenty-four Sweeps in sooty frocks,
Sitting on their jackasses a hunting of the fox.

   Trot, Sweepers, trot, O, trot Sweepers, trot,
   Trot all day down the broad high way,
And go home when its dark with your Donkeys.
     Sweeper creep, Sweeper climb,
     Sweeper ride in the hunting time.
      Tally ho! all in a row.
     Trotting down the middle of the road they go!
      Tally oh! all in a row,
        &c., &c.

Rouge et noir, the blacks they score,
The Reds to-day, they are only four;
Some they quids, and some they smokes,
A blowing of their backy and a cracking of their jokes,
   Trot, sweepers, trot, &c.

"Gently, gentlemen in black,
Don't if you please over-ride the pack" –
Saucy Dick says, "Blow me tight
Be'ant they a coming it quite purlite."
   Trot, sweepers, trot, &c.

Many a slip 'twixt cup and lip,
Hear ye the end of this hunting trip;
Consternation there was great,
When plump they come upon a Turnpike Gate.
   Halt, Sweepers, halt, O, halt Sweepers halt,
   Lack-a-day! if ye cannot pay,
Ye all may go home wi' your Donkeys.
     Sweeper creep, Sweeper climb
     Sweeper ride in the hunting time.
      Who-ho! all in a row
     Stopping in the middle of the Highway-O!
      Who-ho! all in a row,
        &c., &c.

Approaching Kelsall Bar.

Red-coats pass'd and went their way,
Master, he can afford to pay,
Toll for the horses and tax for the hounds,
For he holds in his pocket two thousand pounds.
    Halt, Sweepers, halt, &c.

Sammy Swipes could pay the shot,
But Sammy Swipes would rather not,
"Of cash," says he, "I am never werry flush,
But the little what I have I spends in lush."
    Halt, Sweepers, halt, &c.

Nimble Ned says, "Let I through,
And I makes no charge for your chimly flue:"
"Here's a go," says Billy Ball,
"Billy," says Joe,"it be no go at all."
    Halt, Sweepers, halt, &c.

"Won't you go tick?" the Sweepers said,
The Tollman laughed but shook his head;
"You are stopp'd," say he, "as your betters be,
All along of a 'Difficultie'."
    Halt, Sweepers, halt, &c.

Sitting astern on their donkey's croup,
Holloing all as they went Who-hoop!
Chaffing of their sport wi' the Cheshire pack,
Every one with A Brush went back.
    Trot, Sweepers, trot, O, trot Sweepers, trot,
    With scraper and sack ye may all trot back
And go home to the Slum wi' your Donkeys.
    Sweeper creep, Sweeper, climb
    Sweeper ride in the hunting time.
    Tally ho! all in a row,
        Trotting down the middle of the road they go.
    Tally ho! all in a row,
            &c., &c.

Arley Hall Papers. (Printed as a broadside.)

The Man with one Hunter

THERE are lords who their hunters can count by the score,
Scarce a Squire in the land, but can stable his four;
Like myself, there are few who, too poor to keep two,
Go a-hunting on one, and that an old screw.

One that flaps at a ditch, like a duck in a pond,
Well content if he land me three inches beyond;
If the cop his two fore-legs successfully climb,
His hind ones will follow in due course of time.

I have oft thought it strange, with a harem of wives,
How among them the Turk to keep order contrives;
One wife in an Englishman's house quantum suf.,
But one horse in his stable is not quite enough.

I would sell without grief the last shirt from my back,
Nor care though my coat were cut out of a sack,
If the duns would but leave me a saddle to sit on,
And a horse underneath it with bridle and bit on.

No blot on my scutcheon, a gentleman born
If of lowly descent I were far less forlorn;
I might then to the post of a Huntsman aspire,
Or at least ride as a Whip to some fox-hunting Squire.

Brother Tom, once in deeper distress than myself,
He, without even one, was laid quite on the shelf;
But ere cutting his throat he an heiress addressed,
And at once with a wife and a stud he was blest.

Though through life I have bent to Diana my knee,
She has never bestowed a like favour on me,
Though unmounted herself does the goddess not know,
He now needs a good horse who a-hunting would go.

Ye who own patent mangers, where flyers are fed,
Which the dealer supplies at three hundred a head,
Let a crumb from your stable in charity fall,
Give a mount to the man who can fill but one stall.

Songs and verses, 1879.

Le Gros-Veneur

A MIGHTY great hunter in deed and in name
To our shire long ago with the Conqueror came;
A-hunting he went with his bugle and bow,
And he shouted in Normandy-French "Tally-Ho!"
  The man we now place at the head of our Chace
  Can his pedigree trace from Le Gros-Veneur!

'Tis a maxim by fox-hunters well understood,
That in horses and hounds there is nothing like blood:
So the chief who the fame of our kennel maintains
Should be born with the purest of blood in his veins!
  The man we now place &c.

Old and young with delight shall the Gros-Veneur greet,
The field once again in good fellowship meet,
The shire with one voice shall re-echo our choice,
And again the old pastime all Cheshire rejoice!
  May the sport we ensure many seasons endure,
  And the Chief of our Chace be Le Gros-Veneur!

Though no more, as of yore, a longbow at his back,
Now the Gros-Veneur guides us and governs our pack;
Again let each earth-stopper rise from his bed,
This year they shall all be well fee'd and well fed.
  May the sport &c.

Let Geoffrey with smiles and with shillings restore
Good humour when housewives their poultry deplore,
Well pleas'd, for each goose on which Reynard has prey'd
To find in their pockets a golden egg laid!
  May the sport &c.

Should our chief with the toil of the senate grow pale,
The elixir of life is a ride o'er the vale;
There, of health, says the song, he shall gain a new stock
"Till his pulse beats the seconds as true as a clock."
  May the sport &c.

I defy Norman-dy now to send a Chasseur
Who can ride alongside of our own Gros-Veneur!
And, couching my lance, I will challenge all France
To outvie the bright eye of the LADY CONSTANCE !
  Long, long, may she grace with her presence our Chace,
  The Bride and the Pride of Le Gros-Veneur!

1858. 4th and subsequent editions.

NOTE: Earl Grosvenor, later the 1st Duke of Westminster, was christened Hugh Lupus after the first Palatine Earl of Chester Hugh de Avrincis, surnamed Lupus, Viscount of Avranches, who was buried in the Abbey of St.Werburgh (Chester Cathedral) in AD1101. The Grosvenor family derives its surname according to tradition from *le gros veneur* or chief huntsman in Normandy, an office held by Sir Gilbert Grosvenor when he came to England with the Conqueror. He was a nephew of Hugh Lupus, Earl of Chester.

Some eight generations later a son of Sir Thomas le Grosvenor of Holme in the time of Henry VI married the heiress of John of Eton, who in turn had descended from William de Eton and Richard de Pulford in the time of Henry II. The family thus acquired Eaton. An earlier branch of the Grosvenor family, which died out at the time of Henry VI descended from Robert le Grosvenor, who was granted the Manor of Buddeworth (Little Budworth) by the 5th Earl of Chester.

It was Sir Thomas's father, Sir Robert, who affirmed his right to bear the arms of Sir Gilbert Grosvenor, *Azure, a bend or*, before the Court of Chivalry in 1385. Although his right to the arms was denied to him, the descent he claimed was allowed. He was granted a Garb Or. (The horse of that name proved useless and was sent to the Cape after finishing 4th and last in the Dee Stakes at Chester. Bend Or won The Derby.)

It was Sir Thomas Grosvenor, the 3rd baronet and grandfather of the 1st Earl, who married Miss Mary Davis of Ebury, the London heiress.

A Railway Accident with the Cheshire.
February 5, 1859

I

By the side of Poole Covert last Saturday stood
A hundred good horses, both cocktail and blood;
Nor long stood they idle, three deep in array,
Ere Reynard by Edwards was hollo'd away.

II

Away! over meadow, away! over plough,
Away! down the dingle, away! up the brow!
"If you like not that fence, sir, get out of the way,
If one minute you lose you may lose the whole day."

III

Away! through the evergreens, – laurel and box,
They may screen a cock-robin but not a run fox;
As he pass'd the henroost at the Rookery Hall,
"Excuse me," said pug, "I have no time to call."

IV

The rail to our left and the river in front
Into two rival parties now sever'd we hunt;
I will tell by and by which were right and which wrong,
Meanwhile let us follow the fox with our song.

V

Away! to the Weaver, whose banks are soft sand,
"Look out, boys, ahead, there's a horse-bridge at hand."
One by one the frail plank we cross'd cautiously o'er,
I had time just to count that we numbered a score.

VI

Though fast fox and hounds, there were men, by my troth,
Whose ambition it was to go faster than both;
If that grey in the skurry escap'd a disaster
Little thanks the good animal ow'd to its master.

VII

Now Hornby went crashing through bullfinch and rail
With Brancker beside him on Murray's rat tail;
Two green collars only were seen in this flight,
Squire Warburton one, and the other John White.

VIII

Where was Massey who found us the fox that we run?
Where Philip the father? where Philip the son?
Where was Grosvenor our Guide? where was bold
  Shrewsberie?
We had with us one Earle, *how I wish we had three!*

IX

Where Talbot? where Lyon? though sailing away
They were both sadly out of their bearings that day;
Where Lascelles, de Trafford, Brooke, Corbet, and Court?
They must take return tickets if bent upon sport.

X

Sailors, railers and tailors! what can you now do?
If you hope to nick in, the next station is Crewe;
Second-class well dispers'd, it was only class first
Which, escaping the boiler, came in for the burst!

XI

Away! with red rowel, away! with slack rein
For twenty-five minutes to Wistaston Lane,
Where a check gave relief both to rider and horse,
Where again the split field reunited its force.

XII

From that point we turned back and continued our chace
To the gorse where we found, but more sober the pace;
Reynard skirting Poole Hall, trying sand-earth and drain,
Was at length by the pack, who deserv'd him, o'erta'en.

XIII

While they worry their fox a short word I would say,
Of advice to those riders who rode the wrong way,
Who were forc'd to put up with skim-milk for their fun,
For the skurry had skimm'd off the cream of the run:

XIV

"As a covertside hack you may prudently stick
To the line of the rail, it is easy and quick;
But when fox and fast hounds on a skurry are bent,
The line you should stick to is that of the scent."

4th and subsequent editions.

NOTE: Hounds had met at Oulton that day. The Hornby mentioned in Verse VII was Henry Hornby, later M.P. for Blackburn and created a baronet, no relation to the famous cricketer, Albert Nielson Hornby, who was twelve years old at the time but hunted all his life with the Cheshire Hounds from Parkfield House, Nantwich and known as 'Monkey'. As well as being Captain of Lancashire he was an international rugger player. He had two brothers who also hunted, 'E.K.' who lived at Poole Hall and was a Free Forester and Charles, who died young.

The gentleman referred to in Verse VIII was Hardman Earle of Allerton Tower, a Liverpool merchant created a baronet in 1869.

A Cheshire Bullfight

AT A CALL from the Chair,
Up spoke Farmer Fair;
"Would you know the best cross for the pail
Let your bull be an Ayrshire,
If not, I declare, Sir,
Your dairy will utterly fail."

"No," replied Farmer Wild,
"All the milk will be spoil'd,
If you bring that ere bull to your dairy;
If you wish the pail full,
You must get a Welsh bull,
That is wild like myself, and as hairy."
So betwixt Ayr an Hair,
And betwixt Wild and Fair,
We must drown this dispute in the cup;
For though vastly exciting
This Budworth bullfighting
'Tis betwixt the two bulls a toss up.

4th Edition.

Farmer Oldstyle and Farmer Newstyle

I

"Good day," said Farmer Oldstyle, taking Newstyle by the
    arm;
I be cum to look aboit me, wilt 'ee show me o'er thy farm?
Young Newstyle took his wide awake, and lighted a cigar,
And said: "Won't I astonish you, old-fashioned as you are!

II

"No doubt you have an aneroid? ere starting, you shall see
How truly mine prognosticates what weather there will be."
"I ain't got no such gimcrack, but I knows there'll be a slush
When I see th'oud ram tak' shelter wi' his tail agen a bush."

III

"Allow me first, to show you the analysis I keep,
And the compounds to explain of this experimental heap,
Where hydrogen, and nitrogen, and oxygen abound,
To hasten germination and to fertilize the ground."

IV

"A pratty soight o'larning you have pil'd up of a ruck;
The only name it went by in my feyther's time was muck;
I knows not how that tool you calls a nollysis *may work;*
I turns it when it's rotten, pretty handy wi' a fork."

V

"A famous pen of Cotswolds! Pass your hand along the back –
Fleeces fit for stuffing the Lord Chancellor's woolsack!
For pemiums e'en Inquisitor would own these wethers are *fit;*
If you want to purchase good 'uns you must go to Mr Garfit.

VI

"Two bulls first-rate, of different breeds – the judges all
    protest
Both are so super-excellent, they know not which is best;
Fair, could he see this Ayrshire, would with jealousy be ril'd,
That hairy one's a Welshman, and was bred by Mr Wild."

VII

"Well, well, that lttle hairy bull he shanna be so bad;
But yonder beast I hear a bellowing like mad,
A snortin' fire and smoke out? – be it some big Rooshian gun?
Or be it twenty bullocks squz together into one?"

VIII

"My steam Factotum that, sir, doing all I have to do –
My ploughman, and my reaper, and my jolly thrasher too;
Steam's yet but in its infancy, no mortal man alive
Can tell to what perfection modern farming will arrive.

IX

"Steam, as yet, is but an infant" – He had scarcely said the word
When through the tottering farmstead was a loud explosion
    heard;
The engine dealing death around, destruction and dismay;
Though steam be but an infant, this indeed was no child's
    play.

X

The women screamed like blazes as the blazing hayrick burn'd,
The sucking pigs were in a crack all into crackling turn'd;
Grill'd chickens clog the hen-coop, roasted ducklings choke the
    gutter,
And turkeys round the poultry-yard on devil'd pinions flutter.

XI

Two feet deep in buttermilk, the stoker's two feet lie,
The cook, before she bakes it, finds a finger in the pie;
The labourers for their lost legs were looking round the farm,
They could not lend a hand because they had not got an arm.

XII

Oldstyle, all soot from head to foot, look'd like a big black sheep
Newstyle was thrown upon his own experimental heap:
"That weather-glass," said Oldstyle, "canna be in proper
    fettle,
Or it might as well a tou'd us there was thunder in the kettle."

XIII

"Steam is so expansive." "Ay," said Oldstyle, "so I see;
So expensive, as you call it, that it wunna do for me;
According to my notion, that's a beast that canna pay,
Who champs up for his morning feed a hundred ton o'hay."

XIV

Then to himself, said Oldstyle, as he homewards quickly went,
"I'll tak' no farm where th' doctor's bill be heavier than the
    rent;
I've never in hot water been; steam shanna speed my *plough,*
I would liefer thrash my oats out by the sweat of my own
    brow.

XV

"I neither want to scald my pigs, nor toast my cheese, not I,
Afore the butcher sticks 'em, or the factor comes to buy;
They shanna catch me here again to risk my limbs and loif;
I've naught at whoam to blow me up, except it be my woif."

4th and subsequent Editions..

The Keeper

I

Rufus Knox, his lordship's keeper, is a formidable chap,
So at least think all who listen to his swagger at the tap;
Ain't he up to poachers? ain't he down upon 'em too?
This very night he'd face and fight a dozen of the crew.

II

With the Squire who hunts the country he is ever in disgrace,
For "Vulpicide" is written in red letters on his face;
His oath that in one covert he a brace of foxes saw,
Is the never-failing prelude that foretokens a blank draw.

III

The mousing owl he spares not, flitting through the twilight dim,
The beak it wears, it is, too hook'd a one for him;
In every woodland songster he suspects a secret foe,
His ear no music toucheth, save the roosting pheasant's crow.

IV

His stoppers and his beaters, for the battue day arriv'd,
Behold him in his glory at the head of the brigade;
That day on which a twelvemonth's toil triumphantly is crown'd,
That day to him the pivot upon which the year turns round.

V

There is a spot where birds are shot by fifties as they fly,
If envious of that station you must tip him on the sly;
Conspicious on the slaughtercard if foremost you would be,
That place like other places must be purchas'd with a fee.

5th and subsequent Editions.

The Close of the Season

Spring! I will give you the reason in rhyme
Why for hunting I hold it the pleasantest time,
When the gorse 'gins to blossom, the hazel to sprout,
When Spring flowers and Spring captains together come out.

When with smiles and with sunshine all nature looks gay,
When the fair one, equipped in fresh hunting array,
No splash of mud-dirt to encumber the skirt,
Though no fox should be found, may find leisure to flirt.

When assured of success, ere the steeplechase day,
Jones writes to his tailor imploring delay,
When the silk jacket wins he will pay for the pink.
Is the promise, when written, worth paper and ink?

November's young fox, as yet timid and shy,
O'er a country unknown will scarce venture to fly;
One spared through the Winter to wander astray,
Leads the pack stoutly back to his home far away.

Chill'd by checks and wrong casts, which the scurry impede,
You may chance in December to lose a good steed;
And what rider unvex'd can his temper restrain,
Urging home a tired hunter through darkness and rain!

Trotting homeward in Spring on the hope we rely
That we reach it ere dark with our hunting coat dry;
The horse undistress'd by the work he has done,
The rider well pleased with his place in the run.

This world, can it show a picture of woe
As a frozen-out Master imprison'd in snow?
His feet on the fender he rides his armchair,
Even Baily *avails not to soothe his despair.*

Good sport with good cheer merry Christmas may bring,
But the joy of all joys is a gallop in Spring,
By the thought, when a brook we encounter made bold,
That the stream is less rapid, the water less cold.

When each cheer is by song of sweet birds echoed back,
Their music a prelude to that of the back;
When clouds soft and southerly streak the blue sky,
When the turf is elastic and the scent is breast high.

5th and subsequent Editions.

Tarporley Hunt Song, 1859

NAMES honour'd of old, on our Club-book enroll'd',
It were shame should their successors slight 'em,
They who Horace could quote, and who first of all wrote
On our Tarporley glasses "Quæsitum";
   O, famous Quæsitum!
    Famous in story Quæsitum!
There has passed very nigh a full century by
Since our fathers first fill'd a Quæsitum.

Old Bacchus so jolly, who hates melancholy,
Our founders, how can he requite 'em?
From the land of the vine let the best of his wine
Be reserv'd to o'erflow the Quæsitum;
   O, famous Quæsitum!
    Jolly Bacchus, fill up the Quæsitum!
Whether claret or port, it must be the best sort,
If it fit be to fill a Quæsitum.

The goblet methinks, from which Jupiter drinks,
With thunder-cheer ter repititum,
Since when Juno was gone he turn'd into the Swan,
Should be chang'd for a crystal Quæsitum;
   O, famous Quæsitum!
    Fit for Olympus, Quæsitum!
Cup-bearer Hebe, how happy would she be
With nectar to fill a Quæsitum.

Those who dar'd with rude eye at Diana to spy,
She unkennell'd her pack to affright 'em;
She who smiles with delight on our banquet tonight,
Bids us fill to the chace a Quæsitum;
   Fill, fill the Quæsitum!
    To the heart stirring chace a Quæsitum;
She who sheds her bright beam upon fountain and stream
With her smile shall make bright the Quæsitum

One bumper still let all fox-hunters fill,
'Tis a toast that will fondly excite 'em,
Since the brave can alone claim the fair as their own,
Let us drink to our loves a Quæsitum;
   Fill, fill the Quæsitum!
    A glowing o'erflowing Quæsitum!
From Beauty's sweet lip he who kisses would sip,
With his own must first kiss the Quæsitum.

Again ere I end, all who foxes befriend,
Let a bumper thrice honour'd delight 'em,
May the forward and fast still be up at the last,
Give the slow ones another Quæsitum;
   Fill, fill the Quæsitum!
    To good fellows all a Quæsitum!
Let him fast be or slow, each shall prove ere we go
An excuse for another Quæsitum.

5th and subsequent Editions.

A Modern Stable

BEHOLD the new stable his lordship has built,
Its walls and its stalls painted, varnish'd and gilt;
No prince in his palace, King, Sultan, or Czar,
Was e'er lodg'd in such state as these quadrupeds are.

Pitchfork and bucket, chain buckle and rack,
Burnish'd up till they shine like the coats on their back;
I scarce know on which most applause to bestow,
On the gilding above or the geldings below.

What I marvell'd at most, in the front of each stall
Why a slab of blue slate should be fix'd in the wall?
Why a horse (and the query still puzzles my pate)
Like a schoolboy should stand with his eyes on a slate?

Must the heads of our horses be cramm'd now a-day
With learning as well as their bellies with hay?
Must our yearlings be coach'd till their little go won
The trainer has taught them "to read as they run".

5th and subsequent Editions.

NOTE: The stables are those at Peckforton Castle.

A "Burst" in the Ball Week
JANUARY 19TH, 1860

WE had danc'd the night through,
Till the candles burnt blue,
 But were all in the saddle next morn;
Once again with Tom Rance,
In broad daylight to dance
 To the music of hollo and horn.

We were all giddy still
With the waltz and quadrille,
 When arous'd by the loud "Tally-ho!"
I must tune my fast rhyme
Up to double-quick time,
 For the movement was prestissimo.

The fox by one hound
Near The Smoker was found –
 As he wip'd that dog's nose with his brush,
"I don't mean to die,"
Said bold Reynard, "not I;
 Nor care I for Edwards one rush."

With a fox of such pluck,
'Twas a piece of rare luck
 That no ploughboy to turn him was near;
That no farmer was there
At the gem'men to swear,
 No tailor to head his career.

Some, to lead off the ball,
Get away first of all,
 Some linger too long at pousette
Down the middle some go,
In the deep ditch below,
 Thrown out ere they up again get.

One, pitch'd from his seat,
Was compell'd with wet feet,
 His heels in the gutter to cool;
While his horse, in full swing,
Danc'd a new Highland fling,
 He himself stood and danc'd a pas seul.

"Tell me, Edwards," said one,
When the skurry was done,
 "How long were we running this rig?"
"To keep time, indeed, sir,
I little take heed, sir,
 When dancing the Tally-ho jig.

But the time I can tell,
And the spot I know well,
 Where the huntsman his fox overtook;
Twenty-five minutes good,
When he reach'd Arley Wood,
 Where he died on the banks of the brook.

I could name the few first
Who went best in this burst;
 I could tell how the steady ones rac'd;
But since all were content
With the pace themselves went,
 What matters it where they were plac'd?

If a live fox should run,
As that dead one has done,
 O'er this country again, by good chance,
May I have my fleet bay
For a partner that day,
 And be just where I was in the dance."

5th and subsequent Editions.

London Languor and Country Convalescence.

ONE VOWEL FITLY PLACED WILL SHEW
THE SENSE OF WHAT IS WRIT BELOW.

WHRRSTLSSWHLSTHTMPRVXD;
STRTBLLS, STRTYLLSTHSNSPRPLXD,
WHRCRPRSLFTTHSCRTNST,
FRFDRSWHNTHSHTSWRPRSSD,
SWTLLNVRTHRKPTHRBD;
HRVRFVRDCHKSWRRD;
THRSLPLSSWRHRYS; HRFT,
NFBLD, NVRSTPPDTHSTRT;
THRVRWRHRNRVSDPRSSD;
THRNVRKNWHRTMPLSRST.

HRKNTSKNBRZSHNVRHDS;
WLLHRSHSLPSWLLHRSHFDS;
GRNSHLTRHRTHBCHXTNDS;
TRSDCKTHSCNWHRRSHWNDS.
SHMNDS, SHMNDS, THNWSWLLPNND,
HNCSVNPRWKHRLTTRSSND,
WHNNDLSSHRTHLCHSF,
WHNTHBNTRDRCTWS;
HRSTRNGTHRNWDSWTLLNVR,
WHNWDDDLTHRSTTLHR.

London Languor and Country Convalescence.

WHERE restless wheels the temper vexed,
    Street bells, street yells the sense perplexed ;
Where creepers left the secret nest,
Free feeders when the sheets were pressed,
Sweet Ellen Vere there kept her bed ;
Her ever-fevered cheeks were red ;
There sleepless were her eyes ; her feet,
Enfeebled, never stepped the street ;
There ever were her nerves depressed ;
There never knew her temples rest.

Here Kent's keen breeze she never heeds ;
Well here she sleeps, well here she feeds ;
Green shelter here the beech extends ;
Trees deck the scene where'er she wends.
She mends, she mends, the news well penned
Hence seven per week her letters send,
When needless here the Leeches' fee,
When the bent reed erect we see,
Her strength renewed sweet Ellen Vere,
When wedded let her settle here.

Tarporley Swan-Hopping
November 6th, 1862

WHEN a Swan takes to singing they say she will die,
But our Tarporley Swan proves that legend a lie;
For a hundred years past she has swung at this door,
May she swing there and sing there a thousand years more!

Rara avis in terris *our Swan though not black,*
Though white her own pinions and white her own back,
Still her flock, in November full-feather'd, are seen
Resplendent in plumage of scarlet and green.

Heralds say she is sprung from that White Swan of yore
Which our Sires at Blore Heath to the battlefield bore;
When Quæsitum meritis, *loyal and true,*
Their swords Cheshire men for Queen Margaret *drew.*

To and fro in her flight she has traversed the Vale,
She has lov'd on an ocean of claret to sail;
Whate'er takes her fancy she thinks it no sin,
So her dancing-days, now she's a hundred, begin.

You have heard in your youth of the Butterfly's Ball,
How the birds and the beasts she invited them all;
So the Tarporley Swan, not a whit less gallant,
Invites all her friends to a Soirée dansante.

Lest her flock at the Ball should themselves misbehave,
The old Swan thus a lecture on etiquette gave:
"Though, my sons, o'er the Vale make you light of a fall,
Beware how you make a false step at the Ball.

"You must all in good feather be dress'd for the night,
Let not the Swan necktie be tied overtight;
Each his partner may fan with the tip of his wing,
Patent pumps for web feet will be quite the right thing.

"Expand not your pinions, 'twere folly to try,
In vain would their vastness with crinoline vie.
Let no rude neck outstretch'd o'er the table be seen,
Nor stand dabbling your bills in the supper tureen

"When you sail down the middle, or swim though a dance,
With grace and with stateliness Swan-like, advance,
Let your entrance, your exit no waddle disclose,
But hold all your heads up, and turn out your toes.

"To the counsel convey'd in these motherly words
Give heed and I trust you will all be good birds;
I give you my blessing and bid you begone,
So away to the Ball with you, every one."

5th and all subsequent Editions.

NOTE: The following ten additional verses were excluded, but were originally published in the December issue of *Baily's Magazine* with a full report on the Centenary festivities, the last verse the same as above:

"In the Chase, in the Chair, you to whom we all bow,
On the shelf leave at Calveley your hunting horn now:
You must not shout 'Away' when the dance is begun,
Nor hollo, excited, 'Whoo-hoop' when 'tis done.

"White, the only white bird that I have in my flock,
Though his plumage he varies oft-times as a Jock,
Still among the first flight, to the Ladies' delight,
He may give them a lead in the 'galop' tonight.

"Since the article grown in the States is so dear,
I will show the choice Cotton, home-grown I have here,
And the ladies will own, I may venture to bet,
They have ne'er seen a sample to equal it yet.

"Geoffrey, my son! be this privilege thine,
Taking care that my guests be well furnished with wine;
To insure the champagne be the best you can buy,
You may dip your own bill in a bottle to try.

"I make an exception in favour of one,
And excuse his appearance tonight as a Swan:
Let him come there to teach 'em the humours of France,
And show them how Little dogs, Little Dogs dance.

"And you mighty Tommy! come hither, my dear,
You who cut ducks and drakes on the water at Mere.,
If a well-behaved Swan, I will let you go loose,
But you're no child of mine when you play the wild goose.

"Was a mother with forty such sons ever blest?
Scarce a nook in the shire where they have not a nest;
I have two sons at Tatton who fail not each year
To come home to Mamma for a holiday here.

"I've a Frank at Poole Hall, and at Statham a John,
Very anxious am I to push both of them on;
Perchance at this Ball they may pick up a mate,
For so pretty a pair it is never too late.

"T'other side of the Dee, in Welch Wales far away,
I've a beautiful bird that was bred at Wynnstay;
A fine one at Rufford, a finer at Stafford,
But the finest of all this fine flock is at Trafford,

"From Sir Dicky, who is eldest of all,
From Johnny my second at Withington Hall,
Down to Oulton's young signet, as yet scarcely fledg'd,
To appear at the Ball, one and all, you are pledg'd."

Tarporley Songstress

A VOICE sweet and clear as the voice of a bird,
Last night was at Tarporley suddenly heard;
And a fair apparition was seen at the bar,
Who bewitch'd the whole Club with her tuneful guitar.

The whist table first was upset by her arts,
That singer's sweet voice play'd the deuce with their hearts;
The pack had been shuffled, they thought by Old Nick,
She herself was a trump, and her touch an odd trick.

"We women are lords of creation," she sung,
Down in meek acquiescence their heads they all hung;
Silver shillings dropt in from a crowd of red coats,
They who had it gave gold in exchange for her notes.

Lascelles vow'd she was quite a theatrical star,
Beating time on his box as she touch'd her guitar;
Said, "Compared to this maid, Jenny Lind is a muff,"
Then he gave her a pinch, for he's quite up to snuff.

Then her lyre to "the Captain with whiskers" she strung,
And she look'd at the face of John White as she sung;
Brooke's love was by brandy and water exprest,
And he gave her of course what himself he loved best.

Court paid his court, dropping down on one knee,
Hoping still that once more he a winner might be;
Harry humm'd to himself the "Old Carrion Crow,"
Snapp'd his fingers, and peep'd at the maid on tiptoe.
The heart of young Tomkinson went pit-a-pat,
Frank Massey fell down on his marrow-bones flat:
Said Starkie, whose pulse with emotion was throbbing,
"This wench must have come from the land of 'Tim Bobbin.'"

"I from home," said Dick Simpson, "where fishing abounds,
Will repay with red herrings this dish of soft sounds".
Said Wil'bram, "No money have I to bestow,
But I'll send her to-morrow a bag of 'old Clo.'"

Giving vent to his bliss in an innocent bleat,
The Lyon lay down like a lamb at her feet;
Said France, "If you like little dogs look at me,
For your lap what a sweet litter pet I should be."

Old Geoffrey himself, as his wife was not by,
Gave a nod with his head, and a wink with his eye;
His hand from his heart to his pocket went down,
And squeezing her fingers he gave half-a-crown.

Half-a-crown! in his purse has Squire Aldersey that?
If so, it was more than he had on his hat;
Still, to show his devotion while sweetly she sung,
For the space of five minutes he held his own tongue.

'No more Buxton Waters.' said Johnny, 'for me.
The Doctor may whistle henceforth for his fee.
Better physic by far than the life pills of Parr,
For a gouty old man is a young maid's guitar.'

Applause all bestowed on her music divine,
Some gave her money and some gave her wine;
Some gave her that thing, and some gave her this,
And others, don't mention it, gave her a kiss.

Then smiling she bade the green collars goodnight.,
And at once disappear'd like a magical sprite;
Though to bed they withdrew they all dream't of her still,
Of that nightingale's voice, and its musical thrill.

Save the muse (who of course was aware of it) none
In that Syren's disguise had detected the Swan:
'Twas the Swan! from her perch by enchantment unhitch'd
She who, thus metamorphosed, the Club had bewitch'd.

1864. Arley in Idleness, which also included 'The Spider and the Fly' which REEW composed for his faithful retainer, Peter Burgess.

NOTE: In 1958 Sir Randle Baker Wilbraham found a transcript of this song and sent it to Geoffrey Egerton-Warburton, asking if it was by REEW. He had found it in an envelope addressed to Randle Wilbraham of Rode and embossed 'Wincham Hall', the home of the Townshend family. G.E.W. could not think that it had been written by his grandfather – 'at least I hope not as it seems pretty good rubbish to me.' But it was in fact privately printed in *Arley in Idleness*. It was the last time that Leicestershire White dined at Tarporley.

Dick Simpson was a 'regular' guest and had given the Club an engraved oblong silver snuffbox for its centenary.

There is a reference to marrow bones which used to be a traditional dish at Tarporley and the Club still possesses a dozen silver marrow-bone scoops, all crested and hall-marked from 1750 onwards.

G.E.W.'s reply confirms that there was nothing about the incident in the club records. So who the woman was or whence she came, remains a mystery.

On the Proposed Division of the Cheshire Country, 1865
FARMER DOBBIN AGAIN, OR, IT WONNA DO

Farmer Dobbin! you've heerd talk of him afore now,
(My woif ou's a nursing at whoam a nesh cow),
So a sope o' good woin wi' you green-collar gents,
While I spake up moi mind, and I hope no offence.

T'other day Maister Fair and moisel had a chat,
"Farmer Dobbin," says he, "do ye know what they're at?"
"No," says I – "Well," says he, "I've heerd a strange tale.
They're for starting a new pack o'dogs in the Vale."

That's a fou nut to crack if it beant spoke in jest,
It be worse boi the half than this forrin cow-pest;
So Oi thoug't Oi'd make bowd just to step up to noight,
And to tell you moisel that that cock wonna foight.

I know what loif is, for Oi've lived long enough,
We mun tak as it comes, baith the smooth and the rough;
What! sloice off the Vale? Why Oi'd welly as lief
Have the fat aw cut off from moi Sunday roast-beef.

Maister Fair and moisel, bean't we safe to come down
When we whops o'er them cops, t'other soid Knutsford town?
When Oi've had ov rough roiding a ballyful there,
Then Oi loik in the Vale a tit-bit for th'owd mare.

For our Parliament men it wur aw moighty fine
To score the owd county in two wi' a loin;
Four members, aw reet 'uns, they say to give maith,
Two for the North end and two for the Saith;

But this new fangled split – now, 'Oi'll tell 'em aw four,
If they bean't plump agen it Oi'll back 'em no more;
Sir Philip himsel', nor his brother staitsmen,
They shall nere catch a vote from owd Dobbin agen.

What say crack sportsmen? – Squoir Tollemache? Squoir Glegg?
Squoir Dixon, the longest of aw in the leg?
What says Squoir Geoffrey – a mon of some weight
One who hears pratty 'cute when there's mischief agate.

And them two little birds that floy, hopping the twig,
What think brother Cissy and Guss o' this rig?
Has your huntsman been tould what a loss will befall him?
And what say your poet, low-rate, as you call him?

Owd Sir Harry, he'd canter to Saighton one morn,
And the next be at Tidnock a-woinding his horn;
Sartin sure, could th'owd Manager hear it tawk'd oer,
He would jump from his grave to the saddle once more.

When you run short o'cubs, and fetch foxes from France,
Whoi, dang it, what then mun we do wi' Tom Rance?
Hafe a loaf may be better than no bread at aw,
But you canna scrat back the lost crumbs you let fa'.

The lawyer, he say, before swapping your lands,
You mun cum to his shop wi' a fee in both hands;
The parson, he'd say, it wur sinful downroight,
For before a divorce there must first be a foight.

Your Chairman, tho' absent a bumper desarves,
A hero who never does nothing by halves,
Ask him, and he'll soon finish up the discussion,
He never cut nothing in two but a Russian.

The Fenians they say be a coming red hot,
To blow us i' pieces wi' powder and shot;
"Young Ireland" in toim may owd England upset,
But we donna want here a "Young Cheshire" – not yet.

As to haulving the Hunt betwixt owd pack and new,
Oi'd as soon think o'cutting moi missus in two;
To our Queen and our Country let aw on us stick,
To th'oud Pack, to th'oud Kennel, and four days a wik.

November, 1865. Published in the local press and sung at Tarporley by William Tomkinson (195).

NOTE : This was Lord Grosvenor's last season as Manager and a proposal had been made by him to relinquish a proportion of the Cheshire Hunt's country. Under the heading *THE CHESHIRE COUNTRY:A WORD FROM DAME DOBBIN*, a reply was published: (The author is believed to have been Le Gendre Starkie)

A Word from Dame Dobbin

Noo, maester, yo joost liven up! yo are na goin to doze
Afore, ould mon, Oi've put a rung in your ould fulish nose!
Ye've bin amang the gentle folk 'stead moinding o'er the seed,
And ye've writ a soight o' rubbitch for ev'ryone to read.

Aye! aye! t'coo's doin gradely and eatin o' her meat!
D'ye think as Oi'd tak on wi' ye, if t'coo she wurna reet?
But summat wrang's gat hand o'ye that's na fro' Rusher coom!
Oi' call it t'Cheshire pest! It's caused by allus staan at 'oom!

Oi's bin wi' Harry Newton, and he's a loikely lad!
He's cured the coo wi' t' bottle, and she wor mortal bad!
He's a bit too fond o' hoontin' for a Cheshire farmer's son;
But he's sold his chesnut colt to-day for gude tu hunderd pun!

He says he'll breed some more– it pays wi' judgement an' wi' care –
Aye! Aye! my mon! I asked him that! But he wunna buy t'ould mare!
Says he "Divide the country! It's big enough for tu!
Why, missus, yo moight feed t'ould mare till at last she could na pleugh!

"It 's very foin to say the squoires be all the other way!
The hoont they're very fond of, but at hoontin where be they?
The squoires who roid tak' t'other side. They are the good uld sort!
They knaw those love the ould hoont best thot want the olden spoort!

If the foxes be na rattled, thin the foxes wunna fly!
If t' coverts be too seldom drawn, they'll be drawn blank by and bye!
It t' meet be moiles an' moiles away, my lord he wunna coom!
Fur t' squoires' ball the meet be spoiled if my lord he stops at 'oom!

Ould Sir Harry wur a spoortsman! I'd ha' loiked to hear 'un swear,
If ev'ry fox kept runnin roond an' roond just loik a hare!
He'd precious sune 'a sed 'Divide' if he'd foond that i' December
He wur doin' nout but coob huntin' joost loik as 'twur September!

Squoire Geoffrey, he's a weighty mon – too weighty p'raps to move!
Why should Squoire Dixon's legs, tho' lang, mak' him walk in a groove?
An' as for Squoire Glegg, I's boond thot, 'sportsman ould and true,'
He'll show no fewer foxes tho' the coontry's cut in tu!
Squoire Warburton's agin it! wull, 'the lowrate' he may be!
I rate joost noo, I knaws he is, and the truth he wunna see!"

Another somewhat obscure *Sequel to Farmer Dobbin* was recited at the Penny Readings at Great Budworth in 1868. REEW also wrote a parochial *Further Sequel to Dame Dobbin* as late as 1882, which starts

Sin' the toime I talk on sum ha' flitted sum be dead,
So now I'll tell o' them as we ha' gotten in their stead.
Squoir Arthur Barry one who loike a noightingale can sing
We mun catch him while at whoam lest he agen be takin' wing.

Killing no Murder

I KNOW not – search England round,
If better Huntsman can be found,
A bolder rider or a neater,
When mounted for the field, than Peter;
But this I know, there is not one
So bent on blood as Collison.
Hear how the doctrine he propounds,
All ye who love to follow hounds:–

  Says he,''Since first my horn was blown,
This maxim I have made my own;
Kill if you can with sport; – but still –
Or with it or without it – kill
A feather in my cap to pin,
A fresh one every brush I win!
That fox is doom'd who seeks for rest
In gorse or spinney when distrest;
Though far and fast he may have sped,
He counts for nothing till he's dead.
I hold that Whip not worth his pay,
Who fails to keep him there at bay;
When round and round the covertside
The mounted mob, like madmen, ride,
Now cross him here, now head him there,
While shouts and clamour rend the air
Spare him, the gentle folk may say,
To live and fight another day;
When April ends the hunting year,
How then should I in Bell appear?
Or how my brother Huntsmen face
If short of booking fifty brace?
Excuse me, gentlemen I say,
My hounds have had but two to-day.''

5th and subsequent Editions.

On Peter Collison's late Fall
1868

BAD luck betide that treacherous spot
Where Peter's horse, though at a trot,
Roll'd over, hurling headlong there
A Huntsman whom we ill could spare;
As there he lay and gasped for breath,
Unconscious quite and pale as death,
The clinging hounds around him yell,
And wailing moans their sorrow tell,
Let ——, who over-rides them all,

Take warning by our Huntsman's fall;
When such shall be that rider's fate
(And his it will be soon or late),
They o'er the downfall of their foe
Will not upraise a voice of woe;
When prostrate, if the pack should greet him
With open mouths, 'twill be to eat him.

5th and subsequent Editions.

Hunting Song

OF all the recreations with which mortal man is blest,
Go where he will, fox-hunting still is pleasantest and best;
The hunter knows no sorrow here, the cup of life to him,
A bumper bright of fresh delight fill'd sparkling to the brim.
    Away, away we go,
      With a tally, tally-ho,
  With a tally, tally, tally, tally, tally, tally-ho!

O! is it not – O! is it not – a spirit-stirring sound,
The eager notes from tuneful throats that tell a fox is found?
O! is it not – O! is it not – a pleasant sight to see
The chequer'd pack, tan, white and black, fly scudding o'er
                                           the lea?
      Chorus.

How keen their emulation in the bustle of the burst,
When side by side the foremost ride, each struggling to be first;
Intent on that sweet music which in front delights their ear,
The sobbing loud of the panting crowd they heed not in the rear.
      Chorus.

The field to all is open, whether clad in black or red,
O'er rail and gate the featherweight may thrust his
                                    thoroughbred;
While heavier men, well mounted, though not foremost in the
                                           fray,
If quick to start and stout of heart, need not be far away.
      Chorus.

And since that joy is incomplete which Beauty shuns to share,
Or maid or bride, if skill'd to ride, we fondly welcome there;
Where woodland hills our music fills and echoes sweet the
                                       chorus,
Or when we fly with a scent breast high, and a galloping fox
                                      before us.
      Chorus.

1868. 5th and subsequent Editions.

Tarporley Song
1870

RECALLING the days of old Bluecap and Barry,
Of Bedford and Gloster, George Heron and Sir Harry,
A bumper tonight the Quæsitum shall carry,
    Which nobody can deny.

Tho' his rivals by Meynell on mutton were fed,
When the race o'er the Beacon by Bluecap was led,
A hundred good yards was the winner ahead,
    Which nobody can deny.

The gentry of Cheshire, whate'er their degrees,
Stanleys or Egertons, Leycesters or Leghs,
One and all with green ribbons have garter'd their knees.
    Which nobody can deny

Over grass while the youngsters were skimming the vale,
Down the pavement away went the old ones full sail,
Each green collar flapp'd by a powder'd pigtail,
    Which nobody can deny.

When foxes were flyers and gorse coverts few,
Those hounds of Sir Harry, where thickest it grew,
How they dash'd into Huxley and hustled it through,
    Which nobody can deny.

The sport they began may we still carry on,
And we forty good fellows, who meet at The Swan,
To the green collar stick, tho' our breeches be gone,
    Which nobody can deny.

Still, whether clad in short garments or long,
With a Cotton to sing us a fox-hunting song,
And a Corbet to lead us, we cannot go wrong,
    Which nobody can deny.

5th and subsequent Editions.

Bow-meeting Song
ARLEY HALL, SEPTEMBER 4, 1851

THE tent is pitched, the target reared, the ground is measured out,
For the weak arm sixty paces, and one hundred for the stout!
Come gather ye together then, the youthful and the fair,
And poet's lay, to future day, the victor shall declare!

Let busy fingers lay aside the needle and the thread,
To prick the golden canvas with a pointed arrowhead;
Ye sportsmen quit the stubble, quit, ye fishermen, the stream,
Fame and glory stand before you, brilliant eyes around you beam.

All honour to the long-bow, which many a battle won,
Ere powder blazed and bullet flew, from arquebus or gun;
All honour to the long-bow, which merry men of yore,
With hound and horn at early morn, in greenwood forest bore.

O! famous is the archer's sport. 'twas honoured long ago,
The God of Love, the God of Wit, bore both of them a bow;
Love laughs to-day in Beauty's eye and blushes on her cheek,
And wit is heard in every word, that merry archers speak;

The archer's heart, though, like his bow, a tough and sturdy thing,
Is pliant still and yielding, when affection pulls the string,
All his words and all his actions are like arrows, pointed well
To hit that golden centre, where true love and friendship dwell.

They tell us in that outline with the lips of beauty show,
How cupid found a model for his heart-subduing bow;
The arrows in his quiver are the glances from her eye,
A feather from Love's wing it is, that makes the arrow fly!

3rd and subsequent editions.

The Covertside Phantom

ONE morning in November,
　As the village clock struck ten,
Came trooping to the covertside
　A field of hunting men;
'Twas neither Quorn nor Pytchley horn
　That summon'd our array;
No; we who met were a homely set,
　In a province far away.

As there we stood conversing,
　Much amazement seiz'd the Hunt,
When spick and span, an unknown man
　Rode onwards to the front;
All whisper'd, gazing wonderstruck,
　"Who can this stranger be?"
Forsooth they were, that man and mare,
　A comely sight to see.

The mare was a faultless chesnut
　As was ever strapp'd by groom;
Nor fault could in the man be found,
　Nor flaw in his costume;
A silk cord loop'd the hunting hat,
　The gloves' consummate fit
No crease disturb'd, and burnish'd bright
　Shone stirrup, chain and bit.

The rider's seat was firm and neat
　As rider's seat could be;
The buckskin white was button'd tight,
　And knotted at the knee;
Above the boots' jet polish
　Was a top of tender stain,
Nor brown nor white, but a mixture light
　Of rose-leaves and champagne.

The heart that waistcoat buttons up
　Must be a heart of steel,
As keen as the keenest rowel
　On the spur that decks his heel;
We look'd the stranger over,
　And we gravely shook our heads,
And we felt a sad conviction
　He would cut us into shreds.

A glance I stole from my double sole
　To my coat of faded red;
The scarlet which had once been there
　My countenance o'erspread;
I blush'd with shame – no wonder!
　So completely was the shine
By the man and mare beside me
　Taken out of me and mine.

How his portrait sketch'd for 'Baily'
　Would the sporting world enchant,
By the pen of a Whyte-Melville,
　Or the pencil of a Grant!
An Adonis, scarlet-coated!
　A glorious field Apollo,
May we have pluck and rare good luck,
　When he leads the way, to follow!

So intense my admiration
　(What I thought I dare not say),
But I felt inclin'd in my inmost mind,
　To wish for a blank day,
Lest a piece of such rare metal,
　So elaborately gilt,
Should expose its polish'd surface
　To a scratch by being spilt.

Sad to think, should such a get-up
  By a downfall come to grief;
That a pink of such perfection
  Should become a crumpled leaf!
Sad to think this bird of Paradise
  Should risk its plumage bright
By encounter with a bullfinch,
  Or a mud-stain in its flight!

But all that glisters is not gold,
  However bright it seem;
Ere long a sudden change came o'er
  The spirit of my dream;
No defeat ourselves awaited
  From the man nor from his mount;
No ground for the discomfort
  We had felt on his account.

A fox was found the stirring sound
  That nerv'd us for the fray –
That hollo burst the bubble,
  And the phantom scar'd away;
We cross'd the vale o'er post and rail,
  Up leaps and downward drops;
But where, oh where, was the chesnut mare
  And the man with the tinted tops?

He was not with the foremost,
  As they one and all declare;
Nor was he with the hindmost, –
  He was neither here nor there;
The last, they say, seen of him
  Was in front of the first fence,
And no one e'er could track the mare,
  Or spot the rider thence.

All turquoise and enamel,
  Like a watch tricked up for show,
Though a pretty thing to look at,
  Far too beautiful to go;
He, the man at whose appearance
  We had felt ourselves so small,
Was only the ninth part of one –
  A tailor after all!

His own line when he took it,
  Was by railway ticket ta'en;
First class, a rattling gallop,
  As he homeward went by train;
A horse-box for his hunter,
  And a band-box for himself,
One was shunted into hidlands,
  T'other laid upon the shelf.

5th Edition and subsequent editions.

FIRST published in *Baily's Magazine*, January, 1871, in which REEW added a further verse, somewhat un- complimentary to Jewish tailors. The word 'hidland(s)' is not given in the OED.

The Two Wizards

GIVE ear, ye who dwell in Tarporley Vale,
While I tell you of Beeston a wonderful tale;
Where its crag, castle-crowned, overhanging the steep,
Noddles down like the head of an old man asleep,
A cavern is scoop'd, though unseen by the eye,
In the side of that rock, where it stands high and dry.
There has dwelt for long ages, and there dwelleth still
A Magician – believe it or not as you will;
He was there when Earl Blundevill laid the first stone
Of those walls, now with ivy and moss overgrown;
He was there when King Henry proclaim'd himself Lord,
When he belted his son with the Palatine sword;
He to King Richard gave up this stronghold,
Therein to deposit his jewels and gold;
He was there when the Puritans mounted the steep,
And defied the king's troops from its garrison'd keep;
And there stood this Wizard to witness the fight,
When Rupert's good sword put those rebels to flight.
For two centuries then it was left to decay,
And its walls, weather-beaten, fell piece-meal away,
And his home grew so dull when his fighting was o'er,
The Wizard declared he could live there no more;
Till the thought cross'd his brain that to cheer his lone days
Some playmates the power of his magic might raise.
So at sunrise one morn stepping forth from his cell,
He uplifted his wand and he mutter'd a spell;
And the stones that it touch'd all became kangaroos.
He had round the walls of his cavern inside
The armour of those who had fought there and died;
Transforming those plates which long rust had worn thin,

He fitted each beast with a jacket of skin;
Then he pluck'd from each sword-blade its black leather sheath,
Which he twisted and stuck as a tail underneath.

And there, as a shepherd, sits watching his flock,
Sits this kangaroo-keeper a-perch on his rock,
Invisible still, but his care night and day
Is to feed them and watch lest they wander astray.
When the huntsman his pack has let loose on the hill;
And those hounds all terror-stricken, all riot eschew,
When they hear a strange voice crying, "Ware Kangaroo!"
To this Wizard invisible bidding farewell,
Of another I yet have a story to tell:
No invisible sprite! when he stands full in view,
You will own him a man, and a goodly man too.
He it is who by dint of his magical skill
Uplifted the stones from the high Stanna hill;
Nor paus'd till those fragments, pil'd up to the sky,
Assum'd the fair form of that castle hard by;
He brandish'd his spade, and along the hillside
The ascent by a roadway made easy and wide;
Unlike the hid portal I spoke of before,
Very plain to the eye is his wide-open door;
Where the tiles of the pavement, the stones of the wall
Unceasingly echo a welcome to all.
There are stables where steeds stand by tens in a row,
There are chambers above and vast cellars below;
Each bed in those chambers holds nightly a guest,
Each bin in that cellar is fill'd with the best.

When this Wizard wends forth from his turret'd walls,
Four horses are bitted and led from their stalls,
He mounts and looks down on a team from his box,
All perfect in shape from their heads to their hocks;
The coats that they carry are burnish'd like gold,
Their fire by a touch of his finger controll'd;
A whip for his wand, when their paces he springs,
You might fancy their shoulders were furnish'd with wings;
Away! rough or smooth, whether uphill or down,
Through highway and byeway through village and town!
With ease and that grace with which ladies can wheedle
Stubborn silk though the eye of a delicate needle,
Through the arch with huge portal on either side hung,
He his leaders can thrust whether restive or young;
O'er the bridge at Bate's Mill he can twist at full speed,
Charioteering – which proves him a Wizard indeed.

Faint harp strings at night o'er his castle resound;
Their tone when first heard by the countryfolk round,
They fancied (so far as it pass'd human skill)
That angels were tuning their harps on the hill;
It was strung, I knew well by an angel inside,
The fingers that swept it were those of his bride.

Oft-times they who deal in these magical arts
Bear hatred and malice to men in their hearts;
But to enmity ne'er was this Wizard inclin'd,
A well-dispos'd being to all human kind;
To console the afflicted, the poor to befriend,
Of his magic, is still the sole object and end;
And each cottager's prayer is, that spells such as these
He may long live to work in this Valley of Cheese.

5th and subsequent editions.

NOTE:

REEW's strange reference to kangaroos can only be an obscure allusion for the benefit of his two soldier brothers, who had long since settled in Australia. His younger brother, George Edward, serving in the 51st Regt. (The King's Own Yorkshire Light Infantry) had gone out to guard convicts in Tasmania. On the way they called at Albany, then the capital of Western Australia, where he fell in love with the Governor's daughter, a Miss Spencer, whom he married in 1842 on resigning from the Army. He became a pioneer farmer. In due course his brother Peter retired from the Indian Army, intending to settle in New Zealand. He and his wife called at Albany and were persuaded by George to stay on, moving to South Australia.

Colonel Peter Egerton Warburton was to be created a C.M.G. for the explorations he made into Western Australia, undertaking various adventurous expeditions into the outback. He was the first European to head westwards to the coast from Alice Springs. He was 60 at the time. It was largely as a result of his activities in this field that the name Warburton was given to no less than seven geographical features on the continent, including two townships in new South Wales and Victoria, the Warburton River in S. Australia, two Warburton ranges of mountains, Warburton Creek, *etc.* in Queensland and Mt. Warburton in the Northern Territory.

The second part refers to that wizard of the ribbons, Lord Tollemache (124), and to Peckforton Castle. It is no mean achievement to drive a car at more than 15 m.p.h. over the tricky, twisting Bate's Mill Bridge over the canal between Beeston and Brassey Green, let alone a coach and four at a canter.

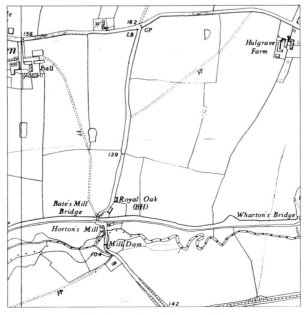

O.S. Map of Bate's Mill Bridge

The Mare and her Master

THOUGH my sight is grown dim, though my arm is grown weak,
Grey hairs on my forehead, and lines on my cheek;
Though the verdure of youth is grown yellow and seer,
I feel my heart throb when November draws near.

I could pardon the wrongs thou hast done me, Old Time!
If thy hand would but help me the stirrup to climb;
The one pleasure left is to gaze on my mare,
Her with whom I lov'd best the excitement to share.

Sound wind and limb, without blemish or speck,
Her rider disabled, her owner a wreck!
Unstripp'd and unsaddled, she seems to ask why;
Unspurr'd and unbooted, I make no reply.

Remembrance then dwells on each hard-ridden run,
On the country we cross'd and the laurels we won;
Fleet limbs once extended, now cribb'd in their stall,
They speak of past triumphs, past gallops recall.

I remember, when baulked of our start at the find,
How we slipp'd undismay'd, through the rabble behind;
No check to befriend us, still tracking the burst,
Till by dint of sheer swiftness the last became first.

And that day I remember, when crossing the bed
Of a deep rolling river, the pack shot ahead;
How the dandies, though cased in their waterproof Peals,
Stood aghast as we stemm'd it, and stuck to their heels.

How ere Jack with his hammer had riven the nail,
And unhing'd the park-gate, we had skimm'd the oak pale;
Over bogs where the hoof of the cocktail stuck fast,
How her foot without sinking Camilla-like pass'd.

I remember though warn'd by the voice of Tom Rance –
"Have a care of that fence" – how we ventur'd the chance;
How we faced it and fell – from the depth of the drain
How we pick'd ourselves up and were with 'em again.

Over meadows of water, through forest of wood,
Over grassland or plough, there is nothing like blood;
Whate'er place I coveted, thou, my good mare,
Despite of all hindrances, landed me there.

The dearest of friends I that man must account,
To whom on her saddle I proffer a mount;
And that friend shall confess that he never yet knew,
Till he handled my pet, what a flyer could do.

Should dealers come down from the Leicestershire vale
And turn with good gold my weight in the scale,
Would I sell thee? not I, for a millionaire's purse!
Through life we are wedded for better for worse.

I can feed thee and pet thee, and finger thy mane,
Though I ne'er throw my leg o'er thy quarters again;
Gold shall ne'er purchase one lock of thy hair,
Death alone shall bereave the old man of his mare.

1871. 5th and subsequent editions.

NOTES: Under its alternative title ***The Old Grey Mare***, it was included in the Hon. F. Lawley's obituary notice of REEW in *Baily's Magazine*, January, 1892. The name Peal refers to the royal bootmakers, PEAL & CO. LTD. of Wigmore St., founded 1791.

A Retort Uncourteous

WHERE London's city skirts the Thames,
In ball-room met two rival dames;
Quoth one: "Why all this youthful sham?
You now are but a has-been, *ma'am."*
"'Tis better far," was the reply,
"To be a has-been *such as I,*
Than still to hang upon the shelf,
A never-was-er *like yourself."*

Epigrams, 3rd Edition.

On a Tame Fox

PARLOUR PET AT DALEFORDS, THE RESIDENCE OF THE
MASTER OF THE CHESHIRE HOUNDS

Squire Corbet! at all seasons
A fox is his delight,
A wild one for the morning,
And a tame one for the night;

For the fox that scours the country
We a green gorse covert raise,
But parlour pug lies warm and snug
In a cover of green baize.

Or in his chair reposing,
Or o'er the saddle bent,
Corbet, wide awake or dozing,
Is never off the scent.

He needs no kirtled housemaid,
The carpet on the stairs
Is dusted by the sweeping
Of the brush that Reynard wears.

This hunting man's housekeeper,
She, without distress of nerves,
Oft amongst the currant jelly
Finds a fox in her preserves.

Bones of chicken ever picking,
This pet, so fed and nurs'd,
Though he never gave a gallop,
He may finish with a burst.

5th and Subsequent Editions.

To comrades of the hunting field, tho' sad to say farewell,
'Tis pleasant still on olden days at Tarporley to dwell;
On friends for whom, alive or dead, our love is unimpair'd,
The mirth and the adventure and the sport that we have shar'd.

The feelings of good fellowship that Tarporley unite,
The honour'd names recorded which made its annals bright.
Old Charley Cholmondeley's portrait and the fashion of our clothes,
In the days of padded neckcloths, breeches green, and silken hose.

The upright form of Delamere, Sir Richard's graceful seat,
The brothers three from Dorfold sprung whom none of us could beat;
The fun with which Bob Grosvenor enliven'd every speech,
The laugh of Charley Wicksted lengthen'd out into a screech.

The classical Quæsitum and the President's hard chair,
Each year's succeeding Patroness whose charms were toasted there;
The inevitable wrangle which the Farmers' Cup provokes,
Sir Watkin cracking biscuits and Sir Harry cracking jokes.

The match in which though Adelaide but held a second place,
No judge was there to certify that Go-by won the race,
The stakes withheld – the winner told jocosely by the Hunt
With nothing else to pocket he must pocket the affront.

Earl Wilton ever foremost amidst Leicestershire high flyers,
Coming down from Melton Mowbray to enlighten Cheshire Squires;
Belgrave, who unbreech'd us, and one fatal afternoon
First clothed us to the ankle in the modern pantaloon.

The foxes which from Huxley have led us many a dance,
Joe Maiden best of huntsman, best of whips old Tommy Rance;
That good old soul, John Dixon, and his lengthy draught of ale,
That mirthful day when "Little Dogs" came home without a tail.

The glory of that gallop which old Oulton Lowe supplied,
The front-rank men of Cheshire charging onward side by side;
The Baron with his spurs at work in rear of the advance,
When Britain, in the field, for once ran clean away from France.

The find at Brindley covert and at Dorfold Hall the kill,
The Breeches left behind us but the brush before us still;
The fox that skimm'd them Tilstone cream – forget we never shall
The score of hunting breeches that were washed in that canal.

And that ill-starr'd disaster when, unconscious of the leap,
I dropp'd into the water of a marl-pit six feet deep;
Enough to damp the keenest – but conceive the fearful sight,
When I found that underneath me lay the body of Jack White.

The harmony infus'd into the rhymes which I had strung,
When first I heard the "Columbine " by James Smith-Barry sung.
While canvas of remembrance of Sir Peter shall prolong,
May the name of his successor be endear'd to you in song.

The carving of the venison when it smok'd upon the board,
The twinkling eye of Johnny Glegg, the chaff of Charley Ford;
The opening of the oysters and the closing of the eyes
In slumber deep – that balmy sleep which midnight cup supplies.

Sir Humphrey and Geof. Shakerley, whose friendship never fails,
Tho' long of two opinions which was heaviest in the scales;
In love of sport as in their weight an even race they run,
So here's a health to both of them and years of future fun.

Old Time, who keeps his own account, however well we wear,
Time whispers "to the old ones you must add another pair,"
May Lascelles in his chosen home long, long a dweller be,
To Philo gorse a bumper, to Sir Philip three times three.

Young inheritors of hunting, ye who would the sport should last,
Think not the chace a hustling race, fit only for the fast;
If sport in modern phrase must be synonymous with speed,
The good old English animal will sink into a weed.

Accept the wish your Laureate leaves behind him ere we part,
That wish shall find an echo in each Cheshire sportsman's heart,
May Time still spare one favour'd pair, tho' other creatures fail,
The Swan that floats above us, and the Fox that skims the Vale!

The snobs who haunt the hunting-field, and rouse the Master's ire,
The fence of fair appearance masking lines of hidden wire;
A straight fox mobb'd and headed by the laggards in the lane,
A good one dug and murder'd, I have seen such sights with pain.

I never kill'd save once a hound, I saw him on his back
With deep remorse – he was, of course, the best one in the pack;
The thought oft-time has griev'd me with a wild fox well away,
That friends right worthy of it should have miss'd the lucky day.

If e'er my favourite covert unexpectedly was blank,
Then silent and dispirited my heart within me sank;
But never till this moment has a tear bedimm'd mine eye,
With sorrow such as now I feel in wishing you Good-bye.

1872. 5th and subsequent Editions.

NOTE: Rowland's letter of resignation was read to the Meeting in 1873 'and universal regret was expressed at its contents' by the 26 Members present, who proceeded to elect him an Honorary Member and the President, Henry Lyon, wrote immediately after the races on the Club's crested writing paper to advise him and report on the races, concluding 'I am very sorry to miss so many old faces. I have the pleasant prospect of proposing several toasts tonight and my only consolation is it is better than having to answer them.'

Home with the Hounds; or, the Huntsman's Lament

OVER-RIDDEN! over-ridden!
  All along of that the check;
When the ditch that gemman slid in,
  Don't I wish he'd broke his neck.
I to hunt my hounds am able,
  Would the field but play me fair;
Mobb'd at Smithfield by the rabble,
  Who a fox could follow there?

Let the tinker ride his kettle,
  Let the tailor ride his goose,
How can hounds to hunting settle
  With the like o' them let loose?
What's the use on't when he scrambles
  Through a run that butchers tit?
Butcher'd fox-hounds for the shambles
  They be neither fat nor fit.

What's the use o' jockies thumping
  Wi' their 'andwhips bits of blood?
Tits by instinct shy of jumping,
  For they could not if they would;
Though the snob, who cannot guide her,
  Mounts the mare as draws his trap;
'Taint the red coat makes the rider,
  Leather boots, nor yet the cap.

They who come their coat to show, they
  Better were at home in bed;
What of hounds and hunting know they?
  Nothing else but "go ahead";
At the Kennel I could train 'em,
  If they would but come to school,
Two and two in couples chain 'em,
  Feed on meal, and keep 'em cool.

Gemmen, gemmen, shame upon 'em,
  Plague my heart out worse than all,
Worse than Bowdon mobs at Dunham,
  Worse than cobblers at Poole Hall;
Spurring at a fence their clippers,
  When the hounds are in the rear!
Reg'lar gemmen! self and whippers
  Tipping reg'lar once a year!

Well! soft solder next I'll try on,
  Rating only riles a swell;
Mister Brancker! Mister Lyon!
  Mister Hornby! – hope you're well;
'Taint the pack that I'm afraid on,
  And I like to see you first,
But when so much steam be laid on
  Beant you fear'd the copper'll burst?

Rantipole, I see'd him sprawling
  Underneath a horse's hoof;
Prudence only heard me calling
  Just in time to keep aloof;
Vulcan lamed for life! Old Victor
  Ne'er again will he show fight;
Venus sin' that gelding kick her,
  Aint he spoilt her beauty quite?

Gentlemen, unto my thinking,
  Should behave themselves as sich;
'Tik'lar when the scent is sinking,
  And the hounds are at a hitch;
How my temper can I master,
  Fretted till I fume and foam?
I can only backwards cast, or
  Blow my horn and take 'em home.

5th and subsequent Editions.

On Hearing that 'The Cheshire' were to hunt Five Days a Week.

"THERE'S luck in odd numbers," says Rory O 'More,
"Five days," says Squire Corbet, "good sport will ensure;"
So, All-fours out of fashion, the game is now Fives,
But who cares what they call it while fox-hunting thrives?

6th Edition.

List of other Hunting Songs from the 5th and 6th Editions:

The Love-Chace.
A 'Meet' at the Hall, and a 'Find' in the Wood.
Newby Ferry. (An overloaded ferryboat capsized crossing the River Ure and six persons, including the Master of the York & Ainsty Hounds, lost their lives, on Feb. 4, 1869.)
A Growl from the Squire of Grumbleton.
'Tis Sixty Years Since.
  The first stanza of this hunting reminiscence goes:

> *"Your heart is fresh as every, Ned,*
> *Although your head be white;*
> *We must crack another bottle, Ned,*
> *Before we say goodnight . . ."*

Ned and Jack recall their Eton and Oxford days and adventures with many a pack, including Cheshire:

> *"And that week with old Sir Harry*
> *Which at Tarporley we spent,*
> *Where Chester's dewy pastures*
> *Are renowned for holding scent;*
> *Where Dorfold's Squire o'er saddle flaps*
> *Unpadded threw his leg,*
> *Where stride for stride, rode side by side*
> *Sir Richard and John Glegg."*

The Stranger's Story, parts one and two, the first verse of which goes:

> *Four frends, all scarlet-coated,*
> *Eager all to join the pack,*
> *At the breakfast board were seated,*
> *Jem and Jerry, Ned and Jack.*

The Lover's Quarrel

Epitaph on the Duke of Wellington's charger.

On Reading in The Times, April 9th, 1860, a critique on the Life of Assheton Smith.

Lines, on reading from the hunting diary of Vernon Delves Broughton, Esq., showing how and where the Duke of Grafton's Hounds killed their Gooseholme fox on 29th November, 1872.

The Roebuck at Toft. *(An old wayside inn removed in 1864)*

and

Welsh Hunting

Hounds belonging to Mr George Thomas of Ystradmynach were being taken home from hunting through the town of Pontypridd in 1869, when the pack suddenly broke away into the shop of Mr Jenkins the Grocer and out again immediately with no less than seven pounds of tallow candles, which they ravenously devoured in the street.

> *WHERE Jenkins, in Wales,*
> *Soap and candles retails,*
> *   The pack in despite of their Whip,*
> *They took up the scent,*
> *And away they went,*
> *   Each one with a tallow dip.*
>
> *With a good seven pounds,*
> *These hungry hounds,*
> *   Away! and away! they go,*
> *While joining the chace,*
> *Follow'd Jenkins' best pace*
> *   Shouting "Tallow! Tallow-Ho!"*

5th and 6th Editions.

On a Thorn Tree planted over the grave of 'Miss Miggs', a Brood Mare

> *WITH a thorn in her side the old mare we inter,*
> *Though alive she ne'er needed the prick of a spur.*
> *Six colts and eight fillies the stock that she bred,*
> *This thorn if it rival the produce she foal'd,*
> *Will be hung in due season with apples of gold;*
> *But Whate'er fruit it bear it will not bear a sloe*
> *For no thorn save a quick thorn can out of her grow.*

5th Edition.

Welsh hunting

Farming and Fox-hunting

FARMERS listen to the ditty
  Of a friend who loves you well;
If you will not, more the pity,
  Nothing but the truth I tell.

Let us while we each our work do
  In good fellowship unite;
Why should we, as Russ and Turk do,
  Fox-hunters and Farmers fight?

If the noble sport decrying,
  Growl you will, we can but laugh;
Freely from the farmstead buying
  Oats, we do not want your chaff.

Spent by what we call a 'splitter',
  Steeds are bedded in the stall.
You who grow such costly litter,
  Men of straw we cannot call.

Selling till the sport is over
  Many a waggon load of hay,
Surely you must live in clover,
  Surely fox-hunting must pay.

Therefore should your fence be broken,
  Post and rail to grief consign'd,
Let no angry word betoken
  Damage to your peace of mind.

Bone-dust sown the pasture sod on,
  Should the surface smooth and flat
By the tramp of hoof be trod on,
  You must make no bones of that.

Should the green wheat in December
  By the field be overrun,
Wait till yellow in September
  Ere ye sue for damage done.

Should the hen-roost robb'd dismay you,
  Reynard guilty of the theft;
Wives be sure the Squire will pay you
  Double for the ducklings left.

Sad indeed though lines of wire be
  Harmless underneath the wave,
From his saddle should the Squire be
  Telegraph'd into his grave.

Plainly by my pen depicted,
  Let the evil and the good,
Profit won or harm inflicted,
  Both be fairly understood.

Each dependent on the weather
  One for scent and one for growth,
Farm and Kennel link'd together,
  Let us drink success to both!

November, 1877. 7th and subsequent editions.

Modern Chivalry

TIME was with sword and battle-axe
  All clad in armour bright,
When cleaving skulls asunder
  Was the business of a knight.

Now chivalry means surgery,
  And spurs are won by him
Who can mend a skull when broken,
  Or piece a fractured limb.

Our knights of old couched lances,
  Drew long swords from the sheath,
Now knighthood couches eye-balls,
  And chivalry draws teeth.

See! rescued from confinement,
  To charm our ravished fight,
Fair ladies are delivered
  By the arm of a true knight.

Behold the knight chirurgeon
  To deeds of blood advance,
A bandage for a banner!
  And a lancet for a lance!

To heroes of the hospital
  The "bloody hand" is due,
But ye heralds bend the fingers,
  Or the fee may tumble through.

The Appleton Thorn

In the Warrington Museum is an allegorical painting on a panel, measuring 3 ft x 2 ft 6 ins. It is of a thorn tree with a young man and a girl dancing round it and it is headed:

Robertus Bateman   *Rowland Egerton Warburton*
me fecit.   A.D. *1880*   *me scriptsit.*

> *This thorn in the year eighteen eighty was set*
> *By the Warburton heir and his bride, Antoinette.*
> *May blessings on both be abundantly shed*
> *And may all those who bawm it as happily wed.*
>
> *This thorn which succeeded the old one blown down,*
> *Stood for fifty-five summers in Appleton town,*
> *There each July as the wenches danced round,*
> *It was bawmed with fresh flowers and with garlands was*
> *   crowned.*
>
> *At Arley whence brought eighteen twenty-five*
> *Once more may it firmly be rooted and thrive.*

This inscription was in the village Club-room at Appleton Thorn and these two lines were over the door of The Thorn public house:

> *You may safely while sober sit under the Thorn*
> *But if drunk overnight it will prick you next morn.*

The old thorn was planted again at Arley three yards South West and three yards East of the back gate, leading out of the park towards Knutsford.

Rowland also wrote a song, to the tune of '*Bonnie Dundee*':

Bawming The Thorn

The Maypole in Spring merry maidens adorn,
Our Midsummer May-day means 'Bawming the Thorn';
On her garlanded throne sits the May Queen alone,
Here each Appleton lad has a queen of his own.
CHORUS
> *Up with fresh garlands this Midsummer morn,*
> *Up with red ribbons on Appleton Thorn,*
> *Come lasses and lads to the Thorn tree to-day*
> *To bawm and shout as ye bawm it hurrah!*

The oak in its strength is the pride of the wood,
The birch bears a twig to make naughty boys do good;
But there grows not a tree which in splendour can vie
With our Thorn tree when bawmed in the month of July.
CHORUS

Kissing under the rose is when nobody sees,
You may under the mistletoe kiss when you please;

No kiss can so sweet as the stolen one be
Which is snatched from a sweetheart when bawming the Tree.
CHORUS

Ye Appleton lads I can promise you this,
When her lips you have pressed with a true lover's kiss,
Woo'd her and won her and made her your bride,
Thenceforth she will ne'er be a thorn in your side.
CHORUS

So, long as this Thorn tree o'shadows the ground,
May sweethearts to bawm it in plenty be found,
And a thousand years hence, when 'tis withered and dead,
May there stand here a Thorn to be bawmed in its stead.
CHORUS

Arley in Idleness.

> NOTE: The word bawming used by REEW has the same meaning as barning, *i.e.* adorning, preferred by the locals. Both are Cheshire dialect. Egerton Leigh wrote another version – *Barning the Appleton Thorn*. The ceremony used to be held on June 29th, St Peter's Day.
>
> It was revived in 1973, when an off-shoot of the Glastonbury Thorn in Somerset was planted at Appleton. A thorn is said to have stood there since AD 1178 when a Cheshire knight, Adam de Dutton, planted one when he came back from the Crusades. He had made a pilgrimage to Glastonbury Abbey to give thanks for his safe return and brought an off-shoot home with him.

Cheshire's Welcome
JANUARY 1881

ERIN once the favoured home
  Of melody and mirth,
The brightest gem of ocean
  And the fairest flower of earth,
Erin where two seasons past
  Allured by horn and hound,
A Royal Huntress sojourned
  And a loving welcome found.

Where rebels now are rulers
  To that land she bids adieu,
She comes where all both great and small
  Are staunch good men and true;
She seeks a shire where loyalty
  In every bosom dwells,
Where Chester's vale full many a tale
  Of merrie hunting tells.

Where we meet not to wage warfare
  With the Palatine Police,
Where friendship and good feeling
  Are preservative of peace,
Where should there be disturbance
  When the fox from covert flies,
We find our compensation
  In the gallop ere he dies.

Whene'er the pack of olden fame
  At Combermere shall meet,
An Empress in the saddle there
  With rapture we will greet,
Who takes, what all would willingly
  To rank and beauty yield,
Alone by right of horsemanship
  Precedence in the field.

Across the Deeside pastures
 With the foremost she will race,
Or lead the way whene'er Wynnstay
 Invites her to the chace;
Or when from Stanner's fir-clad hill
A gallant fox takes flight.
 Though with lightning speed they follow
She will keep the pack in sight.

She quits a court to share the sport
 Which here without annoy
No league to mar the pastime
 She may peaceably enjoy;
That sport so rare unknown elsewhere
 Alone can England give,
And many a year right welcome here
 To share it she may live.

Song Sheet, *Arley in Idleness*, 7th, 8th and 9th Editions. NOTE: This hunting song was dedicated by permission to Her Majesty the Empress of Austria and Queen of Hungary. It was set to music for voice and piano by Edward R. Terry and published in January, 1881, price 4/=. It included the following chorus:

 Away! away! away!
 With a tally tally-ho!
 With a tally,tally,tally,
 Tally tally tally-ho!

List of others in the 7th Edition:

Brother Tom, sequel to The Man with One Hunter
Bought and Sold
An Australian Stag-Hunt, as described by a Northamptonshire sportsman, Melbourne, 1878.
On the Death of Whyte-Melville
Found at Last
A London Ballad
Hush! Hush! Hush!
Epigram on a Hard-riding youth named Taylor.

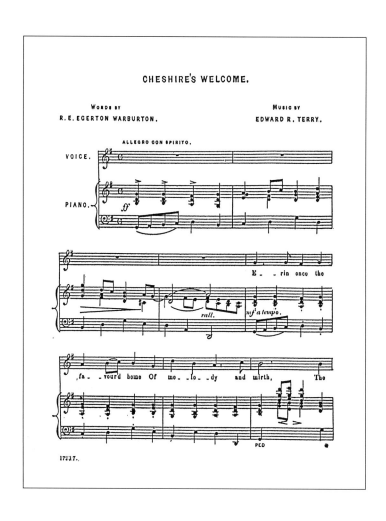

and

Paraphrase by a Master of Hounds

Si j'avance suivez moi; si je recule
Tuez moi; si je tombe vengez moi.

Henri de la Rochejaqueleine

FOLLOW when I take the lead;
Pass me, when I fail in speed;
But I pray you, one and all,
Jump not on me when I fall

In 1883 an illustrated book of sonnets was published. This was one of them:

Addressed to a Lady
who told me, that being ignorant of botany, I could not enjoy my garden.

I love my garden, though I dare confess,
*   While wandering free its fragrant flowers among,*
*   To me is pedantry that unknown tongue*
*   With which vain science mocks their loveliness.*
Perfume and flower I love, nor love I less
*   The fluttering insect, whose light wings are hung*
*   With gold and purple, and the sweet lay sung*
*   By thousand birds who their protector bless.*
Think thou, who wrong'st me thus, how fondly I
*   Gaze on thy features, though unskill'd to speak,*
*   In learned phrase, of their anatomy;*
I love the blush that mantles o'er thy cheek.
*   I love the smile of welcome in thine eye,*
*   Nor how, nor whence, they come care I to seek.*

Drawing or Designing
A True Story

The mistake which the subject of this epigram occurred was in consequence of Sir R. Brooke having desired his architect to obtain the drawing of a badger, the family crest.

Mine host whose company was not first rate
A badger kept for customers to bait.
Ere carved in oak to dect a newell'd stair
To sketch the badger went an artist there.
Quoth he politely 'I would fain inspect
And draw your badger, if you don't object.'
Mine host perplexed made answer when he saw him,
'Sir, where's your dog, if you be come to draw him?'

Arley in Idleness.

To Miss Maude Mainwaring
who had made a bet with the Author whether the Arley or the Peover oak would be first in leaf.

Pleased to receive when I awoke
A sample of your early oak,
More pleased to think the self same day
The post would mine to you convey;
Let neither claim a triumph won,
The race has neck and neck been run.
How Arley and how Peover dwell
In harmony these emblems tell,
Long may each house like either tree
Maintain a friendly rivalry.

Arley in Idleness.

NOTE: Tall and slim, Maud Mainwaring always had a passion for nature and a wonderful way with animals. She was the third daughter of the 2nd Baronet and died unmarried in 1930 at her home, Park Cottage, Sandiway. Sadly in later life she too suffered from blindness. She was Lady Patroness to Capt. Park-Yates in 1880 and was largely responsible for raising the fund from the ladies of the Cheshire Hunt to pay for the stained glass window in his memory at Sandiway Church.

Blindness

No sunbeam smiles upon my weary way,
*   'Tis as though light had ne'er created been,*
*   As though this world and all that is therein,*
*   Still without form and void, in darkness lay.*

One from my side has pass'd unseen away,
*   Snatched from this world of darkness and of sin;*
*   My prayer, my hope that I may likewise win*
*   And share with her the light of endless day.*

As on my way a friendly arm I need
*   To guide my steps, lest they some peril meet,*
*   Some snare encounter as I onward speed,*

My soul a guide in its Redeemer hath;
*   Lord! be Thy word a lantern to my feet,*
*   A light to light me on my heavenward path.*

Arley in Idleness, 1879 and Twenty-Two Sonnets, 1883.

NOTE: REEW altered the first line to:

No rising sunbeam cheers me with its ray,

But blind and lonely though he was he never lost his
irrepressible sense of humour, as may be seen from the
date of this:

Hunting Made Easy
On Sir Watkin Wynn's New Railway Carriage for Hunting.

*In days long ago men their hunters bestrode
And at dawn with the pack to the covert-side rode,
Their morning fox killed ere the clock had struck ten,
Stout foxes were they – may we find such again!
After that when they lay somewhat later in bed
Down the road in mud boots at a canter they sped.
But why to old modes of conveyance hark back,
When this Jubilee year starts a new covert hack:
One that puffs, and although as a whistler well known
In whose movement no want of condition is shown,
Though he feeds not on beans, nor on oats, nor on hay
Many go-downs of water he needs on the way.
One thousand pounds only the price of this steed,
Will not hunting henceforth be made easy indeed?
Now comforts unknown to the past Sportsman abound
For the Master, the Huntsman, the Horse and the Hound.
Now the cook will at once a hot breakfast provide
And your tea be poured out while to covert you glide.
Since no horn need the Huntsman apply to his lips,
He may vary the ride by a smoke with his Whips.
Should anyone study still further his ease
He a hunter may make of this hack if he please;
Should he wish to preserve the new scarlet unstained,
He may sit through the day to his newspaper chained;
Or for further excitement may partners enlist
And prolong the day's sport by a rubber of whist.
Leading men to first class will of course be preferred,
The slow ones may follow behind in a third.*

*A piano, no doubt, in the ladies' saloon,
Will resound with sweet song to a tally-ho tune,
To some their armchair will a side-saddle seem,
A stirrup their footstool, a gallop their dream.
Of this room, who can paint the adornment inside!
Rich borders of lace upon buffalo hide!
Photographed panels, gilt mirrors outspread,
Which the features reflect of fair riders in red.
Still perils there are as we all must allow,
Such as ne'er in the chase were encountered till now.
In the field 'off the line' simply ends in a check –
By 'off the line' here is meant breaking your neck!
Should a man be thrown out, little hope there is then
That howe'er he may strive he will catch 'em again;
Sad indeed should this hunt in a burst be 'blown up',
Though all in at the death, none to hallo who-whoop.*

1887.   REEW, aged 84.

NOTE: Published in *LYRA VENATICA - A Collection
of Hunting Songs*, compiled by John Sherard Reeve, 1906.
With one or two exceptions the contents of this book had
not previously been published and the volume, from
which these lines were copied by the editor at Clonsilla
near Dublin, was a Christmas gift in 1915 to Miss Olivia
Dewhurst (sis.308) from Lord Cholmondeley (222).

Part Two

A Cheshire Miscellany of Sporting verse
selected and annotated by Gordon Fergusson

The Cheshire Hunt
A Song composed by **Charles Wicksted (112)** of Betley Hall, Staffordshire.

1.
COME awake from your slumbers, jump out of your bed,
Drink your tea, mount your hack, and away to Will Head;
For who'd be behind-hand, or like to be late,
When Sir Harry's fleet pack at the cover side wait.
CHORUS
    For who'd be behind-hand, or like to be late,
    When Sir Harry's fleet pack at the coverside wait?

2.
Those sons of old Bedford so prized by George Heron,
So quick at a cast, and so ready to turn;
If with these fast hounds, you'd play a good part,
Both the rider and horse must be quick at a start.
CHORUS

3.
Let the feats of old Bluecap and Wanton shine forth,
Without rival in speed, and unequalled in worth;
Alas (O rare Bluecap) would not fate let thee tarry,
Rever'd to a fault, by the Laird John Smith-Barry.
CHORUS

4.
Hark! hark! they have found him, who would not rejoice,
At the soul stirring sound of old Victor's loud voice;
He's away, I declare, don't you hear there's a halloo,
And now we will see how the gentlemen follow.
CHORUS

5.
But now let me ask who's that thrusting along,
So anxious the first to get out of the throng?
Who's cramming his mare up that steep rotten bank,
With the rein on her neck, and both spurs on her flank?
CHORUS.

6.
There's scarcely a young one, and ne'er an old stager,
For the first twenty minutes can live with the Major;
Tho', supposing this run for a full hour should last,
I hope he'll not find he has started too fast.
CHORUS

7.
Who, glued to his saddle, with his horse seems to fly?
'Tis a Lancashire Lord, who is worth a Jew's eye;
In this run I will wager, he'll keep a front seat,
For unless his horse stops, he will never be beat.
CHORUS

8.
With a seat that's so graceful, and hand that's so light,
Now racing beside him comes Leicestershire White;
Not yet gone to Melton, he this day for his pleasure,
Condescends to be rural, and hunts with the Cheshire.
CHORUS

9.
But who's charging that rasper? – do tell me I beg,
With both hands to his bridle, and swinging his leg
On that very long mare, whose sides are so flat,
With the head of a buffalo, and a tail like a rat?
CHORUS

10.
'Tis the gallant Sir Richard, a rum one to follow,
Who dearly loves lifting the hounds to a halloo;
A straight forward man, who no jealousy knows,
Who forgets all his pains, when a hunting he goes.
CHORUS.

11.

And next snug and quiet, without noise or bother,
On Sheffielder comes the brave Colonel his brother;
He keeps steadily onward, no obstacle fears,
Like those true British heroes, the bold Grenadiers.
    CHORUS.

12.

But who to the field is now making his bow?
'Tis the Squire of Dorfold, on game Harry Gow,
That preserver of foxes, that friend to the sport,
Tho' he proves no preserver of claret and port.
    CHORUS.

13.

And who's that, may I ask, who in purple is clad,
Riding wide of the pack, and tight holding his pad?
'Tis a bruising top sawyer, and if there's a run,
The Rector of Davenham will see all the fun.
    CHORUS.

14.

Now hustling and bustling, and rolling about,
And pushing his way in the midst of the route –
Little Ireland comes, for a front place he strives,
Through rough, and through smooth he his Tilbury drives.
    CHORUS.

15.

Pray get out of the way, at the fence why so tarry?
Don't you see down upon us is coming Sir Harry?
And if you don't mind, you'll perhaps rue the day,
When like Wellington, you were upset by a Grey.
    CHORUS.

16.

This Grey he can't hold, tho' his hand is not weak,
And his bit you may see has a very long cheek;
But if the first flight he can keep in his eye,
To be thereabout he will gallantly try.
    CHORUS.

17.

Now leaving the crowd, our attention we fix
On two knowing sportsmen who're riding with sticks;
The first, so renown'd on the turf, is Squire France,
Who on his young Milo will lead them a dance.
    CHORUS.

18.

The next is John Glegg, and I really don't brag,
When I say no one better can ride a good nag:
A good nag, when he has one, I mean bye and bye,
Do you know of good one? – he's wanting to buy.
    CHORUS.

19.

Now larking along with the foremost you see,
Quite determined to go, Charley Ford on The Pea;
This moment ecstatic, this joy of the chase
His regret for old Paddy can scarcely efface.
    CHORUS

20.

For Walmseley on Paddy has just passed by,
And on him poor Charley did cast a sheep's eye;
But ne'er mind, no pleasure's without its alloy,
And some day you'll again have a good one my boy.
    CHORUS

21.

Who's that – I can't see; – by his figure I know tho',
It can be no other than Hammond on Otho;
If practice makes perfect, he's nothing to fear,
For his nag has been practising many a year.

    CHORUS

22.

Going straight to the hounds, never known to cast wider,
Now comes little Rowley the steeple-chase rider;
Harry Brooke, his antagonist, quiet and steady,
And Stanley who always for business is ready.
    CHORUS.

23.

With old Oulton-Lowe let due honour keep pace,
And long life to Sir Philip, the pride of the chase;
Though its far-fam'd cover be on the decline,
We'll still drink his health in a bumper of wine.
    CHORUS

24.

Then there's Squire Harper, whom some may call slow,
But I've seen him ride when he chooses to go;
Little Jemmy comes next, and of danger shews sense,
For from off his Surveyor he's surveying the fence.
    CHORUS

25.

But the pride of all Cheshire, the bold Delamere,
Alas! I can't shew you, for he's not here;
His collar bone's broken, don't be in a fright,
His spirit's not broken, he'll soon be "all right."
    CHORUS.

26.

And now, having told you the whole of the field,
All Cheshire-men true, to no others they'll yield;
And whilst the sparkling decanters are going their rounds.
Let us drink to Sir Harry and the old Cheshire hounds.
        For who'd be behind-hand, or like to be late,
        When Sir Harry's fleet pack at the coverside wait?

NOTES:

THIS song was composed sometime before 1830, *The Woore Hunt* being written that year by Rowland Egerton Warburton by way of reply. It was subsequently published in 1837 by John Twemlow of Hatherton and when he re-published it in 1846, he dedicated it to the then Manager of the Cheshire Hounds, Mr James Hugh Smith-Barry. Three lithographs were included in the slim quarto volume: a portrait of Bluecap at Marbury, a sketch of Bluecap's monument together with his epitaph and an engraving of Sartorius's painting of the race at Newmarket.

A copy was presented to the Tarporley Hunt Club in 1981 by Elizabeth, wife of Desmond, 10th Viscount Ashbrook, together with a copy of the Sixth Edition of her great grandfather's *Hunting Songs*, in recognition of her husband's membership from 1945 to 1980.

John Twemlow added verses 3 and 23 and composed in Smith-Barry's honour the following couplets:

> SOME *never pull up till they meet with a fall,*
> *Or strive to prevent, till too late to recall;*
> *But rashly advance, without caution or fear,*
> *When at length for their valour they pay very dear.*
>> *But who can be behind-hand, or will be the last,*
>> *After Barry's fleet pack that's so quick at a cast?*

> *Here's health to the Maiden who rides like a man,*
> *Who loves to show sport, and make play when he can;*
> *Who lifts his hounds onward, through covert and field,*
> *Till reynard, dead beat, to his whoo-hoop must yield.*
>> *For who can be behind-hand, or will be last,*
>> *After Barry's fleet pack that's so quick at a cast?*

> *If you look 'fore you leap, you'll ne'er meet with a check,*
> *If you leap 'fore you look, you'll hazard your neck;*
> *But this is cool logic to a fox-hunting youth,*
> *Let spillers and breakdowns then teach him the truth.*
>> *But who can be behind-hand, or will be the last*
>> *After Barry's fleet pack that's so quick at a cast?*

References in the foregoing verses to Members of the Tarporley Hunt Club will be found in the index. Others include: Verse 7. Lord Molyneux, son of the 2nd Earl of Sefton of Croxteth Park, whose family for many years owned an estate at Church Minshull. Verse 14. Ireland Blackburne was mounted by a London horsedealer called Tilbury. Verse 22. Edward John Stanley, later 2nd Lord Stanley of Alderley, according to Hatherton, rather than his younger brother William, who was elected to Tarporley. 'Little Jemmy' in Verse 24 is James Tomkinson of Davenham Cottage, the eldest son of the Rev. James of Dorfold and an officer in the Blues, who died young.

Lord Delamere's fractured clavicle, mentioned in Verse 25, was as a result of a fall when riding in the company of Lord Wilton along a street in the West end of London. For twenty years of his life he had been a star in Leicestershire. Whether or not it was intentional, Wicksted's choice of adjective was highly appropriate. It was Delamere's great great grandmother, Mary Holford, from whom this branch of the Cholmondeley family derived the Vale Royal Estate, granted to Sir Thomas Holcroft by Henry VIII on the Dissolution, and purchased by her two generations later. As a widow Dame Mary Cholmondeley, residing at Holford Hall, was called by James I 'the bold Lady of Cheshire'.

WHEN he lived at Stocken Hall, Rutland, **Field Marshal Thomas Grosvenor**'s favourite horse was called Black Butcher and he and his old groom, Tom Perkins, buried him in a riding in Mawkery Wood nearby, erecting a monument for which his owner composed the following lines:

> WHENE'ER *in Mawkery Wood you hear the sound*
> *Of Lowther's voice encouraging the hound,*
> *Pass ye not heedless by this pile of stones,*
> *For underneath lie honest Butcher's bones;*
> *Black was his colour, yet his nature fair,*
> *'Tis Grosvenor pays this tribute to his worth*
> *A better Hunter ne'er stretched leather girth.*

Chorus of Liberal–minded Foxes
by **Egerton Leigh (214)**

(Met to celebrate the birthday of Geoffrey Shakerley, late Master of the Cheshire Fox-hounds.)

Chorus.
HERE'S to Shakerley's *health, and returns of this day,*
And that we may, like him, live to see it we pray.

1st Fox.
Here's his health! o'er my old wife he sounded the mort,
A regular vixen! one of the wrong sort.

2nd Fox.
Here's his health! of my firstborn his hounds made their grub;
His crimes whitenened my tag – a most dissolute cub.

3rd Fox a real lady.
Here's his health! for he chopped my fat husband in covert;
I'm blest with a younger mate but older lover.

4th Fox.
Here's his health! for as panting I lay in a drain,
Having had quantum suff in a very long run,
He would not let them dig me, on which they were fain,
Saying, 'Leave him alone. he will show some more fun.'

CHORUS
Here's Shakerley's *health! for though we may be sinners,*
He saves us from keepers, and pays for our dinners;
It is he plants our gorse so snug and so warm,
And takes care that traps and nets do us no harm;
When they lay up their cubs, he keeps our wives quiet,
Driving far from our earths all row and all riot;
And a brush *now and then we can very well spare,*
When he gives us a brush so oft during the year.
And may many returns of his birthday be spent!
May he live to a hundred! Who knows more of scent?

Ballads & Legends of Cheshire, 1867.

This is who he was

The following unsigned poem appeared in *Baily's Magazine of Sports and Pastimes* in 1872 and the headline to the verses asked: 'WHO IS HE?'. They were re-published in 1915 in an article on The Cheshire by a mystified G.T.Burrows.

THE meet was at Kelsall, the covert they drew
Ambrose Dixon's – a sure find, as everyone knew.
The run was a clipper for hounds, but the men,
Being stopped by the Gowy, ne'er saw them again;
But they stuck to their fox, being staunch hounds and true
(How gallantly over the country they flew!),

And running a ring of some seven miles round,
Ran into him near the gorse where they found.

Close by was a public, where shirking the run,
A man whose "get-up" was a figure of fun,
While calmly enjoying his twentieth gill,
Heard the hounds, then looked out, and so witnessed the kill.
He rushed to the stable, soon mounted his horse,
And valiantly galloping up to the gorse,
Seized the fox, which at once he triumphantly bore
With frantic "who-oops!" to the public-house door,

His breeches (home-made) were covered with blood;
Like a butcher just fresh from the shambles he stood.
With a huge carving knife he then broke up the fox,
In a style that was anything but orthodox.
When the Master came up, what stories he told,
Quite outrivalling Baron Munchausen the Bold.

He said that he rode to the hounds from the first
To the last of this rattling seven miles burst;
That the overflowed river he cleared at a bound,
That the bogs he skimmed over as though they were sound.
The stiffest of fences were nothing, of course,
To the sixteen-stone man on his £20 horse.

At the Beeston Hotel, while awaiting the train
(His wonderful feat telling over again),
He produced from the skirt of his rotten old pink
Some mangled remains – pooh! – how he did stink! –
And said, "These sweet things as a gift I intend,
With a couple of 'sovs.' to the huntsman to send!"
Then he took his departure. Now "Who is this man?"
All the Hunt wish to know, so tell them who can!

NOTE: The answer is to be found in Harry Rawson's manuscript hunting journal, in the possession of John Boddington (350). Hounds met at Kelsall Bar on January 13th, 1872:

A Gowy fox crossed the river with the hounds at his brush. The result was that, before a soul cd. get to them, they were out of sight – in fact the field & all the authorities were galloping about the country for upwards of an hour looking for them. The line of the chase was as follows. On getting over the river, the point seemed to be Ashton Hayes, but making a turn to the right Reynard ran by Gt.Barrow to Cotton & thence nearly to Wharton. Before reaching Wharton, however, he turned & ran back to Stamford Bridge where he was killed. The only man who saw the finish was Butcher Bill, who was in the Stamford public when the pack returned! Home in disgust. The hounds however were trotted off to Saighton. They didn't find again.

John Tomlinson's Story

(*See* Book One Chapter XIV pp212-4 for account of the Shooting at Dale Ford on All Hallow's Eve, 1873.)

EIGHT of my choral friends and I,
  Made up a tuneful nine,
To serenade Squire Corbet was
  Our innocent design.

We sung two good old English songs,
  And then we rang for beers.
We little thought our staves would bring
  Their staves about our ears.

A single glass of ale apiece
  We looked for, for our carol,
Instead of that he gave us all
  The contents of a barrel.

With one and twenty cruel shots
  My legs are riddled quite,
Nineteen went right into my left,
  The two left in my right.

"Run or I'll shoot, stop or I'll shoot,"
  The mandate changing so,
No longer puzzles me, for I
  Can neither stand nor go.

I did my best to "stop" and "run"
  The night the deed was done in,
And after I myself had stopped,
  I found my legs were running.

We thought to soon be out of range,
  Not reck'ning as we ran,
That pellets fired at Daleford Hall
  Could reach the Calf of Man.

I thought I'd bring an action once,
  But this I must abandon,
The court and jury all would say –
  I'd not a leg to stand on.

Ah, cruel is the Shropshire squire,
  Ah, cruel and severe,
Instead of bringing beer to me,
  He's brought me to my bier.

Though doctors say I'm doing well,
  My end is near; I feel
That what were once two healthy calves,
  Will soon be potted veal.

My pulse is high, my spirits low,
  Nor ease nor rest remains,
By day and night from thigh to heel,
  I'm full of shooting pains.

I make no will for reasons good,
  The reasons good are these –
I've got no legacies to leave
  Nor any leg at ease.

Hurrah for the Old Green Collars!

There were hundreds at Wrenbury Station!
Many a good man and true;
Scarlet coats by the dozen,
Grey and black and blue;
  But hurrah for the old green collars,
  Hurrah for the Cheshire Hounds.

Ah, soon that large field sifted,
Some funk, some shirk, some fall;
But Corbet his good horse lifted
O'er that gate in front of them all.
  For none can beat our Master
  When he hunts the Cheshire Hounds.

We found him in Wrenbury Mosses,
And killed him on Peckforton Hill;
Good-bye to the funkers and shirkers,
We must ride to be with them still;
  Hurrah for the old green collars,
  Hurrah for the Cheshire Hounds.

We raced him for forty minutes,
And never touched a plough;
There were many bold men at starting,
But few of them with us now;
  But most of them wear the green collar,
  All hunt with the Cheshire Hounds.

There's Tollemache boldly cramming,
And Rivers close at his side,
There's many a good man ramming,
And Beatty riding wide;
  Hurrah for the old green collars,
  Hurrah for the Cheshire Hounds.

There's Cole from the land of Erin,
Biddulph from Watkin's Hunt,
Clement Hill from the Shropshire,
All riding up to the front;
  But none can beat the green collars,
  So we'll stick with the Cheshire Hounds.

Payne may be more clever,
Shropshire may have more luck,
But give me the old grass country,
Cheshire for sport and pluck;
  Three cheers for the old green collars,
  Three cheers for the Cheshire Hounds.

I can feel my good horse pulling,
And boldly he cocks his ear,
For he sees the wide brook rushing,
And together we land all clear,
  In company with the green collars,
  Right up to the Cheshire Hounds.

Fortunately the full version has not been found. These verses have been taken from the chapter on The Cheshire from *Hunting Countries* by F.A.Stewart and refer to a wonderful forty minutes in Corbet's day *c.*1875 with a kill in Pennsylvania.

Dream of an old Meltonian
by **William Bromley-Davenport (207)**

I AM old, I am old, and my eyes are grown weaker,
  My beard is as white as the foam on the sea,
Yet pass me the bottle and fill me a beaker,
  A bright brimming toast in a bumper for me!
Back, back through long vistas of time I am wafted
  But the glow at my heart's undiminished in force.
Deep, deep in that heart has fond memory engrafted
  Those quick thirty minutes from Ranksboro' Gorse . . .

Last night in St. Stephen's so wearily sitting,
  (The Member for Boreham sustained the debate,)
Some pitying spirit that round me was flitting
  Vouchsafed a sweet vision my pains to abate.
The Mace, and the Speaker, and House disappearing,
  The leather-clad bench is a thoroughbred horse;
'Tis the whimpering cry of the fox-hound I'm hearing,
  And my 'seat' is a pigskin at Ranksboro' Gorse.

He's away! I can hear the identical holloa!
  I can feel my young thoroughbred strain down the ride,
I can hear the dull thunder of hundreds that follow
  I can see my old comrades in life by my side.
Do I dream? All around me I see the dead riding,
  And voices long silent re-echo with glee;
I can hear the far wail of the Master's vain chiding,
  As vain as the Norseman's reproof to the sea.

Vain indeed! for the bitches are racing before us –
  Not a nose to the ear – not a stern in the air;
And we know by the notes of that modified chorus
  How straight we must ride if we wish to be there!
With a crash o'er the turnpike, and onward I'm sailing,
  Released from the throes of the thundering mass,
Which dispersed right and left as I topped the high railing,
  And shape my own course o'er the billowy grass.

Select is the circle in which I am moving,
  Yet open and free the admission to all;
Still, still more select is that company proving,
  Weeded out by the funker and thinned by the fall!
Yet here all are equal – no class legislation,
  No privilege hinders, no family pride:
In the 'image of war' show the pluck of the nation;
  Ride ancient patrician! democracy, ride!

Oh! gently, my young one; the fence we are nearing
  Is leaning towards us – 'tis hairy and black,
The binders are strong, and necessitate clearing,
  Or the wide ditch beyond will find room for your back.
Well saved! we are over! now far down the pastures
  Of Ashwell the willows betoken the line
Of the dull-flowing stream of historic disasters;
  We must face, my bold young one, the dread Whissendine!

No shallow-dug pan with a hurdle to screen it,
    That cocktail imposture the steeplechase brook!
But the steep broken banks tell us plain, if we mean it,
    The less we shall like it the longer we look.
Then steady my young one, my place I've selected,
    Above the dwarf willow 'tis sound I'll be bail,
With your muscular quarters beneath you collected,
    Prepare for a rush like the 'limited mail'.

Oh! now let me know the full worth of your breeding,
    Brave son of Belzoni, be true to your sires,
Sustain old traditions – remember you're leading
    The cream of the cream in the shire of the shires!
With a quick shortened stride as the distance you measure,
    With a crack of the nostril and cock of the ear,
And a rocketing bound, and we're over, my treasure,
    Twice nine feet of water, and landed all clear!

What! four of us only? are these the survivors
    Of all that rode gaily from Ranksboro' ridge?
I hear the faint splash of a few hardy divers,
    The rest are in hopeless research of a bridge;
Vœ Victis! *the way of the world and the winners!*
    Do we ne'er ride away from a friend in distress?
Alas! we are anti-Samaritan sinners,
    And steaming past Stapleford, onward we press.

Ah! don't they mean mischief, the merciless ladies?
    What fox can escape such implacable foes?
Of the sex cruel slaughter for ever the trade is,
    Whether human or animal – YONDER HE GOES!
Never more for the woodland! his purpose has failed him,
    Though to gain the old shelter he gallantly tries;
In vain the last double, for Jezebel's nailed him;
    WHOO-HOOP! *in the open the veteran dies!*

Yes, four of us only! but is it a vision?
    Dear lost ones, how come ye with morals to mix?
Methought that ye hunted the pastures Elysian,
    And between us there rolled the unjumpable Styx!
Stay, stay but a moment! the grass fields are fading,
    And heavy obscurity palsies my brain;
Through what country, what ploughs and what sloughs am I
                                      wading?
    Alas! 'tis the member for Boreham again!

Oh glory of youth! consolation of age!
    Sublimest of ecstasies under the sun!
Though the veteran may linger too long on the stage,
    Yet he'll drink a last toast to a fox-hunting run.
And oh! young descendants of ancient top-sawyers!
    By your lives to the world their example enforce;
Whether landlord, or parsons, or statesmen or lawyers,
    Ride straight, as they rode it from Ranksboro' Gorse.

Though a rough-riding world may bespatter your breeches,
    Though sorrow may cross you or slander revile,
Though you plunge overhead in misfortune's blind ditches,
    Shun the gap of deception, the handgate of guile;
Oh, avoid them! for there, see the crowd is contending,
    Ignoble the object – ill-mannered the throng;
Shun the miry lane, falsehood, with turns never ending,
    Ride straight for truth's timber, no matter how strong.

I'll pound you safe over! sit steady and quiet;
    Along the sound headland of honesty steer;
Beware the false holloas and juvenile riot,
    Though the oxer of duty be wide, never fear!
And when the run's over of earthly existence,
    And you get safe to ground, you will feel no remorse,
If you ride it – no matter what line or what distance –
    As straight as we rode it from Ranksboro' Gorse.

First published in *Baily's Magazine* in 1876. Verse II has been omitted.

NOTE: Colonel Bromley-Davenport's other best known work is *Lowesby Hall*, his parody of Tennyson's*Locksley Hall*.

Comrades, leave me here a little, while as yet 'tis early morn:
Leave me here, and when you want me, sound upon the bugle horn.

was what Tennyson wrote.

Gilmour, leave me here a little, and when John of Gaunt is drawn,
If you find the raw material, let Jack Morgan blow his horn.

was the opening couplet of Lowesby Hall. Or again:

Many a day from yonder spinney in November moist and chill
Have I watched the wily animal sneak slowly up the hill.

Many a night I've watched the vapours of my last remaining weed,
When my spurs have ceased to animate my apathetic steed.
WM.B.D.

In the Spring a fuller crimsom comes upon the robin's breast; In
the Spring the wanton lapwing gets himself another crest;

In the Spring a livelier iris changes on the burnish'd dove;
In the Spring a young man's fancy lightly turns to thoughts of love.
T.

Even in his day WM.B.D. had good cause to write the following prophesy:

For I looked into its pages, and I read the book of fate,
And saw fox-hunting abolished by an order of the State;

Saw the heavens filled with guano, and the clouds at men's command
Raining down unsavoury liquids for the benefit of land;

Saw the airy navies earthwards bear the planetary swell,
And the long projected railroad from Halifax to Hell;

Saw the landlords yield their acres after centuries of wrongs,
Cotton lords turn country gentlemen in patriotic throngs;

Queen, religion, State abandoned, and the flags of party furled
In the Government of Cobden, and the dotage of the world.

Lines on High Leigh
by The Rev. A. J. Richardson

'TIS an odd state of things that a stranger would see,
If he came on a visit perchance to High Leigh;
To his mind it would cause great confusion and bother,
To find things so mix'd up the one with the other;
Two establishments separate, two Halls, and two Squires,
Two parsons, two chapels, two bells and two choirs!
Whilst the magnates themselves couldn't fairly agree
As to spelling correctly the name of 'High Leigh';
One stoutly insisting on "i" with the "e",
The other on nothing between "e" and "g";
On map and on signpost you'd meet with the "i",
P.O.O.'s were without it and folks wondered why;
Then the agent found out, when he took the big ledger down,
The estates all mix'd up with the farms of Lord Egerton;

And directions for letters and parcels were wrapp'd in
A regular muddle between Colonel and Captain;
For if to "the Hall" they should chance be address'd,
It was doubtful if meant for the "East" or the "West";
But for rights of precedence 'twas doubtful which had 'em,
For neither could trace much further than Adam!
So what you're about, be particular, please,
For Cheshire is full of cats, cheeses and Leighs,
Leghs' of Lyme, Leghs' of Adlington, everything "Legh",
From the innermost bounds to the banks of the Dee;
And from dropping a letter what comes there's no telling,
So you'd best mind your "i", and look after your spelling.

High Leigh, 1879.

WARREN DE TABLEY, the third Baron (1835-1895), was a celebrated Cheshire poet and though not a Member of the Tarporley Hunt Club his home was naturally much frequented by many of its members as guests from time to time in his father's day, especially when his stepmother, the widow of **James Smith-Barry** (147), held court at Tabley. She was an attractive hostess, witty and shrewd with a great personal beauty and lovely smile, in her old age essentially *grande dame*. Formerly Miss Elizabeth Jacson of Newton Bank, Chester, she died aged 93.

This shy and reclusive man was also an eminent botanist and an acknowledged authority on brambles, his *Flora of Cheshire* being published posthumously by his sister, who planted the sprig of blackberry on his grave at Lower Peover.

The book of his collected works runs to 485 pages, but none of his poems are really suitable for this anthology. The nearest is one of four melancholy pages, *The Sale at the Farm*, of which these are the <u>opening</u> lines:

I TRUST the worst is over with this sale.
The old place had a strange look in the crowd:
The jostling and the staring and the creak
Of shuffled feet, the public laugh sent round,
The hammer's clink, the flippant auctioneer,
Number on number lengthening out the day:
Familiar things dishonoured, like old friends

Set up on high to scorning fools: and then
The ache of loss, and some dull sense that they
Would sell me last by parcels, till the dusk
Drew, in December sleet, and all were gone:
And this old wreck bowed at my drooping fire
In gathered shade unfriended and alone.
Bare walls and fixtures here: thus ends the day.

A Day's Ride A Life's Romance
by G. J. Whyte-Melville

WHEN the early dawn is stealing
O'er the moorland edge revealing
All the tender tints of morning ere she flushes into day,
Then beneath her window, shaking
Bit and bridle, while she's waking,
Stands a bonny steed comparisoned to bear my love away;
By hill and holt to follow,
Hound and horn, and huntsman's holloa,
Follow! follow! where they lure us; follow, follow as we may!

When the chase is onward speeding,
With its boldest spirits leading,
When the red is on the rowel, and the foam is on the rein,
Far in front her form is fleeting,
And her gentle heart is beating,
With the rapture of the revel, as it sweeps across the plain;
Then I press by dint of riding
Where my beacon star is guiding,
And the laggard spurring madly hurries after us in vain.

O'er the open still careering
Fence and furrow freely clearing,
Like the winds of heaven leaving little trace of where we pass;
With merry music ringing,
Father Time is surely flinging
Golden sand about the moments as she shakes them from the glass:
Horn and hound are chiming gladly,
Horse and man are vying madly
In the glory of the gallop. Forty minutes on the grass !

Till by yonder group dismounted,
Group that's quickly told and counted,
Hark, the pack are baying fiercely round their quarry lying dead;
So she gathers up her tresses,
And with loving hand caresses
Neck and shoulder of the bonny steed, and homeward turns her head.
But from eyes that shine so brightly
Such a spectacle unsightly
Must be hidden, as we hide each thing of sorrow and of dread.

Every sweet must have its bitter,
And the time has come to quit her,
Oh ! the night is falling darker for the happy day that's done;
Now I wish I were the bridle,
In the fingers of my idol,
Now I wish I were the bonny steed that bore her through the run;
For I fain would still be nearest
To my loveliest and dearest,
And I fain would be the truest slave that ever worshipped one!

NOTE: When Whyte-Melville wrote this, he is said to have been inspired by the Empress of Austria's relationship with Captain W.G. (Bay) Middleton, formerly of the XII Royal Lancers.

Cheshire Chivalry

THESE verses, under the same title as R.E.E.W.'s Hunting Song of 1837, appeared in *The Chester Chronicle* in March, 1882, prior to the departure from Combermere Abbey of the Empress Elisabeth of Austria. There was one verse which was omitted, being considered 'not fair nor true of the original'.

A MASTER of hounds young man,
Master or "order" young man;
A demon, a thruster,
When hounds go a "buster,"
    A stern and determined young man.
                [R.Corbet]

A master of hounds young man,
A placid and calm young man,
There's nothing that ruffles
The great "Mr Puffles"
    But "the hounds over-riding young man."
                [E.W.Park Yates]

A "Lord of the Mere" young man,
An Imperial intriguer young man;
At "Tarporley" glorious,
Always uproarious,
    "Combermere Abbey" young man.
                [Lord Combermere]

A great "Viscount" young man
A jolly and stout young man;
A galloping, following,
Bucketing, holloa'ing,
    Bright green-collar'd young man.
                [Lord Cole]

*   *   *   *   *   *   *   *

A "real" M.P. young man,
Constitutional tory young man;
Never yet has been beat
For a parliament seat
    A truly right-minded young man.
                [Piers Egerton Warburton]

Political "whip" young man,
Wrong headed high minded young man;
In Gladstone believing,
Till time undeceive him,
    A "stick to the party" young man.
                [Lord Richard Grosvenor]

Another "whip" sort of young man,
A "whipper-in" sort of young man;
Breeches and bootikins,
Put on his hunting things,
    A very well-dressed young man.
                [James Tomkinson]

A practical farming young man,
A "Marley Moss" young man;
"Seeds, wheat and clover,
You must not ride over,"
    Cries the Marbury Squire young man.
                [Cudworth Poole]

A "Rookery Baron" young man,
A clever young-headed young man;
As a matter of fact,
He is brimful of tact,
    A remarkably shrewd young man.
                [Baron Wm. von Schröder]

Hospitable "Frank" young man,
"Sticks" never blank young man;
If any, 'tis few
That can handle a cue
    Like the "Worleston pet" young man.
                [Frank Behrens]

A "Cavendish" nice young man,
A "nailer" to hounds young man;
Soubriquet "Fatty",
Always so natty,
    10th Hussars young man.
        [Captain the Hon.Charles Cavendish,
        later Lord Chesham, son-in-law of
        the Duke of Westminster. He and Lady
        Beatrice hunted from Tattenhall Hall.]

One other hunting young,
As hard as a "Rock" young man;
Horsery, foolery,
Larkery, schoolery,
    Dealery "Savage" young man.
                [Lord Rocksavage]

A white-headed "Paget" young man,
A "premature Fossil" young man;
Fox-hunting! Anything!
Pheasants – High rocketting,
    The dream of this old young man.
                [Lord Alexander Paget]

The Season, 1883-1884

A Saturday with Sir Watkin W. Wynn's Hounds
AT WHITCHURCH STATION

YOU *are welcome to boast of the Pytchley and Quorn,*
  All praise to the Cheshire redound,
But long life to Sir Watkin, the strains of whose horn
  Bring a welcome where e'er they resound.
Let the churl and the grumbler for once cast aside
  All sorrow and care, and be gay,
While each bosom is swelling with true British pride,
  For we hunt with Sir Watkin to-day.
      Then haste to the meet, 'tis a pleasure to greet,
      Such a brilliant and sparkling array.

Miss Wynn, [a] on the back of a handsome brown mare,
  Looks cheerful and bright as the morn;
Lady Paget's [b] fine grey, well carries his fare
  In the van, when away they have gone.
From Ireland, where Parnell the sport has destroyed,
  Lady Waterford, [c] here, finds her way;
Mrs Bunbury, too, Misses Hesketh and Lloyd,
  All hunt with Sir Watkin to-day.
      Then haste, &c.

Colonel Lloyd,[d] oh so silent, goes pounding away
  When the hounds are running their best,
Rivers Bulkeley[e] goes cramming, and brooks *no delay*
  While Godsall[f] brims over with jest.
Lord Combermere,[g] too, on a neat hog-maned mare,
  Now rides like a demon, they say,
And Sandford, whose coverts are never known bare,
  And hunt with Sir Watkin to-day.
      Then haste, &c.

There's Paley and Bunbury, both eager to go,
  And Rasbotham,[h] still as a mouse;
The Marquis of Waterford,[c] I'll have you all know,
  Moves his hunter as well as 'The House.'
There's Bibby[i] and Phillips, from Shrewsbury side,
  Clement Hill, too, who never says nay
To a rasper, that happens to come in his stride,
  And all hunt with Sir Watkin to-day.
      Then haste, &c.

John Jones, from Moss Fields, and also his wife,
  And Ethelston, owning Peel's Gorse;
There's Sandbach,[j] for sport just as keen as a knife,
  And Poole[k] on a good looking horse.
Lord Hopetoun[l] and sisters go well to the fore,
  Whilst Parker prefers the highway.
I see Whitmore and wife, Parsons, Darby, and Gore,[m]
  And all hunt with Sir Watkin to-day.
      Then haste, &c.

Misses Bibby and Lonsdale, Mrs Drake and the Squire,
  And Brandreth forsaking his flock;
May Sir Watkin's young heir[a] of hunting ne'er tire,
  A true chip of the finest old block.
Miss Ethelston, too, I must not omit,
  A fondness for sport doth betray;
Captains Beatty[n] and Fife are both looking fit,
  And hunt with Sir Watkin to-day.
      Then haste, &c.

Heywood-Lonsdale[o] preferring a seat on a horse,
  To a seat in 'The House', by the bye,
And Kenyon,[p] from Macefen, renowned for its gorse,
  And Royds from the Cottage close by.
Rocksavage[q] drives up at a deuce of a pace,
  Having lost little time on the way,
Sir Edward Hanmer[r] turns up, with bright smiling face,
  To hunt with Sir Watkin to-day.
      Then haste, &c.

Richard Biddulph and daughters, and Thompson, and Cotes,
  And a stranger or two on smart 'tits',
There's Blew[s] for The Field, engaged taking notes,
  And Walley renowned for his bits.
I see Williams from Edgeley and Cotton from Ash,
  And Dickson who comes a long way,
Messieurs Corbet and Son,[t] drive up with a dash,
  To hunt with Sir Watkin to-day.
      Then haste, &c.

Baron Schröder[u] is there, 'got up' with great care,
  Captain Lloyd looking natty and trim,
I see Harrison there, on his clever brown mare,
  And Vernon,[v] Tom Johnson and Gwynn.
There's pleasant Jack Lloyd[w] leaves his patient behind,
  May heaven preserve them I pray,
And Swann far too leggy for birds of that kind,
  All hunt with Sir Watkin to-day.
      Then haste, &c.

Archie Peel,[x] on a long tail, that gallops, you bet,
  And Davies on one fresh and raw,
There's Brocklehurst[y] smiling, with teeth firmly set,
  And two Etches who follow the law.
Captains Mitford and Spicer are present, on lease,
  And Swetenham sings on his way,
'Brief life is my portion,' away then with grief,
  For we hunt with Sir Watkin to-day.
      Then haste, &c.

Charles Somerset, known by the soubriquet 'Char',
And Tollemache,[z] by friends known as 'Tolly',
Price Angus and Sparrow, who comes from afar,
Don't deem that to hunt is a folly,
Barrow Jones, looking pale, and Radcliffes galore,
And Mousley who takes a bye day,
I see Gresty who charges two guineas or more
For a mount with Sir Watkin to-day.
    Then haste, &c.

Lord Paget[b] who boasts an extremely nice boot,
And Bateman who ne'er makes a noise,
Tinley Barton who wears a peculiar suit,
And Hassall, the keenest of boys.
From Wem Sir Charles Frederick, and tall Captain Harry,
With his daughter who rides a nice bay;
Owen Williams, and Menzies, at home do not tarry,
But hunt with Sir Watkin to-day.
    Then haste, &c.

Captain Cowen[aa] drawn here, as light draws a moth,
And Watson for timber goes 'nap',
I see Bridgeman and Puleston,[bb] both don the black cloth,
Whilst Burton prefers the old cap.
Miss Lovett, come down, by the Cambrian train,
And Whitfield, who farms Sandford way,
Brocklebank on a bay, of Zoedone strain,
All hunt with Sir Watkin to-day.
    Then haste, &c.

Barbour,[cc] and Brassey, and Ormerod are there,
And a Laird, too, of highest degree,
Roscoe, from Broughall, on a dappled-grey mare,
Lady Rock,[q] who goes straight as a bee.
Albert Hornby[dd] ne'er bowled (of that I'll go bail),
For a nag who can gallop and stay,
And Percy 'gangs forrard', like a yacht with wet sail,
All hunt with Sir Watkin to-day.
    Then haste, &c.

Two Howards, from Broughton, and Owen, from Wales,
Gordon-Haughton's from Staffordshire side,
Tayleur has come over, from Drayton-in-Hales,
And Barnes, the V.S., has a ride.
Mainwaring, of Oteley, a would-be M.P,
But 'On, Stanley, on,' barred the way;
Mostyn, Eyton, and others newcomers to me,
All hunt with Sir Watkin to-day.
    Then haste, &c.

That must be Lord Cole,[ee] that I heard him I swear,
Murmur gently, 'Ah! how do ye do;'
Dumville Lees has left off the pursuit of the hare,
And Ward, who stands just six feet two.
Chambres, Starkey,[ff] Stott-Milne, and Mrs H. Lees,
Miss Howard, who each ride a grey,

Doctor Jordison's out, on the best of his 'gees',
And all hunt with Sir Watkin to-day.
    Then haste, &c.

But whom have we here, to the meet coming down,
That 'seat' seems familiar to me;
And so does the hat, the tops of nut brown,
Why bless me, it surely can't be!
It is though, by Jove! for, to life come again,
And as welcome as flowers in May,
The form that I gaze on, belongs to Charles Payne,[gg]
Who cannot keep out of the fray,
    Then haste, &c.

But of those out 'on wheels', I really can't pass.
A lady well-known far and wide,
Who always selects some nice looking lass
To take the small seat by her side.
Mrs Hill I refer to, you may try, but in vain,
To find me a man out to-day
With a knowledge so great of each dirty bye lane,
The 'short cuts', and each bridle way.
    Then haste, &c.

To complete the gay throng, there is yet one more name,
The last, but not least, in my song,
A name well engraved in the annals of fame,
Whose praise is on every tongue;
Sir Watkin I mean, and I know I'm not wrong,
When I say that we all of us pray,
Rejoicing in health, may we see him ere long,
Resume, once again, his old sway.
    Then haste, &c.

All things have an end, and so has my song,
And if it amusement doth yield,
Then I am well paid, but if it's too long,
Lay blame on the size of the 'field'.
But Goodall[gg] and hounds are now ready to start,
So throw your cigar end away,
And button your coat, and thank from your heart,
That you hunt with Sir Watkin to-day.
    Then haste to the meet, 'tis a pleasure to greet
    Such a brilliant and sparkling array.

ASH WOOD
(alias JAMES LEYMOTT ETCHES, a Whitchurch solicitor.)

NOTES:

a. Louise Alexandra married her cousin and heir to her father, the 6th Baronet, the following August. She died in 1911.

b. Hester, 2nd daughter of Lord Combermere (157), married to Lord Alexander Paget (228). Their son, born 1885, succeeded as 6th Marquess of Anglesey.

c. The 5th Marquess of Waterford became Master of the Buckhounds, 1885/85. He suffered a severe sprain in his back from a hunting accident, in consequence of which he was allowed to remain seated when addressing the House of Lords and which caused him eventually to commit suicide. Lady Waterford, his second wife, Blanche, was the Duke of Beaufort's daughter. Their hunting box was at Malpas.

d. Colonel, later Lieut.-Gen., Sir Francis Lloyd of Aston, Salop.

e. Major Charles Rivers Bulkeley of Oak Cottage, Whitchurch.

f. Philip Thomas Godsal of Iscoyd Park.

g. The 2nd Viscount Combermere, aged 63.

h. Lived at Ebnal Grange, Malpas. His nephew, Fulke Walwyn, spent a lot of time with him there and hunted with the Wynnstay.

i. Frank Bibby of Hardwicke Grange and Sansaw, Salop. M.F.H.(N.Shropshire, 1898-1909.) A first cousin once removed of Sir Harold Bibby (324).

j. Samuel Sandbach of Hafodunos, Denbighshire.

k. Cudworth Poole (205) of Marbury Hall, Whitchurch.

l. The 7th Earl of Hopetoun, later 1st Marquess of Linlithgow, then aged 22 and living at Higginsfield, Cholmondeley and a lifelong friend of Lord Rocksavage.

m. The Hon. George Ormsby-Gore, later 3rd Baron Harlech, who for many years lived at The Lodge, Malpas.

n. Captain David Beatty, late IV Hussars, who leased Howbeck Lodge, Nantwich from Lord Shrewsbury, later of Cherry Hill, Malpas and at one time Gardenhurst, Tarporley. Father of Admiral of the Fleet Earl Beatty, his second son.

o. Arthur Pemberton Heywood-Lonsdale of Cloverley, Whitchurch, who bought the Shavington Estate in 1885.

p. The Hon. Edward Kenyon of Maesfen, Salop., then over 70, the younger son of the 2nd Baron and great uncle of the 5th Baron.

q. Lord Rocksavage (222) who in 1879 had married Winifred Ida, the younger daughter of Col. Sir Robert Kingscote, GCVO, KCB

r. Sir Edward Hanmer, Bt. of Bettisfield Park, the 4th Baronet, then over 70.

s. W.C.A.Blew, a prolific writer on hunting and racing, quoted in this volume.

t. H.R.Corbet (189), the then Manager of the South Cheshire Hounds, and his son, Regie, Jnr.(220).

u. Baron Wm.von Schröder (224) of The Rookery, Nantwich. (224).

v Thomas Minshull Vernon of Tushingham Hall.

w. Dr Jack Lloyd of Chirk.

x. Archie Peel, whose uncle was Sir Robert Peel, the 2nd Bart. and Prime Minister. He married the daughter of General Sir Roger Palmer of Cefn Park, which was inherited by their daughter, who was the mother of Lieut.-Col.'Roddy' Fenwick-Palmer, whose step-niece, Cynthia, married Chubb Paterson (322). He lived at The Gerwyn, near Marchwiel, and would think nothing of galloping a hack over to Keele Park to ride work there.

y. Arthur Brocklehurst of Nantwich used to ride a lot of winners at Tarporley and the other local National Hunt meetings.

z. Henry Tollemache (204). Unlikely to have been his father, who was then aged 76.

aa. Most probably Captain Fred Cowan, father of Admiral of the Fleet Sir Walter Cowan, Baronet of the Baltic, and who as a young officer in the 23rd R.W.F had whipped in to the Calpe Hounds at Gibraltar. In his day Sir Watkin himself had had a day with the garrison fox-hounds when his yacht passed through the Strait.

bb. The Rev. Gresley Puleston, (pronounced 'Pilston') later 4th and last Bart., Rector of Worthenbury and author of *The Wynnstay Country*. Sir Richard, the 2nd baronet, of Emral Hall, who established a pack in 1786 and well into the next century hunted much of what was to become the Wynnstay Country.

cc. George Barbour, whose father bought Bolesworth in 1857 and father of Robert Barbour (262).

dd. A.N.Hornby of Parkfield House, Nantwich, international cricketer and Captain of Lancashire.

ee. Lord Cole (218).

ff. Probably Walter Starkey of Wrenbury Hall, after whom Starkey's Gorse is named.

gg. Charles Payne, former Huntsman to Sir Watkin, recently retired after eighteen seasons. His son was Huntsman to the Calpe Hounds, 1874-82.

hh. Frank Goodall, aged 30, had just had eight seasons with the Meath. He was destined to be the last Royal Huntsman of the Queen's Buckhounds (founded *a*.1216, disbanded 1901).

A Lay Of Bangor-On-Dee Steeplechases – 1887

I HATE your Flat racing, give me steeplechasing,
*   And Bangor's the scene of the day.*
Where the meadows so sound are the very best ground
*   For the sport we're enjoying to-day.*
The crowds that are seen are far greater I ween
*   Than ever were seen here before;*
And the card it is longer, the entries are stronger,
*   The starters are better and more;*
The Sweepstakes attractive, the managers active,
*   The bright charming morn are the cause.*
We'll enjoy the great treat, our luncheon we'll eat,
*   It tastes best of all out of doors.*
They are come from Welsh Wales, with its mountains and vales,
*   They are come from the country around;*
In thousands the 'Masses' enjoy with 'the Classes'
*   The fun that is here to be found.*
Wynnstay has a party, its popular Bart., he
*   Is known as a Patron of sport,*
And Combermere's Lord, by Cheshire adored,
*   His experience as Steward has brought.*
There is Sal from the mere he, looks happy and cheery,
*   And the Squire from Bryn-y-Pys Hall,*
And Archie from Gerwyn, and Best from the Berwyn,
*   With Welshers I cannot recall.*
Next the Kaffir I see, and Whitmore from King's Lee,
*   Owen John from the famed Bara Chaws;*
There's Bobby from Cefn, to whom Bangor's a Heaven,
*   He can ride and sit still as a mouse.*
Tho' Althrey is left of its tenant bereft,
*   The old bird and the cygnets are here.*
He has found a new nest with a mate of the best,
*   And has come to enjoy the good cheer.*
From Cholmondeley comes Rock, with of course Arthur Brock,
*   And his dug-up old fossils equine;*
Though good is his jockey, and talented's Rock, he
*   Of winners has not found a mine.*
From the Cottage of Oak, with four quads in the yoke,
*   Rivers Bulkeley arrives on the scene;*
Though his team is but scratch, it would be hard to match,
*   The dash they display o'er the green.*
From Cheshire comes Corbet, you search through the orbit
*   A vulpicide greater to find;*
Young Reg. and his Dad, looking cheery and glad,
*   To use language bad's not inclined.*
Where's Shropshire's keen Master? 'twould be a disaster
*   If hunting was stopped as some say;*
Ah! perish the thought! Here's success to the sport!
*   Our best thanks to Lonsdale we'll pay.*
And Puffles and Dandy, good naturedly bandy
*   Their jokes from the backs of their hacks,*
And an M.P. or two with sensation quite new,
*   For the meeting of holiday smacks.*
From Marbury's Poole, who since he left school,

Has thickened and grown you may bet,
From Cherry Hill's Sandy, who thinks he'll be handy
*   With the daughter of old Etiquette.*
But my muse travels fast, the pace cannot last,
*   So I can't tell you everyone here*
Enniskillen (late Cole) I'd forgot on my soul!
*   Wherever there's Sport he'll be near.*
But 'Borderer' keen, with Price ever Green,
*   Audits the account of the fray,*
Which way the wind Blew, Arundel will tell you
*   In The Field of the next Saturday.*
Now the Wynnstay Light Horse are clearing the Course,
*   And the farmers are saddling their cracks,*
And Holland is there with a thoroughbred mare,
*   That they back as if others were hacks.*
A second race over, and backers in clover.
*   For success still the favourite attends.*
Old pals we meet and we cordially greet
*   Our neighbours, relations, and friends.*
It's luncheon time now, so away from the row
*   And hubbub in Paddock and Ring,*
For I hear the corks pop, and I must have a drop
*   Before further glories I sing.*
So just one more glass to the health of the lass,
*   Each drinks to the flame he admires,*
The niggers are singing, the saddling-bells ringing,
*   The Bookies of odds are the criers.*
The Clerk of the Course runs a very fine horse;
*   His jockey's not Chalk, but of Cotton.*
But he never one minute appears to be in it,
*   And this form must never be forgotten!*
But now for the fun! We must see what's to run
*   For the Sweepstakes, a new race this year,*
See! Sir Watkin is riding, a good horse bestriding,
*   If he cannot quite win he'll be near.*
What sport is this race! And a rattling good pace,
*   The first round has settled the black –*
Sir Watkin is riding and Grosvenor biding,
*   His time with Seymour on the crack –*
The colours flash by, and I'm sorry that I
*   Cannot tell you what's first past the post,*
For I'm lunching again, and, in sparkling Champagne,
*   The health of the rider I'll toast!*
Here's good luck to Chasing, its better than Racing,
*   And Sportsmen like 'Mr.E.Jay',*
Who run on the square should never despair,
*   If they own a sound nag that can stay.*
So Bangor Iscoed, where the silver Dee's flowed,
*   For centuries past to the Sea,*
Of Sport meritorious and rivalry glorious,
*   May your meadows the scene ever be!*

R.K. Mainwaring

NOTE: Bangor-on-Dee Steeplechases, at one time known as the Wynnstay Hunt Meeting and even Bangor Hunt Steeplechases, originated from a match between the Hon. Lloyd Kenyon of Gredington and Mr Richard Myddelton-Biddulph, which took place on February 25th, 1859 at Bangor Meadows. The promoters thought they might as well make a day of it and farmers' and gentlemen's races were arranged to fill up the programme. Thereafter it became an annual event. The principals were the son and heir of the 3rd Lord Kenyon and the Lord Lieutenant of Denbighshire's son from Chirk Castle. The race was won by Biddulph, then a Cornet in the 1st Life Guards.

R.K.Mainwaring, no relation to Sir Harry, was a ferocious looking man with a black beard. He was a handicapper. He also wrote some verses about Gamecock's Grand National victory for 'Mr E. Jay' (E.J. Thornewill of Sandy Brow).

A Chant From North Cheshire

WHEN the farmer's reaped his acres,
  Stored and stacked his golden corn,
Bright the visions then which make us
  Fix the first cub-hunting dawn

Watch the hunters in their boxes,
  Getting back their satin bloom,
Prick their ears at talk of 'foxes'
  Banded forth from groom to groom.

Suddenly they're all attention,
  Leave their oats and look perplexed;
Was it that they heard a mention,
  'Twemlow Gorse on Thursday next?'

When in overnight inspection
  Cubberley goes on his rounds,
Bent on making shrewd selection
  Of his gamest puppy hounds.

Ah, the beauties! how intently
  Scan they all his brooding face,
Waving sterns around him gently,
  With their languid, houndish grace.

Then the early morning chatter,
  Misty movements in the fog;
How they make the cobbles clatter
  As to covertside they jog!

NOTE: The above verses are an excerpt from a poem by *Chanticleer*, published in 1902 in *Baily's Magazine*.

TARPORLEY HUNT MEETING
April 15th, 1903
The Victory of Dreadnought
in the
Cheshire Farmers' Half-Bred Steeplechase
A MEMENTO
respectably dedicated to
S. Challoner, Esq.

"A head like a snake, and a skin like a mouse,
  An eye like a woman, bright, gentle and brown;
With loins and a back that would carry a house.
  And quarters to lift him right over the town."
  MAJOR WHYTE-MELVILLE.

'Tis Tarporley's famous Tournament where famous warriors meet,
To battle for its trophies gained but by brave and fleet.

Cheshire's Half-Bred Steeplechase – The Farmers' – now holds sway,
And warriors nine assemble here to take part in the fray.
'Neath Challoner's popular banner – Fergusson as rider- knight –
Brave DREADNOUGHT, game and speedy, is ready for
  the fight.
Throughout the heat of battle he bravely bears the brunt, While vainly foes are striving he hold his place in front.
Ah, bravo, gallant DREADNOUGHT! Ah Fergusson, well-
  done!
The Challoner Flag's triumphant, the Steeplechase is won! List to the cheers and plaudits as the flag now waves ahead, For on the popular banner a lustre bright is shed!

* * * *

To the Owner, the Trainer,
  Rider-knight, Steed,
We pledge them in bumpers,
  Hurrah for the deed!

The Last Day Of The Season

To one horse, a man, and a cart to the Meet, add two hunters and a groom. Stew slowly over a cold scent for six hours; then serve up for nine minutes. Add a driver with a brougham and pair, and a man to ride second horse home. Result a blank day, bar a vixen.

INGREDIENTS: *4 men, 5 horses, 1 four-wheeled carriage, 1 two-wheeled carriage and 1 girl.*

The girl in question was Miss Olive Cotton-Jodrell, aged 20, hunting from Reaseheath in 1903, the year she was Lady Patroness of the Tarporley Hunt Club (President: Sir Delves Louis Broughton (233)): a comment by her father, Col. Edward Cotton-Jodrell (225).

Her niece Susan was appointed Lady Patroness in 1931 when Sir 'Jock' Delves Broughton was President and again the following year owing to the Club Meeting being cancelled.

A Cheshire Hunt Alphabet – 1923

A IS for Alfred – a noisy old bear,
A devil for whisky and also to swear.
[Alfred Ashton of Tarporley.]

B is for Bobs and Ida his wife, who
has a new baby each year of her life.
[Mr & Mrs Barbour of Bolesworth.]

C is for Cotton and Carter too.
They will sell you a horse which may be a screw.
[Gilbert Cotton and Hamilton Carter, the
Bolesworth agent, who was to marry Mr
Barbour's widow.]

D is for Dewhurst, the wildest of men.
He is fond of his port, his tongue and his pen.
[Major Cyril Dewhurst.]

E is for Eleanor, wife of above,
who is always screaming, ready to shove.

F is for Frank turning crusty, poor fellow.
Make Jimmy field master and he'll be more mellow.
[The Tinsley brothers.]

G is for Gilbert of Walton renown.
His wife is a big one and stretches her gown.
[Sir Gilbert and Lady Greenall.]

H is Herman, that silly old Vic,
Who is fond of the ladies, but not very quick.
[Of Park House, Cholmondeley.]

I is for Isolde, rudely inclined,
With her nose in the air, but we don't really mind.
[Lord Arthur Grosvenor's elder daughter,
who married Jack Alston-Roberts-West.]

J is for Jarmay, who has a large farm.
If he keeps to his Friesians, he won't do much harm.
['Pishta' Jarmay of Bulkeley Hall. His
father was Sir John Jarmay of Petty Pool,
Sandiway, Director of Brunner Mond & Co.]

K is for Kenneth, whose name's on a car.
He likes to go hunting, but does not get far.
[Sir Kenneth Crossley, 2nd Bart., who had
recently bought Combermere.]

L is for Littledale, bold Clara, who
last year killed one horse and this year killed two.
[Wife of J.B. Littledale of Bunbury.]

M is for Midwood, who is trying his hand
As Master in Cheshire – how long will he stand?
[Mr Walter Midwood of Calveley Hall.]

N is for Norman, who says he is broke.
You would hardly believe it to see him at Stoke.
[R.N.H.Verdin of Stoke Hall, Nantwich.]

O is Olivia, who goes to the shires
And likes to have dashes with silly young squires.
[Olivia, daughter of Major Cyril
Dewhurst. She was Lady Patroness in 1925]

P is for Poole, who nobody heeds.
He is always shouting 'ware wheat!' and 'ware seeds!'
[Bryan Davies Poole of Marbury Hall,
Whitchurch.]

Q is for queer ones, there are lots of them here.
And some of them live by the side of the mere.

R is for Rock our staunchest supporter,
Who goes like a bird over timber and water.
[Lord Cholmondeley, who died that
year.]

S is for Straker, whose collar is green,
But not of the sort that ought to be seen.
[Major Ian Straker of the Tynedale, who
had taken Lower Broxton Hall]

T is for Tomkinson of Willington Hall,
Who gets wild when his wife won't return from a ball.
[Always immaculate, Phyllis Tomkinson
cast a spell at this time with
her beauty and her superb
skill as a horsewoman]

U is for Ursula, clever and kind.
She paints the place blue, but we don't really mind.
[Lady Ursula Grosvenor, elder daughter of
the Duke of Westminster]

V is for Violet – has a pack of her own
And kills some hares before they're full grown.
[The Duke of Westminster's second wife,
whom he had married in 1920. In later life, as
the Hon. Mrs Freddie Cripps, she insisted on
wearing a velvet cap, claiming that as she had
been a Master she was entitled to do so]

W is for Wignall, Walter Starkey and Wright.
  The first two can't keep this good huntsman in sight.
    [Fred Wignall, father-in-law of Robin
    Grosvenor, Lord Arthur's son; Walter Starkey
    of Wrenbury; Joe Wright the huntsman.]

X is for Xmas – long past, the season's now over.
  We cannot go hunting because of the clover.

Y is for Yaddie, Tom Royden's stud groom.
  She rides in a snaffle and never has room.
      [One of the two Watson sisters, who lived
      in the Wirral]

Z we cannot manage – it gets us all beat.

Like Jimmy our Master, we beat a retreat.
      [Jimmy Tinsley, the former Master.]

NOTE: Some of the above comments were a little unkind, to say the least. A further dreary edition was written in 1926, but fortunately did not get wide circulation. The only redeeming letter, possibly was 'B':

The Barbours turn out regardless of cost
With little Eliza who never gets lost,
On good sorts of horses well schooled and well made;
A credit the lot are to all kinds of trade.

(That's enough alphabets.– Ed.)

Little Foxes
A PLEA FOR PITY

I dreamed, and lo! in this my dream the cranks had had their way,
Fox-hunting was forbid by law for ever and a day;
No more across the English grass might English sportsmen ride,
No more the scarlet coats be seen at winter covert side.

But what of 'Master Reynolds' whom this law was passed to save
From the death that so befits him as a brigand wild and brave?
Alas! I saw quite clearly what must now become his fate
With none to stand between him and the chicken-farmer's hate.

The shot at dusk, the shot at dawn, the snatched uncertain aim,
The wounds that only slowly kill, the wounds that only maim,
The bitter gripe of poison and the burning, rending pain,
The broken teeth and bleeding jaws that bite the trap in vain.

The roly cubs in summer dawns that scrapped and played amain
Are dying now by inches, for their dam comes not again;
She is lying in a hedgerow with a gin upon her pad,
A broken, bleeding sacrifice to sentiment run mad.

I woke, and knew it but a dream, as yet Mus' Reynolds ran,
As he did before the wolf pack 'ere ever there was man.
I woke, but breathed a little prayer for fear of what impends.
God pity little foxes and save them from their friends!

NOTE: This was published in *Punch*, February 14th, 1929, under the name of Crotchet, the *nom de plume* of Phil Stevenson, Joint Master from 1948-1954 of the Royal Rock, Britain's oldest pack of beagles. Before he died he had a small booklet of his favourite verses printed as *Beagling Ballads and Random Rhymes*. In an article in *Cheshire Life* John Winton described him as having the hunt balladeer's taste for terrible puns and referred to his *Royal Rock Beagles* which goes to the tune of *Clementine* as one of 'the most blood-chilling banality'. This is it:

LITTLE hounds with lovely voices
Singing down the Raby Vale,
See them feather altogether
Sure to-day they cannot fail.
    In the Hundred of the Wirral
    From the Mersey to the Dee
    Saw you ever hounds to clever
    As the famous R.R.B.?

Hark to Minstrel, Hark to Meddler,
Druid joins the glad refrain;
Little Cheerful says an ear full,
Now the chorus swell again
    CHORUS

See the Master, none is faster,
Terence only can compete;
Still aspiring though perspiring,
Toil the field on leaden feet.
    CHORUS

Hark the horn its long note singing,
As the day fades into night;
Hounds are homing in the gloaming,
While the stars are growing bright.
    CHORUS

Lines to a Fox's Mask
by Noël Winterbottom of Tilstone House, later wife of **Col. Anthony Dewhurst (308).**

AND now no more those glazed eyeballs gleam
With senses open, and no more those ears
Up-pricked, can listen, as in byegone years
They heard hound music by the Withy Stream.
Bared are thy teeth that made the last wild strife
Against old Hackler's n'er relenting jaw;
Tired is thy tongue, and still for evermore

Those pads which bore thee well till ceased thy life.
And yet what mem'ries still thine old mask bears
Of fences bold, green fields and ditches wide;
Of brilliant mornings; hacking to the meet . . .
Reynard! whilst gazing thus, e'en now one hears
The loveliest music nature ever sighed:
Hound music, in the Distance soft and sweet.

The Cheshire Forest Hunt Club Toast

To a sportsman in a russet coat
With facings white at chest and throat
Our best laid plans he often mocks
Gentlemen – drink deep – our friend the fox.

[Hugh A. Whittemore, March 25th, 1958 – the date on which the inaugural dinner took place at The Grosvenor Hotel, Chester.

Blue Collars

Blue collars, blue collars, – they'll gallop all day
Blue collars, blue collars, – to show them the way
Blue collars, blue collars, – they all ride so hard
To pull down their fox on the Forest's green sward.

Their Master's a vulpicide of well-known renown,
There's naught that will stop him nor yet bring him down;
When he crosses a pasture all covered in weeds
He'll ring up the farmer and give him some seeds.

Will Welbourne, a game 'un as we have all seen,
He loves all his hounds – no pack is more keen.
Alfred Hopwood a rider as tough as can be
But kept up to scratch by gallant G.B.

Arthur Holden's delight is a good coach and four,
When he's naught else to do he'll take them on tour.
John Stringer the North country tenderly cares
And stops all the foxes out of their lairs.
The cost of all this becomes rather heavy
So he pays for it all from a Grand National levy.

Of some of our Members we hear quite a lot
But quietest of all is our friend Joseph Scott.
Our point-to-point meeting he runs every year
And now is the time to give him a cheer.

Bert Willey (God Bless him) works like a thrall
To dig out subscriptions from both great and small.
When all Wirral farmers are in a ferment,
With some hedges smashed and some hedges bent,
We send for Don Tennant that wonderful fellow
Whose silver tongue quells their hectoring bellow.

High on our list comes Bobby O'Neill
Friend in our need and true as good steel,
A great horseman, Bobby, we all must agree
At Capenhurst ditches he's lovely to see.

Bill Houlbrook's a sportsman with good horses too,
Of his share of winners he's had quite a few.
Over Littleton fences he did love to ride
But as he's grown older he's grown rather wide.

Horace Aitchison, with pleasure we welcome tonight.
He always makes sure his earths are just right.
To hook a good fish is his hobby I'm told,
And he'll ne'er let it slip when once its took hold.

Myself I place last – I cannot claim fame
Except for the foxes bred down Powey Lane.

Let us think for a momemt of those who are gone
Although they have left us, their memory lives on.
Blue collars both, whom we could not spare,
Let's think of them hunting, still hunting here.

Blue colars, blue collars, blue collars are we,
Blue collars, blue collars a brave lot to see.
From rise of the sun till it sets in the West
Not one of us here would give Reynard best.

Note: The founder of the Cheshire Forest Hunt Club was Mr Philip Hunter of Littleton Old Hall and later Portal. He was Chairman of his family seed firm, Hunters of Chester, founded in 1883.

The Morning After

TWO heads on a pillow, one covered in curls,
T'other aching like blazes, around it mist swirls.
Oh wife of my bosom, come lend me thy breast
And gently, so gently this aching head rest.

All night I've been dining with collars of blue,
The wine was superb, the food perfect too.
The Master himself in the President's chair,
The best of my friends were all seated there.
The scene was historic; picture it please
With candlelight flickering on sportsmen like these,
The glint of thy silver reflecting the light
On engraved buttons and shirt fronts so white.
In coats of gay scarlet eleven sat down,
No grumbles were heard, no sign of a frown.
Eleven blue collars so happily met,
We founded our club and I'll take a safe bet
Last night at the Grosvenor history was made
And fears for our hunting quickly allayed;
The anti fox-hunters have had a good run
But damn, say I, we'll still have our fun.

The port circled round, 'twas lovely to see,
Its ruby eye winking, kept winking at me.
So wife of my bosom,, come lend me thy breast
And gently, so gently this aching head rest.

1958   HUGH A.WHITTEMORE

THE following verses were recited by their author, Simon Dewhurst (348) when proposing 'FOX-HUNTING' at Tarporley in 1989:

In Praise of Hunting
– A Revised Version

NOW this is a tale about 'unting
Of which you know a great deal of course;
It tells of Albert Birtwhistle,
'is 'ounds and 'is 'orn and 'is 'orse.

Albert were Master of Fox-'unt
In bygone days of old,
When women all wore bowler 'ats
And did as they was told.

The gentlemen were well turned out
And generally looked the part.
They were 'ardly ever sober,
But were always there at the start.

Albert were a proper little 'itler,
Some said an Ayotollah,
In his shiny black boots and red tailcoat
And 'is slightly off-colour green collar.

'is 'orse were an odd looking creature
With an obstinate mind of 'is own;
Its front end were a kind of piebald
And its back-end a sort of a roan.

Its ears they stuck out at right angles,
As did 'is boney old 'ips;
Its fetlocks were 'airy and stringy,
As were whiskers upon lower lip.

One cold rainy day in December
The field to first covert did ride,
Where they started to munch on their fruitcake
And knock back the whisky on t'side.

As they stood by the side of covert,
Which seemed to go on for miles,
Men relaxed by standing in stirrups,
While gently relieving their piles.

Albert leant down to earthstopper
And said: "Shall we find any foxes?"
Old Bill he stood close an' he whispered:
"You should do, we put in six boxes!"

Just then from the depths of the covert
A bark and a yap did begin.
When the 'orse of a lady quite close to old Albert
Unexpectedly chose to break wind.

The lady went bright puce and stammered:
"I'm sorry" – as a matter of course.
But Albert weren't known for 'is manners
And said "For a moment I thought it were 'orse."

The barking began to get louder
And a fox from the covert did run,
When all of a sudden from middle of wood
They 'eard the bang of a gun.

Now there were two things that 'ad possibly 'appened
And neither were all too pleasant:
The 'untsman could 'ave shot 'imself
Or there was somebody firing at pheasant.

The Master didn't take long to make mind up;
'is face went the colour of coat.
'e belted 'is 'orse across blunt end
And shot towards wood like a stoat.

"Follow me!," he cried out to the 'unt.
And, leading the cavalry charge,
Crashed into wood like a tiger gone mad
With most of the field – by and large.

Standing on ride, in midst of the wood,
Stood a long line of guns, all abreast.
A couple of pheasants 'ad already flown by
An' now they were waiting for rest.

From the thickets in front came a tumult,
Of elephants, one would surmise.
At end of the line Colonel Sidebottom cried:
"Don't shoot till you see the white of their eyes!"

Now this were young Willie's very first shoot,
An' 'e stood there wi' tremblin' knees.
'e thought to 'imself: "What shall I do next?"
When Albert came crashing through trees.

Willie was all of a dither.
As Master thundered right past,
'e turned and fired off both barrels
And knocked 'imself out with the blast.

Albert's 'orse then went bananas;
There were one thing that made him see red,
That were being fired on by shot gun
And peppered up backside wi' lead.

Albert weren't too 'appy neither,
As 'e'd banged 'is 'ead on a tree.
'is 'at had fallen over 'is face
And 'e were finding it hard to see.

There were one thing I'd forgotten to mention
And that were an' 'unt saboteur
Who reckoned he'd take the mornin' off
An' go out for a breath of fresh air.

He smelt pretty bad and 'is air were long,
As 'e prowled through the wood with 'is spray.
And 'e 'adn't a clue of what 'it 'im
As Albert's orse came t'other way.

The rest of the field 'ad charged across ride
And the guns were getting distraught.
They were firing away amid total confusion,
Just like Battle of Agincourt.

The 'unt saboteur 'ad been sniffed by the 'ounds
Who were 'olding the fellow at bay.
Albert and 'orse had bolted through wood
And the fox . . . . had got clean away.

(With apologies to the late Marriott Edgar, whose work was originally performed by Stanley Holloway and Marriott Edgar.)

The Tarporley Hunt Club Dinners

To Tarporley dinners they come in their hordes,
Colonels and Generals, Dukes and some Lords.
Pink coats and green breeches and shirts gleaming white;
When seated in rows it's an elegant sight.

The Members comprise a true sporting band,
And always will welcome the Hunt on their land.
The fences they've jumped is everyone's boast,
"Fox-hunting"'s always the favourite toast.

Secretary Gordon with diligent zeal,
Chooses the menus to suit every meal;
He's very severe, no complaint will he brook,
Now that their Manager's also their cook.

The food is delicious, the wine is superb,
But sadly their drinking, all Members must curb;
It isn't from fear of the next morning's ride.
But due to the Police Car that's lurking outside.

October, 1989   J.E.K.R.

In Thanksgiving for the Life of Doreen Blain-Cole,
who died on December 31st, 1990, aged 76.

(She was a founder Member and the first Secretary of the Cheshire Hunt Supporters' Club.)

As a pale sun rises slowly
    on a new cub-hunting scene
    when you gave us all hot coffee,
    I'll remember you Doreen.

At the Opening Meet in Autumn
    from your vantage at Town's Green
    when you watched the hounds in Pages,
    I'll remember you Doreen.

At the Point-to-Point at Alpraham,
    on racing you were keen,
    on your wagon as a Grand Stand,
    I'll remember you Doreen.

In your little house at Nantwich
    by the Church across the green,
    where we sipped our tea and gossipped
    I'll remember you Doreen.

                    J.E.K.R.

The Cheshire Tally-Ho!

NOW *the leaves of the forest are yellow,*
   Once more we behold the glad pack;
From Ox Heys we go to draw Philo,
   The Field is red chequered with black.
As Coley arrives at the covert,
   All eyes on the hounds as they go,
His cheer by the echo sounds over,
   "Loo in!, Forrard on!, Tally-ho!"
     Away! Away! The Horse Club we go!
     With a tally, tally, tally, Cheshire Tally-ho!

May the names now recorded in metre
   While Hunting endureth survive;
From Saighton comes one they call Peter,
   Whose feats o'er that country still thrive.
At Bradwall there's George the new squire,
   Whilst Master, his brother John Barlow,
O'er grasslands he leads us in Cheshire,
   Whene'er the horn blows: "Tally-ho!"
     Away! Away! The Horse Club we go!
     With a tally, tally, tally, Cheshire Tally-ho!

There's Greenall from Wynnstay all bragging
   The news of the neighbouring hunt,
John Mather renowned for his building,
   And John Warrington e'er ebullient.
From Henbury hails de Ferranti,
   Whose house is the height of Palladio,
The Modernists may all be anti,
   But Prince Charles is pro, "Tally-ho!"
     Away! Away! The Horse Club we go!
     With a tally, tally, tally, Cheshire Tally-ho!

That dogged old soldier named Sayce
   With Bert he'd e'en leap the wide Dee.
We can always be sure of a chase
   When Geoff finds a fox up a tree.
By Moseley to ride in a run,
   Or chukkar with him at polo,
Is a revel, and frolic, and fun.
   There croaks a most true "Tally-ho!"
     Away! Away! The Horse Club we go!
     With a tally, tally, tally, Cheshire Tally-ho!

Is elegant Dawes at the front?
   Is Woolley now back at his Hall?
Without Wilson our screws cannot hunt,
   And here's Bill with a bill for us all.
The Williams make sure we've no worry
   With no wire at Haughton nor Spurstow
There's always an excellent skurry
   And unhindered we go, "Tally-ho!"
     Away! Away! The Horse Club we go!
     With a tally, tally, tally, Cheshire Tally-ho!

John Sellers of Rushton's a goer,
   Though tennis is really his game;
John Goodwin is surely no slower,
   Hospitality Hankelow's fame.
Ferranti flies in from Llanfechan,
   His thunderous horse is not slow,
He's away the moment hounds beckon,
   And the Huntsman he cries: "Tally-ho!".
     Away! Away! The Horse Club we go!
     With a tally, tally, tally, Cheshire Tally-ho!

When Rickie doth fall on a sod,
   E'en then he is ever so cheery.
But oh! To be seventy like Bod –
   He's out 'till the end and ne'er weary.
From Calpe, now Deva, here's Tom,
   Astride the magnificent Waldo,
A mount just as safe as a condom,
   Both jumping they go! Tally-ho!
     Away! Away! The Horse Club we go!
     With a tally, tally, tally, Cheshire Tally-ho!

We sportsmen so keen for the chase
   So gallant there never were other;
We hunt the sly fox at great pace,
   And know the best line from each covert.
None better than we know the art,
   'Cross country e'er long may we go
The Cheshire we love in our heart
   And thrill at the sound "Tally-ho!"
     Away! Away! The Horse Club we go!
     With a tally, tally, tally, Cheshire Tally-ho!

Once again: Away! Away! The Horse Club we go!
     With a tally, tally, tally, Cheshire Tally-ho!

Even yet again and again.

T.P.H.
(with profound apologies to REEW)

NOTE:
The Cheshire Hunt Horse Club Song, first sung by the author of these lines at Bradwall Manor, January 23rd, 1992. This club was formed in 1974 and had its inaugural dinner at the Blue Cap Inn. Restricted to twenty members, its purpose is to provide the horses for the hunt servants. The most recently elected member is Mr Willie Carson, the ex-champion jockey who married a Cheshire girl, since when he has always enjoyed his hunting in Cheshire.

Addenda et Corriegenda

p. 10   All the four sons of the 4th Earl of Barrymore, mentioned in this book, were by his third wife. He also had a son and two daughters by his first wife, the son dying as an infant in 1707.

p. 38   Lord Cole took a seventeen-year-old Scottish heiress, Miss Charlotte Baird, as his bride, thus reducing his financial worries. She was a cousin of Charlotte Baird who married Bay Middleton. The red-headed Lady Cole bore nine children in twelve years, though not all were fathered by her husband. One person said to have cuckholded him was from the family his sister Charlotte married into – the Smith-Barrys.

p. 46   Shavington Hall has mullioned windows and is surprisingly faced with 'lavatory' brick.

p. 112   Another private pack of fox-hounds from about 1785 onwards belonged to the Rector of Myddle, Salop. and later also of Whitchurch, the Rev. Francis Henry Egerton, a scion of the Dukes of Bridgwater and born in 1756, the son of the Bishop of Durham and a life-long bachelor, though he did have one son and four illegitimate daughters.

He wrote a seemingly civil letter asking Mr Thos. Boycott for permission to hunt over his land on the Cheshire/Shropshire border should his hounds run there. The Squire of Hinton sought his agent's advice and received the following reply:

> ... if you give Mr Egerton leave to hunt Hinton, you must give up every idea of having any Game there, as he makes a common practice of hunting on other Peoples Ground and not his own...

Asking him particularly to withhold permisson, the agent continued:

> I may add that every independent person in the Town of Whitchurch – qualified & unqualified unite with me in the request, and I believe I may make a further addition by saying that a few weeks will teach Egerton how insignificent the Duke's and his Property is when put in Competition with a few of the Inhabitants, – this he is aware of & therefore wrote that letter to you.

The Rev. Lord Henry, as he became, held his Rectorship until his death in 1829, succeeding his brother as 8th Earl of Bridgwater in 1823. He took up residence in Paris and in his declining years became very eccentric. He dressed his cats and dogs as ladies and gentlemen, fed them at his table and took them out in his carriage. He also kept rabbits, pigeons and partridges with clipped wings solely for the pleasure he derived from killing a few heads of game for the pot. He even took to wearing a new pair of boots each day and labelling them carefully to remind him where he had been and, by their condition, what the weather was like.

See also Old Oulton Lowe, page 392.

p. 156   In 1873, for the occasion of Lady Grey-Egerton's birthday, the Oulton and Egerton tenantry commissioned George Richmond, RA to paint a portrait of Sir Philip. He is depicted wearing a Club scarf pin in his cravat. It is the earliest known example and the swan emblem is modelled larger than the one eventually adopted.

Sir Philip de Malpas Grey-Egerton, from an engraving of the portrait by George Richmond, referred to on the previous page.

*   *   *

WHITE MISCHIEF AND THE ANGEL OF DEATH.

p. 254 An incident in the Cheshire hunting field concerning Jock Broughton was when his mount got kicked by a horse ridden by a young farmer called Jack Lakin. Soon after as he passed him, Sir Delves brought the butt-end of his heavy hunting whip down on Jack's horse's head so hard that it was pole-axed to the ground. 'That will teach you to come out on a kicker,' he sneered as he went on his way.

As for Diana, Evelyn so loathed his step-mother that, once, when she was coming to stay at Doddington, he persuaded the groom to corn up the pony she would be riding. Sure enough the first time she was out, it bolted sharply. However she was a competent enough horsewoman to ride it into a nearby haystack.

In her twilight years and following Diana, Lady Delamere's death in 1987, a great many people who knew no better have tainted her reputation by branding her as the probable murderess of Joss Erroll. From an impeccable source (totally unconnected with any of the families involved), the woman scorned and the most likely culprit was Alice, the divorced wife of Raymond de Trafford, the third son of Sir Humphrey, the 3rd baronet (230). An American, she had previously been wed to Comte Frédéric de Janzé of Paris, the marriage ending in divorce, and became an established member of the Happy Valley set. Her second marriage was a travesty – she and Raymond going their separate ways after a mere three weeks. She was even once charged with his attempted murder at the Gard du Nord, the judge regarding it as a *crime passionel*. By 1941, she felt jilted as one of Erroll's many conquests and so had motive, means and mentality. Eventually she contracted cancer of the womb, but was that the sole reason she chose to take her own life with *her revolver*, failing at the first attempt? After her death in March, 1943, her suicide note was handed to the Nairobi Police and its contents have yet to be revealed.

Illustration Acknowledgements

THE AUTHOR WISHES TO ACKNOWLEDGE here all those who allowed him to have their paintings, prints, *etc.* photographed and reproduced, including: Her Grace Anne, Duchess of Westminster, His Grace the Duke of Westminster, Lavinia, Marchioness of Cholmondeley, the late Lord Kenyon, Mr Anthony Barbour, the Hon.Mrs Jonathan Forbes, Mr David Greenhough (The Pheasant Inn, Burwardsley), Mr Charles Johnson, Mr David Musgrave, Mr Ross Pigot and Mr C.R.Tomkinson, Mr Richard Prideaux-Brune, Mrs Duncan Simonds, Mrs Anthony Villiers, Mrs G.H.de V.Wilbraham, Mrs Babe Williams. Mr Robin Wilson, Mrs K.Atkinson (Archivist, Lyme Park) and the Manchester City Art Gallery.

The author is also most grateful to the following individuals, institutions, publications and photographers, whose work is reproduced on the pages shown:

Mr Jim Mead, pp viii, 30.

Mr Peter Harding, Tetbury, pp 11-16, 92/3, 135.

Mr Paul Barker (Country Life), pp 33, 40, 41, 57, 71.

Mr Don Williams, Beeston Lodge, Tarporley, pp iv, 48, 73-77, 94, 111, 116, 128, 132, 134, 135, 159, 173, 214, 231, 247, 256, 260, 263, 265, 268, 269, 273, 274, 280, 283, 285, 286, 288, 289, 291, 295, 308.

Mr Andrew Jenkins from his collection of post cards, pp 29, 95, 130, 278, 287.

Mr S.P. Dewhurst, pp 29, 136.

Mr W.G.Fergusson, pp 2, 37, 38, 79, 114, 294, 403.

Baily's Magazine of Sports and Pastimes, engravings, pp 142, 205, 262

British Library Newspaper Library, pp 226, 277.

Cheshire County Record Office, for photocopies on pp 21, 83.

Cheshire Life, pp 22, 53,, 81, 97, 309.

Chester Chronicle (Mr Ken Evans), pp 61, 360.

Clarendon Gallery, Manchester, p 190

Countryman's Gallery, Leicester, p 230.

Courtauld Institute of Art, pp 9, 153.

Illustrated Sporting and Dramatic News, pp 283-285, 306.

The Field, p 118 and **The Field (Guglielmo Galvin)**, p 312.

National Portrait Gallery, pp 6, 24, 78, 102.

Sotheby's, pp 18, 109, 147.

Tate Gallery, p 54

Whitchurch Herald, (courtesy Burleydam W.I. Scrap-book), p 114.

The author has the copyright for the photographs on pp 39, 56, 58, 78, 106, 127, 135, 154, 259, 310, 311, 374, 395.

The artists and sources of other paintings reproduced have in most cases been included with the captions and the author wishes to acknowledge with gratitude the copyright of all concerned.

The illustrations on pp 46, 58, 63, 66-7, 100, 126, 131, 149, 158, 159, 160, 162, 177, 188, 189, 197, 206, 217, 219, 220, 222, 225, 239, 242, 253, 257, 258, 266, 267, 273, 286, 287, 290, 296, 303 and 356 are taken from the *TARPORLEY HUNT CLUB ALBUMS*.

Those on pp 144, 148, 167, 192, 200, 201, 204, 207, 211, and 249 are from the 2nd Viscount Combermere's album of original sketches in the possession of the Tarporley Hunt Club.

Those on pp 26, 31, 33, 51, 53, 59, 66, 67, and 69 are from the Club's Bicentenary Album of Photographs by **Hector Houghton** of Alderley Edge.

PORTRAIT SKETCHES OF CHESHIRE HUNTING MEN is the source for the illustrations on pp 44, 63, 85, 86, 125, 137, 139, 143, 179, 191, 199, 200, 203, 211, 215, 217, 222, 232 and 235.

The drawings on pp 26, 44, 64, 272, 292, 293, 297,

302, 307, 315, 361, 364 and 378 are from *CHESHIRE CATS AND CHEESES*.

The drawings on pp 157 and 161 are from the Hon. Rose Bootle-Wilbraham's scrap-book, courtesy Lt.-Col. Geoffrey Sparrow, and the photographs on p 95 of the author's father, of Lord Enniskillen on pp 279 and those of the King of Spain at Eaton on pp 282–3 are from the late Major Gilbert Cotton's scrap-book.

The painting on p 231 and the line drawings on pp 424, 428, 433, 434, 440, 441, 442, 445, 448 and 444/5 have been done specially for this book by **Elizabeth Scrivener** and those on pp 5 and 151 by **Samantha Hunter**. The drawing on pp 368–373 *passim* are taken from *Hounds are Home* and are by **Gerald Hare**. Those on pp x and 126 are by Lionel Edwards.

Except where otherwise stated in a caption the line drawings and lithographs (by W.Crane, Chester) in BOOK TWO are taken from the 1st and 2nd Editions of *Hunting Songs*. The etchings by *Phiz* (Hablôt K. Browne) on pp 420 to 422 are from the 9th Limited Edition.

Finally a note about **Archibald MacKinnon**, whose work is on pp 92/3 & 260. He was born at Campeltown, the son of a sea captain, and began his career as an engineer before studying oil painting at Edinburgh Academy. His best known work is a giant Crucifixion which he painted on the wall of a cave on Duvaar Island at the entrance to Campbeltown loch. He did it early one morning after a fit of depression, using no scaffolding and tying his brush to a walking stick to reach the top. He told no one about it, but a becalmed yachtsman came across it when he went ashore to stretch his legs. He thought he had seen a vision as the sun shone on it through a crevice and promptly fainted. This was in 1887 and after its discovery MacKinnon admitted it was his work, inspired by a dream. It has been restored three times. Shortly afterwards he moved to Nantwich, where he was remembered as a pawky, kenspeckle man, very Scottish and somewhat henpecked. In 1953 his daughter found a 12' × 9' canvas of the cave painting in the cellar of her home. It was donated to a Salvation Army Home in the South of England. It seems he was never commissioned nor paid for his painting of Tarporley Races, 1890, which he completed in 1896 and signed with his monogram. On his death he left it to a farmer at Woore who had loaned him some money to buy his oils and brushes. The Club missed an opportunity to purchase the canvas after it had been bought by a London dealer in 1970. The name on his tombstone in Middlewich Road cemetery, Nantwich, is given as ARCHIBALD C. C. MACKINNON. He had a studio off Hospital Street and he and his family lived at 7, Laburnum Avenue, a neat little terraced alley off the Crewe road not far from Churche's Mansion.

The finest view in Europe (Revised Version) from a sketch by Nöel Winterbottom. The Pony Club has always had a strong branch in Cheshire.

Index Nominorum

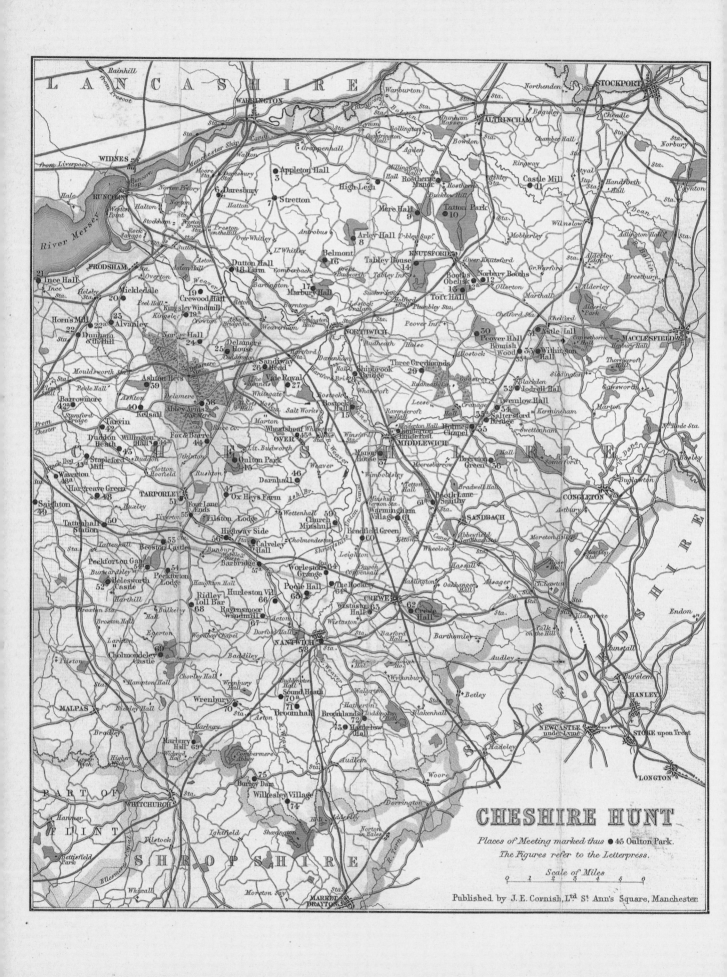

CHESHIRE HUNT

Places of Meeting marked thus ● 45 Oulton Park.
The Figures refer to the Letterpress.

Scale of Miles

Published by J. E. Cornish, Ltd St Ann's Square, Manchester.